Shakespeare

VOLUME 1
THE COMEDIES

Shakespeare

VOLUME 1
THE COMEDIES

AURORA PUBLISHING

Published by
AURORA PUBLISHING
Unit 9C, Bradley Fold Trading Estate
Radcliffe Moor Road, Bradley Fold
Bolton BL2 6RT

Volume 1
ISBN 1-85926-002-0

3 Volume Set
ISBN 1-85926-001-2

Cover design and
production by
MetraDisc Limited
Castleton, Rochdale OL11 3DT

Printed in Guernsey by
Guernsey Press Limited

CONTENTS

THE

TEMPEST

ACT I.

SCENE I. *On a ship at sea : a tempestuous
noise of thunder and lightning heard.*

Enter a Ship-Master *and* a Boatswain.

Ship-Master.

Boatswain !

Boatswain. Here, master : what cheer ?

Ship-Master. Good, speak to the mariners :
fall to 't, yarely, or we run ourselves aground :
bestir, bestir. [*Exit.*

Enter Mariners.

Boatswain. Heigh, my hearts ! cheerly, cheerly,
my hearts ! yare, yare ! Take in the topsail.
Tend to the master's whistle. Blow, till thou
burst thy wind, if room enough !

Enter ALONSO, SEBASTIAN, ANTONIO, FERDINAND,
GONZALO, *and others.*

Alonso. Good boatswain, have care. Where's
the master ? Play the men.

Boatswain. I pray now, keep below.

Antonio. Where is the master, boatswain ?

Boatswain. Do you not hear him ? You mar
our labour : keep your cabins : you do assist
the storm.

Gonzalo. Nay, good, be patient.

Boatswain. When the sea is. Hence ! What
cares these roarers for the name of king ? To
cabin : silence ! trouble us not.

Gonzalo. Good, yet remember whom thou hast
aboard.

Boatswain. None that I more love than myself.
You are a counsellor ; if you can command
these elements to silence, and work the peace
of the present, we will not hand a rope more ;
use your authority : if you cannot, give thanks
you have lived so long, and make yourself
ready in your cabin for the mischance of the
hour, if it so hap. Cheerly, good hearts ! Out
of our way, I say. [*Exit.*

Gonzalo. I have great comfort from this fellow :
methinks he hath no drowning mark upon
him ; his complexion is perfect gallows. Stand
fast, good Fate, to his hanging : make the rope
of his destiny our cable, for our own doth little
advantage. If he be not born to be hanged,
our case is miserable. [*Exeunt.*

Re-enter Boatswain.

Boatswain. Down with the topmast ! yare ! lower,
lower ! Bring her to try with main-course. [*A
cry within.*] A plague upon this howling ! they
are louder than the weather or our office.

Re-enter SEBASTIAN, ANTONIO, *and* GONZALO.

Yet again ! what do you here ? Shall we give
o'er and drown ? Have you a mind to sink ?

Sebastian. A pox o' your throat, you bawling,
blasphemous, incharitable dog !

Boatswain. Work you then.

Antonio. Hang, cur ! hang, you whoreson, in-
solent noisemaker ! We are less afraid to be
drowned than thou art.

Gonzalo. I 'll warrant him for drowning ; though
the ship were no stronger than a nutshell and
as leaky as an unstanched wench.

Boatswain. Lay her a-hold, a-hold ! set her two
courses off to sea again ; lay her off.

Enter Mariners *wet.*

Mariners. All lost ! to prayers, to prayers ! all
lost !

Boatswain. What, must our mouths be cold ?

Gonzalo. The king and prince at prayers ! let 's
assist them.
For our case is as theirs.

Sebastian. I 'm out of patience.

Antonio. We are merely cheated of our lives by
drunkards :
This wide-chapp'd rascal—would thou mightst lie
drowning

The washing of ten tides !
  Gonzalo.   He 'll be hang'd yet,
Though every drop of water swear against it
And gape at widest to glut him.
[*A confused noise within :* ' Mercy on us !—
' We split, we split ! '—' Farewell my wife and
    children ! '—
' Farewell, brother ! '—' We split, we split, we
    split ! ']
  Antonio. Let 's all sink with the king.
  Sebastian. Let 's take leave of him.
              [*Exeunt Antonio and Sebastian.*
  Gonzalo. Now would I give a thousand furlongs
of sea for an acre of barren ground, long heath,
brown furze, any thing. The wills above be
done ! but I would fain die a dry death. [*Exeunt.*

SCENE II. *The island.* *Before* PROSPERO'S *cell.*
      Enter PROSPERO *and* MIRANDA.

  Miranda. If by your art, my dearest father, you
    have
Put the wild waters in this roar, allay them.
The sky, it seems, would pour down stinking
    pitch,
But that the sea, mounting to the welkin's
    cheek,
Dashes the fire out. O, I have suffer'd
With those that I saw suffer : a brave vessel,
Who had, no doubt, some noble creature in her,
Dash'd all to pieces. O, the cry did knock
Against my very heart. Poor souls, they perish'd.
Had I been any god of power, I would
Have sunk the sea within the earth or ere
It should the good ship so have swallow'd and
The fraughting souls within her.
  Prospero.   Be collected :
No more amazement : tell your piteous heart
There 's no harm done.
  Miranda.   O, woe the day !
  Prospero.   No harm.
I have done nothing but in care of thee,
Of thee, my dear one, thee, my daughter, who
Art ignorant of what thou art, nought knowing
Of whence I am, nor that I am more better
Than Prospero, master of a full poor cell,
And thy no greater father.
  Miranda.   More to know
Did never meddle with my thoughts.
  Prospero.   'Tis time
I should inform thee farther. Lend thy hand,
And pluck my magic garment from me. So :
              [*Lays down his mantle.*
Lie there, my art. Wipe thou thine eyes ; have
    comfort.
The direful spectacle of the wreck, which touch'd
The very virtue of compassion in thee,
I have with such provision in mine art
So safely ordered that there is no soul—
No, not so much perdition as an hair
Betid to any creature in the vessel
Which thou heard'st cry, which thou saw'st sink.
  Sit down ;
For thou must now know farther.
  Miranda.   You have often
Begun to tell me what I am, but stopp'd
And left me to a bootless inquisition,
Concluding 'Stay : not yet.'
  Prospero.   The hour 's now come ;
The very minute bids thee ope thine ear :
Obey and be attentive. Canst thou remember
A time before we came unto this cell ?

I do not think thou canst, for then thou wast
    not
Out three years old.
  Miranda.   Certainly, sir, I can.
  Prospero. By what ? by any other house or person?
Of any thing the image tell me that
Hath kept with thy remembrance.
  Miranda.   'Tis far off
And rather like a dream than an assurance
That my remembrance warrants. Had I not
Four or five women once that tended me ?
  Prospero. Thou hadst, and more, Miranda. But
    how is it
That this lives in thy mind ? What seest thou
    else
In the dark backward and abysm of time ?
If thou remember'st aught ere thou camest here,
How thou camest here thou mayst.
  Miranda.   But that I do not.
  Prospero. Twelve year since, Miranda, twelve
    year since,
Thy father was the Duke of Milan and
A prince of power.
  Miranda.   Sir, are not you my father ?
  Prospero. Thy mother was a piece of virtue, and
She said thou wast my daughter ; and thy father
Was Duke of Milan ; and thou his only heir
And princess no worse issued.
  Miranda.   O the heavens !
What foul play had we, that we came from
    thence ?
Or blessed was 't we did ?
  Prospero.   Both, both, my girl:
By foul play, as thou say'st, were we heaved
    thence,
But blessedly holp hither.
  Miranda.   O, my heart bleeds
To think o' the teen that I have turn'd you to,
Which is from my remembrance ! Please you,
    farther.
  Prospero. My brother and thy uncle, call'd
    Antonio—
I pray thee, mark me—that a brother should
Be so perfidious !—he whom next thyself
Of all the world I loved and to him put
The manage of my state ; as at that time
Through all the signories it was the first
And Prospero the prime duke, being so reputed
In dignity, and for the liberal arts
Without a parallel ; those being all my study,
The government I cast upon my brother
And to my state grew stranger, being transported
And rapt in secret studies. Thy false uncle—
Dost thou attend me ?
  Miranda.   Sir, most heedfully.
  Prospero. Being once perfected how to grant
    suits,
How to deny them, who to advance and who
To trash for over-topping, new created
The creatures that were mine, I say, or changed
    'em,
Or else new form'd 'em ; having both the key
Of officer and office, set all hearts i' the state
To what tune pleased his ear ; that now he was
The ivy which had hid my princely trunk,
And suck'd my verdure out on 't. Thou at-
    tend'st not.
  Miranda. O, good sir, I do.
  Prospero.   I pray thee, mark me.
I, thus neglecting worldly ends, all dedicated
To closeness and the bettering of my mind

With that which, but by being so retired,
O'er-prized all popular rate, in my false brother
Awaked an evil nature ; and my trust,
Like a good parent, did beget of him
A falsehood in its contrary as great
As my trust was ; which had indeed no limit,
A confidence sans bound. He being thus lorded,
Not only with what my revenue yielded,
But what my power might else exact, like one
† Who having into truth, by telling of it,
Made such a sinner of his memory,
To credit his own lie, he did believe
He was indeed the duke ; out o' the substitution,
And executing the outward face of royalty,
With all prerogative : hence his ambition grow-
    ing—
Dost thou hear ?
   Miranda.   Your tale, sir, would cure deafness.
   Prospero.   To have no screen between this part
he play'd
And him he play'd it for, he needs will be
Absolute Milan. Me, poor man, my library
Was   dukedom   large   enough :   of   temporal
    royalties
He thinks me now incapable ; confederates—
So dry he was for sway—wi' the King of Naples
To give him annual tribute, do him homage,
Subject his coronet to his crown and bend
The dukedom yet unbow'd—alas, poor Milan !—
To most ignoble stooping.
   Miranda.   O the heavens !
   Prospero.   Mark his condition and the event ;
then tell me
If this might be a brother.
   Miranda.   I should sin
To think but nobly of my grandmother :
Good wombs have borne bad sons.
   Prospero.   Now the condition.
This King of Naples, being an enemy
To me inveterate, hearkens my brother's suit ;
Which was, that he, in lieu o' the premises
Of homage and I know not how much tribute,
Should presently extirpate me and mine
Out of the dukedom and confer fair Milan
With all the honours on my brother : whereon,
A treacherous army levied, one midnight
Fated to the purpose did Antonio open
The gates of Milan, and, i' the dead of darkness,
The ministers for the purpose hurried thence
Me and thy crying self.
   Miranda.   Alack, for pity !
I, not remembering how I cried out then,
Will cry it o'er again ; it is a hint
That wrings mine eyes to 't.
   Prospero.   Hear a little further
And then I 'll bring thee to the present business
Which now 's upon 's ; without the which this
    story
Were most impertinent.
   Miranda.   Wherefore did they not
That hour destroy us ?
   Prospero.   Well demanded, wench :
My   tale   provokes   that   question.   Dear,   they
    durst not,
So dear the love my people bore me, nor set
A mark so bloody on the business, but
With colours fairer painted their foul ends.
In few, they hurried us aboard a bark,
Bore   us   some   leagues   to   sea ;   where   they   pre-
    pared

A rotten carcass of a boat, not rigg'd,
Nor tackle, sail, nor mast ; the very rats
Instinctively have quit it : there they hoist us,
To cry to the sea that roar'd to us, to sigh
To the winds whose pity, sighing back again,
Did us but loving wrong.
   Miranda.   Alack, what trouble
Was I then to you !
   Prospero.   O, a cherubin
Thou wast that did preserve me. Thou didst
    smile,
Infused with a fortitude from heaven,
When I have deck'd the sea with drops full salt,
Under my burthen groan'd ; which raised in
    me
An undergoing stomach, to bear up
Against what should ensue.
   Miranda.   How came we ashore ?
   Prospero.   By Providence divine.
Some food we had and some fresh water that
A noble Neapolitan, Gonzalo,
Out of his charity, who being then appointed
Master of this design, did give us, with
Rich garments, linens, stuffs and necessaries,
Which   since   have   steaded   much ;   so,   of   his
    gentleness,
Knowing I loved my books, he furnish'd me
From mine own library with volumes that
I prize above my dukedom.
   Miranda.   Would I might
But ever see that man !
   Prospero.   Now I arise :   [*Resumes his mantle.*
Sit still, and hear the last of our sea-sorrow.
Here in this island we arrived ; and here
Have I, thy schoolmaster, made thee more
    profit
Than other princesses can that have more time
For vainer hours and tutors not so careful.
   Miranda.   Heavens thank you for 't ! And now,
    I pray you, sir,
For still 'tis beating in my mind, your reason
For raising this sea-storm ?
   Prospero.   Know thus far forth.
By accident most strange, bountiful Fortune,
Now my dear lady, hath mine enemies
Brought to this shore ; and by my prescience
I find my zenith doth depend upon
A most auspicious star, whose influence
If now I court not but omit, my fortunes
Will ever after droop. Here cease more ques-
    tions :
Thou art inclined to sleep ; 'tis a good dulness,
And give it way : I know thou canst not choose.
                              [*Miranda sleeps.*
Come away, servant, come. I am ready now.
Approach, my Ariel, come.

                Enter ARIEL.

   Ariel.   All hail, great master ! grave sir, hail !
    I come
To answer thy best pleasure ; be 't to fly,
To swim, to dive into the fire, to ride
On the curl'd clouds, to thy strong bidding task
Ariel and all his quality.
   Prospero.   Hast thou, spirit,
Perform'd to point the tempest that I bade thee ?
   Ariel.   To every article.
I boarded the king's ship ; now on the beak,
Now in the waist, the deck, in every cabin,
I flamed amazement : sometime I 'ld divide,

And burn in many places ; on the topmast,
The yards and bowsprit, would I flame distinctly,
Then meet and join.   Jove's lightnings the
   precursors
O' the dreadful thunder-claps, more momentary
And sight-outrunning were not ; the fire and
   cracks
Of sulphurous roaring the most mighty Neptune
Seem to besiege and make his bold waves
   tremble,
Yea, his dread trident shake.
Prospero.   My brave spirit !
Who was so firm, so constant, that this coil
Would not infect his reason ?
Ariel.   Not a soul
But felt a fever of the mad and play'd
Some tricks of desperation.   All but mariners
Plunged in the foaming brine and quit the
   vessel,
Then all afire with me : the king's son, Ferdi-
   nand,
With hair up-staring,—then like reeds, not
   hair,—
Was the first man that leap'd ; cried, ' Hell is
   empty,
And all the devils are here .'
Prospero.   Why, that 's my spirit !
But was not this nigh shore ?
Ariel.   Close by, my master.
Prospero.   But are they, Ariel, safe ?
Ariel.   Not a hair perish'd ;
On their sustaining garments not a blemish,
But fresher than before : and, as thou badest me,
In troops I have dispersed them 'bout the isle.
The king's son have I landed by himself ;
Whom I left cooling of the air with sighs
In an odd angle of the isle and sitting,
His arms in this sad knot.
Prospero.   Of the king's ship
The mariners say how thou hast disposed
And all the rest o' the fleet.
Ariel.   Safely in harbour
Is the king's ship ; in the deep nook, where
   once
Thou call'dst me up at midnight to fetch dew
From the still-vex'd Bermoothes, there she 's hid :
The mariners all under hatches stow'd ;
Who, with a charm join'd to their suffer'd
   labour,
I have left asleep : and for the rest o' the fleet
Which I dispersed, they all have met again
And are upon the Mediterranean flote,
Bound sadly home for Naples,
Supposing that they saw the king's ship wreck'd
And his great person perish.
Prospero.   Ariel, thy charge
Exactly is perform'd : but there 's more work.
What is the time o' the day ?
Ariel.   Past the mid season.
Prospero.   At least two glasses.   The time 'twixt
   six and now
Must by us both be spent most preciously.
Ariel.   Is there more toil ? Since thou dost
give me pains,
Let me remember thee what thou hast promised.
Which is not yet perform'd me.
Prospero.   How now ? moody ?
What is't thou canst demand ?
Ariel.   My liberty.
Prospero.   Before the time be out ? no more !

Ariel.   I prithee,
Remember I have done thee worthy service ;
Told thee no lies, made thee no mistakings,
   served
Without or grudge or grumblings : thou didst
   promise
To bate me a full year.
Prospero.   Dost thou forget
From what a torment I did free thee ?
Ariel.   No.
Prospero.   Thou dost, and think'st it much to
   tread the ooze
Of the salt deep,
To run upon the sharp wind of the north,
To do me business in the veins o' the earth
When it is baked with frost.
Ariel.   I do not, sir.
Prospero.   Thou liest, malignant thing ! Hast
   thou forgot
The foul witch Sycorax, who with age and envy
Was grown into a hoop ? hast thou forgot her ?
Ariel.   No, sir.
Prospero.   Thou hast.   Where was she born ?
   speak ; tell me.
Ariel.   Sir, in Argier.
Prospero.   O, was she so ? I must
Once in a month recount what thou hast been,
Which thou forget'st.   This damn'd witch
   Sycorax,
For mischiefs manifold and sorceries terrible
To enter human hearing, from Argier,
Thou know'st, was banish'd : for one thing she
   did
They would not take her life.   Is not this true ?
Ariel.   Ay, sir.
Prospero.   This blue-eyed hag was hither brought
   with child
And here was left by the sailors.   Thou, my
   slave,
As thou report'st thyself, wast then her servant ;
And, for thou wast a spirit too delicate
To act her earthy and abhorr'd commands,
Refusing her grand hests, she did confine thee,
By help of her more potent ministers
And in her most unmitigable rage,
Into a cloven pine ; within which rift
Imprison'd thou didst painfully remain
A dozen years ; within which space she died
And left thee there ; where thou didst vent thy
   groans
As fast as mill-wheels strike.   Then was this
   island—
Save for the son that she did litter here,
A freckled whelp hag-born—not honour'd with
A human shape.
Ariel.   Yes, Caliban her son.
Prospero.   Dull thing, I say so ; he, that Caliban
Whom now I keep in service.   Thou best
   know'st
What torment I did find thee in ; thy groans
Did make wolves howl and penetrate the breasts
Of ever angry bears ; it was a torment
To lay upon the damn'd, which Sycorax
Could not again undo : it was mine art,
When I arrived and heard thee, that made gape
The pine and let thee out.
Ariel.   I thank thee, master.
Prospero.   If thou more murmur'st, I will rend
   an oak
And peg thee in his knotty entrails till
Thou hast howl'd away twelve winters.

Ariel.   Pardon, master ;
I will be correspondent to command
And do my spiriting gently.
   Prospero.   Do so, and after two days
I will discharge thee.
   Ariel.   That 's my noble master !
What shall I do ? say what ; what shall I do ?
   Prospero. Go make thyself like a nymph o' the
    sea ; be subject
To no sight but thine and mine, invisible
To every eyeball else. Go take this shape
And hither come in 't : go, hence with diligence !
                           [Exit Ariel.
Awake, dear heart, awake ! thou hast slept well ;
Awake !
   Miranda. The strangeness of your story put
Heaviness in me.
   Prospero. Shake it off. Come on ;
We'll visit Caliban my slave, who never
Yields us kind answer.
   Miranda.   'Tis a villain, sir,
I do not love to look on.
   Prospero.   But, as 'tis,
We cannot miss him : he does make our fire,
Fetch in our wood and serves in offices
That profit us. What, ho ! slave ! Caliban !
Thou earth, thou ! speak.
   Caliban [*Within*] There 's wood enough within.
   Prospero. Come forth, I say ! there 's other
    business for thee ;
Come, thou tortoise ! when ?

     Re-enter ARIEL *like a water-nymph.*

Fine apparition ! My quaint Ariel,
Hark in thine ear.
   Ariel. My Lord, it shall be done. [*Exit.*
   Prospero. Thou poisonous slave, got by the devil
    himself
Upon thy wicked dam, come forth !

       Enter CALIBAN.

   Caliban. As wicked dew as e'er my mother
    brush'd
With raven's feather from unwholesome fen
Drop on you both ! a south-west blow on ye
And blister you all o'er !
   Prospero. For this, be sure, to-night thou shalt
    have cramps,
Side-stitches that shall pen thy breath up ;
    urchins
Shall, for that vast of night that they may work,
All exercise on thee ; thou shalt be pinch'd
As thick as honeycomb, each pinch more
    stinging
Than bees that made 'em.
   Caliban.   I must eat my dinner.
This island 's mine, by Sycorax my mother,
Which thou takest from me. When thou camest
    first,
Thou strokedst me and madest much of me,
    wouldst give me
Water with berries in 't, and teach me how
To name the bigger light, and how the less,
That burn by day and night : and then I loved thee
And show'd thee all the qualities o' the isle,
The fresh springs, brine-pits, barren place and
    fertile :
Cursed be I that did so ! All the charms
Of Sycorax, toads, beetles, bats, light on you !
For I am all the subjects that you have,

Which first was mine own king : and here you
    sty me
In this hard rock, whiles you do keep from me
The rest o' the island.
   Prospero.   Thou most lying slave,
Whom stripes may move, not kindness ! I have
    used thee,
Filth as thou art, with human care, and lodged
    thee
In mine own cell, till thou didst seek to violate
The honour of my child.
   Caliban. O ho, O ho ! would 't had been done !
Thou didst prevent me ; I had peopled else
This isle with Calibans.
   Prospero.   Abhorred slave,
Which any print of goodness wilt not take,
Being capable of all ill ! I pitied thee,
Took pains to make thee speak, taught thee each
    hour
One thing or other : when thou didst not, savage,
Know thine own meaning, but wouldst gabble like
A thing most brutish, I endow'd thy purposes
With words that made them known. But thy
    vile race,
Though thou didst learn, had that in 't which
    good natures
Could not abide to be with ; therefore wast thou
Deservedly confined into this rock,
Who hadst deserved more than a prison.
   Caliban. You taught me language ; and my
    profit on 't
Is, I know how to curse. The red plague rid you
For learning me your language !
   Prospero.   Hag-seed, hence !
Fetch us in fuel ; and be quick, thou 'rt best,
To answer other business. Shrug'st thou, malice ?
If thou neglect'st or dost unwillingly
What I command, I 'll rack thee with old cramps,
Fill all thy bones with aches, make thee roar
That beasts shall tremble at thy din.
   Caliban.   No, pray thee.
[*Aside*] I must obey : his art is of such power,
It would control my dam's god, Setebos,
And make a vassal of him.
   Prospero. So, slave ; hence ! [*Exit Caliban.*

Re-enter ARIEL, *invisible, playing and singing ;*
      FERDINAND *following.*

        ARIEL's *song*
    Come unto these yellow sands,
      And then take hands :
    Courtsied when you have and kiss'd
      The wild waves whist,
    Foot it featly here and there ;
    And, sweet sprites, the burthen bear.
Burthen [*dispersedly*]. Hark, hark !
                  Bow-wow.
    The watch-dogs bark :
                  Bow-wow.
   Ariel. Hark, hark ! I hear
      The strain of strutting chanticleer
      Cry, Cock-a-diddle-dow.
   Ferdinand. Where should this music be ? i' the
    air or the earth ?
It sounds no more : and, sure, it waits upon
Some god o' the island. Sitting on a bank,
Weeping again the king my father's wreck,
This music crept by me upon the waters,
Allaying both their fury and my passion

With its sweet air : thence I have follow'd it,
Or it hath drawn me rather. But 'tis gone.
No, it begins again.

ARIEL *sings.*

Full fathom five thy father lies ;
　Of his bones are coral made ;
Those are pearls that were his eyes :
　Nothing of him that doth fade
But doth suffer a sea-change
Into something rich and strange.
Sea-nymphs hourly rang his knell :
　　　　　　 Burthen. Ding-dong.
Ariel.　Hark ! now I hear them,—Ding-dong, bell.
Ferdinand.　The ditty does remember my drown'd
　father.
This is no mortal business, nor no sound
That the earth owes. I hear it now above me.
Prospero.　The fringed curtains of thine eye
　advance
And say what thou seest yond.
Miranda.　　　　　 What is 't ? a spirit ?
Lord, how it looks about ! Believe me, sir,
It carries a brave form. But 'tis a spirit.
Prospero.　No, wench ; it eats and sleeps and
　hath such senses
As we have, such. This gallant which thou seest
Was in the wreck ; and, but he 's something
　stain'd
With grief that 's beauty's canker, thou mightst
　call him
A goodly person : he hath lost his fellows
And strays about to find 'em.
Miranda.　　　　　 I might call him
A thing divine, for nothing natural
I ever saw so noble.
Prospero. [*Aside*]　It goes on, I see,
As my soul prompts it. Spirit, fine spirit ? I 'll
　free thee
Within two days for this.
Ferdinand.　　　　 Most sure, the goddess
On whom these airs attend ! Vouchsafe my
　prayer
May know if you remain upon this island ;
And that you will some good instruction give
How I may bear me here : my prime request,
Which I do last pronounce, is, O you wonder !
If you be maid or no ?
Miranda.　　　　 No wonder, sir :
But certainly a maid.
Ferdinand.　　　　 My language ! heavens !
I am the best of them that speak this speech,
Were I but where 'tis spoken.
Prospero.　　　　 How ? the best ?
What wert thou, if the King of Naples heard
　thee ?
Ferdinand.　A single thing, as I am now that
　wonders
To hear thee speak of Naples. He does hear me :
And that he does I weep : myself am Naples,
Who with mine eyes, never since at ebb, beheld
The king my father wreck'd.
Miranda.　　　　 Alack, for mercy !
Ferdinand.　Yes, faith, and all his lords ; the Duke
　of Milan
And his brave son being twain.
Prospero. [*Aside*]　The Duke of Milan
And his more braver daughter could control thee,
If how 'twere fit to do 't. At the first sight
They have changed eyes. Delicate Ariel,

I'll set thee free for this.　[*To Fer.*]　A word,
　good sir ;
I fear you have done yourself some wrong ; a
　word.
Miranda.　Why speaks my father so ungently ?
　This
Is the third man that e'er I saw, the first
That e'er I sigh'd for ; pity move my father
To be inclined my way !
Ferdinand.　　　　 O, if a virgin,
And your affection not gone forth, I 'll make you
The queen of Naples.
Prospero.　　　　 Soft, sir ! one word more.
[*Aside*] They are both in either's powers ; but
　this swift business
I must uneasy make, lest too light winning
Make the prize light.　[*To Fer.*]　One word
　more ; I charge thee
That thou attend me ; thou dost here usurp
The name thou owest not ; and hast put thyself
Upon this island as a spy, to win it
From me, the lord on 't.
Ferdinand.　　　　 No, as I am a man.
Miranda.　There 's nothing ill can dwell in such a
　temple :
If the ill spirit have so fair a house,
Good things will strive to dwell with 't.
Prospero.　　　　 Follow me.
Speak not you for him ; he 's a traitor. Come ;
I 'll manacle thy neck and feet together :
Sea-water shalt thou drink ; thy food shall be
The fresh-brook muscles, wither'd roots and
　husks
Wherein the acorn cradled. Follow.
Ferdinand.　　　　 No ;
I will resist such entertainment till
Mine enemy has more power.
　　　　 [*Draws, and is charmed from moving.*
Miranda.　　　　 O dear father,
Make not too rash a trial of him, for
He 's gentle and not fearful.
Prospero.　　　　 What ? I say,
My foot my tutor ? Put thy sword up, traitor ;
Who makest a show but darest not strike, thy
　conscience
Is so possess'd with guilt ; come from thy ward,
For I can here disarm thee with this stick
And make thy weapon drop.
Miranda.　　　　 Beseech you, father.
Prospero.　Hence ! hang not on my garments.
Miranda.　　　　 Sir, have pity ;
I 'll be his surety.
Prospero.　　　　 Silence ! one word more
Shall make me chide thee, if not hate thee.
　What !
An advocate for an impostor ! hush !
Thou think'st there is no more such shapes as he,
Having seen but him and Caliban : foolish
　wench !
To the most of men this is a Caliban
And they to him are angels.
Miranda.　　　　 My affections
Are then most humble ; I have no ambition
To see a goodlier man.
Prospero.　　　　 Come on ; obey :
Thy nerves are in their infancy again
And have no vigour in them.
Ferdinand.　　　　 So they are :
My spirits, as in a dream, are all bound up.
My father's loss, the weakness which I feel,
The wreck of all my friends, nor this man's threats,

To whom I am subdued, are but light to me,
Might I but through my prison once a day
Behold this maid : all corners else o' the earth
Let liberty make use of ; space enough
Have I in such a prison.
Prospero. [*Aside*] It works. [*To Fer.*] Come on.
Thou hast done well, fine Ariel ! [*To Fer.*]
  Follow me.
[*To Ariel.*] Hark what thou else shalt do me.
Miranda.   Be of comfort ;
My father 's of a better nature, sir,
Than he appears by speech : this is unwonted
Which now came from him.
Prospero.   Thou shalt be as free
As mountain winds : but then exactly do
All points of my command.
Ariel.   To the syllable.
Prospero. Come, follow. Speak not for him.
                                      [*Exeunt.*

ACT II.

SCENE I. *Another part of the island.*

Enter ALONSO, SEBASTIAN, ANTONIO, GONZALO
    ADRIAN, FRANCISCO, *and others.*

Gonzalo.

B eseech you, sir, be merry ; you have cause,
    So have we all, of joy ; for our escape
    Is much beyond our loss. Our hint of woe
Is common ; every day some sailor's wife,
The masters of some merchant and the merchant
Have just our theme of woe ; but for the miracle,
I mean our preservation, few in millions
Can speak like us : then wisely, good sir, weigh
Our sorrow with our comfort.
Alonzo.   Prithee, peace.
Sebastian. He receives comfort like cold porridge.
Antonio. The visitor will not give him o'er so.
Sebastian. Look, he 's winding up the watch of
his wit ; by and by it will strike.
Gonzalo. Sir,—
Sebastian. One : tell.
Gonzalo. When every grief is entertain'd that 's
offer'd,
Comes to the entertainer—
Sebastian. A dollar.
Gonzalo. Dolour comes to him, indeed : you have
spoken truer than you purposed.
Sebastian. You have taken it wiselier than I meant
you should.
Gonzalo. Therefore, my lord,—
Antonio. Fie, what a spendthrift is he of his
tongue !
Alonzo. I prithee, spare.
Gonzalo. Well, I have done ; but yet,—
Sebastian. He will be talking.
Antonio. Which, of he or Adrian, for a good
wager, first begins to crow ?
Sebastian. The old cock.
Antonio. The cockerel.
Sebastian. Done. The wager ?
Antonio. A laughter.
Sebastian. A match !
Adrian. Though this island seem to be desert,—
Sebastian. Ha, ha, ha ! So, you're paid.
Adrian. Uninhabitable and almost inacces-
sible,—
Sebastian. Yet,—
Adrian. Yet,—

Antonio. He could not miss 't.
Adrian. It must needs be of subtle, tender and
delicate temperance.
Antonio. Temperance was a delicate wench.
Sebastian. Ay, and a subtle ; as he most learnedly
delivered.
Adrian. The air breathes upon us here most
sweetly.
Sebastian. As if it had lungs and rotten ones.
Antonio. Or as 'twere perfumed by a fen.
Gonzalo. Here is every thing advantageous to life.
Antonio. True ; save means to live.
Sebastian. Of that there 's none, or little.
Gonzalo. How lush and lusty the grass looks !
how green !
Antonio. The ground indeed is tawny.
Sebastian. With an eye of green in 't.
Antonio. He misses not much.
Sebastian. No ; he doth but mistake the truth
totally.
Gonzalo. But the rarity of it is,—which is indeed
almost, beyond credit,—
Sebastian. As many vouched rarities are.
Gonzalo. That our garments, being, as they were,
drenched in the sea, hold notwithstanding their
freshness and glosses, being rather new-dyed
than stained with salt water.
Antonio. If but one of his pockets could speak,
would it not say he lies ?
Sebastian. Ay, or very falsely pocket up his report.
Gonzalo. Methinks our garments are now as
fresh as when we put them on first in Afric, at
the marriage of the king's fair daughter Claribel
to the King of Tunis.
Sebastian. 'Twas a sweet marriage, and we prosper
well in our return.
Adrian. Tunis was never graced before with
such a paragon to their queen.
Gonzalo. Not since widow Dido's time.
Antonio. Widow ! a pox o' that ! How came that
widow in ? widow Dido !
Sebastian. What if he had said ' widower
Æneas ' too ? Good Lord, how you take it !
Adrian. ' Widow Dido ' said you ? you make me
study of that : she was of Carthage, not of Tunis.
Gonzalo. This Tunis, sir, was Carthage.
Adrian. Carthage ?
Gonzalo. I assure you, Carthage.
Sebastian. His word is more than the miraculous
harp ; he hath raised the wall and houses too.
Antonio. What impossible matter will he make
easy next ?
Sebastian. I think he will carry this island home
in his pocket and give it his son for an apple.
Antonio. And, sowing the kernels of it in the
sea, bring forth more islands.
Gonzalo. Ay.
Antonio. Why, in good time.
Gonzalo. Sir, we were talking that our garments
seem now as fresh as when we were at Tunis at
the marriage of your daughter, who is now queen.
Antonio. And the rarest that e'er came there.
Sebastian. Bate, I beseech you, widow Dido.
Antonio. O, widow Dido ! ay, widow Dido.
Gonzalo. Is not, sir, my doublet as fresh as the
first day I wore it ? I mean, in a sort.
Antonio. That sort was well fished for.
Gonzalo. When I wore it at your daughter's
marriage ?
Alonso. You cram these words into mine ears
against

The stomach of my sense. Would I had never
Married my daughter there ! for, coming thence,
My son is lost and, in my rate, she too,
Who is so far from Italy removed.
I ne'er again shall see her. O thou mine heir
Of Naples and of Milan, what strange fish
Hath made his meal on thee ?
    Francisco.   Sir, he may live :
I saw him beat the surges under him,
And ride upon their backs ; he trod the water,
Whose enmity he flung aside, and breasted
The surge most swoln that met him ; his bold
    head
'Bove the contentious waves he kept, and oar'd
Himself with his good arms in lusty stroke
To the shore, that o'er his wave-worn basis bow'd,
As stooping to relieve him : I not doubt
He came alive to land.
    Alonso.   No, no, he 's gone.
    Sebastian.   Sir, you may thank yourself for this
    great loss,
That would not bless our Europe with your
    daughter,
But rather lose her to an African :
Where she at least is banish'd from your eye,
Who hath cause to wet the grief on 't.
    Alonso.   Prithee, peace.
    Sebastian.   You were kneel'd to and importuned
    otherwise
By all of us, and the fair soul herself
Weigh'd between loathness and obedience, at
Which end o' the beam should bow.   We have
    lost your son,
I fear, for ever : Milan and Naples have
Moe widows in them of this business' making
Than we bring men to comfort them :
The fault 's your own.
    Alonso.   So is the dear'st o' the loss.
    Gonzalo.   My lord Sebastian,
The truth you speak doth lack some gentleness
And time to speak it in : you rub the sore,
When you should bring the plaster.
    Sebastian.   Very well.
    Antonio.   And most chirurgeonly.
    Gonzalo.   It is foul weather in us all, good sir,
When you are cloudy.
    Sebastian.   Foul weather ?
    Antonio.   Very foul.
    Gonzalo.   Had I plantation of this isle, my lord,—
    Antonio.   He' ld sow 't with nettle-seed.
    Sebastian.   Or docks, or mallows.
    Gonzalo.   And were the king on 't, what would I
    do ?
    Sebastian.   'Scape being drunk for want of wine.
    Gonzalo.   I' the commonwealth I would by con-
    traries
Execute all things ; for no kind of traffic
Would I admit ; no name of magistrate ;
Letters should not be known ; riches, poverty,
And use of service, none ; contract, succession,
Bourn, bound of land, tilth, vineyard, none ;
No use of metal, corn, or wine or oil ;
No occupation ; all men idle, all ;
And women too, but innocent and pure ;
No sovereignty :—
    Sebastian.   Yet he would be king on 't.
    Antonio.   The latter end of his commonwealth
forgets the beginning.
    Gonzalo.   All things in common nature should
    produce

Without sweat or endeavour : treason, felony,
Sword, pike, knife, gun, or need of any engine,
Would I not have ; but nature should bring forth,
Of it own kind, all foison, all abundance,
To feed my innocent people.
    Sebastian.   No marrying 'mong his subjects ?
    Antonio.   None, man ; all idle : whores and
    knaves.
    Gonzalo.   I would with such perfection govern,
    sir,
To excel the golden age.
    Sebastian.   God save his majesty !
    Antonio.   Long live Gonzalo !
    Gonzalo.   And,—do you mark me, sir ?
    Alonso.   Prithee, no more : thou dost talk no-
thing to me.
    Gonzalo.   I do well believe your highness ; and
did it to minister occasion to these gentlemen,
who are of such sensible and nimble lungs that
they always use to laugh at nothing.
    Antonio.   'Twas you we laughed at.
    Gonzalo.   Who in this kind of merry fooling am
nothing to you : so you may continue and laugh
at nothing still.
    Antonio.   What a blow was there given !
    Sebastian.   An it had not fallen flat-long.
    Gonzalo.   You are gentlemen of brave mettle ;
you would lift the moon out of her sphere, if she
would continue in it five weeks without changing.

Enter ARIEL, *invisible, playing solemn music.*

    Sebastian.   We would so, and then go a bat-fowling.
    Antonio.   Nay, good my lord, be not angry.
    Gonzalo.   No, I warrant you ; I will not adven-
ture my discretion so weakly. Will you laugh
me asleep, for I am very heavy ?
    Antonio.   Go sleep, and hear us.
           [*All sleep except Alon., Seb., and Ant.*
    Alonso.   What, all so soon asleep ! I wish mine
    eyes
Would, with themselves, shut up my thoughts :
    I find
They are inclined to do so.
    Sebastian.   Please you, sir,
Do not omit the heavy offer of it :
It seldom visits sorrow ; when it doth,
It is a comforter.
    Antonio.   We two, my lord,
Will guard your person while you take your rest,
And watch your safety.
    Alonso.   Thank you. Wondrous heavy.
           [*Alonso sleeps. Exit Ariel.*
    Sebastian.   What a strange drowsiness possesses
    them !
    Antonio.   It is the quality o' the climate.
    Sebastian.   Why
Doth it not then our eyelids sink ? I find not
Myself disposed to sleep.
    Antonio.   Nor I ; my spirits are nimble.
They fell together all, as by consent ;
They dropp'd, as by a thunder-stroke.   What
    might,
Worthy Sebastian ? O, what might ?—No more :—
And yet methinks I see it in thy face,
What thou shouldst be : the occasion speaks thee,
    and
My strong imagination sees a crown
Dropping upon thy head.
    Sebastian.   What, art thou waking ?
    Antonio.   Do you not hear me speak ?
    Sebastian.   I do ; and surely

It is a sleepy language and thou speak'st
Out of thy sleep. What is it thou didst say ?
This is a strange repose, to be asleep
With eyes wide open ; standing, speaking,
　　moving,
And yet so fast asleep.
　　Antonio.　　　　　　Noble Sebastian,
Thou 'let'st thy fortune sleep—die, rather ;
　　wink'st
Whiles thou art waking.
　　Sebastian.　　　　　　Thou dost snore distinctly ;
There 's meaning in thy snores.
　　Antonio. I am more serious than my custom : you
Must be so too, if heed me ; which to do
Trebles thee o'er.
　　Sebastian.　　Well, I am standing water.
　　Antonio. I 'll teach you how to flow.
　　Sebastian.　　　　　　Do so : to ebb
Hereditary sloth instructs me.
　　Antonio.　　　　　O,
If you but knew how you the purpose cherish
Whiles thus you mock it ! how, in stripping it,
You more invest it ! Ebbing men, indeed,
Most often do so near the bottom run
By their own fear or sloth.
　　Sebastian.　　　　Prithee, say on :
The setting of thine eye and cheek proclaim
A matter from thee, and a birth indeed
Which throes thee much to yield.
　　Antonio.　　　　　Thus, sir :
Although this lord of weak remembrance, this,
Who shall be of as little memory
When he is earth'd, hath here almost persuaded,—
For he 's a spirit of persuasion, only
Professes to persuade,—the king his son 's alive,
'Tis as impossible that he 's undrown'd
As he that sleeps here swims.
　　Sebastian.　　　　I have no hope
That he 's undrown'd.
　　Antonio.　　　　O, out of that ' no hope '
What great hope have you ! no hope that way
　　is
Another way so high a hope that even
Ambition cannot pierce a wink beyond,
But doubt discovery there. Will you grant
　　with me
That Ferdinand is drown'd ?
　　Sebastian.　　　　He 's gone.
　　Antonio.　　　　　Then, tell me,
Who 's the next heir of Naples ?
　　Sebastian.　　　　　Claribel.
　　Antonio. She that is queen of Tunis ; she that
　　dwells
Ten leagues beyond man's life ; she that from
　　Naples
Can have no note, unless the sun were post—
The man i' the moon 's too slow—till new-born
　　chins
Be rough and razorable ; she that—from whom ?
We all were sea-swallow'd, though some cast
　　again,
And by that destiny to perform an act
Where of what 's past is prologue, what to come
In yours and my discharge.
　　Sebastian. What stuff is this ! how say you ?
'Tis true, my brother's daughter 's queen of
　　Tunis ;
So is she heir of Naples ; 'twixt which regions
There is some space.
　　Antonio.　　　　A space whose every cubit

Seems to cry out, ' How shall that Claribel
Measure us back to Naples ? Keep in Tunis,
And let Sebastian wake.' Say, this were death
That now hath seized them ; why, they were no
　　worse
Than now they are. There be that can rule
　　Naples
As well as he that sleeps ; lords that can prate
As amply and unnecessarily
As this Gonzalo ; I myself could make
A chough of as deep chat. O, that you bore
The mind that I do ! what a sleep were this
For your advancement ! Do you understand me ?
　　Sebastian. Methinks I do.
　　Antonio.　　　　And how does your content
Tender your own good fortune ?
　　Sebastian.　　　　　I remember
You did supplant your brother Prospero.
　　Antonio.　　　　　　True :
And look how well my garments sit upon me ;
Much feater than before : my brother's servants
Were then my fellows ; now they are my men.
　　Sebastian. But, for your conscience ?
　　Antonio. Ay, sir ; where lies that ? if 'twere a
　　kibe,
'Twould put me to my slipper : but I feel not
This deity in my bosom : twenty consciences,
That stand 'twixt me and Milan, candied be they
And melt ere they molest ! Here lies your
　　brother,
No better than the earth he lies upon,
If he were that which now he 's like, that 's dead :
Whom I, with this obedient steel, three inches
　　of it,
Can lay to bed for ever ; whiles you, doing thus,
To the perpetual wink for aye might put
This ancient morsel, this Sir Prudence, who
Should not upbraid our course. For all the
　　rest,
They 'll take suggestion as a cat laps milk ;
They 'll tell the clock to any business that
We say befits the hour.
　　Sebastian.　　　　Thy case, dear friend,
Shall be my precedent ; as thou got'st Milan,
I'll come by Naples. Draw thy sword : one
　　stroke
Shall free thee from the tribute which thou
　　payest ;
And I the king shall love thee.
　　Antonio.　　　　　Draw together ;
And when I rear my hand, do you the like,
To fall it on Gonzalo.
　　Sebastian. O, but one word. [*They talk apart.*

Re-enter ARIEL, *invisible.*

　　Ariel. My master through his art foresees the
　　danger
That you, his friend, are in ; and sends me
　　forth—
For else his project dies—to keep them living.
　　　　　　　　　　[*Sings in Gonzalo's ear.*
　　　While you here do snoring lie,
　　　Open-eyed conspiracy
　　　　　His time doth take.
　　　If of life you keep a care,
　　　Shake off slumber, and beware :
　　　　　Awake, awake !
　　Antonio. Then let us both be sudden.
　　Gonzalo.　　　　　Now, good angels
Preserve the king.　　　　　　[*They wake.*

Alonso. Why, how now? ho, awake! Why are you drawn?

Wherefore this ghastly looking?

Gonzalo. What 's the matter?

Sebastian. Whiles we stood here securing your repose,
Even now, we heard a hollow burst of bellowing
Like bulls, or rather lions : did 't not wake you?
It struck mine ear most terribly.

Alonso. I heard nothing.

Antonio. O, 'twas a din to fright a monster's ear,
To make an earthquake! sure, it was the roar
Of a whole herd of lions.

Alonso. Heard you this, Gonzalo?

Gonzalo. Upon mine honour, sir, I heard a humming,
And that a strange one too, which did awake me :
I shaked you, sir, and cried : as mine eyes open'd,
I saw their weapons drawn : there was a noise,
That 's verily. 'Tis best we stand upon our guard,
Or that we quit this place : let 's draw our weapons.

Alonso. Lead off this ground ; and let 's make further search
For my poor son.

Gonzalo. Heavens keep him from these beasts!
For he is, sure, i' the island.

Alonso. Lead away.

Ariel. Prospero my lord shall know what I have done :
So, king, go safely on to seek thy son. [*Exeunt.*

SCENE II. *Another part of the island.*

Enter CALIBAN *with a burden of wood. A noise of thunder heard.*

Caliban. All the infections that the sun sucks up
From bogs, fens, flats, on Prosper fall and make him
By inch-meal a disease! His spirits hear me
And yet I needs must curse. But they 'll nor pinch,
Fright me with urchin-shows, pitch me i' the mire,
Nor lead me, like a firebrand, in the dark
Out of my way, unless he bid 'em ; but
For every trifle are they set upon me ;
Sometime like apes that mow and chatter at me
And after bite me, then like hedgehogs which
Lie tumbling in my barefoot way and mount
Their pricks at my footfall ; sometime am I
All wound with adders who with cloven tongues
Do hiss me into madness.

Enter TRINCULO.

Lo, now, lo!
Here comes a spirit of his, and to torment me
For bringing wood in slowly. I 'll fall flat ;
Perchance he will not mind me.

Trinculo. Here 's neither bush nor shrub, to bear off any weather at all, and another storm brewing ; I hear it sing i' the wind : yond same black cloud, yond huge one, looks like a foul bombard that would shed his liquor. If it should thunder as it did before, I know not where to hide my head ; yond same cloud cannot choose but fall by pailfuls. What have we here? a man or a fish? dead or alive? A fish : he smells like a fish ; a very ancient and fish-like smell ; a kind of not of the newest Poor-John. A strange fish! Were I in England now, as once I was, and had but this fish painted, not a holiday fool there but would give a piece of silver : there would this monster make a man ; any strange beast there makes a man : when they will not give a doit to relieve a lame beggar, they will lay out ten to see a dead Indian. Legged, like a man! and his fins like arms! Warm o' my troth! I do now let loose my opinion ; hold it no longer : this is no fish, but an islander, that hath lately suffered by a thunderbolt. [*Thunder.*] Alas, the storm is come again! my best way is to creep under his gaberdine ; there is no other shelter hereabout : misery acquaints a man with strange bed-fellows. I will here shroud till the dregs of the storm be past.

Enter STEPHANO, *singing ; a bottle in his hand.*

Stephano. I shall no more to sea, to sea,
 Here shall I die ashore—
This is a very scurvy tune to sing at a man's funeral : well, here 's my comfort. [*Drinks.*
[*Sings.*
 The master, the swabber, the boatswain and I,
  The gunner and his mate
 Loved Mall, Meg and Marian and Margery,
  But none of us cared for Kate ;
  For she had a tongue with a tang,
  Would cry to a sailor, Go hang!
 She loved not the savour of tar nor of pitch,
 Yet a tailor might scratch her where'er she did itch :
  Then to sea, boys, and let her go hang!
This is a cusrvy tune too : but here's my comfort. [*Drinks.*

Caliban. Do not torment me : Oh!

Stephano. What 's the matter? Have we devils here? Do you put tricks upon 's with savages and men of Ind, ha? I have not 'scaped drowning to be afeard now of your four legs ; for it hath been said, As proper a man as ever went on four legs cannot make him give ground ; and it shall be said so again while Stephano breathes at nostrils.

Caliban. The spirit torments me ; Oh!

Stephano. This is some monster of the isle with four legs, who hath got as I take it, an ague. Where the devil should he learn our language? I will give him some relief, if it be but for that. If I can recover him and keep him tame and get to Naples with him, he 's a present for any emperor that ever trod on neat's-leather.

Caliban. Do not torment me, prithee ; I 'll bring my wood home faster.

Stephano. He 's in his fit now and does not talk after the wisest. He shall taste of my bottle : if he have never drunk wine afore, it will go near to remove his fit. If I can recover him and keep him tame, I will not take too much for him ; he shall pay for him that hath him, and that soundly.

Caliban. Thou dost me yet but little hurt ; thou wilt anon, I know it by thy trembling : now Prosper works upon thee.

Stephano. Come on your ways ; open your mouth ;

here is that which will give language to you, cat: open your mouth; this will shake your shaking, I can tell you, and that soundly: you cannot tell who 's your friend: open your chaps again.

Trinculo. I should know that voice: it should be—but he is drowned; and these are devils: O defend me!

Stephano. Four legs and two voices: a most delicate monster! His forward voice now is to speak well of his friend; his backward voice is to utter foul speeches and to detract. If all the wine in my bottle will recover him, I will help his ague. Come. Amen! I will pour some in thy other mouth.

Trinculo. Stephano!

Stephano. Doth thy other mouth call me? Mercy, mercy! This is a devil, and no monster: I will leave him; I have no long spoon.

Trinculo. Stephano! If thou beest Stephano, touch me and speak to me; for I am Trinculo—be not afeard—thy good friend Trinculo.

Stephano. If thou beest Trinculo, come forth: I 'll pull thee by the lesser legs: if any be Trinculo's legs, these are they. Thou art very Trinculo indeed! How camest thou to be the siege of this moon-calf? can he vent Trinculos?

Trinculo. I took him to be killed with a thunder-stroke. But art thou not drowned, Stephano? I hope now thou art not drowned. Is the storm overblown? I had me under the dead moon-calf's gaberdine for fear of the storm. And art thou living, Stephano? O Stephano, two Neapolitans 'scaped!

Stephano. Prithee, do not turn me about; my stomach is not constant.

Caliban. [*Aside*] These be fine things, an if they be not sprites.
That 's a brave god and bears celestial liquor. I will kneel to him.

Stephano. How didst thou 'scape? How comest thou hither? swear by this bottle how thou camest hither. I escaped upon a butt of sack which the sailors heaved o'erboard, by this bottle! which I made of the bark of a tree with mine own hands since I was cast ashore.

Caliban. I 'll swear upon that bottle to be thy true subject; for the liquor is not earthly.

Stephano. Here; swear then how thou escapedst.

Trinculo. Swum ashore, man, like a duck: I can swim like a duck, I 'll be sworn.

Stephano. Here, kiss the book. Though thou canst swim like a duck, thou art made like a goose.

Trinculo. O Stephano, hast any more of this?

Stephano. The whole butt, man: my cellar is in a rock by the sea-side where my wine is hid. How now, moon-calf! how does thine ague?

Caliban. Hast thou not dropp'd from heaven?

Stephano. Out o' the moon, I do assure thee: I was the man i' the moon when time was.

Caliban. I have seen thee in her and I do adore thee:
My mistress show'd me thee and thy dog and thy bush.

Stephano. Come, swear to that; kiss the book: I will furnish it anon with new contents: swear.

Trinculo. By this good light, this is a very shallow monster! I afeard of him! A very weak monster! The man i' the moon! A

most poor credulous monster! Well drawn, monster, in good sooth!

Caliban. I 'll show thee every fertile inch o' th' island;
And I will kiss thy foot: I prithee, be my god.

Trinculo. By this light, a most perfidious and drunken monster! when 's god's asleep, he 'll rob his bottle.

Caliban. I 'll kiss thy foot; I 'll swear myself thy subject.

Stephano. Come on then; down, and swear.

Trinculo. I shall laugh myself to death at this puppy-headed monster. A most scurvy monster! I could find in my heart to beat him,—

Stephano. Come, kiss.

Trinculo. But that the poor monster 's in drink: an abominable monster!

Caliban. I 'll show thee the best springs; I 'll pluck thee berries;
I 'll fish for thee and get thee wood enough.
A plague upon the tyrant that I serve!
I 'll bear him no more sticks, but follow thee,
Thou wondrous man.

Trinculo. A most ridiculous monster, to make a wonder of a poor drunkard!

Caliban. I prithee, let me bring thee where crabs grow;
And I with my long nails will dig thee pig-nuts;
Show thee a jay's nest and instruct thee how
To snare the nimble marmoset; I 'll bring thee
To clustering filberts and sometimes I 'll get thee
Young scamels from the rock. Wilt thou go with me?

Stephano. I prithee now, lead the way without any more talking. Trinculo, the king and all our company else being drowned, we will inherit here: here; bear my bottle: fellow Trinculo, we 'll fill him by and by again.

Caliban. [*Sings drunkenly*]
Farewell, master; farewell, farewell!

Trinculo. A howling monster; a drunken monster!

Caliban. No more dams I 'll make for fish;
    Nor fetch in firing
    At requiring;
  Nor scrape trencher, nor wash dish:
    'Ban, 'Ban, Cacaliban
    Has a new master: get a new man.
Freedom, hey-day! hey-day, freedom! freedom, hey-day, freedom!

Stephano. O brave monster! lead the way.
[*Exeunt.*

ACT III.

SCENE I. *Before* Prospero's *cell.*

Enter Ferdinand, *bearing a log.*

Ferdinand.

There be some sports are painful, and their labour
  Delight in them sets off: some kinds of baseness
Are nobly undergone and most poor matters
Point to rich ends. This my mean task
Would be as heavy to me as odious, but
The mistress which I serve quickens what 's dead
And makes my labours pleasures: O, she is
Ten times more gentle than her father 's crabbed,
And he 's composed of harshness. I must remove
Some thousands of these logs and pile them up,

Upon a sore injunction : my sweet mistress
Weeps when she sees me work, and says, such baseness
Had never like executor. I forget :
But these sweet thoughts do even refresh my labours,
† Most busy lest, when I do it.

Enter MIRANDA ; and PROSPERO at a distance, unseen.

Miranda.   Alas, now, pray you,
Work not so hard : I would the lightning had
Burnt up those logs that you are enjoin'd to pile !
Pray, set it down and rest you : when this burns,
'Twill weep for having wearied you. My father
Is hard at study ; pray now, rest yourself ;
He 's safe for these three hours.
Ferdinand.   O most dear mistress,
The sun will set before I shall discharge
What I must strive to do.
Miranda.   If you 'll sit down,
I 'll bear your logs the while : pray, give me that ;
I 'll carry it to the pile.
Ferdinand.   No, precious creature :
I had rather crack my sinews, break my back,
Than you should such dishonour undergo,
While I sit lazy by.
Miranda.   It would become me
As well as it does you : and I should do it
With much more ease ; for my good will is to it,
And yours it is against.
Prospero.   Poor worm, thou art infected !
This visitation shows it.
Miranda.   You look wearily.
Ferdinand. No, noble mistress ; 'tis fresh morning with me
When you are by at night. I do beseech you—
Chiefly that I might set it in my prayers—
What is your name ?
Miranda.   Miranda.—O my father,
I have broke your hest to say so !
Ferdinand.   Admired Miranda !
Indeed the top of admiration ! worth
What 's dearest to the world ! Full many a lady
I have eyed with best regard and many a time
The harmony of their tongues hath into bondage
Brought my too diligent ear : for several virtues
Have I liked several women ; never any
With so full soul, but some defect in her
Did quarrel with the noblest grace she owed
And put it to the foil : but you, O you,
So perfect and so peerless, are created
Of every creature's best !
Miranda.   I do not know
One of my sex ; no woman's face remember,
Save, from my glass, mine own ; nor have I seen
More that I may call men than you, good friend,
And my dear father : how features are abroad,
I am skilless of ; but, by my modesty,
The jewel in my dower, I would not wish
Any companion in the world but you,
Nor can imagination form a shape,
Besides yourself, to like of. But I prattle
Something too wildly and my father's precepts
I therein do forget.
Ferdinand.   I am in my condition
A prince, Miranda ; I do think, a king ;
I would, not so !—and would no more endure

This wooden slavery than to suffer
The flesh-fly blow my mouth. Hear my soul speak :
The very instant that I saw you, did
My heart fly to your service ; there resides,
To make me slave to it ; and for your sake
Am I this patient log-man.
Miranda.   Do you love me ?
Ferdinand. O heaven, O earth bear witness to this sound
And crown what I profess with kind event
If I speak true ! if hollowly, invert
What best is boded me to mischief ! I
Beyond all limit of what else i' the world
Do love, prize, honour you.
Miranda.   I am a fool
To weep at what I am glad of.
Prospero.   Fair encounter
Of two most rare affections ! Heavens rain grace
On that which breeds between 'em !
Ferdinand.   Wherefore weep you ?
Miranda. At mine unworthiness that dare not offer
What I desire to give, and much less take
What I shall die to want. But this is trifling ;
And all the more it seeks to hide itself,
The bigger bulk it shows. Hence, bashful cunning !
And prompt me, plain and holy innocence !
I am your wife, if you will marry me ;
If not, I 'll die your maid : to be your fellow
You may deny me : but I 'll be your servant,
Whether you will or no.
Ferdinand.   My mistress, dearest ;
And I thus humble ever.
Miranda.   My husband, then ?
Ferdinand. Ay, with a heart as willing
As bondage e'er of freedom : here 's my hand.
Miranda. And mine, with my heart in 't : and now farewell
Till half an hour hence.
Ferdinand.   A thousand thousand !
     [Exeunt Fer. and Mir. severally.
Prospero. So glad of this as they I cannot be,
Who are surprised withal ; but my rejoicing
At nothing can be more. I 'll to my book,
For yet ere supper-time must I perform
Much business appertaining.   *[Exit.*

SCENE II. *Another part of the island.*

Enter CALIBAN, STEPHANO, and TRINCULO.

Stephano. Tell not me ; when the butt is out, we will drink water ; not a drop before : therefore bear up, and board 'em. Servant-monster, drink to me.
Trinculo. Servant-monster ! the folly of this island ! They say there 's but five upon this isle : we are three of them ; if th' other two be brained like us, the state totters.
Stephano. Drink, servant-monster, when I bid thee : thy eyes are almost set in thy head.
Trinculo. Where should they be set else ? he were a brave monster indeed, if they were set in his tail.
Stephano. My man-monster hath drown'd his tongue in sack : for my part, the sea cannot drown me ; I swam, ere I could recover the shore, five and thirty leagues off and on. By

this light, thou shalt be my lieutenant, monster, or my standard.

Trinculo. Your lieutenant, if you list ; he 's no standard.

Stephano. We 'll not run, Monsieur Monster.

Trinculo. Nor go neither ; but you 'll lie like dogs and yet say nothing neither.

Stephano. Moon-calf, speak once in thy life, if thou beest a good moon-calf.

Caliban. How does thy honour ? Let me lick thy shoe.
I 'll not serve him ; he is not valiant.

Trinculo. Thou liest, most ignorant monster : I am in case to justle a constable. Why, thou deboshed fish, thou, was there ever man a coward that hath drunk so much sack as I to-day ? Wilt thou tell a monstrous lie, being but half a fish and half a monster ?

Caliban. Lo, how he mocks me ! wilt thou let him, my lord ?

Trinculo. ' Lord ' quoth he ! That a monster should be such a natural !

Caliban. Lo, lo, again ! bite him to death, I prithee.

Stephano. Trinculo, keep a good tongue in your head : if you prove a mutineer,—the next tree ! The poor monster 's my subject and he shall not suffer indignity.

Caliban. I thank my noble lord. Wilt thou be pleased to hearken once again to the suit I made to thee ?

Stephano. Marry, will I : kneel and repeat it ; I will stand, and so shall Trinculo.

Enter Ariel, *invisible.*

Caliban. As I told thee before, I am subject to a tyrant, a sorcerer, that by his cunning hath cheated me of the island.

Ariel. Thou liest.

Caliban. Thou liest, thou jesting monkey, thou : I would my valiant master would destroy thee ! I do not lie.

Stephano. Trinculo, if you trouble him any more in 's tale, by this hand, I will supplant some of your teeth.

Trinculo. Why, I said nothing.

Stephano. Mum, then, and no more. Proceed.

Caliban. I say, by sorcery he got this isle ; From me he got it. If thy greatness will Revenge it on him,—for I know thou darest, But this thing dare not,—

Stephano. That 's most certain.

Caliban. Thou 'shalt be lord of it and I 'll serve thee.

Stephano. How now shall this be compassed ? Canst thou bring me to the party ?

Caliban. Yea, yea, my lord : I 'll yield him thee asleep,
Where thou mayst knock a nail into his head.

Ariel. Thou liest ; thou canst not.

Caliban. What a pied ninny 's this ! Thou scurvy patch !
I do beseech thy greatness, give him blows
And take his bottle from him : when that 's gone
He shall drink nought but brine ; for I 'll not show him
Where the quick freshes are.

Stephano. Trinculo, run unto no further danger : interrupt the monster one word further, and, by this hand, I 'll turn my mercy out o' doors and make a stock-fish of thee.

Trinculo. Why, what did I ? I did nothing. I 'll go farther off.

Stephano. Didst thou not say he lied ?

Ariel. Thou liest.

Stephano. Do I so ? Take thou that. [*Beats Trin.*] As you like this, give me the lie another time.

Trinculo. I did not give the lie. Out o' your wits and hearing too ? A pox o' your bottle ! this can sack and drinking do. A murrain on your monster, and the devil take your fingers !

Caliban. Ha, ha, ha !

Stephano. Now, forward with your tale. Prithee, stand farther off.

Caliban. Beat him enough : after a little time I 'll beat him too.

Stephano. Stand farther. Come, proceed.

Caliban. Why, as I told thee, 'tis a custom with him,
I' th' afternoon to sleep : there thou mayst brain him,
Having first seized his books, or with a log
Batter his skull, or paunch him with a stake,
Or cut his wezand with thy knife. Remember
First to possess his books ; for without them
He 's but a sot, as I am, nor hath not
One spirit to command : they all do hate him
As rootedly as I. Burn but his books.
He has brave utensils,—for so he calls them,—
Which, when he has a house, he 'll deck withal.
And that most deeply to consider is
The beauty of his daughter ; he himself
Calls her a nonpareil : I never saw a woman,
But only Sycorax my dam and she ;
But she as far surpasseth Sycorax
As great'st does least.

Stephano.   Is it so brave a lass ?

Caliban. Ay, lord ; she will become thy bed, I warrant,
And bring thee forth brave brood.

Stephano. Monster, I will kill this man : his daughter and I will be king and queen,—save our graces !—and Trinculo and thyself shall be viceroys. Dost thou like the plot, Trinculo ?

Trinculo. Excellent.

Stephano. Give me thy hand : I am sorry I beat thee ; but, while thou livest, keep a good tongue in thy head.

Caliban. Within this half hour will he be asleep : Wilt thou destroy him then ?

Stephano.   Aye, on mine honour.

Ariel. This will I tell my master.

Caliban. Thou makest me merry ; I am full of pleasure :
Let us be jocund : will you troll the catch
You taught me but while-ere ?

Stephano. At thy request, monster, I will do reason, any reason. Come on, Trinculo, let us sing.
[*Sings.*

Flout 'em and scout 'em
And scout 'em and flout 'em ;
Thought is free.

Caliban. That's not the tune.
(*Ariel plays the tune on a tabor and pipe.*)

Stephano. What is this same ?

Trinculo. This is the tune of our catch, played by the picture of Nobody.

Stephano. If thou beest a man, show thyself in thy likeness : if thou beest a devil, take 't as thou list.

Trinculo. O, forgive me my sins !

Stephano. He that dies pays all debts : I defy thee. Mercy upon us !

Caliban. Art thou afeard?
Stephano. No, monster, not I.
Caliban. Be not afeard ; the isle is full of noises
Sounds and sweet airs, that give delight and
  hurt not.
Sometimes a thousand twangling instruments
Will hum about mine ears, and sometime voices
That, if I then had waked after long sleep,
Will make me sleep again : and then, in
  dreaming,
The clouds methought would open and show
  riches
Ready to drop upon me, that, when I waked,
I cried to dream again.
Stephano. This will prove a brave kingdom to me,
where I shall have my music for nothing.
Caliban. When Prospero is destroyed.
Stephano. That shall be by and by : I remember
the story.
Trinculo. The sound is going away ; let 's follow
it, and after do our work.
Stephano. Lead, monster ; we 'll follow. I would I
could see this taborer ; he lays it on.
Trinculo. Wilt come ? I 'll follow, Stephano.
          [*Exeunt.*

SCENE III.   *Another part of the island.*

Enter ALONSO, SEBASTIAN, ANTONIO, GON-
   ZALO, ADRIAN, FRANCISCO, *and others.*

Gonzalo. By'r lakin, I can go no further, sir ;
My old bones ache : here 's a maze trod indeed
Through forth-rights and meanders ! By your
  patience,
I needs must rest me.
Alonso.   Old lord, I cannot blame thee,
Who am myself attach'd with weariness,
To the dulling of my spirits : sit down, and rest.
Even here I will put off my hope and keep it
No longer for my flatterer : he is drown'd
Whom thus we stray to find, and the sea mocks
Our frustrate search on land. Well, let him
  go.
Antonio. [*Aside to Seb.*] I am right glad that
he 's so out of hope.
Do not, for one repulse, forego the purpose
That you resolved to effect.
Sebastian. [*Aside to Ant.*] The next advantage
Will we take throughly.
Antonio. [*Aside to Seb.*] Let it be to-night ;
For, now they are oppress'd with travel, they
Will not, nor cannot, use such vigilance
As when they are fresh.
Sebastian. [*Aside to Ant.*] I say, to-night : no
more.   [*Solemn and strange music.*
Alonso. What harmony is this ? My · good
friends, hark !
Gonzalo. Marvellous sweet music !

Enter PROSPERO *above, invisible. Enter several*
strange Shapes, bringing in a banquet ; they
dance about it with gentle actions of saluta-
tion ; and, inviting the King, &c. to eat,
they depart.
Alonso. Give us kind keepers, heavens ! What
were these ?
Sebastian. A living drollery. Now I will believe
That there are unicorns, that in Arabia
There is one tree, the phœnix' throne, one
  phœnix

At this hour reigning there.
Antonio.   I 'll believe both ;
And what does else want credit, come to me,
And I 'll be sworn 'tis true : travellers ne'er did
  lie,
Though fools at home condemn 'em.
Gonzalo.   If in Naples
I should report this now, would they believe me ?
If I should say, I saw such islanders—
For, certes, these are people of the island—
Who, though they are of monstrous shape, yet,
  note,
Their manners are more gentle-kind than of
Our human generation you shall find
Many, nay, almost any.
Prospero.   [*Aside*] Honest lord,
Thou hast said well ; for some of you there pre-
  sent
Are worse than devils.
Alonso.   I cannot too much muse
Such shapes, such gesture and such sound, ex-
  pressing,
Although they want the use of tongue, a kind
Of excellent dumb discourse.
Prospero.   [*Aside*] Praise in departing.
Francisco. They vanish'd strangely.
Sebastian.   No matter, since
They have left their viands behind ; for we have
  stomachs.
Will 't please you taste of what is here ?
Alonso.   Not I.
Gonzalo. Faith, sir, you need not fear. When
  we were boys,
Who would believe that there were mountaineers
Dew-lapp'd like bulls, whose throats had hang-
  ing at 'em
Wallets of flesh ? or that there were such men
Whose heads stood in their breasts ? which now
we find
Each putter-out of five for one will bring us
Good warrant of.
Alonso.   I will stand to and feed,
Although my last : no matter, since I feel
The best is past. Brother, my lord the duke,
Stand to and do as we.

Thunder and lightning. Enter ARIEL, *like a*
harpy ; claps his wings upon the table ; and,
with a quaint device, the banquet vanishes.

Ariel. You are three men of sin, whom
  Destiny,
That hath to instrument this lower world
And what is in 't, the never-surfeited sea
Hath caused to belch up you ; and on this island
Where man doth not inhabit ; you 'mongst men
Being most unfit to live. I have made you mad ;
And even with such-like valour men hang and
drown
Their proper selves.
          [*Alon., Seb. &c. draw their swords.*
          You fools ! I and my fellows
Are ministers of Fate : the elements,
Of whom your swords are temper'd, may as well
Wound the loud winds, or with bemock'd-at
  stabs
Kill the still-closing waters, as diminish
One dowle that 's in my plume : my fellow-
  ministers
Are like invulnerable. If you could hurt,
Your swords are now too massy for your strengths

And will not be uplifted.   But remember—
For that 's my business to you—that you three
From Milan did supplant good Prospero ;
Exposed unto the sea, which hath requit it,
Him and his innocent child : for which foul deed
The powers, delaying, not forgetting, have
Incensed the seas and shores, yea, all the crea-
    tures,
Against your peace.   Thee of thy son, Alonso,
They have bereft ;   and do pronounce by me
Lingering perdition, worse than any death
Can be at once, shall step by step attend
You and your ways ;   whose wraths to guard you
    from—
Which here, in this most desolate isle, else falls
Upon your heads—is nothing but heart-sorrow
And a clear life ensuing.

He vanishes in thunder ; then, to soft music,
enter the Shapes again, and dance, with
mocks and mows, and carrying out the table.

Prospero.   Bravely the figure of this harpy hast
    thou
Perform'd, my Ariel ;   a grace it had, devouring :
Of my instruction hast thou nothing bated
In what thou hadst to say : so, with good life
And observation strange, my meaner ministers
Their several kinds have done.   My high charms
    work
And these mine enemies are all knit up
In their distractions ;   they now are in my power ;
And in these fits I leave them, while I visit
Young Ferdinand, whom they suppose is drown'd,
And his and mine loved darling.   [*Exit above.*
    Gonzalo.   I' the name of something holy, sir,
        why stand you
In this strange stare ?
    Alonso.   O, it is monstrous, monstrous !
Methought the billows spoke and told me of it ;
The winds did sing it to me, and the thunder,
That deep and dreadful organ-pipe, pronounced
The name of Prosper : it did bass my trespass.
Therefore my son i' the ooze is bedded, and
I 'll seek him deeper than e'er plummet sounded
And with him there lie mudded.   [*Exit.*
    Sebastian.   But one fiend at a time,
I 'll fight their legions o'er.
    Antonio.   I 'll be thy second.
                    [*Exeunt Seb. and Ant.*
    Gonzalo.   All three of them are desperate : their
        great guilt,
Like poison given to work a great time after,
Now 'gins to bite the spirits.   I do beseech you
That are of suppler joints, follow them swiftly
And hinder them from what this ecstasy
May now provoke them to.
    Adrian.   Follow, I pray you.   [*Exeunt.*

ACT IV.

SCENE I.   *Before* Prospero's *cell.*

Enter Prospero, Ferdinand, *and* Miranda.

Prospero.

If I have too austerely punish'd you,
    Your compensation makes amends, for I
    Have given you here a thrid of mine own life,
Or that for which I live ;   who once again
I tender to thy hand : all thy vexations
Were but my trials of thy love, and thou

Hast strangely stood the test :   here, afore Heaven,
I ratify this my rich gift.   O Ferdinand,
Do not smile at me that I boast her off,
For thou shalt find she will outstrip all praise
And make it halt behind her.
    Ferdinand.   I do believe it
Against an oracle.
    Prospero.   Then, as my gift and thine own ac-
        quisition
Worthily purchased, take my daughter :   but
If thou dost break her virgin-knot before
All sanctimonious ceremonies may
With full and holy rite be minister'd,
No sweet aspersion shall the heavens let fall
To make this contract grow ;   but barren hate,
Sour-eyed disdain and discord shall bestrew
The union of your bed with weeds so loathly
That you shall hate it both : therefore take heed,
As Hymen's lamps shall light you.
    Ferdinand.   As I hope
For quiet days, fair issue and long life,
With such love as 'tis now, the murkiest den,
The most opportune place. the strong'st sugges-
    tion
Our worser genius can, shall never melt
Mine honour into lust, to take away
The edge of that day's celebration
When I shall   think, or Phœbus' steeds   are
    founder'd,
Or Night kept chain'd below,
    Prospero.   Fairly spoke.
Sit then and talk with her ;   she is thine own.
What, Ariel !   my industrious servant, Ariel !

Enter Ariel.

    Ariel.   What   would   my   potent master ?   here
        I am.
    Prospero.   Thou and thy meaner fellows your last
        service
Did worthily perform ;   and I must use you
In such another trick.   Go bring the rabble,
O'er whom I give thee power, here to this place :
Incite them to quick motion ;   for I must
Bestow upon the eyes of this young couple
Some vanity of mine art :   it is my promise,
And they expect it from me.
    Ariel.   Presently ?
    Prospero.   Ay, with a twink.
    Ariel.   Before you can say ' come ' and ' go,'
        And breathe twice and cry ' so, so,'
        Each one, tripping on his toe,
        Will be here with mop and mow.
        Do you love me, master ?   no ?
    Prospero.   Dearly, my delicate Ariel.   Do not
        approach
Till thou dost hear me call.
    Ariel.   Well, I conceive.   [*Exit.*
    Prospero.   Look thou be true ;   do not give dalli-
        ance
Too much the rein :   the strongest oaths are straw
To the fire i' the blood :   be more abstemious,
Or else, good night your vow !
    Ferdinand.   I warrant you, sir ;
The white cold virgin snow upon my heart
Abates the ardour of my liver.
    Prospero.   Well.
Now come, my Ariel !   bring a corollary,
Rather than want a spirit :   appear, and pertly !
No tongue !   all eyes !   be silent.   [*Soft music.*

Enter IRIS.

Iris. Ceres, most bounteous lady, thy rich
  leas
Of wheat, rye, barley, vetches, oats and pease ;
Thy turfy mountains, where live nibbling sheep,
And flat meads thatch'd with stover, them to
  keep ;
Thy banks with pioned and twilled brims,
Which spongy April at thy hest betrims,
To make cold nymphs chaste crowns ; and thy
  broom-groves,
Whose shadow the dismissed bachelor loves,
Being lass-lorn ; thy pole-clipt vineyard ;
And thy sea-marge, sterile and rocky-hard,
Where thou thyself dost air ;—the queen o' the
  sky,
Whose watery arch and messenger am I,
Bids thee leave these, and with her sovereign
  grace,
Here on this grass-plot, in this very place,
To come and sport : her peacocks fly amain :
Approach, rich Ceres, her to entertain.

Enter CERES.

Ceres. Hail, many-colour'd messenger, that
  ne'er
Dost disobey the wife of Jupiter ;
Who with thy saffron wings upon my flowers
Diffusest honey-drops, refreshing showers,
And with each end of thy blue bow dost crown
My bosky acres and my unshrubb'd down,
Rich scarf to my proud earth ; why hath thy
  queen
Summon'd me hither, to this short-grass'd
  green ?
Iris. A contract of true love to celebrate ;
And some donation freely to estate
On the blest lovers.
Ceres.   Tell me, heavenly bow,
If Venus or her son, as thou dost know,
Do now attend the queen ? Since they did plot
The means that dusky Dis my daughter got,
Her and her blind boy's scandal'd company
I have forsworn.
Iris.   Of her society
Be not afraid : I met her deity
Cutting the clouds towards Paphos and her son
Dove-drawn with her. Here thought they to
  have done
Some wanton charm upon this man and maid,
Whose vows are, that no bed-right shall be paid
Till Hymen's torch be lighted : but in vain ;
Mars's hot minion is return'd again ;
Her waspish-headed son has broke his arrows,
Swears he will shoot no more but play with
  sparrows
And be a boy right out.
Ceres.   High'st queen of state,
Great Juno, comes ; I know her by her gait.

Enter JUNO.

Juno. How does my bounteous sister ? Go
  with me
To bless this twain, that they may prosperous be
And honour'd in their issue.   [*They sing :*

Juno. Honour, riches, marriage-blessing,
  Long continuance, and increasing,
  Hourly joys be still upon you !
  Juno sings her blessings on you.

Ceres. Earth's increase, foison plenty,
  Barns and garners never empty,
  Vines with clustering bunches growing,
  Plants with goodly burthen bowing ;
  Spring come to you at the farthest
  In the very end of harvest !
  Scarcity and want shall shun you ;
  Ceres' blessing so is on you.
Ferdinand. This is a most majestic-vision, and
Harmonious charmingly. May I be bold
To think these spirits ?
Prospero.   Spirits which by mine art
I have from their confines call'd to enact
My present fancies.
Ferdinand.   Let me live here ever ;
So rare a wonder'd father and a wife
Makes this place Paradise.
      [*Juno and Ceres whisper, and send
            Iris on employment.*
Prospero.   Sweet, now, silence !
Juno and Ceres whisper seriously ;
There 's something else to do : hush, and be
  mute,
Or else our spell is marr'd.
Iris. You nymphs, call'd Naiads, of the
  windring brooks,
With your sedged crowns and ever-harmless
  looks,
Leave your crisp channels and on this green land
Answer your summons ; Juno does command :
Come, temperate nymphs, and help to celebrate
A contract of true love ; be not too late.

Enter certain Nymphs.

You sunburnt sicklemen, of August weary,
Come hither from the furrow and be merry :
Make holiday ; your rye-straw hats put on
And these fresh nymphs encounter every one
In country footing.

  *Enter certain Reapers, properly habited : they
  join with the Nymphs in a graceful dance ;
  towards the end whereof* PROSPERO *starts
  suddenly, and speaks ; after which, to a
  strange, hollow, and confused noise, they
  heavily vanish.*

Prospero. [*Aside*] I had forgot that foul con-
  spiracy
Of the beast Caliban and his confederates
Against my life : the minute of their plot
Is almost come. [*To the Spirits*]. Well done !
  avoid ; no more !
Ferdinand. This is strange : your father 's in some
  passion
That works him strongly.
Miranda.   Never till this day
Saw I him touch'd with anger so distemper'd.
Prospero. You do look, my son, in a moved sort,
As if you were dismay'd : be cheerful, sir.
Our revels now are ended. These our actors,
As I foretold you, were all spirits and
Are melted into air, into thin air :
And, like the baseless fabric of this vision,
The cloud-capp'd towers, the gorgeous palaces,
The solemn temples, the great globe itself,
Yea, all which it inherit, shall dissolve
And, like this insubstantial pageant faded,
Leave not a rack behind. We are such stuff
As dreams are made on, and our little life
Is rounded with a sleep. Sir, I am vex'd ;

Bear with my weakness; my old brain is
   troubled :
Be not disturb'd with my infirmity :
If you be pleased, retire into my cell
And there repose : a turn or two I 'll walk,
To still my beating mind.
   Ferdinand. Miranda. We wish your peace. [*Exeunt.*
   Prospero. Come with a thought. I thank thee,
   Ariel : come.

Enter ARIEL.

   Ariel. Thy thoughts I cleave to. What 's thy
   pleasure ?
   Prospero.   Spirit,
We must prepare to meet with Caliban.
   Ariel. Ay, my commander : when I presented
   Ceres,
I thought to have told thee of it, but I fear'd
Lest I might anger thee.
   Prospero. Say again, where didst thou leave
   these varlets ?
   Ariel. I told you, sir, they were red-hot with
   drinking ;
So full of valour that they smote the air
For breathing in their faces ; beat the ground
For kissing of their feet ; yet always bending
Towards their project. Then I beat my tabor ;
At which, like unback'd colts, they prick'd their
   ears,
Advanced their eyelids, lifted up their noses
As they smelt music ; so I charm'd their ears
That calf-like they my lowing follow'd through
Tooth'd briers, sharp furzes, pricking goss and
   thorns,
Which enter'd their frail shins : at last I left
   them
I' the filthy-mantled pool beyond your cell,
There dancing up to the chins, that the foul lake
O'erstunk their feet.
   Prospero.   This was well done, my bird.
Thy shape invisible retain thou still :
The trumpery in my house, go bring it hither,
For stale to catch these thieves.
   Ariel.   I go, I go.   [*Exit.*
   Prospero. A devil, a born devil, on whose nature
Nurture can never stick ; on whom my pains,
Humanely taken, all, all lost, quite lost ;
And as with age his body uglier grows,
So his mind cankers. I will plague them all,
Even to roaring.

Re-enter ARIEL, *loaden with glistering apparel, &c.*

   Come, hang them on this line.

PROSPERO *and* ARIEL *remain, invisible. Enter*
CALIBAN, STEPHANO, *and* TRINCULO, *all wet.*

   Caliban. Pray you, tread softly, that the blind
mole may not
Hear a foot fall : we now are near his cell.
   Stephano. Monster, your fairy, which you say is a
harmless fairy, has done little better than played
the Jack with us.
   Trinculo. Monster, I do smell all horse-piss ; at
which my nose is in great indignation.
   Stephano. So is mine. Do you hear, monster ? If
I should take a displeasure against you, look
you,—

   Trinculo. Thou wert but a lost monster.
   Caliban. Good my lord, give me thy favour still.
Be patient, for the prize I 'll bring thee to
Shall hoodwink this mischance : therefore speak
softly.
All 's hush'd as midnight yet.
   Trinculo. Ay, but to lose our bottles in the
pool—
   Stephano. There is not only disgrace and dis-
honour in that, monster, but an infinite loss.
   Trinculo. That 's more to me than my wetting :
yet this is your harmless fairy, monster.
   Stephano. I will fetch off my bottle, though I be
o'er ears for my labour.
   Caliban. Prithee, my king, be quiet. See'st thou
here,
This is the mouth o' the cell : no noise, and
enter,
Do that good mischief which may make this
island
Thine own for ever, and I, thy Caliban,
For aye thy foot-licker.
   Stephano. Give me thy hand. I do begin to have
bloody thoughts.
   Trinculo. O king Stephano ! O peer ! O worthy
Stephano ! look what a wardrobe here is for thee !
   Caliban. Let it alone, thou fool ; it is but trash.
   Trinculo. O, ho, monster ! we know what belongs
to a frippery. O king Stephano !
   Stephano. Put off that gown, Trinculo ; by this
hand, I 'll have that gown.
   Trinculo. Thy grace shall have it.
   Caliban. The dropsy drown this fool ! what do
you mean
To dote thus on such luggage ? Let 's alone
And do the murder first : if he awake,
From toe to crown he 'll fill our skins with
pinches,
Make us strange stuff.
   Stephano. Be you quiet, monster. Mistress line,
is not this my jerkin ? Now is the jerkin under
the line : now, jerkin, you are like to lose your
hair and prove a bald jerkin.
   Trinculo. Do, do : we steal by line and level,
an 't like your grace.
   Stephano. I thank thee for that jest ; here 's a
garment for 't : wit shall not go unrewarded
while I am king of this country. ' Steal by line
and level ' is an excellent pass of pate ; there 's
another garment for 't.
   Trinculo. Monster, come, put some lime upon
your fingers, and away with the rest.
   Caliban. I will have none on 't : we shall lose
our time,
And all be turn'd to barnacles, or to apes
With foreheads villanous low.
   Stephano. Monster, lay to your fingers : help to
bear this away where my hogshead of wine is,
or I 'll turn you out of my kingdom : go to,
carry this.
   Trinculo. And this.
   Stephano. Ay, and this.

*A noise of hunters heard. Enter divers Spirits,
   in shape of dogs and hounds, and hunt them
   about,* PROSPERO *and* ARIEL *setting them on.*
   Prospero. Hey, Mountain, hey !
   Ariel. Silver ! there it goes, Silver !
   Prospero. Fury, Fury ! there, Tyrant, there !
   hark ! hark !
                    [*Cal., Ste., and Trin. are driven out.*

Go charge my goblins that they grind their
    joints
With dry convulsions, shorten up their sinews
With aged cramps, and more pinch-spotted
    make them
Than pard or cat o' mountain.
Ariel.   Hark, they roar !
Prospero. Let them be hunted soundly. At this
    hour
Lie at my mercy all mine enemies :
Shortly shall all my labours end, and thou
Shalt have the air at freedom : for a little
Follow, and do me service.   [*Exeunt.*

ACT V.

SCENE I. *Before* PROSPERO'S *cell.*

Enter PROSPERO *in his magic robes, and* ARIEL.

Prospero.

Now does my project gather to a head :
    My charms crack not ; my spirits obey ; and
    time
Goes upright with his carriage. How 's the day ?
Ariel. On the sixth hour ; at which time,
    my lord,
You said our work should cease.
Prospero.   I did say so,
When first I raised the tempest. Say, my spirit,
How fares the king and 's followers ?
Ariel.   Confined together
In the same fashion as you gave in charge,
Just as you left them ; all prisoners, sir,
In the line-grove which weather-fends your cell ;
They cannot budge till your release. The king,
His brother and yours, abide all three distracted
And the remainder mourning over them,
Brimful of sorrow and dismay ; but chiefly
Him that you term'd, sir, ' The good old lord,
    Gonzalo ;'
His tears run down his beard, like winter's drops
From eaves of reeds. Your charm so strongly
    works 'em
That if you now beheld them, your affections
Would become tender.
Prospero.   Dost thou think so, spirit ?
Ariel. Mine would, sir, were I human.
Prospero.   And mine shall.
Hast thou, which art but air, a touch, a feeling
Of their afflictions, and shall not myself,
One of their kind, that relish all as sharply,
Passion as they, be kindlier moved than thou
    art ?
Though with their high wrongs I am struck to
    the quick,
Yet with my nobler reason 'gainst my fury
Do I take part : the rarer action is
In virtue than in vengeance ; they being
    penitent,
The sole drift of my purpose doth extend
Not a frown further. Go release them, Ariel :
My charms I 'll break, their senses I 'll restore,
And they shall be themselves.
Ariel.   I 'll fetch them, sir. [*Exit.*
Prospero. Ye elves of hills, brooks, standing lakes
    and groves,
And ye that on the sands with printless foot
Do chase the ebbing Neptune and do fly him

When he comes back ; you demi-puppets that
By moonshine do the green sour ringlets make,
Whereof the ewe not bites, and you whose pas-
    time
Is to make midnight mushrooms, that rejoice
To hear the solemn curfew ; by whose aid,
Weak masters though ye be, I have bedimm'd
The noontide sun, call'd forth the mutinous
    winds,
And 'twixt the green sea and the azured vault
Set roaring war : to the dread rattling thunder
Have I given fire and rifted Jove's stout oak
With his own bolt ; the strong-based promon-
    tory
Have I made shake and by the spurs pluck'd
    up
The pine and cedar : graves at my command
Have waked their sleepers, oped, and let 'em
    forth
By my so potent art. But this rough magic
I here abjure, and, when I have required
Some heavenly music, which even now I do,
To work mine end upon their senses that
This airy charm is for, I 'll break my staff,
Bury it certain fathoms in the earth,
And deeper than did ever plummet sound
I 'll drown my book.   [*Solemn music.*

Re-enter ARIEL *before : then* ALONSO, *with a
    frantic gesture, attended by* GONZALO ; SE-
    BASTIAN *and* ANTONIO *in like manner, at-
    tended by* ADRIAN *and* FRANCISCO : *they all
    enter the circle which* PROSPERO *had made,
    and there stand charmed : which* PROSPERO
    observing, speaks :

A solemn air and the best comforter
To an unsettled fancy cure thy brains,
Now useless, boil'd within thy skull ! There
    stand,
For you are spell-stopp'd.
Holy Gonzalo, honourable man,
Mine eyes, even sociable to the show of thine,
Fall fellowly drops. The charm dissolves apace,
And as the morning steals upon the night,
Melting the darkness, so their rising senses
Begin to chase the ignorant fumes that mantle
Their clearer reason. O good Gonzalo,
My true preserver, and a loyal sir
To him thou follow'st ! I will pay thy graces
Home both in word and deed. Most cruelly
Didst thou, Alonso, use me and my daughter :
Thy brother was a furtherer in the act.
Thou art pinch'd for 't now, Sebastian. Flesh
    and blood,
You, brother mine, that entertain'd ambition,
Expell'd remorse and nature ; who, with Se-
    bastian,
Whose inward pinches therefore are most strong,
Would here have kill'd your king ; I do forgive
    thee,
Unnatural though thou art. There understanding
Begins to swell, and the approaching tide
Will shortly fill the reasonable shore
That now lies foul and muddy. Not one of them
That yet looks on me, or would know me : Ariel,
Fetch me the hat and rapier in my cell :
I will discase me, and myself present
As I was sometime Milan : quickly, spirit ;
Thou shalt ere long be free.

ARIEL *sings and helps to attire him.*

  Where the bee sucks, there suck I :
  In a cowslip's bell I lie ;
  There I couch when owls do cry.
  On the bat's back do I fly
  After summer merrily.
Merrily, merrily shall I live now
Under the blossom that hangs on the bough.

Prospero. Why, that 's my dainty Ariel ! I shall
 miss thee ;
But yet thou shalt have freedom : so, so, so.
To the king's ship, invisible as thou art :
There shalt thou find the mariners asleep
Under the hatches ; the master and the boat-swain
Being awake, enforce them to this place,
And presently, I prithee.
 Ariel. I drink the air before me, and return
Or ere your pulse twice beat.   [*Exit.*
 Gonzalo. All torment, trouble, wonder and
 amazement
Inhabits here : some heavenly power guide us
Out of this fearful country !
 Prospero.   Behold, sir king,
The wronged Duke of Milan, Prospero :
For more assurance that a living prince
Does now speak to thee, I embrace thy body ;
And to thee and thy company I bid
A hearty welcome.
 Alonso. Whether thou be'st he or no,
Or some enchanted trifle to abuse me,
As late I have been, I not know : thy pulse
Beats as of flesh and blood ; and, since I saw
 thee,
The affliction of my mind amends, with which,
I fear, a madness held me : this must crave,
An if this be at all, a most strange story.
Thy dukedom I resign and do entreat
Thou pardon me my wrongs. But how should
 Prospero
Be living and be here ?
 Prospero. First, noble friend,
Let me embrace thine age, whose honour cannot
Be measured or confined.
 Gonzalo. Whether this be
Or be not, I 'll not swear.
 Prospero. You do yet taste
Some subtilties o' the isle, that will not let you
Believe things certain. Welcome, my friends
all !
[*Aside to Sebastion and Antonio.*] But you, my
 brace of lords, were I so minded,
I here could pluck his highness' frown upon
 you
And justify you traitors : at this time
I will tell no tales.
 Sebastion. [*Aside*] The devil speaks in him.
 Prospero.   No.
For you, most wicked sir, whom to call brother
Would even infect my mouth, I do forgive
Thy rankest fault ; all of them ; and require
My dukedom of thee, which perforce, I know,
Thou must restore.
 Alonso. If thou be'st Prospero,
Give us particulars of thy preservation ;
How thou hast met us here, who three hours
 since
Were wreck'd upon this shore ; where I have
 lost—
How sharp the point of this remembrance is !—

My dear son Ferdinand.
 Prospero.   I am woe for 't, sir.
 Alonso. Irreparable is the loss, and patience
Says it is past her cure.
 Prospero.   I rather think
You have not sought her help, of whose soft
 grace
For the like loss I have her sovereign aid
And rest myself content.
 Alonso.   You the like loss !
 Prospero. As great to me as late ; and, supportable
To make the dear loss, have I means much
 weaker
Than you may call to comfort you, for I
Have lost my daughter.
 Alonso. A daughter ?
O heavens, that they were living both in Naples,
The king and queen there ! that they were, I
 wish
Myself were mudded in that oozy bed
Where my son lies. When did you lose your
 daughter ?
 Prospero. In this last tempest. I perceive, these
 lords
At this encounter do so much admire
That they devour their reason and scarce think
Their eyes do offices of truth, their words
Are natural breath : but, howsoe'er you have
Been justled from your senses, know for certain
That I am Prospero and that very duke
Which was thrust forth of Milan, who most
 strangely
Upon this shore, where you were wreck'd, was
 landed,
To be the lord on 't. No more yet of this ;
For 'tis a chronicle of day by day,
Not a relation for a breakfast nor
Befitting this first meeting. Welcome, sir ;
This cell 's my court : here have I few at-
 tendants
And subjects none abroad : pray you, look in.
My dukedom since you have given me again,
I will requite you with as good a thing ;
At least bring forth a wonder, to content ye
As much as me my dukedom.

Here Prospero discovers FERDINAND *and*
 MIRANDA *playing at chess.*

 Miranda. Sweet lord, you play me false.
 Ferdinand.   No, my dear'st love,
I would not for the world.
 Miranda. Yes, for a score of kingdoms you
 should wrangle,
And I would call it fair play.
 Alonso.   If this prove
A vision of the Island, one dear son
Shall I twice lose.
 Sebastion. A most high miracle !
 Ferdinand. Though the seas threaten, they are
 merciful ;
I have cursed them without cause. [*Kneels.*
 Alonso.   Now all the blessings
Of a glad father compass thee about !
Arise, and say how thou camest here.
 Miranda.   O, wonder !
How many goodly creatures are there here !
How beauteous mankind is ! O brave new
 world,
That has such people in 't !
 Prospero.   'Tis new to thee,

Alonso. What is this maid with whom thou
    wast at play ?
Your eld'st acquaintance cannot be three hours :
Is she the goddess that hath sever'd us,
And brought us thus together ?
    Ferdinand.   Sir, she is mortal ;
But by immortal Providence she's mine :
I chose her when I could not ask my father
For his advice, nor thought I had one.   She
Is daughter to this famous Duke of Milan,
Of whom so often I have heard renown,
But never saw before ; of whom I have
Received a second life ; and second father
This lady makes him to me.
    Alonso.   I am hers :
But, O, how oddly will it sound that I
Must ask my child forgiveness !
    Prospero.   There, sir, stop :
Let us not burthen our remembrance with
A heaviness that 's gone.
    Gonzalo.   I have inly wept
Or should have spoke ere this.   Look down,
    you gods,
And on this couple drop a blessed crown !
For it is you that have chalk'd forth the way
Which brought us hither.
    Alonso.   I say, Amen, Gonzalo !
    Gonzalo.   Was Milan thrust from Milan, that
    his issue
Should become kings of Naples ? O, rejoice
Beyond a common joy, and set it down
With gold on lasting pillars :   In one voyage
Did Claribel her husband find at Tunis
And Ferdinand, her brother, found a wife
Where he himself was lost, Prospero his dukedom
In a poor isle and all of us ourselves
When no man was his own.
    Alonso.   [*To Ferdinand and Miranda.*] Give me
    your hands :
Let grief and sorrow still embrace his heart
That doth not wish you joy !
    Gonzalo.   Be it so ! Amen !

Re-enter ARIEL, *with the* Master *and* Boatswain
        amazedly following.

O, look, sir, look, sir ! here is more of us :
I prophesied, if a gallows were on land,
This fellow could not drown. Now, blasphemy,
That swear'st grace o'erboard, not an oath on
    shore ?
Hast thou no mouth by land ? What is the
    news ?
    Boatswain.   The best news is, that we have safely
    found
Our king and company ; the next, our ship—
Which, but three glasses since, we gave out
    split—
Is tight and yare and bravely rigg'd as when
We first put out to sea.
    Ariel.   [*Aside to Prospero*] Sir, all this service
Have I done since I went.
    Prospero.   [*Aside to Ariel.*] My tricksy spirit !
    Alonso.   These are not natural events : they
    strengthen
From strange to stranger. Say, how came you
    hither ?
    Boatswain.   If I did think, sir, I were well awake,
I 'ld strive to tell you. We were dead of sleep,
And—how we know not—all clapp'd under
    hatches ;

Where but even now with strange and several
    noises
Of roaring, shrieking, howling, jingling chains,
And moe diversity of sounds, all horrible,
We were awaked ; straightway, at liberty ;
Where we, in all her trim, freshly beheld
Our royal, good and gallant ship, our master
Capering to eye her : on a trice, so please you,
Even in a dream, were we divided from them
And were brought moping hither.
    Ariel.   [*Aside to Prospero.*] Was 't well done ?
    Prospero.   [*Aside to Ariel.*] Bravely, my diligence.
    Thou shalt be free.
    Alonso.   This is as strange a maze as e'er men
    trod ;
And there is in this business more than nature
Was ever conduct of : some oracle
Must rectify our knowledge.
    Prospero.   Sir, my liege,
Do not infest your mind with beating on
The strangeness of this business ; at pick'd
    leisure
Which shall be shortly, single I' ll resolve you,
Which to you shall seem probable, of every
These happen'd accidents ; till when, be cheerful
And think of each thing well.   [*Aside to Ariel.*]
    Come hither, spirit :
Set Caliban and his companions free ;
Untie the spell. [*Exit Ariel*]. How fares my
    gracious sir ?
There are yet missing of your company
Some few odd lads that you remember not.

Re-enter ARIEL, *driving in* CALIBAN, STEPHANO
    and TRINCULO, *in their stolen apparel.*

    Stephano.   Every man shift for all the rest, and let
no man take care for himself ; for all is but
fortune. Coragio, bully-monster, coragio !
    Trinculo.   If these be true spies which I wear in
my head, here 's a goodly sight.
    Caliban.   O Setebos, these be brave spirits in-
    deed !
How fine my master is ! I am afraid
He will chastise me.
    Sebastion.   Ha, ha !
What things are these, my lord Antonio ?
Will money buy 'em !
    Antonio.   Very like ; one of them
Is a plain fish, and, no doubt, marketable.
    Prospero.   Mark but the badges of these men,
    my lords,
Then say, if they be true. This mis-shapen
    knave,
His mother was a witch, and one so strong
That could control the moon, make flows and
    ebbs,
And deal in her command without her power.
These three have robb'd me ; and this demi-
    devil—
For he 's a bastard one—had plotted with them
To take my life. Two of these fellows you
Must know and own ; this thing of darkness I
Acknowledge mine.
    Caliban.   I shall be pinch'd to death.
    Alonso.   Is not this Stephano, my drunken
    butler ?
    Sebastion.   He is drunk now : where had he wine ?
    Alonso.   And Trinculo is reeling ripe ; where
should they

Find this grand liquor that hath gilded 'em ?
How camest thou in this pickle ?

Trinculo.   I have been in such a pickle since I
saw you last that, I fear me, will never out of
my bones : I shall not fear fly-blowing.

Sebastion.   Why, how now, Stephano !

Stephano.   O, touch me not ; I am not Stephano,
but a cramp.

Prospero.   You 'ld be king o' the isle, sirrah ?

Stephano.   I should have been a sore one then.

Alonso.   This is a strange thing as e'er I look'd
on.   [*Pointing to Caliban.*

Prospero.   He is as disproportion'd in his manners
As in his shape.   Go, sirrah, to my cell ;
Take with you your companions ; as you look
To have my pardon, trim it handsomely.

Caliban.   Ay, that I will ; and I'll be wise here-
after
And seek for grace.   What a thrice-double ass
Was I, to take this drunkard for a god
And worship this dull fool !

Prospero.   Go to ; away !

Alonso.   Hence, and bestow your luggage where
you found it.

Sebastion.   Or stole it, rather.
             [*Exeunt Caliban, Stephano and Trinculo.*

Prospero.   Sir, I invite your highness and your
train
To my poor cell, where you shall take your rest
For this one night ; which, part of it, I 'll waste
With such discourse as, I not doubt, shall
make it
Go quick away ; the story of my life
And the particular accidents gone by
Since I came to this isle ; and in the morn
I'll bring you to your ship and so to Naples,
Where I have hope to see the nuptial
Of these our dear-beloved solemnized ;

And thence retire me to my Milan, where
Every third thought shall be my grave.

Alonso.   I long
To hear the story of your life, which must
Take the ear strangely.

Prospero.   I 'll deliver all :
And promise you calm seas, auspicious gales
And sail so expeditious that shall catch
Your royal fleet far off. [*Aside to Ari.*] My
        Ariel, chick,
That is thy charge : then to the elements
Be free and fare thou well ! Please you, draw
near.   [*Exeunt.*

EPILOGUE.

Now my charms are all o'erthrown,
And what strength I have 's mine own,
Which is most faint : now, 'tis true,
I must be here confined by you,
Or sent to Naples.   Let me not,
Since I have my dukedom got
And pardon'd the deceiver, dwell
In this bare island by your spell ;
But release me from my bands
With the help of your good hands :
Gentle breath of yours my sails
Must fill, or else my project fails,
Which was to please.   Now I want
Spirits to enforce, art to enchant,
And my ending is despair,
Unless I be relieved by prayer,
Which pierces so that it assaults
Mercy itself and frees all faults.
As you from crimes would pardon'd be,
Let your indulgence set me free.

THE
TWO GENTLEMEN OF VERONA

DRAMATIS PERSONÆ

DUKE OF MILAN, *Father to* Silvia.
VALENTINE, } *The two Gentlemen.*
PROTEUS,   }
ANTONIO, *Father to* Proteus.
THURIO, *a foolish rival to* Valentine.
EGLAMOUR, *Agent for* Silvia *in her escape.*
HOST, *where* Julia *lodges.*
OUTLAWS, *with* Valentine.
SPEED, *a clownish servant to* Valentine.
LAUNCE, *the like to* Proteus.
PANTHINO, *Servant to* Antonio.

JULIA, *beloved of* Proteus.
SILVIA, *beloved of* Valentine.
LUCETTA, *waiting-woman to* Julia.

Servants, Musicians.

SCENE, Verona ; Milan ; The frontiers of
Mantua.

ACT I.

SCENE I. *Verona. An open place.*

Enter VALENTINE *and* PROTEUS.

Valentine.
Cease to persuade, my loving Proteus :
    Home-keeping youth have ever homely wits.
    Were 't not affection chains thy tender days
To the sweet glances of thy honour'd love,
I rather would entreat thy company
To see the wonders of the world abroad
Than, living dully sluggardized at home,
Wear out thy youth with shapeless idleness.
But since thou lovest, love still and thrive therein,
Even as I would when I to love begin.
  Proteus. Wilt thou be gone ? Sweet Valentine, adieu !
Think on thy Proteus, when thou haply seest
Some rare note-worthy object in thy travel :
Wish me partaker in thy happiness
When thou dost meet good hap : and in thy danger,
If ever danger do environ thee,
Commend thy grievance to my holy prayers,
For I will be thy beadsman, Valentine.
  Valentine. And on a love-book pray for my success ?
  Proteus. Upon some book I love I 'll pray for thee.

  Valentine. That 's on some shallow story of deep love :
How young Leander cross'd the Hellespont.
  Proteus. That 's a deep story of a deeper love ;
For he was more than over shoes in love.
  Valentine. 'Tis true; for you are over boots in love,
And yet you never swum the Hellespont.
  Proteus. Over the boots ? nay, give me not the boots.
  Valentine. No, I will not, for it boots thee not.
  Proteus.   What ?
  Valentine. To be in love, where scorn is bought with groans ;
Coy looks with heart-sore sighs: one fading moment's mirth
With twenty watchful, weary, tedious nights :
If haply won, perhaps a hapless gain ;
If lost, why then a grievous labour won ;
However, but a folly bought with wit,
Or else a wit by folly vanquished.
  Proteus. So, by your circumstance, you call me fool.
  Valentine. So, by your circumstance, I fear you 'll prove.
  Proteus. 'Tis love you cavil at : I am not Love.
  Valentine. Love is your master, for he masters you :
And he that is so yoked by a fool,
Methinks, should not be chronicled for wise.
  Proteus. Yet writers say, as in the sweetest bud
The eating canker dwells, so eating love
Inhabits in the finest wits of all.
  Valentine. And writers say, as the most forward bud
Is eaten by the canker ere it blow,
Even so by love the young and tender wit
Is turn'd to folly, blasting in the bud,
Losing his verdure even in the prime
And all the fair effects of future hopes.
But wherefore waste I time to counsel thee
That art a votary to fond desire ?
Once more adieu ! my father at the road
Expects my coming, there to see me shipp'd.
  Proteus. And thither will I bring thee, Valentine.
  Valentine. Sweet Proteus, no ; now let us take our leave.
To Milan let me hear from thee by letters
Of thy success in love and what news else
Betideth here in absence of thy friend ;
And I likewise will visit thee with mine.
  Proteus. All happiness bechance to thee in Milan !
  Valentine. As much to you at home ! and so, farewell.   [*Exit.*
  Proteus. He after honour hunts, I after love :
He leaves his friends to dignify them more ;
I leave myself, my friends and all, for love.

Thou, Julia, thou hast metamorphosed me,
Made me neglect my studies, lose my time,
War with good counsel, set the world at nought ;
Made wit with musing weak, heart sick with
    thought.

Enter Speed.

Speed. Sir Proteus, save you ! Saw you my
    master ?
Proteus. But now he parted hence, to embark
    for Milan.
Speed. Twenty to one then he is shipp'd al-
    ready,
An I have play'd the sheep in losing him.
Proteus. Indeed, a sheep doth very often stray,
An if the shepherd be a while away.
Speed. You conclude that my master is a
shepherd then and I a sheep ?
Proteus. I do.
Speed. Why then, my horns are his horns,
whether I wake or sleep.
Proteus. A silly answer and fitting well a sheep.
Speed. This proves me still a sheep.
Proteus. True ; and thy master a shepherd.
Speed. Nay, that I can deny by a circum-
stance.
Proteus. It shall go hard but I 'll prove it by an-
other.
Speed. The shepherd seeks the sheep, and
not the sheep the shepherd ; but I seek my
master, and my master seeks not me : therefore
I am no sheep.
Proteus. The sheep for fodder follow the shepherd ; the shepherd for food follows not the
sheep : thou for wages followest thy master ;
thy master for wages follows not thee : therefore thou art a sheep.
Speed. Such another proof will make me cry
' baa.'
Proteus. But, dost thou hear ? gavest thou my
letter to Julia ?
Speed. Ay, sir : I, a lost mutton, gave your
letter to her, a laced mutton, and she, a laced
mutton, gave me, a lost mutton, nothing for my
labour.
Proteus. Here 's too small a pasture for such store
of muttons.
Speed. If the ground be overcharged, you
were best stick her.
Proteus. Nay : in that you are astray, 'twere best
pound you.
Speed. Nay, sir, less than a pound shall serve
me for carrying your letter.
Proteus. You mistake ; I mean the pound,—a
pinfold.
Speed. From a pound to a pin ? fold if over
and over,
'Tis threefold too little for carrying a letter to
your lover.
Proteus. But what said she ?
Speed. [*First nodding*] Ay.
Proteus. Nod—Ay—why, that 's noddy.
Speed. You mistook, sir ; I say, she did nod :
and you ask me if she did nod ; and I say,
' Ay.'
Proteus. And that set together is noddy.
Speed. Now you have taken the pains to set
it together, take it for your pains.
Proteus. No, no ; you shall have it for bearing
the letter.

Speed. Well, I perceive I must be fain to bear
with you.
Proteus. Why, sir, how do you bear with me ?
Speed. Marry, sir, the letter, very orderly ;
having nothing but the word ' noddy ' for my
pains.
Proteus. Beshrew me, but you have a quick wit.
Speed. And yet it cannot overtake your slow
purse.
Proteus. Come, come, open the matter in brief :
what said she ?
Speed. Open your purse, that the money and
the matter may be both at once delivered.
Proteus. Well, sir, here is for your pains. What
said she ?
Speed. Truly, sir, I think you 'll hardly win
her.
Proteus. Why, couldst thou perceive so much
from her ?
Speed. Sir, I could perceive nothing at all
from her ; no, not so much as a ducat for delivering your letter : and being so hard to me
that brought your mind, I fear she 'll prove as
hard to you in telling your mind. Give her no
token but stones ; for she 's as hard as steel.
Proteus. What said she ? nothing ?
Speed. No, not so much as ' Take this for
thy pains.' To testify your bounty, I thank
you, you have testerned me ; in requital whereof, henceforth carry your letters yourself : and
so, sir, I 'll commend you to my master.
Proteus. Go, go, be gone, to save your ship from
wreck,
Which cannot perish having thee aboard,
Being destined to a drier death on shore.
                    [*Exit Speed.*
I must go send some better messenger :
I fear my Julia would not deign my lines,
Receiving them from such a worthless post.
                    [*Exit.*

SCENE II.   *The same.   Garden of* Julia's
                house.

Enter Julia *and* Lucetta.

Julia. But say, Lucetta, now we are alone,
Wouldst thou then counsel me to fall in love ?
Lucetta. Ay, madam, so you stumble not un-
heedfully.
Julia. Of all the fair resort of gentlemen
That every day with parle encounter me,
In thy opinion which is worthiest love ?
Lucetta. Please you repeat their names, I 'll
show my mind
According to my shallow simple skill.
Julia. What think'st thou of the fair Sir
Eglamour ?
Lucetta. As of a knight well-spoken, neat and
fine :
But, were I you, he never should be mine.
Julia. What think'st thou of the rich Mercatio ?
Lucetta. Well of his wealth : but of himself, so so.
Julia. What think'st thou of the gentle
Proteus ?
Lucetta. Lord, Lord ! to see what folly reigns
in us !
Julia. How now ! what means this passion at
his name ?
Lucetta. Pardon, dear madam : 'tis a passing
shame

That I, unworthy body as I am,
Should censure thus on lovely gentlemen.

Julia. Why not on Proteus, as of all the rest ?

Lucetta. Then thus : of many good I think him
best.

Julia. Your reason ?

Lucetta. I have no other but a woman's reason ;
I think him so because I think him so.

Julia. And wouldst thou have me cast my
love on him ?

Lucetta. Ay, if you thought your love not cast
away.

Julia. Why he, of all the rest, hath never
moved me.

Lucetta. Yet he, of all the rest, I think, best
loves ye.

Julia. His little speaking shows his love but
small.

Lucetta. Fire that's closest kept burns most of all.

Julia. They do not love that do not show their
love.

Lucetta. O, they love least that let men know
their love.

Julia. I would I knew his mind.

Lucetta. Peruse this paper, madam.

Julia. 'To Julia.' Say, from whom ?

Lucetta. That the contents will show.

Julia. Say, say, who gave it thee ?

Lucetta. Sir Valentine's page ; and sent, I think,
from Proteus.
He would have given it you ; but I, being in
the way,
Did in your name receive it : pardon the fault,
I pray.

Julia. Now, by my modesty, a goodly broker !
Dare you presume to harbour wanton lines ?
To whisper and conspire against my youth ?
Now, trust me, 'tis an office of great worth
And you an officer fit for the place.
There, take the paper : see it be return'd ;
Or else return no more into my sight.

Lucetta. To plead for love deserves more fee
than hate.

Julia. Will ye be gone ?

Lucetta.   That you may ruminate.
                                                    [*Exit.*

Julia. And yet I would I had o'erlooked the
letter :
It were a shame to call her back again
And pray her to a fault for which I chid her.
What a fool is she, that knows I am a maid,
And would not force the letter to my view !
Since maids, in modesty, say 'no' to that
Which they would have the proffer construe 'ay.'
Fie, fie, how wayward is this foolish love
That, like a testy babe, will scratch the nurse
And presently all humbled kiss the rod !
How churlishly I chid Lucetta hence,
When willingly I would have had her here !
How angerly I taught my brow to frown,
When inward joy enforced my heart to smile !
My penance is to call Lucetta back
And ask remission for my folly past.
What ho ! Lucetta !

Re-enter LUCETTA.

Lucetta.   What would your ladyship ?

Julia. Is 't near dinner-time ?

Lucetta.   I would it were,
That you might kill your stomach on your meat
And not upon your maid.

Julia. What is 't that you took up so gingerly ?

Lucetta. Nothing.

Julia. Why didst thou stoop, then ?

Lucetta. To take a paper up that I let fall.

Julia. And is that paper nothing ?

Lucetta. Nothing concerning me.

Julia. Then let it lie for those that it concerns.

Lucetta. Madam, it will not lie where it concerns,
Unless it have a false interpreter.

Julia. Some love of yours hath writ to you in
rhyme.

Lucetta. That I might sing it, madam, to a tune.
Give me a note : your ladyship can set.

Julia. As little by such toys as may be
possible.
Best sing it to the tune of ' Light o' love.'

Lucetta. It is too heavy for so light a tune.

Julia. Heavy ! belike it hath some burden
then ?

Lucetta. Ay, and melodious were it, would you
sing it.

Julia. And why not you ?

Lucetta.   I cannot reach so high.

Julia. Let 's see your song. How now, minion !

Lucetta. Keep tune there still, so you will sing
it out :
And yet methinks I do not like this tune.

Julia. You do not ?

Lucetta.   No, madam ; it is too sharp.

Julia. You, minion, are too saucy.

Lucetta. Nay, now you are too flat
And mar the concord with too harsh a descant :
There wanteth but a mean to fill your song.

Julia. The mean is drown'd with your unruly
bass.

Lucetta. Indeed, I bid the base for Proteus.

Julia. This babble shall not henceforth trouble
me.
Here is a coil with protestation !
                                          [*Tears the letter.*
Go get you gone, and let the papers lie :
You would be fingering them, to anger me.

Lucetta. She makes it strange ; but she would
be best pleased
To be so anger'd with another letter.   [*Exit.*

Julia. Nay, would I were so anger'd with the
same !
O hateful hands, to tear such loving words !
Injurious wasps, to feed on such sweet honey
And kill the bees that yield it with your stings !
I 'll kiss each several paper for amends.
Look, here is writ ' kind Julia.'   Unkind Julia !
As in revenge of thy ingratitude,
I throw thy name against the bruising stones,
Trampling contemptuously on thy disdain.
And here is writ ' love-wounded Proteus.'
Poor wounded name ! my bosom as a bed
Shall lodge thee till thy wound be throughly
heal'd ;
And thus I search it with a sovereign kiss.
But twice or thrice was ' Proteus ' written down.
Be calm, good wind, blow not a word away
Till I have found each letter in the letter,
Except mine own name : that some whirlwind bear
Unto a ragged fearful-hanging rock
And throw it thence into the raging sea !
Lo, here in one line is his name twice writ,
' Poor forlorn Proteus, passionate Proteus,
To the sweet Julia :' that I 'll tear away.

And yet I will not, sith so prettily
He couples it to his complaining names.
Thus will I fold them one upon another :
Now kiss, embrace, contend, do what you will.

Re-enter LUCETTA.

Lucetta. Madam,
Dinner is ready, and your father stays.
Julia. Well, let us go.
Lucetta. What, shall these papers lie like tell-tales here ?
Julia. If you respect them, best to take them up.
Lucetta. Nay, I was taken up for laying them down :
Yet here they shall not lie, for catching cold.
Julia. I see you have a month's mind to them.
Lucetta. Ay, madam, you may say what sights you see ;
I see things too, although you judge I wink.
Julia. Come, come ; will 't please you go ?
                             [*Exeunt.*

SCENE III.   *The same.* ANTONIO's *house.*

Enter ANTONIO *and* PANTHINO.

Antonio. Tell me, Panthino, what sad talk was that
Wherewith my brother held you in the cloister ?
Panthino. 'Twas of his nephew Proteus, your son.
Antonio. Why, what of him ?
Panthino.   He wonder'd that your lordship
Would suffer him to spend his youth at home,
While other men, of slender reputation,
Put forth their sons to seek preferment out :
Some to the wars, to try their fortune there ;
Some to discover islands far away ;
Some to the studious universities.
For any or for all these exercises
He said that Proteus your son was meet,
And did request me to importune you
To let him spend his time no more at home,
Which would be great impeachment to his age,
In having known no travel in his youth.
Antonio. Nor need'st thou much importune me to that
Whereon this month I have been hammering.
I have consider'd well his loss of time
And how he cannot be a perfect man,
Not being tried and tutor'd in the world :
Experience is by industry achieved
And perfected by the swift course of time.
Then tell me, whither were I best to send him ?
Panthino. I think your lordship is not ignorant
How his companion, youthful Valentine,
Attends the emperor in his royal court.
Antonio. I know it well.
Panthino. 'Twere good, I think, your lordship sent him thither :
There shall he practise tilts and tournaments,
Hear sweet discourse, converse with noblemen,
And be in eye of every exercise
Worthy his youth and nobleness of birth.
Antonio. I like thy counsel ; well hast thou advised :
And that thou mayst perceive how well I like it
The execution of it shall make known.
Even with the speediest expedition
I will dispatch him to the emperor's court.
Panthino. To-morrow, may it please you, Don Alphonso

With other gentlemen of good esteem
Are journeying to salute the emperor
And to commend their service to his will.
Antonio. Good company ; with them shall Proteus go :
And, in good time ! now will we break with him.

Enter PROTEUS.

Proteus. Sweet love ! sweet lines ! sweet life !
Here is her hand, the agent of her heart ;
Here is her oath for love, her honour's pawn.
O, that our fathers would applaud our loves,
To seal our happiness with their consents !
O heavenly Julia !
Antonio. How now ! what letter are you reading there ?
Proteus. May 't please your lordship, 'tis a word or two
Of commendations sent from Valentine,
Deliver'd by a friend that came from him.
Antonio. Lend me the letter ; let me see what news.
Proteus. There is no news, my lord, but that he writes
How happily he lives, how well beloved
And daily graced by the emperor ;
Wishing me with him, partner of his fortune.
Antonio. And how stand you affected to his wish ?
Proteus. As one relying on your lordship's will
And not depending on his friendly wish.
Antonio. My will is something sorted with his wish.
Muse not that I thus suddenly proceed ;
For what I will, I will, and there an end.
I am resolved that thou shalt spend some time
With Valentinus in the emperor's court :
What maintenance he from his friends receives,
Like exhibition thou shalt have from me.
To-morrow be in readiness to go :
Excuse it not, for I am peremptory.
Proteus. My lord, I cannot be so soon provided :
Please you, deliberate a day or two.
Antonio. Look, what thou want'st shall be sent after thee :
No more of stay ! to-morrow thou must go.
Come on, Panthino : you shall be employ'd
To hasten on his expedition.
          [*Exeunt Antonio and Panthino.*
Proteus. Thus have I shunn'd the fire for fear of burning,
And drench'd me in the sea, where I am drown'd.
I fear'd to show my father Julia's letter,
Lest he should take exceptions to my love ;
And with the vantage of mine own excuse
Hath he excepted most against my love.
O, how this spring of love resembleth
The uncertain glory of an April day,
Which now shows all the beauty of the sun,
And by and by a cloud takes all away !

Re-enter PANTHINO.

Panthino. Sir Proteus, your father calls for you :
He is in haste ; therefore, I pray you, go.
Proteus. Why, this it is : my heart accords thereto,
And yet a thousand times it answers ' no.'
                             [*Exeunt.*

ACT II.

SCENE I. *Milan. The* DUKE'S *palace.*

Enter VALENTINE *and* SPEED.

Speed.

S ir, your glove.
   Valentine. Not mine ; my gloves are on.
   Speed. Why, then, this may be yours, for
this is but one.
   Valentine. Ha ! let me see : ay, give it me, it 's
mine :
Sweet ornament that decks a thing divine !
Ah, Silvia, Silvia !
   Speed. Madam Silvia ! Madam Silvia !
   Valentine. How now, sirrah ?
   Speed. She is not within hearing, sir.
   Valentine. Why, sir, who bade you call her ?
   Speed. Your worship, sir ; or else I mis-
took.
   Valentine. Well, you 'll still be too forward.
   Speed. And yet I was last chidden for being
too slow.
   Valentine. Go to, sir : tell me, do you know
Madam Silvia ?
   Speed. She that your worship loves ?
   Valentine. Why, how know you that I am in love ?
   Speed. Marry, by these special marks : first,
you have learned, like Sir Proteus, to wreathe
your arms, like a malecontent ; to relish a love-
song, like a robin-redbreast ; to walk alone, like
one that had the pestilence ; to sigh, like a
schoolboy that had lost his A B C ; to weep, like
a young wench that had buried her grandam ;
to fast, like one that takes diet ; to watch, like
one that fears robbing ; to speak puling, like a
beggar at Hallowmas. You were wont, when
you laughed, to crow like a cock ; when you
walked, to walk like one of the lions ; when you
fasted, it was presently after dinner ; when you
looked sadly, it was for want of money : and
now you are metamorphosed with a mistress,
that, when I look on you, I can hardly think
you my master.
   Valentine. Are all these things perceived in me ?
   Speed. They are all perceived without ye.
   Valentine. Without me ? they cannot.
   Speed. Without you ? nay, that 's certain, for,
without you were so simple, none else would :
but you are so without these follies, that these
follies are within you and shine through you like
the water in an urinal, that not an eye that sees
you but is a physician to comment on your
malady.
   Valentine. But tell me, dost thou know my lady
Silvia ?
   Speed. She that you gaze on so as she sits at
supper ?
   Valentine. Hast thou observed that ? even she,
I mean.
   Speed. Why, sir, I know her not.
   Valentine. Dost thou know her by my gazing
on her, and yet knowest her not ?
   Speed. Is she not hard-favoured, sir ?
   Valentine. Not so fair, boy, as well-favoured.
   Speed. Sir, I know that well enough.
   Valentine. What dost thou know ?
   Speed. That she is not so fair as, of you, well
favoured.
   Valentine. I mean that her beauty is exquisite,
but her favour infinite.

   Speed. That 's because the one is painted and
the other out of all count.
   Valentine. How painted ? and how out of count ?
   Speed. Marry, sir, so painted, to make her fair,
that no man counts of her beauty.
   Valentine. How esteemest thou me ? I account
of her beauty.
   Speed. You never saw her since she was de-
formed.
   Valentine. How long hath she been deformed ?
   Speed. Ever since you loved her.
   Valentine. I have loved her ever since I saw her ;
and still I see her beautiful.
   Speed. If you love her, you cannot see her.
   Valentine. Why ?
   Speed. Because Love is blind. O, that you
had mine eyes ; or your own eyes had the lights
they were wont to have when you chid at Sir
Proteus for going ungartered !
   Valentine. What should I see then ?
   Speed. Your own present folly and her
passing deformity : for he, being in love, could
not see to garter his hose, and you, being in
love, cannot see to put on your hose.
   Valentine. Belike, boy, then, you are in love ; for
last morning you could not see to wipe my shoes.
   Speed. True, sir ; I was in love with my bed :
I thank you, you swinged me for my love, which
makes me the bolder to chide you for yours.
   Valentine. In conclusion, I stand affected to her.
   Speed. I would you were set, so your affection
would cease.
   Valentine. Last night she enjoined me to write
some lines to one she loves.
   Speed. And have you ?
   Valentine. I have.
   Speed. Are they not lamely writ ?
   Valentine. No, boy, but as well as I can do them.
Peace ! here she comes.
   Speed. [*Aside*] O excellent motion ! O ex-
ceeding puppet ! Now will he interpret to her.

Enter SILVIA.

   Valentine. Madam and mistress, a thousand
good-morrows.
   Speed. [*Aside*] O, give ye good even ! here 's
a million of manners.
   Silvia. Sir Valentine and servant, to you two
thousand.
   Speed. [*Aside*] He should give her interest,
and she gives it him.
   Valentine. As you enjoin'd me, I have writ your
letter
Unto the secret nameless friend of yours ;
Which I was much unwilling to proceed in
But for my duty to your ladyship.
   Silvia. I thank you, gentle servant : 'tis very
clerkly done.
   Valentine. Now trust me, madam, it came hardly
off ;
For being ignorant to whom it goes
I writ at random, very doubtfully.
   Silvia. Perchance you think too much of so
much pains ?
   Valentine. No, madam ; so it stead you, I will
write,
Please you command, a thousand times as much ;
And yet—
   Silvia. A pretty period ! Well, I guess the sequel ;
And yet I will not name it ; and yet I care not ;

And yet take this again ; and yet I thank you,
Meaning henceforth to trouble you no more.
Speed. [*Aside*] And yet you will ; and yet
another 'yet.'
Valentine. What means your ladyship ? do you
not like it ?
Silvia. Yes, yes : the lines are very quaintly writ ;
But since unwillingly, take them again.
Nay, take them.
Valentine. Madam, they are for you.
Silvia. Ay, ay : you writ them, sir, at my re-
quest ;
But I will none of them ; they are for you ;
I would have had them writ more movingly.
Valentine. Please you, I 'll write your ladyship
another.
Silvia. And when it 's writ, for my sake read
it over,
And if it please you, so ; if not, why, so.
Valentine. If it please me, madam, what then ?
Silvia. Why, if it please you, take it for your
labour :
And so, good morrow, servant.   [*Exit.*
Speed. O jest unseen, inscrutable, invisible,
As a nose on a man's face, or a weathercock on
a steeple !
My master sues to her, and she hath taught her
suitor,
He being her pupil, to become her tutor.
O excellent device ! was there ever heard a
better,
That my master, being scribe, to himself should
write the letter ?
Valentine. How now, sir ? what are you reasoning
with yourself ?
Speed. Nay, I was rhyming : 'tis you that have
the reason.
Valentine. To do what ?
Speed. To be a spokesman from Madam
Silvia.
Valentine. To whom ?
Speed. To yourself : why, she wooes you by
a figure.
Valentine. What figure ?
Speed. By a letter, I should say.
Valentine. Why, she hath not writ to me ?
Speed. What need she, when she hath made
you write to yourself ? Why, do you not perceive
the jest ?
Valentine. No, believe me.
Speed. No believing you, indeed, sir. But
did you perceive her earnest ?
Valentine. She gave me none, except an angry
word.
Speed. Why, she hath given you a letter.
Valentine. That 's the letter I writ to her friend.
Speed. And that letter hath she delivered, and
there an end.
Valentine. I would it were no worse.
Speed. I'll warrant you, 'tis as well :
For often have you writ to her, and she, in
modesty,
Or else for want of idle time, could not again
reply ;
Or fearing else some messenger that might her
mind discover,
Herself hath taught her love himself to write
unto her lover.
All this I speak in print, for in print I found it.
Why muse you, sir ? 'tis dinner-time.

Valentine. I have dined.
Speed. Ay, but hearken, sir ; though the
chameleon Love can feed on the air, I am one
that am nourished by my victuals and would
fain have meat. O, be not like your mistress ;
be moved, be moved.   [*Exeunt.*

SCENE II.   *Verona.   JULIA'S house.*

Enter PROTEUS *and* JULIA.

Proteus. Have patience, gentle Julia.
Julia. I must, where is no remedy.
Proteus. When possibly I can, I will return.
Julia. If you turn not, you will return the
sooner.
Keep this remembrance for thy Julia's sake.
[*Giving a ring.*
Proteus. Why, then, we 'll make exchange ; here,
take you this.
Julia. And seal the bargain with a holy kiss.
Proteus. Here is my hand for my true constancy ;
And when that hour o'erslips me in the day
Wherein I sigh not, Julia, for thy sake,
The next ensuing hour some foul mischance
Torment me for my love's forgetfulness !
My father stays my coming ; answer not ;
The tide is now : nay, not thy tide of tears ;
That tide will stay me longer than I should.
Julia, farewell !   [*Exit Julia.*
What, gone without a word ?
Ay, so true love should do : it cannot speak ;
For truth hath better deeds than words to grace it.

Enter PANTHINO.

Panthino. Sir Proteus, you are stay'd for.
Proteus. Go ; I come, I come.
Alas ! this parting strikes poor lovers dumb.
[*Exeunt.*

SCENE III.   *The same.   A street.*

Enter LAUNCE, *leading a dog.*

Launce. Nay, 'twill be this hour ere I have
done weeping : all the kind of the Launces have
this very fault. I have received my proportion,
like the prodigious son, and am going with Sir
Proteus to the Imperial's court. I think Crab
my dog be the sourest-natured dog that lives :
my mother weeping, my father wailing, my sister
crying, our maid howling, our cat wringing her
hands, and all our house in a great perplexity,
yet did not this cruel-hearted cur shed one tear :
he is a stone, a very pebble stone, and has no more
pity in him than a dog : a Jew would have wept
to have seen our parting ; why, my grandam,
having no eyes, look you, wept herself blind at
my parting. Nay, I 'll show you the manner of
it. This shoe is my father : no, this left shoe is
my father : no, no, this left shoe is my mother :
nay, that cannot be so neither : yes, it is so, it is
so, it hath the worser sole. This shoe, with the
hole in it, is my mother, and this my father ; a
vengeance on 't ! there 'tis : now, sir, this staff
is my sister, for, look you, she is as white as a
lily and as small as a wand : this hat is Nan, our
maid : I am the dog : no, the dog is himself, and
I am the dog—Oh ! the dog is me, and I am myself ; ay, so, so. Now come I to my father ;
Father, your blessing : now should not the shoe
speak a word for weeping : now should I kiss
my father ; well, he weeps on. Now come I to

my mother : O, that she could speak now like a wood woman ! Well, I kiss her ; why, there 's 'tis ; here 's my mother's breath up and down. Now come I to my sister ; mark the moan she makes. Now the dog all this while sheds not a tear nor speaks a word ; but see how I lay the dust with my tears.

Enter PANTHINO.

Panthino. Launce, away, away, aboard ! thy master is shipped and thou art to post after with oars. What 's the matter ? why weepest thou, man ? Away, ass ! you 'll lose the tide, if you tarry any longer.

Launce. It is no matter if the tied were lost ; for it is the unkindest tied that ever any man tied.

Panthino. What 's the unkindest tide ?

Launce. Why, he that 's tied here, Crab, my dog.

Panthino. Tut, man, I mean thou 'lt lose the flood, and, in losing the flood, lose thy voyage, and, in losing thy voyage, lose thy master, and, in losing thy master, lose thy service, and, in losing thy service,—Why dost thou stop my mouth ?

Launce. For fear thou shouldst lose thy tongue.

Panthino. Where should I lose my tongue ?

Launce. In thy tale.

Panthino. In thy tail !

Launce. Lose the tide, and the voyage, and the master, and the service, and the tied ! Why, man, if the river were dry, I am able to fill it with my tears ; if the wind were down, I could drive the boat with my sighs.

Panthino. Come, come away, man ; I was sent to call thee.

Launce. Sir, call me what thou darest.

Panthino. Wilt thou go ?

Launce. Well, I will go.   [*Exeunt.*

SCENE IV. *Milan. The* DUKE'S *palace.*

Enter SILVIA, VALENTINE, THURIO, *and* SPEED.

Silvia. Servant !

Valentine. Mistress ?

Speed. Master, Sir Thurio frowns on you.

Valentine. Ay, boy, it 's for love.

Speed. Not of you.

Valentine. Of my mistress, then.

Speed. 'Twere good you knocked him.   [*Exit.*

Silvia. Servant, you are sad.

Valentine. Indeed, madam, I seem so.

Thurio. Seem you that you are not ?

Valentine. Haply I do.

Thurio. So do counterfeits.

Valentine. So do you.

Thurio. What seem I that I am not ?

Valentine. Wise.

Thurio. What instance of the contrary ?

Valentine. Your folly.

Thurio. And how quote you my folly ?

Valentine. I quote it in your jerkin.

Thurio. My jerkin is a doublet.

Valentine. Well, then, I 'll double your folly.

Thurio. How ?

Silvia. What, angry, Sir Thurio ! do you change colour ?

Valentine. Give him leave, madam ; he is a kind of chameleon.

Thurio. That hath more mind to feed on your blood than live in your air.

Valentine. You have said, sir.

Thurio. Ay, sir, and done too, for this time.

Valentine. I know it well, sir ; you always end ere you begin.

Silvia. A fine volley of words, gentlemen, and quickly shot off.

Valentine. 'Tis indeed, madam ; we thank the giver.

Silvia. Who is that, servant ?

Valentine. Yourself, sweet lady ; for you gave the fire. Sir Thurio borrows his wit from your ladyship's looks, and spends what he borrows kindly in your company.

Thurio. Sir, if you spend word for word with me, I shall make your wit bankrupt.

Valentine. I know it well, sir ; you have an exchequer of words, and, I think, no other treasure to give your followers, for it appears, by their bare liveries, that they live by your bare words.

Silvia. No more, gentlemen, no more : here comes my father.

Enter DUKE.

Duke. Now, daughter Silvia, you are hard beset.
Sir Valentine, your father 's in good health :
What say you to a letter from your friends
Of much good news ?

Valentine. My lord, I will be thankful
To any happy messenger from thence.

Duke. Know ye Don Antonio, your countryman ?

Valentine. Ay, my good lord, I know the gentleman
To be of worth and worthy estimation
And not without desert so well reputed.

Duke. Hath he not a son ?

Valentine. Ay, my good lord ; a son that well deserves
The honour and regard of such a father.

Duke. You know him well ?

Valentine. I know him as myself ; for from our infancy
We have conversed and spent our hours together :
And though myself have been an idle truant,
Omitting the sweet benefit of time
To clothe mine age with angel-like perfection,
Yet hath Sir Proteus, for that 's his name,
Made use and fair advantage of his days ;
His years but young, but his experience old ;
His head unmellow'd, but his judgment ripe ;
And, in a word, for far behind his worth
Comes all the praises that I now bestow,
He is complete in feature and in mind
With all good grace to grace a gentleman.

Duke. Beshrew me, sir, but if he make this good,
He is as worthy for an empress' love
As meet to be an emperor's counsellor.
Well, sir, this gentleman is come to me,
With commendation from great potentates ;
And here he means to spend his time awhile ;
I think 'tis no unwelcome news to you.

Valentine. Should I have wish'd a thing, it had been he.

Duke. Welcome him then according to his worth.

Silvia, I speak to you, and you, Sir Thurio ;
For Valentine, I need not cite him to it :
I will send him hither to you presently.   [*Exit.*
Valentine. This is the gentleman I told your lady-
ship
Had come along with me, but that his mistress
Did hold his eyes lock'd in her crystal looks.
   Silvia. Belike that now she hath enfranchised
them
Upon some other pawn for fealty.
   Valentine. Nay, sure, I think she holds them
prisoners still.
   Silvia. Nay, then he should be blind ; and,
being blind,
How could he see his way to seek out you ?
   Valentine. Why, lady, Love hath twenty pairs of
eyes.
   Thurio. They say that Love hath not an eye
at all.
   Valentine. To see such lovers, Thurio, as yourself :
Upon a homely object Love can wink.
   Silvia. Have done, have done ; here comes the
gentleman.

Enter PROTEUS.   [*Exit* THURIO.

   Valentine. Welcome, dear Proteus ! Mistress, I
beseech you,
Confirm his welcome with some special favour.
   Silvia. His worth is warrant for his welcome
hither,
If this be he you oft have wish'd to hear from.
   Valentine. Mistress, it is : sweet lady, entertain
him
To be my fellow-servant to your ladyship.
   Silvia. Too low a mistress for so high a servant.
   Proteus. Not so, sweet lady : but too mean a
servant
To have a look of such a worthy mistress.
   Valentine. Leave off discourse of disability :
Sweet lady, entertain him for your servant.
   Proteus. My duty will I boast of ; nothing else.
   Silvia. And duty never yet did want his meed :
Servant, you are welcome to a worthless
mistress.
   Proteus. I 'll die on him that says so but your-
self.
   Silvia. That you are welcome ?
   Proteus.   That you are worthless.

Re-enter THURIO.

   Thurio. Madam, my lord your father would
speak with you.
   Silvia. I wait upon his pleasure. Come, Sir
Thurio,
Go with me. Once more, new servant, welcome :
I 'll leave you to confer of home affairs ;
When you have done, we look to hear from you.
   Proteus. We 'll both attend upon your ladyship.
           [*Exeunt Silvia and Thurio.*
   Valentine. Now, tell me, how do all from whence
you came ?
   Proteus. Your friends are well and have them
much commended.
   Valentine. And how do yours ?
   Proteus.   I left them all in health.
   Valentine. How does your lady ? and how thrives
your love ?
   Proteus. My tales of love were wont to weary
you ;
I know you joy not in a love-discourse.

   Valentine. Ay, Proteus, but that life is alter'd
now ;
I have done penance for contemning Love,
Whose high imperious thoughts have punish'd
me
With bitter fasts, with penitential groans,
With nightly tears and daily heart-sore sighs ;
For in revenge of my contempt of love,
Love hath chased sleep from my enthralled eyes
And made them watchers of mine own heart's
sorrow.
O gentle Proteus, Love 's a mighty lord
And hath so humbled me as I confess
There is no woe to his correction
Nor to his service no such joy on earth.
Now no discourse, except it be of love ;
Now can I break my fast, dine, sup and sleep,
Upon the very naked name of love.
   Proteus. Enough ; I read your fortune in your
eye.
Was this the idol that you worship so ?
   Valentine. Even she ; and is she not a heavenly
saint ?
   Proteus. No ; but she is an earthly paragon.
   Valentine. Call her divine.
   Proteus.   I will not flatter her.
   Valentine. O, flatter me ; for love delights in
praises.
   Proteus. When I was sick, you gave me bitter
pills,
And I must minister the like to you.
   Valentine. Then speak the truth by her ; if not
divine,
Yet let her be a principality,
Sovereign to all the creatures on the earth.
   Proteus. Except my mistress.
   Valentine.   Sweet, except not any ;
Except thou wilt except against my love.
   Proteus. Have I not reason to prefer mine own ?
   Valentine. And I will help thee to prefer her too ;
She shall be dignified with this high honour—
To bear my lady's train, lest the base earth
Should from her vesture chance to steal a kiss
And, of so great a favour growing proud,
Disdain to root the summer-swelling flower
And make rough winter everlastingly.
   Proteus. Why, Valentine, what braggardism is
this ?
   Valentine. Pardon me, Proteus ; all I can is
nothing
To her whose worth makes other worthies
nothing ;
She is alone.
   Proteus. Then let her alone.
   Valentine. Not for the world : why, man, she is
mine own,
And I as rich in having such a jewel
As twenty seas, if all their sand were pearl,
The water nectar and the rocks pure gold.
Forgive me that I do not dream on thee,
Because thou see'st me dote upon my love.
My foolish rival, that her father likes
Only for his possessions are so huge,
Is gone with her along, and I must after,
For love, thou know'st, is full of jealousy.
   Proteus. But she loves you ?
   Valentine. Ay, and we are betroth'd : nay, more,
our marriage-hour,
With all the cunning manner of our flight,
Determined of ; how I must climb her window,
The ladder made of cords, and all the means

Plotted and 'greed on for my happiness.
Good Proteus, go with me to my chamber,
In these affairs to aid me with thy counsel.
   Proteus. Go on before; I shall inquire you
     forth:
I must unto the road, to disembark
Some necessaries that I needs must use,
And then I 'll presently attend you.
   Valentine. Will you make haste?
   Proteus. I will.   [*Exit Valentine.*
Even as one heat another heat expels,
Or as one nail by strength drives out another,
So the remembrance of my former love
Is by a newer object quite forgotten.
† Is it mine, or Valentine's praise,
Her true perfection, or my false transgression,
That makes me reasonless to reason thus?
She is fair; and so is Julia that I love—
That I did love, for now my love is thaw'd;
Which, like a waxen image 'gainst a fire,
Bears no impression of the thing it was.
Methinks my zeal to Valentine is cold,
And that I love him not as I was wont.
O, but I love his lady too too much,
And that 's the reason I love him so little.
How shall I dote on her with more advice,
That thus without advice begin to love her!
'Tis but her picture I have yet beheld,
And that hath dazzled my reason's light;
But when I look on her perfections,
There is no reason but I shall be blind.
If I can check my erring love, I will:
If not, to compass her I 'll use my skill.   [*Exit.*

SCENE V. *The same. A street.*

   Enter SPEED *and* LAUNCE *severally.*

   Speed. Launce! by mine honesty, welcome
to Milan!
   Launce. Forswear not thyself, sweet youth,
for I am not welcome. I reckon this always,
that a man is never undone till he be hanged,
nor never welcome to a place till some certain
shot be paid and the hostess say ' Welcome! '
   Speed. Come on, you madcap, I 'll to the
alehouse with you presently; where, for one
shot of five pence, thou shalt have five thousand
welcomes. But, sirrah, how did thy master part
with Madam Julia?
   Launce. Marry, after they closed in earnest,
they parted very fairly in jest.
   Speed. But shall she marry him?
   Launce. No.
   Speed. How then? shall he marry her?
   Launce. No, neither.
   Speed. What, are they broken?
   Launce. No, they are both as whole as a fish.
   Speed. Why, then, how stands the matter
with them?
   Launce. Marry, thus; when it stands well with
him, it stands well with her.
   Speed. What an ass art thou! I understand
thee not.
   Launce. What a block art thou, that thou canst
not! My staff understands me.
   Speed. What thou sayest?
   Launce. Ay, and what I do too: look thee,
I 'll but lean, and my staff understands me.
   Speed. It stands under thee, indeed.
   Launce. Why, stand-under and under-stand is
all one.
   Speed. But tell me true, will 't be a match?

   Launce. Ask my dog: if he say ay, it will;
if he say no, it will; if he shake his tail and say
nothing, it will.
   Speed. The conclusion is then that it will.
   Launce. Thou shalt never get such a secret
from me but by a parable.
   Speed. 'Tis well that I get it so. But,
Launce, how sayest thou, that my master is
become a notable lover?
   Launce. I never knew him otherwise.
   Speed. Than how?
   Launce. A notable lubber, as thou reportest
him to be.
   Speed. Why, thou whoreson ass, thou mis-
takest me.
   Launce. Why, fool, I meant not thee; I
meant thy master.
   Speed. I tell thee, my master is become a
hot lover.
   Launce. Why, I tell thee, I care not though
he burn himself in love. If thou wilt, go with
me to the alehouse; if not, thou art an Hebrew,
a Jew, and not worth the name of a Christian.
   Speed. Why?
   Launce. Because thou hast not so much
charity in thee as to go to the ale with a
Christian. Wilt thou go?
   Speed. At thy service.   [*Exeunt.*

SCENE VI. *The same. The* DUKE's *palace.*

   Enter PROTEUS.

   Proteus. To leave my Julia, shall I be forsworn;
To love fair Silvia, shall I be forsworn;
To wrong my friend, I shall be much forsworn;
And even that power which gave me first my
     oath
Provokes me to this threefold perjury;
Love bade me swear and Love bids me for-
     swear.
O sweet-suggesting Love, if thou hast sinn'd,
Teach me, thy tempted subject, to excuse it!
At first I did adore a twinkling star,
But now I worship a celestial sun.
Unheedful vows may heedfully be broken,
And he wants wit that wants resolved will
To learn his wit to exchange the bad for better.
Fie, fie, unreverend tongue! to call her bad,
Whose sovereignty so oft thou hast preferr'd
With twenty thousand soul-confirming oaths.
I cannot leave to love, and yet I do;
But there I leave to love where I should love.
Julia I lose and Valentine I lose:
If I keep them, I needs must lose myself;
If I lose them, thus find I by their loss
For Valentine myself, for Julia Silvia.
I to myself am dearer than a friend,
For love is still most precious in itself;
And Silvia—witness Heaven, that made her
     fair!—
Shows Julia but a swarthy Ethiope.
I will forget that Julia is alive,
Remembering that my love to her is dead;
And Valentine I 'll hold an enemy,
Aiming at Silvia as a sweeter friend.
I cannot now prove constant to myself,
Without some treachery used to Valentine.
This night he meaneth with a corded ladder
To climb celestial Silvia's chamber-window,
Myself in counsel, his competitor.
Now presently I 'll give her father notice
Of their disguising and pretended flight;

Who, all enraged, will banish Valentine ;
For Thurio, he intends, shall wed his daughter ;
But, Valentine being gone, I 'll quickly cross
By some sly trick blunt Thurio's dull proceeding.
Love, lend me wings to make my purpose swift,
As thou hast lent me wit to plot this drift !
                                                    [*Exit.*

SCENE VII.   *Verona.   JULIA'S house.*

Enter JULIA *and* LUCETTA.

Julia.   Counsel, Lucetta ; gentle girl, assist me ;
And even in kind love I do conjure thee,
Who art the table wherein all my thoughts
Are visibly character'd and engraved,
To lesson me and tell me some good mean
How, with my honour, I may undertake
A journey to my loving Proteus.
Lucetta.   Alas, the way is wearisome and long !
Julia.   A true-devoted pilgrim is not weary
To measure kingdoms with his feeble steps ;
Much less shall she that hath Love's wings to fly,
And when the flight is made to one so dear,
Of such divine perfection, as Sir Proteus.
Lucetta.   Better forbear till Proteus make return.
Julia.   O, know'st thou not his looks are my
     soul's food ?
Pity the dearth that I have pined in,
By longing for that food so long a time.
Didst thou but know the inly touch of love,
Thou wouldst as soon go kindle fire with snow
As seek to quench the fire of love with words.
Lucetta.   I do not seek to quench your love's
     hot fire,
But qualify the fire's extreme rage,
Lest it should burn above the bounds of reason.
Julia.   The more thou damm'st it up, the
     more it burns.
The current that with gentle murmur glides,
Thou know'st, being stopp'd, impatiently doth
     rage ;
But when his fair course is not hindered,
He makes sweet music with the enamell'd
     stones,
Giving a gentle kiss to every sedge
He overtaketh in his pilgrimage,
And so by many winding nooks he strays
With willing sport to the wild ocean.
Then let me go and hinder not my course :
I 'll be as patient as a gentle stream
And make a pastime of each weary step,
Till the last step have brought me to my love ;
And there I 'll rest, as after much turmoil
A blessed soul doth in Elysium.
Lucetta.   But in what habit will you go along ?
Julia.   Not like a woman ; for I would prevent
The loose encounters of lascivious men :
Gentle Lucetta, fit me with such weeds
As may beseem some well-reputed page.
Lucetta.   Why, then, your ladyship must cut
     your hair.
Julia.   No, girl ; I'll knit it up in silken strings
With twenty odd-conceited true-love knots.
To be fantastic may become a youth
Of greater time than I shall show to be.
Lucetta.   What fashion, madam, shall I make
     your breeches ?
Julia.   That fits as well as ' Tell me, good my
     lord,

What compass will you wear your farthingale ? '
Why even what fashion thou best likest,
     Lucetta.
Lucetta.   You must needs have them with a
     codpiece, madam.
Julia.   Out, out, Lucetta ! that will be ill-
     favour'd.
Lucetta.   A round hose, madam, now 's not
     worth a pin,
Unless you have a codpiece to stick pins on.
Julia.   Lucetta, as thou lovest me, let me have
What thou thinkest meet and is most mannerly.
But tell me, wench, how will the world repute
     me
For undertaking so unstaid a journey ?
I fear me, it will make me scandalized.
Lucetta.   If you think so, then stay at home
     and go not.
Julia.   Nay, that I will not.
Lucetta.   Then never dream on infamy, but go.
If Proteus like your journey when you come,
No matter who 's displeased when you are gone :
I fear me, he will scarce be pleased withal.
Julia.   That is the least, Lucetta, of my fear :
A thousand oaths, an ocean of his tears
And instances of infinite of love
Warrant me welcome to my Proteus.
Lucetta.   All these are servants to deceitful men.
Julia.   Base men, that use them to so base
     effect !
But truer stars did govern Proteus' birth ;
His words are bonds, his oaths are oracles,
His love sincere, his thoughts immaculate,
His tears pure messengers sent from his heart,
His heart as far from fraud as heaven from
     earth.
Lucetta.   Pray heaven he prove so, when you
     come to him !
Julia.   Now, as thou lovest me, do him not
     that wrong
To bear a hard opinion of his truth :
Only deserve my love by loving him ;
And presently go with me to my chamber,
To take a note of what I stand in need of,
To furnish me upon my longing journey.
All that is mine I leave at thy dispose,
My goods, my lands, my reputation ;
Only, in lieu thereof, dispatch me hence.
Come, answer not, but to it presently !
I am impatient of my tarriance.   [*Exeunt.*

ACT III.

SCENE I.   *Milan.   The DUKE'S palace.*

Enter DUKE, THURIO, *and* PROTEUS.
         Duke.

S ir Thurio, give us leave, I pray, awhile ;
   We have some secrets to confer about.
                                         [*Exit Thurio.*
Now, tell me, Proteus, what 's your will with
     me ?
Proteus.   My gracious lord, that which I would
     discover
The law of friendship bids me to conceal ;
But when I call to mind your gracious favours
Done to me, undeserving as I am,
My duty pricks me on to utter that
Which else no worldly good should draw from
     me.
Know, worthy prince, Sir Valentine, my friend,

This night intends to steal away your daughter :
Myself am one made privy to the plot.
I know you have determined to bestow her
On Thurio, whom your gentle daughter hates ;
And should she thus be stol'n away from you,
It would be much vexation to your age.
Thus, for my duty's sake, I rather chose
To cross my friend in his intended drift
Than, by concealing it, heap on your head
A pack of sorrows which would press you down,
Being unprevented, to your timeless grave.

Duke. Proteus, I thank thee for thine honest
  care ;
Which to requite, command me while I live.
This love of theirs myself have often seen,
Haply when they have judged me fast asleep,
And oftentimes have purposed to forbid
Sir Valentine her company and my court :
But fearing lest my jealous aim might err
And so unworthily disgrace the man,
A rashness that I ever yet have shunn'd,
I gave him gentle looks, thereby to find
That which thyself hast now disclosed to me.
And, that thou mayst preceive my fear of this,
Knowing that tender youth is soon suggested,
I nightly lodge her in an upper tower,
The key whereof myself have ever kept ;
And thence she cannot be convey'd away.

Proteus. Know, noble lord, they have devised a
  mean
How he her chamber-window will ascend
And with a corded ladder fetch her down ;
For which the youthful lover now is gone
And this way comes he with it presently ;
Where, if it please you, you may intercept him.
But, good my lord, do it so cunningly
That my discovery be not aimed at ;
For love of you, not hate unto my friend,
Hath made me publisher of this pretence.

Duke. Upon mine honour, he shall never
  know
That I had any light from thee of this.

Proteus. Adieu, my lord ; Sir Valentine is
  coming.   [*Exit.*

Enter VALENTINE.

Duke. Sir Valentine, whither away so fast ?
Valentine. Please it your grace, there is a mes-
  senger
That stays to bear my letters to my friends,
And I am going to deliver them.
Duke. Be they of much import ?
Valentine. The tenour of them doth but signify
My health and happy being at your court.
Duke. Nay then, no matter ; stay with me
  awhile ;
I am to break with thee of some affairs
That touch me near, wherein thou must be
  secret.
'Tis not unknown to thee that I have sought
To match my friend Sir Thurio to my daughter.
Valentine. I know it well, my lord ; and, sure, the
  match
Were rich and honourable ; besides, the gentle-
  man
Is full of virtue, bounty, worth and qualities
Beseeming such a wife as your fair daughter :
Cannot your grace win her to fancy him ?
Duke. No, trust me ; she is peevish, sullen,
  froward,
Proud, disobedient, stubborn, lacking duty,

Neither regarding that she is my child
Nor fearing me as if I were her father ;
And, may I say to thee, this pride of hers,
Upon advice, hath drawn my love from her ;
And, where I thought the remnant of mine age
Should have been cherish'd by her child-like
  duty,
I now am full resolved to take a wife
And turn her out to who will take her in :
Then let her beauty be her wedding-dower ;
For me and my possessions she esteems not.

Valentine. What would your grace have me to do
  in this ?
Duke. † There is a lady in Verona here
Whom I affect ; but she is nice and coy
And nought esteems my aged eloquence :
Now therefore would I have thee to my tutor—
For long agone I have forgot to court ;
Besides, the fashion of the time is changed—
How and which way I may bestow myself
To be regarded in her sun-bright eye.
Valentine. Win her with gifts, if she respect not
  words :
Dumb jewels often in their silent kind
More than quick words do move a woman's
  mind.
Duke. But she did scorn a present that I sent
  her.
Valentine. A woman sometimes scorns what best
  contents her.
Send her another ; never give her o'er ;
For scorn at first makes after-love the more.
If she do frown, 'tis not in hate of you,
But rather to beget more love in you :
If she do chide, 'tis not to have you gone ;
For why, the fools are mad, if left alone.
Take no repulse, whatever she doth say ;
For ' get you gone,' she doth not mean ' away !'
Flatter and praise, commend, extol their graces ;
Though ne'er so black, say they have angels'
  faces.
That man that hath a tongue, I say, is no man,
If with his tongue he cannot win a woman.
Duke. But she I mean is promised by her
  friends
Unto a youthful gentleman of worth,
And kept severely from resort of men,
That no man hath access by day to her.
Valentine. Why, then, I would resort to her by
  night.
Duke. Ay, but the doors be lock'd and keys
  kept safe,
That no man hath recourse to her by night.
Valentine. What lets but one may enter at her
  window ?
Duke. Her chamber is aloft, far from the
  ground,
And built so shelving that one cannot climb it
Without apparent hazard of his life.
Valentine. Why then, a ladder quaintly made of
  cords,
To cast up, with a pair of anchoring hooks,
Would serve to scale another Hero's tower,
So bold Leander would adventure it.
Duke. Now, as thou art a gentleman of
  blood,
Advise me where I may have such a ladder.
Valentine. When would you use it ? Pray, sir, tell
  me that.
Duke. This very night ; for Love is like a
  child,

That longs for everything that he can come by.
Valentine. By seven o'clock I 'll get you such a
ladder.
Duke. But, hark thee ; I will go to her alone :
How shall I best convey the ladder thither ?
Valentine. It will be light, my lord, that you may
bear it
Under a cloak that is of any length.
Duke. A cloak as long as thine will serve
the turn ?
Valentine. Ay, my good lord.
Duke.   Then let me see thy cloak :
I 'll get me one of such another length.
Valentine. Why, any cloak will serve the turn, my
lord.
Duke. How shall I fashion me to wear a
cloak ?
I pray thee, let me feel thy cloak upon me.
What letter is this same ? What 's here ? ' To
Silvia ' !
And here an engine fit for my proceeding.
I 'll be so bold to break the seal for once. [*Reads.*
' My thoughts do harbour with my Silvia nightly,
And slaves they are to me that send them
flying :
O, could their master come and go as lightly,
Himself would lodge where senseless they are
lying !
My herald thoughts in thy pure bosom rest
them ;
While I, their king, that hither them impor-
tune,
Do curse the grace that with such grace hath
bless'd them,
Because myself do want my servants' fortune :
I curse myself, for they are sent by me,
That they should harbour where their lord
would be.'
What 's here ?
' Silvia, this night I will enfranchise thee.'
'Tis so ; and here 's the ladder for the purpose.
Why, Phaethon,—for thou art Merops' son,—
Wilt thou aspire to guide the heavenly car
And with thy daring folly burn the world ?
Wilt thou reach stars, because they shine on
thee ?
Go, base intruder ! overweening slave !
Bestow thy fawning smiles on equal mates,
And think my patience, more than thy desert,
Is privilege for thy departure hence :
Thank me for this more than for all the favours
Which all too much I have bestow'd on thee.
But if thou linger in my territories
Longer than swiftest expedition
Will give thee time to leave our royal court,
By heaven ! my wrath shall far exceed the love
I ever bore my daughter or thyself.
Be gone ! I will not hear thy vain excuse ;
But, as thou lovest thy life, make speed from
hence.   [*Exit.*
Valentine. And why not death rather than living
torment ?
To die is to be banish'd from myself ;
And Silvia is myself : banish'd from her
Is self from self : a deadly banishment !
What light is light, if Silvia be not seen ?
What joy is joy, if Silvia be not by ?
Unless it be to think that she is by
And feed upon the shadow of perfection.
Except I be by Silvia in the night,
There is no music in the nightingale ;

Unless I look on Silvia in the day,
There is no day for me to look upon ;
She is my essence, and I leave to be,
If I be not by her fair influence
Foster'd, illumined, cherish'd, kept alive.
I fly not death, to fly his deadly doom :
Tarry I here, I but attend on death :
But, fly I hence, I fly away from life.

Enter PROTEUS *and* LAUNCE.

Proteus. Run, boy, run, run, and seek him out.
Launce. Soho, soho !
Proteus. What seest thou ?
Launce. Him we go to find : there 's not a
hair on 's head but 'tis a Valentine.
Proteus. Valentine ?
Valentine. No.
Proteus. Who then ? his spirit ?
Valentine. Neither.
Proteus. What then ?
Valentine. Nothing.
Launce. Can nothing speak ? Master, shall
I strike ?
Proteus. Who wouldst thou strike ?
Launce. Nothing.
Proteus. Villain, forbear.
Launce. Why, sir, I 'll strike nothing: I pray
you,—
Proteus. Sirrah, I say, forbear. Friend Valen-
tine, a word.
Valentine. My ears are stopt and cannot hear
good news,
So much of bad already hath possess'd them.
Proteus. Then in dumb silence will I bury mine,
For they are harsh, untuneable and bad.
Valentine. Is Silvia dead ?
Proteus. No, Valentine.
Valentine. No Valentine, indeed, for sacred Silvia.
Hath she forsworn me ?
Proteus. No, Valentine.
Valentine. No Valentine, if Silvia have forsworn
me.
What is your news ?
Launce. Sir, there is a proclamation that
you are vanished.
Proteus. That thou art banished—O, that 's the
news !—
From hence, from Silvia and from me thy friend.
Valentine. O, I have fed upon this woe already,
And now excess of it will make me surfeit.
Doth Silvia know that I am banished ?
Proteus. Ay, ay ; and she hath offer'd to the
doom—
Which, unreversed, stands in effectual force—
A sea of melting pearl, which some call tears :
Those at her father's churlish feet she tender'd ;
With them, upon her knees, her humble self ;
Wringing her hands, whose whiteness so be-
came them
As if but now they waxed pale for woe :
But neither bended knees, pure hands held up,
Sad sighs, deep groans, nor silver-shedding tears,
Could penetrate her uncompassionate sire ;
But Valentine, if he be ta'en, must die.
Besides, her intercession chafed him so,
When she for thy repeal was suppliant,
That to close prison he commanded her,
With many bitter threats of biding there.
Valentine. No more ; unless the next word that
thou speak'st
Have some malignant power upon my life :

If so, I pray thee, breathe it in mine ear,
As ending anthem of my endless dolour.
   Proteus. Cease to lament for that thou canst
      not help,
And study help for that which thou lament'st.
Time is the nurse and breeder of all good.
Here if thou stay, thou canst not see thy love ;
Besides, thy staying will abridge thy life.
Hope is a lover's staff ; walk hence with that
And manage it against despairing thoughts.
Thy letters may be here, though thou art hence ;
Which, being writ to me, shall be deliver'd
Even in the milk-white bosom of thy love.
The time now serves not to expostulate :
Come, I 'll convey thee through the city-gate ;
And, ere I part with thee, confer at large
Of all that may concern thy love-affairs.
As thou lovest Silvia, though not for thyself,
Regard thy danger, and along with me !
   Valentine. I pray thee, Launce, an if thou seest
      my boy,
Bid him make haste and meet me at the North-
      gate.
   Proteus. Go, sirrah, find him out. Come,
Valentine.
   Valentine. O my dear Silvia ! Hapless Valentine !
         [*Exeunt Valentine and Proteus.*
   Launce. I am but a fool, look you ; and yet
I have the wit to think my master is a kind of a
knave   but that 's all one, if he be but one
knave. He lives not now that knows me to be
in love ; yet I am in love ; but a team of horse
shall not pluck that from me ; nor who 'tis I
love ; and yet 'tis a woman ; but what woman,
I will not tell myself ; and yet 'tis a milkmaid ;
yet 'tis not a maid, for she hath had gossips ;
yet 'tis a maid, for she is her master's maid, and
serves for wages.   She hath more qualities than
a water-spaniel ; which is much in a bare Christian. [*Pulling out a paper.*] Here is the cate-
log of her condition. ' Imprimis : She can fetch
and carry.' Why, a horse can do no more : nay,
a horse cannot fetch, but only carry ; therefore
is she better than a jade.   ' Item : She can milk ;'
look you, a sweet virtue in a maid with clean
hands.

                 Enter SPEED.

   Speed. How now, Signior Launce ! what
news with your mastership ?
   Launce. With my master's ship ? why, it is at
sea.
   Speed. Well, your old vice still ; mistake
the word.   What news, then, in your paper ?
   Launce. The blackest news that ever thou
heardest.
   Speed. Why, man, how black ?
   Launce. Why, as black as ink.
   Speed. Let me read them.
   Launce. Fie on thee, jolt-head ! thou canst not
read.
   Speed. Thou liest ; I can.
   Launce. I will try thee. Tell me this : who
begot thee ?
   Speed. Marry, the son of my grandfather.
   Launce. O illiterate loiterer ! it was the son
of thy grandmother : this proves that thou
canst not read.
   Speed. Come, fool, come ; try me in thy
paper.

   Launce. There ; and Saint Nicholas be thy
speed !
   Speed. [*Reads*] ' Imprimis : She can milk.'
   Launce. Ay, that she can.
   Speed. ' Item : She brews a good ale.'
   Launce. And   thereof comes   the   proverb :
' Blessing of your heart, you brew good ale.'
   Speed. ' Item : She can sew.'
   Launce. That 's as much as to say, Can
she so ?
   Speed. ' Item : She can knit.'
   Launce. What need a man care for a stock
with a wench, when she can knit him a stock ?
   Speed. ' Item : She can wash and scour.'
   Launce. A special virtue ; for then she need
not be washed and scoured.
   Speed. ' Item : She can spin.'
   Launce. Then may I set the world on wheels,
when she can spin for her living.
   Speed. ' Item : She hath many nameless
virtues.'
   Launce. That 's as much as to say, bastard
virtues ; that, indeed, know not their fathers
and therefore have no names.
   Speed. ' Here follow her vices.'
   Launce. Close at the heels of her virtues.
   Speed. ' Item : She is not to be kissed fast-
ing, in respect of her breath.'
   Launce. Well, that fault may be mended
with a breakfast. Read on.
   Speed. ' Item : She hath a sweet mouth.'
   Launce. That makes amends for her sour
breath.
   Speed. ' Item : She doth talk in her sleep.'
   Launce. It 's no matter for that, so she sleep
not in her talk.
   Speed. ' Item : She is slow in words.'
   Launce. O villain, that set this down among
her vices ! To be slow in words is a woman's
only virtue : I pray thee, out with 't, and place
it for her chief virtue.
   Speed. ' Item : She is proud.'
   Launce. Out with that too ; it was Eve's
legacy, and cannot be ta'en from her.
   Speed. ' Item : She hath no teeth.'
   Launce. I care not for that neither, because
I love crusts.
   Speed. ' Item : She is curst.'
   Launce. Well, the best is, she hath no teeth
to bite.
   Speed. ' Item : She will often praise her
liquor.'
   Launce. If her liquor be good, she shall : if
she will not, I will ; for good things should be
praised.
   Speed. ' Item : She is too liberal.'
   Launce. On her tongue she cannot, for that 's
writ down she is slow of ; of her purse she shall
not, for that I 'll keep shut ; now, of another
thing she may, and that cannot I help. Well,
proceed.
   Speed. ' Item : She hath more hair than wit,
and more faults than hairs, and more wealth
than faults.'
   Launce. Stop there ; I 'll have her : she was
mine, and not mine, twice or thrice in that last
article.   Rehearse that once more.
   Speed. ' Item : She hath more hair than
wit,'—
   Launce. More hair than wit ? It may be :
I 'll prove it. The cover of the salt hides the

salt, and therefore it is more than the salt ; the hair that covers the wit is more than the wit, for the greater hides the less. What 's next ?

Speed. ' And more faults than hairs,'—

Launce. That 's monstrous : O, that that were out !

Speed. ' And more wealth than faults.'

Launce. Why, that word makes the faults gracious. Well, I 'll have her : and if it be a match, as nothing is impossible,—

Speed. What then ?

Launce. Why, then will I tell thee—that thy master stays for thee at the North-gate.

Speed. For me ?

Launce. For thee ! ay, who art thou ? he hath stayed for a better man than thee.

Speed. And must I go to him ?

Launce. Thou must run to him. for thou hast stayed so long that going will scarce serve the turn.

Speed. Why didst not tell me sooner ? pox of your love-letters !   [*Exit.*

Launce. Now will he be swinged for reading my letter ; an unmannerly slave, that will thrust himself into secrets ! I 'll after, to rejoice in the boy's correction.   [*Exit.*

SCENE II. *The same.   The* Duke's *palace.*

Enter Duke *and* Thurio.

Duke. Sir Thurio, fear not but that she will love you,

Now Valentine is banish'd from her sight.

Thurio. Since his exile she hath despised me most,

Forsworn my company and rail'd at me,

That I am desperate of obtaining her.

Duke. This weak impress of love is as a figure

Trenched in ice, which with an hour's heat

Dissolves to water and doth lose his form.

A little time will melt her frozen thoughts

And worthless Valentine shall be forgot.

Enter Proteus.

How now, Sir Proteus ! Is your countryman

According to our proclamation gone ?

Proteus. Gone, my good lord.

Duke. My daughter takes his going grievously.

Proteus. A little time, my lord, will kill that grief.

Duke. So I believe ; but Thurio thinks not so.

Proteus, the good conceit I hold of thee—

For thou hast shown some sign of good desert—

Makes me the better to confer with thee.

Proteus. Longer than I prove loyal to your grace

Let me not live to look upon your grace.

Duke. Thou know'st how willingly I would

The match between Sir Thurio and my daughter.

Proteus. I do, my lord.

Duke. And also, I think, thou art not ignorant

How she opposes her against my will.

Proteus. She did, my lord, when Valentine was here.

Duke. Ay, and perversely she persevers so.

What might we do to make the girl forget

The love of Valentine and love Sir Thurio ?

Proteus. The best way is to slander Valentine

With falsehood, cowardice and poor descent,

Three things that women highly hold in hate.

Duke. Ay, but she 'll think that it is spoke in hate.

Proteus. Ay, if his enemy deliver it :

Therefore it must with circumstance be spoken

By one whom she esteemeth as his friend.

Duke. Then you must undertake to slander him.

Proteus. And that, my lord, I shall be loath to do :

'Tis an ill office for a gentleman,

Especially against his very friend.

Duke. Where your good word cannot advantage him,

Your slander never can endamage him ;

Therefore the office is indifferent,

Being entreated to it by your friend.

Proteus. You have prevail'd, my lord : if I can do it

By aught that I can speak in his dispraise,

She shall not long continue love to him.

But say this weed her love from Valentine,

It follows not that she will love Sir Thurio.

Thurio. Therefore, as you unwind her love from him,

Lest it should ravel and be good to none,

You must provide to bottom it on me ;

Which must be done by praising me as much

As you in worth dispraise Sir Valentine.

Duke. And, Proteus, we dare trust you in this kind,

Because we know, on Valentine's report,

You are already Love's firm votary

And cannot soon revolt and change your mind.

Upon this warrant shall you have access

Where you with Silvia may confer at large ;

For she is lumpish, heavy, melancholy,

And, for your friend's sake, will be glad of you ;

Where you may temper her by your persuasion

To hate young Valentine and love my friend.

Proteus. As much as I can do, I will effect :

But you, Sir Thurio, are not sharp enough ;

You must lay lime to tangle her desires

By wailful sonnets, whose composed rhymes

Should be full-fraught with serviceable vows.

Duke. Ay,

Much is the force of heaven-bred poesy.

Proteus. Say that upon the altar of her beauty

You sacrifice your tears, your sighs, your heart :

Write till your ink be dry, and with your tears

Moist it again, and frame some feeling line

That may discover such integrity :

For Orpheus' lute was strung with poets' sinews,

Whose golden touch could soften steel and stones,

Make tigers tame and huge leviathans

Forsake unsounded deeps to dance on sands.

After your dire-lamenting elegies,

Visit by night your lady's chamber-window

With some sweet concert ; to their instruments

Tune a deploring dump : the night's dead silence

Will well become such sweet-complaining grievance.

This, or else nothing, will inherit her.

Duke. This discipline shows thou hast been in love.

Thurio. And thy advice this night I 'll put in practice.

Therefore, sweet Proteus, my direction-giver,

Let us into the city presently
To sort some gentlemen well skill'd in music.
I have a sonnet that will serve the turn
To give the onset to thy good advice.
Duke. About it, gentlemen !
Proteus. We 'll wait upon your grace till after
supper,
And afterward determine our proceedings.
Duke. Even now about it ! I will pardon
you.   *Exeunt.*

ACT IV.

SCENE I. *The frontiers of Mantua. A forest.*

Enter certain Outlaws.

First Outlaw.

Fellows, stand fast : I see a passenger.
Second Outlaw. If there be ten, shrink not, but
down with 'em.

Enter VALENTINE *and* SPEED.

Third Outlaw. Stand, sir, and throw us that
you have about ye :
If not, we 'll make you sit and rifle you.
Speed. Sir, we are undone ; these are the
villains
That all the travellers do fear so much.
Valentine. My friends,—
First Outlaw. That 's not so, sir : we are your
enemies.
Second Outlaw. Peace ! we 'll hear him.
Third Outlaw. Ay, by my beard, will we, for
he 's a proper man.
Valentine. Then know that I have little wealth to
lose :
A man I am cross'd with adversity ;
My riches are these poor habiliments,
Of which if you should here disfurnish me,
You take the sum and substance that I have.
Second Outlaw. Whither travel you ?
Valentine. To Verona.
First Outlaw. Whence came you ?
Valentine. From Milan.
Third Outlaw. Have you long sojourned there ?
Valentine. Some sixteen months, and longer
might have stay'd,
If crooked fortune had not thwarted me.
First Outlaw. What, were you banish'd thence ?
Valentine. I was.
Second Outlaw. For what offence ?
Valentine. For that which now torments me to
rehearse :
I kill'd a man, whose death I much repent ;
But yet I slew him manfully in fight,
Without false vantage or base treachery.
First Outlaw. Why, ne'er repent it, if it were done
so. ·
But were you banish'd for so small a fault ?
Valentine. I was, and held me glad of such a
doom.
Second Outlaw. Have you the tongues ?
Valentine. My youthful travel therein made me
happy,
Or else I often had been miserable.
Third Outlaw. By the bare scalp of Robin Hood's
fat friar,
This fellow were a king for our wild faction !
First Outlaw. We 'll have him. Sirs, a word.
Speed. Master, be one of them ; it 's an honour-
able kind of thievery.
Valentine. Peace, villain !

Second Outlaw. Tell us this : have you any thing
to take to ?
Valentine. Nothing but my fortune.
Third Outlaw. Know, then, that some of us are
gentlemen,
Such as the fury of ungovern'd youth
Thrust from the company of awful men :
Myself was from Verona banished
For practising to steal away a lady,
An heir, and near allied unto the duke.
Second Outlaw. And I from Mantua, for a gentle-
man,
Who, in my mood, I stabb'd unto the heart.
First Outlaw. And I for such like petty crimes
as these.
But to the purpose—for we cite our faults,
That they may hold excused our lawless lives ;
And partly, seeing you are beautified
With goodly shape and by your own report
A linguist and a man of such perfection
As we do in our quality much want—
Second Outlaw. Indeed, because you are a ban-
ish'd man,
Therefore, above the rest, we parley to you :
Are you content to be our general ?
To make a virtue of necessity
And live, as we do, in this wilderness ?
Third Outlaw. What say'st thou ? wilt thou be
of our consort ?
Say ay, and be the captain of us all :
We 'll do thee homage and be ruled by thee,
Love thee as our commander and our king.
First Outlaw. But if thou scorn our courtesy,
thou diest.
Second Outlaw. Thou shalt not live to brag what
we have offer'd.
Valentine. I take your offer and will live with you,
Provided that you do no outrages
On silly women or poor passengers.
Third Outlaw. No, we detest such vile base
practices.
Come, go with us, we 'll bring thee to our crews,
And show thee all the treasure we have got ;
Which, with ourselves, all rest at thy dispose.
                                      [*Exeunt.*

SCENE II. *Milan. Outside the* DUKE'S
palace, under SILVIA'S *chamber.*

Enter PROTEUS.

Proteus. Already have I been false to Valentine
And now I must be as unjust to Thurio.
Under the colour of commending him,
I have access my own love to prefer :
But Silvia is too fair, too true, too holy,
To be corrupted with my worthless gifts.
When I protest true loyalty to her,
She twits me with my falsehood to my friend ;
When to her beauty I commend my vows,
She bids me think how I have been forsworn
In breaking faith with Julia whom I loved :
And notwithstanding all her sudden quips,
The least whereof would quell a lover's hope,
Yet, spaniel-like, the more she spurns my love,
The more it grows and fawneth on her still.
But here comes Thurio ; now must we to her window,
And give some evening music to her ear.

Enter THURIO *and Musicians.*

Thurio. How now, Sir Proteus, are you crept
before us ?

Proteus. Ay, gentle Thurio : for you know that love
Will creep in service where it cannot go.
Thurio. Ay, but I hope, sir, that you love not here.
Proteus. Sir, but I do ; or else I would be hence.
Thurio. Who ? Silvia ?
Proteus.   Ay, Silvia ; for your sake.
Thurio. I thank you for your own. Now, gentlemen,
Let 's tune, and to it lustily awhile.

Enter, at a distance, Host, *and* Julia *in boy's clothes.*

Host. Now, my young guest, methinks you 're allycholly : I pray you, why is it ?
Julia. Marry, mine host, because I cannot be merry.
Host. Come, we 'll have you merry : I 'll bring you where you shall hear music and see the gentleman that you asked for.
Julia. But shall I hear him speak ?
Host. Ay, that you shall.
Julia. That will be music.   [*Music plays.*
Host. Hark, hark !
Julia. Is he among these ?
Host. Ay : but, peace ! let 's hear 'em.

SONG.

Who is Silvia ? what is she,
    That all our swains commend her ?
Holy, fair and wise is she ;
    The heaven such grace did lend her,
That she might admired be.
Is she kind as she is fair ?
    For beauty lives with kindness.
Love doth to her eyes repair,
    To help him of his blindness,
And, being help'd, inhabits there.
Then to Silvia let us sing,
    That Silvia is excelling ;
She excels each mortal thing
    Upon the dull earth dwelling :
To her let us garland bring.

Host. How now ! are you sadder than you were before ? How do you, man ? the music likes you not.
Julia. You mistake ; the musician likes me not.
Host. Why, my pretty youth ?
Julia. He plays false, father.
Host. How ? out of tune on the strings ?
Julia. Not so ; but yet so false that he grieves my very heart-strings.
Host. You have a quick ear.
Julia. Ay, I would I were deaf ; it makes me have a slow heart.
Host. I perceive you delight not in music.
Julia. Not a whit, when it jars so.
Host. Hark, what fine change is in the music !
Julia. Ay, that change is the spite.
Host. You would have them always play but one thing ?
Julia. I would always have one play but one thing.
But, host, does this Sir Proteus that we talk on
Often resort unto this gentlewoman ?
Host. I tell you what Launce, his man, told me : he loved her out of all nick.
Julia. Where is Launce ?
Host. Gone to seek his dog ; which tomorrow, by his master's command, he must carry for a present to his lady.

Julia. Peace ! stand aside : the company parts
Proteus. Sir Thurio, fear not you : I will so plead
That you shall say my cunning drift excels.
Thurio. Where meet we ?
Proteus.   At Saint Gregory's well.
Thurio.   Farewell.
          [*Exeunt Thurio and Musicians.*

Enter Silvia *above.*
Proteus. Madam, good even to your ladyship.
Silvia. I thank you for your music, gentlemen.
Who is that that spake ?
Proteus. One, lady, if you knew his pure heart's truth,
You would quickly learn to know him by his voice.
Silvia. Sir Proteus as I take it.
Proteus. Sir Proteus, gentle lady, and your servant.
Silvia. What 's your will ?
Proteus.   That I may compass yours.
Silvia. You have your wish ; my will is even this :
That presently you hie you home to bed,
Thou subtle, perjured, false, disloyal man !
Think'st thou I am so shallow, so conceitless,
To be seduced by thy flattery,
That hast deceived so many with thy vows ?
Return, return, and make thy love amends.
For me, by this pale queen of night I swear,
I am so far from granting thy request
That I despise thee for thy wrongful suit,
And by and by intend to chide myself
Even for this time I spend in talking to thee.
Proteus. I grant, sweet love, that I did love a lady ;
But she is dead.
Julia. [*Aside*] 'Twere false, if I should speak it ;
For I am sure she is not buried.
Silvia. Say that she be ; yet Valentine thy friend
Survives ; to whom, thyself art witness,
I am betroth'd ; and art thou not ashamed
To wrong him with thy importunacy ?
Proteus. I likewise hear that Valentine is dead.
Silvia. And so suppose am I ; for in his grave
Assure thyself my love is buried.
Proteus. Sweet lady, let me rake it from the earth.
Silvia. Go to thy lady's grave and call hers thence,
Or, at the least, in hers sepulchre thine.
Julia. [*Aside*] He heard not that.
Proteus. Madam, if your heart be so obdurate,
Vouchsafe me yet your picture for my love,
The picture that is hanging in your chamber ;
To that I 'll speak, to that I 'll sigh and weep :
For since the substance of your perfect self
Is else devoted, I am but a shadow ;
And to your shadow will I make true love.
Julia. [*Aside*] If 'twere a substance, you would, sure, deceive it,
And make it but a shadow, as I am.
Silvia. I am very loath to be your idol, sir :
But since your falsehood shall become you well
To worship shadows and adore false shapes,
Send to me in the morning and I 'll send it :
And so, good rest.
Proteus.   As wretches have o'ernight
That wait for execution in the morn.
          [*Exeunt Proteus and Silvia severally.*
Julia. Host, will you go ?
Host. By my halidom, I was fast asleep.
Julia. Pray you, where lies Sir Proteus ?

Host. Marry, at my house. Trust me, I think
'tis almost day.

Julia. Not so ; but it hath been the longest night
That e'er I watch'd and the most heaviest.

[*Exeunt.*

SCENE III. *The same.*

Enter EGLAMOUR.

Eglamour. This is the hour that Madam Silvia
Entreated me to call and know her mind :
There 's some great matter she 'ld employ me in,
Madam, madam !

Enter SILVIA *above.*

Silvia.   Who calls ?
Eglamour.   Your servant and your friend ;
One that attends your ladyship's command.
Silvia. Sir Eglamour, a thousand times good
morrow.
Eglamour. As many, worthy lady, to yourself :
According to your ladyship's impose,
I am thus early come to know what service
It is your pleasure to command me in.
Silvia. O Eglamour, thou art a gentleman—
Think not I flatter, for I swear I do not—
Valiant, wise, remorseful, well accomplish'd :
Thou art not ignorant what dear good will
I bear unto the banish'd Valentine,
Nor how my father would enforce me marry
Vain Thurio, whom my very soul abhors.
Thyself hast loved ; and I have heard thee say
No grief did ever come so near thy heart
As when thy lady and thy true love died,
Upon whose grave thou vow'dst pure chastity.
Sir Eglamour, I would to Valentine,
To Mantua, where I hear he makes abode ;
And, for the ways are dangerous to pass,
I do desire thy worthy company,
Upon whose faith and honour I repose.
Urge not my father's anger, Eglamour,
But think upon my grief, a lady's grief,
And on the justice of my flying hence,
To keep me from a most unholy match,
Which heaven and fortune still rewards with plagues.
I do desire thee, even from a heart
As full of sorrows as the sea of sands,
To bear me company and go with me :
If not, to hide what I have said to thee,
That I may venture to depart alone.
Eglamour. Madam, I pity much your grievances ;
Which since I know they virtuously are placed,
I give consent to go along with you,
Recking as little what betideth me
As much I wish all good befortune you.
When will you go ?
Silvia.   This evening coming.
Eglamour. Where shall I meet you ?
Silvia.   At Friar Patrick's cell,
Where I intend holy confession.
Eglamour. I will not fail your ladyship. Good
morrow, gentle lady.
Silvia. Good morrow, kind Sir Eglamour.

[*Exeunt severally.*

SCENE IV. *The same.*

Enter LAUNCE, *with his Dog.*

Launce. When a man 's servant shall play the cur
with him, look you, it goes hard : one that I brought
up of a puppy ; one that I saved from drowning,
when three or four of his blind brothers and sisters

went to it. I have taught him, even as one would
say precisely, ' thus I would teach a dog.' I was
sent to deliver him as a present to Mistress Silvia
from my master ; and I came no sooner into the
dining-chamber but he steps me to her trencher
and steals her capon's leg : O, 'tis a foul thing when
a cur cannot keep himself in all companies ! I would
have, as one should say, one that takes upon him
to be a dog indeed, to be, as it were, a dog at all
things. If I had not had more wit than he, to take
a fault upon me that he did, I think verily he had
been hanged for 't ; sure as I live, he had suffered
for 't : you shall judge. He thrusts me himself
into the company of three or four gentlemanlike
dogs, under the duke's table : he had not been
there—bless the mark !—a pissing while, but all
the chamber smelt him. ' Out with the dog ! ' says
one : ' What cur is that ? ' says another : ' Whip
him out ' says the third : ' Hang him up ' says the
duke. I, having been acquainted with the smell
before, knew it was Crab, and goes me to the fellow
that whips the dogs : ' Friend,' quoth I, ' you
mean to whip the dog ? ' ' Ay, marry, do I,' quoth
he. ' You do him the more wrong,' quoth I ;
' 'twas I did the thing you wot of.' He makes me
no more ado, but whips me out of the chamber.
How many masters would do this for his servant ?
Nay, I'll be sworn, I have sat in the stocks for puddings
he hath stolen, otherwise he had been executed ;
I have stood on the pillory for geese he hath killed,
otherwise he had suffered for 't. Thou thinkest
not of this now. Nay, I remember the trick you
served me when I took my leave of Madam Silvia :
did not I bid thee still mark me and do as I do ?
when didst thou see me heave up my leg and make
water against a gentlewoman's farthingale ? didst
thou ever see me do such a trick ?

Enter PROTEUS *and* JULIA.

Proteus. Sebastian is thy name ? I like thee well
And will employ thee in some service presently.
Julia. In what you please : I 'll do what I can.
Proteus. I hope thou wilt. [*To Launce*] How
now, you whoreson peasant !
Where have you been these two days loitering ?
Launce. Marry, sir, I carried Mistress Silvia the
dog you bade me.
Proteus. And what says she to my little jewel ?
Launce. Marry, she says your dog was a cur,
and tells you currish thanks is good enough for such
a present.
Proteus. But she received my dog ?
Launce. No, indeed, did she not : here have I
brought him back again.
Proteus. What, didst thou offer her this from me ?
Launce. Ay, sir ; the other squirrel was stolen
from me by the hangman boys in the market-place :
and then I offered her mine own, who is a dog as
big as ten of yours, and therefore the gift the greater.
Proteus. Go get thee hence, and find my dog again,
Or ne'er return again into my sight.
Away, I say ! stay'st thou to vex me here ?

[*Exit Launce.*

A slave, that still an end turns me to shame !
Sebastian, I have entertained thee,
Partly that I have need of such a youth
That can with some discretion do my business,
For 'tis no trusting to yond foolish lout,
But chiefly for thy face and thy behaviour,
Which, if my augury deceive me not,
Witness good bringing up, fortune and truth :

Therefore know thou, for this I entertain thee.
Go presently and take this ring with thee,
Deliver it to Madam Silvia :
She loved me well deliver'd it to me.
 Julia. It seems you loved not her, to leave her
token.
She is dead, belike ?
 Proteus.   Not so ; I think she lives.
 Julia. Alas !
 Proteus. Why dost thou cry ' alas ' ?
 Julia   I cannot choose
But pity her.
 Proteus. Wherefore shouldst thou pity her ?
 Julia. Because methinks that she loved you as
well
As you do love your lady Silvia :
She dreams on him that has forgot her love ;
You dote on her that cares not for your love.
'Tis pity love should be so contrary ;
And thinking on it makes me cry ' alas ! '
 Proteus. Well, give her that ring and therewithal
This letter. That 's her chamber. Tell my lady
I claim the promise for her heavenly picture.
Your message done, hie home unto my chamber,
Where thou shalt find me, sad and solitary.
           [*Exit.*
 Julia. How many women would do such a
message ?
Alas, poor Proteus ! thou hast entertain'd
A fox to be the shepherd of thy lambs.
Alas, poor fool ! why do I pity him
That with his very heart despiseth me ?
Because he loves her, he despiseth me ;
Because I love him, I must pity him.
This ring I gave him when he parted from me,
To bind him to remember my good will ;
And now am I, unhappy messenger,
To plead for that which I would not obtain,
To carry that which I would have refused,
To praise his faith which I would have dispraised.
I am my master's true-confirmed love ;
But cannot be true servant to my master,
Unless I prove false traitor to myself.
Yet will I woo for him, but yet so coldly
As, heaven it knows, I would not have him speed.

Enter SILVIA, *attended.*

Gentlewoman, good day ! I pray you, be my mean
To bring me where to speak with Madam Silvia.
 Silvia. What would you with her, if that I be she ?
 Julia. If you be she. I do entreat your patience
To hear me speak the message I am sent on.
 Silvia. From whom ?
 Julia. From my master, Sir Proteus, madam.
 Silvia. O, he sends you for a picture.
 Julia. Ay, madam.
 Silvia. Ursula, bring my picture there.
Go give your master this : tell him from me,
One Julia, that his changing thoughts forget,
Would better fit his chamber than this shadow.
 Julia. Madam, please you peruse this letter.—
Pardon me, madam ; I have unadvised
Deliver'd you a paper that I should not :
This is the letter to your ladyship.
 Silvia. I pray thee, let me look on that again.
 Julia. It may not be ; good madam, pardon me.
 Silvia. There, hold !
I will not look upon your master's lines :
I know they are stuff'd with protestations
And full of new-found oaths ; which he will break
As easily as I do tear his paper.

 Julia. Madam, he sends your ladyship this ring.
 Silvia. The more shame for him that he sends it
me ;
For I have heard him say a thousand times
His Julia gave it him at his departure.
Though his false finger have profaned the ring,
Mine shall not do his Julia so much wrong.
 Julia. She thanks you.
 Silvia. What say'st thou ?
 Julia. I thank you, madam, that you tender her.
Poor gentlewoman ! my master wrongs her much.
 Silvia. Dost thou know her ?
 Julia. Almost as well as I do know myself :
To think upon her woes I do protest
That I have wept a hundred several times.
 Silvia. Belike she thinks that Proteus hath for-
sook her.
 Julia. I think she doth ; and that 's her cause of
sorrow.
 Silvia. Is she not passing fair ?
 Julia. She hath been fairer, madam, than she is :
When she did think my master loved her well,
She, in my judgement, was as fair as you ;
But since she did neglect her looking-glass
And threw her sun-expelling mask away,
The air hath starved the roses in her cheeks
And pinch'd the lily-tincture of her face,
That now she is become as black as I.
 Silvia. How tall was she ?
 Julia. About my stature ; for at Pentecost,
When all our pageants of delight were play'd,
Our youth got me to play the woman's part,
And I was trimm'd in Madam Julia's gown,
Which served me as fit, by all men's judgements,
As if the garment had been made for me :
Therefore I know she is about my height.
And at that time I made her weep agood,
For I did play a lamentable part :
Madam, 'twas Ariadne passioning
For Theseus' perjury and unjust flight ;
Which I so lively acted with my tears
That my poor mistress, moved therewithal,
Wept bitterly ; and would I might be dead
If I in thought felt not her very sorrow !
 Silvia. She is beholding to thee, gentle youth.
Alas, poor lady, desolate and left !
I weep myself to think upon thy words.
Here, youth, there is my purse ; I give thee this
For thy sweet mistress' sake, because thou lovest her.
Farewell.   [*Exit Silvia, with attendants.*
 Julia. And she shall thank you for 't, if e'er you
know her.
A virtuous gentlewoman, mild and beautiful !
I hope my master's suit will be but cold,
Since she respects my mistress' love so much.
Alas, how love can trifle with itself !
Here is her picture : let me see ; I think,
If I had such a tire, this face of mine
Were full as lovely as is this of hers :
And yet the painter flatter'd her a little,
Unless I flatter with myself too much.
Her hair is auburn, mine is perfect yellow :
If that be all the difference in his love,
I'll get me such a colour'd periwig.
Her eyes are grey as glass, and so are mine :
Ay, but her forehead 's low, and mine 's as high.
What should it be that he respects in her
But I can make respective in myself,
If this fond Love were not a blinded god ?
Come, shadow, come, and take this shadow up,
For 'tis thy rival. O thou senseless form,

Thou shalt be worshipp'd, kiss'd, loved and adored !
And, were there sense in his idolatry,
My substance should be statue in thy stead.
I 'll use thee kindly for thy mistress' sake,
That used me so ; or else, by Jove I vow,
I should have scratch'd out your unseeing eyes,
To make my master out of love with thee !
                                          [Exit.

ACT V.

SCENE I. *Milan. An abbey.*

Enter EGLAMOUR.

Eglamour.

The sun begins to gild the western sky ;
  And now it is about the very hour
  That Silvia, at Friar Patrick's cell, should
    meet me.
She will not fail, for lovers break not hours,
Unless it be to come before their time ;
So much they spur their expedition.
See where she comes.

Enter SILVIA.

             Lady, a happy evening !
Silvia. Amen, amen ! Go on, good Eglamour,
Out at the postern by the abbey-wall :
I fear I am attended by some spies.
Eglamour. Fear not : the forest is not three
  leagues off ;
If we recover that, we are sure enough.
                             [Exeunt.

SCENE II. *The same. The* DUKE'S *palace.*

Enter THURIO, PROTEUS, *and* JULIA.

Thurio. Sir Proteus, what says Silvia to my suit ?
Proteus. O, sir, I find her milder than she was ;
And yet she takes exceptions at your person.
Thurio. What, that my leg is too long ?
Proteus. No ; that it is too little.
Thurio. I 'll wear a boot, to make it somewhat
  rounder.
Julia. [*Aside*] But love will not be spurr'd to what
  it loathes.
Thurio. What says she to my face ?
Proteus. She says it is a fair one.
Thurio. Nay, then the wanton lies ; my face is
  black.
Proteus. But pearls are fair ; and the old saying
  is,
Black men are pearls in beauteous ladies' eyes.
Julia. [*Aside*] 'Tis true ; such pearls as put out
  ladies' eyes :
For I had rather wink than look on them.
Thurio. How likes she my discourse ?
Proteus. Ill, when you talk of war.
Thurio. But well, when I discourse of love and
  peace ?
Julia. [*Aside*] But better, indeed, when you hold
  your peace.
Thurio. What says she to my valour ?
Proteus. O, sir, she makes no doubt of that.
Julia. [*Aside*] She need not, when she knows it
  cowardice.
Thurio. What says she to my birth ?
Proteus. That you are well derived.
Julia. [*Aside*] True ; from a gentleman to a fool.
Thurio. Considers she my possessions ?
Proteus. O, ay ; and pities them.
Thurio. Wherefore ?
Julia. [*Aside*] That such an ass should owe them.

Proteus. That they are out by lease.
Julia. Here comes the duke.

Enter DUKE.

Duke. How now, Sir Proteus ! how now,
  Thurio !
Which of you saw Sir Eglamour of late ?
Thurio. Not I.
Proteus.   Nor I.
Duke.   Saw you my daughter ?
Proteus.   Neither.
Duke. Why then,
She 's fled unto that peasant Valentine ;
And Eglamour is in her company.
'Tis true ; for Friar Laurence met them both,
As he in penance wander'd through the forest ;
Him he knew well, and guess'd that it was she,
But, being mask'd; he was not sure of it ;
Besides, she did intend confession
At Patrick's cell this even ; and there she was not ;
These likelihoods confirm her flight from hence.
Therefore, I pray you, stand not to discourse,
But mount you presently and meet with me
Upon the rising of the mountain-foot
That leads toward Mantua, whither they are fled :
Dispatch, sweet gentlemen, and follow me.
                                    [Exit.
Thurio. Why, this it is to be a peevish girl,
That flies her fortune when it follows her.
I 'll after, more to be revenged on Eglamour
Than for the love of reckless Silvia.   *[Exit.*
Proteus. And I will follow, more for Silvia's love
Than hate of Eglamour that goes with her.
                                    [Exit.
Julia. And I will follow, more to cross that love
Than hate for Silvia that is gone for love.
                                    [Exit.

SCENE III. *The frontiers of Mantua.*
                The forest.

Enter Outlaws *with* SILVIA.

First Outlaw. Come, come,
Be patient ; we must bring you to our captain.
Silvia. A thousand more mischance than this one
Have learn'd me how to brook this patiently.
Second Outlaw. Come, bring her away.
First Outlaw. Where is the gentleman that was
  with her ?
Third Outlaw. Being nimble-footed, he hath
  outrun us,
But Moyses and Valerius follow him.
Go thou with her to the west end of the wood ;
There is our captain : we 'll follow him that 's fled ;
The thicket is beset ; he cannot 'scape.
First Outlaw. Come, I must bring you to our
  captain's cave :
Fear not ; he bears an honourable mind,
And will not use a woman lawlessly.
Silvia. O Valentine, this I endure for thee !
                                  [Exeunt.

SCENE IV. *Another part of the forest.*

Enter VALENTINE.

Valentine. How use doth breed a habit in a man !
This shadowy desert, unfrequented woods,
I better brook than flourishing peopled towns :
Here can I sit alone, unseen of any,

And to the nightingale's complaining notes
Tune my distresses and record my woes.
O thou that dost inhabit in my breast,
Leave not the mansion so long tenantless,
Lest, growing ruinous, the building fall
And leave no memory of what it was !
Repair me with thy presence, Silvia ;
Thou gentle nymph, cherish thy forlorn swain !
What halloing and what stir is this to-day ?
These are my mates, that make their wills their law,
Have some unhappy passenger in chase.
They love me well ; yet I have much to do
To keep them from uncivil outrages.
Withdraw thee, Valentine ; who 's this comes here ?

Enter PROTEUS, SILVIA, *and* JULIA.

Proteus.   Madam, this service I have done for you,
Though you respect not aught your servant doth,
To hazard life and rescue you from him
That would have forced your honour and your
    love ;
Vouchsafe me, for my meed, but one fair look ;
A smaller boon than this I cannot beg
And less than this, I am sure, you cannot give.
Valentine.   [*Aside*] How like a dream is this I
    see and hear !
Love, lend me patience to forbear a while.
Silvia.   O miserable, unhappy that I am !
Proteus.   Unhappy were you, madam, ere I came ;
But by my coming I have made you happy.
Silvia.   By thy approach thou makest me most
    unhappy.
Julia.   [*Aside*] And me, when he approacheth
    to your presence.
Silvia.   Had I been seized by a hungry lion,
I would have been a breakfast to the beast,
Rather than have false Proteus rescue me.
O, Heaven be judge how I love Valentine,
Whose life 's as tender to me as my soul !
And full as much, for more there cannot be,
I do detest false perjured Proteus.
Therefore be gone ; solicit me no more.
Proteus.   What dangerous action, stood it next to
    death,
Would I not undergo for one calm look !
O, 'tis the curse in love, and still approved,
When women cannot love where they 're beloved !
Silvia.   When Proteus cannot love where he 's
    beloved.
Read over Julia's heart, thy first best love,
For whose dear sake thou didst then rend thy faith
Into a thousand oaths ; and all those oaths
Descended into perjury, to love me.
Thou hast no faith left now, unless thou 'dst two ;
And that 's far worse than none ; better have none
Than plural faith which is too much by one :
Thou counterfeit to thy true friend !
Proteus.   In love
Who respects friend ?
Silvia.   All men but Proteus.
Proteus.   Nay, if the gentle spirit of moving words
Can no way change you to a milder form,
I 'll woo you like a soldier, at arms' end,
And love you 'gainst the nature of love,—force ye.
Silvia.   O heaven !
Proteus.   I 'll force thee yield to my desire.
Valentine.   Ruffian, let go that rude uncivil touch,
Thou friend of an ill fashion !
Proteus.   Valentine !
Valentine.   Thou common friend, that 's without
    faith or love,

For such is a friend now ; treacherous man !
Thou hast beguiled my hopes ; nought but mine eye
Could have persuaded me : now I dare not say
I have one friend alive ; thou wouldst disprove me.
Who should be trusted, when one's own right hand
Is perjured to the bosom ? Proteus,
I am sorry I must never trust thee more,
But count the world a stranger for thy sake.
The private wound is deepest : O time most accurst,
'Mongst all foes that a friend should be the worst !
Proteus.   My shame and guilt confounds me.
Forgive me, Valentine : if hearty sorrow
Be a sufficient ransom for offence,
I tender 't here ; I do as truly suffer
As e'er I did commit.
Valentine.   Then I am paid ;
And once again I do receive thee honest.
Who by repentance is not satisfied
Is nor of heaven nor earth, for these are pleased.
By penitence the Eternal's wrath 's appeased :
And, that my love may appear plain and free,
All that was mine in Silvia I give thee.
Julia.   O me unhappy !   [*Swoons.*
Proteus.   Look to the boy.
Valentine.   Why, boy ! why, wag ! how now !
what 's the matter ? Look up ; speak.
Julia.   O good sir, my master charged me to
deliver a ring to Madam Silvia, which, out of my
neglect, was never done.
Proteus.   Where is that ring, boy ?
Julia.   Here 'tis ; this is it.
Proteus.   How ! let me see :
Why, this is the ring I gave to Julia.
Julia.   O, cry you mercy, sir, I have mistook :
This is the ring you sent to Silvia.
Proteus.   But how comest thou by this ring ? At
    my depart
I gave this unto Julia.
Julia.   And Julia herself did give it me ;
And Julia herself hath brought it hither.
Proteus.   How ! Julia !
Julia.   Behold her that gave aim to all thy oaths,
And entertain'd 'em deeply in her heart.
How oft hast thou with perjury cleft the root !
O Proteus, let this habit make thee blush !
Be thou ashamed that I have took upon me
Such an immodest raiment, if shame live
In a disguise of love :
It is the lesser blot, modesty finds,
Women to change their shapes than men their minds.
Proteus.   Than men their minds ! 'tis true. O
    heaven ! were man
But constant, he were perfect. That one error
Fills him with faults ; makes him run through all
    the sins :
Inconstancy falls off ere it begins.
What is in Silvia's face, but I may spy
More fresh in Julia's with a constant eye ?
Valentine.   Come, come, a hand from either :
Let me be blest to make this happy close ;
'Twere pity two such friends should be long foes.
Proteus.   Bear witness, Heaven, I have my wish
    for ever.
Julia.   And I mine.

Enter Outlaws, *with* DUKE *and* THURIO.

Outlaws.   A prize, a prize, a prize !
Valentine.   Forbear, forbear, I say ! it is my lord
    the duke.
Your grace is welcome to a man disgraced,

Banished Valentine.
 Duke.   Sir Valentine !
 Thurio. Yonder is Silvia ; and Silvia 's mine.
 Valentine. Thurio, give back, or else embrace thy
  death ;
Come not within the measure of my wrath ;
Do not name Silvia thine ; if once again,
† Verona shall not hold thee. Here she stands :
Take but possession of her with a touch :
I dare thee but to breathe upon my love.
 Thurio. Sir Valentine, I care not for her, I :
I hold him but a fool that will endanger
His body for a girl that loves him not :
I claim her not, and therefore she is thine.
 Duke. The more degenerate and base art thou,
To make such means for her as thou hast done
And leave her on such slight conditions.
Now, by the honour of my ancestry,
I do applaud thy spirit, Valentine,
And think thee worthy of an empress' love :
Know then, I here forget all former griefs,
Cancel all grudge, repeal thee home again,
Plead a new state in thy unrival'd merit,
To which I thus subscribe : Sir Valentine,
Thou art a gentleman and well derived ;
Take thou thy Silvia, for thou hast deserved her.
 Valentine. I thank your grace ; the gift hath made
  me happy.
I now beseech you, for your daughter's sake,
To grant one boon that I shall ask of you.

 Duke. I grant it, for thine own, whate'er it be.
 Valentine. These banish'd men that I have kept
  withal
Are men endued with worthy qualities :
Forgive them what they have committed here
And let them be recall'd from their exile :
They are reformed, civil, full of good
And fit for great employment, worthy lord.
 Duke. Thou hast prevail'd ; I pardon them and
  thee :
Dispose of them as thou know'st their deserts.
Come, let us go : we will include all jars
With triumphs, mirth and rare solemnity.
 Valentine. And, as we walk along, I dare be bold
With our discourse to make your grace to smile.
What think you of this page, my Lord ?
 Duke. I think the boy hath grace in him ; he
  blushes.
 Valentine. I warrant you, my lord, more grace
  than boy.
 Duke. What mean you by that saying ?
 Valentine. Please you, I 'll tell you as we pass
  along,
That you will wonder what hath fortuned.
Come, Proteus ; 'tis your penance but to hear
The story of your loves discovered :
That done, our day of marriage shall be yours ;
One feast, one house, one mutual happiness.
            [*Exeunt.*

THE

MERRY WIVES OF WINDSOR

DRAMATIS PERSONÆ

SIR JOHN FALSTAFF.

FENTON, *a gentleman.*

SHALLOW, *a country justice.*

SLENDER, *cousin to* Shallow.

FORD, } *two gentlemen dwelling at Windsor.*
PAGE, }

WILLIAM PAGE, *a boy, son to* Page

SIR HUGH EVANS, *a Welsh parson.*

DOCTOR CAIUS, *a French physician.*

Host of the Garter Inn.

BARDOLPH, }
PISTOL, } *sharpers attending on* Falstaff.
NYM, }

ROBIN, *page to* Falstaff.

SIMPLE, *servant to* Slender.

RUGBY, *servant to* Doctor Caius.

MISTRESS FORD.

MISTRESS PAGE.

ANNE PAGE, *her daughter.*

MISTRESS QUICKLY, *servant to* Doctor Caius.

Servants to Page, Ford, &c.

SCENE : Windsor, and the neighbourhood.

ACT I.

SCENE I. *Windsor. Before* PAGE'S *house.*

Enter JUSTICE SHALLOW, SLENDER, *and* SIR
HUGH EVANS.

Shallow.

Sir Hugh, persuade me not ; I will make a
Star-chamber matter of it : if he were twenty
Sir John Falstaffs, he shall not abuse Robert
Shallow, esquire.

Slender. In the county of Gloucester, justice of
peace and ' Coram.'

Shallow. Ay, cousin Slender, and ' Custalorum.'

Slender. Ay, and ' Rato-lorum ' too ; and a
gentleman born, master parson ; who writes himself
' Armigero,' in any bill, warrant, quittance, or
obligation, ' Armigero.'

Shallow. Ay, that I do ; and have done any time
these three hundred years.

Slender. All his successors gone before him hath
done 't ; and all his ancestors that come after him
may : they may give the dozen white luces in their
coat.

Shallow. It is an old coat.

Evans. The dozen white louses do become an
old coat well ; it agrees well, passant ; it is a familiar
beast to man, and signifies love.

Shallow. The luce is the fresh fish ; the salt fish
is an old coat.

Slender. I may quarter, coz.

Shallow. You may, by marrying.

Evans. It is marring indeed, if he quarter it.

Shallow. Not a whit.

Evans. Yes, py'r lady ; if he has a quarter of
your coat, there is but three skirts for yourself, in
my simple conjectures : but that is all one. If Sir
John Falstaff have committed disparagements unto
you, I am of the church, and will be glad to do my
benevolence to make atonements and compremises
between you.

Shallow. The council shall hear it ; it is a riot.

Evans. It is not meet the council hear a riot ;
there is no fear of Got in a riot : the council, look
you, shall desire to hear the fear of Got, and not to
hear a riot ; take your vizaments in that.

Shallow. Ha ! o' my life, if I were young again,
the sword should end it.

Evans. It is petter that friends is the sword, and
end it : and there is also another device in my prain,
which peradventure prings goot discretions with it :
there is Anne Page, which is daughter to Master
Thomas Page, which is pretty virginity.

Slender. Mistress Anne Page ? She has brown
hair, and speaks small like a woman.

Evans. It is that fery person for all the orld, as
just as you will desire ; and seven hundred pounds
of moneys, and gold and silver, is her grandsire
upon his death's-bed—Got deliver to a joyful resur-
rections !—give, when she is able to overtake seventeen years old : it were a goot motion if we leave
our pribbles and prabbles, and desire a marriage
between Master Abraham and Mistress Anne Page.

Slender. Did her grandsire leave her seven hundred pound ?

Evans. Ay, and her father is make her a petter
penny.

Slender. I know the young gentlewoman ; she
has good gifts.

Evans. Seven hundred pounds and possibilities
is goot gifts.

Shallow. Well, let us see honest Master Page.
Is Falstaff there ?

Evans. Shall I tell you a lie ? I do despise a
liar as I do despise one that is false, or as I despise
one that is not true. The knight, Sir John, is there ;
and, I beseech you, be ruled by your well-willers.
I will peat the door for Master Page. [*Knocks*]
What, hoa ! Got pless your house here !

Page. [*Within*] Who 's there ?

Enter PAGE.

Evans. Here is Got's plessing, and your friend, and Justice Shallow; and here young Master Slender, that peradventures shall tell you another tale, if matters grow to your likings.

Page. I am glad to see your worships well. I thank you for my venison, Master Shallow.

Shallow. Master Page, I am glad to see you: much good do it your good heart ! I wished your venison better ; it was ill killed. How doth good Mistress Page?—and I thank you always with my heart, la ! with my heart.

Page. Sir, I thank you.

Shallow. Sir, I thank you ; by yea and no, I do.

Page. I am glad to see you, good Master Slender.

Slender. How does your fallow greyhound, sir ? I heard say he was outrun on Cotsall.

Page. It could not be judged, sir.

Slender. You 'll not confess, you 'll not confess.

Shallow. That he will not. 'Tis your fault, 'tis your fault ; 'tis a good dog.

Page. A cur, sir.

Shallow. Sir, he 's a good dog, and a fair dog : can there be more said ? he is good and fair. Is Sir John Falstaff here ?

Page. Sir, he is within ; and I would I could do a good office between you.

Evans. It is spoke as a Christians ought to speak.

Shallow. He hath wronged me, Master Page.

Page. Sir, he doth in some sort confess it.

Shallow. If it be confessed, it is not redressed : is not that so, Master Page ? He hath wronged me ; indeed he hath ; at a word, he hath, believe me : Robert Shallow, esquire, saith, he is wronged.

Page. Here comes Sir John.

Enter SIR JOHN FALSTAFF, BARDOLPH, NYM, *and* PISTOL.

Falstaff. Now, Master Shallow, you 'll complain of me to the king ?

Shallow. Knight, you have beaten my men, killed my deer, and broke open my lodge.

Falstaff. But not kissed your keeper's daughter ?

Shallow. Tut, a pin ! this shall be answered.

Falstaff. I will answer it straight ; I have done all this. That is now answered.

Shallow. The council shall know this.

Falstaff. 'Twere better for you if it were known in counsel : you 'll be laughed at.

Evans. Pauca verba, Sir John ; goot worts.

Falstaff. Good worts ! good cabbage. Slender, I broke your head : what matter have you against me ?

Slender. Marry, sir, I have matter in my head against you ; and against your cony-catching rascals, Bardolph, Nym, and Pistol.

Bardolph. You Banbury cheese !

Slender. Ay, it is no matter.

Pistol. How now, Mephostophilus !

Slender. Ay, it is no matter.

Nym. Slice, I say ! pauca, pauca : slice ! that 's my humour.

Slender. Where 's Simple, my man ? Can you tell, cousin ?

Evans. Peace, I pray you. Now let us understand. There is three umpires in this matter, as I understand ; that is, Master Page, fidelicet Master Page ; and there is myself, fidelicet myself ; and the three party is, lastly and finally, mine host of the Garter.

Page. We three, to hear it and end it between them.

Evans. Fery goot : I will make a prief of it in my note-book ; and we will afterwards ork upon the cause with as great discreetly as we can.

Falstaff. Pistol !

Pistol. He hears with ears.

Evans. The tevil and his tam ! what phrase is this, ' He hears with ear ' ? why, it is affectations.

Falstaff. Pistol, did you pick Master Slender's purse ?

Slender. Ay, by these gloves, did he, or I would I might never come in mine own great chamber again else, of seven groats in mill-sixpences, and two Edward shovel-boards, that cost me two shilling and two pence a-piece of Yead Miller, by these gloves.

Falstaff. Is this true, Pistol ?

Evans. No ; it is false, if it is a pick-purse.

Pistol. Ha, thou mountain-foreigner ! Sir John and master mine, I combat challenge of this latten bilbo. Word of denial in thy labras here ! Word of denial : froth and scum, thou liest !

Slender. By these gloves, then, 'twas he.

Nym. Be advised, sir, and pass good humours : I will say ' marry trap ' with you, if you run the nuthook's humour on me ; that is the very note of it.

Slender. By this hat, then, he in the red face had it ; for though I cannot remember what I did when you made me drunk, yet I am not altogether an ass.

Falstaff. What say you, Scarlet and John ?

Bardolph. Why, sir, for my part, I say the gentleman had drunk himself out of his five sentences.

Evans. It is his five senses : fie, what the ignorance is !

Bardolph. And being fap, sir, was, as they say, cashiered ; and so conclusions passed the careires.

Slender. Ay, you spake in Latin then too ; but 'tis no matter : I 'll ne'er be drunk whilst I live again, but in honest, civil, godly company, for this trick : if I be drunk, I 'll be drunk with those that have the fear of God, and not with drunken knaves.

Evans. So Got udge me, that is a virtuous mind.

Falstaff. You hear all these matters denied, gentlemen ; you hear it.

Enter ANNE PAGE, *with wine ;* MISTRESS FORD *and* MISTRESS PAGE, *following.*

Page. Nay, daughter, carry the wine in ; we 'll drink within.   [*Exit Anne Page.*

Slender. O heaven ! this is Mistress Anne Page.

Page. How now, Mistress Ford !

Falstaff. Mistress Ford, by my troth, you are very well met : by your leave, good mistress.
                                                  [*Kisses her.*

Page. Wife, bid these gentlemen welcome. Come, we have a hot venison pasty to dinner : come, gentlemen, I hope we shall drink down all unkindness.
      [*Exeunt all except Shallow, Slender, and Evans.*

Slender. I had rather than forty shillings I had my Book of Songs and Sonnets here.

Enter SIMPLE.

How now, Simple ! where have you been ? I must wait on myself, must I ? You have not the Book of Riddles about you, have you ?

Simpl.   Book of Riddles ! why, did you not lend it to Alce Sho, :ake upon All-hallowmas last, a fortnight afore Michaelmas ?

Shallow.   Come, coz ; come, coz ; we stay for you. A word with you, coz ; marry, this, coz : there is, as 'twere, a tender, a kind of tender, made afar off by Sir Hugh here.   Do you understand me ?

Slender.   Ay, sir, you shall find me reasonable ; if it be so, I shall do that that is reason.

Shallow.   Nay, but understand me.

Slender.   So I do, sir.

Evans.   Give ear to his motions, Master Slender : I will description the matter to you, if you be capacity of it.

Slender.   Nay, I will do as my cousin Shallow says : I pray you, pardon me ; he 's a justice of peace in his country, simple though I stand here.

Evans.   But that is not the question : the question is concerning your marriage.

Shallow.   Ay, there 's the point, sir.

Evans.   Marry, is it ; the very point of it ; to Mistress Anne Page.

Slender.   Why, if it be so, I will marry her upon any reasonable demands.

Evans.   But can you affection the 'oman ? Let us command to know that of your mouth or of your lips ; for divers philosophers hold that the lips is parcel of the mouth.   Therefore, precisely, can you carry your good will to the maid ?

Shallow.   Cousin Abraham Slender, can you love her ?

Slender.   I hope, sir, I will do as it shall become one that would do reason.

Evans.   Nay, Got's lords and his ladies ! you must speak possitable, if you can carry her your desires towards her.

Shallow.   That you must.   Will you, upon good dowry, marry her ?

Slender.   I will do a greater thing than that, upon your request, cousin, in any reason.

Shallow.   Nay, conceive me, conceive me, sweet coz : what I do is to pleasure you, coz.   Can you love the maid ?

Slender.   I will marry her, sir, at your request : but if there be no great love in the beginning, yet heaven may decrease it upon better acquaintance, when we are married and have more occasion to know one another ; I hope, upon familiarity will grow more contempt : but if you say, ' Marry her,' I will marry her ; that I am freely dissolved, and dissolutely.

Evans.   It is a fery discretion answer ; save the fall is in the ort ' dissolutely :' the ort is, according to our meaning, ' resolutely :' his meaning is good.

Shallow.   Ay, I think my cousin meant well.

Slender.   Ay, or else I would I might be hanged, la !

Shallow.   Here comes fair Mistress Anne.

Re-enter ANNE PAGE.

Would I were young for your sake, Mistress Anne !

Anne.   The dinner is on the table : my father desires your worships' company.

Shallow.   I will wait on him, fair Mistress Anne.

Evans.   Od's plessed will ! I will not be absence at the grace.

[*Exeunt Shallow and Evans.*

Anne.   Will 't please your worship to come in, sir?

Slender.   No, I thank you, forsooth, heartily ; I am very well.

Anne.   The dinner attends you, sir.

Slender.   I am not a-hungry, I thank you, forsooth.   Go, sirrah, for all you are my man, go wait upon my cousin Shallow.   [*Exit Simple.*] A justice of peace sometime may be beholding to his friend for a man.   I keep but three men and a boy yet, till my mother be dead : but what though ? yet I live like a poor gentleman born.

Anne.   I may not go in without your worship : they will not sit till you come.

Slender.   I' faith, I 'll eat nothing : I thank you as much as though I did.

Anne.   I pray you, sir, walk in.

Slender.   I had rather walk here, I thank you. I bruised my shin th' other day with playing at sword and dagger with a master of fence ; three veneys for a dish of stewed prunes ; and, by my troth, I cannot abide the smell of hot meat since. Why do your dogs bark so ? be there bears i' the town ?

Anne.   I think there are, sir ;   I heard them talked of.

Slender.   I love the sport well ; but I shall as soon quarrel at it as any man in England. You are afraid, if you see the bear loose, are you not ?

Anne.   Ay, indeed, sir.

Slender.   That 's meat and drink to me, now. I have seen Sackerson loose twenty times, and have taken him by the chain ; but, I warrant you, the women have so cried and shrieked at it, that it passed : but women, indeed, cannot abide 'em ; they are very ill-favoured rough things.

Re-enter PAGE.

Page.   Come, gentle Master Slender, come ;   we stay for you.

Slender.   I 'll eat nothing, I thank you, sir.

Page.   By cock and pie, you shall not choose, sir ! come, come.

Slender.   Nay, pray you, lead the way.

Page.   Come on, sir.

Slender.   Mistress Anne, yourself shall go first.

Anne.   Not I, sir ;   pray you, keep on.

Slender.   Truly, I will not go first ; truly, la ! I will not go you that wrong.

Anne.   I pray you, sir.

Slender.   I 'll rather be unmannerly than troublesome.   You do yourself wrong, indeed, la !

[*Exeunt.*

SCENE II.   *The same.*

Enter SIR HUGH EVANS *and* SIMPLE.

Evans.   Go your ways, and ask of Doctor Caius' house which is the way : and there dwells one Mistress Quickly, which is in the manner of his nurse, or his dry nurse, or his cook, or his laundry, his washer, and his wringer.

Simple.   Well, sir.

Evans.   Nay, it is petter yet.   Give her this letter ; for it is a 'oman that altogether 's acquaintance with Mistress Anne Page : and the letter is, to desire and require her to solicit your master's desires to Mistress Anne Page.   I pray you, be gone : I will make an end of my dinner ; there 's pippins and cheese to come.

[*Exeunt.*

SCENE III.   *A room in the Carter Inn.*

Enter FALSTAFF, HOST, BARDOLPH, NYM, PISTOL, *and* ROBIN.

Falstaff.   Mine host of the Garter !

Host. What says my bully-rook? speak scholarly and wisely.

Falstaff. Truly, mine host, I must turn away some of my followers.

Host. Discard, bully Hercules; cashier: let them wag; trot, trot.

Falstaff. I sit at ten pounds a week.

Host. Thou 'rt an emperor, Cæsar, Keisar, and Pheezar. I will entertain Bardolph; he shall draw, he shall tap: said I well, bully Hector?

Falstaff. Do so, good mine host.

Host. I have spoke; let him follow. [*To Bardolph*]. Let me see thee froth and lime: I am at a word: follow. [*Exit.*

Falstaff. Bardolph, follow him. A tapster is a good trade: an old cloak makes a new jerkin; a withered serving-man a fresh tapster. Go; adieu.

Bardolph. It is a life that I have desired: I will thrive.

Pistol. O base Hungarian wight! wilt thou the spigot wield? [*Exit Bardolph.*

Nym. He was gotten in drink: is not the humour conceited?

Falstaff. I am glad I am so acquit of this tinder-box: his thefts were too open; his filching was like an unskilful singer; he kept not time.

Nym. The good humour is to steal at a minute's rest.

Pistol. 'Convey,' the wise it call. 'Steal!' foh! a fico for the phrase!

Falstaff. Well, sirs, I am almost out at heels.

Pistol. Why, then, let kibes ensue.

Falstaff. There is no remedy; I must cony-catch; I must shift.

Pistol. Young ravens must have food.

Falstaff. Which of you know Ford of this town?

Pistol. I ken the wight: he is of substance good.

Falstaff. My honest lads, I will tell you what I am about.

Pistol. Two yards, and more.

Falstaff. No quips now, Pistol! Indeed, I am in the waist two yards about; but I am now about no waste; I am about thrift. Briefly, I do mean to make love to Ford's wife: I spy entertainment in her; she discourses, she carves, she gives the leer of invitation: I can construe the action of her familiar style; and the hardest voice of her behaviour, to be Englished rightly, is 'I am Sir John Falstaff's.'

Pistol. He hath studied her will, and translated her will, out of honesty into English.

Nym. The anchor is deep: will that humour pass?

Falstaff. Now, the report goes she has all the rule of her husband's purse: he hath a legion of angels.

Pistol. As many devils entertain; and 'To her, boy,' say I.

Nym. The humour rises; it is good: humour me the angels.

Falstaff. I have writ me here a letter to her: and here another to Page's wife, who even now gave me good eyes too, examined my parts with most judicious œillades; sometimes the beam of her view gilded my foot, sometimes my portly belly.

Pistol. Then did the sun on dunghill shine.

Nym. I thank thee for that humour.

Falstaff. O, she did so course o'er my exteriors with such a greedy intention, that the appetite of her eye did seem to scorch me up like a burning-glass! Here 's another letter to her: she bears the purse too; she is a region in Guiana, all gold and bounty. I will be cheater to them both, and they shall be exchequers to me; they shall be my East and West Indies, and I will trade to them both. Go bear thou this letter to Mistress Page; and thou this to Mistress Ford: we will thrive, lads, we will thrive.

Pistol. Shall I Sir Pandarus of Troy become, And by my side wear steel? then, Lucifer take all!

Nym. I will run no base humour: here, take the humour-letter: I will keep the haviour of reputation.

Falstaff. [*To Robin*] Hold, sirrah, bear you these letters tightly;
Sail like my pinnace to these golden shores.
Rogues, hence, avaunt! vanish like hailstones, go;
Trudge, plod away o' the hoof; seek shelter, pack!
Falstaff will learn the humour of the age,
French thrift, you rogues; myself and skirted page.
[*Exeunt Falstaff and Robin.*

Pistol. Let vultures gripe thy guts! for gourd and fullam holds,
And high and low beguiles the rich and poor:
Tester I 'll have in pouch when thou shalt lack,
Base Phrygian Turk!

Nym. I have operations which be humours of revenge.

Pistol. Wilt thou revenge?

Nym. By welkin and her star!

Pistol. With wit or steel?

Nym. With both the humours, I:
I will discuss the humour of this love to Page.

Pistol. And I to Ford shall eke unfold
How Falstaff, varlet vile,
His dove will prove, his gold will hold,
And his soft couch defile.

Nym. My humour shall not cool: I will incense Page to deal with poison; I will possess him with yellowness, for the † revolt of mine is dangerous: that is my true humour.

Pistol. Thou art the Mars of malecontents: I second thee; troop on. [*Exeunt.*

SCENE IV. *A room in* DOCTOR CAIUS'S *house.*

Enter MISTRESS QUICKLY, SIMPLE, *and* RUGBY.

Quickly. What, John Rugby! I pray thee, go to the casement, and see if you can see my master, Master Doctor Caius, coming. If he do, i' faith, and find any body in the house, here will be an old abusing of God's patience and the king's English.

Rugby. I 'll go watch.

Quickly. Go; and we 'll have a posset for 't soon at night, in faith, at the latter end of a sea-coal fire. [*Exit Rugby.*] An honest, willing, kind fellow, as ever servant shall come in house withal, and, I warrant you, no tell-tale nor no breed-bate: his worst fault is, that he is given to prayer; he is something peevish that way: but nobody but has his fault; but let that pass. Peter Simple, you say your name is?

Simple. Ay, for fault of a better.

Quickly. And Master Slender 's your master?

Simple. Ay, forsooth.

Quickly. Does he not wear a great round beard, like a glover's paring-knife?

Simple. No, forsooth: he hath but a little wee face, with a little yellow beard, a Cain-coloured beard.

Quickly. A softly-sprighted man, is he not?

Simple. Ay, forsooth : but he is as tall a man of his hands as any is between this and his head ; he hath fought with a warrener.

Quickly. How say you? O, I should remember him : does he not hold up his head, as it were, and strut in his gait?

Simple. Yes, indeed, does he.

Quickly. Well, heaven send Anne Page no worse fortune ! Tell Master Parson Evans I will do what I can for your master : Anne is a good girl, and I wish—

Re-enter RUGBY.

Rugby. Out, alas ! here comes my master.

Quickly. We shall all be shent. Run in here, good young man ; go into this closet : he will not stay long. [*Shuts Simple in the closet.*] What, John Rugby ! John ! what, John, I say ! Go, John, go inquire for my master ; I doubt he be not well, that he comes not home.

[*Singing*] And down, down, adown-a, &c.

Enter DOCTOR CAIUS.

Caius. Vat is you sing? I do not like des toys. Pray you, go and vetch me in my closet un boitier vert, a box, a green-a box : do intend vat I speak? a green-a box.

Quickly. Ay, forsooth ; I 'll fetch it you. [*Aside*] I am glad he went not in himself : if he had found the young man, he would have been horn-mad.

Caius. Fe, fe, fe, fe ! ma foi, il fait fort chaud. Je m'en vais a la cour—la grande affaire.

Quickly. Is it this, sir?

Caius. Oui : mette le au mon pocket : depeche, quickly. Vere is dat knave Rugby?

Quickly. What, John Rugby ! John !

Rugby. Here, sir !

Caius. You are John Rugby, and you are Jack Rugby. Come, take-a your rapier, and come after my heel to the court.

Rugby. 'Tis ready, sir, here in the porch.

Caius. By my trot, I tarry too long. Od's me ! Qu'ai-j'oublie ! dere is some simples in my closet, dat I 'll not for the varld I shall leave behind.

Quickly. Ay me, he 'll find the young man there, and be mad !

Caius. O diable, diable ! vat is in my closet? Villain ! larron ! [*Pulling Simple out.*] Rugby, my rapier !

Quickly. Good master, be content.

Caius. Wherefore shall I be content-a?

Quickly. The young man is an honest man.

Caius. What shall dat honest man do in my closet? dere is no honest man dat shall come in my closet.

Quickly. I beseech you, be not so phlegmatic. Hear the truth of it : he came of an errand to me from Parson Hugh.

Caius. Vell.

Simple. Ay, forsooth ; to desire her to—

Quickly. Peace, I pray you.

Caius. Peace-a your tongue. Speak-a your tale.

Simple. To desire this honest gentlewoman, your maid, to speak a good word to Mistress Anne Page for my master in the way of marriage.

Quickly. This is all, indeed, la ! but I 'll ne'er put my finger in the fire, and need not.

Caius. Sir Hugh send-a you? Rugby, baille me some paper. Tarry you a little-a while.

[*Writes.*

Quickly. [*Aside to Simple*] I am glad he is so quiet : if he had been throughly moved, you should have heard him so loud and so melancholy. But notwithstanding, man, I 'll do you your master what good I can : and the very yea and the no is, the French doctor, my master,—I may call him my master, look you, for I keep his house ; and I wash, wring, brew, bake, scour, dress meat and drink, make the beds, and do all myself,—

Simple. [*Aside to Quickly*] 'Tis a great charge to come under one body's hand.

Quickly. [*Aside to Simple*] Are you avised o' that? you shall find it a great charge : and to be up early and down late ; but notwithstanding,—to tell you in your ear ; I would have no words of it,— my master himself is in love with Mistress Anne Page : but notwithstanding that, I know Anne's mind,—that 's neither here nor there.

Caius. You jack'nape, give-a this letter to Sir Hugh ; by gar, it is a shallenge : I will cut his troat in de park ; and I will teach a scurvy jack-a-nape priest to meddle or make. You may be gone ; it is not good you tarry here. By gar, I will cut all his two stones ; by gar, he shall not have a stone to throw at his dog.

[*Exit Simple.*

Quickly. Alas, he speaks but for his friend.

Caius. It is no matter-a ver dat ; do not you tell-a me dat I shall have Anne Page for myself? By gar, I vill kill de Jack priest ; and I have appointed mine host of de Jarteer to measure our weapon. By gar, I will myself have Anne Page.

Quickly. Sir, the maid loves you, and all shall be well. We must give folks leave to prate : what, the good-jer !

Caius. Rugby, come to the court with me. By gar, if I have not Anne Page, I shall turn your head out of my door. Follow my heels, Rugby.

[*Exeunt Caius and Rugby.*

Quickly. You shall have An fool's-head of your own. No, I know Anne's mind for that : never a woman in Windsor knows more of Anne's mind than I do ; nor can do more than I do with her, I thank heaven.

Fenton. [*Within*] Who 's within there? ho !

Quickly. Who 's there, I trow ! Come near the house, I pray you.

Enter FENTON.

Fenton. How now, good woman ! how dost thou?

Quickly. The better that it pleases your good worship to ask.

Fenton. What news? how does pretty Mistress Anne?

Quickly. In truth, sir, and she is pretty, and honest, and gentle ; and one that is your friend, I can tell you that by the way ; I praise heaven for it.

Fenton. Shall I do any good, thinkest thou? shall I not lose my suit?

Quickly. Troth, sir, all is in his hands above : but notwithstanding, Master Fenton, I 'll be sworn on a book, she loves you. Have not your worship a wart above your eye?

Fenton. Yes, marry, have I ; what of that?

Quickly. Well, thereby hangs a tale : good faith, it is such another Nan ; but, I detest, an honest maid as ever broke bread : we had, an hour's talk of that wart. I shall never laugh but in that maid's company ! But indeed she is given too much to allicholy and musing : but for you—well, go to.

Fenton. Well, I shall see her to-day. Hold, there 's money for thee ; let me have thy voice in my behalf : if thou seest her before me, commend me.

Quickly. Will I ? i' faith, that we will ; and I will tell your worship more of the wart the next time we have confidence ; and of other wooers.

Fenton. Well, farewell ; I am in great haste now.

Quickly. Farewell to your worship. [*Exit Fenton.*] Truly, an honest gentleman : but Anne loves him not ; for I know Anne's mind as well as another does. Out upon 't ! what have I forgot ?   [*Exit.*

ACT II.

SCENE I. *Before* PAGE'S *house.*

Enter MISTRESS PAGE, *with a letter.*

Mrs Page.

W hat, have I scaped love-letters in the holi-day-time of my beauty, and am I now a subject for them ? Let me see.   [*Reads.*
' Ask me no reason why I love you ; for though Love use Reason for his physician, he admits him not for his counsellor. You are not young, no more am I ; go to then, there 's sympathy : you are merry, so am I ; ha, ha ! then there 's more sympathy : you love sack, and so do I ; would you desire better sympathy ? Let it suffice thee, Mistress Page,—at the least, if the love of soldier can suffice,—that I love thee. I will not say, pity me ; 'tis not a soldier-like phrase · but I say, love me. By me,
Thine own true knight,
By day or night,
Or any kind of light,
With all his might
For thee to fight,   JOHN FALSTAFF.'
What a Herod of Jewry is this ! O wicked, wicked world ! One that is well-nigh worn to pieces with age to show himself a young gallant ! What an unweighed behaviour hath this Flemish drunkard picked—with the devil's name !—out of my con-versation, that he dares in this manner assay me ? Why, he hath not been thrice in my company ! What should I say to him ? I was then frugal of my mirth : Heaven forgive me ! Why, I 'll exhibit a bill in the parliament for the putting down of men. How shall I be revenged on him ? for revenged I will be, as sure as his guts are made of puddings.

Enter MISTRESS FORD.

Mrs Ford. Mistress Page ! trust me, I was going to your house.

Mrs Page. And, trust me, I was coming to you. You look very ill.

Mrs Ford. Nay, I 'll ne'er believe that ; I have to show to the contrary.

Mrs Page. Faith, but you do, in my mind.

Mrs Ford. Well, I do then ; yet I say I could show you to the contrary. O Mistress Page, give me some counsel !

Mrs Page. What 's the matter, woman ?

Mrs Ford. O woman, if it were not for one trifling respect, I could come to such honour !

Mrs Page. Hang the trifle, woman ! take the honour. What is it ? dispense with trifles ; what is it ?

Mrs Ford. If I would but go to hell for an eternal moment or so, I could be knighted.

Mrs Page. What ? thou liest ! Sir Alice Ford ! These knights will hack ; and so thou shouldst not alter the article of thy gentry.

Mrs Ford. We burn daylight : here, read, read; perceive how I might be knighted. I shall think the worse of fat men, as long as I have an eye to make difference of men's liking : and yet he would not swear ; praised women's modesty ; and gave such orderly and well-behaved reproof to all un-comeliness, that I would have sworn his disposition would have gone to the truth of his words ; but they do no more adhere and keep place together than the Hundredth Psalm to the tune of ' Green Sleeves.' What tempest, I trow, threw this whale, with so many tuns of oil in his belly, ashore at Windsor ? How shall I be revenged on him ? I think the best way were to entertain him with hope, till the wicked fire of lust have melted him in his own grease. Did you ever hear the like ?

Mrs Page. Letter for letter, but that the name of Page and Ford differs ! To thy great comfort in this mystery of ill opinions, here 's the twin-brother of thy letter : but let thine inherit first ; for, I protest, mine never shall. I warrant he hath a thousand of these letters, writ with blank space for different names,—sure, more,—and these are of the second edition : he will print them, out of doubt ; for he cares not what he puts into the press, when he would put us two. I had rather be a giantess, and lie under Mount Pelion. Well, I will find you twenty lascivious turtles ere one chaste man.

Mrs Ford. Why, this is the very same ; the very hand, the very words. What doth he think of us ?

Mrs Page. Nay, I know not : it makes me almost ready to wrangle with mine own honesty. I 'll entertain myself like one that I am not acquainted withal ; for, sure, unless he know some strain in me, that I know not myself, he would never have boarded me in this fury.

Mrs Ford. ' Boarding,' call you it ? I 'll be sure to keep him above deck.

Mrs Page. So will I : if he come under my hatches, I 'll never to sea again. Let 's be revenged on him : let 's appoint him a meeting ; give him a show of comfort in his suit and lead him on with a fine-baited delay, till he hath pawned his horse to mine host of the Garter.

Mrs Ford. Nay, I will consent to act any villany against him, that may not sully the chariness of our honesty. O, that my husband saw this letter ! it would give eternal food to his jealousy.

Mrs Page. Why, look where he comes ; and my good man too: he 's as far from jealousy as I am from giving him cause ; and that I hope is an un-measurable distance.

Mrs Ford. You are the happier woman.

Mrs Page. Let 's consult together against this greasy knight. Come hither.   [*They retire.*

Enter FORD *with* PISTOL, *and* PAGE *with* NYM.

Ford. Well, I hope it be not so.

Pistol. Hope is a curtal dog in some affairs : Sir John affects thy wife.

Ford. Why, sir, my wife is not young.

Pistol. He wooes both high and low, both rich and poor,
Both young and old, one with another, Ford ;
He loves the gallimaufry : Ford, perpend.

Ford. Love my wife !

Pistol. With liver burning hot. Prevent, or go
thou,
Like Sir Actæon he, with Ringwood at thy heels :
O, odious is the name !

Ford. What name, sir ?

Pistol. The horn, I say. Farewell.
Take heed, have open eye, for thieves do foot by
night :
Take heed, ere summer comes or cuckoo-birds do
sing.
Away, Sir Corporal Nym !
Believe it, Page ; he speaks sense.   [*Exit.*

Ford. [*Aside*] I will be patient ; I will find
out this.

Nym. [*To Page*] And this is true ; I like not
the humour of lying. He hath wronged me in some
humours : I should have borne the humoured
letter to her ; but I have a sword and it shall bite
upon my necessity. He loves your wife ; there 's
the short and the long. My name is Corporal
Nym ; I speak and I avouch ; 'tis true : my name
is Nym and Falstaff loves your wife. Adieu. I
love not the humour of bread and cheese, and
there 's the humour of it. Adieu.   [*Exit.*

Page. 'The humour of it,' quoth a' ! here 's a
fellow frights English out of his wits.

Ford. I will seek out Falstaff.

Page. I never heard such a drawling, affecting
rogue.

Ford. If I do find it : well.

Page. I will not believe such a Cataian, though
the priest o' the town commended him for a true
man.

Ford. 'Twas a good sensible fellow : well.

Page. How now, Meg !
    [*Mrs Page and Mrs Ford come forward.*

Mrs Page. Whither go you, George ? Hark you.

Mrs Ford. How now, sweet Frank ! why art
thou melancholy ?

Ford. I melancholy ! I am not melancholy.
Get you home, go.

Mrs Ford. Faith, thou hast some crotchets in
thy head. Now, will you go, Mistress Page ?

Mrs Page. Have with you. You 'll come to
dinner, George. [*Aside to Mrs Ford*] Look who
comes yonder : she shall be our messenger to this
paltry knight.

Mrs Ford. [*Aside to Mrs Page*] Trust me, I
thought on her : she 'll fit it.

Enter MISTRESS QUICKLY.

Mrs Page. You are come to see my daughter
Anne ?

Quickly. Ay, forsooth ; and, I pray, how does
good Mistress Anne ?

Mrs Page. Go in with us and see : we have an
hour's talk with you.
    [*Exeunt Mrs Page, Mrs Ford, and Mrs Quickly.*

Page. How now, Master Ford !

Ford. You heard what this knave told me, did
you not ?

Page. Yes : and you heard what the other told
me ?

Ford. Do you think there is truth in them ?

Page. Hang 'em, slaves ! I do not think the
knight would offer it : but these that accuse him in
his intent towards our wives are a yoke of his dis-
carded men ; very rogues, now they be out of service.

Ford. Were they his men ?

Page. Marry, were they.

Ford. I like it never the better for that. Does
he lie at the Garter ?

Page. Ay, marry, does he. If he should intend
this voyage towards my wife, I would turn her loose
to him ; and what he gets more of her than sharp
words, let it lie on my head.

Ford. I do not misdoubt my wife ; but I would
be loath to turn them together. A man may be
too confident : I would have nothing lie on my
head : I cannot be thus satisfied.

Page. Look where my ranting host of the Garter
comes : there is either liquor in his pate or money in
his purse when he looks so merrily.

Enter HOST.

How now, mine host !

Host. How now, bully-rook ! thou 'rt a gentleman. Cavaleiro-justice, I say !

Enter SHALLOW.

Shallow. I follow, mine host, I follow. Good
even and twenty, good Master Page ! Master Page,
will you go with us ? we have sport in hand.

Host. Tell him, cavaleiro-justice ; tell him,
bully-rook.

Shallow. Sir, there is a fray to be fought between
Sir Hugh the Welsh priest and Caius the French
doctor.

Ford. Good mine host o' the Garter, a word
with you.   [*Drawing him aside.*

Host. What sayest thou, my bully-rook ?

Shallow. [*To Page*] Will you go with us to behold it ? My merry host hath had the measuring
of their weapons ; and, I think, hath appointed
them contrary places ; for, believe me, I hear the
parson is no jester. Hark, I will tell you what
our sport shall be.
    [*They converse apart.*

Host. Hast thou no suit against my knight, my
guest-cavaleire ?

Ford. None, I protest : but I 'll give you a pottle
of burnt sack to give me recourse to him and tell
him my name is Brook ; only for a jest.

Host. My hand, bully ; thou shalt have egress
and regress ;—said I well ?—and thy name shall
be Brook. It is a merry knight. Will you go,
† An-heires ?

Shallow. Have with you, mine host.

Page. I have heard the Frenchman hath good
skill in his rapier.

Shallow. Tut, sir, I could have told you more.
In these times you stand on distance, your passes,
stoccadoes, and I know not what : 'tis the heart,
Master Page ; 'tis here, 'tis here. I have seen the
time with my long sword I would have made you
four tall fellows skip like rats.

Host. Here, boys, here, here ! shall we wag ?

Page. Have with you. I had rather hear them
scold than fight.
    [*Exeunt Host, Shallow, and Page.*

Ford. Though Page be a secure fool, and stands
so firmly on his wife's frailty, yet I cannot put off
my opinion so easily : she was in his company at
Page's house ; and what they made there, I know
not. Well, I will look further into 't : and I have a
disguise to sound Falstaff. If I find her honest,
I lose not my labour ; if she be otherwise, 'tis labour
well bestowed.   [*Exit.*

SCENE II. *A room in the Garter Inn.*

Enter FALSTAFF *and* PISTOL.

Falstaff. I will not lend thee a penny.

Pistol. Why, then the world 's mine oyster, Which I with sword will open.

Falstaff. Not a penny. I have been content, sir, you should lay my countenance to pawn : I have grated upon my good friends for three reprieves for you and your coach-fellow Nym ; or else you had looked through the grate, like a geminy of baboons. I am damned in hell for swearing to gentlemen my friends, you were good soldiers and tall fellows ; and when Mistress Bridget lost the handle of her fan, I took 't upon mine honour thou hadst it not.

Pistol. Didst not thou share ? hadst thou not fifteen pence ?

Falstaff. Reason, you rogue, reason : thinkest thou I 'll endanger my soul gratis ? At a word, hang no more about me, I am no gibbet for you. Go. A short knife and a throng ! To your manor of Pickt-hatch ! Go. You 'll not bear a letter for me, you rogue ! you stand upon your honour ! Why, thou unconfinable baseness, it is as much as I can do to keep the terms of my honour precise : I, I, I myself sometimes, leaving the fear of God on the left hand and hiding mine honour in my necessity, am fain to shuffle, to hedge and to lurch ; and yet you, rogue, will ensconce your rags, your cat-a-mountain looks, your red-lattice phrases, and your bold-beating oaths, under the shelter of your honour ! You will not do it, you !

Pistol. I do relent : what would thou more of man ?

Enter ROBIN.

Robin. Sir, here 's a woman would speak with you.

Falstaff. Let her approach.

Enter MISTRESS QUICKLY.

Quickly. Give your worship good morrow.

Falstaff. Good morrow, good wife.

Quickly. Not so, an 't please your worship.

Falstaff. Good maid, then.

Quickly. I 'll be sworn, As my mother was, the first hour I was born.

Falstaff. I do believe the swearer. What with me ?

Quickly. Shall I vouchsafe your worship a word or two ?

Falstaff. Two thousand, fair woman : and I 'll vouchsafe thee the hearing.

Quickly. There is one Mistress Ford, sir :—I pray, come a little nearer this ways :—I myself dwell with Master Doctor Caius,—

Falstaff. Well, on : Mistress Ford, you say,—

Quickly. Your worship says very true : I pray your worship, come a little nearer this ways.

Falstaff. I warrant thee, nobody hears ; mine own people, mine own people.

Quickly. Are they so ? God bless them and make them his servants !

Falstaff. Well, Mistress Ford ; what of her ?

Quickly. Why, sir, she 's a good creature. Lord, Lord ! your worship 's a wanton ! Well, heaven forgive you and all of us, I pray !

Falstaff. Mistress Ford ; come, Mistress Ford.

Quickly. Marry, this is the short and the long of it ; you have brought her into such a canaries as 'tis wonderful. The best courtier of them all, when the court lay at Windsor, could never have brought her to such a canary. Yet there has been knights, and lords, and gentlemen, with their coaches, I warrant you, coach after coach, letter after letter, gift after gift ; smelling so sweetly, all musk, and so rushling, I warrant you, in silk and gold ; and in such alligant terms ; and in such wine and sugar of the best and the fairest, that would have won any woman's heart ; and, I warrant you, they could never get an eye-wink of her : I had myself twenty angels given me this morning ; but I defy all angels, in any such sort, as they say, but in the way of honesty : and, I warrant you, they could never get her so much as sip on a cup with the proudest of them all : and yet there has been earls, nay, which is more, pensioners ; but, I warrant you, all is one with her.

Falstaff. But what says she to me ? be brief, my good she-Mercury.

Quickly. Marry, she hath received your letter, for the which she thanks you a thousand times ; and she gives you to notify that her husband will be absence from his house between ten and eleven.

Falstaff. Ten and eleven ?

Quickly. Ay, forsooth ; and then you may come and see the picture, she says, that you wot of : Master Ford, her husband, will be from home. Alas ! the sweet woman leads an ill life with him : he 's a very jealousy man : she leads a very frampold life with him, good heart.

Falstaff. Ten and eleven. Woman, commend me to her ; I will not fail her.

Quickly. Why, you say well. But I have another messenger to your worship. Mistress Page hath her hearty commendations to you too : and let me tell you in your ear, she 's as fartuous a civil modest wife, and one, I tell you, that will not miss you morning nor evening prayer, as any is in Windsor, whoe'er be the other : and she bade me tell your worship that her husband is seldom from home ; but she hopes there will come a time. I never knew a woman so dote upon a man : surely I think you have charms, la ; yes, in truth.

Falstaff. Not I, I assure thee : setting the attraction of my good parts aside I have no other charms.

Quickly. Blessing on your heart for 't !

Falstaff. But, I pray thee, tell me this : has Ford's wife and Page's wife acquainted each other how they love me ?

Quickly. That were a jest indeed ! they have not so little grace, I hope : that were a trick indeed ! But Mistress Page would desire you to send her your little page, of all loves : her husband has a marvellous infection to the little page ; and truly Master Page is an honest man. Never a wife in Windsor leads a better life than she does : do what she will, say what she will, take all, pay all, go to bed when she list, rise when she list, all is as she will : and truly she deserves it ; for if there be a kind woman in Windsor, she is one. You must send her your page ; no remedy.

Falstaff. Why, I will.

Quickly. Nay, but do so, then : and, look you, he may come and go between you both ; and in any case have a nay-word, that you may know one another's mind, and the boy never need to understand any thing ; for 'tis not good that children should know any wickedness : old folks, you know, have discretion, as they say, and know the world.

Falstaff. Fare thee well : commend me to them both : there 's my purse ; I am yet thy debtor. Boy, go along with this woman. [*Exeunt Mistress Quickly and Robin.*] This news distracts me !

Pistol. This punk is one of Cupid's carriers : Clap on more sails ; pursue ; up with your fights : Give fire : she is my prize, or ocean whelm them all !
[*Exit.*

Falstaff. Sayest thou so, old Jack ? go thy ways ; I 'll make more of thy old body than I have done. Will they yet look after thee ? Wilt thou, after the expense of so much money, be now a gainer ? Good body, I thank thee. Let them say 'tis grossly done ; so it be fairly done, no matter.

Enter BARDOLPH.

Bardolph. Sir John, there 's one Master Brook below would fain speak with you, and be acquainted with you ; and hath sent your worship a morning's draught of sack.

Falstaff. Brook is his name ?

Bardolph. Ay, sir.

Falstaff. Call him in. [*Exit Bardolph.*] Such Brooks are welcome to me, that o'erflow such liquor. Ah, ha ! Mistress Ford and Mistress Page, have I encompassed you ? go to ; via !

Re-enter BARDOLPH, *with* FORD *disguised.*

Ford. Bless you, sir !

Falstaff. And you, sir! Would you speak with me ?

Ford. I make bold to press with so little preparation upon you.

Falstaff. You 're welcome. What 's your will ? Give us leave, drawer. [*Exit Bardolph.*

Ford. Sir, I am a gentleman that have spent much ; my name is Brook.

Falstaff. Good Master Brook, I desire more acquaintance of you.

Ford. Good Sir John, I sue for yours : not to charge you ; for I must let you understand I think myself in better plight for a lender than you are : The which hath something emboldened me to this unseasoned intrusion ; for they say, if money go before, all ways do lie open.

Falstaff. Money is a good soldier, sir, and will on.

Ford. Troth, and I have a bag of money here troubles me : if you will help to bear it, Sir John, take all, or half, for easing me of the carriage.

Falstaff. Sir, I know not how I may deserve to be your porter.

Ford. I will tell you, sir, if you will give me the hearing.

Falstaff. Speak, good Master Brook : I shall be glad to be your servant.

Ford. Sir, I hear you are a scholar,—I will be brief with you,—and you have been a man long known to me, though I had never so good means, as desire, to make myself acquainted with you. I shall discover a thing to you, wherein I must very much lay open mine own imperfection : but, good Sir John, as you have one eye upon my follies, as you hear them unfolded, turn another into the register of your own ; that I may pass with a reproof the easier, sith you yourself know how easy it is to be such an offender.

Falstaff. Very well, sir ; proceed.

Ford. There is a gentlewoman in this town ; her husband's name is Ford.

Falstaff. Well, sir.

Ford. I have long loved her, and, I protest to you, bestowed much on her ; followed her with a doting observance ; engrossed opportunities to meet her ; fee'd every slight occasion that could but niggardly give me sight of her ; not only bought many presents to give her, but have given largely to many to know what she would have given ; briefly, I have pursued her as love hath pursued me ; which hath been on the wing of all occasions. But whatsoever I have merited, either in my mind or in my means, meed, I am sure, I have received none ; unless experience be a jewel that I have purchased at an infinite rate, and that hath taught me to say this :
' Love like a shadow flies when substance love pursues ;
Pursuing that that flies, and flying what pursues.'

Falstaff. Have you received no promise of satisfaction at her hands ?

Ford. Never.

Falstaff. Have you importuned her to such a purpose ?

Ford. Never.

Falstaff. Of what quality was your love, then ?

Ford. Like a fair house built on another man's ground ; so that I have lost my edifice by mistaking the place where I erected it.

Falstaff. To what purpose have you unfolded this to me ?

Ford. When I have told you that, I have told you all. Some say, that though she appear honest to me, yet in other places she enlargeth her mirth so far that there is shrewd construction made of her. Now, Sir John, here is the heart of my purpose : you are a gentleman of excellent breeding, admirable discourse, of great admittance, authentic in your place and person, generally allowed for your many war-like, court-like, and learned preparations.

Falstaff. O, sir !

Ford. Believe it, for you know it. There is money ; spend it, spend it ; spend more ; spend all I have ; only give me so much of your time in exchange of it, as to lay an amiable siege to the honesty of this Ford's wife : use your art of wooing ; win her to consent to you : if any man may, you may as soon as any.

Falstaff. Would it apply well to the vehemency of your affection, that I should win what you would enjoy ? Methinks you prescribe to yourself very preposterously.

Ford. O, understand my drift. She dwells so securely on the excellency of her honour, that the folly of my soul dares not present itself : she is too bright to be looked against. Now, could I come to her with any detection in my hand, my desires had instance and argument to commend themselves : I could drive her then from the ward of her purity, her reputation, her marriage-vow, and a thousand other her defences, which now are too too strongly embattled against me. What say you to 't, Sir John ?

Falstaff. Master Brook, I will first make bold with your money ; next, give me your hand ; and last, as I am a gentleman, you shall, if you will, enjoy Ford's wife.

Ford. O good sir !

Falstaff. I say you shall.

Ford. Want no money, Sir John ; you shall want none.

Falstaff. Want no Mistress Ford, Master Brook ; you shall want none. I shall be with her, I may tell you, by her own appointment ; even as you came in to me, her assistant or go-between parted from me : I say I shall be with her between ten and eleven ; for at that time the jealous rascally knave her husband will be forth. Come you to me at night ; you shall know how I speed.

Ford. I am blest in your acquaintance. Do you know Ford, sir ?

Falstaff. Hang him, poor cuckoldly knave ! I know him not : yet I wrong him to call him poor ; they say the jealous wittolly knave hath masses of money ; for the which his wife seems to me well-favoured. I will use her as the key of the cuckoldly rogue's coffer ; and there 's my harvest-home.

Ford. I would you knew Ford, sir, that you might avoid him if you saw him.

Falstaff. Hang him, mechanical salt-butter rogue ! I will stare him out of his wits ; I will awe him with my cudgel : it shall hang like a meteor o'er the cuckold's horns. Master Brook, thou shalt know I will predominate over the peasant, and thou shalt lie with his wife. Come to me soon at night. Ford's a knave, and I will aggravate his style ; thou, Master Brook, shalt know him for knave and cuckold. Come to me soon at night.   [*Exit.*

Ford. What a damned Epicurean rascal is this ! My heart is ready to crack with impatience. Who says this is improvident jealousy ? my wife hath sent to him ; the hour is fixed ; the match is made. Would any man have thought this ? See the hell of having a false woman ! My bed shall be abused, my coffers ransacked, my reputation gnawn at ; and I shall not only receive this villanous wrong, but stand under the adoption of abominable terms, and by him that does me this wrong. Terms ! names ! Amaimon sounds well ; Lucifer, well ; Barbason, well ; yet they are devils' additions, the names of fiends : but Cuckold ! Wittol !—Cuckold ! the devil himself hath not such a name. Page is an ass, a secure ass : he will trust his wife ; he will not be jealous. I will rather trust a Fleming with my butter, Parson Hugh the Welshman with my cheese, an Irishman with my aqua-vitæ bottle, or a thief to walk my ambling gelding, than my wife with herself : then she plots, then she ruminates, then she devises ; and what they think in their hearts they may effect, they will break their hearts but they will effect. God be praised for my jealousy ! Eleven o'clock the hour. I will prevent this, detect my wife, be revenged on Falstaff, and laugh at Page. I will about it ; better three hours too soon that a minute too late. Fie, fie, fie ! cuckold, cuckold ! cuckold !   [*Exit.*

SCENE III. *A field near Windsor.*

Enter CAIUS *and* RUGBY.

Caius. Jack Rugby !

Rugby. Sir ?

Caius. Vat is de clock, Jack ?

Rugby. 'Tis past the hour, sir, that Sir Hugh promised to meet.

Caius. By gar, he has save his soul, dat he is no come ; he has pray his Pible well, dat he is no come : by gar, Jack Rugby, he is dead already, if he be come.

Rugby. He is wise, sir ; he knew your worship would kill him, if he came.

Caius. By gar, de herring is no dead so as I vill kill him. Take your rapier, Jack ; I vill tell you how I vill kill him.

Rugby. Alas, sir, I cannot fence.

Caius. Villany, take your rapier.

Rugby. Forbear ; here 's company.

Enter HOST, SHALLOW, SLENDER, *and* PAGE.

Host. Bless thee, bully doctor !

Shallow. Save you, Master Doctor Caius !

Page. Now, good master doctor !

Slender. Give you good morrow, sir.

Caius. Vat be all you, one, two, tree, four, come for ?

Host. To see thee fight, to see thee foin, to see thee traverse ; to see thee here, to see thee there ; to see thee pass thy punto, thy stock, thy reverse, thy distance, thy montant. Is he dead, my Ethiopian? is he dead, my Francisco ? ha, bully ! What says my Æsculapius ? my Galen ? my heart of elder ? ha ! is he dead, bully stale ? is he dead ?

Caius. By gar, he is de coward Jack priest of de vorld ; he is not show his face.

Host. Thou art a Castalion-King-Urinal. Hector of Greece, my boy !

Caius. I pray you, bear vitness that me have stay six or seven, two, tree hours for him, and he is no come.

Shallow. He is the wiser man, master doctor : he is a curer of souls, and you a curer of bodies ; if you should fight, you go against the hair of your professions. Is it not true, Master Page ?

Page. Master Shallow, you have yourself been a great fighter, though now a man of peace.

Shallow. Bodykins, Paster Page, though I now be old and of the peace, if I see a sword out, my finger itches to make one. Though we are justices and doctors and churchmen, Master Page, we have some salt of our youth in us ; we are the sons of women, Master Page.

Page. 'Tis true, Master Shallow.

Shallow. It will be found so, Master Page. Master Doctor Caius, I am come to fetch you home. I am sworn of the peace : you have showed yourself a wise physician, and Sir Hugh hath shown himself a wise and patient churchman. You must go with me, master doctor.

Host. Pardon, guest-justice. A word, Mounseur Mockwater.

Caius. Mock-vater ! vat is dat ?

Host. Mock-water, in our English tongue, is valour, bully.

Caius. By gar, den, I have as mush mock-vater as de Englishman. Scurvy jack-dog priest ! by gar, me vill cut his ears.

Host. He will clapper-claw thee tightly, bully.

Caius. Clapper-de-claw ! vat is dat ?

Host. That is, he will make thee amends.

Caius. By gar, me do look he shall clapper-de-claw me ; for, by gar, me vill have it.

Host. And I will provoke him to 't, or let him wag.

Caius. Me tank you for dat.

Host. And, moreover, bully,—but first, master guest, and Master Page, and eke Cavaleiro Slender, go you through the town to Frogmore.

                            [*Aside to them.*

Page. Sir Hugh is there, is he ?

Host. He is there : see what humour he is in ; and I will bring the doctor about by the fields. Will it do well ?

Shallow. We will do it.

Page, Shallow, and Slender. Adieu, good master doctor.   [*Exeunt Page, Shallow, and Slender.*

Caius. By gar, me vill kill de priest ; for he speak for a jack-an-ape to Anne Page.

Host. Let him die : sheathe thy impatience, throw cold water on thy choler : go about the fields with me through Frogmore : I will bring thee where Mistress Anne Page is, at a farmhouse a-feasting ; and thou shalt woo her. Cried I aim ? said I well ?

Caius. By gar, me dank you vor dat : by gar, I love you ; and I shall procure-a you de good guest, de earl, de knight, de lords, de gentlemen, my patients.

Host. For the which I will be thy adversary toward Anne Page. Said I well ?

Caius. By gar, 'tis good ; vell said.

Host. Let us wag, then.

Caius. Come at my heels, Jack Rugby.

[*Exeunt.*

ACT III.

SCENE I. *A field near Frogmore.*

Enter Sir Hugh Evans *and* Simple.

Evans.

I pray you now, good Master Slender's serving-man, and friend Simple by your name, which way have you looked for Master Caius, that calls himself doctor of physic ?

Simple. Marry, sir, the pittie-ward, the park-ward, every way ; old Windsor way, and every way but the town way.

Evans. I most fehemently desire you you will also look that way.

Simple. I will, sir.   [*Exit.*

Evans. 'Pless my soul, how full of chollors I am, and trempling of mind ! I shall be glad if he have deceived me. How melancholies I am ! I will knog his urinals about his knave's costard when I have good opportunities for the ork. 'Pless my soul !   [*Sings.*

To shallow rivers, to whose falls
Melodious birds sings madrigals ;
There will we make our peds of roses,
And a thousand fragrant posies.
To shallow—

Mercy on me ! I have a great dispositions to cry.
          [*Sings.*

Melodious birds sing madrigals—
When as I sat in Pabylon—
And a thousand vagram posies.
To shallow &c.

Re-enter Simple.

Simple. Yonder he is coming, this way, Sir Hugh.

Evans. He 's welcome.   [*Sings.*

To shallow rivers, to whose falls—
Heaven prosper the right ! What weapons is he ?

Simple. No weapons, sir. There comes my master, Master Shallow, and another gentleman, from Frogmore, over the stile, this way.

Evans. Pray you, give me my gown ; or else keep it in your arms.

Enter Page, Shallow, *and* Slender.

Shallow. How now, master Parson ! Good mor-row, good Sir Hugh. Keep a gamester from the dice, and a good student from his book, and it is wonderful.

Slender. [*Aside*] Ah, sweet Anne Page !

Page. 'Save you, good Sir Hugh !

Evans. 'Pless you from his mercy sake, all of you !

Shallow. What, the sword and the word ! do you study them both, master parson ?

Page. And youthful still ! in your doublet and hose this raw rheumatic day !

Evans. There is reasons and causes for it.

Page. We are come to you to do a good office, master parson.

Evans. Fery well : what is it ?

Page. Yonder is a most reverend gentleman, who, belike having received wrong by some person, is at most odds with his own gravity and patience that ever you saw.

Shallow. I have lived fourscore years and up-ward ; I never heard a man of his place, gravity and learning, so wide of his own respect.

Evans. What is he ?

Page. I think you know him ; Master Doctor Caius, the renowned French physician.

Evans. Got's will, and his passion of my heart ! I had as lief you would tell me of a mess of porridge.

Page. Why ?

Evans. He has no more knowledge in Hibocrates and Galen,—and he is a knave besides ; a cowardly knave as you would desires to be acquainted withal.

Page. I warrant you, he 's the man should fight with him.

Slender. [*Aside*] O sweet Anne Page !

Shallow. It appears so by his weapons. Keep them asunder : here comes Doctor Caius.

Enter Host, Caius, *and* Rugby.

Page. Nay, good master parson, keep in your weapon.

Shallow. So do you, good master doctor.

Host. Disarm them, and let them question : let them keep their limbs whole and hack our English.

Caius. I pray you, let-a me speak a word with your ear. Vherefore vill you not meet-a me ?

Evans. [*Aside to Caius*] Pray you, use your patience : in good time.

Caius. By gar, you are de coward, de Jack dog, John ape.

Evans. [*Aside to Caius*] Pray you, let us not be laughing-stocks to other men's humours : I desire you in friendship, and I will one way or other make you amends. [*Aloud*] I will knog your urinals about your knave's cogscomb for missing your meetings and appointments.

Caius. Diable ! Jack Rugby,—mine host de Jarteer,—have I not stay for him to kill him ? have I not, at de place I did appoint ?

Evans. As I am a Christians soul now, look you, this is the place appointed : I 'll be judgement by mine host of the Garter.

Host. Peace, I say, Gallia and Gaul, French and Welsh, soul-curer and body-curer !

Caius. Ay, dat is very good : excellent.

Host. Peace, I say ! hear mine host of the Garter. Am I politic ? am I subtle ? am I a Machiavel ? Shall I lose my doctor ? no ; he gives me the potions and the motions. Shall I lose my parson, my priest, my Sir Hugh ? no : he gives me the proverbs and the no-verbs. Give me thy hand, terrestrial ; so. Give me thy hand, celestial ; so. Boys of art, I have deceived you both ; I have directed you to wrong places : your hearts are mighty, your skins are whole, and let burnt sack be the issue. Come, lay their swords to pawn. Follow me, lads of peace ; follow, follow, follow.

Shallow. Trust me, a mad host. Follow, gen-tlemen, follow.

Slender. [*Aside*] O sweet Anne Page !
[*Exeunt Shallow, Slender, Page, and Host.*
Caius. Ha, do I perceive dat ? have you make-a
de sot of us, ha, ha ?
Evans. This is well ; he has made us his vlouting-
stog. I desire you that we may be friends ; and
let us knog our prains together to be revenge on this
same scall, scurvy, cogging companion, the host of
the Garter.
Caius. By gar, with all my heart. He promise
to bring me where is Anne Page ; by gar, he deceive
me too.
Evans. Well, I will smite his noddles. Pray you,
follow.   [*Exeunt.*

SCENE II. *A street.*

Enter MISTRESS PAGE *and* ROBIN.

Mrs Page. Nay, keep your way, little gal'ant ;
you were wont to be a follower, but now you are a
leader. Whether had you rather lead mine eyes, or
eye your master's heels ?
Robin. I had rather, forsooth, go before you like
a man than follow him like a dwarf.
Mrs Page. O, you are a flattering boy : now I
see you 'll be a courtier.

Enter FORD.

Ford. Well met, Mistress Page. Whither go
you ?
Mrs Page. Truly, sir, to see your wife. Is she
at home ?
Ford. Ay ; and as idle as she may hang together,
for want of company. I think, if your husbands
were dead, you two would marry.
Mrs Page. Be sure of that,—two other husbands.
Ford. Where had you this pretty weathercock ?
Mrs Page. I cannot tell what the dickens his
name is my husband had him of. What do you call
your knight's name, sirrah ?
Robin. Sir John Falstaff.
Ford. Sir John Falstaff !
Mrs Page. He, he ; I can never hit on 's name.
There is such a league between my good man and
he ! Is your wife at home indeed ?
Ford. Indeed she is.
Mrs Page. By your leave, sir : I am sick till
I see her.   [*Exeunt Mrs Page and Robin.*
Ford. Has Page any brains ? hath he any eyes ?
hath he any thinking ? Sure, they sleep ; he hath
no use of them. Why, this boy will carry a letter
twenty mile, as easy as a cannon will shoot point-
blank twelve score. He pieces out his wife's inclination ; he gives her folly motion and advantage :
and now she 's going to my wife, and Falstaff's boy
with her. A man may hear this shower sing in the
wind. And Falstaff's boy with her ! Good plots,
they are laid ; and our revolted wives share damnation together. Well ; I will take him, then torture
my wife, pluck the borrowed veil of modesty from
the so seeming Mistress Page, divulge Page himself
for a secure and wilful Actæon ; and to these
violent proceedings all my neighbours shall cry aim.
[*Clock heard.*] The clock gives me my cue, and
my assurance bids me search : there I shall find
Falstaff : I shall be rather praised for this than
mocked ; for it is as positive as the earth is firm
that Falstaff is there : I will go.

Enter PAGE, SHALLOW, SLENDER, HOST, SIR
HUGH EVANS, CAIUS, *and* RUGBY.

Shallow, Page, etc. Well met, Master Ford.
Ford. Trust me, a good knot : I have good cheer
at home ; I pray you all go with me.
Shallow. I must excuse myself, Master Ford.
Slender. And so must I, sir : we have appointed
to dine with Mistress Anne, and I would not break
with her for more money than I 'll speak of.
Shallow. We have lingered about a match between Anne Page and my cousin Slender, and this
day we shall have our answer.
Slender. I hope I have your good will, father
Page.
Page. You have, Master Slender ; I stand wholly
for you : but my wife, master doctor, is for you
altogether.
Caius. Ay, be-gar ; and de maid is love-a me :
my nursh-a Quickly tell me so mush.
Host. What say you to young Master Fenton ?
he capers, he dances, he has eyes of youth, he writes
verses, he speaks holiday, he smells April and May :
he will carry 't, he will carry 't ; 'tis in his buttons ;
he will carry 't.
Page. Not by my consent, I promise you. The
gentleman is of no having : he kept company with
the wild prince and Poins ; he is of too high a region ;
he knows too much. No, he shall not knit a knot in
his fortunes with the finger of my substance : if he
take her, let him take her simply ; the wealth I have
waits on my consent, and my consent goes not that
way.
Ford. I beseech you heartily, some of you go
home with me to dinner : besides your cheer, you
shall have sport ; I will show you a monster. Master
doctor, you shall go ; so shall you, Master Page ;
and you, Sir Hugh.
Shallow. Well, fare you well : we shall have the
freer wooing at Master Page's.
[*Exeunt Shallow and Slender.*
Caius. Go home, John Rugby ; I come anon.
[*Exit Rugby.*
Host. Farewell, my hearts : I will to my honest
knight Falstaff, and drink canary with him. [*Exit.*
Ford. [*Aside*] I think I shall drink in pipe-wine
first with him ; I 'll make him dance. Will you
go, gentles ?
All. Have with you to see this monster.
[*Exeunt.*

SCENE III. *A room in* FORD'S *house.*

Enter MISTRESS FORD *and* MISTRESS PAGE.

Mrs Ford. What, John ! What, Robert !
Mrs Page. Quickly, quickly ! Is the buck-
basket—
Mrs Ford. I warrant. What, Robin, I say !

Enter Servants *with a basket.*

Mrs Page. Come, come, come.
Mrs Ford. Here, set it down.
Mrs Page. Give your men the charge ; we
must be brief.
Mrs Ford. Marry, as I told you before, John
and Robert, be ready here hard by in the grew-house :
and when I suddenly call you, come forth, and
without any pause or staggering take this basket
on your shoulders : that done, trudge with it in all

haste, and carry it among the whitsters in Datchet-mead, and there empty it in the muddy ditch close by the Thames side.

Mrs Page. You will do it ?

Mrs Ford. I ha' told them over and over ; they lack no direction. Be gone, and come when you are called. [*Exeunt Servants.*

Mrs Page. Here comes little Robin.

Enter ROBIN.

Mrs Ford. How now, my eyas-musket ! what news with you ?

Robin. My master, Sir John, is come in at your back-door, Mistress Ford, and requests your company.

Mrs Page. You little Jack-a-Lent, have you been true to us ?

Robin. Ay, I 'll be sworn. My master knows not of your being here and hath threatened to put me into everlasting liberty if I tell you of it ; for he swears he 'll turn me away.

Mrs Page. Thou 'rt a good boy : this secrecy of thine shall be a tailor to thee and shall make thee a new doublet and hose. I 'll go hide me.

Mrs Ford. Do so. Go tell thy master I am alone. [*Exit Robin.*] Mistress Page, remember you your cue.

Mrs Page. I warrant thee ; if I do not act it, hiss me. [*Exit.*

Mrs Ford. Go to, then : we 'll use this unwhole-some humidity, this gross watery pumpion ; we 'll teach him to know turtles from jays.

Enter FALSTAFF.

Falstaff. Have I caught thee, my heavenly jewel ? Why, now let me die, for I have lived long enough : this is the period of my ambition : O this blessed hour !

Mrs Ford. O sweet Sir John !

Falstaff. Mistress Ford, I cannot cog, I cannot prate, Mistress Ford. Now shall I sin in my wish : I would thy husband were dead : I 'll speak it before the best lord ; I would make thee my lady.

Mrs Ford. I your lady, Sir John ! alas, I should be a pitiful lady !

Falstaff. Let the court of France show me such another. I see how thine eye would emulate the diamond : thou hast the right arched beauty of the brow that becomes the ship-tire, the tire-valiant, or any tire of Venetian admittance.

Mrs Ford. A plain kerchief, Sir John : my brows become nothing else ; nor that well neither.

Falstaff. By the Lord, thou art a traitor to say so : thou wouldst make an absolute courtier ; and the firm fixture of thy foot would give an excellent motion to thy gait in a semi-circled farthingale. I see what thou wert, if Fortune thy foe were not, Nature thy friend. Come, thou canst not hide it.

Mrs Ford. Believe me, there 's no such thing in me.

Falstaff. What made me love thee ? let that per-suade thee there 's something extraordinary in thee. Come, I cannot cog and say thou art this and that, like a many of these lisping hawthorn-buds, that come like women in men's apparel, and smell like Bucklersbury in simple time ; I cannot : but I love thee ; none but thee ; and thou deservest it.

Mrs Ford. Do not betray me, sir. I fear you love Mistress Page.

Falstaff. Thou mightst as well say I love to walk by the Counter-gate, which is as hateful to me as the reek of a lime-kiln.

Mrs Ford. Well, heaven knows how I love you ; and you shall one day find it.

Falstaff. Keep in that mind ; I 'll deserve it.

Mrs Ford. Nay, I must tell you, so you do ; or else I could not be in that mind.

Robin. [*Within*] Mistress Ford, Mistress Ford ! here 's Mistress Page at the door, sweating and blowing and looking wildly, and would needs speak with you presently.

Falstaff. She shall not see me : I will ensconce me behind the arras.

Mrs Ford. Pray you, do so ; she 's a very tattling woman. [*Falstaff hides himself.*

Re-enter MISTRESS PAGE *and* ROBIN.

What 's the matter ? how now !

Mrs Page. O Mistress Ford, what have you done ? You 're shamed, you 're overthrown, you 're undone for ever !

Mrs Ford. What 's the matter, good Mistress Page ?

Mrs Page. O well-a-day, Mistress Ford ! having an honest man to your husband, to give him such cause of suspicion !

Mrs Ford. What cause of suspicion ?

Mrs Page. What cause of suspicion ! Out upon you ! how am I mistook in you !

Mrs Ford. Why, alas, what 's the matter ?

Mrs Page. Your husband's coming hither, woman, with all the officers in Windsor, to search for a gentleman that he says is here now in the house by your consent, to take an ill advantage of his absence : you are undone.

Mrs Ford. 'Tis not so, I hope.

Mrs Page. Pray heaven it be not so, that you have such a man here ! but 'tis most certain your husband's coming, with half Windsor at his heels, to search for such a one. I come before to tell you. If you know yourself clear, why, I am glad of it ; but if you have a friend here, convey, convey him out. Be not amazed ; call all your senses to you ; defend your reputation, or bid farewell to your good life for ever.

Mrs Ford. What shall I do ? There is a gentle-man my dear friend ; and I fear not mine own shame so much as his peril : I had rather than a thousand pound he were out of the house.

Mrs Page. For shame ! never stand ' you had rather ' and ' you had rather : ' your husband's here at hand ; bethink you of some conveyance : in the house you cannot hide him. O, how have you deceived me ! Look, here is a basket : if he be of any reasonable stature, he may creep in here ; and throw foul linen upon him, as if it were going to bucking : or—it is whiting-time—send him by your two men to Datchet-mead.

Mrs Ford. He 's too big to go in there. What shall I do ?

Falstaff. [*Coming forward*] Let me see 't, let me see 't, O, let me see 't ! I 'll in, I 'll in. Follow your friend's counsel. I 'll in.

Mrs Page. What, Sir John Falstaff ! Are these your letters, knight ?

Falstaff. I love thee. Help me away. Let me creep in here. I 'll never—

[*Gets into the basket ; they cover him with foul linen.*

Mrs Page. Help to cover your master, boy. Call your men, Mistress Ford. You dissembling knight !

Mrs Ford. What, John ! Robert ! John !
[*Exit Robin.*

Re-enter Servants.

Go take up these clothes here quickly. Where 's
the cowl-staff ? look, how you drumble ! Carry
them to the laundress in Datchet-mead ; quickly,
come.

Enter FORD, PAGE, CAIUS, *and* SIR HUGH
EVANS.

Ford. Pray you, come near : if I suspect without
cause, why then make sport at me ; then let me
be your jest ; I deserve it. How now ! whither
bear you this ?
Servants. To the laundress, forsooth.
Mrs Ford. Why, what have you to do whither
they bear it ? You were best meddle with buck-
washing.
Ford. Buck ! I would I could wash myself of
the buck ! Buck, buck, buck ! Ay, buck ; I warrant
you, buck ; and of the season too, it shall appear.
[*Exeunt Servants with the basket.*] Gentlemen, I
have dreamed to-night ; I 'll tell you my dream.
Here, here, here be my keys : ascend my chambers ;
search, seek, find out : I 'll warrant we'll unkennel
the fox. Let me stop this way first. [*Locking the
door.*] So, now uncape.
Page. Good Master Ford, be contented : you
wrong yourself too much.
Ford. True, Master Page. Up, gentlemen ; you
shall see sport anon : follow me, gentlemen.
[*Exit.*
Evans. This is fery fantastical humours and
jealousies.
Caius. By gar, 'tis no the fashion of France ;
it is not jealous in France.
Page. Nay, follow him, gentlemen ; see the
issue of his search.
[*Exeunt Page, Caius, and Evans.*
Mrs Page. Is there not a double excellency
in this ?
Mrs Ford. I know not which pleases me better,
that my husband is deceived, or Sir John.
Mrs Page. What a taking was he in when your
husband asked who was in the basket !
Mrs Ford. I am half afraid he will have need of
washing ; so throwing him into the water will do
him a benefit.
Mrs Page. Hang him, dishonest rascal ! I
would all of the same strain were in the same distress.
Mrs Ford. I think my husband hath some special
suspicion of Falstaff's being here ; for I never saw
him so gross in his jealousy till now.
Mrs Page. I will lay a plot to try that ; and we
will yet have more tricks with Falstaff : his dissolute
disease will scarce obey this medicine.
Mrs Ford. Shall we send that foolish carrion,
Mistress Quickly, to him, and excuse his throwing
into the water ; and give him another hope, to
betray him to another punishment ?
Mrs Page. We will do it : let him be sent for
to-morrow, eight o'clock, to have amends.

Re-enter FORD, PAGE, CAIUS, *and* SIR HUGH
EVANS.

Ford. I cannot find him : may be the knave
bragged of that he could not compass.

Mrs Page [*Aside to Mrs Ford*] Heard you
that ?
Mrs Ford. You use me well, Master Ford,
do you ?
Ford. Ay, I do so.
Mrs Ford. Heaven make you better than your
thoughts !
Ford. Amen !
Mrs Page. You do yourself mighty wrong,
Master Ford.
Ford. Ay, ay ; I must bear it.
Evans. If there be any pody in the house, and
in the chambers, and in the coffers, and in the presses
heaven forgive my sins at the day of judgement !
Caius. By gar, nor I too : there is no bodies.
Page. Fie, fie, Master Ford ! are you not asham-
ed ? What spirit, what devil suggests this imagina-
tion ? I would not ha' your distemper in this kind
for the wealth of Windsor Castle.
Ford. 'Tis my fault, Master Page : I suffer for it.
Evans. You suffer for a pad conscience : your
wife is as honest a 'omans as I will desires among
five thousand, and five hundred too.
Caius. By gar, I see 'tis an honest woman.
Ford. Well, I promised you a dinner. Come,
come, walk in the Park : I pray you, pardon me ;
I will hereafter make known to you why I have
done this. Come, wife ; come, Mistress Page. I
pray you, pardon me ; pray heartily, pardon me.
Page. Let 's go in, gentlemen ; but, trust me,
we 'll mock him. I do invite you to-morrow morning
to my house to breakfast : after, we 'll a-birding
together ; I have a fine hawk for the bush. Shall
it be so ?
Ford. Any thing.
Evans. If there is one, I shall make two in the
company.
Caius. If dere be one or two, I shall make-a the
turd.
Ford. Pray you, go, Master Page.
Evans. I pray you, now, remembrance to-morrow
on the lousy knave, mine host.
Caius. Dat is good ; by gar, with all my heart !
Evans. A lousy knave, to have his gibes and
his mockeries ! [*Exeunt.*

SCENE IV. *A room in* PAGE's *house.*

Enter FENTON *and* ANNE PAGE.

Fenton. I see I cannot get thy father's love ;
Therefore no more turn me to him, sweet Nan.
Anne. Alas, how then ?
Fenton. Why, thou must be thyself.
He doth object I am too great of birth ;
And that, my state being gall'd with my expense,
I seek to heal it only by his wealth :
Besides these, other bars he lays before me,
My riots past, my wild societies ;
And tells me 'tis a thing impossible
I should love thee but as a property.
Anne. May be he tells you true.
Fenton. No, heaven so speed me in my time to
come !
Albeit I will confess thy father's wealth
Was the first motive that I woo'd thee, Anne :
Yet, wooing thee, I found thee of more value
Than stamps in gold or sums in sealed bags ;
And 'tis the very riches of thyself
That now I aim at.

Anne.   Gentle Master Fenton,
Yet seek my father's love ; still seek it, sir :
If opportunity and humblest suit
Cannot attain it, why, then,—hark you hither !
                        [*They converse apart.*

Enter SHALLOW, SLENDER, *and* MISTRESS
                        QUICKLY.

Shallow.   Break their talk, Mistress Quickly : my
kinsman shall speak for himself.
Slender.   I 'll make a shaft or a bolt on 't : 'slid,
'tis but venturing.
Shallow.   Be not dismayed.
Slender.   No, she shall not dismay me : I care
not for that, but that I am afeard.
Quickly.   Hark ye ;   Master Slender would
speak a word with you.
Anne.   I come to him. [*Aside*] This is my
        father's choice.
O, what a world of vile ill-favour'd faults
Looks handsome in three hundred pounds a-year !
Quickly.   And how does good Master Fenton ?
Pray you, a word with you.
Shallow.   She 's coming ; to her, coz.   O boy,
thou hadst a father !
Slender.   I had a father, Mistress Anne ; my uncle
can tell you good jests of him. Pray you, uncle,
tell Mistress Anne the jest, how my father stole
two geese out of a pen, good uncle.   41
Shallow.   Mistress Anne, my cousin loves you.
Slender.   Ay, that I do ; as well as I love any
woman in Gloucestershire.
Shallow.   He will maintain you like a gentlewoman.
Slender.   Ay, that I will, come cut and long-tail,
under the degree of a squire.
Shallow.   He will make you a hundred and fifty
pounds jointure.
Anne.   Good Master Shallow, let him woo for
himself.
Shallow.   Marry, I thank you for it ; I thank you
for that good comfort. She calls you, coz : I 'll
leave you.
Anne.   Now, Master Slender,—
Slender.   Now, good Mistress Anne,—
Anne.   What is your will ?
Slender.   My will ! 'od's heartlings, that 's a pretty
jest indeed ! I ne'er made my will yet, I thank
heaven ; I am not such a sickly creature, I give
heaven praise.
Anne.   I mean, Master Slender, what would you
with me ?
Slender.   Truly, for mine own part, I would little
or nothing with you. Your father and my uncle
hath made motions : if it be my luck, so ; if not,
happy man be his dole ! They can tell you how
things go better than I can : you may ask your
father ; here he comes.

Enter PAGE *and* MISTRESS PAGE.

Page.   Now, Master Slender : love him, daughter
Anne.
Why, how now ! what does Master Fenton here ?
You wrong me, sir, thus still to haunt my house :
I told you, sir, my daughter is disposed of.
Fenton.   Nay, Master Page, be not impatient.
Mrs Page.   Good Master Fenton, come not to
my child.
Page.   She is no match for you.
Fenton.   Sir, will you hear me ?

Page.   No, good Master Fenton.
Come, Master Shallow ; come, son Slender, in.
Knowing my mind, you wrong me, Master Fenton.
                [*Exeunt Page, Shallow, and Slender.*
Quickly.   Speak to Mistress Page.
Fenton.   Good Mistress Page, for that I love
        your daughter
In such a righteous fashion as I do,
Perforce, against all checks, rebukes and manners,
I must advance the colours of my love
And not retire : let me have your good will.
Anne.   Good mother, do not marry me to yond
fool.
Mrs Page.   I mean it not ; I seek you a better
husband.
Quickly.   That 's my master, master doctor.
Anne.   Alas, I had rather be set quick i' the earth
And bowl'd to death with turnips !
Mrs Page.   Come, trouble not yourself. Good
Master Fenton,
I will not be your friend nor enemy :
My daughter will I question how she loves you,
And as I find her, so am I affected.
Till then farewell, sir : she must needs go in ;
Her father will be angry.
Fenton.   Farewell, gentle mistress :   farewell,
Nan.   [*Exeunt Mrs Page and Anne.*
Quickly.   This is my doing, now : ' Nay,' said
I, ' will you cast away your child on a fool, and a
physician ? Look on Master Fenton : ' this is my
doing.
Fenton.   I thank thee ; and I pray thee, once
to-night.
Give my sweet Nan this ring : there 's for thy pains.
Quickly.   Now heaven send thee good fortune !
[*Exit Fenton.*]   A kind heart he hath : a woman
would run through fire and water for such a kind
heart. But yet I would my master had Mistress
Anne ; or I would Master Slender had her : or,
in sooth, I would Master Fenton, had her : I will
do what I can for them all three ; for so I have
promised, and I 'll be as good as my word ; but
speciously for Master Fenton. Well, I must of
another errand to Sir John Falstaff from my two
mistresses : what a beast am I to slack it !   [*Exit.*

SCENE V.   *A room in the Garter Inn.*

Enter FALSTAFF *and* BARDOLPH.

Falstaff.   Bardolph, I say,—
Bardolph.   Here, sir.
Falstaff.   Go fetch me a quart of sack ; put a toast
in 't. [*Exit Bardolph.*] Have I lived to be carried
in a basket, like a barrow of butcher's offal, and to
be thrown in the Thames ? Well, if I be served such
another trick, I 'll have my brains ta'en out and
buttered, and give them to a dog for a new year's
gift. The rogues slighted me into the river with as
little remorse as they would have drowned a blind
bitch's puppies, fifteen i' the litter : and you may
know by my size that I have a kind of alacrity in
sinking ; if the bottom were as deep as hell, I should
down. I had been drowned, but that the shore was
shelvy and shallow,—a death that I abhor ; for the
water swells a man ; and what a thing should I
have been when I had been swelled ! I should have
been a mountain of mummy.

Re-enter BARDOLPH *with sack.*

Bardolph.   Here 's Mistress Quickly, sir, to speak
with you.

Falstaff. Come, let me pour in some sack to the Thames water; for my belly 's as cold as if I had swallowed snowballs for pills to cool the reins. Call her in.

Bardolph. Come in, woman!

Enter MISTRESS QUICKLY.

Quickly. By your leave; I cry you mercy: give your worship good morrow.

Falstaff. Take away these chalices. Go brew me a pottle of sack finely.

Bardolph. With eggs, sir?

Falstaff. Simple of itself; I 'll no pullet-sperm in my brewage. [*Exit Bardolph.*] How now!

Quickly. Marry, sir, I come to your worship from Mistress Ford.

Falstaff. Mistress Ford! I have had ford enough; I was thrown into the ford; I have my belly full of ford.

Quickly. Alas the day! good heart, that was not her fault: she does so take on with her men; they mistook their erection.

Falstaff. So did I mine, to build upon a foolish woman's promise.

Quickly. Well, she laments, sir, for it, that it would yearn your heart to see it. Her husband goes this morning a-birding; she desires you once more to come to her between eight and nine: I must carry her word quickly: she 'll make you amends, I warrant you.

Falstaff. Well, I will visit her: tell her so; and bid her think what a man is: let her consider his frailty, and then judge of my merit.

Quickly. I will tell her.

Falstaff. Do so. Between nine and ten, sayest thou?

Quickly. Eight and nine, sir.

Falstaff. Well, be gone: I will not miss her.

Quickly. Peace be with you, sir.   [*Exit.*

Falstaff. I marvel I hear not of Master Brook; he sent me word to stay within: I like his money well. O, here he comes.

Enter FORD.

Ford. Bless you, sir!

Falstaff. Now, Master Brook, you come to know what hath passed between me and Ford's wife?

Ford. That, indeed, Sir John, is my business.

Falstaff. Master Brook, I will not lie to you: I was at her house the hour she appointed me.

Ford. And sped you, sir?

Falstaff. Very ill-favouredly, Master Brook.

Ford. How so, sir? Did she change her determination?

Falstaff. No, Master Brook: but the peaking Cornuto her husband, Master Brook, dwelling in a continual 'larum of jealousy, comes me in the instant of our encounter, after we had embraced, kissed, protested, and, as it were, spoke the prologue of our comedy; and at his heels a rabble of his companions, thither provoked and instigated by his distemper, and, forsooth, to search his house for his wife's love.

Ford. What, while you were there?

Falstaff. While I was there.

Ford. And did he search for you, and could not find you?

Falstaff. You shall hear. As good luck would have it, comes in one Mistress Page; gives intelligence of Ford's approach; and, in her invention and Ford's wife's distraction, they conveyed me into a buck-basket.

Ford. A buck-basket!

Falstaff. By the Lord, a buck-basket! rammed me in with foul shirts and smocks, socks, foul stockings, greasy napkins; that, Master Brook, there was the rankest compound of villanous smell that ever offended nostril.

Ford. And how long lay you there?

Falstaff. Nay, you shall hear, Master Brook, what I have suffered to bring this woman to evil for your good. Being thus crammed in the basket, a couple of Ford's knaves, his hinds, were called forth by their mistress to carry me in the name of foul clothes to Datchet-lane: they took me on their shoulders; met the jealous knave their master in the door, who asked them once or twice what they had in their basket: I quaked for fear, lest the lunatic knave would have searched it; but fate, ordaining he should be a cuckold, held his hand. Well: on went he for a search, and away went I for foul clothes. But mark the sequel, Master Brook: I suffered the pangs of three several deaths; first, an intolerable fright, to be detected with a jealous rotten bell-wether; next, to be compassed, like a good bilbo, in the circumference of a peck, hilt to point, heel to head; and then, to be stopped in, like a strong distillation, with stinking clothes that fretted in their own grease: think of that,—a man of my kidney,—think of that,—that am as subject to heat as butter; a man of continual dissolution and thaw: it was a miracle to 'scape suffocation. And in the height of this bath, when I was more than half stewed in grease, like a Dutch dish, to be thrown into the Thames, and cooled, glowing hot, in that surge, like a horse-shoe; think of that,—hissing hot,—think of that, Master Brook.

Ford. In good sadness, sir, I am sorry that for my sake you have suffered all this. My suit then is desperate; you 'll undertake her no more?

Falstaff. Master Brook, I will be thrown into Etna, as I have been into Thames, ere I will leave her thus. Her husband is this morning gone a-birding: I have received from her another embassy of meeting; 'twixt eight and nine is the hour, Master Brook.

Ford. 'Tis past eight already, sir.

Falstaff. Is it? I will then address me to my appointment. Come to me at your convenient leisure, and you shall know how I speed; and the conclusion shall be crowned with your enjoying her. Adieu. You shall have her, Master Brook; Master Brook, you shall cuckold Ford.   [*Exit.*

Ford. Hum! ha! is this a vision? is this a dream? do I sleep? Master Ford, awake! awake, Master Ford! there 's a hole made in your best coat, Master Ford. This 'tis to be married! this 'tis to have linen and buck-baskets! Well, I will proclaim myself what I am: I will now take the lecher; he is at my house; he cannot 'scape me; 'tis impossible he should; he cannot creep into a halfpenny purse, nor into a pepper-box: but, lest the devil that guides him should aid him, I will search impossible places. Though what I am I cannot avoid, yet to be what I would not shall not make me tame: if I have horns to make one mad, let the proverb go with me: I 'll be horn-mad. [*Exit.*

ACT IV.

SCENE I. *A street.*

Enter MISTRESS PAGE, MISTRESS QUICKLY,
and WILLIAM.

Mrs Page.

Is he at Master Ford's already, think'st thou ?
Quickly. Sure he is by this, or will be presently :
but, truly, he is very courageous mad about
his throwing into the water. Mistress Ford desires
you to come suddenly.
Mrs Page. I 'll be with her by and by ; I 'll but
bring my young man here to school. Look, where
his master comes ; 'tis a playing-day, I see.

Enter SIR HUGH EVANS.

How now, Sir Hugh ! no school to-day ?
Evans. No ; Master Slender is let the boys
leave to play.
Quickly. Blessing of his heart !
Mrs Page. Sir Hugh, my husband says my son
profits nothing in the world at his book. I pray
you, ask him some questions in his accidence.
Evans. Come hither, William ; hold up your
head ; come.
Mrs Page. Come on, sirrah ; hold up your
head ; answer your master, be not afraid.
Evans. William, how many numbers is in nouns ?
William. Two.
Quickly. Truly, I thought there had been one
number more, because they say, ' 'Od's nouns.'
Evans. Peace your tattlings ! What is ' fair,'
William ?
William. Pulcher.
Quickly. Polecats ! there are fairer things than
polecats, sure.
Evans. You are a very simplicity 'oman : I pray
you, peace. What is ' lapis,' William ?
William. A stone.
Evans. And what is ' a stone,' William ?
William. A pebble.
Evans. No, it is ' lapis : ' I pray you, remember
in your prain.
William. Lapis.
Evans. That is a good William. What is he,
William, that does lend articles ?
William. Articles are borrowed of the pronoun,
and be thus declined, Singulariter, nominativo,
hic, hæc, hoc.
Evans. Nominativo, hig, hag, hog ; pray you,
mark : genitivo, hujus. Well, what is your accusa-
tive case ?
William. Accusativo, hinc.
Evans. I pray you, have your remembrance,
child ; accusativo, hung, hang, hog.
Quickly. ' Hang-hog ' is Latin for bacon, I
warrant you.
Evans. Leave your prabbles, 'oman. What is
the focative case, William ?
William. O,—vocativo, O.
Evans. Remember, William ; focative is caret.
Quickly. And that 's a good root.
Evans. 'Oman, forbear.
Mrs Page. Peace !
Evans. What is your genitive case plural,
William ?
William. Genitive case !
Evans. Ay.

William. Genitive,—horum, harum, horum.
Quickly. Vengeance of Jenny's case ! fie on her !
never name her, child, if she be a whore.
Evans. For shame, 'oman.
Quickly. You do ill to teach the child such words :
he teaches him to hick and to hack, which they 'll
do fast enough of themselves, and to call ' horum : '
fie upon you !
Evans. 'Oman, art thou lunatics ? hast thou no
understandings for thy cases and the numbers of the
genders ? Thou art as foolish Christian creatures
as I would desires.
Mrs Page. Prithee, hold thy peace.
Evans. Show me now, William, some declensions
of your pronouns.
William. Forsooth, I have forgot.
Evans. It is qui, quæ, quod : if you forget
your ' quies,' your ' quæs,' and your ' quods,'
you must be preeches. Go your ways, and play ; go.
Mrs Page. He is a better scholar than I thought
he was.
Evans. He is a good sprag memory. Farewell,
Mistress Page.
Mrs Page. Adieu, good Sir Hugh.
[*Exit Sir Hugh.*]
Get you home, boy. Come, we stay too long.
[*Exeunt.*

SCENE II. *A room in* FORD'S *house.*

Enter FALSTAFF *and* MISTRESS FORD.

Falstaff. Mistress Ford, your sorrow hath eaten
up my sufferance. I see you are obsequious in
your love, and I profess requital to a hair's breadth ;
not only, Mistress Ford, in the simple office of love,
but in all the accoutrement, complement and ceremony of it. But are you sure of your husband now ?
Mrs Ford. He 's a-birding, sweet Sir John.
Mrs Page. [*Within*] What ho, gossip Ford !
what, ho !
Mrs Ford. Step into the chamber, Sir John.
[*Exit Falstaff.*

Enter MISTRESS PAGE.

Mrs Page. How now, sweetheart ! who 's at
home besides yourself ?
Mrs Ford. Why, none but mine own people.
Mrs Page. Indeed !
Mrs Ford. No, certainly. [*Aside to her*] Speak
louder.
Mrs Page. Truly, I am so glad you have nobody
here.
Mrs Ford. Why ?
Mrs Page. Why, woman, your husband is in
his old lunes again : he so takes on yonder with my
husband ; so rails against all married mankind ;
so curses all Eve's daughters, of what complexion
soever ; and so buffets himself on the forehead,
crying, ' Peer out, peer out ! ' that any madness I
ever yet beheld seemed but tameness, civility and
patience, to this his distemper he is in now : I am
glad the fat knight is not here.
Mrs Ford. Why, does he talk of him ?
Mrs Page. Of none but him ; and swears he was
carried out, the last time he searched for him, in a
basket ; protests to my husband he is now here,
and hath drawn him and the rest of their company
from their sport, to make another experiment of his
suspicion : but I am glad the knight is not here ;
now he shall see his own foolery.

Mrs Ford. How near is he, Mistress Page?
Mrs Page. Hard by; at street end; he will be here anon.
Mrs Ford. I am undone! The knight is here.
Mrs Page. Why then you are utterly shamed, and he 's but a dead man. What a woman are you! —Away with him, away with him! better shame than murder.
Mrs Ford. Which way should he go? how should I bestow him? Shall I put him into the basket again?

Re-enter FALSTAFF.

Falstaff. No, I 'll come no more i' the basket. May I not go out ere he come?
Mrs Page. Alas, three of Master Ford's brothers watch the door with pistols, that none shall issue out; otherwise you might slip away ere he came. But what make you here?
Falstaff. What shall I do? I 'll creep up into the chimney.
Mrs Ford. There they always use to discharge their birding-pieces. Creep into the kiln-hole.
Falstaff. Where is it?
Mrs Ford. He will seek there, on my word. Neither press, coffer, chest, trunk, well, vault, but he hath an abstract for the remembrance of such places, and goes to them by his note: there is no hiding you in the house.
Falstaff. I 'll go out then.
Mrs Page. If you go out in your own semblance, you die, Sir John. Unless you go out disguised—
Mrs Ford. How might we disguise him?
Mrs Page. Alas the day, I know not! There is no woman's gown big enough for him; otherwise he might put on a hat, a muffler and a kerchief, and so escape.
Falstaff. Good hearts, devise something; any extremity rather than a mischief.
Mrs Ford. My maid's aunt, the fat woman of Brentford, has a gown above.
Mrs Page. On my word, it will serve him; she 's as big as he is: and there 's her thrummed hat and her muffler too. Run up, Sir John.
Mrs Ford. Go, go, sweet Sir John: Mistress Page and I will look some linen for your head.
Mrs Page. Quick, quick! we 'll come dress you straight: put on the gown the while.
                                            [*Exit Falstaff.*
Mrs Ford. I would my husband would meet him in this shape: he cannot abide the old woman of Brentford; he swears she 's a witch; forbade her my house and hath threatened to beat her.
Mrs Page. Heaven guide him to thy husband's cudgel, and the devil guide his cudgel afterwards!
Mrs Ford. But is my husband coming?
Mrs Page. Ay, in good sadness, is he; and talks of the basket too, howsoever he hath had intelligence.
Mrs Ford. We 'll try that; for I 'll appoint my men to carry the basket again, to meet him at the door with it, as they did last time.
Mrs Page. Nay, but he 'll be here presently; let 's go dress him like the witch of Brentford.
Mrs Ford. I 'll first direct my men what they shall do with the basket. Go up; I 'll bring linen for him straight.   [*Exit.*
Mrs Page. Hang him, dishonest varlet! we cannot misuse him enough.
We 'll leave a proof, by that which we will do,
Wives may be merry, and yet honest too:

We do not act that often jest and laugh;
'Tis old, but true, Still swine eats all the draff.
                                            [*Exit.*

Re-enter MISTRESS FORD *with two* Servants.

Mrs Ford. Go, sirs, take the basket again on your shoulders: your master is hard at door; if he bid you set it down, obey him: quickly, dispatch.   [*Exit.*
First Servant. Come, come, take it up.
Second Servant. Pray heaven it be not full of knight again.
First Servant. I hope not; I had as lief bear so much lead.

Enter FORD, PAGE, SHALLOW, CAIUS, *and*
SIR HUGH EVANS.

Ford. Ay, but if it prove true, Master Page, have you any way then to unfool me again? Set down the basket, villain! Somebody call my wife. Youth in a basket! O you pandarly rascals! there 's a knot, a ging, a pack, a conspiracy against me: now shall the devil be shamed. What, wife, I say! Come, come forth! Behold what honest clothes you send forth to bleaching!
Page. Why, this passes, Master Ford; you are not to go loose any longer; you must be pinioned.
Evans. Why, this is lunatics! this is mad as a mad dog!
Shallow. Indeed, Master Ford, this is not well, indeed.
Ford. So say I too, sir.

Re-enter MISTRESS FORD.

Come hither, Mistress Ford; Mistress Ford, the honest woman, the modest wife, the virtuous creature, that hath the jealous fool to her husband! I suspect without cause, mistress, do I?
Mrs Ford. Heaven be my witness you do, if you suspect me in any dishonesty.
Ford. Well said, brazen-face! hold it out. Come forth, sirrah!
                        [*Pulling clothes out of the basket.*
Page. This passes!
Mrs Ford. Are you not ashamed? let the clothes alone.
Ford. I shall find you anon.
Evans. 'Tis unreasonable! Will you take up your wife's clothes? Come away.
Ford. Empty the basket, I say!
Mrs Ford. Why, man, why?
Ford. Master Page, as I am a man, there was one conveyed out of my house yesterday in this basket: why may not he be there again? In my house I am sure he is: my intelligence is true; my jealousy is reasonable. Pluck me out all the linen.
Mrs Ford. If you find a man there, he shall die a flea's death.
Page. Here 's no man.
Shallow. By my fidelity, this is not well, Master Ford; this wrongs you.
Evans. Master Ford, you must pray, and not follow the imaginations of your own heart: this is jealousies.
Ford. Well, he 's not here I seek for.
Page. No, nor nowhere else but in your brain.

Ford. Help to search my house this one time. If I find not what I seek, show no colour for my extremity ; let me for ever be your table-sport ; let them say of me, ' As jealous as Ford, that searched a hollow walnut for his wife's leman.' Satisfy me once more ; once more search with me.

Mrs Ford. What, ho, Mistress Page ! come you and the old woman down ; my husband will come into the chamber.

Ford. Old woman ! what old woman 's that ?

Mrs Ford. Why, it is my maid's aunt of Brent- 179
ford.

Ford. A witch, a quean, an old cozening quean ! Have I not forbid her my house ? She comes of errands, does she ? We are simple men ; we do not know what 's brought to pass under the profession of fortune-telling. She works by charms, by spells, by the figure, and such daubery as this is, beyond our element : we know nothing. Come down, you witch, you hag, you ; come down, I say !

Mrs Ford. Nay, good, sweet husband ! Good gentlemen, let him not strike the old woman.

Re-enter FALSTAFF *in woman's clothes, and*
MISTRESS PAGE.

Mrs Page. Come, Mother Prat ; come, give me your hand.

Ford. I 'll prat her. [*Beating him*] Out of my door, you witch, you hag, you baggage, you polecat, you ronyon ! out, out ! I 'll conjure you, I 'll fortune-tell you. [*Exit Falstaff.*

Mrs Page. Are you not ashamed ? I think you have killed the poor woman.

Mrs Ford. Nay, he will do it. 'Tis a goodly credit for you.

Ford. Hang her, witch !

Evans. By yea and no, I think the 'oman is a witch indeed : I like not when a 'oman has a great peard ; I spy a great peard under his muffler.

Ford. Will you follow, gentlemen ? I beseech you, follow ; see but the issue of my jealousy : if I cry out thus upon no trail, never trust me when I open again.

Page. Let 's obey his humour a little further : come, gentlemen.

[*Exeunt Ford, Page, Shallow, Caius, and Evans.*

Mrs Page. Trust me, he beat him most pitifully.

Mrs Ford. Nay, by the mass, that he did not ; he beat him most unpitifully, methought.

Mrs Page. I 'll have the cudgel hallowed and hung o'er the altar ; it hath done meritorious service.

Mrs Ford. What think you ? may we, with the warrant of womanhood and the witness of a good conscience, pursue him with any further revenge ?

Mrs Page. The spirit of wantonness is, sure, scared out of him : if the devil have him not in fee-simple, with fine and recovery, he will never, I think, in the way of waste, attempt us again.

Mrs Ford. Shall we tell our husbands how we have served him ?

Mrs Page. Yes, by all means ; if it be but to scrape the figures out of your husband's brains. If they can find in their hearts the poor unvirtuous fat knight shall be any further afflicted, we two will still be the ministers.

Mrs Ford. I 'll warrant they 'll have him publicly shamed : and methinks there would be no period to the jest, should he not be publicly shamed.

Mrs Page. Come, to the forge with it then ; shape it : I would not have things cool. [*Exeunt.*

SCENE III.   *A room in the Garter Inn.*

Enter HOST *and* BARDOLPH.

Bardolph. Sir, the Germans desire to have three of your horses : the duke himself will be tomorrow at court, and they are going to meet him.

Host. What duke should that be comes so secretly ? I hear not of him in the court. Let me speak with the gentlemen : they speak English ?

Bardolph. Ay, sir ; I 'll call them to you.

Host. They shall have my horses ; but I 'll make them pay ; I 'll sauce them : they have had my house a week at command ; I have turned away my other guests : they must come off ; I 'll sauce them. Come. [*Exeunt.*

SCENE IV.   *A room in* FORD'S *house.*

Enter PAGE, FORD, MISTRESS PAGE, MISTRESS
FORD, *and* SIR HUGH EVANS.

Evans. 'Tis one of the best discretions of a 'oman as ever I did look upon.

Page. And did he send you both these letters at an instant ?

Mrs Page. Within a quarter of an hour.

Ford. Pardon me, wife. Henceforth do what thou wilt ;
I rather will suspect the sun with cold
Than thee with wantonness : now doth thy honour stand,
In him that was of late an heretic,
As firm as faith.

Page.   'Tis well, 'tis well ; no more :
Be not as extreme in submission
As in offence,
But let our plot go forward : let our wives
Yet once again, to make us public sport,
Appoint a meeting with this old fat fellow,
Where we may take him and disgrace him for it.

Ford. There is no better way than that they spoke of.

Page. How ? to send him word they 'll meet him in the park at midnight ? Fie, fie ! he 'll never come.

Evans. You say he has been thrown in the rivers and has been grievously peaten as an old 'oman : methinks there should be terrors in him that he should not come ; methinks his flesh is punished, he shall have no desires.

Page. So think I too.

Mrs Ford. Devise but how you 'll use him when he comes,
And let us two devise to bring him thither.

Mrs Page. There is an old tale goes that Herne the hunter,
Sometime a keeper here in Windsor forest,
Doth all the winter-time, at still midnight,
Walk round about an oak, with great ragg'd horns ;
And there he blasts the tree and takes the cattle
And makes milch-kine yield blood and shakes a chain
In a most hideous and dreadful manner :
You have heard of such a spirit, and well you know
The superstitious idle-headed eld
Received and did deliver to our age
This tale of Herne the hunter for a truth.

Page. Why, yet there want not many that do fear
In deep of night to walk by this Herne's oak :
But what of this ?

Mrs Ford.   Marry, this is our device ;
That Falstaff at that oak shall meet with us.

Page. Well, let it not be doubted but he 'll come :
And in this shape when you have brought him thither,
What shall be done with him ? what is your plot ?
   Mrs Page. That likewise have we thought upon, and thus :
Nan Page my daughter and my little son
And three or four more of their growth we 'll dress
Like urchins, ouphes and fairies, green and white,
With rounds of waxen tapers on their heads,
And rattles in their hands : upon a sudden,
As Falstaff, she and I, are newly met,
Let them from forth a sawpit rush at once
With some diffused song : upon their sight,
We two in great amazedness will fly :
Then let them all encircle him about
And, fairy-like, to pinch the unclean knight,
And ask him why, that hour of fairy revel,
In their so sacred paths he dares to tread
In shape profane.
   Mrs Ford. And till he tell the truth,
Let the supposed fairies pinch him sound
And burn him with their tapers.
   Mrs Page.   The truth being known,
We 'll all present ourselves, dis-horn the spirit,
And mock him home to Windsor.
   Ford.   The children must
Be practised well to this, or they 'll ne'er do 't.
   Evans. I will teach the children their behaviours ;
and I will be like a jack-an-apes also, to burn the
knight with my taber.
   Ford. That will be excellent. I 'll go buy them
vizards.
   Mrs Page. My Nan shall be the queen of all
the fairies,
Finely attired in a robe of white.
   Page. That silk will I go buy. [*Aside*] And in
that time
Shall Master Slender steal my Nan away
And marry her at Eton. · Go send to Falstaff straight.
   Ford. Nay, I 'll to him again in name of Brook :
He 'll tell me all his purpose : sure, he 'll come.
   Mrs Page. Fear not you that. Go get us pro-
perties
And tricking for our fairies.
   Evans. Let us about it : it is admirable pleasures
and fery honest knaveries.
               [*Exeunt Page, Ford, and Evans.*
   Mrs Page. Go, Mistress Ford,
Send quickly to Sir John, to know his mind.
                    [*Exit Mrs Ford.*
I 'll to the doctor : he hath my good will,
And none but he, to marry with Nan Page.
That Slender, though well landed, is an idiot ;
And he my husband best of all affects.
The doctor is well money'd, and his friends
Potent at court : he, none but he, shall have her,
Though twenty thousand worthier come to crave
   her.   [*Exit.*

SCENE V.   *A room in the Garter Inn.*

       Enter HOST *and* SIMPLE.

   Host. What wouldst thou have, boor ? what,
thick-skin ? speak, breathe, discuss ; brief, short,
quick, snap.
   Simple. Marry, sir, I come to speak with Sir
John Falstaff from Master Slender.
   Host. There 's his chamber, his house, his castle,
his standing-bed and truckle-bed ; 'tis painted about

with the story of the Prodigal, fresh and new. Go
knock and call ; he 'll speak like an Anthropop-
haginian unto thee : knock, I say.
   Simple. There 's an old woman, a fat woman,
gone up into his chamber : I 'll be so bold as stay,
sir, till she come down ; I come to speak with her,
indeed.
   Host. Ha ! a fat woman ! the knight may be
robbed : I 'll call. Bully Knight ! bully Sir John !
speak from thy lungs military : art thou there ? it
is thine host, thine Ephesian, calls.
   Falstaff. [*Above*] How now, mine host !
   Host. Here 's a Bohemian-Tartar tarries the
coming down of thy fat woman. Let her descend,
bully, let her descend ; my chambers are honourable :
fie ! privacy ? fie !

          Enter FALSTAFF.

   Falstaff. There was, mine host, an old fat woman
even now with me ; but she 's gone.
   Simple. Pray you, sir, was 't not the wise woman
of Brentford ?
   Falstaff. Ay, marry, was it, mussel-shell : what
would you with her ?
   Simple. My master, sir, Master Slender, sent to
her, seeing her go thorough the streets, to know,
sir, whether one Nym, sir, that beguiled him of a
chain, had the chain or no.
   Falstaff. I spake with the old woman about it.
   Simple. And what says she, I pray, sir ?
   Falstaff. Marry, she says that the very same man
that beguiled Master Slender of his chain cozened
him of it.
   Simple. I would I could have spoken with the
woman herself ; I had other things to have spoken
with her too from him.
   Falstaff. What are they ? let us know.
   Host. Ay, come ; quick.
   Simple. I may not conceal them, sir.
   Host. Conceal them, or thou diest.
   Simple. Why, sir, they were nothing but about
Mistress Anne Page ; to know if it were my master's
fortune to have her or no.
   Falstaff. 'Tis, 'tis his fortune.
   Simple. What, sir ?
   Falstaff. To have her, or no. Go ; say the
woman told me so.
   Simple. May I be bold to say so, sir ?
   Falstaff. Ay, sir ; like who more bold.
   Simple. I thank your worship : I shall make my
master glad with these tidings.   [*Exit.*
   Host. Thou art clerkly, thou art clerkly, Sir
John. Was there a wise woman with thee ?
   Falstaff. Ay, that there was, mine host ; one that
hath taught me more wit than ever I learned before
in my life ; and I paid nothing for it neither, but
was paid for my learning.

          Enter BARDOLPH.

   Bardolph. Out, alas, sir ! cozenage, mere cozenage !
   Host. Where be my horses ? speak well of
them, varletto.
   Bardolph. Run away with the cozeners ; for so
soon as I came beyond Eton, they threw me off from
behind one of them, in a slough of mire ; and set
spurs and away, like three German devils, three
Doctor Faustuses.
   Host. They are gone but to meet the duke,
villain : do not say they be fled ; Germans are
honest men.

Enter SIR HUGH EVANS.

Evans. Where is mine host?
Host. What is the matter, sir?
Evans. Have a care of your entertainments : there is a friend of mine come to town, tells me there is three cozen-germans that has cozened all the hosts of Readins, of Maidenhead, of Colebrook, of horses and money. I tell you for good will, look you : you are wise and full of gibes and vlouting-stocks, and 'tis not convenient you should be cozened. Fare you well.   [*Exit.*

Enter DOCTOR CAIUS.

Caius. Vere is mine host de Jarteer?
Host. Here, master doctor, in perplexity and doubtful dilemma.
Caius. I cannot tell vat is dat : but it is tell-a me dat you make grand preparation for a duke de Jamany : by my trot, dere is no duke dat the court is know to come. I tell you for good vill : adieu.
                                               [*Exit.*
Host. Hue and cry, villain, go! Assist me, knight. I am undone! Fly, run, hue and cry, villain! I am undone! [*Exeunt Host and Bardolph.*
Falstaff. I would all the world might be cozened ; for I have been cozened and beaten too. If it should come to the ear of the court, how I have been transformed and how my transformation hath been washed and cudgelled, they would melt me out of my fat drop by drop and liquor fishermen's boots with me : I warrant they would whip me with their fine wits till I were as crestfallen as a dried pear. I never prospered since I forswore myself at primero. Well, if my wind were but long enough to say my prayers, I would repent.

Enter MISTRESS QUICKLY.

Now, whence come you?
Quickly. From the two parties, forsooth.
Falstaff. The devil take one party and his dam the other! and so they shall be both bestowed. I have suffered more for their sakes, more than the villanous inconstancy of man's disposition is able to bear.
Quickly. And have not they suffered? Yes, I warrant ; speciously one of them ; Mistress Ford, good heart, is beaten black and blue, that you cannot see a white spot about her.
Falstaff. What tellest thou me of black and blue? I was beaten myself into all the colours of the rainbow ; and I was like to be apprehended for the witch of Brentford : but that my admirable dexterity of wit, my counterfeiting the action of an old woman, delivered me, the knave constable had set me i' the stocks, i' the common stocks, for a witch.
Quickly. Sir, let me speak with you in your chamber : you shall hear how things go ; and, I warrant, to your content. Here is a letter will say somewhat. Good hearts, what ado here is to bring you together! Sure, one of you does not serve heaven well, that you are so crossed.
Falstaff. Come up into my chamber.   [*Exeunt.*

SCENE VI.   *Another room in the Garter Inn.*

Enter FENTON *and* HOST.

Host. Master Fenton, talk not to me ; my mind is heavy : I will give over all.

Fenton. Yet hear me speak. Assist me in my purpose,
And, as I am a gentleman, I'll give thee
A hundred pounds in gold more than your loss.
Host. I will hear you, Master Fenton ; and I will at the least keep your counsel.
Fenton. From time to time I have acquainted you
With the dear love I bear to fair Anne Page ;
Who mutually hath answer'd my affection,
So far forth as herself might be her chooser,
Even to my wish : I have a letter from her
Of such contents as you will wonder at ;
The mirth whereof so larded with my matter,
That neither singly can be manifested,
Without the show of both ; fat Falstaff
Hath a great scene : the image of the jest
I'll show you here at large. Hark, good mine host.
To-night at Herne's oak, just 'twixt twelve and one,
Must my sweet Nan present the Fairy Queen ;
The purpose why, is here : in which disguise,
While other jests are something rank on foot,
Her father hath commanded her to slip
Away with Slender and with him at Eton
Immediately to marry : she hath consented :
Now, sir,
Her mother, ever strong against that match
And firm for Doctor Caius, hath appointed
That he shall likewise shuffle her away,
While other sports are tasking of their minds,
And at the deanery, where a priest attends,
Straight marry her : to this her mother's plot
She seemingly obedient likewise hath
Made promise to the doctor. Now, thus it rests :
Her father means she shall be all in white,
And in that habit, when Slender sees his time
To take her by the hand and bid her go,
She shall go with him : her mother hath intended,
The better to denote her to the doctor,
For they must all be mask'd and vizarded,
That quaint in green she shall be loose enrobed,
With ribands pendent, flaring 'bout her head ;
And when the doctor spies his vantage ripe,
To pinch her by the hand, and, on that token,
The maid hath given consent to go with him.
Host. Which means she to deceive, father or mother?
Fenton. Both, my good host, to go along with me :
And here it rests, that you'll procure the vicar
To stay for me at church 'twixt twelve and one,
And, in the lawful name of marrying,
To give our hearts united ceremony.
Host. Well, husband your device ; I'll to the vicar ;
Bring you the maid, you shall not lack a priest.
Fenton. So shall I evermore be bound to thee ;
Besides, I'll make a present recompense.   [*Exeunt.*

ACT V.

SCENE I.   *A room in the Garter Inn.*

Enter FALSTAFF *and* MISTRESS QUICKLY.

Falstaff.

P rithee, no more prattling ; go. I'll hold. This is the third time ; I hope good luck lies in odd numbers. Away! go. They say there is divinity in odd numbers, either in nativity, chance, or death. Away!
Quickly. I'll provide you a chain ; and I'll do what I can to get you a pair of horns.

Falstaff. Away, I say ; time wears : hold up your head, and mince.   [*Exit Mistress Quickly.*

Enter FORD.

How now, Master Brook ! Master Brook, the matter will be known to-night, or never. Be you in the Park about midnight, at Herne's oak, and you shall see wonders.

Ford. Went you not to her yesterday, sir, as you told me you had appointed ?

Falstaff. I went to her, Master Brook, as you see, like a poor old man : but I came from her, Master Brook, like a poor old woman. That same knave Ford, her husband, hath the finest mad devil of jealousy in him, Master Brook, that ever governed frenzy. I will tell you : he beat me grievously, in the shape of a woman ; for in the shape of man, Master Brook, I fear not Goliath with a weaver's beam ; because I know also life is a shuttle. I am in haste ; go along with me : I 'll tell you all, Master Brook. Since I plucked geese, played truant and whipped top, I knew not what 'twas to be beaten till lately. Follow me : I 'll tell you strange things of this knave Ford, on whom to-night I will be revenged, and I will deliver his wife into your hand. Follow. Strange things in hand, Master Brook ! Follow.   [*Exeunt.*

SCENE II.   *Windsor Park.*

Enter PAGE, SHALLOW, *and* SLENDER.

Page. Come, come ; we 'll couch i' the castle-ditch till we see the light of our fairies. Remember, son Slender, my daughter.

Slender. Ay, forsooth ; I have spoke with her and we have a nay-word how to know one another : I come to her in white, and cry ' mum ; ' she cries ' budget ; ' and by that we know one another.

Shallow. That 's good too : but what needs either your ' mum ' or her ' budget ? ' the white will decipher her well enough. It hath struck ten o'clock.

Page. The night is dark ; light and spirits will become it well. Heaven prosper our sport ! No man means evil but the devil, and we shall know him by his horns. Let 's away ; follow me.   [*Exeunt.*

SCENE III.   *A street leading to the Park.*

Enter MISTRESS PAGE, MISTRESS FORD, *and* DOCTOR CAIUS.

Mrs Page. Master Doctor, my daughter is in green : when you see your time, take her by the hand, away with her to the deanery, and dispatch it quickly. Go before into the Park : we two must go together.

Caius. I know vat I have to do. Adieu.

Mrs Page. Fare you well, sir.   [*Exit Caius.*] My husband will not rejoice so much at the abuse of Falstaff as he will chafe at the doctor's marrying my daughter : but 'tis no matter ; better a little chiding than a great deal of heart-break.

Mrs Ford. Where is Nan now and her troop of fairies, and the Welsh devil Hugh ?

Mrs Page. They are all couched in a pit hard by Herne's oak, with obscured lights ; which, at the very instant of Falstaff's and our meeting, they will at once display to the night.

Mrs Ford. That cannot choose but amaze him.

Mrs Page. If he be not amazed, he will be mocked; if he be amazed, he will every way be mocked.

Mrs Ford. We 'll betray him finely.

Mrs Page. Against such lewdsters and their lechery. Those that betray them do no treachery.

Mrs Ford. The hour draws on. To the oak, to the oak !   [*Exeunt.*

SCENE IV.   *Windsor Park.*

Enter SIR HUGH EVANS *disguised, with others as Fairies.*

Evans. Trib, trib, fairies ; come ; and remember your parts : be pold, I pray you ; follow me into the pit ; and when I give the watch 'ords, do as I pid you : come, come ; trib, trib.   [*Exeunt.*

SCENE V.   *Another part of the Park.*

Enter FALSTAFF *disguised as Herne.*

Falstaff. The Windsor bell hath struck twelve ; the minute draws on. Now, the hot blooded gods assist me ! Remember, Jove, thou wast a bull for thy Europa ; love set on thy horns. O powerful love ! that, in some respects, makes a beast a man, in some other, a man a beast. You were also, Jupiter, a swan for the love of Leda. O omnipotent Love ! how near the god drew to the complexion of a goose ! A fault done first in the form of a beast. O Jove, a beastly fault ! And then another fault in the semblance of a fowl ; think on 't, Jove ; a foul fault ! When gods have hot backs, what shall poor men do ? For me, I am here a Windsor stag ; and the fattest, I think, i' the forest. Send me a cool rut-time, Jove, or who can blame me to piss my tallow ? Who comes here ? my doe ?

Enter MISTRESS FORD *and* MISTRESS PAGE.

Mrs Ford. Sir John ! art thou there, my deer ? my male deer ?

Falstaff. My doe with the black scut ! Let the sky rain potatoes ; let it thunder to the tune of Green Sleeves, hail kissing-comfits and snow eringoes ; let there come a tempest of provocation, I will shelter me here.

Mrs Ford. Mistress Page is come with me, sweetheart.

Falstaff. Divide me like a bribe buck, each a haunch : I will keep my sides to myself, my shoulders for the fellow of this walk, and my horns I bequeath your husbands. Am I a woodman, ha ? Speak I like Herne the hunter ? Why, now is Cupid a child of conscience ; he makes restitution. As I am a true spirit, welcome !   [*Noise within.*

Mrs Page. Alas, what noise ?

Mrs Ford. Heaven forgive our sins !

Falstaff. What should this be ?

Mrs Ford. }
Mrs Page. } Away, away !   [*They run off.*

Falstaff. I think the devil will not have me damned, lest the oil that 's in me should set hell on fire ; he would never else cross me thus.

Enter SIR HUGH EVANS, *disguised as before* : PISTOL, *as Hobgoblin* ; MISTRESS QUICKLY, ANNE PAGE, *and others, as Fairies, with tapers.*

Quickly. Fairies, black, grey, green, and white, You moonshine revellers, and shades of night,

You orphan heirs of fixed destiny,
Attend your office and your quality.
Crier Hobgoblin, make the fairy oyes.
Pistol. Elves, list your names ; silence, you
    airy toys.
Cricket, to Windsor chimneys shalt thou leap :
Where fires thou find'st unraked and hearths unswept,
There pinch the maids as blue as bilberry :
Our radiant queen hates sluts and sluttery.
    Falstaff. They are fairies ; he that speaks to them
    shall die :
I 'll wink and couch : no man their works must eye.
                                [*Lies down upon his face.*

Evans. Where 's Bede ? Go you, and where you
    find a maid
That, ere she sleep, has thrice her prayers said,
Raise up the organs of her fantasy ;
Sleep she as sound as careless infancy :
But those as sleep and think not on their sins,
Pinch them, arms, legs, backs, shoulders, sides and
    shins.
Quickly. About, about ;
Search Windsor Castle, elves, within and out :
Strew good luck, ouphes, on every sacred room :
That it may stand till the perpetual doom,
In state as wholesome as in state 'tis fit,
Worthy the owner, and the owner it.
The several chairs of order look you scour
With juice of balm and every precious flower :
Each fair instalment, coat, and several crest,
With loyal blazon, evermore be blest !
And nightly, meadow-fairies, look you sing,
Like to the Garter's compass, in a ring :
The expressure that it bears, green let it be,
More fertile-fresh than all the field to see ;
And ' Honi soit qui mal y pense ' write
In emerald tufts, flowers purple, blue, and white ;
Like sapphire, pearl and rich embroidery,
Buckled below fair knighthood's bending knee :
Fairies use flowers for their charactery.
Away ; disperse : but till 'tis one o'clock,
Our dance of custom round about the oak
Of Herne the hunter, let us not forget.
Evans. Pray you, lock hand in hand ; yourselves
    in order set ;
And twenty glow-worms shall our lanterns be,
To guide our measure round about the tree.
But, stay ; I smell a man of middle-earth.
Falstaff. Heavens defend me from that Welsh
    fairy, lest he transform me to a piece of cheese !
Pistol. Vile worm, thou wast o'erlook'd even in
    thy birth.
Quickly. With trial-fire touch me his finger-end :
If he be chaste, the flame will back descend
And turn him to no pain ; but if he start,
It is the flesh of a corrupted heart.
Pistol. A trial, come.
Evans.   Come, will this wood take fire ?
                        [*They burn him with their tapers.*
Falstaff. Oh, Oh, Oh !
Quickly. Corrupt, corrupt, and tainted in desire !
About him, fairies ; sing a scornful rhyme ;
And, as you trip, still pinch him to your time.

                    SONG.

Fie on sinful fantasy !
Fie on lust and luxury !
Lust is but a bloody fire,
Kindled with unchaste desire,
Fed in heart, whose flames aspire

As thoughts do blow them, higher and higher.
Pinch him, fairies, mutually ;
Pinch him for his villany ;
Pinch him, and burn him, and turn him about,
Till candles and starlight and moonshine be out.

During this song they pinch FALSTAFF. DOCTOR
CAIUS *comes one way, and steals away a boy
in green ;* SLENDER, *another way, and takes
off a boy in white : and* FENTON *comes,
and steals away Mrs* ANNE PAGE. *A noise
of hunting is heard within. All the Fairies
run away.* FALSTAFF *pulls off his buck's-
head, and rises,*

Enter PAGE, FORD, MISTRESS PAGE *and*
        MISTRESS FORD.

Page. Nay, do not fly ; I think we have watch'd
    you now :
Will none but Herne the hunter serve your turn ?
Mrs Page. I pray you, come, hold up the jest
    no higher.
Now, good Sir John, how like you Windsor wives ?
See you these, husband ? do not these fair yokes
Become the forest better than the town ?
Ford. Now, sir, who 's a cuckold now ? Master
Brook, Falstaff 's a knave, a cuckoldly knave ; here
are his horns, Master Brook : and, Master Brook,
he hath enjoyed nothing of Ford's but his buck-
basket, his cudgel, and twenty pounds of money,
which must be paid to Master Brook ; his horses
are arrested for it, Master Brook.
Mrs Ford. Sir John, we have had ill luck ; we
could never meet. I will never take you for my
love again ; but I will always count you my deer.
Falstaff. I do begin to perceive that I am made
an ass.
Ford. Ay, and an ox too : both the proofs are
extant.
Falstaff. And these are not fairies ? I was three or
four times in the thought they were not fairies
and yet the guiltiness of my mind, the sudden surprise
of my powers, drove the grossness of the foppery
into a received belief, in despite of the teeth of all
rhyme and reason, that they were fairies. See now
how wit may be made a Jack-a-Lent, when 'tis upon
ill employment !
Evans. Sir John Falstaff, serve Got, and leave
your desires, and fairies will not pinse you.
Ford. Well said, fairy Hugh.
Evans. And leave your jealousies too, I pray you.
Ford. I will never mistrust my wife again, till
thou art able to woo her in good English.
Falstaff. Have I laid my brain in the sun and
dried it, that it wants matter to prevent so gross
o'erreaching as this ? Am I ridden with a Welsh
goat too ? shall I have a coxcomb of frize ? 'Tis
time I were choked with a piece of toasted cheese.
Evans. Seese is not good to give putter ; your
belly is all putter.
Falstaff. ' Seese ' and ' putter ' ! have I lived to
stand at the taunt of one that makes fritters of
English ? This is enough to be the decay of lust and
late-walking through the realm.
Mrs Page. Why, Sir John, do you think, though
we would have thrust virtue out of our hearts by
the head and shoulders and have given ourselves
without scruple to hell, that ever the devil could
have made you our delight ?
Ford. What, a hodge-pudding ? a bag of flax ?

Mrs Page. A puffed man ?

Page. Old, cold, withered and of intolerable entrails ?

Ford. And one that is as slanderous as Satan ?

Page. And as poor as Job ?

Ford. And as wicked as his wife ?

Evans. And given to fornications, and to taverns and sack and wine and metheglins, and to drinkings and swearings and starings, pribbles and prabbles ?

Falstaff. Well, I am your theme : you have the start of me ; I am dejected ; I am not able to answer the Welsh flannel ; ignorance itself is a plummet o'er me : use me as you will.

Ford. Marry, sir, we 'll bring you to Windsor, to one Master Brook, that you have cozened of money, to whom you should have been a pandar : over and above that you have suffered, I think to repay that money will be a biting affliction.

Page. Yet be cheerful, knight : thou shalt eat a posset to-night at my house ; where I will desire thee to laugh at my wife, that now laughs at thee : tell her Master Slender hath married her daughter.

Mrs Page. [*Aside*] Doctors doubt that : if Anne Page be my daughter, she is, by this, Doctor Caius' wife.

Enter SLENDER.

Slender. Whoa, ho ! ho, father Page !

Page. Son, how now ! how now, son ! have you dispatched ?

Slender. Dispatched ! I 'll make the best in Gloucestershire know on 't ; would I were hanged, la, else !

Page. Of what, son ?

Slender. I came yonder at Eton to marry Mistress Anne Page, and she 's a great lubberly boy. If it had not been i' the church, I would have swinged him, or he should have swinged me. If I did not think it had been Anne Page, would I might never stir !—and 'tis a post-master's boy.

Page. Upon my life, then, you took the wrong.

Slender. What need you tell me that ? I think so, when I took a boy for a girl. If I had been married to him, for all he was in woman's apparel, I would not have had him.

Page. Why, this is your own folly. Did not I tell you how you should know my daughter by her garments ?

Slender. I went to her in white, and cried ' mum ' and she cried ' budget,' as Anne and I had appointed ; and yet it was not Anne, but a postmaster's boy.

Mrs Page. Good George, be not angry : I knew of your purpose ; turned my daughter into green ; and, indeed, she is now with the doctor at the deanery, and there married.

Enter CAIUS.

Caius. Vere is Mistress Page ? By gar, I am cozened · I ha' married un garçon, a boy : un paysan, by gar, a boy ; it is not Anne Page . by gar, I am cozened.

Mrs Page. Why, did you take her in green ?

Caius. Ay, by gar, and 'tis a boy . by gar, I 'll raise all Windsor.   [*Exit.*

Ford. This is strange. Who hath got the right Anne ?

Page. My heart misgives me : here comes Master Fenton.

Enter FENTON *and* ANNE PAGE.

How now, Master Fenton !

Anne. Pardon, good father ! good my mother, pardon !

Page. Now, mistress, how chance you went not with Master Slender ?

Mrs Page. Why went you not with master doctor, maid ?

Fenton. You do amaze her · hear the truth of it.
You would have married her most shamefully,
Where there was no proportion held in love.
The truth is, she and I, long since contracted,
Are now so sure that nothing can dissolve us.
The offence is holy that she hath committed ;
And this deceit loses the name of craft,
Of disobedience, or unduteous title,
Since therein she doth evitate and shun
A thousand irreligious cursed hours,
Which forced marriage would have brought upon her.

Ford. Stand not amazed ; here is no remedy :
In love the heavens themselves do guide the state ;
Money buys lands, and wives are sold by fate.

Falstaff. I am glad, though you have ta'en a special stand to strike at me, that your arrow hath glanced.

Page. Well, what remedy ? Fenton, heaven give thee joy !
What cannot be eschew'd must be embraced.

Falstaff. When night dogs run, all sorts of deer are chased.

Mrs Page. Well, I will muse no further. Master Fenton,
Heaven give you many, many merry days !
Good husband, let us every one go home,
And laugh this sport o'er by a country fire :
Sir John and all.

Ford.   Let it be so. Sir John,
To Master Brook you yet shall hold your word :
For he to-night shall lie with Mistress Ford.
                                        [*Exeunt.*

MEASURE FOR MEASURE

DRAMATIS PERSONÆ

VINCENTIO, the Duke.
ANGELO, *Deputy*.
ESCALUS, *an ancient Lord*.
CLAUDIO, *a young gentleman*.
LUCIO, *a fantastic*.
Two other gentlemen.
PROVOST.
THOMAS, } *two friars*.
PETER,
A Justice.
VARRIUS.
ELBOW, *a simple constable*.
FROTH, *a foolish gentleman*.
POMPEY, *servant to* Mistress Overdone.
ABHORSON, *an executioner*.
BARNARDINE, *a dissolute prisoner*.

ISABELLA, *sister to* Claudio.
MARIANA, *betrothed to* Angelo.
JULIET, *beloved of* Claudio.
FRANCISCA, *a nun*.
MISTRESS OVERDONE, *a bawd*.

Lords, Officers, Citizens, Boy, *and* Attendants.

SCENE : Vienna.

ACT I.

SCENE I. *An apartment in the* DUKE'S *palace*.

Enter DUKE, ESCALUS, Lords *and* Attendants.

Duke.

Escalus.
    Escalus. My lord.
    Duke. Of government the properties to unfold,
Would seem in me to affect speech and discourse ;
Since I am put to know that your own science
Exceeds, in that, the lists of all advice
My strength can give you : then no more remains,
† But that to your sufficiency . . . . .
. . . . as your worth is able,
And let them work. The nature of our people,
Our city's institutions, and the terms
For common justice, you 're as pregnant in
As art and practice hath enriched any
That we remember. There is our commission,
From which we would not have you warp. Call
    hither,

I say, bid come before us Angelo.
                            [*Exit an Attendant.*
What figure of us think you he will bear ?
For you must know, we have with special soul
Elected him our absence to supply,
Lent him our terror, dress'd him with our love,
And given his deputation all the organs
Of our own power : what think you of it ?
    Escalus. If any in Vienna be of worth
To undergo such ample grace and honour,
It is Lord Angelo.
    Duke.   Look where he comes.

Enter ANGELO.

    Angelo. Always obedient to your grace's will,
I come to know your pleasure.
    Duke.   Angelo,
There is a kind of character in thy life,
That to the observer doth thy history
Fully unfold. Thyself and thy belongings
Are not thine own so proper as to waste
Thyself upon thy virtues, they on thee.
Heaven doth with us as we with torches do,
Not light them for themselves ; for if our virtues
Did not go forth of us 'twere all alike
As if we had them not. Spirits are not finely touch'd
But to fine issues, nor Nature never lends
The smallest scruple of her excellence
But, like a thrifty goddess, she determines
Herself the glory of a creditor,
Both thanks and use. But I do bend my speech
To one that can my part in him advertise ;
Hold therefore, Angelo :—
In our remove be thou at full ourself ;
Mortality and mercy in Vienna
Live in thy tongue and heart : old Escalus,
Though first in question, is thy secondary.
Take thy commission.
    Angelo.   Now, good my lord,
Let there be some more test made of my metal,
Before so noble and so great a figure
Be stamp'd upon it.
    Duke.   No more evasion :
We have with a leaven'd and prepared choice
Proceeded to you ; therefore take your honours.
Our haste from hence is of so quick condition
That it prefers itself and leaves unquestion'd
Matters of needful value. We shall write to you,
As time and our concernings shall importune,
How it goes with us, and do look to know
What doth befall you here. So, fare you well :
To the hopeful execution do I leave you
Of your commissions.
    Angelo.   Yet give leave, my lord,
That we may bring you something on the way.
    Duke. My haste may not admit it ;
Nor need you, on mine honour, have to do
With any scruple ; your scope is as mine own,

So to enforce or qualify the laws
As to your soul seems good.   Give me your hand :
I 'll privily away.   I love the people,
But do not like to stage me to their eyes :
Though it do well, I do not relish well
Their loud applause and Aves vehement ;
Nor do I think the man of safe discretion
That does affect it.   Once more, fare you well.

Angelo.   The heavens give safety to your purposes !

Escalus.   Lead forth and bring you back in
happiness !

Duke.   I thank you.   Fare you well.   [*Exit.*

Escalus.   I shall desire you, sir, to give me leave
To have free speech with you ; and it concerns me
To look into the bottom of my place :
A power I have, but of what strength and nature
I am not yet instructed.

Angelo.   'Tis so with me.   Let us withdraw to-
gether,
And we may soon our satisfaction have
Touching that point.

Escalus.   I 'll wait upon your honour.   [*Exeunt.*

SCENE II.   *A street.*

Enter LUCIO *and two* Gentlemen.

Lucio.   If the duke with the other dukes come
not to composition with the King of Hungary, why
then all the dukes fall upon the king.

First Gentleman.   Heaven grant us its peace, but
not the King of Hungary's !

Second Gentleman.   Amen.

Lucio.   Thou concludest like the sanctimonious
pirate, that went to sea with the Ten Command-
ments, but scraped one out of the table.

Second Gentleman.   ' Thou shalt not steal ' ?

Lucio.   Ay, that he razed.

First Gentleman.   Why, 'twas a commandment to
command the captain and all the rest from their
functions : they put forth to steal.   There 's not a
soldier of us all, that, in the thanksgiving before
meat, do relish the petition well that prays for peace.

Second Gentleman.   I never heard any soldier
dislike it.

Lucio.   I believe thee ; for I think thou never
wast where grace was said.

Second Gentleman.   No ? a dozen times at least.

First Gentleman.   What, in metre ?

Lucio.   In any proportion or in any language.

First Gentleman.   I think, or in any religion.

Lucio.   Ay, why not ?   Grace is grace, despite
of all controversy : as, for example, thou thyself art
a wicked villain, despite of all grace.

First Gentleman.   Well, there went but a pair of
shears between us.

Lucio.   I grant : as there may between the lists
and the velvet.   Thou art the list.

First Gentleman.   And thou the velvet : thou art
good velvet ; thou 'rt a three-piled piece, I warrant
thee : I had as lief be a list of an English kersey as
be piled, as thou art piled, for a French velvet.   Do
I speak feelingly now ?

Lucio.   I think thou dost ; and, indeed, with
most painful feeling of thy speech : I will, out of
thine own confession, learn to begin thy health ;
but, whilst I live, forget to drink after thee.

First Gentleman.   I think I have done myself
wrong, have I not ?

Second Gentleman.   Yes, that thou hast, whether
thou art tainted or free.

Lucio.   Behold, behold, where Madam Mitigation comes !   I have purchased as many diseases
under her roof as come to—

Second Gentleman.   To what, I pray ?

Lucio.   Judge.

Second Gentleman.   To three thousand dolours
a year.

First Gentleman.   Ay, and more.

Lucio.   A French crown more.

First Gentleman.   Thou art always figuring diseases in me ; but thou art full of error ; I am sound.

Lucio.   Nay, not as one would say, healthy ;
but so sound as things that are hollow : thy bones
are hollow ; impiety has made a feast of thee.

Enter MISTRESS OVERDONE.

First Gentleman.   How now ! which of your hips
has the most profound sciatica ?

Mrs Overdone.   Well, well ; there 's one yonder
arrested and carried to prison was worth five thousand
of you all.

Second Gentleman.   Who 's that, I pray thee ?

Mrs Overdone.   Marry, sir, that 's Claudio,
Signior Claudio.

First Gentleman.   Claudio to prison ?   'tis not so.

Mrs Overdone.   Nay, but I know 'tis so : I saw
him arrested, saw him carried away ; and, which is
more, within these three days his head to be chopped
off.

Lucio.   But, after all this fooling, I would not
have it so.   Art thou sure of this ?

Mrs Overdone.   I am too sure of it : and it is for
getting Madam Julietta with child.

Lucio.   Believe me, this may be : he promised
to meet me two hours since, and he was ever precise
in promise-keeping.

Second Gentleman.   Besides, you know, it draws
something near to the speech we had to such a
purpose.

First Gentleman.   But, most of all, agreeing with
the proclamation.

Lucio.   Away ! let 's go learn the truth of it.
            [*Exeunt Lucio and Gentlemen.*

Mrs Overdone.   Thus, what with the war, what
with the sweat, what with the gallows and what
with poverty, I am custom shrunk.

Enter POMPEY.

How now ! what 's the news with you ?

Pompey.   Yonder man is carried to prison.

Mrs Overdone.   Well ; what has he done ?

Pompey.   A woman.

Mrs Overdone.   But what 's his offence ?

Pompey.   Groping for trouts in a peculiar river.

Mrs Overdone.   What, is there a maid with child
by him ?

Pompey.   No, but there 's a woman with maid by
him.   You have not heard of the proclamation,
have you ?

Mrs Overdone.   What proclamation, man ?

Pompey.   All houses in the suburbs of Vienna
must be plucked down.

Mrs Overdone.   And what shall become of those
in the city ?

Pompey.   They shall stand for seed : they had
gone down too, but that a wise burgher put in for
them.

Mrs Overdone.   But shall all our houses of resort
in the suburbs be pulled down ?

Pompey.   To the ground, mistress.

Mrs Overdone. Why, here 's a change indeed in the commonwealth ! What shall become of me ?

Pompey. Come ; fear not you : good counsellors lack no clients : though you change your place, you need not change your trade ; I 'll be your tapster still. Courage ! there will be pity taken on you : you that have worn your eyes almost out in the service, you will be considered.

Mrs Overdone. What 's to do here, Thomas tapster ? let 's withdraw.

Pompey. Here comes Signior Claudio, led by the provost to prison ; and there 's Madam Juliet.

[*Exeunt.*

Enter PROVOST, CLAUDIO, JULIET, *and*
Officers.

Claudio. Fellow, why dost thou show me thus to the world ?
Bear me to prison, where I am committed.

Provost. I do it not in evil disposition,
But from Lord Angelo by special charge.

Claudio. Thus can the demigod Authority
Make us pay down for our offence by weight
The words of heaven ; on whom it will, it will ;
On whom it will not, so ; yet still 'tis just.

Re-enter LUCIO *and two* Gentlemen.

Lucio. Why, how now, Claudio ! whence comes this restraint ?

Claudio. From too much liberty, my Lucio, liberty :
As surfeit is the father of much fast,
So every scope by the immoderate use
Turns to restraint. Our natures do pursue,
Like rats that ravin down their proper bane,
A thirsty evil ; and when we drink we die.

Lucio. If I could speak so wisely under an arrest, I would send for certain of my creditors : and yet, to say the truth, I had as lief have the foppery of freedom as the morality of imprisonment. What 's thy offence, Claudio ?

Claudio. What but to speak of would offend again.

Lucio. What, is 't murder ?

Claudio. No.

Lucio. Lechery ?

Claudio. Call it so.

Provost. Away, sir ! you must go.

Claudio. One word, good friend. Lucio, a word with you.

Lucio. A hundred, if they 'll do you any good. Is lechery so look'd after ?

Claudio. Thus stands it with me : upon a true contract
I got possession of Julietta's bed :
You know the lady ; she is fast my wife,
Save that we do the denunciation lack
Of outward order : this we came not to,
Only for propagation of a dower
Remaining in the coffer of her friends,
From whom we thought it meet to hide our love
Till time had made them for us. But it chances
The stealth of our most mutual entertainment
With character too gross is writ on Juliet.

Lucio. With child, perhaps ?

Claudio.   Unhappily, even so.
And the new deputy now for the duke—
Whether it be the fault and glimpse of newness,
Or whether that the body public be

A horse whereon the governor doth ride,
Who, newly in the seat, that it may know
He can command, lets it straight feel the spur ;
Whether the tyranny be in his place,
Or in his eminence that fills it up,
I stagger in :—but this new governor
Awakes me all the enrolled penalties
Which have like unscour'd armour, hung by the wall
So long that nineteen zodiacs have gone round
And none of them been worn : and, for a name,
Now puts the drowsy and neglected act
Freshly on me : 'tis surely for a name.

Lucio. I warrant it is : and thy head stands so tickle on thy shoulders that a milkmaid, if she be in love, may sigh it off. Send after the duke and appeal to him.

Claudio. I have done so, but he 's not to be found.
I prithee, Lucio, do me this kind service :
This day my sister should the cloister enter
And there receive her approbation :
Acquaint her with the danger of my state ;
Implore her, in my voice, that she make friends
To the strict deputy ; bid herself assay him :
I have great hope in that ; for in her youth
There is a prone and speechless dialect,
Such as move men ; beside, she hath prosperous art
When she will play with reason and discourse,
And well she can persuade.

Lucio. I pray she may : as well for the encouragement of the like, which else would stand under grievous imposition, as for the enjoying of thy life, who I would be sorry should be thus foolishly lost at a game of tick-tack. I 'll to her.

Claudio. I thank you, good friend Lucio.

Lucio. Within two hours.

Claudio.   Come, officer, away !
[*Exeunt.*

SCENE III.   *A monastery.*

Enter DUKE *and* FRIAR THOMAS.

Duke. No, holy father ; throw away that thought ;
Believe not that the dribbling dart of love
Can pierce a complete bosom. Why I desire thee
To give me secret harbour, hath a purpose
More grave and wrinkled than the aims and ends
Of burning youth.

Friar Thomas. May your grace speak of it ?

Duke. My holy sir, none better knows than you
How I have ever loved the life removed
And held in idle price to haunt assemblies
Where youth, and cost, and witless bravery keeps.
I have deliver'd to Lord Angelo,
A man of stricture and firm abstinence,
My absolute power and place here in Vienna,
And he supposes me travell'd to Poland ;
For so I have strew'd it in the common ear,
And so it is received. Now, pious sir,
You will demand of me why I do this ?

Friar Thomas. Gladly, my lord.

Duke. We have strict statutes and most biting laws,
The needful bits and curbs to headstrong weeds,
Which for this nineteen years we have let slip ;
Even like an o'ergrown lion in a cave,
That goes not out to prey. Now, as fond fathers,
Having bound up the threatening twigs of birch,
Only to stick it in their children's sight
For terror, not to use, in time the rod

Becomes more mock'd than fear'd ; so our decrees,
Dead to infliction, to themselves are dead ;
And liberty plucks justice by the nose ;
The baby beats the nurse, and quite athwart
Goes all decorum.
   Friar Thomas.   It rested in your grace
To unloose this tied-up justice when you pleased :
And it in you more dreadful would have seem'd
Than in Lord Angelo.
   Duke.   I do fear, too dreadful :
Sith 'twas my fault to give the people scope,
'Twould be my tyranny to strike and gall them
For what I bid them do : for we bid this be done,
When evil deeds have their permissive pass
And not the punishment. Therefore indeed, my
    father,
I have on Angelo imposed the office ;
Who may, in the ambush of my name, strike home,
† And yet my nature never in the fight
To do in slander. And to behold his sway,
I will, as 'twere a brother of your order,
Visit both prince and people : therefore, I prithee,
Supply me with the habit and instruct me
How I may formally in person bear me
Like a true friar. Moe reasons for this action
At our more leisure shall I render you ;
Only, this one : Lord Angelo is precise ;
Stands at a guard with envy ; scarce confesses
That his blood flows, or that his appetite
Is more to bread than stone : hence shall we see,
If power change purpose, what our seemers be.
                              [Exeunt.

SCENE IV. *A nunnery.*

Enter ISABELLA *and* FRANCISCA.

  Isabella. And have you nuns no farther privi-
leges ?
  Francisca. Are not these large enough ?
  Isabella. Yes, truly : I speak not as desiring
more ;
But rather wishing a more strict restraint
Upon the sisterhood, the votarists of Saint Clare.
  Lucio. [*Within*]   Ho ! Peace be in this place !
  Isabella.   Who 's that which calls ?
  Francisca. It is a man's voice. Gentle Isabella,
Turn you the key, and know his business of him ;
You may, I may not ; you are yet unsworn.
When you have vow'd, you must not speak with
    men
But in the presence of the prioress :
Then, if you speak, you must not show your face,
Or, if you show your face, you must not speak.
He calls again ; I pray you, answer him.   [*Exit.*
  Isabella. Peace and prosperity! Who is 't that
calls ?

Enter LUCIO.

  Lucio. Hail, virgin, if you be, as those cheek-
roses
Proclaim you are no less ! Can you so stead me
As bring me to the sight of Isabella,
A novice of this place and the fair sister
To her unhappy brother Claudio ?
  Isabella. Why ' her unhappy brother ' ? let me
ask,
The rather for I now must make you know
I am that Isabella and his sister.
  Lucio. Gentle and fair, your brother kindly
greets you :

Not to be weary with you, he 's in prison.
  Isabella. Woe me ! for what ?
  Lucio. For that which, if myself might be his
judge,
He should receive his punishment in thanks :
He hath got his friend with child.
  Isabella. Sir, make me not your story.
  Lucio.   It is true.
I would not—though 'tis my familiar sin
With maids to seem the lapwing and to jest,
Tongue far from heart—play with all virgins so :
I hold you as a thing ensky'd and sainted,
By your renouncement an immortal spirit,
And to be talk'd with in sincerity,
As with a saint.
  Isabella. You do blaspheme the good in mocking
me.
  Lucio. Do not believe it. Fewness and truth,
'tis thus :
Your brother and his lover have embraced :
As those that feed grow full, as blossoming time
That from the seedness the bare fallow brings
To teeming foison, even so her plenteous womb
Expresseth his full tilth and husbandry.
  Isabella. Some one with child by him ? My
cousin Juliet ?
  Lucio. Is she your cousin ?
  Isabella. Adoptedly ; as school-maids change
their names
By vain though apt affection.
  Lucio.   She it is.
  Isabella. O, let him marry her.
  Lucio.   This is the point.
The duke is very strangely gone from hence ;
Bore many gentlemen, myself being one,
In hand and hope of action : but we do learn
By those that know the very nerves of state,
His givings-out were of an infinite distance
From his true-meant design. Upon his place,
And with full line of his authority,
Governs Lord Angelo ; a man whose blood
Is very snow-broth ; one who never feels
The wanton stings and motions of the sense,
But doth rebate and blunt his natural edge
With profits of the mind, study and fast.
He—to give fear to use and liberty,
Which have for long run by the hideous law,
As mice by lions—hath pick'd out an act,
Under whose heavy sense your brother's life
Falls into forfeit : he arrests him on it ;
And follows close the rigour of the statute,
To make him an example. All hope is gone,
Unless you have the grace by your fair prayer
To soften Angelo : and that 's my pith of business
'Twixt you and your poor brother.
  Isabella. Doth he so seek his life ?
  Lucio.   Has censured him
Already ; and, as I hear, the provost hath
A warrant for his execution.
  Isabella. Alas ! what poor ability 's in me
To do him good ?
  Lucio.   Assay the power you have.
  Isabella. My power ? Alas, I doubt—
  Lucio.   Our doubts are traitors
And make us lose the good we oft might win
By fearing to attempt. Go to Lord Angelo,
And let him learn to know, when maidens sue,
Men give like gods ; but when they weep and
kneel,
All their petitions are as freely theirs
As they themselves would owe them.

Isabella. I 'll see what I can do.
Lucio.   But speedily.
Isabella. I will about it straight ;
No longer staying but to give the mother
Notice of my affair. I humbly thank you :
Commend me to my brother : soon at night
I 'll send him certain word of my success.
Lucio. I take my leave of you.
Isabella.   Good sir, adieu.
                                            [*Exeunt.*

ACT II.

SCENE I. *A hall in* ANGELO's *house.*

Enter ANGELO, ESCALUS, *and a* Justice, Provost,
Officers, *and other* Attendants, *behind.*

Angelo.

We must not make a scarecrow of the law,
Setting it up to fear the birds of prey,
And let it keep one shape, till custom make it
Their perch and not their terror.
Escalus.   Ay, but yet
Let us be keen, and rather cut a little,
Than fall, and bruise to death. Alas, this gentleman,
Whom I would save, had a most noble father !
Let but your honour know,
Whom I believe to be most strait in virtue,
That, in the working of your own affections,
Had time cohered with place or place with wishing,
Or that the resolute acting of your blood
Could have attain'd the effect of your own purpose,
Whether you had not sometime in your life
Err'd in this point which now you censure him,
And pull'd the law upon you.
Angelo. 'Tis one thing to be tempted, Escalus,
Another thing to fall. I not deny,
The jury, passing on the prisoner's life,
May in the sworn twelve have a thief or two
Guiltier than him† they try. What 's open made to
        justice,
That justice seizes : what know the laws
That thieves do pass on thieves ? 'Tis very pregnant,
The jewel that we find, we stoop and take 't
Because we see it ; but what we do not see
We tread upon, and never think of it.
You may not so extenuate his offence
For I have had such faults ; but rather tell me,
When I, that censure him, do so offend,
Let mine own judgement pattern out my death,
And nothing come in partial. Sir, he must die.
Escalus. Be it as your wisdom will.
Angelo.   Where is the provost ?
Provost. Here, if it like your honour.
Angelo.   See that Claudio
Be executed by nine to-morrow morning :
Bring him his confessor, let him be prepared ;
For that 's the utmost of his pilgrimage.
                                        [*Exit Provost.*
Escalus. [*Aside*] Well, heaven forgive him !
    and forgive us all !
Some rise by sin, and some by virtue fall :
† Some run from brakes of ice, and answer none :
And some condemned for a fault alone.

Enter ELBOW, *and* Officers *with* FROTH *and*
        POMPEY.

Elbow. Come, bring them away : if these be
good people in a commonweal that do nothing but
use their abuses in common houses, I know no law :
bring them away.
Angelo. How now, sir ! What 's your name ?
and what 's the matter ?
Elbow. If it please your honour, I am the poor
duke's constable, and my name is Elbow : I do
lean upon justice, sir, and do bring in here before
your good honour two notorious benefactors.
Angelo. Benefactors ? Well ; what benefactors
are they ? are they not malefactors ?
Elbow. If it please your honour, I know not well
what they are ; but precise villans they are, that I
am sure of ; and void of all profanation in the world
that good Christians ought to have.
Escalus. This comes off well ; here 's a wise officer.
Angelo. Go to : what quality are they of ? Elbow
is your name ? why dost thou not speak, Elbow ?
Pompey. He cannot, sir ; he 's out at elbow.
Angelo. What are you, sir ?
Elbow. He, sir ! a tapster, sir ; parcel-bawd ; one
that serves a bad woman ; whose house, sir, was,
as they say, plucked down in the suburbs ; and now
she professes a hot-house, which, I think, is a very
ill house too.
Escalus. How know you that ?
Elbow. My wife, sir, whom I detest before
heaven and your honour,—
Escalus. How ? thy wife ?
Elbow. Ay, sir ; whom, I thank heaven, is an
honest woman,—
Escalus. Dost thou detest her therefore ?
Elbow. I say, sir, I will detest myself also, as
well as she, that this house, if it be not a bawd's
house, it is pity of her life, for it is a naughty house
Escalus. How dost thou know that, constable ?
Elbow. Marry, sir, by my wife ; who, if she had
been a woman cardinally given, might have been
accused in fornication, adultery, and all unclean-
liness there.
Escalus. By the woman's means ?
Elbow. Ay, sir, by Mistress Overdone's means :
but as she spit in his face, so she defied him.
Pompey. Sir, if it please your honour, this is
not so.
Elbow. Prove it before these varlets here, thou
honourable man ; prove it.
Escalus. Do you hear how he misplaces ?
Pompey. Sir, she came in great with child ; and
longing, saving your honour's reverence, for stewed
prunes ; sir, we had but two in the house, which
at that very distant time stood, as it were, in a fruit-
dish, a dish of some three-pence ; your honours have
seen such dishes ; they are not China dishes, but
very good dishes,—
Escalus. Go to, go to : no matter for the dish,
sir.
Pompey. No, indeed, sir, not of a pin ; you are
therein in the right : but to the point. As I say,
this Mistress Elbow, being, as I say, with child,
and being great-bellied, and longing, as I said, for
prunes ; and having but two in the dish, as I said,
Master Froth here, this very man, having eaten the
rest, as I said, and, as I say, paying for them very
honestly ; for, as you know, Master Froth, I could
not give you three-pence again.
Froth. No, indeed.
Pompey. Very well ; you being then, if you be
remembered, cracking the stones of the foresaid
prunes,—
Froth. Ay, so I did indeed.

Pompey. Why, very well ; I telling you then, if you be remembered, that such a one and such a one were past cure of the thing you wot of, unless they kept very good diet, as I told you,—

Froth. All this is true.

Pompey. Why, very well, then,—

Escalus. Come, you are a tedious fool : to the purpose. What was done to Elbow's wife, that he hath cause to complain of ? Come me to what was done to her.

Pompey. Sir, your honour cannot come to that yet.

Escalus. No, sir, nor I mean it not.

Pompey. Sir, but you shall come to it, by your honour's leave. And, I beseech you, look into Master Froth here, sir ; a man of fourscore pound a year ; whose father died at Hallowmas : was 't not at Hallowmas, Master Froth ?

Froth. All-hallond eve.

Pompey. Why, very well ; I hope here be truths. He, sir, sitting, as I say, in a lower chair, sir ; 'twas in the Bunch of Grapes, where indeed you have a delight to sit, have you not ?

Froth. I have so ; because it is an open room and good for winter.

Pompey. Why, very well, then ; I hope here be truths.

Angelo. This will last out a night in Russia, When nights are longest there : I 'll take my leave, And leave you to the hearing of the cause ; Hoping you 'll find good cause to whip them all.

Escalus. I think no less. Good morrow to your lordship.   [*Exit Angelo.*

Now, sir, come on : what was done to Elbow's wife, once more ?

Pompey. Once, sir ? there was nothing done to her once.

Elbow. I beseech you, sir, ask him what this man did to my wife.

Pompey. I beseech your honour, ask me.

Escalus. Well, sir ; what did this gentleman to her ?

Pompey. I beseech you, sir, look in this gentleman's face. Good Master Froth, look upon his honour ; 'tis for a good purpose. Doth your honour mark his face ?

Escalus. Ay, sir, very well.

Pompey. Nay, I beseech you, mark it well.

Escalus. Well, I do so.

Pompey. Doth your honour see any harm in his face ?

Escalus. Why, no.

Pompey. I 'll be supposed upon a book, his face is the worst thing about him. Good, then ; if his face be the worst thing about him, how could Master Froth do the constable's wife any harm ? I would know that of your honour.

Escalus. He 's in the right. Constable, what say you to it ?

Elbow. First, an it like you, the house is a respected house ; next, this is a respected fellow ; and his mistress is a respected woman.

Pompey. By this hand, sir, his wife is a more respected person than any of us all.

Elbow. Varlet, thou liest ; thou liest, wicked varlet ! the time is yet to come that she was ever respected with man, woman, or child.

Pompey. Sir, she was respected with him before he married with her.

Escalus. Which is the wiser here ? Justice or Iniquity ? Is this true ?

Elbow. O thou caitiff ! O thou varlet ! O thou wicked Hannibal ! I respected with her before I was married to her ! If ever I was respected with her, or she with me, let not your worship think me the poor duke's officer. Prove this, thou wicked Hannibal, or I 'll have mine action of battery on thee.

Escalus. If he took you a box o' the ear, you might have your action of slander too.

Elbow. Marry, I thank your good worship for it. What is 't your worship's pleasure I shall do with this wicked caitiff ?

Escalus. Truly, officer, because he hath some offences in him that thou wouldst discover if thou couldst, let him continue in his courses till thou knowest what they are.

Elbow. Marry, I thank your worship for it. Thou seest, thou wicked varlet, now, what 's come upon thee : thou art to continue now, thou varlet ; thou art to continue.

Escalus. Where were you born, friend ?

Froth. Here in Vienna, sir.

Escalus. Are you of fourscore pounds a year ?

Froth. Yes, an 't please you, sir.

Escalus. So. What trade are you of, sir ?

Pompey. A tapster ; a poor widow's tapster.

Escalus. Your mistress' name ?

Pompey. Mistress Overdone.

Escalus. Hath she had any more than one husband ?

Pompey. Nine, sir ; Overdone by the last.

Escalus. Nine ! Come hither to me, Master Froth. Master Froth, I would not have you acquainted with tapsters : they will draw you, Master Froth, and you will hang them. Get you gone, and let me hear no more of you.

Froth. I thank your worship. For mine own part, I never come into any room in a taphouse, but I am drawn in.

Escalus. Well, no more of it, Master Froth : farewell. [*Exit Froth.*] Come you hither to me, Master tapster. What 's your name, Master tapster ?

Pompey. Pompey.

Escalus. What else ?

Pompey. Bum, sir.

Escalus. Troth, and your bum is the greatest thing about you : so that in the beastliest sense you are Pompey the Great. Pompey, you are partly a bawd, Pompey, howsoever you colour it in being a tapster, are you not ? come, tell me true : it shall be the better for you.

Pompey. Truly, sir, I am a poor fellow that would live.

Escalus. How would you live, Pompey ? by being a bawd ? What do you think of the trade, Pompey ? is it a lawful trade ?

Pompey. If the law would allow it, sir.

Escalus. But the law will not allow it, Pompey ; nor it shall not be allowed in Vienna.

Pompey. Does your worship mean to geld and splay all the youth of the city ?

Escalus. No, Pompey.

Pompey. Truly, sir, in my poor opinion, they will to 't then. If your worship will take order for the drabs and the knaves, you need not to fear the bawds.

Escalus. There are pretty orders beginning, I can tell you : it is but heading and hanging.

Pompey. If you head and hang all that offend that way but for ten year together, you 'll be glad to give out a commission for more heads : if this law hold in Vienna ten year, I 'll rent the fairest

house in it after three-pence a bay : if you live to
see this come to pass, say Pompey told you so.

Escalus. Thank you, good Pompey ; and, in
requital of your prophecy, hark you, I advise you,
let me not find you before me again upon any complaint whatsoever ; no, not for dwelling where
you do : if I do, Pompey, I shall beat you to your
tent, and prove a shrewd Cæsar to you ; in plain
dealing, Pompey, I shall have you whipt : so, for
this time, Pompey, fare you well.

Pompey. I thank your worship for your good
counsel : [*Aside*] but I shall follow it as the flesh
and fortune shall better determine.
Whip me ? no, no ; let carman whip his jade :
The valiant heart 's not whipt out of his trade.
                                             [*Exit.*

Escalus. Come hither to me, Master Elbow ;
come hither, Master constable. How long have
you been in this place of constable ?

Elbow. Seven year and a half, sir.

Escalus. I thought, by your readiness in the
office, you had continued in it some time. You
say, seven years together ?

Elbow. And a half, sir.

Escalus. Alas, it hath been great pains to you.
They do you wrong to put you so oft upon 't : are
there not men in your ward sufficient to serve it ?

Elbow. Faith, sir, few of any wit in such matters :
as they are chosen, they are glad to choose me for
them ; I do it for some piece of money, and go
through with all.

Escalus. Look you bring me in the names of
some six or seven, the most sufficient of your parish.

Elbow. To your worship's house, sir ?

Escalus. To my house. Fare you well.
                                         [*Exit Elbow.*
What 's o'clock, think you ?

Justice. Eleven, sir.

Escalus. I pray you home to dinner with me.

Justice. I humbly thank you.

Escalus. It grieves me for the death of Claudio ;
But there 's no remedy.

Justice. Lord Angelo is severe.

Escalus.   It is but needful :
Mercy is not itself, that oft looks so ;
Pardon is still the nurse of second woe :
But yet,—poor Claudio ! There is no remedy.
Come, sir.   [*Exeunt.*

SCENE II.   *Another room in the same.*

Enter PROVOST *and a* Servant.

Servant. He 's hearing of a cause ; he will come
straight :
I 'll tell him of you.

Provost.   Pray you, do.   [*Exit Servant.*]
          I 'll know
His pleasure ; may be he will relent. Alas,
He hath but as offended in a dream !
All sects, all ages smack of this vice ; and he
To die for 't !

Enter ANGELO.

Angelo.   Now, what 's the matter, provost ?

Provost. Is it your will Claudio shall die to-
morrow ?

Angelo. Did not I tell thee yea ? hadst thou not
order ?
Why dost thou ask again ?

Provost.   Lest I might be too rash :
Under your good correction, I have seen,
When, after execution, judgement hath
Repented o'er his doom.

Angelo.   Go to ; let that be mine :
Do you your office, or give up your place,
And you shall well be spared.

Provost.   I crave your honour's pardon.
What shall be done, sir, with the groaning Juliet ?
She 's very near her hour.

Angelo.   Dispose of her
To some more fitter place, and that with speed.

Re-enter Servant.

Servant. Here is the sister of the man condemn'd
Desires access to you.

Angelo.   Hath he a sister ?

Provost. Ay, my good lord ; a very virtuous
maid,
And to be shortly of a sisterhood,
If not already.

Angelo. Well, let her be admitted.
                                     [*Exit Servant.*
See you the fornicatress be removed :
Let her have needful, but not lavish, means ;
There shall be order for 't.

Enter ISABELLA *and* LUCIO.

Provost.   God save your honour !

Angelo. Stay a little while. [*To Isabella*] You 're
welcome : what 's your will ?

Isabella. I am a woeful suitor to your honour,
Please but your honour hear me.

Angelo.   Well ; what 's your suit ?

Isabella. There is a vice that most I do abhor,
And most desire should meet the blow of justice ;
For which I would not plead, but that I must ;
For which I must not plead, but that I am
At war 'twixt will and will not.

Angelo.   Well ; the matter ?

Isabella. I have a brother is condemn'd to die :
I do beseech you, let it be his fault,
And not my brother.

Provost. [*Aside*] Heaven give thee moving graces!

Angelo. Condemn the fault, and not the actor
of it ?
Why, every fault 's condemn'd ere it be done :
Mine were the very cipher of a function,
To fine the faults whose fine stands in record,
And let go by the actor.

Isabella.   O just but severe law !
I had a brother, then. Heaven keep your honour !

Lucio. [*Aside to Isabella*] Give 't not o'er so :
to him again, entreat him ;
Kneel down before him, hang upon his gown ;
You are too cold ; if you should need a pin,
You could not with more tame a tongue desire it :
To him, I say !

Isabella. Must he needs die ?

Angelo.   Maiden, no remedy.

Isabella. Yes ; I do think that you might pardon
him,
And neither heaven nor man grieve at the mercy.

Angelo. I will not do 't.

Isabella.   But can you, if you would ?

Angelo. Look, what I will not, that I cannot do.

Isabella. But might you do 't, and do the world
no wrong,
If so your heart were touch'd with that remorse
As mine is to him ?

Angelo. He 's sentenced ; 'tis too late.
Lucio. [*Aside to Isabella*] You are too cold.
Isabella. Too late? why, no , I, that do speak a word,
May call it back again. Well, believe this,
No ceremony that to great ones 'longs,
Not the king's crown, nor the deputed sword,
The marshall's truncheon, nor the judge's robe,
Become them with one half so good a grace
As mercy does.
If he had been as you and you as he,
You would have slipt like him ; but he, like you,
Would not have been so stern.
Angelo. Pray you, be gone.
Isabella. I would to heaven I had your potency,
And you were Isabel ! should it then be thus?
No ; I would tell what 'twere to be a judge,
And what a prisoner.
Lucio. [*Aside to Isabella*] Ay, touch him ; there 's the vein.
Angelo. Your brother is a forfeit of the law,
And you but waste your words.
Isabella. Alas, alas !
Why, all the souls that were were forfeit once ;
And He that might the vantage best have took
Found out the remedy. How would you be,
If He, which is the top of judgement, should
But judge you as you are ? O, think on that ;
And mercy then will breathe within your lips,
Like man new made.
Angelo. Be you content, fair maid ;
It is the law, not I condemn your brother :
Were he my kinsman, brother, or my son,
If should be thus with him : he must die to-morrow.
Isabella. To-morrow ! O, that 's sudden! Spare him, spare him !
He 's not prepared for death. Even for our kitchens
We kill the fowl of season : shall we serve heaven
With less respect than we do minister
To our gross selves? Good, good my lord, bethink you ;
Who is it that hath died for this offence?
There 's many have committed it.
Lucio. [*Aside to Isabella*] Ay, well said.
Angelo. The law hath not been dead, though it hath slept :
Those many had not dared to do that evil,
If the first that did the edict infringe
Had answer'd for his deed . now 'tis awake,
Takes note of what is done ; and, like a prophet,
Looks in a glass, that shows what future evils,
Either new, or by remissness new-conceived,
And so in progress to be hatch'd and born,
Are now to have no successive degrees,
But, ere they live, to end.
Isabella. Yet show some pity.
Angelo. I show it most of all when I show justice ;
For then I pity those I do not know,
Which a dismiss'd offence would after gall ;
And do him right that, answering one foul wrong,
Lives not to act another. Be satisfied ;
Your brother dies to-morrow ; be content.
Isabella. So you must be the first that gives this sentence,
And he, that suffers. O, it is excellent
To have a giant's strength ; but it is tyrannous
To use it like a giant.
Lucio. [*Aside to Isabella*] That 's well said.
Isabella. Could great men thunder
As Jove himself does, Jove would ne'er be quiet,
For every pelting, petty officer

Would use his heaven for thunder ;
Nothing but thunder ! Merciful Heaven,
Thou rather with thy sharp and sulphurous bolt
Split'st the unwedgeable and gnarled oak
Than the soft myrtle : but man, proud man,
Drest in a little brief authority,
Most ignorant of what he 's most assured,
His glassy essence, like an angry ape,
Plays such fantastic tricks before high heaven
As make the angels weep ; who, with our spleens,
Would all themselves laugh mortal.
Lucio. [*Aside to Isabella*] O, to him, to him, wench ! he will relent ;
He 's coming ; I perceive 't.
Provost. [*Aside*] Pray heaven she win him !
Isabella. We cannot weigh our brother with ourself :
Great men may jest with saints ; 'tis wit in them,
But in the less foul profanation.
Lucio. Thou 'rt i' the right, girl ; more o' that.
Isabella. That in the captain's but a choleric word,
Which in the soldier is flat blasphemy.
Lucio. [*Aside to Isabella*] Art avised o' that ? more on 't.
Angelo. Why do you put these sayings upon me?
Isabella. Because authority, though it err like others,
Hath yet a kind of medicine in itself,
That skins the vice o' the top. Go to your bosom ;
Knock there, and ask your heart what it doth know
That 's like my brother's fault : if it confess
A natural guiltiness such as is his,
Let it not sound a thought upon your tongue
Against my brother's life.
Angelo. [*Aside*] She speaks, and 'tis
Such sense, that my sense breeds with it. Fare you well.
Isabella. Gentle my lord, turn back.
Angelo. I will bethink me : come again to-morrow.
Isabella. Hark how I 'll bribe you : good my lord, turn back.
Angelo. How ! bribe me?
Isabella. Ay, with such gifts that heaven shall share with you.
Lucio. [*Aside to Isabella*] You had marr'd all else.
Isabella. Not with fond shekels of the tested gold,
Or stones whose rates are either rich or poor
As fancy values them ; but with true prayers
That shall be up at heaven and enter there
Ere sun-rise, prayers from preserved souls,
From fasting maids whose minds are dedicate
To nothing temporal.
Angelo. Well ; come to me to-morrow.
Lucio. [*Aside to Isabella*] Go to ; 'tis well ; away !
Isabella. Heaven keep your honour safe !
Angelo. [*Aside*] Amen :
For I am that way going to temptation,
Where prayers cross.
Isabella. At what hour to-morrow
Shall I attend your lordship?
Angelo. At any time 'fore noon.
Isabella. 'Save your honour !
[*Exeunt Isabella, Lucio, and Provost.*
Angelo. From thee, even from thy virtue !
What 's this, what 's this? Is this her fault or mine?
The tempter or the tempted, who sins most?
Ha !

Not she ; nor doth she tempt : but it is I
That, lying by the violet in the sun,
Do as the carrion does, not as the flower,
Corrupt with virtuous season. Can it be
That modesty may more betray our sense
Than woman's lightness? Having waste ground
      enough,
Shall we desire to raze the sanctuary
And pitch our evils there ? O, fie, fie, fie !
What dost thou, or what art thou, Angelo ?
Dost thou desire her foully for those things
That make her good ? O, let her brother live :
Thieves for their robbery have authority
When judges steal themselves. What, do I love her,
That I desire to hear her speak again,
And feast upon her eyes ? What is 't I dream on ?
O cunning enemy, that, to catch a saint,
With saints dost bait thy hook ! Most dangerous
Is that temptation that doth goad us on
To sin in loving virtue : never could the strumpet,
With all her double vigour, art and nature,
Once stir my temper ; but this virtuous maid
Subdues me quite. Ever till now,
When men were fond, I smiled and wonder'd how.
                                        [*Exit*.

SCENE III. *A room in a prison.*

Enter, severally, DUKE *disguised as a friar,
and* PROVOST.

Duke. Hail to you, provost ? so I think you are.
Provost. I am the provost. What 's your will,
      good friar ?
Duke. Bound by my charity and my blest order,
I come to visit the afflicted spirits
Here in the prison. Do me the common right
To let me see them and to make me know
The nature of their crimes, that I may minister
To them accordingly.
Provost. I would do more than that, if more
were needful.

Enter JULIET.

Look, here comes one : a gentlewoman of mine,
Who, falling in the flaws of her own youth,
Hath blister'd her report : she is with child ;
And he that got it, sentenced ; a young man
More fit to do another such offence
Than die for this.
Duke. When must he die ?
Provost.   As I do think, to-morrow.
I have provided for you : stay awhile,   [*To Juliet.*
And you shall be conducted.
Duke. Repent you, fair one, of the sin you carry ?
Juliet. I do ; and bear the shame most patiently.
Duke. I 'll teach you how you shall arraign your
      conscience,
And try your penitence, if it be sound,
Or hollowly put on.
Juliet.   I 'll gladly learn.
Duke. Love you the man that wrong'd you ?
Juliet. Yes, as I love the woman that wrong'd him.
Duke. So then it seems your most offenceful act
Was mutually committed ?
Juliet.   Mutually.
Duke. Then was your sin of heavier kind than
his.
Juliet. I do confess it, and repent it, father.

Duke. 'Tis meet so, daughter : but lest you do
      repent,
As that the sin hath brought you to this shame,
Which sorrow is always toward ourselves, not heaven,
Showing we would not spare heaven as we love it,
But as we stand in fear,—
Juliet. I do repent me, as it is an evil,
And take the shame with joy.
Duke.   There rest.
Your partner, as I hear, must die to-morrow,
And I am going with instruction to him.
Grace go with you, Benedicite !   [*Exit.*
Juliet. ' Must die to-morrow !   O injurious love,
That respites me a life, whose very comfort
Is still a dying horror !
Provost.   'Tis pity of him.   [*Exeunt.*

SCENE IV. *A room in* ANGELO'S *house.*

Enter ANGELO.

Angelo. When I would pray and think, I think
      and pray
To several subjects. Heaven hath my empty words ;
Whilst my invention, hearing not my tongue,
Anchors on Isabel : Heaven in my mouth,
As if I did but only chew his name ;
And in my heart the strong and swelling evil
Of my conception. The state, whereon I studied,
Is like a good thing, being often read,
Grown fear'd and tedious ; yea, my gravity,
Wherein—let no man hear me—I take pride,
Could I with boot change for an idle plume,
Which the air beats for vain. O place, O form,
How often dost thou with thy case, thy habit,
Wrench awe from fools and tie the wiser souls
To thy false seeming ! Blood, thou art blood :
Let 's write good angel on the devil's horn ;
'Tis not the devil's crest.

Enter a Servant.

                    How now ! who 's there ?
Servant. One Isabel, a sister, desires access to you.
Angelo. Teach her the way. [*Exit Servant*]. O
      heavens !
Why does my blood thus muster to my heart,
Making both it unable for itself,
And dispossessing all my other parts
Of necessary fitness ?
So play the foolish throngs with one that swoons ;
Come all to help him, and so stop the air
By which he should revive : and even so
The general, subject to a well-wish'd king,
Quit their own part, and in obsequious fondness
Crowd to his presence, where their untaught love
Must needs appear offence.

Enter ISABELLA.

                    How now, fair maid ?
Isabella. I am come to know your pleasure.
Angelo. That you might know it, would much
      better please me
Than to demand what 'tis. Your brother cannot
      live.
Isabella. Even so. Heaven keep your honour !
Angelo. Yet may he live a while ; and, it may be,
As long as you or I : yet he must die.
Isabella. Under your sentence ?
Angelo. Yea.

Isabella. When, I beseech you? that in his reprieve,
Longer or shorter, he may be so fitted
That his soul sicken not.
Angelo. Ha ! fie, these filthy vices ! It were as good
To pardon him that hath from nature stolen
A man already made, as to remit
Their saucy sweetness that do coin heaven's image
In stamps that are forbid : 'tis all as easy
Falsely to take away a life true made
As to put metal in restrained means
To make a false one.
Isabella. 'Tis set down so in heaven, but not in earth.
Angelo. Say you so ? then I shall pose you quickly.
Which had you rather, that the most just law
Now took your brother's life ; or, to redeem him,
Give up your body to such sweet uncleanness
As she that he hath stain'd ?
Isabella.　　　　　Sir, believe this,
I had rather give my body than my soul.
Angelo. I talk not of your soul : our compell'd sins
Stand more for number than for accompt.
Isabella.　　　　　How say you ?
Angelo. Nay, I 'll not warrant that ; for I can speak
Against the thing I say. Answer to this :
I, now the voice of the recorded law,
Pronounce a sentence on your brother's life :
Might there not be a charity in sin
To save this brother's life ?
Isabella.　　　　　Please you to do 't,
I 'll take it as a peril to my soul,
It is no sin at all, but charity.
Angelo. Pleased you to do 't at peril of your soul,
Were equal poise of sin and charity.
Isabella. That I do beg his life, if it be sin,
Heaven let me bear it ! you granting of my suit,
If that be sin, I 'll make it my morn prayer
To have it added to the faults of mine,
And nothing of your answer.
Angelo.　　　　　Nay, but hear me.
Your sense pursues not mine : either you are ignorant,
Or seem so craftily ; and that 's not good.
Isabella. Let me be ignorant, and in nothing good,
But graciously to know I am no better.
Angelo. Thus wisdom wishes to appear most bright
When it doth tax itself ; as these black masks
Proclaim an enshield beauty ten times louder
Than beauty could, display'd. But mark me ;
To be received plain, I 'll speak more gross :
Your brother is to die.
Isabella. So.
Angelo. And his offence is so, as it appears,
Accountant to the law upon that pain.
Isabella. True.
Angelo. Admit no other way to save his life,—
As I subscribe not that, nor any other,
But in the loss of question,—that you, his sister,
Finding yourself desired of such a person,
Whose credit with the judge, or own great place,
Could fetch your brother from the manacles
Of the all-building law ; and that there were
No earthly mean to save him, but that either
You must lay down the treasures of your body
To this supposed, or else to let him suffer ;
What would you do ?

Isabella. As much for my poor brother as myself :
That is, were I under the terms of death,
The impression of keen whips I 'ld wear as rubies,
And strip myself to death, as to a bed
That longing have been sick for, ere I 'ld yield
My body up to shame.
Angelo. Then must your brother die.
Isabella. And 'twere the cheaper way :
Better it were a brother died at once,
Than that a sister, by redeeming him,
Should die for ever.
Angelo. Were not you then as cruel as the sentence
That you have slander'd so ?
Isabella. Ignomy in ransom and free pardon
Are of two houses : lawful mercy
Is nothing kin to foul redemption.
Angelo. You seem'd of late to make the law a tyrant ;
And rather proved the sliding of your brother
A merriment than a vice.
Isabella. O, pardon me, my lord ; it oft falls out,
To have what we would have, we speak not what we mean :
I something do excuse the thing I hate,
For his advantage that I dearly love.
Angelo. We are all frail.
Isabella.　　　　　Else let my brother die,
If not a feodary, but only he
Owe and succeed thy weakness.
Angelo. Nay, women are frail too.
Isabella. Ay, as the glasses where they view themselves ;
Which are as easy broke as they make forms.
Women ! Help Heaven ! men their creation mar
In profiting by them. Nay, call us ten times frail ;
For we are soft as our complexions are,
And credulous to false prints.
Angelo.　　　　　I think it well :
And from this testimony of your own sex,—
Since I suppose we are made to be no stronger
Than faults may shake our frames,—let me be bold ;
I do arrest your words. Be that you are,
That is, a woman ; if you be more, you 're none ;
If you be one, as you are well express'd
By all external warrants, show it now,
By putting on the destined livery.
Isabella. I have no tongue but one : gentle my lord,
Let me entreat you speak the former language.
Angelo. Plainly conceive, I love you.
Isabella. My brother did love Juliet,
And you tell me that he shall die for it.
Angelo. He shall not, Isabel, if you give me love.
Isabella. I know your virtue hath a license in 't,
Which seems a little fouler than it is,
To pluck on others.
Angelo.　　　　　Believe me, on mine honour,
My words express my purpose.
Isabella. Ha ! little honour to be much believed,
And most pernicious purpose ! Seeming, seeming !
I will proclaim thee, Angelo ; look for 't :
Sign me a present pardon for my brother,
Or with an outstretch'd throat I 'll tell the world aloud
What man thou art.
Angelo.　　　　　Who will believe thee, Isabel ?
My unsoil'd name, the austereness of my life,
My vouch against you, and my place i' the state,
Will so your accusation overweigh,
That you shall stifle in your own report
And smell of calumny, I have begun,

And now I give my sensual race the rein :
Fit thy consent to my sharp appetite ;
Lay by all nicety and prolixious blushes,
That banish what they sue for ; redeem thy brother
By yielding up thy body to my will ;
Or else he must not only die the death,
But thy unkindness shall his death draw out
To lingering sufferance. Answer me to-morrow,
Or, by the affection that now guides me most,
I 'll prove a tyrant to him. As for you,
Say what you can, my false o'erweighs your true.
                                        [*Exit.*
Isabella. To whom should I complain ? Did I
    tell this,
Who would believe me ? O perilous mouths,
That bear in them one and the self-same tongue,
Either of condemnation or approof ;
Bidding the law make court'sy to their will ;
Hooking both right and wrong to the appetitie,
To follow as it draws ! I 'll to my brother :
Though he hath fall'n by prompture of the blood,
Yet hath he in him such a mind of honour,
That, had he twenty heads to tender down
On twenty bloody blocks, he 'ld yield them up,
Before his sister should her body stoop
To such abhorr'd pollution.
Then, Isabel, live chaste, and, brother, die :
More than our brother is our chastity.
I 'll tell him yet of Angelo's request,
And fit his mind to death, for his soul's rest.
                                        [*Exit.*

ACT III.

SCENE I.   *A room in the prison.*

Enter DUKE *disguised as before,* CLAUDIO,
and PROVOST.

Duke.
So then you hope of pardon from Lord Angelo ?
Claudio. The miserable have no other medicine
    But only hope :
I 've hope to live, and am prepared to die.
Duke. Be absolute for death ; either death or
    life
Shall thereby be the sweeter. Reason thus with
    life :
If I do lose thee, I do lose a thing
That none but fools would keep : a breath thou art,
Servile to all the skyey influences.
That dost this habitation, where thou keep'st,
Hourly afflict : merely, thou art death's fool ;
For him thou labour'st by thy flight to shun
And yet runn'st toward him still. Thou art not
    noble ;
For all the accommodations that thou bear'st
Are nursed by basensss. Thou'rt by no means
    valiant ;
For thou dost fear the soft and tender fork
Of a poor worm. Thy best of rest is sleep,
And that thou oft provokest ; yet grossly fear'st
Thy death, which is no more. Thou art not thyself ;
For thou exist'st on many a thousand grains
That issue out of dust. Happy thou art not ;
For what thou hast not, still thou strivest to get,
And what thou hast, forget 'st. Thou art not certain ;
For thy complexion shifts to strange effects,
After the moon. If thou art rich, thou 'rt poor ;
For, like an ass whose back with ingots bows,
Thou bear'st thy heavy riches but a journey,
And death unloads thee. Friend hast thou none ;

For thine own bowels, which do call thee sire,
The mere effusion of thy proper loins,
Do curse the gout, serpigo, and the rheum,
For ending thee no sooner. Thou hast nor youth
    nor age,
But, as it were, an after-dinner's sleep,
Dreaming on both ; for all thy blessed youth
Becomes as aged, and doth beg the alms
Of palsied eld ; and when thou art old and rich,
Thou hast neither heat, affection, limb, nor beauty,
To make thy riches pleasant. What 's yet in this
That bears the name of life ? Yet in this life
Lie hid moe thousand deaths : yet death we fear,
That makes these odds all even.
    Claudio.   I humbly thank you.
To sue to live, I find I seek to die ;
And, seeking death, find life : let it come on.
Isabella. [*Within*] What, ho ! Peace here ; grace
    and good company !
Provost. Who 's there ? come in : the wish de-
    serves a welcome.
Duke. Dear sir, ere long I 'll visit you again.
Claudio. Most holy sir, I thank you.

Enter ISABELLA.

Isabella. My business is a word or two with
    Claudio.
Provost. And very welcome. Look, signior,
    here 's your sister.
Duke. Provost, a word with you.
Provost. As many as you please.
Duke.' Bring me to hear them speak, where I
may be concealed.
                    [*Exeunt Duke and Provost.*
Claudio. Now, sister, what 's the comfort ?
Isabella.   Why,
As all comforts are ; most good, most good indeed.
Lord Angelo, having affairs to heaven,
Intends you for his swift ambassador,
Where you shall be an everlasting leiger :
Therefore your best appointment make with speed ;
To-morrow you set on.
Claudio.   Is there no remedy ?
Isabella. None, but such remedy as, to save a
    head,
To cleave a heart in twain.
Claudio.   But is there any ?
Isabella. Yes, brother, you may live :
There is a devilish mercy in the judge,
If you 'll implore it, that will free your life,
But fetter you till death.
Claudio.   Perpetual durance ?
Isabella. Ay, just ; perpetual durance, a restraint,
Though all the world's vastidity you had,
To a determined scope.
Claudio.   But in what nature ?
Isabella. In such a one as, you consenting to 't,
Would bark your honour from that trunk you bear,
And leave you naked.
Claudio.   Let me know the point.
Isabella. O, I do fear thee, Claudio ; and I
    quake,
Lest thou a feverous life shouldst entertain,
And six or seven winters more respect
Than a perpetual honour. Darest thou die ?
The sense of death is most in apprehension ;
And the poor beetle, that we tread upon,
In corporal sufferance finds a pang as great
As when a giant dies.
Claudio.   Why give you me this shame ?
Think you I can a resolution fetch

From flowery tenderness ? If I must die,
I will encounter darkness as a bride,
And hug it in mine arms.
　Isabella.　There spake my brother ; there my
　　father's grave
Did utter forth a voice.　Yes, thou must die :
Thou art too noble to conserve a life
In base appliances.　This outward-sainted deputy,
Whose settled visage and deliberate word
Nips youth i' the head and follies doth emmew
As falcon doth the fowl, is yet a devil ;
His filth within being cast, he would appear
A pond as deep as hell.
　Claudio.　　　　　　The prenzie Angelo !
　Isabella.　O, 'tis the cunning livery of hell,
The damned'st body to invest and cover
In prenzie guards !　Dost thou think, Claudio ?
If I would yield him my virginity,
Thou mightst be freed.
　Claudio.　　　　　O heavens ! it cannot be.
　Isabella.　Yes, he would give 't thee, from this
　　rank offence,
So to offend him still.　This night 's the time
That I should do what I abhor to name,
Or else thou diest to-morrow.
　Claudio.　　　　　Thou shalt not do 't.
　Isabella.　O, were it but my life,
I 'ld throw it down for your deliverance
As frankly as a pin.
　Claudio.　　　　Thanks, dear Isabel.
　Isabella.　Be ready, Claudio, for your death to-
　　morrow.
　Claudio.　Yes.　Has he affections in him,
That thus can make him bite the law by the nose,
When he would force it ?　Sure, it is no sin ;
Or of the deadly seven it is the least.
　Isabella.　Which is the least ?
　Claudio.　If it were damnable, he being so wise,
Why would he for the momentary trick
Be perdurably fined ?　O Isabel !
　Isabella.　What says my brother ?
　Claudio.　　　　　Death is a fearful thing.
　Isabella.　And shamed life a hateful.
　Claudio.　Ay, but to die, and go we know not
　　where ;
To lie in cold obstruction and to rot ;
This sensible warm motion to become
A kneaded clod ; and the delighted spirit
To bathe in fiery floods, or to reside
In thrilling region of thick-ribbed ice ;
To be imprison'd in the viewless winds,
And blown with restless violence round about
The pendent world ; or to be worse than worst
Of those that lawless and uncertain thought
Imagine howling : 'tis too horrible !
The weariest and most loathed worldly life
That age, ache, penury and imprisonment
Can lay on nature is a paradise
To what we fear of death.
　Isabella.　Alas, alas !
　Claudio.　　　　　Sweet sister, let me live :
What sin you do to save a brother's life,
Nature dispenses with the deed so far
That it becomes a virtue.
　Isabella.　　　　　O you beast !
O faithless coward ! O dishonest wretch !
Wilt thou be made a man out of my vice ?
Is 't not a kind of incest, to take life
From thine own sister's shame ?　What should I
　　think ?
Heaven shield my mother play'd my father fair !

For such a warped slip of wilderness
Ne'er issued from his blood.　Take my defiance !
Die, perish !　Might but my bending down
Reprieve thee from thy fate, it should proceed :
I 'll pray a thousand prayers for thy death,
No word to save thee.
　Claudio.　Nay, hear me, Isabel.
　Isabella.　　　　O, fie, fie, fie !
Thy sin 's not accidental, but a trade.
Mercy to thee would prove itself a bawd :
'Tis best that thou diest quickly.
　Claudio.　　　　O hear me, Isabella !

Re-enter DUKE.

　Duke.　Vouchsafe a word, young sister, but one
　　word.
　Isabella.　What is your will ?
　Duke.　Might you dispense with your leisure,
I would by and by have some speech with you : the
satisfaction I would require is likewise your own
benefit.
　Isabella.　I have no superfluous leisure ; my stay
must be stolen out of other affairs ; but I will attend
you a while.　　　　　　　　　　　[*Walks apart.*
　Duke.　Son, I have overheard what hath passed
between you and your sister.　Angelo had never
the purpose to corrupt her ; only he hath made
an assay of her virtue to practise his judgement
with the disposition of natures : she, having the
truth of honour in her, hath made him that gracious denial which he is most glad to receive.　I
am confessor to Angelo, and I know this to be true ;
therefore prepare yourself to death : do not satisfy
your resolution with hopes that are fallible : to-
morrow you must die ; go to your knees and make
ready.
　Claudio.　Let me ask my sister pardon.　I am so
out of love with life that I will sue to be rid of it.
　Duke.　Hold you there : farewell.　[*Exit Claudio.*]
Provost, a word with you !

Re-enter PROVOST.

　Provost.　What 's your will, father ?
　Duke.　That now you are come, you will be gone.
Leave me awhile with the maid : my mind promises
with my habit no loss shall touch her by my company.
　Provost.　In good time.
　　　　　[*Exit Provost.　Isabella comes forward.*
　Duke.　The hand that hath made you fair hath
made you good : the goodness that is cheap in
beauty makes beauty brief in goodness ; but grace,
being the soul of your complexion, shall keep the
body of it ever fair.　The assault that Angelo hath
made to you, fortune hath conveyed to my understanding ; and, but that frailty hath examples for
his falling, I should wonder at Angelo.　How will
you do to content this substitute, and to save your
brother ?
　Isabella.　I am now going to resolve him : I had
rather my brother die by the law than my son should
be unlawfully born.　But, O, how much is the good
duke deceived in Angelo !　If ever he return and I
can speak to him, I will open my lips in vain, or
discover his government.
　Duke.　That shall not be much amiss : yet, as
the matter now stands, he will avoid your accusation ;
he made trial of you only.　Therefore fasten your
ear on my advisings : to the love I have in doing
good a remedy presents itself.　I do make myself

believe that you may most uprighteously do a poor wronged lady a merited benefit ; redeem your brother from the angry law ; do no stain to your own gracious person ; and much please the absent duke, if peradventure he shall ever return to have hearing of this business.

Isabella. Let me hear you speak farther. I have spirit to do any thing that appears not foul in the truth of my spirit.

Duke. Virtue is bold, and goodness never fearful. Have you not heard speak of Mariana, the sister of Frederick the great soldier who miscarried at sea ?

Isabella. I have heard of the lady, and good words went with her name.

Duke. She should this Angelo have married ; was affianced to her by oath, and the nuptial appointed : between which time of the contract and limit of the solemnity, her brother Frederick was wrecked at sea, having in that perished vessel the dowry of his sister. But mark how heavily this befell to the poor gentlewoman : there she lost a noble and renowned brother, in his love toward her ever most kind and natural ; with him, the portion and sinew of her fortune, her marriage-dowry ; with both, her combinate husband, this well-seeming Angelo.

Isabella. Can this be so ? did Angelo so leave her ?

Duke. Left her in her tears, and dried not one of them with his comfort ; swallowed his vow whole, pretending in her discoveries of dishonour : in few, bestowed her on her own lamentation, which she yet wears for his sake ; and he, a marble to her tears, is washed with them, but relents not.

Isabella. What a merit were it in death to take this poor maid from the world ! What corruption in this life, that it will let this man live ! But how out of this can she avail ?

Duke. It is a rupture that you may easily heal : and the cure of it not only saves your brother, but keeps you from dishonour in doing it.

Isabella. Show me how, good father.

Duke. This forenamed maid hath yet in her the continuance of her first affection : this unjust unkindness, that in all reason should have quenched her love, hath, like an impediment in the current, made it more violent and unruly. Go you to Angelo ; answer his requiring with a plausible obedience ; agree with his demands to the point ; only refer yourself to this advantage, first, that your stay with him may not be long ; that the time may have all shadow and silence in it ; and the place answer to convenience. This being granted in course,—and now follows all,—we shall advise this wronged maid to stead up your appointment, go in your place ; if the encounter acknowledge itself hereafter, it may compel him to her recompense : and here, by this, is your brother saved, your honour untainted, the poor Mariana advantaged, and the corrupt deputy scaled. The maid will I frame and make fit for his attempt. If you think well to carry this as you may, the doubleness of the benefit defends the deceit from reproof. What think you of it ?

Isabella. The image of it gives me content already ; and I trust it will grow to a most prosperous perfection.

Duke. It lies much to your holding up. Haste you speedily to Angelo : if for this night he entreat you to his bed, give him promise of satisfaction. I will presently to Saint Luke's : there, at the moated grange, resides this dejected Mariana. At that place call upon me ; and dispatch with Angelo, that it may be quickly.

Isabella. I thank you for this comfort. Fare you well, good father.   [*Exeunt severally.*

SCENE II.   *The street before the prison.*

Enter, on one side, DUKE *disguised as before ; on the other,* ELBOW, *and* Officers *with* POMPEY.

Elbow. Nay, if there be no remedy for it, but that you will needs buy and sell men and women like beasts, we shall have all the world drink brown and white bastard.

Duke. O heavens ! what stuff is here ?

Pompey. 'Twas never merry world since, of two usuries, the merriest was put down, and the worser allowed by order of law a furred gown to keep him warm ; and furred with fox and lamb-skins too, to signify, that craft, being richer than innocency, stands for the facing.

Elbow. Come your way, sir. 'Bless you, good father friar.

Duke. And you, good brother father. What offence hath this man made you, sir ?

Elbow. Marry, sir, he hath offended the law : and, sir, we take him to be a thief too, sir ; for we have found upon him, sir, a strange picklock, which we have sent to the deputy.

Duke. Fie, sirrah ! a bawd, a wicked bawd !
The evil that thou causest to be done,
That is thy means to live. Do thou but think
What 'tis to cram a maw or clothe a back
From such a filthy vice : say to thyself,
From their abominable and beastly touches
I drink, I eat, array myself, and live.
Canst thou believe thy living is a life,
So stinkingly depending ? Go mend, go mend.

Pompey. Indeed, it does stink in some sort, sir ; but yet, sir, I would prove—

Duke. Nay, if the devil have given thee proofs for sin,
Thou wilt prove his. Take him to prison, officer :
Correction and instruction must both work
Ere this rude beast will profit.

Elbow. He must before the deputy, sir ; he has given him warning : the deputy cannot abide a whoremaster : if he be a whoremonger, and comes before him, he were as good go a mile on his errand.

Duke. That we were all, as some would seem to be,
† From our faults, as faults from seeming, free !

Elbow. His neck will come to your waist,—a cord, sir.

Pompey. I spy comfort ; I cry bail. Here 's a gentleman and a friend of mine.

Enter LUCIO.

Lucio. How now, noble Pompey ! What, at the wheels of Cæsar ? art thou led in triumph ? What, is there none of Pygmalion's images, newly made woman, to be had now, for putting the hand in the pocket and extracting it clutched ? What reply, ha ? What sayest thou to this tune, matter and method ? Is it not drowned i' the last rain, ha ? What sayest thou, Trot ? Is the world as it was, man ? Which is the way ? Is it sad, and few words ? or how ? The trick of it ?

Duke. Still thus, and thus ; still worse !

Lucio. How doth my dear morsel, thy mistress ? Procures she still, ha ?

Pompey. Troth, sir, she had eaten up all her beef, and she is herself in the tub.

Lucio. Why, 'tis good; it is the right of it; it must be so: ever your fresh whore and your powdered bawd: an unshunned consequence; it must be so. Art going to prison, Pompey?

Pompey. Yes, faith, sir.

Lucio. Why, 'tis not amiss, Pompey. Farewell: go say I sent thee thither. For debt, Pompey? or how?

Elbow. For being a bawd, for being a bawd.

Lucio. Well, then, imprison him: if imprisonment be the due of a bawd, why, 'tis his right: bawd is he doubtless, and of antiquity too; bawd-born. Farewell, good Pompey. Commend me to the prison, Pompey: you will turn good husband now, Pompey; you will keep the house.

Pompey. I hope, sir, your good worship will be my bail.

Lucio. No, indeed, will I not, Pompey; it is not the wear. I will pray, Pompey, to increase your bondage: if you take it not patiently, why, your mettle is the more. Adieu, trusty Pompey. 'Bless you, friar.

Duke. And you.

Lucio. Does Bridget paint still, Pompey, ha?

Elbow. Come your ways, sir; come.

Pompey. You will not bail me, then, sir?

Lucio. Then, Pompey, nor now. What news abroad, friar? what news?

Elbow. Come your ways, sir; come.

Lucio. Go to kennel, Pompey; go. [*Exeunt Elbow, Pompey and Officers.*] What news, friar, of the duke?

Duke. I know none. Can you tell me of any?

Lucio. Some say he is with the Emperor of Russia; other some, he is in Rome: but where is he, think you?

Duke. I know not where; but wheresoever, I wish him well.

Lucio. It was a mad fantastical trick of him to steal from the state, and usurp the beggary he was never born to. Lord Angelo dukes it well in his absence; he puts transgression to 't.

Duke. He does well in 't.

Lucio. A little more lenity to lechery would do no harm in him: something too crabbed that way, friar.

Duke. It is too general a vice, and severity must cure it.

Lucio. Yes, in good sooth, the vice is of a great kindred; it is well allied: but it is impossible to extirp it quite, friar, till eating and drinking be put down. They say this Angelo was not made by man and woman after this downright way of creation: is it true, think you?

Duke. How should he be made, then?

Lucio. Some report a sea-maid spawned him; some, that he was begot between two stockfishes. But it is certain that when he makes water his urine is congealed ice; that I know to be true: † and he is a motion generative; that 's infallible.

Duke. You are pleasant, sir, and speak apace.

Lucio. Why, what a ruthless thing is this in him, for the rebellion of a codpiece to take away the life of a man! Would the duke that is absent have done this? Ere he would have hanged a man for the getting a hundred bastards, he would have paid for the nursing a thousand: he had some feeling of the sport; he knew the service, and that instructed him to mercy.

Duke. I never heard the absent duke much

detected for women; he was not inclined that way.

Lucio. O, sir, you are deceived.

Duke. 'Tis not possible.

Lucio. Who, not the duke? yes, your beggar of fifty; and his use was to put a ducat in her clack-dish: the duke had crotchets in him. He would be drunk too; that let me inform you.

Duke. You do him wrong, surely.

Lucio. Sir, I was an inward of his. A shy fellow was the duke: and I believe I know the cause of his withdrawing.

Duke. What, I prithee, might be the cause?

Lucio. No, pardon; 'tis a secret must be locked within the teeth and the lips: but this I can let you understand, the greater file of the subject held the duke to be wise.

Duke. Wise! why, no question but he was.

Lucio. A very superficial, ignorant, unweighing fellow.

Duke. Either this is envy in you, folly, or mistaking: the very stream of his life and the business he hath helmed must upon a warranted need give him a better proclamation. Let him be but testimonied in his own bringings-forth, and he shall appear to the envious a scholar, a statesman and a soldier. Therefore you speak unskilfully; or if your knowledge be more it is much darkened in your malice.

Lucio. Sir, I know him, and I love him.

Duke. Love talks with better knowledge, and knowledge with dearer love.

Lucio. Come, sir, I know what I know.

Duke. I can hardly believe that, since you know not what you speak. But, if ever the duke return, as our prayers are he may, let me desire you to make your answer before him. If it be honest you have spoke, you have courage to maintain it: I am bound to call upon you; and, I pray you, your name?

Lucio. Sir, my name is Lucio; well known to the duke.

Duke. He shall know you better, sir, if I may live to report you.

Lucio. I fear you not.

Duke. O, you hope the duke will return no more; or you imagine me too unhurtful an opposite. But indeed I can do you little harm; you 'll forswear this again.

Lucio. I 'll be hanged first: thou art deceived in me, friar. But no more of this. Canst thou tell if Claudio die to-morrow or no?

Duke. Why should he die, sir?

Lucio. Why? For filling a bottle with a tundish. I would the duke we talk of were returned again: this ungenitured agent will unpeople the province with continency; sparrows must not build in his house-eaves, because they are lecherous. The duke yet would have dark deeds darkly answered; he would never bring them to light: would he were returned! Marry, this Claudio is condemned for untrussing. Farewell, good friar: I prithee, pray for me. The duke, I say to thee again, would eat mutton on Fridays. He 's not past it yet, and I say to thee, he would mouth with a beggar, though she smelt brown bread and garlic: say that I said so. Farewell.　　　　　　　　　　　[*Exit.*

Duke. No might nor greatness in mortality Can censure 'scape; back-wounding calumny The whitest virtue strikes. What kings so strong Can tie the gall up in the slanderous tongue? But who comes here?

Enter Escalus, Provost, *and* Officers *with*
Mistress Overdone.

Escalus. Go ; away with her to prison !
Mrs Overdone. Good my lord, be good to me ;
your honour is accounted a merciful man ; good
my lord.
Escalus. Double and treble admonition, and
still forfeit in the same kind ! This would make
mercy swear and play the tyrant.
Provost. A bawd of eleven years' continuance,
may it please your honour.
Mrs Overdone. My lord, this is one Lucio's
information against me. Mistress Kate Keepdown
was with child by him in the duke's time ; he promised
her marriage : his child is a year and a quarter old,
come Philip and Jacob : I have kept it myself ; and
see how he goes about to abuse me !
Escalus. That fellow is a fellow of much license :
let him be called before us. Away with her to
prison ! Go to ; no more words. [*Exeunt Officers
with Mistress Overdone.*] Provost, my brother
Angelo will not be altered ; Claudio must die to-
morrow : let him be furnished with divines, and
have all charitable preparation. If my brother
wrought by my pity, it should not be so with him.
Provost. So please you, this friar hath been with
him, and advised him for the entertainment of
death.
Escalus. Good even, good father.
Duke. Bliss and goodness on you !
Escalus. Of whence are you ?
Duke. Not of this country, though my chance
is now
To use it for my time : I am a brother
Of gracious order, late come from the See
In special business from his holiness.
Escalus. What news abroad i' the world ?
Duke. None, but that there is so great a fever
on goodness, that the dissolution of it must cure
it : novelty is only in request ; and it is as dangerous
to be aged in any kind of course, as it is virtuous
to be constant in any undertaking. There is scarce
truth enough alive to make societies secure ; but
security enough to make fellowships accurst : much
upon this riddle runs the wisdom of the world.
This news is old enough, yet it is every day's news.
I pray you, sir, of what disposition was the duke ?
Escalus. One that, above all other strifes, con-
tended especially to know himself.
Duke. What pleasure was he given to ?
Escalus. Rather rejoicing to see another merry,
than merry at any thing which professed to make
him rejoice : a gentleman of all temperance. But
leave we him to his events, with a prayer they may
prove prosperous ; and let me desire to know how
you find Claudio prepared. I am made to understand that you have lent him visitation.
Duke. He professes to have received no sinister
measure from his judge, but most willingly humbles
himself to the determination of justice : yet had
he framed to himself, by the instruction of his frailty,
many deceiving promises of life ; which I by my
good leisure have discredited to him, and now is
he resolved to die.
Escalus. You have paid the heavens your function,
and the prisoner the very debt of your calling. I
have laboured for the poor gentleman to the extremest shore of my modesty : but my brother
justice have I found so severe, that he hath forced
me to tell him he is indeed Justice.

Duke. If his own life answer the straitness of
his proceeding, it shall become him well ; wherein
if he chance to fail, he hath sentenced himself.
Escalus. I am going to visit the prisoner. Fare
you well.
Duke. Peace be with you !
                              [*Exeunt Escalus and Provost.*]
He who the sword of heaven will bear
Should be as holy as severe ;
Pattern in himself to know,
† Grace to stand, and virtue go ;
More nor less to others paying
Than by self-offences weighing.
Shame to him whose cruel striking
Kills for faults of his own liking !
Twice treble shame on Angelo,
To weed my vice and let his grow !
O, what may man within him hide,
Though angel on the outward side !
† How may likeness made in crimes,
Making practice on the times,
To draw with idle spiders' strings
Most ponderous and substantial things !
Craft against vice I must apply :
With Angelo to-night shall lie
His old betrothed but despised ;
† So disguise shall, by the disguised,
Pay with falsehood false exacting,
And perform an old contracting.   [*Exit.*

ACT IV.

SCENE I. *.The moated grange at* St. Luke's.

Enter Mariana *and a* Boy.

Boy *sings.*

T ake, O, take those lips away,
 That so sweetly were forsworn ;
 And those eyes, the break of day,
 Lights that do mislead the morn :
But my kisses bring again, bring again ;
Seals of love, but seal'd in vain, seal'd in vain.
Mariana. Break off thy song, and haste thee
 quick away :
Here comes a man of comfort, whose advice
Hath often still'd my brawling discontent.
                                        [*Exit Boy.*

Enter Duke *disguised as before.*

I cry you mercy, sir ; and well could wish
You had not found me here so musical :
Let me excuse me, and believe me so,
My mirth it much displeased, but pleased my woe.
Duke. 'Tis good ; though music oft hath such
 a charm
To make bad good, and good provoke to harm.
I pray you, tell me, hath any body inquired for me
here to-day ? much upon this time have I promised
here to meet.
Mariana. You have not been inquired after : I
have sat here all day.

Enter Isabella.

Duke. I do constantly believe you. The time
is come even now. I shall crave your forbearance
a little · may be I will call upon you anon, for some
advantage to yourself.
Mariana. I am always bound to you.   [*Exit.*

Duke.   Very well met, and well come.
What is the news from this good deputy ?
Isabella.   He hath a garden circummured with
brick,
Whose western side is with a vineyard back'd ;
And to that vineyard is a planched gate,
That makes his opening with this bigger key :
This other doth command a little door
Which from the vineyard to the garden leads ;
There have I made my promise
Upon the heavy middle of the night
To call upon him.
Duke.   But shall you on your knowledge find
this way ?
Isabella.   I have ta'en a due and wary note upon 't :
With whispering and most guilty diligence,
In action all of precept, he did show me
The way twice o'er.
Duke.   Are there no other tokens
Between you 'greed concerning her observance ?
Isabella.   No, none, but only a repair i' the dark ;
And that I have possess'd him my most stay
Can be but brief ; for I have made him know
I have a servant comes with me along,
That stays upon me, whose persuasion is
I come about my brother.
Duke.   'Tis well borne up.
I have not yet made known to Mariana
A word of this.   What, ho !   within !   come forth !

Re-enter MARIANA.

I pray you, be acquainted with this maid ;
She comes to do you good.
Isabella.   I do desire the like.
Duke.   Do you persuade yourself that I respect
you ?
Mariana.   Good friar, I know you do, and have
found it.
Duke.   Take, then, this your companion by the
hand,
Who hath a story ready for your ear.
I shall attend your leisure : but make haste ;
The vaporous night approaches.
Mariana.   Will 't please you walk aside ?
                        [*Exeunt Mariana and Isabella.*
Duke.   O place and greatness !   millions of false
eyes
Are stuck upon thee : volumes of report
Run with these false and most contrarious quests
Upon thy doings : thousand escapes of wit
Make thee the father of their idle dreams
And rack thee in their fancies.

Re-enter MARIANA *and* ISABELLA.

                        Welcome, how agreed ?
Isabella.   She 'll take the enterprise upon her,
father,
If you advise it.
Duke.   It is not my consent,
But my entreaty too.
Isabella.   Little have you to say
When you depart from him, but, soft and low,
' Remember now my brother.'
Mariana.   Fear me not.
Duke.   Nor, gentle daughter, fear you not at all.
He is your husband on a pre-contract :
To bring you thus together, 'tis no sin,
Sith that the justice of your title to him
Doth flourish the deceit.   Come, let us go :

Our corn 's to reap, for yet our tithe 's to sow.
                        [*Exeunt.*

SCENE II.   *A room in the prison.*

Enter PROVOST *and* POMPEY.

Provost.   Come hither, sirrah.   Can you cut off
a man's head ?
Pompey.   If the man be a bachelor, sir, I can ;
but if he be a married man, he 's his wife's head,
and I can never cut off a woman's head.
Provost.   Come, sir, leave me your snatches, and
yield me a direct answer.   To-morrow morning
are to die Claudio and Barnardine.   Here is in our
prison a common executioner, who in his office
lacks a helper : if you will take it on you to assist
him, it shall redeem you from your gyves ; if not,
you shall have your full time of imprisonment and
your deliverance with an unpitied whipping, for
you have been a notorious bawd.
Pompey.   Sir, I have been an unlawful bawd
time out of mind ; but yet I will be content to be a
lawful hangman.   I would be glad to receive some
instruction from my fellow partner.
Provost.   What, ho !   Abhorson !   Where 's Abhorson, there ?

Enter ABHORSON.

Abhorson.   Do you call, sir ?
Provost.   Sirrah, here 's a fellow will help you
to-morrow in your execution.   If you think it meet,
compound with him by the year, and let him abide
here with you ;   if not, use him for the present and
dismiss him.   He cannot plead his estimation with
you ;   he hath been a bawd.
Abhorson.   A bawd, sir ? fie upon him !   he will
discredit our mystery.
Provost.   Go to, sir ;   you weigh equally ;   a
feather will turn the scale.   [*Exit.*
Pompey.   Pray, sir, by your good favour,—for
surely, sir, a good favour you have, but that you
having a hanging look,—do you call, sir, your
occupation a mystery ?
Abhorson.   Ay, sir ;   a mystery.
Pompey.   Painting, sir, I have heard say, is a
mystery ;   and your whores, sir, being members
of my occupation, using painting, do prove my
occupation a mystery :   but what mystery there
should be in hanging, if I should be hanged, I cannot
imagine.
Abhorson.   Sir, it is a mystery.
Pompey.   Proof ?
Abhorson.   Every true man's apparel fits your
thief · if it be too little for your thief, your true
man thinks it big enough ; if it be too big for your
thief, your thief thinks it little enough : so every
true man's apparel fits your thief.

Re-enter PROVOST.

Provost.   Are you agreed ?
Pompey.   Sir, I will serve him ;   for I do find
your hangman is a more penitent trade than your
bawd ;   he doth oftener ask forgiveness.
Provost.   You, sirrah, provide your block and
your axe to-morrow four o'clock.
Abhorson.   Come on, bawd ;   I will instruct thee
in my trade ;   follow.
Pompey.   I do desire to learn, sir :   and I hope,
if you have occasion to use me for your own turn.

you shall find me yare ; for truly, sir, for your
kindness I owe you a good turn.
Provost. Call hither Barnardine and Claudio :
          [*Exeunt Pompey and Abhorson.*]
The one has my pity ; not a jot the other,
Being a murderer, though he were my brother.

Enter CLAUDIO.

Look, here 's the warrant, Claudio, for thy death :
'Tis now dead midnight, and by eight to-morrow
Thou must be made immortal. Where 's Barnardine ?
  Claudio. As fast lock'd up in sleep as guiltless
    labour
When it lies starkly in the traveller's bones :
He will not wake.
  Provost.   Who can do good on him ?
Well, go, prepare yourself. [*Knocking within.*]
  But, hark, what noise ?
Heaven give your spirits comfort ! [*Exit Claudio.*]
  By and by.
I hope it is some pardon or reprieve
For the most gentle Claudio.

Enter DUKE *disguised as before.*

                    Welcome, father.
  Duke. The best and wholesomest spirits of the
    night
Envelope you, good Provost ! Who call'd here of
    late ?
  Provost. None, since the curfew rung.
  Duke. Not Isabel ?
  Provost. No.
  Duke.   They will, then, ere 't be long.
  Provost. What comfort is for Claudio ?
  Duke. There 's some in hope.
  Provost.   It is a bitter deputy.
  Duke. Not so, not so ; his life is parallel'd
Even with the stroke and line of his great justice :
He doth with holy abstinence subdue
That in himself which he spurs on his power
To qualify in others : were he meal'd with that
Which he corrects, then were he tyrannous ;
But this being so, he 's just.   [*Knocking within.*]
              Now are they come.
                    [*Exit Provost.*]
This is a gentle provost : seldom when
The steeled gaoler is the friend of men.
                    [*Knocking within.*]
How now! what noise ? That spirit 's possess'd
    with haste
That wounds the unsisting postern with these strokes.

Re-enter PROVOST.

  Provost. There he must stay until the officer
Arise to let him in : he is call'd up.
  Duke. Have you no countermand for Claudio
    yet,
But he must die to-morrow ?
  Provost.   None, sir, none.
  Duke. As near the dawning, provost, as it is,
You shall hear more ere morning.
  Provost.   Happily
You something know ; yet I believe there comes
No countermand ; no such example have we :
Besides, upon the very siege of justice
Lord Angelo hath to the public ear
Profess'd the contrary.

Enter a MESSENGER.

                    This is his lordship 's man.
  Duke. And here comes Claudio's pardon.
  Messenger. [*Giving a paper.*] My lord hath sent
you this note ; and by me this further charge, that
you swerve not from the smallest article of it, neither
in time, matter, or other circumstance. Good
morrow ; for, as I take it, it is almost day.
  Provost. I shall obey him. [*Exit Messenger.*]
  Duke. [*Aside*] This is his pardon, purchased
    by such sin
For which the pardoner himself is in.
Hence hath offence his quick celerity,
When it is borne in high authority :
When vice makes mercy, mercy 's so extended,
That for the fault's love is the offender friended.
Now, sir, what news ?
  Provost. I told you. Lord Angelo, belike thinking
me remiss in mine office, awakens me with this
unwonted putting-on ; methinks strangely, for he
hath not used it before.
  Duke. Pray you, let 's hear.
  Provost [Reads]
  ' Whatsoever you may hear to the contrary, let
Claudio be executed by four of the clock ; and in
the afternoon Barnardine : for my better satisfaction,
let me have Claudio's head sent me by five. Let
this be duly performed ; with a thought that more
depends on it than we must yet deliver. Thus fail
not to do your office, as you will answer it at your
peril.'
What say you to this, sir ?
  Duke. What is that Barnardine who is to be
executed in the afternoon ?
  Provost. A Bohemian born, but here nursed up
and bred ; one that is a prisoner nine years old.
  Duke. How came it that the absent duke had
not either delivered him to his liberty or executed
him ? I have heard it was ever his manner to do
so.
  Provost. His friends still wrought reprieves for
him : and, indeed, his fact, till now in the government of Lord Angelo, came not to an undoubtful
proof.
  Duke. It is now apparent ?
  Provost. Most manifest, and not denied by himself.
  Duke. Hath he borne himself penitently in
prison ? how seems he to be touched ?
  Provost. A man that apprehends death no more
dreadfully but as a drunken sleep ; careless, reckless,
and fearless of what 's past, present, or to come ;
insensible of mortality, and desperately mortal.
  Duke. He wants advice.
  Provost. He will hear none : he hath evermore
had the liberty of the prison ; give him leave to
escape hence, he would not : drunk many times a
day, if not many days entirely drunk. We have
very oft awaked him, as if to carry him to execution,
and showed him a seeming warrant for it : it hath
not moved him at all.
  Duke. More of him anon. There is written in
your brow, provost, honesty and constancy : if I
read it not truly, my ancient skill beguiles me ; but,
in the boldness of my cunning, I will lay my self in
hazard. Claudio, whom here you have warrant
to execute, is no greater forfeit to the law than
Angelo, who hath sentenced him. To make you
understand this in a manifested effect, I crave but
four days' respite ; for the which you are to do me
both a present and a dangerous courtesy.
  Provost. Pray, sir, in what ?

Duke. In the delaying death.

Provost. Alack, how may I do it, having the hour limited, and an express command, under penalty, to deliver his head in the view of Angelo? I may make my case as Claudio's, to cross this in the smallest.

Duke. By the vow of mine order I warrant you, if my instructions may be your guide. Let this Barnardine be this morning executed, and his head borne to Angelo.

Provost. Angelo hath seen them both, and will discover the favour.

Duke. O, death 's a great disguiser; and you may add to it. Shave the head, and tie the beard; and say it was the desire of the penitent to be so bared before his death : you know the course is common. If anything fall to you upon this, more than thanks and good fortune, by the saint whom I profess, I will plead against it with my life.

Provost. Pardon me, good father; it is against my oath.

Duke. Were you sworn to the duke, or to the deputy?

Provost. To him, and to his substitutes.

Duke. You will think you have made no offence, if the duke avouch the justice of your dealing?

Provost. But what likelihood is in that?

Duke. Not a resemblance, but a certainty. Yet since I see you fearful, that neither my coat, integrity, nor persuasion can with ease attempt you, I will go further than I meant, to pluck all fears out of you. Look you, sir, here is the hand and seal of the duke : you know the character, I doubt not; and the signet is not strange to you.

Provost. I know them both.

Duke. The contents of this is the return of the duke : you shall anon over-read it at your pleasure; where you shall find, within these two days he will be here. This is a thing that Angelo knows not; for he this very day receives letters of strange tenour; perchance of the duke's death; perchance entering into some monastery; but, by chance, nothing of what is writ. Look, the unfolding star calls up the shepherd. Put not yourself into amazement how these things should be : all difficulties are but easy when they are known. Call your executioner, and off with Barnardine's head : I will give him a present shrift and advise him for a better place. Yet you are amazed; but this shall absolutely resolve you. Come away; it is almost clear dawn.   [*Exeunt.*

SCENE III.   *Another room in the same.*

Enter POMPEY.

Pompey. I am as well acquainted here as I was in our house of profession : one would think it were Mistress Overdone's own house, for here be many of her old customers. First, here 's young Master Rash; he 's in for a commodity of brown paper and old ginger, nine-score and seventeen pounds; of which he made five marks, ready money : marry, then ginger was not much in request, for the old women were all dead. Then is there here one Master Caper, at the suit of Master Three-pile the mercer, for some four suits of peach-coloured satin, which now peaches him a beggar. Then have we here young Dizy, and young Master Deep-vow, and Master Copper-spur, and Master Starve-lackey the rapier and dagger man, and young Drop-heir that killed lusty Pudding and Master Forthlight

the tilter, and brave Master Shooty the great traveller, and wild Half-can that stabbed Pots, and, I think, forty more : all great doers in our trade, and are now ' for the Lord's sake.'

Enter ABHORSON.

Abhorson. Sirrah, bring Barnardine hither.

Pompey. Master Barnardine ! you must rise and be hanged, Master Barnardine !

Abhorson. What, ho, Barnardine !

Barnardine. [*Within*] A pox o' your throats ! Who makes that noise there? What are you?

Pompey. Your friends, sir; the hangman. You must be so good, sir, to rise and be put to death.

Barnardine. [*Within*] Away, you rogue, away ! I am sleepy.

Abhorson. Tell him he must awake, and that quickly too.

Pompey. Pray, Master Barnardine, awake till you are executed, and sleep afterwards.

Abhorson. Go in to him, and fetch him out.

Pompey. He is coming, sir, he is coming; I hear his straw rustle.

Abhorson. Is the axe upon the block, sirrah?

Pompey. Very ready, sir.

Enter BARNARDINE.

Barnardine. How now, Abhorson? what 's the news with you?

Abhorson. Truly, sir, I would desire you to clap into your prayers; for, look you, the warrant 's come.

Barnardine. You rogue, I have been drinking all night; I am not fitted for 't.

Pompey. O, the better, sir; for he that drinks all night, and is hanged betimes in the morning, may sleep the sounder all the next day.

Abhorson. Look you, sir; here comes your ghostly father : do we jest now, think you?

Enter DUKE *disguised as before.*

Duke. Sir, induced by my charity, and hearing how hastily you are to depart, I am come to advise you, comfort you and pray with you.

Barnardine. Friar, not I : I have been drinking hard all night, and I will have more time to prepare me, or they shall beat out my brains with billets : I will not consent to die this day, that 's certain.

Duke. O, sir, you must : and therefore I beseech you Look forward on the journey you shall go.

Barnardine. I swear I will not die to-day for any man's persuasion.

Duke. But hear you.

Barnardine. Not a word : if you have anything to say to me, come to my ward; for thence will not I to-day.   [*Exit.*

Duke. Unfit to live or die : O gravel heart! After him, fellows; bring him to the block.

[*Exeunt Abhorson and Pompey.*

Enter PROVOST.

Provost. Now, sir, how do you find the prisoner?

Duke. A creature unprepared, unmeet for death; And to transport him in the mind he is Were damnable.

Provost.   Here in the prison, father,
There died this morning of a cruel fever
One Ragozine, a most notorious pirate,
A man of Claudio's years ; his beard and head
Just of his colour.   What if we do omit
This reprobate till he were well inclined ;
And satisfy the deputy with the visage
Of Ragozine, more like to Claudio ?
    Duke.   O, 'tis an accident that heaven provides !
Dispatch it presently ; the hour draws on
Prefix'd by Angelo : see this be done,
And sent according to command ; whiles I
Persuade this rude wretch willingly to die.
    Provost. This shall be done, good father, presently.
But Barnardine must die this afternoon :
And how shall we continue Claudio,
To save me from the danger that might come
If he were known alive ?
    Duke.   Let this be done.
Put them in secret holds, both Barnardine and
    Claudio :
Ere twice the sun hath made his journal greeting
To the under generation, you shall find
Your safety manifested.
    Provost. I am your free dependant.
    Duke.   Quick, dispatch, and send the head to
    Angelo.   [*Exit Provost.*
Now will I write letters to Angelo,—
The provost, he shall bear them,—whose contents
Shall witness to him I am near at home,
And that, by great injunctions, I am bound
To enter publicly : him I 'll desire
To meet me at the consecrated fount
A league below the city ; and from thence,
By cold gradation and well-balanced form,
We shall proceed with Angelo.

Re-enter PROVOST.

    Provost. Here is the head ; I 'll carry it myself.
    Duke.   Convenient is it.   Make a swift return ;
For I would commune with you of such things
That want no ears but yours.
    Provost.   I 'll make all speed.   [*Exit.*
    Isabella. [*Within*] Peace, ho, be here !
    Duke.   The tongue of Isabel.   She 's come to
    know
If yet her brother's pardon be come hither :
But I will keep her ignorant of her good,
To make her heavenly comforts of despair,
When it is least expected.

Enter ISABELLA.

    Isabella.   Ho, by your leave !
    Duke.   Good morning to you, fair and gracious
    daughter.
    Isabella. The better, given me by so holy a man.
Hath yet the deputy sent my brother's pardon ?
    Duke.   He hath released him, Isabel, from the
    world :
His head is off and sent to Angelo.
    Isabella. Nay, but it is not so.
    Duke.   It is no other : show your wisdom,
    daughter,
In your close patience.
    Isabella. O, I will to him and pluck out his eyes !
    Duke.   You shall not be admitted to his sight.
    Isabella. Unhappy Claudio ! wretched Isabel !
Injurious world ! most damned Angelo !
    Duke.   This nor hurts him nor profits you a jot ;
Forbear it therefore ; give your cause to heaven.

Mark what I say, which you shall find
By every syllable a faithful verity :
The duke comes home to-morrow ; nay, dry your
    eyes ;
One of our convent, and his confessor,
Gives me this instance : already he hath carried
Notice to Escalus and Angelo,
Who do prepare to meet him at the gates,
There to give up their power. If you can, pace
    your wisdom
In that good path that I would wish it go,
And you shall have your bosom on this wretch,
Grace of the duke, revenges to your heart,
And general honour.
    Isabella.   I am directed by you.
    Duke.   This letter, then, to Friar Peter give ;
'Tis that he sent me of the duke's return :
Say, by this token, I desire his company
At Mariana's house to-night.   Her cause and yours
I 'll perfect him withal, and he shall bring you
Before the duke, and to the head of Angelo
Accuse him home and home.   For my poor self,
I am combined by a sacred vow
And shall be absent.   Wend you with this letter :
Command these fretting waters from your eyes
With a light heart ; trust not my holy order,
If I pervert your course.   Who 's here ?

Enter LUCIO.

    Lucio.   Good even. Friar, where 's the provost ?
    Duke.   Not within, sir.
    Lucio.   O pretty Isabella, I am pale at mine
heart to see thine eyes so red : thou must be patient.
I am fain to dine and sup with water and bran ;
I dare not for my head fill my belly ; one fruitful
meal would set me to 't.   But they say the duke
will be here to-morrow. By my troth, Isabel, I
loved the duke : if the old fantastical duke of
dark corners had been at home, he had lived.
                                    [*Exit Isabella.*
    Duke.   Sir, the duke is marvellous little beholding
to your reports ; but the best is, he lives not in
them.
    Lucio.   Friar, thou knowest not the duke so well
as I do : he 's a better woodman than thou takest
him for.
    Duke.   Well, you 'll answer this one day. Fare
ye well.
    Lucio.   Nay, tarry ; I 'll go along with thee :
I can tell thee pretty tales of the duke.
    Duke.   You have told me too many of him
already, sir, if they be true ; if not true, none were
enough.
    Lucio.   I was once before him for getting a wench
with child.
    Duke.   Did you such a thing ?
    Lucio.   Yes, marry, did I : but I was fain to
forswear it ; they would else have married me to
the rotten medlar.
    Duke.   Sir, your company is fairer than honest.
Rest you well.
    Lucio.   By my troth, I 'll go with thee to the lane 's
end : if bawdy talk offend you, we 'll have very little
of it. Nay, friar, I am a kind of burr ; I shall stick.
                                    [*Exeunt.*

SCENE IV.   *A room in* ANGELO'S *house.*

Enter ANGELO *and* ESCALUS.

    Escalus. Every letter he hath writ hath disvouched other.

Angelo. In most uneven and distracted manner.
His actions show much like to madness : pray
heaven his wisdom be not tainted ! And why meet
him at the gates, and redeliver our authorities there ?
Escalus. I guess not.
Angelo. And why should we proclaim it in an
hour before his entering, that if any crave redress
of injustice, they should exhibit their petitions in
the street ?
Escalus. He shows his reason for that : to have
a dispatch of complaints, and to deliver us from
devices hereafter, which shall then have no power
to stand against us.
Angelo. Well, I beseech you, let it be proclaimed
betimes i' the morn ; I'll call you at your house :
give notice to such men of sort and suit as are to
meet him.
Escalus. I shall, sir. Fare you well.
Angelo. Good night.   [*Exit Escalus.*
This deed unshapes me quite, makes me unpregnant
And dull to all proceedings. A deflower'd maid !
And by an eminent body that enforced
The law against it ! But that her tender shame
Will not proclaim against her maiden loss,
How might she tongue me ! Yet reason dares her
no ;
For my authority bears of a credent bulk,
That no particular scandal once can touch
But it confounds the breather. He should have
lived,
Save that his riotous youth, with dangerous sense,
Might in the times to come have ta'en revenge,
By so receiving a dishonour'd life
With ransom of such shame. Would yet he had
lived !
Alack, when once our grace we have forgot,
Nothing goes right : we would, and we would not.
                                             [*Exit.*

SCENE V.   *Fields without the town.*

Enter DUKE *in his own habit, and* FRIAR PETER.

Duke. These letters at fit time deliver me :
                                    [*Giving letters.*
The provost knows our purpose and our plot.
The matter being afoot, keep your instruction,
And hold you ever to our special drift ;
Though sometimes you do blench from this to that,
As cause doth minister. Go call at Flavius' house,
And tell him where I stay : give the like notice
To Valentinus, Rowland, and to Crassus,
And bid them bring the trumpets to the gate ;
But send me Flavius first.
Friar Peter. It shall be speeded well.   [*Exit.*

Enter VARRIUS.

Duke. I thank thee, Varrius ; thou hast made
good haste :
Come, we will walk. There's other of our friends
Will greet us here anon, my gentle Varrius. [*Exeunt.*

SCENE VI.   *Street near the city gate.*

Enter ISABELLA *and* MARIANA.

Isabella. To speak so indirectly I am loath :
I would say the truth ; but to accuse him so,
That is your part : yet I am advised to do it ;
He says, to veil full purpose.

Mariana.   Be ruled by him.
Isabella. Besides, he tells me that, if peradventure
He speak against me on the adverse side,
I should not think it strange ; for 'tis a physic
That's bitter to sweet end.
Mariana. I would Friar Peter—
Isabella.   O, peace ! the friar is come.

Enter FRIAR PETER.

Friar Peter. Come, I have found you out a stand
most fit,
Where you may have such vantage on the duke,
He shall not pass you. Twice have the trumpets
sounded ;
The generous and gravest citizens
Have hent the gates, and very near upon
The duke is entering : therefore, hence, away !
                                             [*Exeunt.*

ACT V.

SCENE I.   *The city gate.*

MARIANA *veiled,* ISABELLA, *and* FRIAR PETER, *at
    their stand. Enter* DUKE, VARRIUS, LORDS,
    ANGELO, ESCALUS, LUCIO, PROVOST, OFFICERS,
    and CITIZENS, *at several doors.*

Duke.
My very worthy cousin, fairly met !
    Our old and faithful friend, we are glad to
    see you.
Angelo. } Happy return be to your royal grace !
Escalus.
Duke. Many and hearty thankings to you both.
We have made inquiry of you ; and we hear
Such goodness of your justice, that our soul
Cannot but yield you forth to public thanks,
Forerunning your requital.
Angelo.   You make my bonds still greater.
Duke. O, your desert speaks loud ; and I
should wrong it,
To lock it in the wards of covert bosom,
When it deserves, with characters of brass,
A forted residence 'gainst the tooth of time
And razure of oblivion. Give me your hand,
And let the subject see, to make them know
That outward courtesies would fain proclaim
Favours that keep within. Come, Escalus,
You must walk by us on our other hand ;
And good supporters are you.

FRIAR PETER and ISABELLA *come forward.*

Friar Peter. Now is your time : speak loud and
kneel before him.
Isabella. Justice, O royal duke ! Vail your regard
Upon a wrong'd, I would fain have said, a maid !
O worthy prince, dishonour not your eye
By throwing it on any other object
Till you have heard me in my true complaint
And given me justice, justice, justice, justice !
Duke. Relate your wrongs ; in what ? by whom ?
be brief.
Here is Lord Angelo shall give you justice :
Reveal yourself to him.
Isabella.   O worthy duke,
You bid me seek redemption of the devil :
Hear me yourself ; for that which I must speak
Must either punish me, not being believed,
Or wring redress from you. Hear me, O hear me,
here !

Angelo. My lord, her wits, I fear me, are not firm :
She hath been a suitor to me for her brother
Cut off by course of justice,—
Isabella.   By course of justice !
Angelo. And she will speak most bitterly and
    strange.
Isabella. Most strange, but yet most truly, will
    I speak :
That Angelo 's forsworn ; is it not strange ?
That Angelo 's a murderer ; is 't not strange?
That Angelo is an adulterous thief,
An hypocrite, a virgin-violator ;
Is it not strange and strange ?
Duke.   Nay, it is ten times strange.
Isabella. It is not truer he is Angelo
Than this is all as true as it is strange :
Nay, it is ten times true ; for truth is truth
To the end of reckoning.
Duke.   Away with her ! Poor soul,
She speaks this in the infirmity of sense.
Isabella.   O prince, I conjure thee, as thou be-
    lievest
There is another comfort than this world,
That thou neglect me not, with that opinion
That I am touch'd with madness ! Make not im-
    possible
That which but seems unlike : 'tis not impossible
But one, the wicked'st caitiff on the ground,
May seem as shy, as grave, as just, as absolute
As Angelo ; even so may Angelo,
In all his dressings, characts, titles, forms,
Be an arch-villain ; believe it, royal prince :
If he be less, he 's nothing ; but he 's more,
Had I more name for badness.
Duke.   By mine honesty,
If she be mad,—as I believe no other,—
Her madness hath the oddest frame of sense,
Such a dependency of thing on thing,
As e'er I heard in madness.
Isabella.   O gracious duke,
Harp not on that, nor do not banish reason
For inequality ; but let your reason serve
To make the truth appear where it seems hid,
And hide the false seems true.
Duke.   Many that are not mad
Have, sure, more lack of reason. What would
    you say ?
Isabella. I am the sister of one Claudio,
Condemn'd upon the act of fornication
To lose his head ; condemn'd by Angelo :
I, in probation of a sisterhood,
Was sent to by my brother ; one Lucio
As then the messenger,—
Lucio.   That 's I, an 't like your grace :
I came to her from Claudio, and desired her
To try her gracious fortune with Lord Angelo
For her poor brother's pardon.
Isabella.   That 's he indeed.
Duke. You were not bid to speak.
Lucio.   No, my good lord ;
Nor wish'd to hold my peace.
Duke.   I wish you now, then ;
Pray you, take note of it : and when you have
A business for yourself, pray heaven you then
Be perfect.
Lucio. I warrant your honour.
Duke. The warrant 's for yourself ; take heed
    to 't.
Isabella. This gentleman told somewhat of my
    tale,—
Lucio. Right.

Duke. It may be right ; but you are i' the wrong
To speak before your time. Proceed.
Isabella.   I went
To this pernicious caitiff deputy,—
Duke. That 's somewhat madly spoken.
Isabella.   Pardon it ;
The phrase is to the matter.
Duke. Mended again. The matter ; proceed.
Isabella. In brief, to set the needless process by,
How I persuaded, how I pray'd, and kneel'd,
How he refell'd me, and how I replied,—
For this was of much length,—the vile conclusion
I now begin with grief and shame to utter :
He would not, but by gift of my chaste body
To his concupiscible intemperate lust,
Release my brother ; and, after much debatement,
My sisterly remorse confutes mine honour,
And I did yield to him : but the next morn betimes,
His purpose surfeiting, he sends a warrant
For my poor brother's head.
Duke.   This is most likely !
Isabella. O, that it were as like as it is true !
Duke. By heaven, fond wretch, thou know'st
    not what thou speak'st,
Or else thou art suborn'd against his honour
In hateful practice. First, his integrity
Stands without blemish. Next, it imports no reason
That with such vehemency he should pursue
Faults proper to himself : if he had so offended,
He would have weigh'd thy brother by himself
And not have cut him off. Some one hath set
    you on :
Confess the truth, and say by whose advice
Thou camest here to complain.
Isabella.   And is this all ?
Then, O you blessed ministers above,
Keep me in patience, and with ripen'd time
Unfold the evil which is here wrapt up
In countenance ! Heaven shield your grace from woe,
As I, thus wrong'd, hence unbelieved go !
Duke. I know you 'ld fain be gone. An officer!
To prison with her ! Shall we thus permit
A blasting and a scandalous breath to fall
On him so near us ? This needs must be a practice.
Who knew of your intent and coming hither ?
Isabella. One that I would were here, Friar
    Lodowick.
Duke. A ghostly father, belike. Who knows that
    Lodowick ?
Lucio. My lord, I know him ; 'tis a meddling
    friar ;
I do not like the man : had he been lay, my lord,
For certain words he spake against your grace
In your retirement, I had swinged him soundly.
Duke. Words against me ! this is a good friar,
    belike !
And to set on this wretched woman here
Against our substitute ! Let this friar be found.
Lucio. But yesternight, my lord, she and that
    friar,
I saw them at the prison : a saucy friar,
A very scurvy fellow.
Friar Peter. Blessed be your royal grace !
I have stood by, my lord, and I have heard
Your royal ear abused. First, hath this woman
Most wrongfully accused your substitute,
Who is as free from touch or soil with her
As she from one ungot.
Duke.   We did believe no less.
Know you that Friar Lodowick that she speaks of ?

Friar Peter. I know him for a man divine and
    holy ;
Not scurvy, nor a temporary meddler,
As he 's reported by this gentleman ;
And, on my trust, a man that never yet
Did, as he vouches, misreport your grace.
    Lucio. My lord, most villanously ; believe it.
    Friar Peter. Well, he in time may come to clear
himself ;
But at this instant he is sick, my lord,
Of a strange fever. Upon his mere request,
Being come to knowledge that there was complaint
Intended 'gainst Lord Angelo, came I hither,
To speak, as from his mouth, what he doth know
Is true and false ; and what he with his oath
And all probation will make up full clear,
Whensoever he 's convented. First, for this woman,
To justify this worthy nobleman,
So vulgarly and personally accused,
Her shall you hear disproved to her eyes,
Till she herself confess it.
    Duke.   Good friar, let 's hear it.
        [*Isabella is carried off guarded ; and
                    Mariana comes forward.*
Do you not smile at this, Lord Angelo ?
O heaven, the vanity of wretched fools !
Give us some seats. Come, cousin Angelo ;
In this I 'll be impartial ; be you judge
Of your own cause. Is this the witness, friar ?
First, let her show her face, and after speak.
    Mariana. Pardon, my lord ; I will not show my
    face
Until my husband bid me.
    Duke. What, are you married ?
    Mariana. No, my lord.
    Duke. Are you a maid ?
    Mariana. No, my lord.
    Duke. A widow, then ?
    Mariana. Neither, my lord.
    Duke. Why, you are nothing then : neither
maid, widow, nor wife ?
    Lucio. My lord, she may be a punk ; for many
of them are neither maid, widow, nor wife.
    Duke. Silence that fellow : I would he had some
    cause
To prattle for himself.
    Lucio. Well, my lord.
    Mariana. My lord, I do confess I ne'er was
    married ;
And I confess besides I am no maid :
I have known my husband ; yet my husband
Knows not that ever he knew me.
    Lucio. He was drunk then, my lord : it can be
no better.
    Duke. For the benefit of silence, would thou wert
so too !
    Lucio. Well, my lord.
    Duke. This is no witness for Lord Angelo.
    Mariana. Now I come to 't, my lord :
She that accuses him of fornication,
In self-same manner doth accuse my husband,
And charges him, my lord, with such a time
When I 'll depose I had him in mine arms
With all the effect of love.
    Angelo. Charges she more than me ?
    Mariana.   Not that I know.
    Duke. No ? you say your husband.
    Mariana. Why, just, my lord, and that is Angelo,
Who thinks he knows that he ne'er knew my body,
But knows he thinks that he knows Isabel's.

    Angelo. This is a strange abuse. Let 's see thy
    face.
    Mariana. My husband bids me ; now I will
unmask.   [*Unveiling.*
This is that face, thou cruel Angelo,
Which once thou sworest was worth the looking on ;
This is the hand which, with a vow'd contract,
Was fast belock'd in thine ; this is the body
That took away the match from Isabel,
And did supply thee at thy garden-house
In her imagined person.
    Duke.   Know you this woman ?
    Lucio. Carnally, she says.
    Duke.   Sirrah, no more !
    Lucio. Enough, my lord.
    Angelo. My lord, I must confess I know this
    woman :
And five years since there was some speech of
    marriage
Betwixt myself and her ; which was broke off,
Partly for that her promised proportions
Came short of composition, but in chief
For that her reputation was disvalued
In levity : since which time of five years
I never spake with her, saw her, nor heard from her,
Upon my faith and honour.
    Mariana.   Noble prince,
As there comes light from heaven and words from
    breath,
As there is sense in truth and truth in virtue,
I am affianced this man's wife as strongly
As words could make up vows : and, my good lord,
But Tuesday night last gone in 's garden-house
He knew me as a wife. As this is true,
Let me in safety raise me from my knees ;
Or else for ever be confixed here,
A marble monument !
    Angelo.   I did but smile till now :
Now, good my lord, give me the scope of justice ;
My patience here is touch'd. I do perceive
These poor informal women are no more
But instruments of some more mightier member
That sets them on : let me have way, my lord,
To find this practice out.
    Duke.   Ay, with my heart ;
And punish them to your height of pleasure.
Thou foolish friar, and thou pernicious woman,
Compact with her that 's gone, think'st thou thy
    oaths,
Though they would swear down each particular saint,
Were testimonies against his worth and credit
That 's seal'd in approbation ? You, Lord Escalus,
Sit with my cousin ; lend him your kind pains
To find out this abuse, whence 'tis derived.
There is another friar that set them on ;
Let him be sent for.
    Friar Peter. Would he were here, my lord ! for
he indeed
Hath set the women on to this complaint :
Your provost knows the place where he abides
And he may fetch him.
    Duke. Go do it instantly.   [*Exit Provost.*
And you, my noble and well-warranted cousin,
Whom it concerns to hear this matter forth,
Do with your injuries as seems you best,
In any chastisement : I for a while will leave you ;
But stir not you till you have well determined
Upon these slanderers.
    Escalus. My lord, we 'll do it throughly.
                              [*Exit Duke.*
Signior Lucio, did not you say you knew that

Friar Lodowick to be a dishonest person ?

Lucio. ' Cucullus non facit monachum : ' honest in nothing but in his clothes ; and one that hath spoke most villanous speeches of the duke.

Escalus. We shall entreat you to abide here till he come and enforce them against him : we shall find this friar a notable fellow.

Lucio. As any in Vienna, on my word.

Escalus. Call that same Isabel here once again : I would speak with her.   [*Exit an Attendant.*] Pray you, my lord, give me leave to question ; you shall see how I 'll handle her.

Lucio. Not better than he, by her own report.

Escalus. Say you ?

Lucio. Marry, sir, I think, if you handled her privately, she would sooner confess : perchance, publicly, she 'll be ashamed.

Escalus. I will go darkly to work with her.

Lucio. That's the way ; for women are light at midnight.

Re-enter OFFICERS *with* ISABELLA ; *and* PROVOST *with the* DUKE *in his friar's habit.*

Escalus. Come on, mistress : here 's a gentle-woman denies all that you have said.

Lucio. My lord, here comes the rascal I spoke of ; here with the provost.

Escalus. In very good time : speak not you to him till we call upon you.

Lucio. Mum.

Escalus. Come, sir : did you set these women on to slander Lord Angelo ? they have confessed you did.

Duke. 'Tis false.

Escalus. How ! know you where you are ?

Duke. Respect to your great place ! and let the devil
Be sometime honour'd for his burning throne !
Where is the duke ? 'tis he should hear me speak.

Escalus. The duke 's in us ; and we will hear you speak :
Look you speak justly.

Duke. Boldly, at least. But, O, poor souls,
Come you to seek the lamb here of the fox ?
Good night to your redress ! Is the duke gone ?
Then is your cause gone too. The duke 's unjust,
Thus to retort your manifest appeal,
And put your trial in the villain's mouth
Which here you come to accuse.

Lucio. This is the rascal ; this is he I spoke of.

Escalus. Why, thou unreverend and unhallow'd friar,
Is 't not enough thou hast suborn'd these women
To accuse this worthy man, but, in foul mouth
And in the witness of his proper ear,
To call him villain ? and then to glance from him
To the duke himself, to tax him with injustice ?
Take him hence ; to the rack with him! We 'll touse you
Joint by joint, but we will know his purpose.
What, ' unjust ' ! .

Duke.   Be not so hot ; the duke
Dare no more stretch this finger of mine than he
Dare rack his own : his subject am I not,
Nor here provincial. My business in this state
Made me a looker on here in Vienna,
Where I have seen corruption boil and bubble
Till it o'er-run the stew ; laws for all faults,
But faults so countenanced, that the strong statutes
Stand like the forfeits in a barber's shop,
As much in mock as mark.

Escalus. Slander to the state ! Away with him to prison !

Angelo. What can you vouch against him, Signior Lucio ?
Is this the man that you did tell us of ?

Lucio. 'Tis he, my lord. Come hither, good-man baldpate : do you know me ?

Duke. I remember you, sir, by the sound of your voice : I met you at the prison, in the absence of the duke.

Lucio. O, did you so ? And do you remember what you said of the duke ?

Duke. Most notedly, sir.

Lucio. Do you so, sir ? And was the duke a fleshmonger, a fool, and a coward, as you then reported him to be ?

Duke. You must, sir, change persons with me, ere you make that my report : you, indeed, spoke of of him ; and much more, much worse.

Lucio. O thou damnable fellow ! Did not I pluck thee by the nose for thy speeches ?

Duke. I protest I love the duke as I love myself.

Angelo. Hark, how the villain would close now, after his treasonable abuses !

Escalus. Such a fellow is not to be talked withal. Away with him to prison ! Where is the provost ? Away with him to prison ! lay bolts enough upon him : let him speak no more. Away with those giglots too, and with the other confederate companion !

Duke. [*To Provost*] Stay, sir ; stay awhile.

Angelo. What, resists he ? Help him, Lucio.

Lucio. Come, sir ; come, sir ; come, sir ; foh, sir ! Why, you bald-pated, lying rascal, you must be hooded, must you ? Show your knave's visage, with a pox to you ! show your sheep-biting face, and be hanged an hour ! Will 't not off ?
            [*Pulls off the friar's hood, and discovers the Duke.*

Duke. Thou art the first knave that e'er madest a duke.
First, provost, let me bail these gentle three.
[*To Lucio*] Sneak not away, sir ; for the friar and you
Must have a word anon. Lay hold on him.

Lucio. This may prove worse than hanging.

Duke. [*To Escalus*] What you have spoke I pardon : sit you down :
We 'll borrow place of him. [*To Angelo*] Sir, by your leave.
Hast thou or word, or wit, or impudence,
That yet can do thee office ? If thou hast,
Rely upon it till my tale be heard,
And hold no longer out.

Angelo.   O my dread lord,
I should be guiltier than my guiltiness,
To think I can be undiscernible,
When I perceive your grace, like power divine,
Hath look'd upon my passes. Then, good prince,
No longer session hold upon my shame,
But let my trial be mine own confession :
Immediate sentence then and sequent death
Is all the grace I beg.

Duke.   Come hither, Mariana.
Say, wast thou e'er contracted to this woman ?

Angelo. I was, my lord.

Duke. Go take her hence, and marry her instantly.
Do you the office, friar : which consummate,
Return him here again. Go with him, provost.
            [*Exeunt Angelo, Mariana, Friar Peter and Provost.*

Escalus. My lord, I am more amazed at his
      dishonour
Than at the strangeness of it.
Duke.   Come hither, Isabel.
Your friar is now your prince : as I was then
Advertising and holy to your business,
Not changing heart with habit, I am still
Attorney'd at your service.
Isabella.   O, give me pardon,
That I, your vassal, have employ'd and pain'd
Your unknown sovereignty !
Duke.   You are pardon'd, Isabel :
And now, dear maid, be you as free to us.
Your brother's death, I know, sits at your heart ;
And you may marvel why I obscured myself,
Labouring to save his life, and would not rather
Make rash remonstrance of my hidden power
Than let him so be lost. O most kind maid,
It was the swift celerity of his death,
Which I did think with slower foot came on,
That brain'd my purpose. But, peace be with him !
That life is better life, past fearing death,
Than that which lives to fear : make it your comfort,
So happy is your brother.
Isabella.   I do, my lord.

Re-enter ANGELO, MARIANA, FRIAR PETER, *and*
      PROVOST.

Duke. For this new-married man approaching
      here,
Whose salt imagination yet hath wrong'd
Your well defended honour, you must pardon
For Mariana's sake : but as he adjudged your
      brother,—
Being criminal, in double violation
Of sacred chastity and of promise-breach
Thereon dependent, for your brother's life,—
The very mercy of the law cries out
Most audible, even from his proper tongue,
' An Angelo for Claudio, death for death ! '
Haste still pays haste, and leisure answers leisure ;
Like doth quit like, and MEASURE still FOR MEASURE.
Then, Angelo, thy fault 's thus manifested ;
Which, though thou wouldst deny, denies thee
      vantage.
We do condemn thee to the very block
Where Claudio stoop'd to death, and with like haste.
Away with him !
Mariana.   O my most gracious lord,
I hope you will not mock me with a husband.
Duke. It is your husband mock'd you with a
      husband.
Consenting to the safeguard of your honour,
I thought your marriage fit ; else imputation,
For that he knew you, might reproach your life
And choke your good to come : for his possessions,
Although by confiscation they are ours,
We do instate and widow you withal,
To buy you a better husband.
Mariana.   O my dear lord,
I crave no other, nor no better man.
Duke. Never crave him ; we are definitive.
Mariana. Gentle my liege,—   [*Kneeling.*
Duke.   You do but lose your labour.
Away with him to death ! [*To Lucio*] Now, sir,
      to you.
Mariana. O my good lord ! Sweet Isabel, take
      my part ;
Lend me your knees, and all my life to come
I 'll lend you all my life to do you service.

Duke. Against all sense you do importune her :
Should she kneel down in mercy of this fact,
Her brother's ghost his paved bed would break,
And take her hence in horror.
Mariana.   Isabel,
Sweet Isabel, do yet but kneel by me ;
Hold up your hands, say nothing ; I 'll speak all.
They say, best men are moulded out of faults ;
And, for the most, become much more the better
For being a little bad : so may my husband,
O Isabel, will you not lend a knee ?
Duke. He dies for Claudio's death.
Isabella.   Most bounteous sir, [*Kneeling.*
Look, if it please you, on this man condemn'd,
As if my brother lived : I partly think
A due sincerity govern'd his deeds,
Till he did look on me : since it is so,
Let him not die. My brother had but justice,
In that he did the thing for which he died :
For Angelo,
His act did not o'ertake his bad intent,
And must be buried but as an intent
That perish'd by the way : thoughts are no subjects ;
Intents but merely thoughts.
Mariana.   Merely, my lord.
Duke. Your suit 's unprofitable ; stand up, I say.
I have bethought me of another fault.
Provost, how came it Claudio was beheaded
At an unusual hour ?
Provost.   It was commanded so.
Duke. Had you a special warrant for the deed ?
Provost. No, my good lord ; it was by private
      message.
Duke. For which I do discharge you of your
      office :
Give up your keys.
Provost.   Pardon me, noble lord :
I thought it was a fault, but knew it not ;
Yet did repent me, after more advice :
For testimony whereof, one in the prison,
That should by private order else have died,
I have reserved alive.
Duke.   What 's he ?
Provost.   His name is Barnardine.
Duke. I would thou hadst done so by Claudio.
Go fetch him hither ; let me look upon him.
                          [*Exit Provost.*
Escalus. I am sorry, one so learned and so wise
As you, Lord Angelo, have still appear'd,
Should slip so grossly, both in the heat of blood,
And lack of temper'd judgement afterward.
Angelo. I am sorry that such sorrow I procure :
And so deep sticks it in my penitent heart
That I crave death more willingly than mercy ;
'Tis my deserving, and I do entreat it.

Re-enter PROVOST, *with* BARNARDINE,
      CLAUDIO *muffled, and* JULIET.

Duke. Which is that Barnardine ?
Provost.   This, my lord.
Duke. There was a friar told me of this man.
Sirrah, thou art said to have a stubborn soul,
That apprehends no further than this world,
And squarest thy life according. Thou'rt condemn'd:
But, for those earthly faults, I quit them all ;
And pray thee take this mercy to provide
For better times to come. Friar, advise him ;
I leave him to your hand. What muffled fellow 's
      that ?

Provost. This is another prisoner that I saved,
Who should have died when Claudio lost his head ;
As like almost to Claudio as himself.
                              [*Unmuffles Claudio.*
Duke. [*To Isabella*] If he be like your brother,
      for his sake
Is he pardon'd ; and, for your lovely sake,
Give me your hand and say you will be mine,
He is my brother too : but fitter time for that.
By this Lord Angelo perceives he 's safe ;
Methinks I see a quickening in his eye.
Well, Angelo, your evil quits you well :
Look that you love your wife ; her worth worth
      yours.
I find an apt remission in myself ;
And yet here 's one in place I cannot pardon.
[*To Lucio*] You, sirrah, that knew me for a fool, a
      coward,
One all of luxury, an ass, a madman ;
Wherein have I so deserved of you,
That you extol me thus ?
    Lucio. 'Faith, my lord, I spoke it but according
to the trick. If you will hang me for it, you may ;
but I had rather it would please you I might be
whipt.
    Duke. Whipt first, sir, and hanged after.
Proclaim it, provost, round about the city,
Is any woman wrong'd by this lewd fellow,
As I have heard him swear himself there 's one
Whom he begot with child, let her appear,

And he shall marry her : the nuptial finish'd,
Let him be whipt and hang'd.
    Lucio. I beseech your highness, do not marry me
to a whore. Your highness said even now, I made
you a duke : good my lord, do not recompense
me in making me a cuckold.
    Duke. Upon mine honour, thou shalt marry her.
Thy slanders I forgive ; and therewithal
Remit thy other forfeits. Take him to prison ;
And see our pleasure herein is executed.
    Lucio. Marrying a punk, my lord, is pressing to
death, whipping, and hanging.
    Duke. Slandering a prince deserves it.
                        [*Exeunt Officers with Lucio.*
She, Claudio, that you wrong'd, look you restore.
Joy to you, Mariana ! Love her, Angelo :
I have confess'd her and I know her virtue.
Thanks, good friend Escalus, for thy much goodness :
There 's more behind that is more gratulate,
Thanks, provost, for thy care and secrecy :
We shall employ thee in a worthier place.
Forgive him, Angelo, that brought you home
The head of Ragozine for Claudio's :
The offence pardons itself. Dear Isabel,
I have a motion much imports your good ;
Whereto if you 'll a willing ear incline,
What 's mine is yours and what is yours is mine.
So, bring us to our palace ; where we 'll show
What 's yet behind, that 's meet you all should
know.   [*Exeunt.*

THE

COMEDY OF ERRORS

DRAMATIS PERSONÆ

SOLINUS, duke of Ephesus.
ÆGEON, a merchant of Syracuse.
ANTIPHOLUS of Ephesus, } twin brothers, and sons to
ANTIPHOLUS of Syracuse, } Ægeon and Æmilia.
DROMIO of Ephesus, } twin brothers, and attendants
DROMIO of Syracuse, } on the two Antipholuses.
BALTHAZAR, a merchant.
ANGELO, a goldsmith.
First Merchant, friend to Antipholus of Syracuse.
Second Merchant, to whom Angelo is a debtor.
PINCH, a schoolmaster.

ÆMILIA, wife to Ægeon, an abbess at Ephesus.
ADRIANA, wife to Antipholus of Ephesus.
LUCIANA, her sister.
LUCE, servant to Adriana.
A Courtezan.

Gaoler, Officers, and other Attendants.

SCENE : Ephesus.

ACT I.

SCENE I. A hall in the DUKE's palace.

Enter DUKE, ÆGEON, Gaoler, Officers, and other
Attendants.

Ægeon.

Proceed, Solinus, to procure my fall
And by the doom of death end woes and all.
    Duke. Merchant of Syracusa, plead no
more ;
I am not partial to infringe our laws :
The enmity and discord which of late
Sprung from the rancorous outrage of your duke
To merchants, our well-dealing countrymen,
Who wanting guilders to redeem their lives
Have seal'd his rigorous statutes with their bloods,
Excludes all pity from our threatening looks.
For, since the mortal and intestine jars
'Twixt thy seditious countrymen and us,
It hath in solemn synods been decreed,
Both by the Syracusians and ourselves,
To admit no traffic to our adverse towns :
Nay, more,
If any born at Ephesus be seen
At any Syracusian marts and fairs ;
Again : if any Syracusian born
Come to the bay of Ephesus, he dies,
His goods confiscate to the duke's dispose,
Unless a thousand marks be levied,
To quit the penalty and to ransom him.
Thy substance, valued at the highest rate,
Cannot amount unto a hundred marks ;
Therefore by law thou art condemn'd to die.
    Ægeon. Yet this my comfort : when your words
are done,
My woes end likewise with the evening sun.
    Duke. Well, Syracusian, say in brief the cause
Why thou departed'st from thy native home
And for what cause thou camest to Ephesus.
    Ægeon. A heavier task could not have been
imposed
Than I to speak my griefs unspeakable :
Yet, that the world may witness that my end
Was wrought by nature, not by vile offence,
I 'll utter what my sorrow gives me leave.
In Syracusa was I born, and wed
Unto a woman, happy but for me,
And by me, had not our hap been bad.
With her I lived in joy ; our wealth increased
By prosperous voyages I often made
To Epidamnum ; till my factor's death
And the great care of goods at random left
Drew me from kind embracements of my spouse :
From whom my absence was not six months old
Before herself, almost at fainting under
The pleasing punishment that women bear,
Had made provision for her following me
And soon and safe arrived where I was.
There had she not been long but she became
A joyful mother of two goodly sons ;
And, which was strange, the one so like the other
As could not be distinguish'd but by names.
That very hour and in the self-same inn
A meaner woman was delivered
Of such a burden, male twins, both alike :
Those, for their parents were exceeding poor,
I bought and brought up to attend my sons.
My wife, not meanly proud of two such boys,
Made daily motions for our home return :
Unwilling I agreed ; alas ! too soon
We came aboard.
A league from Epidamnum had we sail'd,
Before the always wind-obeying deep
Gave any tragic instance of our harm :
But longer did we not retain much hope ;
For what obscured light the heavens did grant
Did but convey unto our fearful minds
A doubtful warrant of immediate death ;
Which though myself would gladly have embraced,
Yet the incessant weepings of my wife,
Weeping before for what she saw must come,
And piteous plainings of the pretty babes,

That mourn'd for fashion, ignorant what to fear,
Forced me to seek delays for them and me.
And this it was, for other means was none :
The sailors sought for safety by our boat,
And left the ship, then sinking-ripe, to us :
My wife, more careful for the latter-born,
Had fasten'd him unto a small spare mast,
Such as seafaring men provide for storms ;
To him one of the other twins was bound,
Whilst I had been like heedful of the other :
The children thus disposed, my wife and I,
Fixing our eyes on whom our care was fix'd,
Fasten'd ourselves at either end the mast ;
And floating straight, obedient to the stream,
Was carried towards Corinth, as we thought.
At length the sun, gazing upon the earth,
Dispersed those vapours that offended us ;
And, by the benefit of his wished light,
The seas wax'd calm, and we discovered
Two ships from far making amain to us,
Of Corinth that, of Epidaurus this :
But ere they came,—O, let me say no more !
Gather the sequel by that went before.
    Duke. Nay, forward, old man ; do not break
    off so ;
For we may pity, though not pardon thee.
    Ægeon. O, had the gods done so, I had not now
Worthily term'd them merciless to us !
For, ere the ships could meet by twice five leagues,
We were encounter'd by a mighty rock ;
Which being violently borne upon,
Our helpful ship was splitted in the midst ;
So that, in this unjust divorce of us,
Fortune had left to both of us alike
What to delight in, what to sorrow for.
Her part, poor soul ! seeming as burdened
With lesser weight but not with lesser woe,
Was carried with more speed before the wind ;
And in our sight they three were taken up
By fishermen of Corinth, as we thought.
At length, another ship had seized on us ;
And, knowing whom it was their hap to save,
Gave healthful welcome to their shipwreck'd guests ;
And would have reft the fishers of their prey,
Had not their bark been very slow of sail ;
And therefore homeward did they bend their course.
Thus have you heard me sever'd from my bliss,
That by misfortunes was my life prolong'd,
To tell sad stories of my own mishaps.
    Duke. And, for the sake of them thou sorrowest
    for,
Do me the favour to dilate at full
What hath befall'n of them and thee till now.
    Ægeon. My youngest boy, and yet my eldest care,
At eighteen years became inquisitive
After his brother : and importuned me
That his attendant—so his case was like,
Reft of his brother, but retain'd his name—
Might bear him company in the quest of him :
Whom whilst I labour'd of a love to see,
I hazarded the loss of whom I loved.
Five summers have I spent in furthest Greece,
Roaming clean through the bounds of Asia,
And, coasting homeward, came to Ephesus ;
Hopeless to find, yet loath to leave unsought
Or that or any place that harbours men.
But here must end the story of my life ;
And happy were I in my timely death,
Could all my travels warrant me they live.
    Duke. Hapless Ægeon, whom the fates have
    mark'd

To bear the extremity of dire mishap !
Now, trust me, were it not against our laws,
Against my crown, my oath, my dignity,
Which princes, would they, may not disannul,
My soul should sue as advocate for thee.
But, though thou art adjudged to the death
And passed sentence may not be recall'd
But to our honour's great disparagement,
Yet I will favour thee in what I can.
Therefore, merchant, I 'll limit thee this day
To seek thy life by beneficial help :
Try all the friends thou hast in Ephesus ;
Beg thou, or borrow, to make up the sum,
And live ; if no, then thou art doom'd to die
Gaoler, take him to thy custody.
    Gaoler. I will, my lord.
    Ægeon. Hopeless and helpless doth Ægeon wend,
But to procrastinate his lifeless end.   *[Exeunt.*

SCENE II.   *The Mart.*

Enter ANTIPHOLUS *of Syracuse,* DROMIO *of Syracuse,
and* First Merchant.
    First Merchant. Therefore give out you are of
    Epidamnum,
Lest that your goods too soon be confiscate.
This very day a Syracusian merchant
Is apprehended for arrival here ;
And not being able to buy out his life
According to the statute of the town
Dies ere the weary sun set in the west.
There is your money that I had to keep.
    Antipholus of Syracuse. Go bear it to the Centaur,
where we host,
And stay there, Dromio, till I come to thee.
Within this hour it will be dinner-time :
Till that, I 'll view the manners of the town,
Peruse the traders, gaze upon the buildings,
And then return and sleep within mine inn,
For with long travel I am stiff and weary.
Get thee away.
    Dromio of Syracuse. Many a man would take
    you at your word,
And go indeed, having so good a mean.   *[Exit.*
    Antipholus of Syracuse. A trusty villain, sir, that
    very oft,
When I am dull with care and melancholy,
Lightens my humour with his merry jests.
What, will you walk with me about the town,
And then go to my inn and dine with me ?
    First Merchant. I am invited, sir, to certain
    merchants,
Of whom I hope to make much benefit :
I crave your pardon. Soon at five o'clock,
Please you, I 'll meet with you upon the mart
And afterward consort you till bed-time :
My present business calls me from you now.
    Antipholus of Syracuse. Farewell till then : I will
    go lose myself
And wander up and down to view the city.
    First Merchant. Sir, I commend you to your own
    content.   *[Exit.*
    Antipholus of Syracuse. He that commends me to
    mine own content
Commends me to the thing I cannot get.
I to the world am like a drop of water
That in the ocean seeks another drop,
Who, falling there to find his fellow forth,
Unseen, inquisitive, confounds himself :
So I, to find a mother and a brother,
In quest of them, unhappy, lose myself.

Enter DROMIO *of Ephesus.*
Here comes the almanac of my true date.
What now ? how chance thou art return'd so soon ?
Dromio of Ephesus. Return'd so soon ! rather
  approach'd too late :
The capon burns, the pig falls from the spit,
The clock hath strucken twelve upon the bell ;
My mistress made it one upon my cheek :
She is so hot because the meat is cold ;
The meat is cold because you come not home ;
You come not home because you have no stomach ;
You have no stomach having broke your fast ;
But we that know what 'tis to fast and pray
Are penitent for your default to-day.
Antipholus of Syracuse. Stop in your wind, sir :
  tell me this, I pray :
Where have you left the money that I gave you ?
Dromio of Ephesus. O—sixpence, that I had o'
  Wednesday last
To pay the saddler for my mistress' crupper ?
The saddler had it, sir ; I kept it not.
Antipholus of Syracuse. I am not in a sportive
  humour now :
Tell me, and dally not, where is the money ?
We being strangers here, how darest thou trust
So great a charge from thine own custody ?
Dromio of Ephesus. I pray you, jest, sir, as you
  sit at dinner :
I from my mistress come to you in post ;
If I return, I shall be post indeed,
For she will score your fault upon my pate.
Methinks your maw, like mine, should be your clock
And strike you home without a messenger.
Antipholus of Syracuse. Come, Dromio, come,
  these jests are out of season ;
Reserve them till a merrier hour than this.
Where is the gold I gave in charge to thee ?
Dromio of Ephesus. To me, sir ? why, you gave
  no gold to me.
Antipholus of Syracuse. Come on, sir knave,
  have done your foolishness
And tell me how thou hast disposed thy charge.
Dromio of Ephesus. My charge was but to fetch
  you from the mart
Home to your house, the Phœnix, sir, to dinner :
My mistress and her sister stays for you.
Antipholus of Syracuse. Now, as I am a Christian,
  answer me
In what safe place you have bestow'd my money,
Or I shall break that merry sconce of yours
That stands on tricks when I am undisposed :
Where is the thousand marks thou hadst of me ?
Dromio of Ephesus. I have some marks of yours
  upon my pate,
Some of my mistress' marks upon my shoulders,
But not a thousand marks between you both.
If I should pay your worship those again,
Perchance you will not bear them patiently.
Antipholus of Syracuse. Thy mistress' marks ?
  what mistress, slave, hast thou ?
Dromio of Ephesus. Your worship's wife, my
  mistress at the Phœnix ;
She that doth fast till you come home to dinner
And prays that you will hie you home to dinner.
Antipholus of Syracuse. What, wilt thou flout
  me thus unto my face,
Being forbid ? There, take you that, sir knave.
Dromio of Ephesus. What mean you, sir ? for
  God's sake, hold your hands!
Nay, an you will not, sir, I 'll take my heels.
                                          [*Exit.*

Antipholus of Syracuse. Upon my life, by some
  device or other
The villain is o'er-raught of all my money.
They say this town is full of cozenage,
As, nimble jugglers that deceive the eye,
Dark-working sorcerers that change the mind,
Soul-killing witches that deform the body,
Disguised cheaters, prating mountebanks,
And many such-like liberties of sin :
If it prove so, I will be gone the sooner.
I 'll to the Centaur, to go seek this slave :
I greatly fear my money is not safe.   [*Exit.*

ACT II.

SCENE I.   *The house of* ANTIPHOLUS *of Ephesus.*

Enter ADRIANA *and* LUCIANA.

Adriana.
Neither my husband nor the slave return'd,
  That in such haste I sent to seek his master !
  Sure, Luciana, it is two o'clock.
Luciana. Perhaps some merchant hath invited
  him
And from the mart he 's somewhere gone to dinner.
Good sister, let us dine and never fret :
A man is master of his liberty :
Time is their master, and when they see time
They 'll go or come : if so, be patient, sister.
Adriana. Why should their liberty than ours be
  more ?
Luciana. Because their business still lies out o'
  door.
Adriana. Look, when I serve him so, he takes it
  ill.
Luciana. O, know he is the bridle of your will.
Adriana. There 's none but asses will be bridled
  so.
Luciana. Why, headstrong liberty is lash'd with
  woe.
There 's nothing situate under heaven's eye
But hath his bound, in earth, in sea, in sky :
The beasts, the fishes and the winged fowls
Are their males' subjects and at their controls :
Men, more divine, the masters of all these,
Lords of the wide world and wild watery seas,
Indued with intellectual sense and souls,
Of more pre-eminence than fish and fowls,
Are masters to their females, and their lords :
Then let your will attend on their accords.
Adriana. This servitude makes you to keep
  unwed.
Luciana. Not this, but troubles of the marriage-
  bed.
Adriana. But, were you wedded, you would bear
  some sway.
Luciata. Ere I learn love, I 'll practise to obey.
Adriana. How if your husband start some other
  where ?
Luciana. Till he come home again, I would for-
  bear.
Adriana. Patience unmoved ! no marvel though
  she pause ;
They can be meek that have no other cause.
A wretched soul, bruised with adversity,
We bid be quiet when we hear it cry ;
But were we burden'd with like weight of pain,
As much or more we should ourselves complain :
So thou, that hast no unkind mate to grieve thee,

With urging helpless patience wouldst relieve me ;
But, if thou live to see like right bereft,
This fool-begg'd patience in thee will be left.
Luciana. Well, I will marry one day, but to try.
Here comes your man ; now is your husband nigh.

Enter DROMIO *of Ephesus.*

Adriana. Say, is your tardy master now at hand ?
Dromio of Ephesus. Nay, he 's at two hands with
me, and that my two ears can witness.
Adriana. Say, didst thou speak with him ? know'st
thou his mind ?
Dromio of Ephesus. Ay, ay, he told his mind upon
mine ear :
Beshrew his hand, I scarce could understand it.
Luciana. Spake he so doubtfully, thou couldst
not feel his meaning ?
Dromio of Ephesus. Nay, he struck so plainly, I
could too well feel his blows ; and withal so doubt-
fully that I could scarce understand them.
Adriana. But say, I prithee, is he coming home ?
It seems he hath great care to please his wife.
Dromio of Ephesus. Why, mistress, sure my
master is horn-mad.
Adriana. Horn-mad, thou villain !
Dromio of Ephesus.   I mean not cuckold-mad ;
But, sure, he is stark mad.
When I desired him to come home to dinner,
He ask'd me for a thousand marks in gold :
' 'Tis dinner-time,' quoth I ; ' My gold ! ' quoth he :
' Your meat doth burn,' quoth I ; ' My gold ! '
  quoth he :
' Will you come home ? ' quoth I ; ' My gold ! '
  quoth he,
' Where is the thousand marks I gave thee, villain ? '
' The pig,' quoth I, ' is burn'd ; ' ' My gold ! ' quoth
  he :
' My mistress, sir,' quoth I ; ' Hang up thy mistress !
I know not thy mistress ; out on thy mistress ! '
Luciana. Quoth who ?
Dromio of Ephesus. Quoth my master :
' I know,' quoth he, ' no house, no wife, no mis-
  tress.'
So that my errand, due unto my tongue,
I thank him, I bare home upon my shoulders ;
For, in conclusion, he did beat me there.
Adriana. Go back again, thou slave, and fetch
him home.
Dromio of Ephesus. Go back again, and be new
beaten home ?
For God's sake, send some other messenger.
Adriana. Back, slave, or I will break thy pate
across.
Dromio of Ephesus. And he will bless that cross
with other beating :
Between you I shall have a holy head.
Adriana. Hence, prating peasant ! fetch thy
master home.
Dromio of Ephesus. Am I so round with you as
you with me,
That like a football you do spurn me thus ?
You spurn me hence, and he will spurn me hither :
If I last in this service, you must case me in leather.
                                        [*Exit.*
Luciana. Fie, how impatience loureth in your
face !
Adriana. His company must do his minions
grace,
Whilst I at home starve for a merry look.
Hath homely age the alluring beauty took

From my poor cheek ? then he hath wasted it :
Are my discourses dull ? barren my wit ?
If voluble and sharp discourse be marr'd,
Unkindness blunts it more than marble hard :
Do their gay vestments his affections bait ?
That 's not my fault ; he 's master of my state :
What ruins are in me that can be found,
By him not ruin'd ? then is he the ground
Of my defeatures. My decayed fair
A sunny look of his would soon repair :
But, too unruly deer, he breaks the pale
And feeds from home ; poor I am but his stale.
Luciana. Self-harming jealousy ! fie, beat it
hence !
Adriana. Unfeeling fools can with such wrongs
dispense.
I know his eye doth homage otherwhere ;
Or else what lets it but he would be here ?
Sister, you know he promised me a chain ;
Would that alone, alone he would detain,
So he would keep fair quarter with his bed !
I see the jewel best enamelled
Will lose his beauty ; yet the gold bides still,
That others touch, and often touching will
† Wear gold : and no man that hath a name,
By falsehood and corruption doth it shame.
Since that my beauty cannot please his eye,
I 'll weep what 's left away, and weeping die.
Luciana. How many fond fools serve mad
jealousy !   [*Exeunt.*

SCENE II. *A public place.*

Enter ANTIPHOLUS *of Syracuse.*

Antipholus of Syracuse. The gold I gave to Dromio
is laid up
Safe at the Centaur ; and the heedful slave
Is wander'd forth, in care to seek me out
By computation and mine host's report,
I could not speak with Dromio since at first
I sent him from the mart. See, here he comes.

Enter DROMIO *of Syracuse.*

How now, sir ! is your merry humour alter'd ?
As you love strokes, so jest with me again.
You know no Centaur ? you received no gold ?
Your mistress sent to have me home to dinner ?
My house was at the Phœnix ? Wast thou mad,
That thus so madly thou didst answer me ?
Dromio of Syracuse. What answer, sir ? when
spake I such a word ?
Antipholus of Syracuse. Even now, even here, not
half an hour since.
Dromio of Syracuse. I did not see you since you
sent me hence,
Home to the Centaur, with the gold you gave me.
Antipholus of Syracuse. Villain, thou didst deny
the gold's receipt
And told'st me of a mistress and a dinner ;
For which, I hope, thou felt'st I was displeased.
Dromio of Syracuse. I am glad to see you in this
merry vein :
What means this jest ? I pray you, master, tell me.
Antipholus of Syracuse. Yea, dost thou jeer and
flout me in the teeth ?
Think'st thou I jest ? Hold, take thou that, and
that.   [*Beating him.*
Dromio of Syracuse. Hold, sir, for God's sake !
now your jest is earnest :
Upon what bargain do you give it me ?

Antipholus of Syracuse.   Because that I familiarly
   sometimes
Do use you for my fool and chat with you,
Your sauciness will jest upon my love
And make a common of my serious hours.
When the sun shines let foolish gnats make sport,
But creep in crannies when he hides his beams.
If you will jest with me, know my aspect
And fashion your demeanour to my looks,
Or I will beat this method in your sconce.
Dromio of Syracuse.   Sconce call you it? so you
would leave battering, I had rather have it a head:
an you use these blows long, I must get a sconce
for my head and insconce it too; or else I shall
seek my wit in my shoulders. But, I pray, sir, why
am I beaten?
Antipholus of Syracuse.   Dost thou not know?
Dromio of Syracuse.   Nothing, sir, but that I am
beaten.
Antipholus of Syracuse.   Shall I tell you why?
Dromio of Syracuse.   Ay, sir, and wherefore; for
they say every why hath a wherefore.
Antipholus of Syracuse.   Why, first,—for flouting
me; and then, wherefore,—
For urging it the second time to me.
Dromio of Syracuse.   Was there ever any man
thus beaten out of season,
When in the why and the wherefore is neither rhyme
   nor reason?
Well, sir, I thank you.
Antipholus of Syracuse.   Thank me, sir! for
what?
Dromio of Syracuse.   Marry, sir, for this some-
thing that you gave me for nothing.
Antipholus of Syracuse.   I'll make you amends
next, to give you nothing for something. But say,
sir, is it dinner-time?
Dromio of Syracuse.   No, sir: I think the meat
wants that I have.
Antipholus of Syracuse.   In good time, sir; what's
that?
Dromio of Syracuse.   Basting.
Antipholus of Syracuse.   Well, sir, then 'twill be
dry.
Dromio of Syracuse.   If it be, sir, I pray you, eat
none of it.
Antipholus of Syracuse.   Your reason?
Dromio of Syracuse.   Lest it make you choleric
and purchase me another dry basting.
Antipholus of Syracuse.   Well, sir, learn to jest in
good time: there's a time for all things.
Dromio of Syracuse.   I durst have denied that,
before you were so choleric.
Antipholus of Syracuse.   By what rule, sir?
Dromio of Syracuse.   Marry, sir, by a rule as
plain as the plain bald pate of father Time himself.
Antipholus of Syracuse.   Let's hear it.
Dromio of Syracuse.   There's no time for a man
to recover his hair that grows bald by nature.
Antipholus of Syracuse.   May he not do it by
fine and recovery?
Dromio of Syracuse.   Yes, to pay a fine for a
periwig and recover the lost hair of another man.
Antipholus of Syracuse.   Why is Time such a
niggard of hair, being, as it is, so plentiful an excrement?
Dromio of Syracuse.   Because it is a blessing that
he bestows on beasts; and what he hath scanted
men in hair he hath given them in wit.
Antipholus of Syracuse.   Why, but there's many a
man hath more hair than wit.

Dromio of Syracuse.   Not a man of those but he
hath the wit to lose his hair.
Antipholus of Syracuse.   Why, thou didst conclude
hairy men plain dealers without wit.
Dromio of Syracuse.   The plain dealer, the sooner
lost: yet he loseth it in a kind of jollity.
Antipholus of Syracuse.   For what reason?
Dromio of Syracuse.   For two; and sound ones
too.
Antipholus of Syracuse.   Nay, not sound, I pray
you.
Dromio of Syracuse.   Sure ones then.
Antipholus of Syracuse.   Nay, not sure, in a thing
falsing.
Dromio of Syracuse.   Certain ones then.
Antipholus of Syracuse.   Name them.
Dromio of Syracuse.   The one, to save the money
that he spends in tiring; the other that at dinner they
should not drop in his porridge.
Antipholus of Syracuse.   You would all this time
have proved there is no time for all things.
Dromio of Syracuse.   Marry, and did, sir; namely,
no time to recover hair lost by nature.
Antipholus of Syracuse.   But your reason was not
substantial, why there is no time to recover.
Dromio of Syracuse.   Thus I mend it: Time
himself is bald and therefore to the world's end
will have bald followers.
Antipholus of Syracuse.   I knew 'twould be a
bald conclusion:
But, soft! who wafts us yonder?

Enter ADRIANA *and* LUCIANA.

Adriana.   Ay, ay, Antipholus, look strange and
   frown:
Some other mistress hath thy sweet aspects;
I am not Adriana nor thy wife.
The time was once when thou unurged wouldst vow
That never words were music to thine ear,
That never object pleasing in thine eye,
That never touch well welcome to thy hand,
That never meat sweet-savour'd in thy taste,
Unless I spake, or look'd, or touch'd, or carved to
   thee.
How comes it now, my husband, O, how comes it,
That thou art thus estranged from thyself?
Thyself I call it, being strange to me,
That, undividable, incorporate,
Am better than thy dear self's better part.
Ah, do not tear away thyself from me!
For know, my love, as easy mayst thou fall
A drop of water in the breaking gulf
And take unmingled thence that drop again,
Without addition or diminishing,
As take from me thyself and not me too.
How dearly would it touch thee to the quick,
Shouldst thou but hear I were licentious
And that this body, consecrate to thee,
By ruffian lust should be contaminate!
Wouldst thou not spit at me and spurn at me
And hurl the name of husband in my face
And tear the stain'd skin off my harlot-brow
And from my false hand cut the wedding-ring
And break it with a deep-divorcing vow?
I know thou canst; and therefore see thou do it.
I am possess'd with an adulterate blot;
My blood is mingled with the crime of lust:
For if we two be one and thou play false,
I do digest the poison of thy flesh,
Being strumpeted by thy contagion.

Keep then fair league and truce with thy true bed ;
I live unstain'd, thou undishonoured.
Antipholus of Syracuse.   Plead you to me, fair
    dame ?   I know you not :
In Ephesus I am but two hours old,
As strange unto your town as to your talk ;
Who, every word by all my wit being scann'd,
Want wit in all one word to understand.
Luciana.   Fie, brother ! how the world is changed
    with you !
When were you wont to use my sister thus ?
She sent for you by Dromio home to dinner.
Antipholus of Syracuse.   By Dromio ?
Dromio of Syracuse.   By me ?
Adriana.   By thee ;   and this thou didst return
    from him,
That he did buffet thee and in his blows
Denied my house for his, me for his wife.
Antipholus of Syracuse.   Did you converse, sir,
    with this gentlewoman ?
What is the course and drift of your compact ?
Dromio of Syracuse.   I, sir ?   I never saw her till
    this time.
Antipholus of Syracuse.   Villain, thou liest ; for
    even her very words
Didst thou deliver to me on the mart.
Dromio of Syracuse.   I never spake with her in
    all my life.
Antipholus of Syracuse.   How can she thus then
    call us by our names ?
Unless it be by inspiration.
Adriana.   How ill agrees it with your gravity
To counterfeit thus grossly with your slave,
Abetting him to thwart me in my mood !
Be it my wrong you are from me exempt,
But wrong not that wrong with a more contempt.
Come, I will fasten on this sleeve of thine :
Thou art an elm, my husband, I a vine,
Whose weakness married to thy stronger state
Makes me with thy strength to communicate :
If aught possess thee from me, it is dross,
Usurping ivy, brier, or idle moss ;
Who, all for want of pruning, with intrusion
Infect thy sap and live on thy confusion.
Antipholus of Syracuse.   To me she speaks ; she
    moves me for her theme :
What, was I married to her in my dream ?
Or sleep I now and think I hear all this ?
What error drives our eyes and ears amiss ?
Until I know this sure uncertainty,
I 'll entertain the offer'd fallacy.
Luciana.   Dromio, go bid the servants spread for
    dinner.
Dromio of Syracuse.   O, for my beads ! I cross me
    for a sinner.
This is the fairy land : O spite of spites !
We talk with goblins, owls and sprites :
If we obey them not, this will ensue,
They 'll suck our breath or pinch us black and blue.
Luciana.   Why pratest thou to thyself and an-
    swer' st not ?
Dromio, thou drone, thou snail, thou slug, thou sot !
Dromio of Syracuse.   I am transformed, master,
    am I not ?
Antipholus of Syracuse.   I think thou art in mind,
    and so am I.
Dromio of Syracuse.   Nay, master, both in mind
    and in my shape.
Antipholus of Syracuse.   Thou hast thine own form.
Dromio of Syracuse.   No, I am an ape.

Luciana.   If thou art changed to aught, 'tis to an
    ass.
Dromio of Syracuse.   'Tis true ; she rides me and
    I long for grass.
'Tis so, I am an ass ;   else it could never be
But I should know her as well as she knows me.
Adriana.   Come, come, no longer will I be a fool,
To put the finger in the eye and weep,
Whilst man and master laugh my woes to scorn.
Come, sir, to dinner.   Dromio, keep the gate.
Husband, I 'll dine above with you to-day
And shrive you of a thousand idle pranks.
Sirrah, if any ask you for your master,
Say he dines forth and let no creature enter.
Come, sister.   Dromio, play the porter well.
Antipholus of Syracuse.   Am I in earth, in heaven,
    or in hell ?
Sleeping or waking ?   mad or well-advised ?
Known unto these, and to myself disguised !
I 'll say as they say and persever so
And in this mist at all adventures go.
Dromio of Syracuse.   Master, shall I be porter
    at the gate ?
Adriana.   Ay ;   and let none enter, lest I break
    your pate.
Luciana.   Come, come, Antipholus, we dine too
    late.   [*Exeunt.*

ACT III.

SCENE I.   *Before the house of* Antipholus *of*
            Ephesus.

Enter Antipholus *of Ephesus,* Dromio *of Ephesus,*
            Angelo, *and* Balthazar.

Antipholus of Ephesus.

Good Signior Angelo, you must excuse us all ;
    My wife is shrewish, when I keep not hours :
    Say that I linger'd with you at your shop
To see the making of her carcanet
And that to-morrow you will bring it home.
But here 's a villain that would face me down
He met me on the mart and that I beat him
And charged him with a thousand marks in gold
And that I did deny my wife and house.
Thou drunkard, thou, what didst thou mean by this ?
Dromio of Ephesus.   Say what you will, sir, but I
    know what I know ;
That you beat me at the mart, I have your hand to
    show :
If the skin were parchment and the blows you gave
    were ink,
Your own handwriting would tell you what I think.
Antipholus of Ephesus.   I think thou art an ass.
Dromio of Ephesus.   Marry, so it doth appear
By the wrongs I suffer and the blows I bear.
I should kick, being kick'd ; and, being at that pass,
You would keep from my heels and beware of an ass.
Antipholus of Ephesus.   You 're sad, Signior
    Balthazar : pray God our cheer
May answer my good will and your good welcome
    here.
Balthazar.   I hold your dainties cheap, sir, and
    your welcome dear.
Antipholus of Ephesus.   O, Signior Balthazar, either
    at flesh or fish,
A table full of welcome makes scarce one dainty dish.
Balthazar.   Good meat, sir, is common ; that
    every churl affords.
Antipholus of Ephesus.   And welcome more com-
    mon ; for that 's nothing but words.

Balthazar. Small cheer and great welcome makes
a merry feast.
Antipholus of Ephesus. Ay to a niggardly host and
more sparing guest :
But though my cates be mean, take them in good
part ;
Better cheer may you have, but not with better heart.
But, soft ! my door is lock'd. Go bid them let us in.
Dromio of Ephesus. Maud, Bridget, Marian,
Cicely, Gillian, Ginn !
Dromio of Syracuse. [*Within*] Mome, malt-horse,
capon, coxcomb, idiot, patch !
Either get thee from the door or sit down at the hatch.
Dost thou conjure for wenches, that thou call'st for
such store,
When one is one too many ? Go get thee from the
door.
Dromio of Ephesus. What patch is made our
porter ? My master stays in the street.
Dromio of Syracuse. [*Within*] Let him walk from
whence he came, lest he catch cold on 's feet.
Antipholus of Ephesus. Who talks within there ?
ho, open the door !
Dromio of Syracuse. [*Within*] Right, sir ; I 'll
tell you when, an you 'll tell me wherefore.
Antipholus of Ephesus. Wherefore ? for my dinner :
I have not dined to-day.
Dromio of Syracuse. [*Within*] Nor to-day here
you must not ; come again when you may.
Antipholus of Ephesus. What art thou that keepest
me out from the house I owe ?
Dromio of Syracuse. [*Within*] The porter for
this time, sir, and my name is Dromio.
Dromio of Ephesus. O villain ! thou hast stolen
both mine office and my name.
The one ne'er got me credit, the other mickle blame.
If thou hadst been Dromio to-day in my place,
Thou wouldst have changed thy face for a name or
thy name for an ass.
Luce. [*Within*] What a coil is there, Dromio ?
who are those at the gate ?
Dromio of Ephesus. Let my master in, Luce.
Luce. [*Within*] Faith, no ; he comes too late :
And so tell your master.
Dromio of Ephesus. O Lord, I must laugh !
Have at you with a proverb—Shall I set in my staff ?
Luce. [*Within*] Have at you with another ;
that 's—When ? can you tell ?
Dromio of Syracuse. [*Within*] If thy name be
call'd Luce,—Luce, thou hast answer'd him well.
Antipholus of Ephesus. Do you hear, you minion ?
you 'll let us in, I hope ?
Luce. [*Within*] I thought to have ask'd you.
Dromio of Syracuse. [*Within*] And you said no.
Dromio of Ephesus. So, come, help : well struck !
there was blow for blow.
Antipholus of Ephesus. Thou baggage, let me in.
Luce. [*Within*] Can you tell for whose sake ?
Dromio of Ephesus. Master, knock the door hard.
Luce. [*Within*] Let him knock till it ache.
Antipholus of Ephesus. You 'll cry for this,
minion, if I beat the door down.
Luce. [*Within*] What needs all that, and a pair
of stocks in the town ?
Adriana. [*Within*] Who is that at the door that
keeps all this noise ?
Dromio of Syracuse. [*Within*] By my troth,
your town is troubled with unruly boys.
Antipholus of Ephesus. Are you there, wife ? you
might have come before.
Adriana. [*Within*] Your wife, sir knave ! go

get you from the door.
Dromio of Ephesus. If you went in pain, master,
this ' knave ' would go sore.
Angelo. Here is neither cheer, sir, nor welcome :
we would fain have either.
Balthazar. In debating which was best, we shall
part with neither.
Dromio of Ephesus. They stand at the door,
master ; bid them welcome hither.
Antipholus of Ephesus. There is something in
the wind, that we cannot get in.
Dromio of Ephesus. You would say so, master,
if your garments were thin.
Your cake there is warm within ; you stand here in
the cold :
It would make a man mad as a buck, to be so bought
and sold.
Antipholus of Ephesus. Go fetch me something :
I 'll break ope the gate.
Dromio of Syracuse. [*Within*] Break any break-
ing here, and I 'll break your knave's pate.
Dromio of Ephesus. A man may break a word
with you, sir, and words are but wind,
Ay, and break it in your face, so he break it not
behind.
Dromio of Syracuse. [*Within*] It seems thou
want'st breaking : out upon thee, hind !
Dromio of Ephesus. Here 's too much ' out upon
thee ! ' I pray thee, let me in.
Dromio of Syracuse. [*Within*] Ay, when fowls
have no feathers and fish have no fin.
Antipholus of Ephesus. Well, I 'll break in : go
borrow me a crow.
Dromio of Ephesus. A crow without feather ?
Master, mean you so ?
For a fish without a fin, there 's a fowl without a
feather :
If a crow help us in, sirrah, we 'll pluck a crow
together.
Antipholus of Ephesus. Go get thee gone ; fetch
me an iron crow.
Balthazar. Have patience, sir ; O, let it not be so !
Herein you war against your reputation
And draw within the compass of suspect
The unviolated honour of your wife.
Once this,—your long experience of her wisdom,
Her sober virtue, years and modesty,
Plead on her part some cause to you unknown ;
And doubt not, sir, but she will well excuse
Why at this time the doors are made against you.
Be ruled by me : depart in patience,
And let us to the Tiger all to dinner,
And about evening come yourself alone
To know the reason of this strange restraint.
If by strong hand you offer to break in
Now in the stirring passage of the day,
A vulgar comment will be made of it,
And that supposed by the common rout
Against your yet ungalled estimation
That may with foul intrusion enter in
And dwell upon your grave when you are dead ;
For slander lives upon succession,
For ever housed where it gets possession.
Antipholus of Ephesus. You have prevail'd : I
will depart in quiet,
And, in despite of mirth, mean to be merry.
I know a wench of excellent discourse,
Pretty and witty, wild and yet, too, gentle :
There will we dine. This woman that I mean,
My wife—but, I protest, without desert—
Hath oftentimes upbraided me withal :

To her will we to dinner. [*To Angelo*] Get you
    home
And fetch the chain ; by this I know 'tis made :
Bring it, I pray you, to the Porpentine ;
For there 's the house : that chain will I bestow—
Be it for nothing but to spite my wife—
Upon mine hostess there : good sir, make haste.
Since mine own doors refuse to entertain me,
I 'll knock elsewhere, to see if they 'll disdain me.
    Angelo. I 'll meet you at that place some hour
    hence.
    Antipholus of Ephesus. Do so. This jest shall
    cost me some expense.   [*Exeunt.*

SCENE II.   *The same.*

Enter LUCIANA *and* ANTIPHOLUS *of Syracuse.*

    Luciana. And may it be that you have quite
    forgot
A husband's office ? shall, Antipholus,
Even in the spring of love, thy love-springs rot ?
Shall love, in building, grow so ruinous ?
If you did wed my sister for her wealth,
    Then for her wealth's sake use her with more
    kindness :
Or if you like elsewhere, do it by stealth ;
    Muffle your false love with some show of blindness :
Let not my sister read it in your eye ;
    Be not thy tongue thy own shame's orator ;
Look sweet, speak fair, become disloyalty ;
    Apparel vice like virtue's harbinger ;
Bear a fair presence, though your heart be tainted ;
    Teach sin the carriage of a holy saint ;
Be secret-false : what need she be acquainted ?
    What simple thief brags of his own attaint ?
'Tis double wrong, to truant with your bed
And let her read it in thy looks at board :
Shame hath a bastard fame, well managed ;
    Ill deeds are doubled with an evil word.
Alas, poor women ! make us but believe,
    Being compact of credit, that you love us ;
Though others have the arm, show us the sleeve ;
    We in your motion turn and you may move us.
Then, gentle brother, get you in again ;
    Comfort my sister, cheer her, call her wife :
'Tis holy sport to be a little vain,
    When the sweet breath of flattery conquers strife.
    Antipholus of Syracuse. Sweet mistress,—what
    your name is else, I know not,
Nor by what wonder you do hit of mine,—
Less in your knowledge and your grace you show not
Than our earth's wonder, more than earth divine.
Teach me, dear creature, how to think and speak ;
    Lay open to my earthy-gross conceit,
Smother'd in errors, feeble, shallow, weak,
    The folded meaning of your words' deceit.
Against my soul's pure truth why labour you
To make it wander in an unknown field ?
Are you a god ? would you create me new ?
Transform me then, and to your power I 'll yield.
But if that I am I, then well I know
    Your weeping sister is no wife of mine,
Nor to her bed no homage do I owe :
    Far more, far more to you do I decline.
O, train me not, sweet mermaid, with thy note,
    To drown me in thy sister's flood of tears :
Sing, siren, for thyself and I will dote :
    Spread o'er the silver waves thy golden hairs,
And as a bed I 'll take them and there lie,
    And in that glorious supposition think

He gains by death that hath such means to die :
Let Love, being light, be drowned if she sink !
    Luciana. What, are you mad, that you do reason
    so ?
    Antipholus of Syracuse. Not mad, but mated ;
    how, I do not know.
    Luciana. It is a fault that springeth from your eye.
    Antipholus of Syracuse. For gazing on your beams,
    fair sun, being by.
    Luciana. Gaze where you should, and that will
    clear your sight.
    Antipholus of Syracuse. As good to wink, sweet
    love, as look on night.
    Luciana. Why call you me love ? call my sister so.
    Antipholus of Syracuse. Thy sister's sister.
    Luciana.   That 's my sister.
    Antipholus of Syracuse.   No ;
It is thyself, mine own self's better part,
Mine eye's clear eye, my dear heart's dearer heart,
My food, my fortune and my sweet hope's aim,
My sole earth's heaven and my heaven's claim.
    Luciana. All this my sister is, or else should be.
    Antipholus of Syracuse. Call thyself sister, sweet,
    for I am thee.
Thee will I love and with thee lead my life :
Thou hast no husband yet nor I no wife.
Give me thy hand.
    Luciana.   O, soft, sir ! hold you still :
I 'll fetch my sister, to get her good will.   [*Exit.*

Enter DROMIO *of Syracuse.*

    Antipholus of Syracuse. Why, how now, Dromio !
where runn'st thou so fast ?
    Dromio of Syracuse. Do you know me, sir ? am
I Dromio ? am I your man ? am I myself ?
    Antipholus of Syracuse. Thy art Dromio, thou art
my man, thou art thyself.
    Dromio of Syracuse. I am an ass, I am a woman's
man and besides myself.
    Antipholus of Syracuse. What woman's man ? and
how besides thyself ?
    Dromio of Syracuse. Marry, sir, besides myself,
I am due to a woman ; one that claims me, one that
haunts me, one that will have me.
    Antipholus of Syracuse. What claim lays she to
thee ?
    Dromio of Syracuse. Marry, sir, such claim as
you would lay to your horse ; and she would have
me as a beast : not that, I being a beast, she would
have me ; but that she, being a very beastly creature,
lays claim to me.
    Antipholus of Syracuse. What is she ?
    Dromio of Syracuse. A very reverent body ; ay,
such a one as a man may not speak of without he
say ' Sir-reverence.' I have but lean luck in the
match, and yet is she a wondrous fat marriage.
    Antipholus of Syracuse. How dost thou mean a
fat marriage ?
    Dromio of Syracuse. Marry, sir, she 's the kitchen
wench and all grease ; and I know not what use to
put her to but to make a lamp of her and run from
her by her own light. I warrant, her rags and the
tallow in them will burn a Poland winter : if she
lives till doomsday, she 'll burn a week longer than
the whole world.
    Antipholus of Syracuse. What complexion is she
of ?
    Dromio of Syracuse. Swart, like my shoe, but her
face nothing like so clean kept : for why, she sweats ;
a man may go over shoes in the grime of it.

Antipholus of Syracuse. That 's a fault that water will mend.

Dromio of Syracuse. No, sir, 'tis in grain ; Noah's flood could not do it.

Antipholus of Syracuse. What 's her name ?

Dromio of Syracuse. Nell, sir ; but her name and three quarters, that 's an ell and three quarters, will not measure her from hip to hip.

Antipholus of Syracuse. Then she bears some breadth ?

Dromio of Syracuse. No longer from head to foot than from hip to hip : she is spherical, like a globe ; I could find out countries in her.

Antipholus of Syracuse. In what part of her body stands Ireland ?

Dromio of Syracuse. Marry, sir, in her buttocks : I found it out by the bogs.

Antipholus of Syracuse. Where Scotland ?

Dromio of Syracuse. I found it by the barrenness ; hard in the palm of the hand.

Antipholus of Syracuse. Where France ?

Dromio of Syracuse. In her forehead ; armed and reverted, making war against her hair.

Antipholus of Syracuse. Where England ?

Dromio of Syracuse. I looked for the chalky cliffs, but I could find no whiteness in them ; but I guess it stood in her chin, by the salt rheum that ran between France and it.

Antipholus of Syracuse. Where Spain ?

Dromio of Syracuse. Faith, I saw it not ; but I felt it hot in her breath.

Antipholus of Syracuse. Where America, the Indies ?

Dromio of Syracuse. Oh, sir, upon her nose, all o'er embellished with rubies, carbuncles, sapphires, declining their rich aspect to the hot breath of Spain ; who sent whole armadoes of caracks to be ballast at her nose.

Antipholus of Syracuse. Where stood Belgia, the Netherlands ?

Dromio of Syracuse. Oh, sir, I did not look so low. To conclude, this drudge, or diviner, laid claim to me ; called me Dromio ; swore I was assured to her ; told me what privy marks I had about me, as, the mark of my shoulder, the mole in my neck, the great wart on my left arm, that I amazed ran from her as a witch :

And, I think, if my breast had not been made of
      faith and my heart of steel,
She had transform'd me to a curtal dog and made me
      turn i' the wheel.

Antipholus of Syracuse. Go hie thee presently,
      post to the road :
An if the wind blow any way from shore,
I will not harbour in this town to-night :
If any bark put forth, come to the mart,
Where I will walk till thou return to me.
If every one knows us and we know none,
'Tis time, I think, to trudge, pack and be gone.

Dromio of Syracuse. As from a bear a man would
      run for life,
So fly I from her that would be my wife.   [*Exit.*

Antipholus of Syracuse. There 's none but witches
      to inhabit here ;
And therefore 'tis high time that I were hence.
She that doth call me husband, even my soul
Doth for a wife abhor. But her fair sister,
Possess'd with such a gentle sovereign grace,
Of such enchanting presence and discourse,
Hath almost made me traitor to myself :
But, lest myself be guilty to self-wrong,

I 'll stop mine ears against the mermaid's song.

Enter ANGELO *with the chain.*

Angelo. Master Antipholus,—

Antipholus of Syracuse. Ay, that 's my name.

Angelo. I know it well, sir : lo, here is the chain.
I thought to have ta'en you at the Porpentine :
The chain unfinish'd made me stay thus long.

Antipholus of Syracuse. What is your will that I
      shall do with this ?

Angelo. What please yourself, sir : I have made
      it for you.

Antipholus of Syracuse. Made it for me, sir ! I
      bespoke it not.

Angelo. Not once, nor twice, but twenty times
      you have.
Go home with it and please your wife withal ;
And soon at supper-time I 'll visit you
And then receive my money for the chain.

Antipholus of Syracuse. I pray you, sir, receive
      the money now,
For fear you ne'er see chain nor money more.

Angelo. You are a merry man, sir : fare you
      well.   [*Exit.*

Antipholus of Syracuse. What I should think of
      this, I cannot tell :
But this I think, there 's no man is so vain
That would refuse so fair an offer'd chain.
I see a man here needs not live by shifts,
When in the streets he meets such golden gifts.
I 'll to the mart and there for Dromio stay :
If any ship put out, then straight away.   [*Exit.*

ACT IV.

SCENE I. *A public place.*

Enter Second Merchant, ANGELO, *and an* Officer.

Second Merchant.

Y
ou know since Pentecost the sum is due,
And since I have not much importuned you ;
Nor now I had not, but that I am bound
To Persia and want guilders for my voyage :
Therefore make present satisfaction,
Or I 'll attach you by this officer.

Angelo. Even just the sum that I do owe to you
Is growing to me by Antipholus,
And in the instant that I met with you
He had of me a chain : at five o'clock
I shall receive the money for the same.
Pleaseth you walk with me down to his house,
I will discharge my bond and thank you too.

Enter ANTIPHOLUS *of Ephesus and* DROMIO *of*
      Ephesus *from the courtezan's.*

Officer. That labour may you save : see where
      he comes.

Antipholus of Ephesus. While I go to the gold-
      smith's house, go thou
And buy a rope's end : that will I bestow
Among my wife and her confederates,
For locking me out of my doors by day,
But, soft ! I see the goldsmith. Get thee gone ;
Buy thou a rope and bring it home to me.

Dromio of Ephesus. I buy a thousand pound a
      year : I buy a rope.   [*Exit.*

Antipholus of Ephesus. A man is well holp up
      that trusts to you :

I promised your presence and the chain ;
But neither chain nor goldsmith came to me.
Belike you thought our love would last too long,
If it were chain'd together, and therefore came not.
  Angelo. Saving your merry humour, here 's the
    note
How much your chain weighs to the utmost carat,
The fineness of the gold and chargeful fashion,
Which doth amount to three odd ducats more
Than I stand debted to this gentleman :
I pray you, see him presently discharged,
For he is bound to sea and stays but for it.
  Antipholus of Ephesus. I am not furnish'd with
    the present money ;
Besides, I have some business in the town.
Good signior, take the stranger to my house
And with you take the chain and bid my wife
Disburse the sum on the receipt thereof :
Perchance I will be there as soon as you.
  Angelo. Then you will bring the chain to her
    yourself ?
  Antipholus of Ephesus. No ; bear it with you,
    lest I come not time enough.
  Angelo. Well, sir, I will. Have you the chain
    about you ?
  Antipholus of Ephesus. An if I have not, sir, I
    hope you have ;
Or else you may return without your money.
  Angelo. Nay, come, I pray you, sir, give me the
    chain :
Both wind and tide stays for this gentleman,
And I, to blame, have held him here too long.
  Antipholus of Ephesus. Good Lord ! you use this
    dalliance to excuse
Your breach of promise to the Porpentine.
I should have chid you for not bringing it,
But, like a shrew, you first begin to brawl.
  Second Merchant. The hour steals on ; I pray you,
    sir, dispatch.
  Angelo. You hear how he importunes me ;—
    the chain !
  Antipholus of Ephesus. Why, give it to my wife
    and fetch your money.
  Angelo. Come, come, you know I gave it you
    even now.
Either send the chain or send me by some token.
  Antipholus of Ephesus. Fie, now you run this
    humour out of breath,
Come, where 's the chain ? I pray you, let me see it.
  Second Merchant. My business cannot brook this
    dalliance.
Good sir, say whether you 'll answer me or no :
If not, I 'll leave him to the officer.
  Antipholus of Ephesus. I answer you ! what
    should I answer you ?
  Angelo. The money that you owe me for the
    chain.
  Antipholus of Ephesus. I owe you none till I
    receive the chain.
  Angelo. You know I gave it you half an hour
    since.
  Antipholus of Ephesus. You gave me none : you
    wrong me much to say so.
  Angelo. You wrong me more, sir, in denying it :
Consider how it stands upon my credit.
  Second Merchant. Well, officer, arrest him at my
    suit.
  Officer. I do ; and charge you in the duke's name
    to obey me.
  Angelo. This touches me in reputation.
Either consent to pay this sum for me

Or I attach you by this officer.
  Antipholus of Ephesus. Consent to pay thee that
    I never had !
Arrest me, foolish fellow, if thou darest.
  Angelo. Here is thy fee ; arrest him, officer.
I would not spare my brother in this case,
If he should scorn me so apparently.
  Officer. I do arrest you, sir : you hear the suit.
  Antipholus of Ephesus. I do obey thee till I give
    thee bail.
But, sirrah, you shall buy this sport as dear
As all the metal in your shop will answer.
  Angelo. Sir, sir, I shall have law in Ephesus,
To your notorious shame ; I doubt it not.

    Enter DROMIO *of Syracuse, from the bay.*

  Dromio of Syracuse. Master, there is a bark of
    Epidamnum
That stays but till her owner comes aboard
And then, sir, she bears away. Our fraughtage, sir,
I have convey'd aboard and I have bought
The oil, the balsamum and aqua-vitæ.
The ship is in her trim : the merry wind
Blows fair from land : they stay for nought at all
But for their owner, master, and yourself.
  Antipholus of Ephesus. How now ! a madman !
    why, thou peevish sheep,
What ship of Epidamnum stays for me ?
  Dromio of Syracuse. A ship you sent me to, to
    hire waftage.
  Antipholus of Ephesus. Thou drunken slave, I
    sent thee for a rope
And told thee to what purpose and what end.
  Dromio of Syracuse. You sent me for a rope's end
    as soon :
You sent me to the bay, sir, for a bark.
  Antipholus of Ephesus. I will debate this matter
    at more leisure
And teach your ears to list me with more heed.
To Adriana, villain, hie thee straight :
Give her this key, and tell her, in the desk
That 's cover'd o'er with Turkish tapestry
There is a purse of ducats ; let her send it :
Tell her I am arrested in the street
And that shall bail me : hie thee, slave, be gone !
On, officer, to prison till it come.

    [*Exeunt Second Merchant, Angelo,*
    Officer, and Antipholus of Ephesus.
  Dromio of Syracuse. To Adriana ! that is where
    we dined,
Where Dowsabel did claim me for her husband :
She is too big, I hope, for me to compass.
Thither I must, although against my will,
For servants must their masters' minds fulfil.

                      [*Exit.*

SCENE II. *The house of* ANTIPHOLUS *of Ephesus.*

    Enter ADRIANA *and* LUCIANA.

  Adriana. Ah, Luciana, did he tempt thee so ?
    Mightst thou perceive austerely in his eye
That he did plead in earnest ? yea or no ?
Look'd he or red or pale, or sad or merrily ?
What observation madest thou in this case
Of his heart's meteors tilting in his face ?
  Luciana. First he denied you had in him no right.
  Adriana. He meant he did me none ; the more
    my spite.

Luciana. Then swore he that he was a stranger here.
Adriana. And true he swore, though yet forsworn he were.
Luciana. Then pleaded I for you.
Adriana.   And what said he ?
Luciana. That love I begg'd for you he begg'd of me.
Adriana. With what persuasion did he tempt thy love ?
Luciana. With words that in an honest suit might move.
First he did praise my beauty, then my speech.
Adriana. Didst speak him fair ?
Luciana.   Have patience, I beseech.
Adriana. I cannot, nor I will not, hold me still ;
My tongue, though not my heart, shall have his will.
He is deformed, crooked, old and sere,
Ill-faced, worse bodied, shapeless everywhere ;
Vicious, ungentle, foolish, blunt, unkind,
Stigmatical in making, worse in mind.
Luciana. Who would be jealous then of such a one ?
No evil lost is wail'd when it is gone.
Adriana. Ah, but I think him better than I say,
And yet would herein others' eyes were worse.
Far from her nest the lapwing cries away :
My heart prays for him, though my tongue do curse.

Enter DROMIO *of Syracuse.*

Dromio of Syracuse. Here ! go ; the desk, the purse ! sweet, now, make haste.
Luciana. How hast thou lost thy breath ?
Dromio of Syracuse.   By running fast.
Adriana. Where is thy master, Dromio ? is he well ?
Dromio of Syracuse. No, he 's in Tartar limbo, worse than hell.
† A devil in an everlasting garment hath him ;
One whose hard heart is button'd up with steel ;
A fiend, a fury, pitiless and rough ;
A wolf, nay, worse, a fellow all in buff ;
A back-friend, a shoulder-clapper, one that countermands
The passages of alleys, creeks and narrow lands ;
A hound that runs counter and yet draws dryfoot well ;
One that before the judgement carries poor souls to hell.
Adriana. Why, man, what is the matter ?
Dromio of Syracuse. I do not know the matter : he is 'rested on the case.
Adriana. What, is he arrested ? Tell me at whose suit.
Dromio of Syracuse. I know not at whose suit he is arrested well ;
But he 's in a suit of buff which 'rested him, that can I tell.
Will you send him, mistress, redemption, the money in his desk ?
Adriana. Go fetch it, sister. [*Exit Luciana.*]
This I wonder at,
That he, unknown to me, should be in debt.
Tell me, was he arrested on a band ?
Dromio of Syracuse. Not on a band, but on a stronger thing ;
A chain, a chain ! Do you not hear it ring ?
Adriana. What, the chain ?
Dromio of Syracuse. No, no, the bell : 'tis time that I were gone :

It was two ere I left him, and now the clock strikes one.
Adriana. The hours come back ! that did I never hear.
Dromio of Syracuse. O, yes ; if any hour meet a sergeant, a' turns back for very fear.
Adriana. As if Time were in debt ! how fondly dost thou reason !
Dromio of Syracuse. Time is a very bankrupt and owes more than he 's worth to season.
Nay, he 's a thief too : have you not heard men say,
That Time comes stealing on by night and day ?
If Time be in debt and theft, and a sergeant in the way,
Hath he not reason to turn back an hour in a day ?

Re-enter LUCIANA *with a purse.*

Adriana. Go, Dromio ; there 's the money, bear it straight,
And bring thy master home immediately.
Come, sister : I am press'd down with conceit—
Conceit, my comfort and my injury.   [*Exeunt.*

SCENE III.   *A public place.*

Enter ANTIPHOLUS *of Syracuse.*

Antipholus of Syracuse. There 's not a man I meet but doth salute me
As if I were their well-acquainted friend ;
And every one doth call me by my name.
Some tender money to me ; some invite me ;
Some other give me thanks for kindnesses ;
Some offer me commodities to buy :
Even now a tailor call'd me in his shop
And show'd me silks that he had bought for me
And therewithal took measure of my body.
Sure, these are but imaginary wiles
And Lapland sorcerers inhabit here.

Enter DROMIO *of Syracuse.*

Dromio of Syracuse. Master, here 's the gold you sent me for. What, have you got the picture of old Adam new-apparelled ?
Antipholus of Syracuse. What gold is this ? what Adam dost thou mean ?
Dromio of Syracuse. Not that Adam that kept the Paradise, but that Adam that keeps the prison : he that goes in the calf's skin that was killed, for the Prodigal ; he that came behind you, sir, like an evil angel, and bid you forsake your liberty.
Antipholus of Syracuse. I understand thee not.
Dromio of Syracuse. No ? why, 'tis a plain case : he that went, like a bass-viol, in a case of leather ; the man, sir, that, when gentlemen are tired, gives them a sob and 'rests them ; he, sir, that takes pity on decayed men and gives them suits of durance ; he that sets up his rest to do more exploits with his mace than a morris-pike.
Antipholus of Syracuse. What, thou meanest an officer ?
Dromio of Syracuse. Ay, sir, the sergeant of the band ; he that brings any man to answer it that breaks his band ; one that thinks a man always going to bed and says ' God give you good rest ! '
Antipholus of Syracuse. Well, sir, there rest in your foolery,
Is there any ship puts forth to-night ? may we be gone ?

Dromio of Syracuse. Why, sir I brought you word an hour since that the bark Expedition put forth to-night ; and then were you hindered by the sergeant, to tarry for the hoy Delay. Here are the angels that you sent for to deliver you.
Antipholus of Syracuse. The fellow is distract, and so am I ;
And here we wander in illusions :
Some blessed power deliver us from hence !

Enter a Courtezan.

Courtezan. Well met, well met, Master Antipholus.
I see, sir, you have found the goldsmith now :
Is that the chain you promised me to-day ?
Antipholus of Syracuse. Satan, avoid ! I charge thee, tempt me not.
Dromio of Syracuse. Master, is this Mistress Satan ?
Antipholus of Syracuse. It is the devil.
Dromio of Syracuse. Nay, she is worse, she is the devil's dam ; and here she comes in the habit of a light wench : and thereof comes that the wenches say ' God damn me ; ' that 's as much to say ' God make me a light wench.' It is written, they appear to men like angels of light : light is an effect of fire, and fire will burn ; ergo, light wenches will burn. Come not near her.
Courtezan. Your man and you are marvellous merry, sir.
Will you go with me ? We 'll mend our dinner here ?
Dromio of Syracuse. Master, if you do, expect spoonmeat : or bespeak a long spoon.
Antipholus of Syracuse. Why, Dromio ?
Dromio of Syracuse. Marry, he must have a long spoon that must eat with the devil.
Antipholus of Syracuse. Avoid then, fiend ! what tell'st thou me of supping ?
Thou art, as you are all, a sorceress :
I conjure thee to leave me and be gone.
Courtezan. Give me the ring of mine you had at dinner,
Or, for my diamond, the chain you promised,
And I 'll be gone, sir, and not trouble you.
Dromio of Syracuse. Some devils ask but the parings of one's nail,
A rush, a hair, a drop of blood, a pin,
A nut, a cherry-stone ;
But she, more covetous, would have a chain.
Master, be wise : an if you give it her,
The devil will shake her chain and fright us with it.
Courtezan. I pray you, sir, my ring, or else the chain :
I hope you do not mean to cheat me so.
Antipholus of Syracuse. Avaunt, thou witch !
Come, Dromio, let us go.
Dromio of Syracuse. ' Fly pride,' says the peacock : mistress, that you know.
                                    [*Exeunt Ant. S. and Dro. S.*
Courtezan. Now, out of doubt Antipholus is mad,
Else would he never so demean himself.
A ring he hath of mine worth forty ducats,
And for the same he promised me a chain :
Both one and other he denies me now.
The reason that I gather he is mad,
Besides this present instance of his rage,
Is a mad tale he told to-day at dinner,
Of his own doors being shut against his entrance.
Belike his wife, acquainted with his fits,
On purpose shut the doors agains this way.

My way is now to hie home to his house,
And tell his wife that, being lunatic,
He rush'd into my house and took perforce
My ring away. This course I fittest choose ;
For forty ducats is too much to lose.   [*Exit.*

SCENE IV. *A street.*

Enter Antipholus *of Ephesus and the* Officer.

Antipholus of Ephesus. Fear me not, man ; I will not break away :
I 'll give thee, ere I leave thee, so much money,
To warrant thee, as I am 'rested for.
My wife is in a wayward mood to-day,
And will not lightly trust the messenger.
That I should be attach'd in Ephesus,
I tell you, 'twill sound harshly in her ears.

Enter Dromio *of Ephesus with a rope's-end.*

Here comes my man ; I think he brings the money.
How now, sir ! have you that I sent you for ?
Dromio of Ephesus. Here's that, I warrant you, will pay them all.
Antipholus of Ephesus. But where 's the money ?
Dromio of Ephesus. Why, sir, I gave the money for the rope.
Antipholus of Ephesus. Five hundred ducats, villain, for a rope ?
Dromio of Ephesus. I 'll serve you, sir, five hundred at the rate.
Antipholus of Ephesus. To what end did I bid thee hie thee home ?
Dromio of Ephesus. To a rope's-end, sir ; and to that end am I returned.
Antipholus of Ephesus. And to that end, sir, I will welcome you.   [*Beating him.*
Officer. Good sir, be patient.
Dromio of Ephesus. Nay, 'tis for me to be patient ; I am in adversity.
Officer. Good now, hold thy tongue.
Dromio of Ephesus. Nay, rather persuade him to hold his hands.
Antipholus of Ephesus. Thou whoreson, senseless villain !
Dromio of Ephesus. I would I were senseless, sir, that I might not feel your blows.
Antipholus of Ephesus. Thou art sensible in nothing but blows, and so is an ass.
Dromio of Ephesus. I am an ass, indeed ; you may prove it by my long ears. I have served him from the hour of my nativity to this instant, and have nothing at his hands for my service but blows. When I am cold, he heats me with beating ; when I am warm, he cools me with beating : I am waked with it when I sleep ; raised with it when I sit ; driven out of doors with it when I go from home ; welcomed home with it when I return : nay, I bear it on my shoulders, as a beggar wont her brat ; and, I think, when he hath lamed me, I shall beg with it from door to door.
Antipholus of Ephesus. Come, go along ; my wife is coming yonder.

Enter Adriana, Luciana, *the* Courtezan, *and* Pinch.

Dromio of Ephesus. Mistress ' respice finem, respect your end ; or rather, † the prophecy like the parrot, ' beware the rope's-end.'

Antipholus of Ephesus. Wilt thou still talk?
                     [*Beating him.*
Courtezan. How say you now? is not your
husband mad?
Adriana. His incivility confirms no less.
Good Doctor Pinch, you are a conjurer ;
Establish him in his true sense again,
And I will please you what you will demand.
Luciana. Alas, how fiery and how sharp he looks !
Courtezan. Mark how he trembles in his ecstasy !
Pinch. Give me your hand and let me feel your
pulse.
Antipholus of Ephesus. There is my hand, and
let it feel your ear.   [*Striking him.*
Pinch. I charge thee, Satan, housed within this
man,
To yield possession to my holy prayers
And to thy state of darkness hie thee straight :
I conjure thee by all the saints in heaven !
   Antipholus of Ephesus. Peace, doting wizard,
peace ! I am not mad.
   Adriana. O, that thou wert not, poor distressed
soul !
   Antipholus of Ephesus. You minion, you, are
these your customers ?
Did this companion with the saffron face
Revel and feast it at my house to-day,
Whilst upon me the guilty doors were shut
And I denied to enter in my house ?
   Adriana. O husband, God doth know you dined
at home ;
Where would you had remain'd until this time,
Free from these slanders and this open shame !
   Antipholus of Ephesus. Dined at home ! Thou
villain, what sayest thou ?
   Dromio of Ephesus. Sir, sooth to say, you did
not dine at home.
   Antipholus of Ephesus. Were not my doors lock'd
up and I shut out ?
   Dromio of Ephesus. Perdie, your doors were
lock'd and you shut out.
   Antipholus of Ephesus. And did not she herself
revile me there ?
   Dromio of Ephesus. Sans fable, she herself reviled
you there.
   Antipholus of Ephesus. Did not her kitchen-maid
rail, taunt and scorn me ?
   Dromio of Ephesus. Certes, she did ; the kitchen-
vestal scorn'd you.
   Antipholus of Ephesus. And did not I in rage
depart from thence ?
   Dromio of Ephesus. In verity you did ; my bones
bear witness,
That since have felt the vigour of his rage.
   Adriana. Is 't good to soothe him in these con-
traries ?
   Pinch. It is no shame : the fellow finds his vein
And yielding to him humours well his frenzy.
   Antipholus of Ephesus. Thou hast suborn'd the
goldsmith to arrest me.
   Adriana. Alas, I sent you money to redeem you,
By Dromio here, who came in haste for it.
   Dromio of Ephesus. Money by me ! heart and
good-will you might ;
But surely, master, not a rag of money.
   Antipholus of Ephesus. Went'st not thou to her
for a purse of ducats ?
   Adriana. He came to me and I deliver'd it.
   Luciana. And I am witness with her that she did.
   Dromio of Ephesus. God and the rope-maker
bear me witness

That I was sent for nothing but a rope !
   Pinch. Mistress, both man and master is possess'd;
I know it by their pale and deadly looks :
They must be bound and laid in some dark room.
   Antipholus of Ephesus. Say, wherefore didst
thou lock me forth to-day ?
And why dost thou deny the bag of gold ?
   Adriana. I did not, gentle husband, lock thee
forth.
   Dromio of Ephesus. And, gentle master, I received
no gold ;
But I confess, sir, that we were lock'd out.
   Adriana. Dissembling villain, thou speak'st false
in both.
   Antipholus of Ephesus. Dissembling harlot, thou
art false in all
And art confederate with a damned pack
To make a loathsome abject scorn of me :
But with these nails I 'll pluck out these false eyes
That would behold in me this shameful sport.

*Enter three or four, and offer to bind him. He
strives.*

   Adriana. O, bind him, bind him ! let him not
come near me.
   Pinch. More company ! The fiend is strong
within him.
   Luciana. Ay me, poor man, how pale and wan
he looks !
   Antipholus of Ephesus. What, will you murder
me ? Thou gaoler, thou,
I am thy prisoner : wilt thou suffer them
To make a rescue ?
   Officer.   Masters, let him go :
He is my prisoner, and you shall not have him.
   Pinch. Go bind this man, for he is frantic too.
                  [*They offer to bind Dromio E.*
   Adriana. What wilt thou do, thou peevish officer ?
Hast thou delight to see a wretched man
Do outrage and displeasure to himself ?
   Officer. He is my prisoner : if I let him go,
The debt he owes will be required of me.
   Adriana. I will discharge thee ere I go from thee :
Bear me forthwith unto his creditor
And, knowing how the debt grows, I will pay it.
Good master doctor, see him safe convey'd
Home to my house. O most unhappy day !
   Antipholus of Ephesus. O most unhappy strumpet!
   Dromio of Ephesus. Master, I am here enter'd
in bond for you.
   Antipholus of Ephesus. Out on thee, villain !
wherefore dost thou mad me ?
   Dromio of Ephesus. Will you be bound for
nothing ? be mad, good master : cry ' The devil !'
   Luciana. God help, poor souls, how idly they
talk !
   Adriana. Go bear him hence. Sister, go you with
me.   [*Exeunt all but Adriana, Luciana, Officer
                               and Courtezan.*]
Say now, whose suit is he arrested at ?
   Officer. One Angelo, a goldsmith : do you know
him ?
   Adriana. I know the man. What is the sum he
owes ?
   Officer. Two hundred ducats.
   Adriana.   Say, how grows it due ?
   Officer. Due for a chain your husband had of
him.
   Adriana. He did bespeak a chain for me, but
had it not.

Courtezan. When as your husband all in rage
to-day
Came to my house and took away my ring—
The ring I saw upon his finger now—
Straight after did I meet him with a chain.
Adriana. It may be so, but I did never see it.
Come, gaoler, bring me where the goldsmith is :
I long to know the truth hereof at large.

Enter ANTIPHOLUS *of Syracuse with his rapier
drawn, and* DROMIO *of Syracuse.*

Luciana. God, for thy mercy ! they are loose
again.
Adriana. And come with naked swords.
Let 's call more help to have them bound again.
Officer. Away ! they 'll kill us.
                    [*Exeunt all but Ant. S. and Dro. S.*
Antipholus of Syracuse. I see these witches are
afraid of swords.
Dromio of Syracuse. She that would be your wife
now ran from you.
Antipholus of Syracuse. Come to the Centaur ;
fetch our stuff from thence :
I long that we were safe and sound aboard.
Dromio of Syracuse. Faith, stay here this night ;
they will surely do us no harm : you saw they speak
us fair, give us gold : methinks they are such a
gentle nation that, but for the mountain of mad
flesh that claims marriage of me, I could find in my
heart to stay here still and turn witch.
Antipholus of Syracuse. I will not stay to-night
for all the town ;
Therefore away, to get our stuff aboard.   [*Exeunt.*

ACT V.

SCENE I.   *A street before a Priory.*

Enter Second Merchant *and* ANGELO.

Angelo.
I am sorry, sir, that I have hinder'd you ;
  But, I protest, he had the chain of me,
  Though most dishonestly he doth deny it.
Second Merchant. How is the man esteem'd
here in the city ?
Angelo. Of very reverend reputation, sir,
Of credit infinite, highly beloved,
Second to none that lives here in the city :
His word might bear my wealth at any time.
Second Merchant. Speak softly : yonder, as I
think, he walks.

Enter ANTIPHOLUS *of Syracuse and* DROMIO *of
Syracuse.*

Angelo. 'Tis so ; and that self chain about his
neck
Which he forswore most monstrously to have.
Good sir, draw near to me, I 'll speak to him.
Signior Antipholus, I wonder much
That you would put me to this shame and trouble ;
And, not without some scandal to yourself,
With circumstance and oaths so to deny
This chain which now you wear so openly :
Beside the charge, the shame, imprisonment,
You have done wrong to this my honest friend,
Who, but for staying on our controversy,
Had hoisted sail and put to sea to-day :
This chain you had of me ; can you deny it ?

Antipholus of Syracuse. I think I had ; I never
did deny it.
Second Merchant. Yes, that you did, sir, and
forswore it too.
Antipholus of Syracuse. Who heard me to deny
it or forswear it ?
Second Merchant. These ears of mine, thou
know'st, did hear thee.
Fie on thee, wretch ! 'tis pity that thou livest
To walk where any honest men resort.
Antipholus of Syracuse. Thou art a villain to
impeach me thus :
I 'll prove mine honour and mine honesty
Against thee presently, if thou darest stand.
Second Merchant. I dare, and do defy thee for a
villain.   [*They draw.*

Enter ADRIANA, LUCIANA, *the* Courtezan, *and others.*

Adriana. Hold, hurt him not, for God's sake !
he is mad.
Some get within him, take his sword away :
Bind Dromio too, and bear them to my house.
Dromio of Syracuse. Run, master, run ; for
God's sake, take a house !
This is some priory. In, or we are spoil'd !
    [*Exeunt Ant. of S., and Drom. of S. to the Priory.*

Enter the Lady Abbess.

Lady Abbess. Be quiet, people. Wherefore throng
you hither ?
Adriana. To fetch my poor distracted husband
hence.
Let us come in, that we may bind him fast
And bear him home for his recovery.
Angelo. I knew he was not in his perfect wits.
Second Merchant. I am sorry now that I did
draw on him.
Lady Abbess. How long hath this possession
held the man ?
Adriana. This week he hath been heavy, sour,
sad,
And much different from the man he was ;
But till this afternoon his passion
Ne'er brake into extremity of rage.
Lady Abbess. Hath he not lost much wealth by
wreck of sea ?
Buried some dear friend ? Hath not else his eye
Stray'd his affection in unlawful love ?
A sin prevailing much in youthful men,
Who give their eyes the liberty of gazing.
Which of these sorrows is he subject to ?
Adriana. To none of these, except it be the last ;
Namely, some love that drew him oft from home.
Lady Abbess. You should for that have repre-
hended him.
Adriana. Why, so I did,
Lady Abbess.   Ay, but not rough enough.
Adriana. As roughly as my modesty would let
me.
Lady Abbess. Haply, in private.
Adriana.   And in assemblies too.
Lady Abbess. Ay, but not enough.
Adriana. It was the copy of our conference :
In bed he slept not for my urging it ;
At board he fed not for my urging it ;
Alone, it was the subject of my theme ;
In company I often glanced it ;
Still did I tell him it was vile and bad.
Lady Abbess. And thereof came it that the man
was mad :

The venom clamours of a jealous woman
Poisons more deadly than a mad dog's tooth.
It seems his sleeps were hinder'd by thy railing,
And thereof comes it that his head is light.
Thou say'st his meat was sauced with thy upbraidings :
Unquiet meals make ill digestions ;
There of the raging fire of fever bred ;
And what 's a fever but a fit of madness ?
Thou say'st his sports were hinder'd by thy brawls :
Sweet recreation barr'd, what doth ensue
But moody and dull melancholy,
Kinsman to grim and comfortless despair,
And at her heels a huge infectious troop
Of pale distemperatures and foes to life ?
In food, in sport and life-preserving rest
To be disturb'd, would mad or man or beast :
The consequence is then thy jealous fits
Have scared thy husband from the use of wits.
   Luciana.   She never reprehended him but mildly,
When he demean'd himself rough, rude and wildly.
Why bear you these rebukes and answer not ?
   Adriana.   She did betray me to my own reproof.
Good people, enter and lay hold on him.
   Lady Abbess.   No, not a creature enters in my
house.
   Adriana.   Then let your servants bring my husband
forth.
   Lady Abbess.   Neither : he took this place for
sanctuary,
And it shall privilege him from your hands
Till I have brought him to his wits again,
Or lose my labour in assaying it.
   Adriana.   I will attend my husband, be his nurse,
Diet his sickness, for it is my office,
And will have no attorney but myself ;
And therefore let me have him home with me.
   Lady Abbess.   Be patient ; for I will not let him
stir
Till I have used the approved means I have,
With wholesome syrups, drugs and holy prayers,
To make of him a formal man again :
It is a branch and parcel of mine oath,
A charitable duty of my order.
Therefore depart and leave him here with me.
   Adriana.   I will not hence and leave my husband
here :
And ill it doth beseem your holiness
To separate the husband and the wife.
   Lady Abbess.   Be quiet and depart : thou shalt
not have him.   [*Exit.*
   Luciana.   Complain unto the duke of this in-
dignity.
   Adriana.   Come, go : I will fall prostrate at his
feet
And never rise until my tears and prayers
Have won his grace to come in person hither
And take perforce my husband from the abbess.
   Second Merchant.   By this, I think, the dial points
at five :
Anon, I 'm sure, the duke himself in person
Comes this way to the melancholy vale,
The place of death and sorry execution,
Behind the ditches of the abbey here.
   Angelo.   Upon what cause ?
   Second Merchant.   To see a reverend Syracusian
merchant,
Who put unluckily into this bay
Against the laws and statutes of this town,
Beheaded publicly for his offence.
   Angelo.   See where they come : we will behold
his death.

   Luciana.   Kneel to the duke before he pass the
abbey.

Enter DUKE, *attended ;* ÆGEON *bareheaded :
with the* Headsman *and other* Officers.

   Duke.   Yet once again proclaim it publicly,
If any friend will pay the sum for him,
He shall not die ; so much we tender him.
   Adriana.   Justice, most sacred duke, against the
abbess !
   Duke.   · She is a virtuous and a reverend lady :
It cannot be that she hath done thee wrong.
   Adriana.   May it please your grace, Antipholus
my husband,
Whom I made lord of me and all I had,
At your important letters,—this ill day
A most outrageous fit of madness took him ;
That desperately he hurried through the street,—
With him his bondman, all as mad as he,—
Doing displeasure to the citizens
By rushing in their houses, bearing thence
Rings, jewels, anything his rage did like.
Once did I get him bound and sent him home,
Whilst to take order for the wrongs I went
That here and there his fury had committed.
Anon, I wot not by what strong escape,
He broke from those that had the guard of him ;
And with his mad attendant and himself,
Each one with ireful passion, with drawn swords,
Met us again and madly bent on us
Chased us away, till raising of more aid
We came again to bind them.   Then they fled
Into this abbey, whither we pursued them :
And here the abbess shuts the gates on us
And will not suffer us to fetch him out,
Nor send him forth that we may bear him hence.
Therefore, most gracious duke, with thy command
Let him be brought forth and borne hence for help.
   Duke.   Long since thy husband served me in
my wars,
And I to thee engaged a prince's word,
When thou didst make him master of thy bed,
To do him all the grace and good I could.
Go, some of you, knock at the abbey-gate
And bid the lady abbess come to me.
I will determine this before I stir.

Enter a Servant.

   Servant.   O mistress, mistress, shift and save
yourself !
My master and his man are both broke loose,
Beaten the maids a-row and bound the doctor,
Whose beard they have singed off with brands of
fire ;
And ever, as it blazed, they threw on him
Great pails of puddled mire to quench the hair :
My master preaches patience to him and the while
His man with scissors nicks him like a fool,
And sure, unless you send some present help,
Between them both they will kill the conjurer.
   Adriana.   Peace, fool ! thy master and his man
are here,
And that is false thou dost report to us.
   Servant.   Mistress, upon my life, I tell you true ;
I have not breathed almost since I did see it.
He cries for you and vows, if he can take you,
To scorch your face and to disfigure you.
                                      [*Cry within.*
Hark, hark ! I hear him, mistress : fly, be gone !

Duke. Come, stand by me ; fear nothing.
Guard with halberds !
Adriana. Ay me, it is my husband ! Witness you,
That he is borne about invisible :
Even now we housed him in the abbey here ;
And now he 's there, past thought of human reason.

Enter ANTIPHOLUS of Ephesus *and* DROMIO of
Ephesus.

Antipholus of Ephesus. Justice, most gracious
duke, O, grant me justice !
Even for the service that long since I did thee,
When I bestrid thee in the wars and took
Deep scars to save thy life ; even for the blood
That then I lost for thee, now grant me justice.
Ægeon. Unless the fear of death doth make me
dote,
I see my son Antipholus and Dromio.
Antipholus of Ephesus. Justice, sweet prince,
against that woman there !
She whom thou gavest to me to be my wife,
That hath abused and dishonour'd me
Even in the strength and height of injury !
Beyond imagination is the wrong
That she this day hath shameless thrown on me.
Duke. Discover how, and thou shalt find me just.
Antipholus of Ephesus. This day, great duke, she
shut the doors upon me,
While she with harlots feasted in my house.
Duke. A grievous fault ! Say, woman, didst
thou so ?
Adriana. No, my good lord : myself, he and my
sister
To-day did dine together. So befall my soul
As this is false he burdens me withal !
Luciana. Ne'er may I look on day, nor sleep on
night,
But she tells to your highness simple truth !
Angelo. O perjured woman ! They are both
forsworn :
In this the madman justly chargeth them.
Antipholus of Ephesus. My liege, I am advised
what I say,
Neither disturbed with the effect of wine,
Nor heady-rash, provoked with raging ire,
Albeit my wrongs might make one wiser mad.
This woman lock'd me out this day from dinner :
That goldsmith there, were he not pack'd with her,
Could witness it, for he was with me then ;
Who parted with me to go fetch a chain,
Promising to bring it to the Porpentine,
Where Balthazar and I did dine together.
Our dinner done, and he not coming thither,
I went to seek him : in the street I met him
And in his company that gentleman.
There did this perjured goldsmith swear me down
That I this day of him received the chain,
Which, God he knows, I saw not : for the which
He did arrest me with an officer.
I did obey, and sent my peasant home
For certain ducats : he with none return'd.
Then fairly I bespoke the officer
To go in person with me to my house.
By the way we met
My wife, her sister, and a rabble more
Of vile confederates. Along with them
They brought one Pinch, a hungry lean-faced villain,
A mere anatomy, a mountebank,
A threadbare juggler and a fortune-teller,
A needy, hollow-eyed, sharp-looking wretch,
A living-dead man : this pernicious slave

Forsooth, took on him as a conjurer,
And, gazing in mine eyes, feeling my pulse,
And with no face, as 'twere, outfacing me,
Cries out, I was possess'd. Then all together
They fell upon me, bound me, bore me thence
And in a dark and dankish vault at home
They left me and my man, both bound together ;
Till, gnawing with my teeth my bonds in sunder,
I gain'd my freedom and immediately
Ran hither to your grace ; whom I beseech
To give me ample satisfaction
For these deep shames and great indignities.
Angelo. My lord, in truth, thus far I witness
with him,
That he dined not at home, but was lock'd out.
Duke. But had he such a chain of thee or no ?
Angelo. He had, my lord : and when he ran in
here,
These people saw the chain about his neck.
Second Merchant. Besides, I will be sworn these
ears of mine
Heard you confess you had the chain of him
After you first forswore it on the mart :
And thereupon I drew my sword on you ;
And then you fled into this abbey here,
From whence, I think, you are come by miracle.
Antipholus of Ephesus. I never came within these
abbey-walls,
Nor ever didst thou draw thy sword on me :
I never saw the chain, so help me Heaven !
And this is false you burden me withal.
Duke. Why, what an intricate impeach is this !
I think you all have drunk of Circe's cup.
If here you housed him, here he would have been ;
If he were mad, he would not plead so coldly :
You say he dined at home ; the goldsmith here
Denies that saying. Sirrah, what say you ?
Dromio of Ephesus. Sir, he dined with her there,
at the Porpentine.
Courtezan. He did, and from my finger snatch'd
that ring.
Antipholus of Ephesus. 'Tis true, my liege ; this
ring I had of her.
Duke. Saw'st thou him enter at the abbey here ?
Courtezan. As sure, my liege, as I do see your
grace.
Duke. Why, this is strange. Go call the abbess
hither.
I think you are all mated or stark mad.
                        [*Exit one to the Abbess.*
Ægeon. Most mighty duke, vouchsafe me speak
a word :
Haply I see a friend will save my life
And pay the sum that may deliver me.
Duke. Speak freely, Syracusian, what thou wilt.
Ægeon. Is not your name, sir, call'd Antipholus ?
And is not that your bondman, Dromio ?
Dromio of Ephesus. Within this hour I was his
bondman, sir,
But he, I thank him, gnaw'd in two my cords :
Now am I Dromio and his man unbound.
Ægeon. I am sure you both of you remember me.
Dromio of Ephesus. Ourselves we do remember,
sir, by you ;
For lately we were bound, as you are now.
You are not Pinch's patient, are you, sir ?
Ægeon. Why look you strange on me ? you know
me well.
Antipholus of Ephesus. I never saw you in my
life till now.

Ægeon. O, grief hath changed me since you saw me last,
And careful hours with time's deformed hand
Have written strange defeatures in my face :
But tell me yet, dost thou not know my voice ?
Antipholus of Ephesus. Neither.
Ægeon. Dromio, nor thou ?
Dromio of Ephesus. No, trust me, sir, nor I.
Ægeon. I am sure thou dost.
Dromio of Ephesus. Ay, sir, but I am sure I do not ; and whatsoever a man denies, you are now bound to believe him.
Ægeon. Not know my voice ! O time's extremity,
Hast thou so crack'd and splitted my poor tongue
In seven short years, that here my only son
Knows not my feeble key of untuned cares ?
Though now this grained face of mine be hid
In sap-consuming winter's drizzled snow
And all the conduits of my blood froze up,
Yet hath my night of life some memory,
My wasting lamps some fading glimmer left,
My dull deaf ears a little use to hear :
All these old witnesses—I cannot err—
Tell me thou art my son Antipholus.
Antipholus of Ephesus. I never saw my father in my life.
Ægeon. But seven years since, in Syracusa, boy,
Thou know'st we parted : but perhaps, my son,
Thou shamest to acknowledge me in misery.
Antipholus of Ephesus. The duke and all that know me in the city
Can witness with me that it is not so :
I ne'er saw Syracusa in my life.
Duke. I tell thee, Syracusian, twenty years
Have I been patron to Antipholus,
During which time he ne'er saw Syracusa :
I see thy age and dangers make thee dote.

Re-enter Abbess *with* ANTIPHOLUS *of Syracuse and* DROMIO *of Syracuse.*

Abbess. Most mighty duke, behold a man much wrong'd. [*All gather to see them.*
Adriana. I see two husbands, or mine eyes deceive me.
Duke. One of these men is Genius to the other ;
And so of these. Which is the natural man,
And which the spirit ? who deciphers them ?
Dromio of Syracuse. I, sir, am Dromio : command him away.
Dromio of Ephesus. I, sir, am Dromio : pray, let me stay.
Antipholus of Syracuse. Ægeon art thou not ? or else his ghost ?
Dromio of Syracuse. O, my old master ! who hath bound him here ?
Abbess. Whoever bound him, I will loose his bonds
And gain a husband by his liberty.
Speak, old Ægeon, if thou be'st the man
That hadst a wife once call'd Æmilia
That bore thee at a burden two fair sons :
O, if thou be'st the same Ægeon, speak,
And speak unto the same Æmilia !
Ægeon. If I dream not, thou art Æmilia :
If thou art she, tell me where is that son
That floated with thee on the fatal raft ?
Abbess. By men of Epidamnum he and I
And the twin Dromio all were taken up ;
But by and by rude fishermen of Corinth
By force took Dromio and my son from them

And me they left with those of Epidamnum.
What then became of them I cannot tell ;
I to this fortune that you see me in.
Duke. Why, here begins his morning story right :
These two Antipholuses, these two so like,
And these two Dromios, one in semblance,—
Besides her urging of her wreck at sea,—
These are the parents to these children,
Which accidentally are met together.
Antipholus, thou camest from Corinth first ?
Antipholus of Syracuse. No, sir, not I ; I came from Syracuse.
Duke. Stay, stand apart ; I know not which is which.
Antipholus of Ephesus. I came from Corinth, my most gracious lord,—
Dromio of Ephesus. And I with him.
Antipholus of Ephesus. Brought to this town by that most famous warrior,
Duke Menaphon, your most renowned uncle.
Adriana. Which of you did dine with me to-day ?
Antipholus of Syracuse. I, gentle mistress.
Adriana. And are not you my husband ?
Antipholus of Ephesus. No ; I say nay to that.
Antipholus of Syracuse. And so do I ; yet did she call me so :
And this fair gentlewoman, her sister here,
Did call me brother. [*To Luciana*] What I told you then,
I hope I shall have leisure to make good ;
If this be not a dream I see and hear.
Angelo. That is the chain, sir, which you had of me.
Antipholus of Syracuse. I think it be, sir ; I deny it not.
Antipholus of Ephesus. And you, sir, for this chain arrested me.
Angelo. I think I did, sir ; I deny it not.
Adriana. I sent you money, sir, to be your bail,
By Dromio ; but I think he brought it not.
Dromio of Ephesus. No, none by me.
Antipholus of Syracuse. This purse of ducats I received from you
And Dromio my man did bring them me.
I see we still did meet each other's man,
And I was ta'en for him, and he for me,
And thereupon these ERRORS are arose.
Antipholus of Ephesus. These ducats pawn I for my father here.
Duke. It shall not need ; thy father hath his life.
Courtezan. Sir, I must have that diamond from you.
Antipholus of Ephesus. There, take it ; and much thanks for my good cheer.
Abbess. Renowned duke, vouchsafe to take the pains
To go with us into the abbey here
And hear at large discoursed all our fortunes :
And all that are assembled in this place,
That by this sympathized one day's error
Have suffer'd wrong, go keep us company,
And we shall make full satisfaction.
Thirty-three years have I but gone in travail
Of you, my sons ; and till this present hour
My heavy burthen ne'er delivered.
The duke, my husband and my children both,
And you the calendars of their nativity,
Go to a gossips' feast, and go with me ;
After so long grief, such festivity !

Duke. With all my heart, I 'll gossip at this feast.

[*Exeunt all but Antipholus of Syracuse, Antipholus of Ephesus, Dromio of Syracuse, and Dromio of Ephesus.*

Dromio of Syracuse. Master, shall I fetch your stuff from shipboard ?

Antipholus of Ephesus. Dromio, what stuff of mine hast thou embark'd ?

Dromio of Syracuse. Your goods that lay at host, sir, in the Centaur.

Antipholus of Syracuse. He speaks to me. I am your master, Dromio :
Come, go with us ; we 'll look to that anon :
Embrace thy brother there ; rejoice with him.

[*Exeunt Antipholus of Syracuse and Antipholus of Ephesus.*

Dromio of Syracuse. There is a fat friend at your master's house,
That kitchen'd me for you to-day at dinner :
She now shall be my sister, not my wife.

Dromio of Ephesus. Methinks you are my glass, and not my brother :
I see by you I am a sweet-faced youth.
Will you walk in to see their gossiping ?

Dromio of Syracuse. Not I, sir ; you are my elder.

Dromio of Ephesus. That 's a question : how shall we try it ?

Dromio of Syracuse. We 'll draw cuts for the senior : till then lead thou first.

Dromio of Ephesus. Nay, then, thus :
We came into the world like brother and brother ;
And now let 's go hand in hand, not one before another. [*Exeunt.*

MUCH ADO ABOUT NOTHING

DRAMATIS PERSONÆ

DON PEDRO, *prince of Arragon.*
DON JOHN, *his bastard brother.*
CLAUDIO, *a young lord of Florence.*
BENEDICK, *a young lord of Padua.*
LEONATO, *governor of Messina.*
ANTONIO, *his brother.*
BALTHASAR, *attendant on* DON PEDRO.
CONRADE, } *followers of* DON JOHN.
BORACHIO, }
FRIAR FRANCIS.
DOGBERRY, *a constable.*
VERGES, *a headborough.*
A Sexton.
A Boy.

HERO, *daughter to* LEONATO.
BEATRICE, *niece to* LEONATO.
MARGARET, } *gentlewomen attending on* HERO.
URSULA, }

Messengers, Watch, Attendants, &c.

SCENE : Messina.

ACT I.

SCENE I. *Before* LEONATO'S *house.*

Enter LEONATO, HERO, *and* BEATRICE, *with a* Messenger.

Leonato.

I learn in this letter that Don Peter of Arragon comes this night to Messina.
Messenger. He is very nearby this : he was not three leagues off when I left him.
Leonato. How many gentlemen have you lost in this action ?
Messenger. But few of any sort, and none of name.
Leonato. A victory is twice itself when the achiever brings home full numbers. I find here that Don Peter hath bestowed much honour on a young Florentine called Claudio.
Messenger. Much deserved on his part and equally remembered by Don Pedro : he hath borne himself beyond the promise of his age, doing, in the figure of a lamb, the feats of a lion : he hath indeed better bettered expectation than you must expect of me to tell you how.
Leonato. He hath an uncle here in Messina will be very much glad of it.

Messenger. I have already delivered him letters and there appears much joy in him ; even so much that joy could not show itself modest enough without a badge of bitterness.
Leonato. Did he break out into tears ?
Messenger. In great measure.
Leonato. A kind overflow of kindness : there are no faces truer than those that are so washed. How much better is it to weep at joy than to joy at weeping !
Beatrice. I pray you, is Signior Mountanto returned from the wars or no ?
Messenger. I know none of that name, lady : there was none such in the army of any sort.
Leonato. What is he that you ask for, niece ?
Hero. My cousin means Signior Benedick of Padua.
Messenger. O, he 's returned ; and as pleasant as ever he was.
Beatrice. He set up his bills here in Messina and challenged Cupid at the flight ; and my uncle's fool, reading the challenge, subscribed for Cupid, and challenged him at the bird-bolt. I pray you, how many hath he killed and eaten in these wars ? But how many hath he killed ? for indeed I promised to eat all of his killing.
Leonato. Faith, niece, you tax Signior Benedick too much ; but he 'll be meet with you, I doubt it not.
Messenger. He hath done good service, lady, in these wars.
Beatrice. You had musty victual, and he hath holp to eat it : he is a very valiant trencherman ; he hath an excellent stomach.
Messenger. And a good soldier too, lady.
Beatrice. And a good soldier to a lady : but what is he to a lord ?
Messenger. A lord to a lord, a man to a man ; stuffed with all honourable virtues.
Beatrice. It is so, indeed ; he is no less than a stuffed man : but for the stuffing,—well, we are all mortal.
Leonato. You must not, sir, mistake my niece. There is a kind of merry war betwixt Signior Benedick and her : they never meet but there 's a skirmish of wit between them.
Beatrice. Alas ! he gets nothing by that. In our last conflict four of his five wits went halting off, and now is the whole man governed with one : so that if he have wit enough to keep himself warm, let him bear it for a difference between himself and his horse ; for it is all the wealth that he hath left, to be known a reasonable creature. Who is his companion now ? He hath every month a new sworn brother.
Messenger. Is 't possible ?
Beatrice. Very easily possible : he wears his faith but as the fashion of his hat ; it ever changes with the next block.
Messenger. I see, lady, the gentleman is not in your books.

Beatrice. No ; an he were, I would burn my study. But, I pray you, who is his companion ? Is there no young squarer now that will make a voyage with him to the devil ?

Messenger. He is most in the company of the right noble Claudio.

Beatrice. O Lord, he will hang upon him like a disease : he is sooner caught than the pestilence, and the taker runs presently mad. God help the noble Claudio ! if he have caught the Benedick, it will cost him a thousand pound ere a' be cured.

Messenger. I will hold friends with you, lady.

Beatrice. Do, good friend.

Leonato. You will never run mad, niece.

Beatrice. No, not till a hot January.

Messenger. Don Pedro is approached.

Enter Don Pedro, Don John, Claudio, Benedick, *and* Bathasar.

Don Pedro. Good Signior Leonato, you are come to meet your trouble : the fashion of the world is to avoid cost, and you encounter it.

Leonato. Never came trouble to my house in the likeness of your grace : for trouble being gone, comfort should remain ; but when you depart from me, sorrow abides and happiness takes his leave.

Don Pedro. You embrace your charge too willingly. I think this is your daughter.

Leonato. Her mother hath many times told me so.

Benedick. Were you in doubt, sir, that you asked her ?

Leonato. Signior Benedick, no ; for then were you a child.

Don Pedro. You have it full, Benedick : we may guess by this what you are, being a man. Truly, the lady fathers herself. Be happy, lady ; for you are like an honourable father.

Benedick. If Signior Leonato be her father, she would not have his head on her shoulders for all Messina, as like him as she is.

Beatrice. I wonder that you will still be talking, Signior Benedick : nobody marks you.

Benedick. What, my dear Lady Disdain ! are you yet living ?

Beatrice. Is it possible disdain should die while she hath such meet food to feed it as Signior Benedick ? Courtesy itself must convert to disdain, if you come in her presence.

Benedick. Then is courtesy a turncoat. But it is certain I am loved of all ladies, only you excepted : and I would I could find in my heart that I had not a hard heart ; for, truly, I love none.

Beatrice. A dear happiness to women : they would else have been troubled with a pernicious suitor. I thank God and my cold blood, I am of your humour for that : I had rather hear my dog bark at a crow than a man swear he loves me.

Benedick. God keep your ladyship still in that mind ! so some gentleman or other shall 'scape a predestinate scratched face.

Beatrice. Scratching could not make it worse, an 'twere such a face as yours were.

Benedick. Well, you are a rare parrot-teacher.

Beatrice. A bird of my tongue is better than a beast of yours.

Benedick. I would my horse had the speed of your tongue, and so good a continuer. But keep your way, i' God's name ; I have done.

Beatrice. You always end with a jade's trick : I know you of old.

Don Pedro. That is the sum of all, Leonato. Signior Claudio and Signior Benedick, my dear friend Leonato hath invited you all. I tell him we shall stay here at the least a month ; and he heartily prays some occasion may detain us longer. I dare swear he is no hypocrite, but prays from his heart.

Leonato. If you swear, my lord, you shall not be forsworn. [*To Don John*] Let me bid you welcome, my lord : being reconciled to the prince your brother, I owe you all duty.

Don John. I thank you : I am not of many words, but I thank you.

Leonato. Please it your grace lead on ?

Don Pedro. Your hand, Leonato ; we will go together.

[*Exeunt all except Benedick and Claudio.*

Claudio. Benedick, didst thou note the daughter of Signior Leonato ?

Benedick. I noted her not ; but I looked on her.

Claudio. Is she not a modest young lady ?

Benedick. Do you question me, as an honest man should do, for my simple true judgement : or would you have me speak after my custom, as being a professed tyrant to their sex ?

Claudio. No ; I pray thee speak in sober judgement.

Benedick. Why, i' faith, methinks she 's too low for a high praise, too brown for a fair praise and too little for a great praise : only this commendation I can afford her, that were she other than she is, she were unhandsome ; and being no other but as she is, I do not like her.

Claudio. Thou thinkest I am in sport : I pray thee tell me truly how thou likest her.

Benedick. Would you buy her, that you inquire after her ?

Claudio. Can the world buy such a jewel ?

Benedick. Yea, and a case to put it into. But speak you this with a sad brow ? or do you play the flouting Jack, to tell us Cupid is a good hare-finder and Vulcan a rare carpenter ? Come, in what key shall a man take you, to go in the song ?

Claudio. In mine eye she is the sweetest lady that ever I looked on.

Benedick. I can see yet without spectacles and I see no such matter : there 's her cousin, an she were not possessed with a fury, exceeds her as much in beauty as the first of May doth the last of December. But I hope you have no intent to turn husband, have you ?

Claudio. I would scarce trust myself, though I had sworn the contrary, if Hero would be my wife.

Benedick. Is 't come to this ? In faith, hath not the world one man but he will wear his cap with suspicion ? Shall I never see a bachelor of threescore again ? Go to, i' faith ; an thou wilt needs thrust thy neck into a yoke, wear the print of it and sigh away Sundays. Look ; Don Pedro is returned to seek you.

Re-enter Don Pedro.

Don Pedro. What secret hath held you here, that you followed not to Leonato's ?

Benedick. I would your grace would constrain me to tell.

Don Pedro. I charge thee on thy allegiance.

Benedick. You hear, Count Claudio : I can be secret as a dumb man ; I would have you think so ; but, on my allegiance, mark you this, on my allegiance. He is in love. With who ? now that is your grace's

part. Mark how short his answer is ;—With Hero,
Leonato's short daughter.

Claudio. If this were so, so were it uttered.

Benedick. Like the old tale, my lord : ' it is not
so, nor 'twas not so, but, indeed, God forbid it
should be so.'

Claudio. If my passion change not shortly, God
forbid it should be otherwise.

Don Pedro. Amen, if you love her ; for the lady
is very well worthy.

Claudio. You speak this to fetch me in, my lord.

Don Pedro. By my troth, I speak my thought.

Claudio. And, in faith, my lord, I spoke mine.

Benedick. And, by my two faiths and troths, my
lord, I spoke mine.

Claudio. That I love her, I feel.

Don Pedro. That she is worthy, I know.

Benedick. That I neither feel how she should be
loved nor know how she should be worthy, is the
opinion that fire cannot melt out of me : I will die
in it at the stake.

Don Pedro. Thou wast ever an obstinate heretic
in the despite of beauty.

Claudio. And never could maintain his part but
in the force of his will.

Benedick. That a woman conceived me, I thank
her ; that she brought me up, I likewise give her
most humble thanks : but that I will have a recheat
winded in my forehead, or hang my bugle in an
invisible baldrick, all women shall pardon me.
Because I will not do them the wrong to mistrust
any, I will do myself the right to trust none ; and the
fine is, for the which I may go the finer, I will live a
bachelor.

Don Pedro. I shall see thee, ere I die, look pale
with love.

Benedick. With anger, with sickness, or with
hunger, my lord, not with love : prove that ever I
lose more blood with love than I will get again with
drinking, pick out mine eyes with a ballad-maker's
pen, and hang me up at the door of a brothel-house
for the sign of blind Cupid.

Don Pedro. Well, if ever thou dost fall from this
faith, thou wilt prove a notable argument.

Benedick. If I do, hang me in a bottle like a cat
and shoot at me ; and he that hits me, let him be
clapped on the shoulder, and called Adam.

Don Pedro. Well, as time shall try :
' In time the savage bull doth bear the yoke.'

Benedick. The savage bull may ; but if ever the
sensible Benedick bear it, pluck off the bull's horns
and set them in my forehead : and let me be vilely
painted, and in such great letters as they write ' Here
is good horse to hire,' let them signify under my sign
' Here you may see Benedick the married man.'

Claudio. If this should ever happen, thou wouldst
be horn-mad.

Don Pedro. Nay, if Cupid have not spent all his
quiver in Venice, thou wilt quake for this shortly.

Benedick. I look for an earthquake too, then.

Don Pedro. Well, you will temporize with the
hours. In the meantime, good Signior Benedick,
repair to Leonato's : commend me to him and tell
him I will not fail him at supper ; for indeed he hath
made great preparation.

Benedick. I have almost matter enough in me for
such an embassage ; and so I commit you—

Claudio. To the tuition of God : From my house,
if I had it,—

Don Pedro. The sixth of July : Your loving friend,
Benedick.

Benedick. Nay, mock not, mock not. The body
of your discourse is sometime guarded with fragments,
and the guards are but slightly basted on neither :
ere you flout old ends any further, examine your
conscience : and so I leave you.   [*Exit.*

Claudio. My liege, your highness now may do
me good.

Don Pedro. My love is thine to teach : teach it
but how,
And thou shalt see how apt it is to learn
Any hard lesson that may do thee good.

Claudio. Hath Leonato any son, my lord ?

Don Pedro. No child but Hero ; she 's his only
heir.
Dost thou affect her, Claudio ?

Claudio.   O, my lord,
When you went onward on this ended action,
I look'd upon her with a soldier's eye,
That liked, but had a rougher task in hand
Than to drive liking to the name of love :
But now I am return'd and that war-thoughts
Have left their places vacant, in their rooms
Come thronging soft and delicate desires,
All prompting me how fair young Hero is,
Saying, I liked her ere I went to wars.

Don Pedro. Thou wilt be like a lover presently
And tire the hearer with a book of words,
If thou dost love fair Hero, cherish it,
And I will break with her and with her father
And thou shalt have her. Was 't not to this end
That thou began'st to twist so fine a story ?

Claudio. How sweetly do you minister to love,
That know love's grief by his complexion !
But lest my liking might too sudden seem,
I would have salved it with a longer treatise.

Don Pedro. What need the bridge much broader
than the flood ?
The fairest grant is the necessity.
Look, what will serve is fit : 'tis once, thou lovest,
And I will fit thee with the remedy.
I know we shall have revelling to-night ;
I will assume thy part in some disguise
And tell fair Hero I am Claudio,
And in her bosom I 'll unclasp my heart
And take her hearing prisoner with the force
And strong encounter of my amorous tale ;
Then after to her father will I break ;
And the conclusion is, she shall be thine.
In practice let us put it presently.   [*Exeunt.*

SCENE II.   *A room in* LEONATO'S *house.*

Enter LEONATO *and* ANTONIO, *meeting.*

Leonato. How now, brother ! Where is my
cousin, your son ? hath he provided this music ?

Antonio. He is very busy about it. But, brother,
I can tell you strange news that you yet dreamt
not of.

Leonato. Are they good ?

Antonio. As the event stamps them : but they
have a good cover ; they show well outward. The
prince and Count Claudio, walking in a thick-
pleached alley in mine orchard, were thus much
overheard by a man of mine : the prince discovered
to Claudio that he loved my niece your daughter
and meant to acknowledge it this night in a dance ;
and if he found her accordant, he meant to take the
present time by the top and instantly break with
you of it.

Leonato. Hath the fellow any wit that told you
this ?

Antonio. A good sharp fellow : I will send for him ; and question him yourself.

Leonato. No, no ; we will hold it as a dream till it appear itself : but I will acquaint my daughter withal, that she may be the better prepared for an answer, if peradventure this be true. Go you and tell her of it. [*Enter attendants.*] Cousins, you know what you have to do. O, I cry you mercy, friend ; go you with me, and I will use your skill. Good cousin, have a care this busy time. [*Exeunt.*

SCENE III. *The same.*

Enter DON JOHN *and* CONRADE.

Conrade. What the good-year, my lord ! why are you thus out of measure sad ?

Don John. There is no measure in the occasion that breeds ; therefore the sadness is without limit.

Conrade. You should hear reason.

Don John. And when I have heard it, what blessing brings it ?

Conrade. If not a present remedy, at least a patient sufferance.

Don John. I wonder that thou, being, as thou sayest thou art, born under Saturn, goest about to apply a moral medicine to a mortifying mischief. I cannot hide what I am : I must be sad when I have cause and smile at no man's jests, eat when I have stomach and wait for no man's leisure, sleep when I am drowsy and tend on no man's business, laugh when I am merry and claw no man in his humour.

Conrade. Yea, but you must not make the full show of this till you may do it without controlment. You have of late stood out against your brother, and he hath ta'en you newly into his grace ; where it is impossible you should take true root but by the fair weather that you make yourself : it is needful that you frame the season for your own harvest.

Don John. I had rather be a canker in a hedge than a rose in his grace, and it better fits my blood to be disdained of all than to fashion a carriage to rob love from any : in this, though I cannot be said to be a flattering honest man, it must not be denied but I am a plain-dealing villain. I am trusted with a muzzle and enfranchised with a clog ; therefore I have decreed not to sing in my cage. If I had my mouth, I would bite ; if I had my liberty, I would do my liking : in the meantime let me be that I am and seek not to alter me.

Conrade. Can you make no use of your discontent ?

Don John. I make all use of it, for I use it only. Who comes here ?

Enter BORACHIO.

What news, Borachio ?

Borachio. I came yonder from a great supper : the prince your brother is royally entertained by Leonato ; and I can give you intelligence of an intended marriage.

Don John. Will it serve for any model to build mischief on ? What is he for a fool that betroths himself to unquietness ?

Borachio. Marry, it is your brother's right hand.

Don John. Who ? the most exquisite Claudio ?

Borachio. Even he.

Don John. A proper squire ! And who, and who ? which way looks he ?

Borachio. Marry, on Hero, the daughter and heir of Leonato.

Don John. A very forward March-chick ! How came you to this ?

Borachio. Being entertained for a perfumer, as I was smoking a musty room, comes me the prince and Claudio, hand in hand, in sad conference : I whipt me behind the arras ; and there heard it agreed upon that the prince should woo Hero for himself, and having obtained her, give her to Count Claudio.

Don John. Come, come, let us thither : this may prove food to my displeasure. That young start-up hath all the glory of my overthrow : if I can cross him any way, I bless myself every way. You are both sure, and will assist me ?

Conrade. To the death, my lord.

Don John. Let us to the great supper : their cheer is the greater that I am subdued. Would the cook were of my mind ! Shall we go prove what 's to be done ?

Borachio. We 'll wait upon your lordship.

[*Exeunt.*

ACT II.

SCENE I. *A hall in* LEONATO'S *house.*

Enter LEONATO, ANTONIO, HERO, BEATRICE, *and others.*

Leonato.

W AS not Count John here at supper ?

Antonio. I saw him not.

Beatrice. How tartly that gentleman looks ! I never can see him but I am heart-burned an hour after.

Hero. He is of a very melancholy disposition.

Beatrice. He were an excellent man that were made just in the midway between him and Benedick : the one is too like an image and says nothing, and the other too like my lady's eldest son, evermore tattling.

Leonato. Then half Signior Benedick's tongue in Count John's mouth, and half Count John's melancholy in Signior Benedick's face,—

Beatrice. With a good leg and a good foot, uncle, and money enough in his purse, such a man would win any woman in the world, if a' could get her good-will.

Leonato. By my troth, niece, thou wilt never get thee a husband, if thou be so shrewd of thy tongue.

Antonio. In faith, she's too curst.

Beatrice. Too curst is more than curst : I shall lessen God's sending that way ; for it is said, ' God sends a curst cow short horns ;' but to a cow too curst he sends none.

Leonato. So, by being too curst, God will send you no horns.

Beatrice. Just, if he send me no husband ; for the which blessing I am at him upon my knees every morning and evening. Lord, I could not endure a husband with a beard on his face : I had rather lie in the woollen.

Leonato. You may light on a husband that hath no beard.

Beatrice. What should I do with him ? dress him in my apparel and make him my waiting-gentlewoman ? He that hath a beard is more than a youth, and he that hath no beard is less than a man : and he that is more than a youth is not for me, and he that is less than a man, I am not for him : therefore I will even take sixpence in earnest of the bear-ward, and lead his apes into hell.

Leonato. Well, then, go you into hell?

Beatrice. No, but to the gate; and there will the devil meet me, like an old cuckold, with horns on his head, and say ' Get you to heaven, Beatrice, get you to heaven; here 's no place for you maids : ' so deliver I up my apes, and away to Saint Peter for the heavens; he shows me where the bachelors sit, and there live we as merry as the day is long.

Antonio. [*To Hero*] Well, niece, I trust you will be ruled by your father.

Beatrice. Yes, faith; it is my cousin's duty to make curtsy and say ' Father, as it please you.' But yet for all that, cousin, let him be a handsome fellow, or else make another curtsy and say ' Father, as it please me.'

Leonato. Well, niece, I hope to see you one day fitted with a husband.

Beatrice. Not till God make men of some other metal than earth. Would it not grieve a woman to be overmastered with a piece of valiant dust? to make an account of her life to a clod of wayward marl? No, uncle, I 'll none : Adam's sons are my brethren; and, truly, I hold it a sin to match in my kindred.

Leonato. Daughter, remember what I told you : if the prince do solicit you in that kind, you know your answer.

Beatrice. The fault will be in the music, cousin, if you be not wooed in good time : if the prince be too important, tell him there is measure in every thing and so dance out the answer. For, hear me, Hero : wooing, wedding, and repenting, is as a Scotch jig, a measure, and a cinque pace : the first suit is hot and hasty, like a Scotch jig, and full as fantastical; the wedding, mannerly-modest, as a measure, full of state and ancientry; and then comes repentance and, with his bad legs, falls into the cinque pace faster and faster, till he sink into his grave.

Leonato. Cousin, you apprehend passing shrewdly.

Beatrice. I have a good eye, uncle; I can see a church by daylight.

Leonato. The revellers are entering, brother : make good room.   [*All put on their masks.*

Enter DON PEDRO, CLAUDIO, BENEDICK, BAL-
THASAR, DON JOHN, BORACHIO, MARGARET,
URSULA, *and others, masked.*

Don Pedro. Lady, will you walk about with your friend?

Hero. So you walk softly and look sweetly and say nothing, I am yours for the walk; and especially when I walk away.

Don Pedro. With me in your company?

Hero. I may say so, when I please.

Don Pedro. And when please you to say so?

Hero. When I like your favour; for God defend the lute should be like the case !

Don Pedro. My visor is Philemon's roof; within the house is Jove.

Hero. Why, then, your visor should be thatched.

Don Pedro. Speak low, if you speak love.
                              [*Drawing her aside.*

Balthasar. Well, I would you did like me.

Margaret. So would not I, for your own sake; for I have many ill qualities.

Balthasar. Which is one?

Margaret. I say my prayers aloud.

Balthasar. I love you the better : the hearers may cry, Amen.

Margaret. God match me with a good dancer !

Balthasar. Amen.

Margaret. And God keep him out of my sight when the dance is done ! Answer, clerk.

Balthasar. No more words : the clerk is answered.

Ursula. I know you well enough; you are Signior Antonio.

Antonio. At a word, I am not.

Ursula. I know you by the waggling of your head.

Antonio. To tell you true, I counterfeit him.

Ursula. You could never do him so ill-well, unless you were the very man. Here 's his dry hand up and down : you are he, you are he.

Antonio. At a word, I am not.

Ursula. Come, come, do you think I do not know you by your excellent wit? can virtue hide itself? Go to, mum, you are he : graces will appear, and there's an end.

Beatrice. Will you not tell me who told you so?

Benedick. No, you shall pardon me.

Beatrice. Nor will you not tell me who you are?

Benedick. Not now.

Beatrice. That I was disdainful, and that I had my good wit out of the ' Hundred Merry Tales : ' —well, this was Signior Benedick that said so.

Benedick. What 's he?

Beatrice. I am sure you know him well enough.

Benedick. Not I, believe me.

Beatrice. Did he never make you laugh?

Benedick. I pray you, what is he?

Beatrice. Why, he is the prince's jester : a very dull fool; only his gift is in devising impossible slanders : none but libertines delight in him; and the commendation is not in his wit, but in his villany; for he both pleases men and angers them, and then they laugh at him and beat him. I am sure he is in the fleet : I would he had boarded me.

Benedick. When I know the gentleman, I 'll tell him what you say.

Beatrice. Do, do : he 'll but break a comparison or two on me; which, peradventure not marked or not laughed at, strikes him into melancholy; and then there 's a partridge wing saved, for the fool will eat no supper that night. [*Music.*] We must follow the leaders.

Benedick. In every good thing.

Beatrice. Nay, if they lead to any ill, I will leave them at the next turning.

              [*Dance. Then exeunt all except Don
                  John, Borachio, and Claudio.*

Don John. Sure my brother is amorous on Hero and hath withdrawn her father to break with him about it. The ladies follow her and but one visor remains.

Borachio. And that is Claudio : I know him by his bearing.

Don John. Are not you Signior Benedick?

Claudio. You know me well; I am he.

Don John. Signior, you are very near my brother in his love : he is enamoured on Hero; I pray you, dissuade him from her : she is no equal for his birth : you may do the part of an honest man in it.

Claudio. How know you he loves her?

Don John. I heard him swear his affection.

Borachio. So did I too; and he swore he would marry her to-night.

Don John. Come, let us to the banquet.

              [*Exeunt Don John and Borachio.*

Claudio. Thus answer I in name of Benedick,
But hear these ills news with the ears of Claudio.
'Tis certain so; the prince wooes for himself.

Friendship is constant in all other things
Save in the office and affairs of love :
Therefore all hearts in love use their own tongues ;
Let every eye negotiate for itself
And trust no agent ; for beauty is a witch
Against whose charms faith melteth into blood.
This is an accident of hourly proof,
Which I mistrusted not.   Farewell, therefore, Hero !

Re-enter BENEDICK.

Benedick.   Count Claudio ?
Claudio.   Yea, the same.
Benedick.   Come, will you go with me ?
Claudio.   Whither ?
Benedick.   Even to the next willow, about your
own business, county.   What fashion will you wear
the garland of ? about your neck, like an usurer's
chain ? or under your arm, like a lieutenant's scarf ?
You must wear it one way, for the prince hath got
your Hero.
Claudio.   I wish him joy of her.
Benedick.   Why, that 's spoken like an honest
drovier : so they sell bullocks.   But did you think
the prince would have served you thus ?
Claudio.   I pray you, leave me.
Benedick.   Ho ! now you strike like the blind
man : 'twas the boy that stole your meat, and you 'll
beat the post.
Claudio.   If it will not be, I 'll leave you.   [*Exit.*
Benedick.   Alas, poor hurt fowl ! now will he
creep into sedges.   But that my Lady Beatrice should
know me, and not know me !   The prince's fool !
Ha ? It may be I go under that title because I am
merry.   Yea, but so I am apt to do myself wrong ;
I am not so reputed : it is the base, though bitter,
disposition of Beatrice that puts the world into her
person, and so gives me out.   Well, I 'll be revenged
as I may.

Re-enter DON PEDRO.

Don Pedro.   Now, signior, where 's the count ?
did you see him ?
Benedick.   Troth, my lord, I have played the part
of Lady Fame.   I found here as melancholy
as a lodge in a warren : I told him, and I think I
told him true, that your grace had got the good will
of this young lady ; and I offered him my company
to a willow-tree, either to make him a garland, as
being forsaken, or to bind him up a rod, as being
worthy to be whipped.
Don Pedro.   To be whipped !   What 's his fault ?
Benedick.   The flat transgression of a school-boy,
who, being overjoyed with finding a birds' nest,
shows it his companion, and he steals it.
Don Pedro.   Wilt thou make a trust a transgression ?   The transgression is in the stealer.
Benedick.   Yet it had not been amiss the rod had
been made, and the garland too ; for the garland
he might have worn himself, and the rod he might
have bestowed on you, who, as I take it, have stolen
his birds' nest.
Don Pedro.   I will but teach them to sing, and
restore them to the owner.
Benedick.   If their singing answer your saying,
by my faith, you say honestly.
Don Pedro.   The Lady Beatrice hath a quarrel
to you : the gentleman that danced with her told
her she is much wronged by you.
Benedick.   O, she misused me past the endurance

of a block !   an oak but with one green leaf on it
would have answered her ; my very visor began to
assume life and scold with her.   She told me, not
thinking I had been myself, that I was the prince's
jester, that I was duller than a great thaw ; huddling
jest upon jest with such impossible conveyance
upon me that I stood like a man at a mark, with a
whole army shooting at me.   She speaks poniards,
and every word stabs : if her breath were as terrible
as her terminations, there were no living near her ;
she would infect to the north star.   I would not
marry her, though she were endowed with all that
Adam had left him before he transgressed : she would
have made Hercules have turned spit, yea, and have
cleft his club to make the fire too.   Come, talk not
of her : you shall find her the infernal Ate in good
apparel.   I would to God some scholar would
conjure her ; for certainly, while she is here, a man
may live as quiet in hell as in a sanctuary ; and
people sin upon purpose, because they would go
thither ; so, indeed, all disquiet, horror and per-
turbation follows her.
Don Pedro.   Look, here she comes.

Re-enter CLAUDIO, BEATRICE, HERO, *and* LEONATO.

Benedick.   Will your grace command me any
service to the world's end ?   I will go on the slightest
errand now to the Antipodes that you can devise
to send me on ; I will fetch you a toothpicker now
from the furthest inch of Asia, bring you the length
of Prester John's foot, fetch you a hair off the great
Cham's beard, do you any embassage to the Pigmies,
rather than hold three words' conference with this
harpy.   You have no employment for me ?
Don Pedro.   None, but to desire your good
company.
Benedick.   O God, sir, here 's a dish I love not :
I cannot endure my Lady Tongue.   [*Exit.*
Don Pedro.   Come, lady, come ; you have lost
the heart of Signior Benedick.
Beatrice.   Indeed, my lord, he lent it me awhile ;
and I gave him use for it, a double heart for his
single one : marry, once before he won it of me with
false dice, therefore your grace may well say I have
lost it.
Don Pedro.   You have put him down, lady, you
have put him down.
Beatrice.   So I would not he should do me, my
lord, lest I should prove the mother of fools.   I
have brought Count Claudio, whom you sent me
to seek.
Don Pedro.   Why, how now, count !   wherefore
are you sad ?
Claudio.   Not sad, my lord.
Don Pedro.   How then ? sick ?
Claudio.   Neither, my lord.
Beatrice.   The count is neither sad, nor sick, nor
merry, nor well ; but civil count, civil as an orange,
and something of that jealous complexion.
Don Pedro.   I' faith, lady, I think your blazon
to be true ; though, I 'll be sworn, if he be so, his
conceit is false.   Here, Claudio, I have wooed in
thy name, and fair Hero is won : I have broke with
her father, and his good will obtained : name the
day of marriage, and God give thee joy !
Leonato.   Count, take of me my daughter, and
with her my fortunes : his grace hath made the
match, and all grace say Amen to it.
Beatrice.   Speak, count, 'tis your cue.
Claudio.   Silence is the perfectest herald of joy :

I were but little happy, if I could say how much. Lady, as you are mine, I am yours : I give away myself for you and dote upon the exchange.

Beatrice. Speak, cousin ; or, if you cannot, stop his mouth with a kiss, and let not him speak neither.

Don Pedro. In faith, lady, you have a merry heart.

Beatrice. Yea, my lord ; I thank it, poor fool, it keeps on the windy side of care. My cousin tells him in his ear that he is in her heart.

Claudio. And so she doth, cousin.

Beatrice. Good Lord, for alliance ! Thus goes every one to the world but I, and I am sunburnt ; I may sit in a corner and cry heigh-ho for a husband !

Don Pedro. Lady Beatrice, I will get you one.

Beatrice. I would rather have one of your father's getting. Hath your grace ne'er a brother like you ? Your father got excellent husbands, if a maid could come by them.

Don Pedro. Will you have me, lady ?

Beatrice. No, my lord, unless I might have another for working-days : your grace is too costly to wear every day. But, I beseech your grace, pardon me : I was born to speak all mirth and no matter.

Don Pedro. Your silence most offends me, and to be merry best becomes you ; for, out of question, you were born in a merry hour.

Beatrice. No, sure, my lord, my mother cried ; but then there was a star danced, and under that was I born. Cousins, God give you joy !

Leonato. Niece, will you look to those things I told you of ?

Beatrice. I cry you mercy, uncle. By your grace's pardon.   [*Exit.*

Don Pedro. By my troth, a pleasant-spirited lady.

Leonato. There 's little of the melancholy element in her, my lord : she is never sad but when she sleeps, and not ever sad then ; for I have heard my daughter say, she hath often dreamed of unhappiness and waked herself with laughing.

Don Pedro. She cannot endure to hear tell of a husband.

Leonato. O, by no means : she mocks all her wooers out of suit.

Don Pedro. She were an excellent wife for Benedick.

Leonato. O Lord, my lord, if they were but a week married, they would talk themselves mad.

Don Pedro. County Claudio, when mean you to go to church ?

Claudio. To-morrow, my lord : time goes on crutches till love have all his rites.

Leonato. Not till Monday, my dear son, which is hence a just seven-night ; and a time too brief, too, to have all things answer my mind.

Don Pedro. Come, you shake the head at so long a breathing : but, I warrant thee, Claudio, the time shall not go dully by us. I will in the interim undertake one of Hercules' labours ; which is, to bring Signior Benedick and the Lady Beatrice into a mountain of affection the one with the other. I would fain have it a match, and I doubt not but to fashion it, if you three will but minister such assistance as I shall give you direction.

Leonato. My lord, I am for you, though it cost me ten nights' watchings.

Claudio. And I, my lord.

Don Pedro. And you too, gentle Hero ?

Hero. I will do any modest office, my lord, to help my cousin to a good husband.

Don Pedro. And Benedick is not the unhope-fullest husband that I know. Thus far can I praise him ; he is of a noble strain, of approved valour and confirmed honesty. I will teach you how to humour your cousin, that she shall fall in love with Benedick ; and I, with your two helps, will so practise on Benedick that, in despite of his quick wit and his queasy stomach, he shall fall in love with Beatrice. If we can do this, Cupid is no longer an archer : his glory shall be ours, for we are the only love-gods. Go in with me, and I will tell you my drift.   [*Exeunt.*

SCENE II. *The same.*

Enter DON JOHN *and* BORACHIO.

Don John. It is so ; the Count Claudio shall marry the daughter of Leonato.

Borachio. Yea, my lord ; but I can cross it.

Don John. Any bar, any cross, any impediment will be medicinable to me : I am sick in displeasure to him, and whatsoever comes athwart his affection ranges evenly with mine. How canst thou cross this marriage ?

Borachio. Not honestly, my lord ; but so covertly that no dishonesty shall appear in me.

Don John. Show me briefly how.

Borachio. I think I told your lordship a year since, how much I am in the favour of Margaret, the waiting gentlewoman to Hero.

Don John. I remember.

Borachio. I can, at any unseasonable instant of the night, appoint her to look out at her lady's chamber-window.

Don John. What life is in that, to be the death of this marriage ?

Borachio. The poison of that lies in you to temper. Go you to the prince your brother ; spare not to tell him that he hath wronged his honour in marrying the renowned Claudio—whose estimation do you mightily hold up—to a contaminated stale, such a one as Hero.

Don John. What proof shall I make of that ?

Borachio. Proof enough to misuse the prince, to vex Claudio, to undo Hero and kill Leonato. Look you for any other issue ?

Don John. Only to despite them, I will endeavour any thing.

Borachio. Go, then ; find me a meet hour to draw Don Pedro and the Count Claudio alone : tell them that you know that Hero loves me ; intend a kind of zeal both to the prince and Claudio, as,—in love of your brother's honour, who hath made this match, and his friend's reputation, who is thus like to be cozened with the semblance of a maid, —that you have discovered thus. They will scarcely believe this without trial : offer them instances ; which shall bear no less likelihood than to see me at her chamber-window, hear me † call Margaret Hero, hear Margaret term me Claudio ; and bring them to see this the very night before the intended wedding,—for in the meantime I will so fashion the matter that Hero shall be absent,—and there shall appear such seeming truth of Hero's disloyalty that jealousy shall be called assurance and all the preparation overthrown.

Don John. Grow this to what adverse issue it can, I will put it in practice. Be cunning in the working this, and thy fee is a thousand ducats.

Borachio. Be you constant in the accusation, and my cunning shall not shame me.

Don John. I will presently go learn their day of marriage.   [*Exeunt.*

SCENE III. LEONATO'S *orchard.*

Enter BENEDICK.

Benedick. Boy !

Enter Boy.

Boy. Signior ?
Benedick. In my chamber-window lies a book :
bring it hither to me in the orchard.
Boy. I am here already, sir.
Benedick. I know that ; but I would have thee
hence, and here again. [*Exit Boy.*] I do much
wonder that one man, seeing how much another
man is a fool when he dedicates his behaviours to
love, will, after he hath laughed at such shallow
follies in others, become the argument of his own
scorn by falling in love : and such a man is Claudio.
I have known when there was no music with him
but the drum and the fife ; and now had he rather
hear the tabor and the pipe : I have known when
he would have walked ten mile a-foot to see a good
armour ; and now will he lie ten nights awake,
carving the fashion of a new doublet. He was wont
to speak plain and to the purpose, like an honest
man and a soldier ; and now is he turned ortho-
graphy ; his words are a very fantastical banquet,
just so many strange dishes. May I be so converted
and see with these eyes ? I cannot tell ; I think not :
I will not be sworn but love may transform me to
an oyster ; but I 'll take my oath on it, till he have
made an oyster of me, he shall never make me such
a fool. One woman is fair, yet I am well ; another
is wise, yet I am well ; another virtuous, yet I am
well ; but till all graces be in one woman, one woman
shall not come in my grace. Rich she shall be,
that 's certain ; wise, or I 'll none ; virtuous, or I 'll
never cheapen her ; fair, or I 'll never look on her ;
mild, or come not near me ; noble, or not I for an
angel ; of good discourse, an excellent musician,
and her hair shall be of what colour it please God.
Ha ! the prince and Monsieur Love ! I will hide
me in the arbour.   [*Withdraws.*

Enter DON PEDRO, CLAUDIO, *and* LEONATO.

Don Pedro. Come, shall we hear this music?
Claudio. Yea, my good lord. How still the
evening is,
As hush'd on purpose to grace harmony !
Don Pedro. See you where Benedick hath hid
himself?
Claudio. O, very well, my lord : the music ended,
We 'll fit the kid-fox with a pennyworth.

Enter BALTHASAR *with Music*

Don Pedro. Come, Balthasar, we 'll hear that
song again.
Balthasar. O, good my lord, tax not so bad a
voice
To slander music any more than once.
Don Pedro. It is the witness still of excellency
To put a strange face on his own perfection.
I pray thee, sing, and let me woo no more.
Balthasar. Because you talk of wooing, I will
sing ;
Since many a wooer doth commence his suit
To her he thinks not worthy, yet he wooes,
Yet will he swear he loves.

Don Pedro.   Now, pray thee, come ;
Or, if thou wilt hold longer argument,
Do it in notes.
Balthasar. Note this before my notes ;
There 's not a note of mine but 's worth the noting.
Don Pedro. Why, these are very crotchets that
he speaks ;
Notes, notes, forsooth, and nothing.   [*Air.*
Benedick. Now, divine air ! now is his soul
ravished ! Is it not strange that sheeps' guts should
hale souls out of men's bodies ? Well, a horn for
my money, when all 's done.

The Song

Balthasar. Sigh no more, ladies, sigh no more,
      Men were deceivers ever,
    One foot in sea and one on shore,
      To one thing constant never :
    Then sigh not so, but let them go,
      And be you blithe and bonny,
    Converting all your sounds of woe
      Into Hey nonny, nonny.

    Sing no more ditties, sing no moe,
      Of dumps so dull and heavy ;
    The fraud of men was ever so,
      Since summer first was leavy :
    Then sigh not so, &c.

Don Pedro. By my troth, a good song.
Balthasar. And an ill singer, my lord.
Don Pedro. Ha, no, no, faith ; thou singest well
enough for a shift.
Benedick. An he had been a dog that should have
howled thus, they would have hanged him : and I
pray God his bad voice bode no mischief. I had as
lief have heard the night-raven, come what plague
could have come after it.
Don Pedro. Yea, marry, dost thou hear, Balthasar ? I pray thee, get us some excellent music ;
for to-morrow night we would have it at the Lady
Hero's chamber-window.
Balthasar. The best I can, my lord.
Don Pedro. Do so ; farewell. [*Exit Balthasar.*]
Come hither, Leonato. What was it you told me
of to-day, that your niece Beatrice was in love with
Signior Benedick ?
Claudio. O, ay : stalk on, stalk on ; the fowl
sits. I did never think that lady would have loved
any man.
Leonato. No, nor I neither ; but most wonderful
that she should so dote on Signior Benedick, whom
she hath in all outward behaviours seemed ever to
abhor.
Benedick. Is 't possible ? Sits the wind in that
corner ?
Leonato. By my troth, my lord, I cannot tell
what to think of it but that she loves him with an
enraged affection : it is past the infinite of thought.
Don Pedro. May be she doth but counterfeit.
Claudio. Faith, like enough.
Leonato. O God, counterfeit ! There was never
counterfeit of passion came so near the life of passion
as she discovers it.
Don Pedro. Why, what effects of passion shows
she ?
Claudio. Bait the hook well ; this fish will bite.
Leonato. What effects, my lord ? She will sit
you, you heard my daughter tell you how.
Claudio. She did, indeed.
Don Pedro. How, how, I pray you ? You amaze
me : I would have thought her spirit had been
invincible against all assaults of affection.

Leonato. I would have sworn it had, my lord ; especially against Benedick.

Benedick. I should think this a gull, but that the white-bearded fellow speaks it : knavery cannot, sure, hide himself in such reverence.

Claudio. He hath ta'en the infection : hold it up.

Don Pedro. Hath she made her affection known to Benedick ?

Leonato. No ; and swears she never will : that 's her torment.

Claudio. 'Tis true, indeed ; so your daughter says : ' Shall I,' says she, ' that have so oft encountered him with scorn, write to him that I love him ? '

Leonato. This says she now when she is beginning to write to him ; for she 'll be up twenty times a night, and there will she sit in her smock till she have writ a sheet of paper : my daughter tells us all.

Claudio. Now you talk of a sheet of paper, I remember a pretty jest your daughter told us of.

Leonato. O, when she had writ it and was reading it over, she found Benedick and Beatrice between the sheet ?

Claudio. That.

Leonato. O, she tore the letter into a thousand halfpence ; railed at herself, that she should be so immodest to write to one that she knew would flout her ; ' I measure him,' says she, ' by my own spirit ; for I should flout him, if he writ to me ; yea, though I love him, I should.'

Claudio. Then down upon her knees she falls, weeps, sobs, beats her heart, tears her hair, prays, curses ; ' O sweet Benedick ! God give me patience ! '

Leonato. She doth indeed : my daughter says so : and the ecstasy hath so much overborne her that my daughter is sometime afeard she will do a desperate outrage to herself : it is very true.

Don Pedro. It were good that Benedick knew of it by some other, if she will not discover it.

Claudio. To what end ? He would make but a sport of it and torment the poor lady worse.

Don Pedro. An he should, it were an alms to hang him. She 's an excellent sweet lady : and, out of all suspicion, she is virtuous.

Claudio. And she is exceeding wise.

Don Pedro. In every thing but in loving Benedick.

Leonato. O, my lord, wisdom and blood combating in so tender a body, we have ten proofs to one that blood hath the victory. I am sorry for her, as I have just cause, being her uncle and her guardian.

Don Pedro. I would she had bestowed this dotage on me : I would have daffed all other respects and made her half myself. I pray you, tell Benedick of it, and hear what a' will say.

Leonato. Were it good, think you ?

Claudio. Hero thinks surely she will die ; for she says she will die, if he love her not, and she will die, ere she make her love known, and she will die, if he woo her, rather than she will bate one breath of her accustomed crossness.

Don Pedro. She doth well : if she should make tender of her love, 'tis very possible he 'll scorn it ; for the man, as you know all, hath a contemptible spirit.

Claudio. He is a very proper man.

Don Pedro. He hath indeed a good outward happiness.

Claudio. Before God ! and, in my mind, very wise.

Don Pedro. He doth indeed show some sparks that are like wit.

Claudio. And I take him to be valiant.

Don Pedro. As Hector, I assure you : and in the managing of quarrels you may say he is wise ; for either he avoids them with great discretion, or undertakes them with a most Christian-like fear.

Leonato. If he do fear God, a' must necessarily keep peace : if he break the peace, he ought to enter into a quarrel with fear and trembling.

Don Pedro. And so will he do ; for the man doth fear God, howsoever it seems not in him by some large jests he will make. Well, I am sorry for your niece. Shall we go seek Benedick, and tell him of her love ?

Claudio. Never tell him, my lord : let her wear it out with good counsel.

Leonato. Nay, that 's impossible : she may wear her heart out first.

Don Pedro. Well, we will hear further of it by your daughter : let it cool the while. I love Benedick well ; and I could wish he would modestly examine himself, to see how much he is unworthy so good a lady.

Leonato. My lord, will you walk ? dinner is ready.

Claudio. If he do not dote on her upon this, I will never trust my expectation.

Don Pedro. Let there be the same net spread for her ; and that must your daughter and her gentlewomen carry. The sport will be, when they hold one an opinion of another's dotage, and no such matter : that 's the scene that I would see, which will be merely a dumb-show. Let us send her to call him in to dinner.

[*Exeunt Don Pedro, Claudio, and Leonato.*

Benedick. [*Coming forward*] This can be no trick : the conference was sadly borne. They have the truth of this from Hero. They seem to pity the lady : it seems their affections have their full bent. Love me ! why, it must be requited. I hear how I am censured : they say I will bear myself proudly, if I perceive the love come from her ; they say too that she will rather die than give any sign of affection. I did never think to marry : I must not seem proud : happy are they that hear their detractions and can put them to mending. They say the lady is fair ; 'tis a truth, I can bear them witness ; and virtuous, 'tis so, I cannot reprove it ; and wise, but for loving me ; by my troth, it is no addition to her wit, nor no great argument of her folly, for I will be horribly in love with her. I may chance have some odd quirks and remnants of wit broken on me, because I have railed so long against marriage : but doth not the appetite alter ? a man loves the meat in his youth that he cannot endure in his age. Shall quips and sentences and these paper bullets of the brain awe a man from the career of his humour ? No, the world must be peopled. When I said I would die a bachelor, I did not think I should live till I were married. Here comes Beatrice. By this day ! she 's a fair lady : I do spy some marks of love in her.

Enter BEATRICE.

Beatrice. Against my will I am sent to bid you come in to dinner.

Benedick. Fair Beatrice, I thank you for your pains.

Beatrice. I took no more pains for those thanks than you take pains to thank me : if it had been painful, I would not have come.

Benedick. You take pleasure then in the message ?

Beatrice. Yea, just so much as you may take upon a knife's point and choke a daw withal. You have no stomach, signior : fare you well.   [*Exit.*

Benedick. Ha ! ' Against my will I am sent to bid you come in to dinner ; ' there 's a double meaning in that. ' I took no more pains for those thanks than you took pains to thank me ; ' that 's as much as to say, Any pains that I take for you is as easy as thanks. If I do not take pity of her, I am a villain ; if I do not love her, I am a Jew. I will go get her picture.   [*Exit.*

ACT III.

SCENE I.   LEONATO's *garden.*

Enter HERO, MARGARET, *and* URSULA.

Hero.

Good Margaret, run thee to the parlour ;
    There shalt thou find my cousin Beatrice
    Proposing with the prince and Claudio :
Whisper her ear and tell her, I and Ursula
Walk in the orchard and our whole discourse
Is all of her ; say that thou overheard'st us ;
And bid her steal into the pleached bower,
Where honeysuckles, ripen'd by the sun,
Forbid the sun to enter, like favourites,
Made proud by princes, that advance their pride
Against that power that bred it : there will she hide her,
To listen our purpose. This is thy office ;
Bear thee well in it and leave us alone.
   Margaret. I 'll make her come, I warrant you, presently.   [*Exit.*
   Hero. Now, Ursula, when Beatrice doth come,
As we do trace this alley up and down,
Our talk must only be of Benedick.
When I do name him, let it be thy part
To praise him more than ever man did merit :
My talk to thee must be how Benedick
Is sick in love with Beatrice. Of this matter
Is little Cupid's crafty arrow made,
That only wounds by hearsay.

Enter BEATRICE, *behind.*

                Now begin ;
For look where Beatrice, like a lapwing, runs
Close by the ground, to hear our conference.
   Ursula. The pleasant'st angling is to see the fish
Cut with her golden oars the silver stream,
And greedily devour the treacherous bait :
So angle we for Beatrice ; who even now
Is couched in the woodbine coverture.
Fear you not my part of the dialogue.
   Hero. Then go we near her, that her ear lose nothing
Of the false sweet bait that we lay for it.
                [*Approaching the bower.*
No, truly, Ursula, she is too disdainful ;
I know her spirits are as coy and wild
As haggerds of the rock.
   Ursula.   But are you sure
That Benedick loves Beatrice so entirely ?
   Hero. So says the prince and my new-trothed lord.
   Ursula. And did they bid you tell her of it, madam?
   Hero. They did entreat me to acquaint her of it ;
But I persuaded them, if they loved Benedick,
To wish him wrestle with affection,
And never to let Beatrice know of it.
   Ursula. Why did you so ? Doth not the gentleman
Deserve as full as fortunate a bed

As ever Beatrice shall couch upon ?
   Hero. O god of love ! I know he doth deserve
As much as may be yielded to a man :
But Nature never framed a woman's heart
Of prouder stuff than that of Beatrice ;
Disdain and scorn ride sparkling in her eyes,
Misprising what they look on, and her wit
Values itself so highly that to her
All matter else seems weak : she cannot love,
Nor take no shape nor project of affection,
She is so self-endeared.
   Ursula.   Sure, I think so ;
And therefore certainly it were not good
She knew his love, lest she make sport at it.
   Hero. Why, you speak truth. I never yet saw man,
How wise, how noble, young, how rarely featured,
But she would spell him backward : if fair-faced,
She would swear the gentleman should be her sister ;
If black, why, Nature, drawing of an antique,
Made a foul blot ; if tall, a lance ill-headed ;
If low, an agate very vilely cut ;
If speaking, why, a vane blown with all winds ;
If silent, why, a block moved with none.
So turns she every man the wrong side out
And never gives to truth and virtue that
Which simpleness and merit purchaseth.
   Ursula. Sure, sure, such carping is not commendable.
   Hero. No, not to be so odd and from all fashions
As Beatrice is, cannot be commendable :
But who dare tell her so ? If I should speak,
She would mock me into air ; O, she would laugh me
Out of myself, press me to death with wit.
Therefore let Benedick, like cover'd fire,
Consume away in sighs, waste inwardly :
It were a better death than die with mocks,
Which is as bad as die with tickling.
   Ursula. Yet tell her of it : hear what she will say.
   Hero. No ; rather I will go to Benedick
And counsel him to fight against his passion.
And, truly, I 'll devise some honest slanders
To stain my cousin with : one doth not know
How much an ill word may empoison liking.
   Ursula. O, do not do your cousin such a wrong.
She cannot be so much without true judgement—
Having so swift and excellent a wit
As she is prized to have—as to refuse
So rare a gentleman as Signior Benedick.
   Hero. He is the only man of Italy,
Always excepted my dear Claudio.
   Ursula. I pray you, be not angry with me, madam,
Speaking my fancy : Signior Benedick,
For shape, for bearing, argument and valour,
Goes foremost in report through Italy.
   Hero. Indeed, he hath an excellent good name.
   Ursula. His excellence did earn it, ere he had it.
When are you married, madam ?
   Hero. Why, every day, to-morrow. Come, go in :
I 'll show thee some attires, and have thy counsel
Which is the best to furnish me to-morrow.
   Ursula. She 's limed, I warrant you : we have caught her, madam.
   Hero. If it proves so, then loving goes by haps :
Some Cupid kills with arrows, some with traps.
              [*Exeunt Hero and Ursula.*
   Beatrice. [*Coming forward*] What fire is in mine ears ? Can this be true ?
Stand I condemn'd for pride and scorn so much ?
Contempt, farewell ! and maiden pride, adieu !
No glory lives behind the back of such.

And, Benedick, love on ; I will requite thee,
Taming my wild heart to thy loving hand :
If thou dost love, my kindness shall incite thee
To bind our loves up in a holy band ;
For others say thou dost deserve, and I
Believe it better than reportingly.   [Exit.

SCENE II. *A room in* LEONATO's *house.*

Enter DON PEDRO, CLAUDIO, BENEDICK, *and* LEONATO

Don Pedro. I do but stay till your marriage be
consummate, and then go I toward Arragon.
Claudio. I 'll bring you thither, my lord, if
you 'll vouchsafe me.
Don Pedro. Nay, that would be as great a soil
in the new gloss of your marriage as to show a child
his new coat and forbid him to wear it. I will only
be bold with Benedick for his company ; for, from
the crown of his head to the sole of his foot, he is
all mirth : he hath twice or thrice cut Cupid's bow-
string and the little hangman dare not shoot at him ;
he hath a heart as sound as a bell and his tongue is
the clapper, for what his heart thinks his tongue
speaks.
Benedick. Gallants, I am not as I have been.
Leonato. So say I : methinks you are sadder.
Claudio. I hope he be in love.
Don Pedro. Hang him, truant ! there 's no true
drop of blood in him, to be truly touched with love :
if he be sad, he wants money.
Benedick. I have the toothache.
Don Pedro. Draw it.
Benedick. Hang it !
Claudio. You must hang it first, and draw it
afterwards.
Don Pedro. What ! sigh for the toothache ?
Leonato. Where is but a humour or a worm.
Benedick. Well, every one can master a grief but
he that has it.
Claudio. Yet say I, he is in love.
Don Pedro. There is no appearance of fancy in
him, unless it be a fancy that he hath to strange
disguises ; as, to be a Dutchman to-day, a Frenchman to-morrow, or in the shape of two countries
at once, as, a German from the waist downward, all
slops, and a Spaniard from the hip upward, no
doublet. Unless he have a fancy to this foolery,
as it appears he hath, he is no fool for fancy, as
you would have it appear he is.
Claudio. If he be not in love with some woman,
there is no believing old signs : a' brushes his hat
o' mornings ; what should that bode ?
Don Pedro. Hath any man seen him at the barber's ?
Claudio. No, but the barber's man hath been
seen with him, and the old ornament of his cheek
hath already stuffed tennis-balls.
Leonato. Indeed, he looks younger than he did,
by the loss of a beard.
Don Pedro. Nay, a' rubs himself with civet :
can you smell him out by that ?
Claudio. That 's as much as to say, the sweet
youth 's in love.
Don Pedro. The greatest note of it is his melancholy.
Claudio. And when was he wont to wash his face ?
Don Pedro. Yea, or to paint himself? for the
which, I hear what they say of him.
Claudio. Nay, but his jesting spirit ; which is
now crept into a lute-string and now governed by
stops.

Don Pedro. Indeed, that tells a heavy tale for
him : conclude, conclude he is in love.
Claudio. Nay, but I know who loves him.
Don Pedro. That would I know too : I warrant,
one that knows him not.
Claudio. Yes, and his ill conditions ; and, in
despite of all, dies for him.
Don Pedro. She shall be buried with her face
upwards.
Benedick. Yet is this no charm for the toothache.
Old signior, walk aside with me : I have studied
eight or nine wise words to speak to you, which
these hobby-horses must not hear.
          [*Exeunt Benedick and Leonato.*
Don Pedro. For my life, to break with him about
Beatrice.
Claudio. 'Tis even so. Hero and Margaret have
by this played their parts with Beatrice ; and then
the two bears will not bite one another when they
meet.

Enter DON JOHN.

Don John. My lord and brother, God save you !
Don Pedro. Good den, brother.
Don John. If your leisure served, I would speak
with you.
Don Pedro. In private ?
Don John. If it please you : yet Count Claudio
may hear ; for what I would speak of concerns him.
Don Pedro. What 's the matter ?
Don John. [*To Claudio*] Means your lordship
to be married to-morrow ?
Don Pedro. You know he does.
Don John. I know not that, when he knows what
I know.
Claudio. If there be any impediment, I pray you
discover it.
Don John. You may think I love you not : let
that appear hereafter, and aim better at me by that
I now will manifest. For my brother, I think he
holds you well, and in dearness of heart hath holp
to effect your ensuing marriage ;—surely suit ill
spent and labour ill bestowed.
Don Pedro. Why, what 's the matter ?
Don John. I came hither to tell you ; and, circumstances shortened, for she has been too long a
talking of, the lady is disloyal.
Claudio. Who, Hero ?
Don John. Even she ; Leonato's Hero, your
Hero, every man's Hero.
Claudio. Disloyal ?
Don John. The word is too good to paint out
her wickedness ; I could say she were worse : think
you of a worse title, and I will fit her to it. Wonder
not till further warrant : go but with me to-night,
you shall see her chamber-window entered, even the
night before her wedding-day : if you love her then,
to-morrow wed her ; but it would better fit your
honour to change your mind.
Claudio. May this be so ?
Don Pedro. I will not think it.
Don John. If you dare not trust that you see,
confess not that you know : if you will follow me,
I will show you enough : and when you have seen
more and heard more, proceed accordingly.
Claudio. If I see any thing to-night why I should
not marry her to-morrow, in the congregation,
where I should wed, there will I shame her.
Don Pedro. And, as I wooed for thee to obtain
her, I will join with thee to disgrace her.
Don John. I will disparage her no farther till

you are my witnesses : bear it coldly but till midnight, and let the issue show itself.

Don Pedro. O day untowardly turned !

Claudio. O mischief strangely thwarting !

Don John. O plague right well prevented ! so
will you say when you have seen the sequel. [*Exeunt.*

SCENE III. *A street.*

Enter DOGBERRY *and* VERGES *with the* Watch.

Dogberry. Are you good men and true ?

Verges. Yea, or else it were pity but they should
suffer salvation, body and soul.

Dogberry. Nay, that were a punishment too good
for them, if they should have any allegiance in them,
being chosen for the prince's watch.

Verges. Well, give them their charge, neighbour
Dogberry.

Dogberry. First, who think you the most desart-
less man to be constable ?

First Watch. Hugh Otecake, sir, or George
Seacole ; for they can write and read.

Dogberry. Come hither, neighbour Seacole. God
hath blessed you with a good name : to be a well-
favoured man is the gift of fortune ; but to write
and read comes by nature.

Second Watch. Both which, master constable,—

Dogberry. You have : I knew it would be your
answer. Well, for your favour, sir, why, give God
thanks, and make no boast of it ; and for your writing and reading, let that appear when there is no
need of such vanity. You are thought here to be
the most senseless and fit man for the constable of
the watch ; therefore bear you the lantern. This is
your charge : you shall comprehend all vagrom men ;
you are to bid any man stand, in the prince's name.

Second Watch. How if a' will not stand ?

Dogberry. Why, then, take no note of him, but
let him go ; and presently call the rest of the watch
together and thank God you are rid of a knave.

Verges. If he will not stand when he is bidden,
he is none of the prince's subjects.

Dogberry. True, and they are to meddle with
none but the prince's subjects. You shall also make
no noise in the streets ; for for the watch to babble
and to talk is most tolerable and not to be endured.

Watch. We will rather sleep than talk : we know
what belongs to a watch.

Dogberry. Why, you speak like an ancient and
most quiet watchman ; for I cannot see how sleeping
should offend : only, have a care that your bills
be not stolen. Well, you are to call at all the ale-
houses, and bid those that are drunk get them to bed.

Watch. How if they will not ?

Dogberry. Why, then, let them alone till they are
sober : if they make you not then the better answer,
you may say they are not the men you took them for.

Watch. Well, sir.

Dogberry. If you meet a thief, you may suspect
him, by virtue of your office, to be no true man ;
and, for such kind of men, the less you meddle or
make with them, why, the more is for your honesty.

Watch. If we know him to be a thief, shall we
not lay hands on him ?

Dogberry. Truly, by your office, you may ; but
I think they that touch pitch will be defiled : the
most peaceable way for you, if you do take a thief,
is to let him show himself what he is and steal out
of your company.

Verges. You have been always called a merciful
man, partner.

Dogberry. Truly, I would not hang a dog by my
will, much more a man who hath any honesty in him.

Verges. If you hear a child cry in the night, you
must call to the nurse and bid her still it.

Watch. How if the nurse be asleep and will not
hear us ?

Dogberry. Why, then, depart in peace, and let
the child wake her with crying ; for the ewe that
will not hear her lamb when it baes will never answer
a calf when he bleats.

Verges. 'Tis very true.

Dogberry. This is the end of the charge :—you,
constable, are to present the prince's own person :
if you meet the prince in the night, you may stay
him.

Verges. Nay, by'r lady, that I think a' cannot.

Dogberry. Five shillings to one on 't, with any
man that knows the statues, he may stay him :
marry, not without the prince be willing ; for, indeed,
the watch ought to offend no man ; and it is an offence
to stay a man against his will.

Verges. By'r lady, I think it be so.

Dogberry. Ha, ah, ha ! Well, masters, good
night : an there be any matter of weight chances,
call up me : keep your fellows' counsels and your
own ; and good night. Come, neighbour.

Watch. Well, masters, we hear our charge :
let us go sit here upon the church-bench till two,
and then all to bed.

Dogberry. One word more, honest neighbours.
I pray you, watch about Signior Leonato's door ;
for the wedding being there to-morrow, there is a
great coil to-night. Adieu : be vigitant, I beseech
you.   [*Exeunt Dogberry and Verges.*

Enter BORACHIO *and* CONRADE.

Borachio. What, Conrade !

Watch. [*Aside*] Peace ! stir not.

Borachio. Conrade, I say !

Conrade. Here, man ; I am at thy elbow.

Borachio. Mass, and my elbow itched ; I thought
there would a scab follow.

Conrade. I will owe thee an answer for that :
and now forward with thy tale.

Borachio. Stand thee close, then, under this
pent-house, for it drizzles rain ; and I will, like a
true drunkard, utter all to thee.

Watch. [*Aside*] Some treason, masters : yet
stand close.

Borachio. Therefore know I have earned of Don
John a thousand ducats.

Conrade. Is it possible that any villany should
be so dear ?

Borachio. Thou shouldst rather ask if it were
possible any villany should be so rich ; for when
rich villains have need of poor ones, poor ones may
make what price they will.

Conrade. I wonder at it.

Borachio. That shows thou art unconfirmed.
Thou knowest that the fashion of a doublet, or a
hat, or a cloak, is nothing to a man.

Conrade. Yes, it is apparel.

Borachio. I mean, the fashion.

Conrade. Yes, the fashion is the fashion.

Borachio. Tush! I may as well say the fool 's
the fool. But seest thou not what a deformed thief
this fashion is ?

Watch. [*Aside*] I know that Deformed ; a' has
been a vile thief this seven year ; a' goes up and
down like a gentleman : I remember his name.

Borachio. Didst thou not hear somebody ?

Conrade. No ; 'twas the vane on the house.

Borachio. Seest thou not, I say, what a deformed thief this fashion is ? how giddily a' turns about all the hot bloods between fourteen and five-and-thirty ? sometimes fashioning them like Pharaoh's soldiers in the reechy painting, sometime like god Bel's priests in the old church-window, sometime like the shaven Hercules in the smirched worm-eaten tapestry, where his codpiece seems as massy as his club ?

Conrade. All this I see ; and I see that the fashion wears out more apparel than the man. But art not thou thyself giddy with the fashion too, that thou hast shifted out of thy tale into telling me of the fashion ?

Borachio. Not so, neither : but know that I have to-night wooed Margaret, the Lady Hero's gentle-woman, by the name of Hero : she leans me out at her mistress' chamber-window, bids me a thousand times good-night—I tell this tale vilely :—I should first tell thee how the prince, Claudio and my master, planted and placed and possessed by my master Don John, saw afar off in the orchard this amiable encounter.

Conrade. And thought they Margaret was Hero ?

Borachio. Two of them did, the prince and Claudio ; but the devil my master knew she was Margaret ; and partly by his oaths, which first possessed them, partly by the dark night, which did deceive them, but chiefly by my villany, which did confirm any slander that Don John had made, away went Claudio enraged ; swore he would meet her, as he was appointed, next morning at the temple, and there, before the whole congregation, shame her with what he saw o'er night and send her home again without a husband.

First Watch. We charge you, in the prince's name, stand !

Second Watch. Call up the right master con-stable. We have here recovered the most dangerous piece of lechery that ever was known in the common-wealth.

First Watch. And one Deformed is one of them : I know him ; a' wears a lock.

Conrade. Masters, masters,—

Second Watch. You 'll be made bring Deformed forth, I warrant you.

Conrade. Masters,—

First Watch. Never speak : we charge you let us obey you to go with us.

Borachio. We are like to prove a goodly com-modity, being taken up of these men's bills.

Conrade. A commodity in question, I warrant you. Come, we 'll obey you.   [*Exeunt.*

SCENE IV. HERO's *apartment.*

Enter HERO, MARGARET, *and* URSULA.

Hero. Good Ursula, wake my cousin Beatrice, and desire her to rise.

Ursula. I will, lady.

Hero. And bid her come hither.

Ursula. Well.   [*Exit.*

Margaret. Troth, I think your other rabato were better.

Hero. No, pray thee, good Meg, I 'll wear this.

Margaret. By my troth, 's not so good ; and I warrant your cousin will say so.

Hero. My cousin 's a fool, and thou art another : I 'll wear none but this.

Margaret. I like the new tire within excellently, if the hair were a thought browner ; and your

gown 's a most rare fashion, i' faith. I saw the Duchess of Milan's gown, that they praise so.

Hero. O, that exceeds, they say.

Margaret. By my troth, 's but a night-gown in respect of yours : cloth o' gold, and cuts, and laced with silver, set with pearls, down sleeves, side sleeves, and skirts, round underborne with a bluish tinsel ; but for a fine, quaint, graceful and excellent fashion, yours is worth ten on 't.

Hero. God give me joy to wear it ! for my heart is exceeding heavy.

Margaret. 'Twill be heavier soon by the weight of a man.

Hero. Fie upon thee ! art not ashamed ?

Margaret. Of what, lady ? of speaking honour-ably ? Is not marriage honourable in a beggar ? Is not your lord honourable without marriage ? I think you would have me say, ' saving your reverence, a husband ' : an bad thinking do not wrest true speaking, I 'll offend nobody : is there any harm in ' the heavier for a husband ' ? None, I think, an it be the right husband and the right wife ; otherwise 'tis light, and not heavy : ask my Lady Beatrice else ; here she comes.

Enter BEATRICE.

Hero. Good morrow, coz.

Beatrice. Good morrow, sweet Hero.

Hero. Why, how now ? do you speak in the sick tune ?

Beatrice. I am out of all other tune, methinks.

Margaret. Clap 's into ' Light o' love ;' that goes without a burden : do you sing it, and I 'll dance it.

Beatrice. Ye light o' love, with your heels ! then, if your husband have stables enough, you 'll see he shall lack no barns.

Margaret. O illegitimate construction ! I scorn that with my heels.

Beatrice. 'Tis almost five o'clock, cousin ; 'tis time you were ready. By my troth, I am exceeding ill : heigh-ho !

Margaret. For a hawk, a horse, or a husband ?

Beatrice. For the letter that begins them all, H.

Margaret. Well, an you be not turned Turk, there 's no more sailing by the star.

Beatrice. What means the fool, trow ?

Margaret. Nothing I ; but God send every one their heart's desire !

Hero. These gloves the count sent me ; they are an excellent perfume.

Beatrice. I am stuffed, cousin ; I cannot smell.

Margaret. A maid, and stuffed ! there 's goodly catching of cold.

Beatrice. O, God help me ! God help me ! how long have you professed apprehension ?

Margaret. Ever since you left it. Doth not my wit become me rarely ?

Beatrice. It is not seen enough, you should wear it in your cap. By my troth, I am sick.

Margaret. Get you some of this distilled Carduus Benedictus, and lay it to your heart : it is the only thing for a qualm.

Hero. There thou prickest her with a thistle.

Beatrice. Benedictus ! why Benedictus ? you have some moral in this Benedictus.

Margaret. Moral ! no, by my troth, I have no moral meaning ; I meant, plain holy-thistle. You may think perchance that I think you are in love : nay, by'r lady, I am not such a fool to think what I list, nor I list not to think what I can, nor indeed I cannot think, if I would think my heart out of thinking, that you are in love or that you will be in love or that you can be in love. Yet Benedick was such another, and now is he become a man : he swore he would never marry, and yet now, in despite of his heart, he eats his meat without grudging : and how you may be converted I know not, but methinks you look with your eyes as other women do.

Beatrice. What pace is this that thy tongue keeps ?
Margaret. Not a false gallop.

Re-enter URSULA.

Ursula. Madam, withdraw : the prince, the count, Signior Benedick, Don John, and all the gallants of the town, are come to fetch you to church.
Hero. Help to dress me, good coz, good Meg, good Ursula.   [*Exeunt.*

SCENE V. *Another room in* LEONATO'S *house.*

Enter LEONATO, *with* DOGBERRY *and* VERGES.

Leonato. What would you with me, honest neighbour ?
Dogberry. Marry, sir, I would have some confidence with you that decerns you nearly.
Leonato. Brief, I pray you ; for you see it is a busy time with me.
Dogberry. Marry, this it is, sir.
Verges. Yes, in truth it is, sir.
Leonato. What is it, my good friends ?
Dogberry. Goodman Verges, sir, speaks a little off the matter : an old man, sir, and his wits are not so blunt as, God help, I would desire they were ; but, in faith, honest as the skin between his brows.
Verges. Yes, I thank God I am as honest as any man living that is an old man and no honester than I.
Dogberry. Comparisons are odorous : palabras, neighbour Verges.
Leonato. Neighbours, you are tedious.
Dogberry. It pleases your worship to say so, but we are the poor duke's officers ; but truly, for mine own part, if I were as tedious as a king, I could find it in my heart to bestow it all of your worship.
Leonato. All thy tediousness on me, ah ?
Dogberry. Yea, an 'twere a thousand pound more than 'tis ; for I hear as good exclamation on your worship as of any man in the city ; and though I be but a poor man, I am glad to hear it.
Verges. And so am I.
Leonato. I would fain know what you have to say.
Verges. Marry, sir, our watch to-night, excepting your worship's presence, ha' ta'en a couple of as arrant knaves as any in Messina.
Dogberry. A good old man, sir ; he will be talking : as they say, When the age is in, the wit is out : God help us ! it is a world to see. Well said, i' faith, neighbour Verges : well, God 's a good man ; an two men ride of a horse, one must ride behind. An honest soul, i' faith, sir ; by my troth he is, as ever broke bread ; but God is to be worshipped ; all men are not alike ; alas, good neighbour !
Leonato. Indeed, neighbour, he comes too shor of you.
Dogberry. Gifts that God gives.
Leonato. I must leave you.
Dogberry. One word, sir : our watch, sir, have indeed comprehended two aspicious persons, and we would have them this morning examined before your worship.

Leonato. Take their examination yourself and bring it me : I am now in great haste, as it may appear unto you.
Dogberry. It shall be suffigance.
Leonato. Drink some wine ere you go : fare you well.

Enter a Messenger.

Messenger. My lord, they stay for you to give your daughter to her husband.
Leonato. I 'll wait upon them : I am ready.
    [*Exeunt Leonato and Messenger.*
Dogberry. Go, good partner, go, get you to Francis Seacole ; bid him bring his pen and inkhorn to the gaol : we are now to examination these men.
Verges. And we must do it wisely.
Dogberry. We will spare for no wit, I warrant you ; here 's that shall drive some of them to a noncome : only get the learned writer to set down our excommunication and meet me at the gaol.
    [*Exeunt.*

ACT IV.

SCENE I. *A church.*

Enter DON PEDRO, DON JOHN, LEONATO, FRIAR FRANCIS, CLAUDIO, BENEDICK, HERO, BEATRICE, *and attendants.*

Leonato.

Come, Friar Francis, be brief ; only to the plain form of marriage, and you shall recount their particular duties afterwards.
Friar. You come hither, my lord, to marry this lady.
Claudio. No.
Leonato. To be married to her : friar, you come to marry her.
Friar. Lady, you come hither to be married to this count.
Hero. I do.
Friar. If either of you know any inward impediment why you should not be conjoined, I charge you, on your souls, to utter it.
Claudio. Know you any, Hero ?
Hero. None, my lord.
Friar. Know you any, count ?
Leonato. I dare make his answer, none.
Claudio. O, what men dare do ! what men may do ! what men daily do, not knowing what they do !
Benedick. How now ! interjections ? Why, then, some be of laughing, as, ah, ha, he !
Claudio. Stand thee by, friar. Father, by your leave :
Will you with free and unconstrained soul
Give me this maid, your daughter ?
Leonato. As freely, son, as God did give her me.
Claudio. And what have I to give you back, whose worth
May counterpoise this rich and precious gift ?
Don Pedro. Nothing, unless you render her again.
Claudio. Sweet prince, you learn me noble thankfulness.
There, Leonato, take her back again :
Give not this rotten orange to your friend ;
She 's but the sign and semblance of her honour.
Behold how like a maid she blushes here !
O, what authority and show of truth
Can cunning sin cover itself withal !
Comes not that blood as modest evidence

To witness simple virtue ? Would you not swear,
All you that see her, that she were a maid,
By these exterior shows ? But she is none :
She knows the heat of a luxurious bed ;
Her blush is guiltiness, not modesty.

Leonato. What do you mean, my lord ?

Claudio.   Not to be married,
Not to knit my soul to an approved wanton.

Leonato. Dear my lord, if you, in your own proof,
Have vanquish'd the resistance of her youth,
And made defeat of her virginity,—

Claudio. I know what you would say : if I have
known her,
You will say she did embrace me as a husband,
And so extenuate the 'forehand sin :
No, Leonato,
I never tempted her with word too large ;
But, as a brother to his sister, show'd
Bashful sincerity and comely love.

Hero. And seem'd I ever otherwise to you ?

Claudio. Out on thee ! Seeming ! I will write
against it :
You seem to me as Dian in her orb,
As chaste as is the bud ere it be blown ;
But you are more intemperate in your blood
Than Venus, or those pamper'd animals
That rage in savage sensuality.

Hero. Is my lord well, that he doth speak so
wide ?

Leonato. Sweet prince, why speak not you ?

Don Pedro.   What should I speak ?
I stand dishonour'd, that have gone about
To link my dear friend to a common stale.

Leonato. Are these things spoken, or do I but
dream ?

Don John. Sir, they are spoken, and these things
are true.

Benedick. This looks not like a nuptial.

Hero.   True ! O God !

Claudio. Leonato, stand I here ?
Is this the prince ? is this the prince's brother ?
is this face Hero's ? are our eyes our own ?

Leonato. All this is so : but what of this, my
lord ?

Claudio. Let me but move one question to your
daughter :
And, by that fatherly and kindly power
That you have in her, bid her answer truly.

Leonato. I charge thee do so, as thou art my
child.

Hero. O, God defend me ! how am I beset !
What kind of catechising call you this ?

Claudio. To make you answer truly to your
name.

Hero. Is it not Hero ? Who can blot that name
With any just reproach ?

Claudio.   Marry, that can Hero ;
Hero itself can blot out Hero's virtue.
What man was he talk'd with you yesternight
Out at your window betwixt twelve and one ?
Now, if you are a maid, answer to this.

Hero. I talk'd with no man at that hour, my lord.

Don Pedro. Why, then are you no maiden.
Leonato,
I am sorry you must hear : upon mine honour,
Myself, my brother and this grieved count
Did see her, hear her, at that hour last night
Talk with a ruffian at her chamber-window ;
Who hath indeed, most like a liberal villain,
Confess'd the vile encounters they have had
A thousand times in secret.

Don John. Fie, fie ! they are not to be named,
my lord,
Not to be spoke of :
There is not chastity enough in language
Without offence to utter them. Thus, pretty lady,
I am sorry for thy much misgovernment.

Claudio. O Hero, what a Hero hadst thou been,
If half thy outward graces had been placed
About thy thoughts and counsels of thy heart !
But fare thee well, most foul, most fair ! farewell,
Thou pure impiety and impious purity !
For thee I 'll lock up all the gates of love,
And on my eyelids shall conjecture hang,
To turn all beauty into thoughts of harm,
And never shall it more be gracious.

Leonato. Hath no man's dagger here a point
for me ?   [*Hero swoons.*

Beatrice. Why, how now, cousin ! wherefore
sink you down ?

Don John. Come, let us go. These things, come
thus to light,
Smother her spirits up.
    [*Exeunt Don Pedro, Don John, and Claudio.*

Benedick. How doth the lady ?

Beatrice.   Dead, I think. Help, uncle !
Hero ! why, Hero ! Uncle ! Signior Benedick !
Friar !

Leonato. O Fate ! take not away thy heavy hand.
Death is the fairest cover for her shame
That may be wish'd for.

Beatrice.   How now, cousin Hero ?

Friar. Have comfort, lady.

Leonato. Dost thou look up ?

Friar. Yea, wherefore should she not ?

Leonato. Wherefore ! Why, doth not every
earthly thing
Cry shame upon her ? Could she here deny
The story that is printed in her blood ?
Do not live, Hero ; do not ope thine eyes ;
For, did I think thou wouldst not quickly die,
Thought I thy spirits were stronger than thy shames,
Myself would, on the rearward of reproaches,
Strike at thy life. Grieved I, I had but one ?
Chid I for that at frugal nature's frame ?
O, one too much by thee ! Why had I one ?
Why ever wast thou lovely in my eyes ?
Why had I not with charitable hand
Took up a beggar's issue at my gates,
Who smirched thus and mired with infamy,
I might have said ' No part of it is mine :
This shame derives itself from unknown loins ' ?
But mine and mine I loved and mine I praised
And mine that I was proud on, mine so much
That I myself was to myself not mine,
Valuing of her,—why, she, O, she is fallen
Into a pit of ink, that the wide sea
Hath drops too few to wash her clean again
And salt too little which may season give
To her foul-tainted flesh !

Benedick.   Sir, sir, be patient.
For my part, I am so attired in wonder,
I know not what to say.

Beatrice. O, on my soul, my cousin is belied !

Benedick. Lady, were you her bedfellow last
night ?

Beatrice. No, truly not ; although, until last
night,
I have this twelvemonth been her bedfellow.

Leonato. Confirm'd, confirm'd ! O, that is
stronger made
Which was before barr'd up with ribs of iron !

Would the two princes lie, and Claudio lie,
Who loved her so, that, speaking of her foulness,
Wash'd it with tears ! Hence from her ! let her die.
  Friar. Hear me a little ; for I have only been
Silent so long and given way unto
† This course of fortune . . . .
By noting of the lady I have mark'd
A thousand blushing apparitions
To start into her face, a thousand innocent shames
In angel whiteness beat away those blushes ;
And in her eye there hath appear'd a fire,
To burn the errors that these princes hold
Against her maiden truth. Call me a fool ;
Trust not my reading nor my observations,
Which with experimental seal doth warrant
The tenour of my book ; trust not my age,
My reverence, calling, nor divinity,
If this sweet lady lie not guiltless here
Under some biting error.
  Leonato.   Friar, it cannot be.
Thou seest that all the grace that she hath left
Is that she will not add to her damnation
A sin of perjury ; she not denies it :
Why seek'st thou then to cover with excuse
That which appears in proper nakedness ?
  Friar. Lady, what man is he you are accused of ?
  Hero. They know that do accuse me : I know
none :
If I know more of any man alive
Than that which maiden modesty doth warrant,
Let all my sins lack mercy ! O my father,
Prove you that any man with me conversed
At hours unmeet, or that I yesternight
Maintain'd the change of words with any creature,
Refuse me, hate me, torture me to death !
  Friar. There is some strange misprision in the
princes.
  Benedick. Two of them have the very bent of
honour ;
And if their wisdoms be misled in this,
The practice of it lives in John the bastard,
Whose spirits toil in frame of villanies.
  Leonato. I know not. If they speak but truth
of her,
These hands shall tear her ; if they wrong her honour,
The proudest of them shall well hear of it.
Time hath not yet so dried this blood of mine,
Nor age so eat up my invention,
Nor fortune made such havoc of my means,
Nor my bad life reft me so much of friends,
But they shall find, awaked in such a kind,
Both strength of limb and policy of mind,
Ability in means and choice of friends,
To quit me of them throughly.
  Friar.   Pause awhile,
And let my counsel sway you in this case,
Your daughter here the princes left for dead :
Let her awhile be secretly kept in,
And publish it that she is dead indeed ;
Maintain a mourning ostentation
And on your family's old monument
Hang mournful epitaphs and do all rites
That appertain unto a burial.
  Leonato. What shall become of this ? what will
this do ?
  Friar. Marry, this well carried shall on her behalf
Change slander to remorse ; that is some good :
But not for that dream I on this strange course,
But on this travail look for greater birth.
She dying, as it must be so maintain'd,
Upon the instant that she was accused,

Shall be lamented, pitied and excused
Of every hearer : for it so falls out
That what we have we prize not to the worth
Whiles we enjoy it, but being lack'd and lost,
Why, then we rack the value, then we find
The virtue that possession would not show us
Whiles it was ours. So will it fare with Claudio :
When he shall hear she died upon his words,
The idea of her life shall sweetly creep
Into his study of imagination,
And every lovely organ of her life
Shall come apparell'd in more precious habit,
More moving-delicate and full of life,
Into the eye and prospect of his soul,
Than when she lived indeed ; then shall he mourn,
If ever love had interest in his liver,
And wish he had not so accused her,
No, though he thought his accusation true.
Let this be so, and doubt not but success
Will fashion the event in better shape
Than I can lay it down in likelihood.
But if all aim but this be levell'd false,
The supposition of the lady's death
Will quench the wonder of her infamy :
And if it sort not well, you may conceal her,
As best befits her wounded reputation,
In some reclusive and religious life,
Out of all eyes, tongues, minds and injuries.
  Benedick. Signior Leonato, let the friar advise
you :
And though you know my inwardness and love
Is very much unto the prince and Claudio,
Yet, by mine honour, I will deal in this
As secretly and justly as your soul
Should with your body.
  Leonato.   Being that I flow in grief,
The smallest twine may lead me.
  Friar. 'Tis well consented : presently away ;
For to strange sores strangely they strain the cure.
Come, lady, die to live ; this wedding-day
  Perhaps is but prolong'd : have patience and
  endure.
                    [*Exeunt all but Benedick and Beatrice.*
  Benedick. Lady Beatrice, have you wept all this
while ?
  Beatrice. Yea, and I will weep a while longer.
  Benedick. I will not desire that.
  Beatrice. You have no reason ; I do it freely.
  Benedick. Surely I do believe your fair cousin is
wronged.
  Beatrice. Ah, how much might the man deserve
of me that would right her !
  Benedick. Is there any way to show such friend-
ship ?
  Beatrice. A very even way, but no such friend.
  Benedick. May a man do it ?
  Beatrice. It is a man's office, but not yours.
  Benedick. I do love nothing in the world so well
as you : is not that strange ?
  Beatrice. As strange as the thing I know not.
It were as possible for me to say I loved nothing
so well as you : but believe me not ; and yet I lie
not ; I confess nothing, nor I deny nothing. I am
sorry for my cousin.
  Benedick. By my sword, Beatrice, thou lovest me.
  Beatrice. Do not swear, and eat it.
  Benedick. I will swear by it that you love me ; and
I will make him eat it that says I love not you.
  Beatrice. Will you not eat your word ?
  Benedick. With no sauce that can be devised to
it. I protest I love thee.

Beatrice. Why, then, God forgive me !

Benedick. What offence, sweet Beatrice ?

Beatrice. You have stayed me in a happy hour : I was about to protest I loved you.

Benedick. And do it with all thy heart.

Beatrice. I love you with so much of my heart that none is left to protest.

Benedick. Come, bid me do any thing for thee.

Beatrice. Kill Claudio.

Benedick. Ha ! not for the wide world.

Beatrice. You kill me to deny it. Farewell.

Benedick. Tarry, sweet Beatrice.

Beatrice. I am gone, though I am here : there is no love in you : nay, I pray you, let me go.

Benedick. Beatrice,—

Beatrice. In faith, I will go.

Benedick. We 'll be friends first.

Beatrice. You dare easier be friends with me than fight with mine enemy.

Benedick. Is Claudio thine enemy ?

Beatrice. Is he not approved in the height a villain, that hath slandered, scorned, dishonoured my kinswoman ? O that I were a man ! What, bear her in hand until they come to take hands ; and then, with public accusation, uncovered slander, unmitigated rancour,—O God, that I were a man ! I would eat his heart in the market-place.

Benedick. Hear me, Beatrice,—

Beatrice. Talk with a man out at a window ! A proper saying !

Benedick. Nay, but, Beatrice,—

Beatrice. Sweet Hero ! She is wronged, she is slandered, she 's undone.

Benedick. Beat—

Beatrice. Princes and counties ! Surely, a princely testimony, a goodly count, Count Comfect ; a sweet gallant, surely ! O that I were a man for his sake ! or that I had any friend would be a man for my sake ! But manhood is melted into courtesies, valour into compliment, and men are only turned into tongue, and trim ones too : he is now as valiant as Hercules that only tells a lie and swears it. I cannot be a man with wishing, therefore I will die a woman with grieving.

Benedick. Tarry, good Beatrice. By this hand, I love thee.

Beatrice. Use it for my love some other way than swearing by it.

Benedick. Think you in your soul the Count Claudio hath wronged Hero ?

Beatrice. Yea, as sure as I have a thought or a soul.

Benedick. Enough, I am engaged ; I will challenge him. I will kiss your hand, and so I leave you: By this hand, Claudio shall render me a dear account. As you hear of me, so think of me. Go, comfort your cousin : I must say she is dead : and so, farewell.   [*Exeunt.*

SCENE II. *A prison.*

Enter DOGBERRY, VERGES, *and* Sexton, *in gowns ; and the* Watch, *with* CONRADE *and* BORACHIO.

Dogberry. Is our whole dissembly appeared ?

Verges. O, a stool and a cushion for the sexton.

Sexton. Which be the malefactors ?

Dogberry. Marry, that am I and my partner.

Verges. Nay, that 's certain ; we have the ex-hibition to examine.

Sexton. But which are the offenders that are to be examined ? let them come before master constable.

Dogberry. Yea, marry, let them come before me. What is your name, friend ?

Borachio. Borachio.

Dogberry. Pray, write down, Borachio. Yours, sirrah ?

Conrade. I am a gentleman, sir, and my name is Conrade.

Dogberry. Write down, master gentleman Con-rade. Masters, do you serve God ?

Conrade. } Yea, sir, we hope.
Borachio.

Dogberry. Write down, that they hope they serve God : and write God first ; for God defend but God should go before such villains ! Masters, it is proved already that you are little better than false knaves ; and it will go near to be thought so shortly. How answer you for yourselves ?

Conrade. Marry, sir, we say we are none.

Dogberry. A marvellous witty fellow, I assure you ; but I will go about with him. Come you hither, sirrah ; a word in your ear : sir, I say to you, it is thought you are false knaves.

Borachio. Sir, I say to you we are none.

Dogberry. Well, stand aside. 'Fore God, they are both in a tale. Have you writ down, that they are none ?

Sexton. Master constable, you go not the way to examine : you must call forth the watch that are their accusers.

Dogberry. Yea, marry, that 's the eftest way. Let the watch come forth. Masters, I charge you, in the prince's name, accuse these men.

First Watch. This man said, sir, that Don John, the prince's brother, was a villain.

Dogberry. Write down Prince John a villain. Why, this is flat perjury, to call a prince's brother villain.

Borachio. Master constable,—

Dogberry. Pray thee, fellow, peace : I do not like thy look, I promise thee.

Sexton. What heard you him say else ?

Second Watch. Marry, that he had received a thousand ducats of Don John for accusing the Lady Hero wrongfully.

Dogberry. Flat burglary as ever was committed.

Verges. Yea, by mass, that it is.

Sexton. What else, fellow ?

First Watch. And that Count Claudio did mean, upon his words, to disgrace Hero before the whole assembly, and not marry her.

Dogberry. O villain ! thou wilt be condemned into everlasting redemption for this.

Sexton. What else ?

Watch. This is all.

Sexton. And this is more, masters, than you can deny. Prince John is this morning secretly stolen away ; Hero was in this manner accused, in this very manner refused, and upon the grief of this suddenly died. Master constable, let these men be bound, and brought to Leonato's : I will go before and show him their examination.   [*Exit.*

Dogberry. Come, let them be opinioned.

Verges. † Let them be in the hands—

Conrade. Off, coxcomb !

Dogberry. God 's my life, where 's the sexton ? let him write down the prince's officer coxcomb. Come, bind them. Thou naughty varlet !

Conrade. Away ! you are an ass, you are an ass.

Dogberry. Dost thou not suspect my place ? dost thou not suspect my years ? O that he were here to write me down an ass ! But, masters, remember

that I am an ass ; though it be not written down,
yet forget not that I am an ass. No, thou villain,
thou art full of piety, as shall be proved upon thee
by good witness. I am a wise fellow, and, which
is more, an officer, and, which is more, a house-
holder, and, which is more, as pretty a piece of flesh
as any is in Messina, and one that knows the law,
go to ; and a rich fellow enough, go to ; and a
fellow that hath had losses, and one that hath two
gowns and every thing handsome about him. Bring
him away. O that I had been writ down an ass !
                                         [*Exeunt.*

ACT V.

SCENE I. *Before* LEONATO'S *house.*

Enter LEONATO *and* ANTONIO.

Antonio

If you go on thus, you will kill yourself ;
    And 'tis not wisdom thus to second grief
    Against yourself.
Leonato.   I pray thee, cease thy counsel,
Which falls into mine ears as profitless
As water in a sieve : give not me counsel ;
Nor let no comforter delight mine ear
But such a one whose wrongs do suit with mine.
Bring me a father that so loved his child,
Whose joy of her is overwhelm'd like mine,
And bid him speak of patience ;
Measure his woe the length and breadth of mine
And let it answer every strain for strain,
As thus for thus and such a grief for such,
In every lineament, branch, shape, and form :
If such a one will smile and stroke his beard,
† Bid sorrow wag, cry ' hem ! ' when he should
        groan,
Patch grief with proverbs, make misfortune drunk
With candle-wasters ; bring him yet to me,
And I of him will gather patience.
But there is no such man : for, brother, men
Can counsel and speak comfort to that grief
Which they themselves not feel ; but, tasting it,
Their counsel turns to passion, which before
Would give preceptial medicine to rage,
Fetter strong madness in a silken thread,
Charm ache with air and agony with words :
No, no ; 'tis all men's office to speak patience
To those that wring under the load of sorrow,
But no man's virtue nor sufficiency
To be so moral when he shall endure
The like himself. Therefore give me no counsel :
My griefs cry louder than advertisement.
Antonio. Therein do men from children nothing
    differ.
Leonato. I pray thee, peace. I will be flesh and
    blood ;
For there was never yet philosopher
That could endure the toothache patiently,
However they have writ the style of gods
And made a push at chance and sufferance.
Antonio. Yet bend not all the harm upon your-
    self ;
Make those that do offend you suffer too.
Leonato. There thou speak'st reason : nay, I
    will do so.
My soul doth tell me Hero is belied ;
And that shall Claudio know ; so shall the prince
And all of them that thus dishonour her.
Antonio. Here comes the prince and Claudio
    hastily.

Enter DON PEDRO *and* CLAUDIO.

Don Pedro. Good den, good den.
Claudio.   Good day to both of you.
Leonato. Hear you, my lords,—
Don Pedro.   We have some haste, Leonato.
Leonato. Some haste, my lord ! well, fare you
    well, my lord :
Are you so hasty now ? well, all is one.
Don Pedro. Nay, do not quarrel with us, good
    old man.
Antonio. If he could right himself with quarrelling,
Some of us would lie low.
Claudio.   Who wrongs him ?
Leonato. Marry, thou dost wrong me ; thou
    dissembler, thou :—
Nay, never lay thy hand upon thy sword ;
I fear thee not.
Claudio.   Marry, beshrew my hand,
If it should give your age such cause of fear :
In faith, my hand meant nothing to my sword.
Leonato. Tush, tush, man ; never fleer and jest
    at me :
I speak not like a dotard nor a fool,
As under privilege of age to brag
What I have done being young, or what would do
Were I not old. Know, Claudio, to thy head,
Thou hast so wrong'd mine innocent child and me
That I am forced to lay my reverence by
And, with grey hairs and bruise of many days,
Do challenge thee to trial of a man.
I say thou hast belied mine innocent child ;
Thy slander hath gone through and through her
    heart,
And she lies buried with her ancestors ;
O, in a tomb where never scandal slept,
Save this of hers, framed by thy villany !
Claudio. My villany ?
Leonato.   Thine, Claudio ; thine, I say.
Don Pedro. You say not right, old man.
Leonato.   My lord, my lord,
I 'll prove it on his body, if he dare,
Despite his nice fence and his active practice,
His May of youth and bloom of lustihood.
Claudio. Away ! I will not have to do with you.
Leonato. Canst thou so daff me ? Thou hast
    kill'd my child :
If thou kill'st me, boy, thou shalt kill a man.
Antonio. He shall kill two of us, and men indeed :
But that 's no matter ; let him kill one first ;
Win me and wear me ; let him answer me.
Come, follow me, boy ; come, sir boy, come, follow
    me :
Sir boy, I 'll whip you from your foining fence ;
Nay, as I am a gentleman, I will.
Leonato. Brother,—
Antonio. Content yourself. God knows I loved
    my niece ;
And she is dead, slander'd to death by villains,
That dare as well answer a man indeed
As I dare take a serpent by the tongue :
Boys, apes, braggarts, Jacks, milksops !
Leonato.   Brother Antony,—
Antonio. Hold you content. What, man ! I
    know them, yea,
And what they weigh, even to the utmost scruple,—
Scambling, out-facing, fashion-monging boys,
That lie and cog and flout, deprave and slander,
Go anticly, show outward hideousness,
And speak off half a dozen dangerous words,
How they might hurt their enemies, if they durst :
And this is all.

Leonato.   But, brother Antony,—
Antonio.   Come, 'tis no matter :
Do not you meddle ; let me deal in this.
Don Pedro.   Gentlemen both, we will not wake
your patience.
My heart is sorry for your daughter's death :
But, on my honour, she was charged with nothing
But what was true and very full of proof.
Leonato.   My lord, my lord,—
Don Pedro.   I will not hear you.
Leonato.   No ? Come, brother ; away ! I will
be heard.
Antonio.   And shall, or some of us will smart
for it.   [*Exeunt Leonato and Antonio.*
Don Pedro.   See, see ; here comes the man we
went to seek.

Enter BENEDICK.

Claudio.   Now, signior, what news ?
Benedick.   Good day, my lord.
Don Pedro.   Welcome, signior : you are almost
come to part almost a fray.
Claudio.   We had like to have had our two noses
snapped off with two old men without teeth.
Don Pedro.   Leonato and his brother. What
thinkest thou ? Had we fought, I doubt we should
have been too young for them.
Benedick.   In a false quarrel there is no true
valour. I came to seek you both.
Claudio.   We have been up and down to seek
thee ; for we are high-proof melancholy and would
fain have it beaten away. Wilt thou use thy wit ?
Benedick.   It is in my scabbard ; shall I draw it ?
Don Pedro.   Dost thou wear thy wit by thy side ?
Claudio.   Never any did so, though very many
have been beside their wit. I will bid thee draw, as
we do the minstrels ; draw, to pleasure us.
Don Pedro.   As I am an honest man, he looks
pale. Art thou sick, or angry ?
Claudio.   What, courage, man ! What though
care killed a cat, thou hast mettle enough in thee to
kill care.
Benedick.   Sir, I shall meet your wit in the career,
an you charge it against me. I pray you choose
another subject.
Claudio.   Nay, then, give him another staff ;
this last was broke cross.
Don Pedro.   By this light, he changes more and
more : I think he be angry indeed.
Claudio.   If he be, he knows how to turn his
girdle.
Benedick.   Shall I speak a word in your ear ?
Claudio.   God bless me from a challenge !
Benedick.   [*Aside to Claudio*] You are a villain ;
I jest not : I will make it good how you dare, with
what you dare, and when you dare. Do me right,
or I will protest your cowardice. You have killed
a sweet lady, and her death shall fall heavy on you.
Let me hear from you.
Claudio.   Well, I will meet you, so I may have
good cheer.
Don Pedro.   What, a feast, a feast ?
Claudio.   I' faith, I thank him ; he hath bid me
to a calf's head and a capon ; the which if I do not
carve most curiously, say my knife 's naught. Shall
I not find a woodcock too ?
Benedick.   Sir, your wit ambles well ; it goes
easily.
Don Pedro.   I 'll tell thee how Beatrice praised
thy wit the other day. I said, thou hadst a fine
wit : ' True,' said she, ' a fine little one.' ' No,' said

I, ' a great wit : ' ' Right,' says she, ' a great gross
one.' ' Nay,' said I, ' a good wit : ' ' Just,' said she,
' it hurts nobody.' ' Nay,' said I, ' the gentleman is
wise : ' ' Certain,' said she, ' a wise gentleman.'
' Nay,' said I, ' he hath the tongues : ' ' That I
believe,' said she, ' for he swore a thing to me on
Monday night, which he forswore on Tuesday
morning ; there 's a double tongue ; there 's two
tongues.' Thus did she, an hour together, trans-
shape thy particular virtues : yet at last she concluded with a sigh, thou wast the properest man in
Italy.
Claudio.   For the which she wept heartily and
said she cared not.
Don Pedro.   Yea, that she did ; but yet, for all
that, an if she did not hate him deadly, she would
love him dearly : the old man's daughter told us
all.
Claudio.   All, all ; and, moreover God saw him
when he was hid in the garden.
Don Pedro.   But when shall we set the savage
bull's horns on the sensible Benedick's head ?
Claudio.   Yea, and text underneath, ' Here dwells
Benedick the married man ' ?
Benedick.   Fare you well, boy : you know my
mind. I will leave you now to your gossip-like
humour : you break jests as braggarts do their
blades, which, God be thanked, hurt not. My
lord, for your many courtesies I thank you : I must
discontinue your company : your brother the bastard
is fled from Messina : you have among you killed
a sweet and innocent lady. For my Lord Lackbeard
there, he and I shall meet : and, till then, peace be
with him.   [*Exit.*
Don Pedro.   He is in earnest.
Claudio.   In most profound earnest ; and, I 'll
warrant you, for the love of Beatrice.
Don Pedro.   And hath challenged thee.
Claudio.   Most sincerely.
Don Pedro.   What a pretty thing man is when he
goes in his doublet and hose and leaves off his wit !
Claudio.   He is then a giant to an ape ; but then
is an ape a doctor to such a man.
Don Pedro.   But, soft you, let me be : pluck up,
my heart, and be sad. Did he not say, my brother
was fled ?

Enter DOGBERRY, VERGES, *and the* Watch, *with* CONRADE *and* BORACHIO.

Dogberry.   Come you, sir : if justice cannot tame
you, she shall ne'er weigh more reasons in her
balance : nay, an you be a cursing hypocrite once,
you must be looked to.
Don Pedro.   How now ? two of my brother's
men bound ! Borachio one !
Claudio.   Hearken after their offence, my lord.
Don Pedro.   Officers, what offence have these men
done ?
Dogberry.   Marry, sir, they have committed false
report ; moreover, they have spoken untruths ;
secondarily, they are slanders ; sixth and lastly,
they have belied a lady ; thirdly, they have verified
unjust things ; and, to conclude, they are lying
knaves.
Don Pedro.   First, I ask thee what they have done ;
thirdly, I ask thee what 's their offence ; sixth and
lastly, why they are committed ; and, to conclude,
what you lay to their charge.
Claudio.   Rightly reasoned, and in his own
division ; and, by my troth, there 's one meaning
well suited.

Don Pedro. Who have you offended, masters, that you are thus bound to your answer ? this learned constable is too cunning to be understood : what 's your offence ?

Borachio. Sweet prince, let me go no farther to mine answer : do you hear me, and let this count kill me. I have deceived even your very eyes : what your wisdoms could not discover, these shallow fools have brought to light ; who in the night overheard me confessing to this man how Don John your brother incensed me to slander the Lady Hero, how you were brought into the orchard and saw me court Margaret in Hero's garments, how you disgraced her, when you should marry her : my villany they have upon record ; which I had rather seal with my death than repeat over to my shame. The lady is dead upon mine and my master's false accusation ; and, briefly, I desire nothing but the reward of a villain.

Don Pedro. Runs not this speech like iron through your blood ?

Claudio. I have drunk poison whiles he utter'd it.

Don Pedro. But did my brother set thee on to this ?

Borachio. Yea, and paid me richly for the practice of it.

Don Pedro. He is composed and framed of treachery :
And fled he is upon this villany.

Claudio. Sweet Hero ! now thy image doth appear
In the rare semblance that I loved it first.

Dogberry. Come, bring away the plaintiffs : by this time our sexton hath reformed Signior Leonato of the matter : and, masters, do not forget to specify, when time and place shall serve, that I am an ass.

Verges. Here, here comes master Signior Leonato, and the sexton too.

Re-enter LEONATO *and* ANTONIO, *with the* Sexton.

Leonato. Which is the villain ? let me see his eyes,
That, when I note another man like him,
I may avoid him : which of these is he ?

Borachio. If you would know your wronger, look on me.

Leonato. Art thou the slave that with thy breath hast kill'd
Mine innocent child ?

Borachio.   Yea, even I alone.

Leonato. No, not so, villain ; thou beliest thyself :
Here stand a pair of honourable men ;
A third is fled, that had a hand in it.
I thank you, princes, for my daughter's death :
Record it with your high and worthy deeds :
'Twas bravely done, if you bethink you of it.

Claudio. I know not how to pray your patience ;
Yet I must speak. Choose your revenge yourself ;
Impose me to what penance your invention
Can lay upon my sin : yet sinn'd I not
But in mistaking.

Don Pedro. By my soul, nor I :
And yet, to satisfy this good old man,
I would bend under any heavy weight
That he 'll enjoin me to.

Leonato. I cannot bid you bid my daughter live ;
That were impossible ; but, I pray you both,
Possess the people in Messina here
How innocent she died ; and if your love
Can labour aught in sad invention,
Hang her an epitaph upon her tomb

And sing it to her bones, sing it to-night :
To-morrow morning come you to my house,
And since you could not be my son-in-law,
Be yet my nephew : my brother hath a daughter,
Almost the copy of my child that 's dead,
And she alone is heir to both of us :
Give her the right you should have given her cousin,
And so dies my revenge.

Claudio.   O noble sir,
Your over-kindness doth wring tears from me !
I do embrace your offer ; and dispose
For henceforth of poor Claudio.

Leonato. To-morrow then I will expect your coming ;
To-night I take my leave. This naughty man
Shall face to face be brought to Margaret,
Who I believe was pack'd in all this wrong,
Hired to it by your brother.

Borachio.   No, by my soul, she was not,
Nor knew not what she did when she spoke to me,
But always hath been just and virtuous
In any thing that I do know by her.

Dogberry. Moreover, sir, which indeed is not under white and black, this plaintiff here, the offender, did call me ass : I beseech you, let it be remembered in his punishment. And also, the watch heard them talk of one Deformed : they say he wears a key in his ear and a lock hanging by it, and borrows money in God's name, the which he hath used so long and never paid that now men grow hard-hearted and will lend nothing for God's sake : pray you, examine him upon that point.

Leonato. I thank thee for thy care and honest pains.

Dogberry. Your worship speaks like a most thankful and reverend youth ; and I praise God for you.

Leonato. There 's for thy pains.

Dogberry. God save the foundation !

Leonato. Go, I discharge thee of thy prisoner, and I thank thee.

Dogberry. I leave an arrant knave with your worship ; which I beseech your worship to correct yourself, for the example of others. God keep your worship ! I wish your worship well ; God restore you to health ! I humbly give you leave to depart ; and if a merry meeting may be wished, God prohibit it ! Come, neighbour.

[*Exeunt Dogberry and Verges.*

Leonato. Until to-morrow morning, lords, farewell.

Antonio. Farewell, my lords : we look for you to-morrow.

Don Pedro. We will not fail.

Claudio.   To-night I 'll mourn with Hero.

Leonato. [*To the Watch*] Bring you these fellows on. We 'll talk with Margaret,
How her acquaintance grew with this lewd fellow.

[*Exeunt, severally.*

SCENE II. LEONATO'S *garden.*

Enter BENEDICK *and* MARGARET, *meeting.*

Benedick. Pray thee, sweet Mistress Margaret, deserve well at my hands by helping me to the speech of Beatrice.

Margaret. Will you then write me a sonnet in praise of my beauty ?

Benedick. In so high a style, Margaret, that no man living shall come over it ; for, in most comely truth, thou deservest it.

Margaret. To have no man come over me ! why, shall I always keep below stairs ?

Benedick. Thy wit is as quick as the greyhound's mouth ; it catches.

Margaret. And yours as blunt as the fencer's foils, which hit, but hurt not.

Benedick. A most manly wit, Margaret ; it will not hurt a woman : and so, I pray thee, call Beatrice : I give thee the bucklers.

Margaret. Give us the swords; we have bucklers of our own.

Benedick. If you use them, Margaret, you must put in the pikes with a vice ; and they are dangerous weapons for maids.

Margaret. Well, I will call Beatrice to you, who I think hath legs.

Benedick. And therefore will come.

[*Exit Margaret.*

[*Sings*]   The god of love,
          That sits above,
And knows me, and knows me,
     How pitiful I deserve,—

I mean in singing ; but in loving, Leander the good swimmer, Troilus the first employer of pandars, and a whole bookful of these quondam carpet-mongers, whose names yet run smoothly in the even road of a blank verse, why, they were never so truly turned over and over as my poor self in love. Marry, I cannot show it in rhyme ; I have tried : I can find out no rhyme to 'lady' but 'baby,' an innocent rhyme ; for 'scorn,' 'horn,' a hard rhyme ; for 'school,' 'fool,' a babbling rhyme ; very ominous endings : no, I was not born under a rhyming planet, nor I cannot woo in festival terms.

Enter BEATRICE.

Sweet Beatrice, wouldst thou come when I called thee ?

Beatrice. Yea, signior, and depart when you bid me.

Benedick. O, stay but till then !

Beatrice. 'Then' is spoken ; fare you well now : and yet, ere I go, let me go with that I came ; which is, with knowing what hath passed between you and Claudio.

Benedick. Only foul words ; and thereupon I will kiss thee.

Beatrice. Foul words is but foul wind, and foul wind is but foul breath, and foul breath is noisome ; therefore I will depart unkissed.

Benedick. Thou hast frighted the word out of his right sense, so forcible is thy wit. But I must tell thee plainly, Claudio undergoes my challenge : and either I must shortly hear from him, or I will subscribe him a coward. And, I pray thee now, tell me for which of my bad parts didst thou first fall in love with me ?

Beatrice. For them all together ; which maintained so politic a state of evil that they will not admit any good part to intermingle with them. But for which of my good parts did you first suffer love for me ?

Benedick. Suffer love ! a good epithet ! I do suffer love indeed, for I love thee against my will.

Beatrice. In spite of your heart, I think ; alas, poor heart ! If you spite it for my sake, I will spite it for yours ; for I will never love that which my friend hates.

Benedick. Thou and I are too wise to woo peaceably.

Beatrice. It appears not in this confession : there 's not one wise man among twenty that will praise himself.

Benedick. An old, an old instance, Beatrice, that lived in the time of good neighbours. If a man do not erect in this age his own tomb ere he dies, he shall live no longer in monument than the bell rings and the widow weeps.

Beatrice. And how long is that, think you ?

Benedick. Question : why, an hour in clamour and a quarter in rheum : therefore is it most expedient for the wise, if Don Worm, his conscience, find no impediment to the contrary, to be the trumpet of his own virtues, as I am to myself. So much for praising myself, who, I myself will bear witness, is praiseworthy : and now tell me, how doth your cousin ?

Beatrice. Very ill.

Benedick. And how do you ?

Beatrice. Very ill too.

Benedick. Serve God, love me and mend. There will I leave you too, for here comes one in haste.

Enter URSULA.

Ursula. Madam, you must come to your uncle. Yonder 's old coil at home : it is proved my Lady Hero hath been falsely accused ; and the prince and Claudio mightily abused ; and Don John is the author of all, who is fled and gone. Will you come presently?

Beatrice. Will you go hear this news, signior ?

Benedick. I will live in thy heart, die in thy lap and be buried in thy eyes ; and moreover I will go with thee to thy uncle's.   [*Exeunt.*

SCENE III. *A church.*

Enter DON PEDRO, CLAUDIO, *and three or four with tapers.*

Claudio. Is this the monument of Leonato ?

A Lord. It is, my lord.

Claudio. [*Reading out of a scroll*]
     Done to death by slanderous tongues
          Was the Hero that here lies :
     Death, in guerdon of her wrongs,
          Gives her fame which never dies.
So the life that died with shame
Lives in death with glorious fame.

Hang thou there upon the tomb,
Praising her when I am dumb.
Now, music, sound, and sing your solemn hymn.

SONG.

     Pardon, goddess of the night,
     Those that slew thy virgin knight ;
     For the which, with songs of woe,
     Round about her tomb they go.
          Midnight, assist our moan ;
          Help us to sigh and groan,
               Heavily, heavily :
          Graves, yawn and yield your dead,
          Till death be uttered,
               Heavily, heavily.

Claudio. Now, unto thy bones good night !
Yearly will I do this rite.

Don Pedro. Good morrow, masters ; put your torches out :
The wolves have prey'd ; and look, the gentle day,
Before the wheels of Phœbus, round about
Dapples the drowsy east with spots of grey.
Thanks to you all, and leave us : fare you well.

Claudio. Good morrow, masters : each his
several way.
Don Pedro. Come, let us hence, and put on other
weeds ;
And then to Leonato's we will go.
Claudio. And Hymen now with luckier issue
speed 's
Than this for whom we render'd up this woe.
                                    [*Exeunt.*

SCENE IV. *A room in* LEONATO'S *house.*

Enter LEONATO, ANTONIO, BENEDICK, BEATRICE,
    MARGARET, URSULA, FRIAR FRANCIS, *and* HERO.

Friar. Did I not tell you she was innocent ?
Leonato. So are the prince and Claudio, who
accused her
Upon the error that you heard debated :
But Margaret was in some fault for this,
Although against her will, as it appears
In the true course of all the question.
Antonio. Well, I am glad that all things sort so
well.
Benedick. And so am I, being else by faith en-
forced
To call young Claudio to a reckoning for it.
Leonato. Well, daughter, and you gentlewomen
all,
Withdraw into a chamber by yourselves,
And when I send for you, come hither mask'd.
                                [*Exeunt Ladies.*
The prince and Claudio promised by this hour
To visit me. You know your office, brother :
You must be father to your brother's daughter,
And give her to young Claudio.
Antonio. Which I will do with confirm'd coun-
tenance.
Benedick. Friar, I must entreat your pains, I
think.
Friar. To do what, signior ?
Benedick. To bind me, or undo me ; one of
them.
Signior Leonato, truth it is, good signior,
Your niece regards me with an eye of favour.
Leonato. That eye my daughter lent her : 'tis
most true.
Benedick. And I do with an eye of love requite her.
Leonato. The sight whereof I think you had
from me,
From Claudio and the prince : but what 's your will ?
Benedick. Your answer, sir, is enigmatical :
But, for my will, my will is your good will
May stand with ours, this day to be conjoin'd
In the state of honourable marriage :
In which, good friar, I shall desire your help.
Leonato. My heart is with your liking.
Friar.   And my help.
Here comes the prince and Claudio.

Enter DON PEDRO *and* CLAUDIO, *and two or three
    others.*

Don Pedro. Good morrow to this fair assembly.
Leonato. Good morrow, prince ; good morrow,
Claudio :
We here attend you. Are you yet determined
To-day to marry with my brother's daughter ?
Claudio. I 'll hold my mind, were she an Ethiope.
Leonato. Call her forth, brother ; here 's the
friar ready.   [*Exit Antonio.*
Don Pedro. Good morrow, Benedick. Why,
what 's the matter,

That you have such a February face,
So full of frost, of storm and cloudiness ?
Claudio. I think he thinks upon the savage bull.
Tush, fear not, man ; we 'll tip thy horns with gold
And all Europa shall rejoice at thee,
As once Europa did at lusty Jove,
When he would play the noble beast in love.
Benedick. Bull Jove, sir, had an amiable horn ;
And some such strange bull leap'd your father's cow,
And got a calf in that same noble feat
Much like to you, for you have just his bleat.
Claudio. For this I owe you : here comes other
reckonings.

Re-enter ANTONIO, *with the* Ladies *masked.*

Which is the lady I must seize upon ?
Antonio. This same is she, and I do give you her.
Claudio. Why, then she 's mine. Sweet, let me
see your face.
Leonato. No, that you shall not, till you take her
hand
Before this friar and swear to marry her.
Claudio. Give me your hand : before this holy
friar,
I am your husband, if you like of me.
Hero. And when I lived, I was your other wife :
                                    [*Unmasking.*
And when you loved, you were my other husband.
Claudio. Another Hero !
Hero.   Nothing certainer :
One Hero died defiled, but I do live,
And surely as I live, I am a maid.
Don Pedro. The former Hero ! Hero that is
dead !
Leonato. She died, my lord, but whiles her slander
lived.
Friar. All this amazement can I qualify ;
When after that the holy rites are ended,
I 'll tell you largely of fair Hero's death :
Meantime let wonder seem familiar,
And to the chapel let us presently.
Benedick. Soft and fair, friar. Which is Beatrice?
Beatrice. [*Unmasking*] I answer to that name.
    What is your will ?
Benedick. Do not you love me ?
Beatrice.   Why, no ; no more than reason.
Benedick. Why, then your uncle and the prince
and Claudio
Have been deceived ; they swore you did.
Beatrice. Do not you love me ?
Benedick.   Troth, no ; no more than reason.
Beatrice. Why, then my cousin Margaret and
Ursula
Are much deceived ; for they did swear you did.
Benedick. They swore that you were almost sick
for me.
Beatrice. They swore that you were well-nigh
dead for me.
Benedick. 'Tis no such matter. Then you do
not love me ?
Beatrice. No, truly, but in friendly recompense.
Leonato. Come, cousin, I am sure you love the
gentleman.
Claudio. And I 'll be sworn upon 't that he loves
her ;
For here 's a paper written in his hand,
A halting sonnet of his own pure brain,
Fashion'd to Beatrice.
Hero.   And here 's another
Writ in my cousin's hand, stolen from her pocket,
Containing her affection unto Benedick.

Benedick. A miracle ! here 's our own hands against our hearts. Come, I will have thee ; but, by this light, I take thee for pity.

Beatrice. I would not deny you ; but, by this good day, I yield upon great persuasion ; and partly to save your life, for I was told you were in a consumption.

Benedick. Peace ! I will stop your mouth.

[Kissing her.

Don Pedro. How dost thou, Benedick, the married man ?

Benedick. I 'll tell thee what, prince ; a college of wit-crackers cannot flout me out of my humour. Dost thou think I care for a satire or an epigram ? No : if a man will be beaten with brains, a' shall wear nothing handsome about him. In brief, since I do purpose to marry, I will think nothing to any purpose that the world can say against it ; and therefore never flout at me for what I have said against it ; for man is a giddy thing, and this is my conclusion. For thy part, Claudio, I did think to have beaten thee : but in that thou art like to be my kinsman, live unbruised and love my cousin.

Claudio. I had well hoped thou wouldst have denied Beatrice, that I might have cudgelled thee out of thy single life, to make thee a double-dealer ; which, out of question, thou wilt be, if my cousin do not look exceeding narrowly to thee.

Benedick. Come, come, we are friends : let 's have a dance ere we are married, that we may lighten our own hearts and our wives' heels.

Leonato. We 'll have dancing afterward.

Benedick. First, of my word ; therefore play, music. Prince, thou art sad ; get thee a wife, get thee a wife : there is no staff more reverend than one tipped with horn.

Enter a Messenger.

Messenger. My lord, your brother John is ta'en in flight.
And brought with armed men back to Messina.

Benedick. Think not on him till to-morrow : I 'll devise thee brave punishments for him. Strike up, pipers.   *[Dance.*

[Exeunt.

LOVE'S LABOUR'S LOST

DRAMATIS PERSONÆ

FERDINAND, king of Navarre.

BIRON, }
LONGAVILLE, } lords attending on the King.
DUMAIN, }

BOYET, } lords attending on the Princess of
MERCADE, } France.

DON ADRIANO DE ARMADO, a fantastical Spaniard.

SIR NATHANIEL, a curate.

HOLOFERNES, a schoolmaster.

DULL, a constable.

COSTARD, a clown.

MOTH, page to Armado.

A FORESTER.

The PRINCESS of France.

ROSALINE, }
MARIA, } ladies attending on the Princess.
KATHARINE, }

JAQUENETTA, a country wench.

Lords, Attendants, &c.

SCENE : Navarre.

ACT I.

SCENE I. *The king of Navarre's park.*

Enter FERDINAND, *king of* NAVARRE, BIRON,
LONGAVILLE, *and* DUMAIN.

King.

Let fame, that all hunt after in their lives,
Live register'd upon our brazen tombs
And then grace us in the disgrace of death ;
When, spite of cormorant devouring Time,
The endeavour of this present breath may buy
That honour which shall bate his scythe's keen edge
And make us heirs of all eternity.
Therefore, brave conquerors,—for so you are,
That war against your own affections
And the huge army of the world's desires,—
Our late edict shall strongly stand in force :
Navarre shall be the wonder of the world ;
Our court shall be a little Academe,
Still and contemplative in living art.
You three, Biron, Dumain, and Longaville,
Have sworn for three years' term to live with me
My fellow-scholars and to keep those statutes
That are recorded in this schedule here :
Your oaths are pass'd ; and now subscribe your
    names,
That his own hand may strike his honour down
That violates the smallest branch herein :

If you are arm'd to do as sworn to do,
Subscribe to your deep oaths, and keep it too.
    Longaville. I am resolved ; 'tis but a three years'
        fast :
The mind shall banquet, though the body pine :
Fat paunches have lean pates, and dainty bits
Make rich the ribs, but bankrupt quite the wits.
    Dumain. My loving lord, Dumain is mortified :
The grosser manner of these world's delights
He throws upon the gross world's baser slaves :
To love, to wealth, to pomp, I pine and die ;
With all these living in philosophy.
    Biron. I can but say their protestation over ;
So much, dear liege, I have already sworn,
That is, to live and study here three years.
But there are other strict observances ;
As, not to see a woman in that term,
Which I hope well is not enrolled there ;
And one day in a week to touch no food
And but one meal on every day beside,
The which I hope is not enrolled there ;
And then, to sleep but three hours in the night,
And not be seen to wink of all the day—
When I was wont to think no harm all night
And make a dark night too of half the day—
Which I hope well is not enrolled there :
O, these are barren tasks, too hard to keep,
Not to see ladies, study, fast, not sleep !
    King. Your oath is pass'd to pass away from
        these.
    Biron. Let me say no, my liege, an if you please:
I only swore to study with your grace
And stay here in your court for three years' space.
    Longaville. You swore to that, Biron, and to
        the rest.
    Biron. By yea and nay, sir, then I swore in jest.
What is the end of study ? let me know.
    King. Why, that to know, which else we should
        not know.
    Biron. Things hid and barr'd, you mean, from
        common sense ?
    King. Ay, that is study's god-like recompense.
    Biron. Come on, then ; I will swear to study so,
To know the thing I am forbid to know :
As thus,—to study where I well may dine,
    When I to feast expressly am forbid ;
Or study where to meet some mistress fine,
    When mistresses from common sense are hid ;
Or, having sworn too hard a keeping oath,
Study to break it and not break my troth.
If study's gain be thus and this be so,
Study knows that which yet it doth not know :
Swear me to this, and I will ne'er say no.
    King. These be the stops that hinder study quite
And train our intellects to vain delight.
    Biron. Why, all delights are vain ; but that
        most vain,
Which with pain purchased doth inherit pain :
As, painfully to pore upon a book

To seek the light of truth ; while truth the while
Doth falsely blind the eyesight of his look :
Light seeking light doth light of light beguile :
So, ere you find where light in darkness lies,
Your light grows dark by losing of your eyes.
Study me how to please the eye indeed
　　By fixing it upon a fairer eye,
Who dazzling so, that eye shall be his heed
　　And give him light that it was blinded by.
Study is like the heaven's glorious sun
　　That will not be deep-search'd with saucy looks :
Small have continual plodders ever won
　　Save base authority from others' books.
These earthly godfathers of heaven's lights
　　That give a name to every fixed star
Have no more profit of their shining nights
　　Than those that walk and wot not what they are.
Too much to know is to know nought but fame ;
And every godfather can give a name.
　　King. How well he 's read, to reason against
　　　　reading !
　　Dumain. Proceeded well, to stop all good pro-
　　　　ceeding !
　　Longaville. He weeds the corn and still lets grow
　　　　the weeding.
　　Biron. The spring is near when green geese are
　　　　a-breeding.
　　Dumain. How follows that ?
　　Biron. 　　　　　　　　Fit in his place and time.
　　Dumain. In reason nothing.
　　Biron. 　　　　　　Something then in rhyme.
　　King. Biron is like an envious sneaping frost
　　　　That bites the first-born infants of the
　　　　spring.
　　Biron. Well, say I am ; why should proud
　　　　summer boast
　　　　Before the birds have any cause to sing ?
Why should I joy in any abortive birth ?
At Christmas I no more desire a rose
Than wish a snow in May's new-fangled mirth
But like of each thing that in season grows.
So you, to study now it is too late,
Climb o'er the house to unlock the little gate.
　　King. Well, sit you out : go home, Biron :
　　　　adieu.
　　Biron. No, my good lord ; I have sworn to stay
　　　　with you :
And though I have for barbarism spoke more
Than for that angel knowledge you can say,
Yet confident I 'll keep what I have swore
And bide the penance of each three years' day.
Give me the paper ; let me read the same ;
And to the strict'st decrees I 'll write my name.
　　King. How well this yielding rescues thee from
　　　　shame !
　　Biron [*reads*]. ' Item, That no woman shall
come within a mile of my court : ' Hath this been
proclaimed ?
　　Longaville. Four days ago.
　　Biron. Let 's see the penalty. [*Reads*] ' On
pain of losing her tongue.' Who devised this penalty ?
　　Longaville. Marry, that did I.
　　Biron. Sweet lord, and why ?
　　Longaville. To fright them hence with that dread
penalty.
　　Biron. A dangerous law against gentility !
　　[*Reads*] ' Item, If any man be seen to talk with
a woman within the term of three years, he shall
endure such public shame as the rest of the court
can possibly devise.'
This article, my liege, yourself must break ;

For well you know here comes in embassy
The French king's daughter with yourself to speak—
　　A maid of grace and complete majesty—
About surrender up of Aquitaine
To her decrepit, sick and bedrid father :
Therefore this article is made in vain,
　　Or vainly comes the admired princess hither.
　　King. What say you, lords ? why, this was quite
forgot.
　　Biron. So study evermore is overshot :
While it doth study to have what it would
It doth forget to do the thing it should,
And when it hath the thing it hunteth most,
'Tis won as towns with fire, so won, so lost.
　　King. We must of force dispense with this decree :
She must lie here on mere necessity.
　　Biron. Necessity will make us all forsworn
　　Three thousand times within this three years
　　space ;
For every man with his affects is born,
　　Not by might master'd but by special grace :
If I break faith, this word shall speak for me ;
I am forsworn on ' mere necessity.'
So to the laws at large I write my name :
　　　　　　　　　　　　　　　　　　[*Subscribes.*
　　And he that breaks them in the least degree
Stands in attainder of eternal shame :
　　Suggestions are to other as to me ;
But I believe, although I seem so loath,
I am the last that will last keep his oath.
But is there no quick recreation granted ?
　　King. Ay, that there is. Our court, you know, is
　　　　haunted
With a refined traveller of Spain ;
A man in all the world's new fashion planted,
　　That hath a mint of phrases in his brain ;
One whom the music of his own vain tongue
　　Doth ravish like enchanting harmony ;
A man of complements, whom right and wrong
　　Have chose as umpire of their mutiny :
This child of fancy that Armado hight
　　For interim to our studies shall relate
In high-born words the worth of many a knight
　　From tawny Spain lost in the world's debate.
How you delight, my lords, I know not, I ;
But, I protest, I love to hear him lie
And I will use him for my minstrelsy.
　　Biron. Armado is a most illustrious wight,
A man of fire-new words, fashion's own knight.
　　Longaville. Costard the swain and he shall be our
　　　　sport ;
And so to study, three years is but short.

　　　　Enter DULL *with a letter, and* COSTARD.

　　Dull. Which is the duke's own person ?
　　Biron. This, fellow : what wouldst ?
　　Dull. I myself reprehend his own person, for I
am his grace's tharborough : but I would see his
own person in flesh and blood.
　　Biron. This is he.
　　Dull. Signior Arme—Arme—commends you.
There 's villany abroad : this letter will tell you
more.
　　Costard. Sir, the contempts thereof are as touch-
ing me.
　　King. A letter from the magnificent Armado.
　　Biron. How low soever the matter, I hope in
God for high words.
　　Longaville. A high hope for a low heaven : God
grant us patience !
　　Biron. To hear ? or forbear laughing ?

Longaville. To hear meekly, sir, and to laugh moderately ; or to forbear both.

Biron. Well, sir, be it as the style shall give us cause to climb in the merriness.

Costard. The matter is to me, sir, as concerning Jaquenetta. The manner of it is, I was taken with the manner.

Biron. In what manner ?

Costard. In manner and form following, sir ; all those three : I was seen with her in the manorhouse, sitting with her upon the form, and taken following her into the park ; which, put together, is in manner and form following. Now, sir, for the manner,—it is the manner of a man to speak to a woman : for the form,—in some form.

Biron. For the following, sir ?

Costard. As it shall follow in my correction and God defend the right !

King. Will you hear this letter with attention ?

Biron. As we would hear an oracle.

Costard. Such is the simplicity of man to hearken after the flesh.

King [*reads*]. Great deputy, the welkin's vicegerent and sole dominator of Navarre, my soul's earth's god, and body's fostering patron.'

Costard. Not a word of Costard yet.

King [*reads*]. ' So it is,'—

Costard. It may be so : but if he say it is so, he is, in telling true, but so.

King. Peace !

Costard. Be to me and every man that dares not fight !

King. No words !

Costard. Of other men's secrets, I beseech you.

King [*reads*]. ' So it is, besieged with sable-coloured melancholy, did commend the black-oppressing humour to the most wholesome physic of thy health-giving air ; and, as I am a gentleman, betook myself to walk. The time when. About the sixth hour ; when beasts most graze, birds best peck, and men sit down to that nourishment which is called supper : so much for the time when. Now for the ground which ; which, I mean, I walked upon : it is ycleped thy park. Then for the place where ; where, I mean, I did encounter that obscene and most preposterous event, that draweth from my snow-white pen the ebon-coloured ink, which here thou viewest, beholdest, surveyest, or seest : but to the place where ; it standeth north-north-east and by east from the west corner of thy curious-knotted garden : there did I see that low-spirited swain. that base minnow of thy mirth,'—

Costard. Me ?

King [*reads*]. ' that unlettered small-knowing soul,'—

Costard. Me ?

King [*reads*]. ' that shallow vassal,'—

Costard. Still me ?

King [*reads*]. ' which, as I remember, hight Costard,—

Costard. O, me !

King [*reads*]. ' sorted and consorted, contrary to thy established proclaimed edict and continent canon, which with,—O, with—but with this I passion to say wherewith,—

Costard. With a wench.

King [*reads*]. ' with a child of our grandmother Eve, a female ; or, for thy more sweet understanding, a woman. Him I, as my ever-esteemed duty pricks me on, have sent to thee, to receive the meed of punishment, by thy sweet grace's officer, Anthony Dull ; a man of good repute, carriage, bearing, and estimation.'

Dull. Me, an 't shall please you ; I am Anthony Dull.

King [*reads*]. ' For Jaquenetta,—so is the weaker vessel called which I apprehended with the aforesaid swain,—I keep her as a vessel of thy law's fury ; and shall, at the least of thy sweet notice, bring her to trial. Thine, in all compliments of devoted and heart-burning heat of duty.

　　　　　　　　　　Don Adriano de Armado.'

Biron. This is not so well as I looked for, but the best that ever I heard.

King. Ay, the best for the worst. But, sirrah, what say you to this ?

Costard. Sir, I confess the wench.

King. Did you hear the proclamation ?

Costard. I do confess much of the hearing it, but little of the marking of it.

King. It was proclaimed a year's imprisonment, to be taken with a wench.

Costard. I was taken with none, sir : I was taken with a damsel.

King. Well, it was proclaimed ' damsel.'

Costard. This was no damsel neither, sir ; she was a virgin.

King. It is so varied too ; for it was proclaimed ' virgin.'

Costard. If it were, I deny her virginity : I was taken with a maid.

King. This maid will not serve your turn, sir.

Costard. This maid will serve my turn, sir.

King. Sir, I will pronounce your sentence : you shall fast a week with bran and water.

Costard. I had rather pray a month with mutton and porridge.

King. And Don Armado shall be your keeper. My Lord Biron, see him deliver'd o'er : And go we, lords, to put in practice that Which each to other hath so strongly sworn.

　　　[*Exeunt King, Longaville, and Dumain.*

Biron. I 'll lay my head to any good man's hat, These oaths and laws will prove an idle scorn. Sirrah, come on.

Costard. I suffer for the truth, sir ; for true it is, I was taken with Jaquenetta, and Jaquenetta is a true girl ; and therefore welcome the sour cup of prosperity ! Affliction may one day smile again ; and till then, sit thee down, sorrow !　　　[*Exeunt*

SCENE II.　*The same.*

Enter Armado *and* Moth.

Armado. Boy, what sign is it when a man of great spirit grows melancholy ?

Moth. A great sign, sir, that he will look sad.

Armado. Why, sadness is one and the self-same thing, dear imp.

Moth. No, no ; O Lord, sir, no.

Armado. How canst thou part sadness and melancholy, my tender juvenal ?

Moth. By a familiar demonstration of the working, my tough senior.

Armado. Why tough senior ? why tough senior ?

Moth. Why tender juvenal ? why tender juvenal ?

Armado. I spoke it, tender juvenal, as a congruent epitheton appertaining to thy young days. which we may nominate tender.

Moth. And I, tough senior, as an appertinent title to your old time, which we may name tough.

Armado. Pretty and apt.

Moth. How mean you, sir? I pretty, and my saying apt? or I apt, and my saying pretty?
Armado. Thou pretty, because little.
Moth. Little pretty, because little. Wherefore apt?
Armado. And therefore apt, because quick.
Moth. Speak you this in my praise, master?
Armado. In thy condign praise.
Moth. I will praise an eel with the same praise.
Armado. What, that an eel is ingenious?
Moth. That an eel is quick.
Armado. I do say thou art quick in answers: thou heatest my blood.
Moth. I am answered, sir.
Armado. I love not to be crossed.
Moth. [*Aside*] He speaks the mere contrary; crosses love not him.
Armado. I have promised to study three years with the duke.
Moth. You may do it in an hour, sir.
Armado. Impossible.
Moth. How many is one thrice told?
Armado. I am ill at reckoning; it fitteth the spirit of a tapster.
Moth. You are a gentleman and a gamester, sir.
Armado. I confess both: they are both the varnish of a complete man.
Moth. Then, I am sure, you know how much the gross sum of deuce-ace amounts to.
Armado. It doth amount to one more than two.
Moth. Which the base vulgar do call three.
Armado. True.
Moth. Why, sir, is this such a piece of study? Now here is three studied, ere ye 'll thrice wink: and how easy it is to put ' years ' to the word ' three,' and study three years in two words, the dancing horse will tell you.
Armado. A most fine figure!
Moth. To prove you a cipher.
Armado. I will hereupon confess I am in love: and as it is base for a soldier to love, so am I in love with a base wench. If drawing my sword against the humour of affection would deliver me from the reprobate thought of it, I would take Desire prisoner, and ransom him to any French courtier for a new-devised courtesy. I think scorn to sigh; methinks I should outswear Cupid. Comfort me, boy: what great men have been in love?
Moth. Hercules, master.
Armado. Most sweet Hercules! More authority, dear boy, name more; and, sweet my child, let them be men of good repute and carriage.
Moth. Samson, master: he was a man of good carriage, great carriage, for he carried the town-gates on his back like a porter: and he was in love.
Armado. O well-knit Samson! strong-jointed Samson! I do excel thee in my rapier as much as thou didst me in carrying gates. I am in love too. Who was Samson's love, my dear Moth?
Moth. A woman, master.
Armado. Of what complexion?
Moth. Of all the four, or the three, or the two, or one of the four.
Armado. Tell me precisely of what complexion.
Moth. Of the sea-water green, sir.
Armado. Is that one of the four complexions?
Moth. As I have read, sir; and the best of them too.
Armado. Green indeed is the colour of lovers; but to have a love of that colour, methinks Samson had small reason for it. He surely affected her for

her wit.
Moth. It was so, sir; for she had a green wit.
Armado. My love is most immaculate white and red.
Moth. Most maculate thoughts, master, are masked under such colours.
Armado. Define, define, well-educated infant.
Moth. My father's wit and my mother's tongue, assist me!
Armado. Sweet invocation of a child; most pretty and pathetical!
Moth. If she be made of white and red,
    Her faults will ne'er be known,
  For blushing cheeks by faults are bred
    And fears by pale white shown:
  Then if she fear, or be to blame,
    By this you shall not know,
  For still her cheeks possess the same
    Which native she doth owe.
A dangerous rhyme, master, against the reason of white and red.
Armado. Is there not a ballad, boy, of the King and the Beggar?
Moth. The world was very guilty of such a ballad some three ages since: but I think now 'tis not to be found; or, if it were, it would neither serve for the writing nor the tune.
Armado. I will have that subject newly writ o'er, that I may example my digression by some mighty precedent. Boy, I do love that country girl that I took in the park with the rational hind Costard: she deserves well.
Moth. [*Aside*] To be whipped; and yet a better love than my master.
Armado. Sing, boy; my spirit grows heavy in love.
Moth. And that 's great marvel, loving a light wench.
Armado. I say, sing.
Moth. Forbear till this company be past.

Enter DULL, COSTARD, *and* JAQUENETTA.

Dull. Sir, the duke's pleasure is, that you keep Costard safe: and you must suffer him to take no delight nor no penance; but a' must fast three days a week. For this damsel, I must keep her at the park: she is allowed for the day-woman. Fare you well.
Armado. I do betray myself with blushing. Maid!
Jaquenetta. Man?
Armado. I will visit thee at the lodge.
Jaquenetta. That 's hereby.
Armado. I know where it is situate.
Jaquenetta. Lord, how wise you are!
Armado. I will tell thee wonders.
Jaquenetta. With that face?
Armado. I love thee.
Jaquenetta. So I heard you say.
Armado. And so, farewell.
Jaquenetta. Fair weather after you!
Dull. Come, Jaquenetta, away!
        [*Exeunt Dull and Jaquenetta.*
Armado. Villain, thou shalt fast for thy offences ere thou be pardoned.
Costard. Well, sir, I hope, when I do it, I shall do it on a full stomach.
Armado. Thou shalt be heavily punished.
Costard. I am more bound to you than your fellows, for they are but lightly rewarded.
Armado. Take away this villain; shut him up.

Moth. Come, you transgressing slave ; away !

Costard. Let me not be pent up. sir : I will fast, being loose.

Moth. No. sir ; that were fast and loose : thou shalt to prison.

Costard. Well, if ever I do see the merry days of desolation that I have seen, some shall see.

Moth. What shall some see ?

Costard. Nay. nothing, Master Moth, but what they look upon. It is not for prisoners to be too silent in their words ; and therefore I will say nothing: I thank God I have as little patience as another man : and therefore I can be quiet.

[Exeunt Moth and Costard.

Armado. I do affect the very ground, which is base, where her shoe, which is baser, guided by her foot, which is basest, doth tread. I shall be forsworn, which is a great argument of falsehood, if I love. And how can that be true love which is falsely attempted ? Love is a familiar : Love is a devil : there is no evil angel but Love.   Yet was Samson so tempted, and he had an excellent strength ; yet was Solomon so seduced, and he had a very good wit. Cupid's butt-shaft is too hard for Hercules' club ; and therefore too much odds for a Spaniard's rapier. The first and second cause will not serve my turn ; the passado he respects not, the duello he regards not : his disgrace is to be called boy : but his glory is to subdue men. Adieu, valour ! rust, rapier ! be still, drum ! for your manager is in love ; yea, he loveth. Assist me, some extemporal god of rhyme, for I am sure I shall turn sonnet. Devise, wit ; write, pen ; for I am for whole volumes in folio.   *[Exit.*

ACT II.

SCENE I. *The same.*

Enter the Princess of France, Rosaline, Maria, Katharine, Boyet, Lords, *and other* Attendants.

Boyet.

Now, madam, summon up your dearest spirits :
    Consider who the king your father sends,
    To whom he sends, and what 's his embassy :
Yourself, held precious in the world's esteem,
To parley with the sole inheritor
Of all perfections that a man may owe,
Matchless Navarre ; the plea of no less weight
Than Aquitaine, a dowry for a queen.
Be now as prodigal of all dear grace
As Nature was in making graces dear
When she did starve the general world beside
And prodigally gave them all to you.

Princess. Good Lord Boyet, my beauty, though
    but mean,
Needs not be painted flourish of your praise :
Beauty is bought by judgement of the eye,
Not utter'd by base sale of chapmen's tongues :
I am less proud to hear you tell my worth
Than you much willing to be counted wise
In spending your wit in the praise of mine.
But now to task the tasker : good Boyet,
You are not ignorant, all-telling fame
Doth noise abroad, Navarre hath made a vow,
Till painful study shall outwear three years,
No woman may approach his silent court :
Therefore to 's seemeth it a needful course,
Before we enter his forbidden gates,
To know his pleasure ; and in that behalf,
Bold of your worthiness, we single you
As our best-moving fair solicitor.

Tell him, the daughter of the King of France,
On serious business, craving quick dispatch,
Importunes personal conference with his grace :
Haste, signify so much ; while we attend,
Like humble-visaged suitors, his high will.

Boyet. Proud of employment, willingly I go.

Princess. All pride is willing pride, and yours
    is so.   *[Exit Boyet.*
Who are the votaries, my loving lords,
That are vow-fellows with this virtuous duke ?

First Lord. Lord Longaville is one.

Princess.   Know you the man ?

Maria. I know him. madam ; at a marriage-
    feast,
Between Lord Perigort and the beauteous heir
Of Jaques Falconbridge, solemnized
In Normandy, saw I this Longaville :
A man of sovereign parts he is esteem'd ;
Well fitted in arts. glorious in arms :
Nothing becomes him ill that he would well.
The only soil of his fair virtue's gloss,
If virtue's gloss will stain with any soil,
Is a sharp wit match'd with too blunt a will ;
Whose edge hath power to cut, whose will still wills
It should none spare that come within his power.

Princess. Some merry mocking lord, belike : is 't
    so ?

Maria. They say so most that most his humours
    know.

Princess. Such short-lived wits do wither as they
    grow.
Who are the rest ?

Katharine. The young Dumain ; a well-accom-
    plished youth,
Of all that virtue love for virtue loved ;
Most power to do most harm, least knowing ill ;
For he hath wit to make an ill shape good,
And shape to win grace though he had no wit.
I saw him at the Duke Alençon's once ;
And much too little of that good I saw
Is my report to his great worthiness.

Rosaline. Another of these students at that time
Was there with him, if I have heard a truth.
Biron they call him ; but a merrier man,
Within the limit of becoming mirth,
I never spent an hour's talk withal :
His eye begets occasion for his wit ;
For every object that the one doth catch
The other turns to a mirth-moving jest,
Which his fair tongue, conceit's expositor,
Delivers in such apt and gracious words
That aged ears play truant at his tales
And younger hearings are quite ravished ;
So sweet and voluble is his discourse.

Princess. God bless my ladies ! are they all in love,
That every one her own hath garnished
With such bedecking ornaments of praise ?

First Lord. Here comes Boyet.

Re-enter Boyet.

Princess.   Now, what admittance, lord ?

Boyet. Navarre had notice of your fair approach ;
And he and his competitors in oath
Were all address'd to meet you, gentle lady,
Before I came. Marry, thus much I have learnt :
He rather means to lodge you in the field,
Like one that comes here to besiege his court.
Than seek a dispensation for his oath,
To let you enter his unpeopled house.
Here comes Navarre.

Enter KING, LONGAVILLE, DUMAIN, BIRON, *and*
             Attendants.

King. Fair princess, welcome to the court of
Navarre.
Princess. ' Fair ' I give you back again ; and
' welcome ' I have not yet : the roof of this court
is too high to be yours ; and welcome to the wide
fields too base to be mine.
King. You shall be welcome, madam, to my
court.
Princess. I will be welcome, then : conduct me
thither.
King. Hear me, dear lady ; I have sworn an oath.
Princess. Our Lady help my lord ! he 'll be for-
sworn.
King. Not for the world, fair madam, by my will.
Princess. Why, will shall break it ; will and
nothing else.
King. Your ladyship is ignorant what it is.
Princess. Were my lord so, his ignorance were
wise,
Where now his knowledge must prove ignorance,
I hear your grace hath sworn out house-keeping :
'Tis deadly sin to keep that oath, my lord,
And sin to break it.
But pardon me, I am too sudden-bold :
To teach a teacher ill beseemeth me.
Vouchsafe to read the purpose of my coming,
And suddenly resolve me in my suit.
King. Madam, I will, if suddenly I may.
Princess. You will the sooner, that I were away ;
For you 'll prove perjured if you make me stay.
Biron. Did not I dance with you in Brabant once ?
Rosaline. Did not I dance with you in Brabant
once ?
Biron. I know you did.
Rosaline. How needless was it then to ask the
question !
Biron. You must not be so quick.
Rosaline. 'Tis 'long of you that spur me with
such questions.
Biron. Your wit 's too hot, it speeds too fast,
'twill tire,
Rosaline. Not till it leave the rider in the mire.
Biron. What time o' day ?
Rosaline. The hour that fools should ask.
Biron. Now fair befall your mask !
Rosaline. Fair fall the face it covers !
Biron. And send you many lovers !
Rosaline. Amen, so you be none.
Biron. Nay, then will I be gone.
King. Madam, your father here doth intimate
The payment of a hundred thousand crowns ;
Being but the one half of an entire sum
Disbursed by my father in his wars.
But say that he or we, as neither have,
Received that sum, yet there remains unpaid
A hundred thousand more; in surety of the which,
One part of Aquitaine is bound to us,
Although not valued to the money's worth.
If then the king your father will restore
But that one half which is unsatisfied,
We will give up our right in Aquitaine,
And hold fair friendship with his majesty.
But that, it seems, he little purposeth,
For here he doth demand to have repaid
A hundred thousand crowns ; and not demands,
On payment of a hundred thousand crowns,
To have his title live in Aquitaine ;
Which we much rather had depart withal
And have the money by our father lent

Than Aquitaine so gelded as it is.
Dear princess, were not his requests so far
From reason's yielding, your fair self should make
A yielding 'gainst some reason in my breast
And go well satisfied to France again.
Princess. You do the king my father too much
    wrong
And wrong the reputation of your name,
In so unseeming to confess receipt
Of that which hath so faithfully been paid.
King. I do protest I never heard of it ;
And if you prove it, I 'll repay it back
Or yield up Aquitaine.
Princess.   We arrest your word.
Boyet, you can produce acquittances
For such a sum from special officers
Of Charles his father.
King.   Satisfy me so.
Boyet. So please your grace, the packet is not
come
Where that and other specialties are bound :
To-morrow you shall have a sight of them.
King. It shall suffice me : at which interview
All liberal reason I will yield unto.
Meantime receive such welcome at my hand
As honour without breach of honour may
Make tender of to thy true worthiness :
You may not come, fair princess, in my gates ;
But here without you shall be so received
As you shall deem yourself lodged in my heart,
Though so denied fair harbour in my house.
Your own good thoughts excuse me, and farewell :
To-morrow shall we visit you again.
Princess. Sweet health and fair desires consort
    your grace !
King. Thy own wish wish I thee in every place !
                             [*Exit.*
Biron. Lady, I will commend you to mine own
heart.
Rosaline. Pray you, do my commendations ; I
would be glad to see it.
Biron. I would you heard it groan.
Rosaline. Is the fool sick ?
Biron. Sick at the heart.
Rosaline. Alack, let it blood.
Biron. Would that do it good ?
Rosaline. My physic says ' ay.'
Biron. Will you prick 't with your eye ?
Rosaline. No point, with my knife.
Biron. Now, God save thy life !
Rosaline. And yours from long living !
Biron. I cannot stay thanksgiving.   [*Retiring.*
Dumain. Sir, I pray you, a word : what lady is
that same ?
Boyet. The heir of Alencon, Katharine her name.
Dumain. A gallant lady. Monsieur, fare you
well.   [*Exit.*
Longaville. I beseech you a word : what is she in
the white ?
Boyet. A woman sometimes, an you saw her in
the light.
Longaville. Perchance light in the light. I desire
her name.
Boyet. She hath but one for herself ; to desire
that were a shame.
Longaville. Pray you, sir, whose daughter ?
Boyet. Her mother's, I have heard.
Longaville. God's blessing on your beard !
Boyet. Good sir, be not offended.
She is an heir of Falconbridge.

Longaville.   Nay, my choler is ended.
She is a most sweet lady.
Boyet.   Not unlike, sir, that may be.
                                    [*Exit Longaville.*
Biron.   What 's her name in the cap ?
Boyet.   Rosaline, by good hap.
Biron.   Is she wedded or no ?
Boyet.   To her will, sir, or so.
Biron.   You are welcome, sir : adieu.
Boyet.   Farewell to me, sir, and welcome to you.
                                    [*Exit Biron.*
Maria.   That last is Biron, the merry mad-cap
   lord :
Not a word with him but a jest.
Boyet.   And every jest but a word.
Princess.   It was well done of you to take him at
   his word.
Boyet.   I was as willing to grapple as he was to
   board.
Maria.   Two hot sheeps, marry.
Boyet.   And wherefore not ships?
No sheep, sweet lamb, unless we feed on your lips.
Maria.   You sheep, and I pasture : shall that
   finish the jest ?
Boyet.   So you grant pasture for me.
                              [*Offering to kiss her.*
Maria.   No so, gentle beast :
My lips are no common, though several they be.
Boyet.   Belonging to whom ?
Maria.   To my fortunes and me.
Princess.   Good wits will be jangling ; but, gentles,
   agree :
This civil war of wits were much better used
On Navarre and his book-men ; for here 'tis abused.
Boyet.   If my observation, which very seldom lies,
By the heart's still rhetoric disclosed with eyes,
Deceive me not now, Navarre is infected.
Princess.   With what ?
Boyet.   With that which we lovers entitle affected.
Princess.   Your reason ?
Boyet.   Why, all his behaviours did make their
   retire
To the court of his eye, peeping thorough desire :
His heart, like an agate, with your print impress'd,
Proud with his form, in his eye pride express'd :
His tongue, all impatient to speak and not see,
Did stumble with haste in his eyesight to be ;
All senses to that sense did make their repair,
To feel only looking on fairest of fair :
Methought all his senses were lock'd in his eye,
As jewels in crystal for some prince to buy ;
Who, tendering their own worth from where they
   were glass'd,
Did point you to buy them, along as you pass'd :
His face's own margent did quote such amazes
That all eyes saw his eyes enchanted with gazes.
I 'll give you Aquitaine and all that is his,
An you give him for my sake but one loving kiss.
Princess.   Come to our pavilion : Boyet is dis-
   posed.
Boyet.   But to speak that in words which his
   eye hath disclosed.
I only have made a mouth of his eye,
By adding a tongue which I know will not lie.
Rosaline.   Thou art an old love-monger and
   speakest skilfully.
Maria.   He is Cupid's grandfather and learns
   news of him.
Rosaline.   Then was Venus like her mother, for
   her father is but grim.
Boyet.   Do you hear, my mad wenches ?

Maria.   No.
Boyet.   What, then, do you see ?
Rosaline.   Ay, our way to be gone.
Boyet.   You are too hard for me.
                                    [*Exeunt.*

ACT III.

SCENE I.   *The same.*

Enter ARMADO *and* MOTH.

Armado.

Warble, child ; make passionate my sense of
   hearing.
   Moth.   Concolinel.   [*Singing.*
Armado.   Sweet air ! Go, tenderness of years ;
take this key, give enlargement to the swain, bring
him festinately hither : I must employ him in a
letter to my love.
   Moth.   Master, will you win your love with a
French brawl ?
Armado.   How meanest thou ? brawling in
French ?
   Moth.   No, my complete master : but to jig off
a tune at the tongue's end canary to it with your
feet, humour it with turning up your eyelids, sigh a
note and sing a note, sometime through the throat,
as if you swallowed love with singing love, sometime
through the nose, as if you snuffed up love by smelling
love ; with your hat penthouse-like o'er the shop of
your eyes ; with your arms crossed on your thin-
belly doublet like a rabbit on a spit ; or your hands
in your pocket like a man after the old painting ;
and keep not too long in one tune, but a snip and
away. These are complements, these are humours ;
these betray nice wenches, that would be betrayed
without these ; and make them men of note—do
you note me ?—that most are affected to these.
   Armado.   How hast thou purchased this experience ?
   Moth.   By my penny of observation.
   Armado.   But O,—but O,—
   Moth.   ' The hobby-horse is forgot.'
   Armado.   Callest thou my love ' hobby-horse ' ?
   Moth.   No, master ; the hobby-horse is but a
colt, and your love perhaps a hackney. But have
you forgot your love ?
   Armado.   Almost I had.
   Moth.   Negligent student ! learn her by heart.
   Armado.   By heart and in heart, boy.
   Moth.   And out of heart, master : all those three
I will prove.
   Armado.   What wilt thou prove ?
   Moth.   A man, if I live ; and this, by, in, and
without, upon the instant : by heart you love her,
because your heart cannot come by her ; in heart
you love her, because your heart is in love with her ;
and out of heart you love her, being out of heart
that you cannot enjoy her.
   Armado.   I am all these three.
   Moth.   And three times as much more, and yet
nothing at all.
   Armado.   Fetch hither the swain : he must carry
me a letter.
   Moth.   A message well sympathized ; a horse to
be ambassador for an ass.
   Armado.   Ha, ha ! what sayest thou ?
   Moth.   Marry, sir, you must send the ass upon
the horse, for he is very slow-gaited. But I go.
   Armado.   The way is but short : away !
   Moth.   As swift as lead, sir.
   Armado.   The meaning, pretty ingenious ?
Is not lead a metal heavy, dull, and slow ?

Moth. Minimè, honest master ; or rather, master, no.

Armado. I say lead is slow.

Moth. You are too swift, sir, to say so : Is that lead slow which is fired from a gun ?

Armado. Sweet smoke of rhetoric !
He reputes me a cannon ; and the bullet, that 's he : I shoot thee at the swain.

Moth. Thump then and I flee. [*Exit.*

Armado. A most acute juvenal ; volable and free of grace !
By thy favour, sweet welkin, I must sigh in thy face : Most rude melancholy, valour gives thee place. My herald is return'd.

Re-enter MOTH *with* COSTARD.

Moth. A wonder, master ! here 's a costard broken in a shin.

Armado. Some enigma, some riddle : come, thy l'envoy ; begin.

Costard. No egma, no riddle. no l'envoy ; no salve † in the mail, sir : O, sir, plantain, a plain plantain ! no l'envoy, no l'envoy ; no salve, sir, but a plantain !

Armado. By virtue, thou enforcest laughter ; thy silly thought my spleen ; the heaving of my lungs provokes me to ridiculous smiling. O, pardon me my stars ! Doth the inconsiderate take salve for l'envoy, and the word l'envoy for a salve ?

Moth. Do the wise think them other ? is not l'envoy a salve ?

Armado. No, page : it is an epilogue or discourse, to make plain
Some obscure precedence that hath tofore been sain.
I will example it :
    The fox, the ape and the humble-bee,
      Were still at odds, being but three.
There 's the moral. Now the l'envoy.

Moth. I will add the l'envoy. Say the moral again.

Armado. The fox, the ape, the humble-bee,
      Were still at odds, being but three.

Moth. Until the goose came out of door,
      And stay'd the odds by adding four.
Now will I begin your moral and do you follow with my l'envoy.
    The fox, the ape and the humble-bee,
      Were still at odds, being but three.

Armado. Until the goose came out of door,
      Staying the odds by adding four.

Moth. A good l'envoy, ending in the goose : would you desire more ?

Costard. The boy hath sold him a bargain, a goose, that 'r flat.
Sir, your pennyworth is good, an your goose be fat.
To sell a bargain well is as cunning as fast and loose :
Let me see ; a fat l'envoy ; ay, that 's a fat goose.

Armado. Come hither, come hither. How did this argument begin ?

Moth. By saying that a costard was broken in a shin.
Then call'd you for the l'envoy.

Costard. True, and I for a plantain : thus came your argument in ;
Then the boy's fat l'envoy, the goose that you bought ;
And he ended the market.

Armado. But tell me ; how was there a costard broken in a shin ?

Moth. I will tell you sensibly.

Costard. Thou hast no feeling of it, Moth ; I will speak that l'envoy :
I Costard, running out, that was safely within,
Fell over the threshold. and broke my shin.

Armado. We will talk no more of this matter.

Costard. Till there be more matter in the shin.

Armado. Sirrah Costard, I will enfranchise thee.

Costard. O, marry me to one Frances ! I smell some l'envoy, some goose, in this.

Armado. By my sweet soul, I mean setting thee at liberty. enfreedoming thy person : thou wert immured, restrained, captivated, bound.

Costard. True, true ; and now you will be my purgation and let me loose.

Armado. I give thee thy liberty, set thee from durance ; and, in lieu thereof, impose on thee nothing but this : bear this significant [*giving a letter*] to the country maid Jaquenetta : there is remuneration ; for the best ward of mine honour is rewarding my dependents. Moth, follow. [*Exit.*

Moth. Like the sequel, I. Signior Costard, adieu.

Costard. My sweet ounce of man's flesh ! my incony Jew ! [*Exit Moth.*
Now will I look to his remuneration. Remuneration ! O, that 's the Latin word for three farthings . three farthings—remuneration.—' What 's the price of this inkle ? '—' One penny,'—' No, I 'll give you a remuneration :' why, it carries it. Remuneration ! why, it is a fairer name than French crown. I will never buy and sell out of this word.

Enter BIRON.

Biron. O, my good knave Costard ! exceedingly well met.

Costard. Pray you, sir, how much carnation ribbon may a man buy for a remuneration ?

Biron. What is a remuneration ?

Costard. Marry, sir, halfpenny farthing.

Biron. Why, then, three-farthing worth of silk.

Costard. I thank your worship : God be wi' you !

Biron. Stay, slave , I must employ thee :
As thou wilt win my favour, good my knave,
Do one thing for me that I shall entreat.

Costard. When would you have it done, sir ?

Biron. This afternoon.

Costard. Well, I will do it, sir : fare you well.

Biron. Thou knowest not what it is.

Costard. I shall know, sir. when I have done it.

Biron. Why, villain, thou must know first.

Costard. I will come to your worship to-morrow morning.

Biron. It must be done this afternoon.
Hark, slave, it is but this :
The princess comes to hunt here in the park,
And in her train there is a gentle lady ;
When tongues speak sweetly, then they name her name,
And Rosaline they call her : ask for her ;
And to her white hand see thou do commend
This seal'd-up counsel. There 's thy guerdon ; go.
            [*Giving him a shilling.*

Costard. Gardon, O sweet gardon ! better than remuneration, a 'leven-pence farthing better : most sweet gardon ! I will do it, sir, in print. Gardon ! Remuneration ! [*Exit.*

Biron. And I, forsooth, in love ! I, that have been love's whip ;
A very beadle to a humorous sigh ;
A critic, nay, a night-watch constable ;
A domineering pedant o'er the boy ;
Than whom no mortal so magnificent !

This wimpled, whining, purblind, wayward boy ;
This senior-junior, giant-dwarf, Dan Cupid ;
Regent of love-rhymes, lord of folded arms,
The anointed sovereign of sighs and groans,
Liege of all loiterers and malcontents,
Dread prince of plackets, king of codpieces,
Sole imperator and great general
Of trotting 'paritors :—O my little heart !—
And I to be a corporal of his field,
And wear his colours like a tumbler's hoop !
What, I ! I love ! I sue ! I seek a wife !
A woman, that is like a German clock,
Still a-repairing, ever out of frame,
And never going aright, being a watch,
But being watch'd that it may still go right !
Nay, to be perjured, which is worst of all ;
And, among three, to love the worst of all ;
A wightly wanton with a velvet brow,
With two pitch-balls stuck in her face for eyes ;
Ay, and, by heaven, one that will do the deed
Though Argus were her eunuch and her guard :
And I to sigh for her ! to watch for her !
To pray for her ! Go to ; it is a plague
That Cupid will impose for my neglect
Of his almighty dreadful little might.
Well, I will love, write, sigh, pray, sue and groan :
Some men must love my lady and some Joan.
                                        [*Exit.*

ACT IV.

SCENE I. *The same.*

Enter the Princess, *and her train, a* Forester, Boyet,
Rosaline, Maria, *and* Katharine.

Princess.

W   as that the king, that spurr'd his horse
            so hard
Against the steep uprising of the hill ?
Boyet. I know not ; but I think it was not he.
Princess. Whoe'er a' was, a' show'd a mounting
mind.
Well, lords, to-day we will have our despatch :
On Saturday we will return to France.
Then, forester, my friend, where is the bush
That we must stand and play the murderer in ?
Forester. Hereby, upon the edge of yonder
coppice ;
A stand where you may make the fairest shoot.
Princess. I thank my beauty, I am fair that
shoot,
And thereupon thou speak'st the fairest shoot.
Forester. Pardon me, madam, for I meant not so.
Princess. What, what ? first praise me and again
say no ?
O short-lived pride ! Not fair ? alack for woe !
Forester. Yes, madam, fair.
Princess.   Nay, never paint me now :
Where fair is not, praise cannot mend the brow,
Here, good my glass, take this for telling true :
Fair payment for foul words is more than due.
Forester. Nothing but fair is that which you in-
herit.
Princess. See, see, my beauty will be saved by
merit !
O heresy in fair, fit for these days !
A giving hand, though foul, shall have fair praise.
But come, the bow : now mercy goes to kill,
And shooting well is then accounted ill.
Thus will I save my credit in the shoot :
Not wounding, pity would not let me do 't :

If wounding, then it was to show my skill,
That more for praise than purpose meant to kill.
And out of question so it is sometimes,
Glory grows guilty of detested crimes,
When, for fame's sake, for praise, an outward part,
We bend to that the working of the heart ;
As I for praise alone now seek to spill
The poor deer's blood, that my heart means no ill.
Boyet. Do not curst wives hold that self-sover-
    eignty
Only for praise sake, when they strive to be
Lords o'er their lords ?
Princess. Only for praise : and praise we may
afford
To any lady that subdues a lord.
Boyet. Here comes a member of the common-
wealth.

Enter Costard.

Costard. God dig-you-den all ! Pray you which
is the head lady ?
Princess. Thou shalt know her, fellow, by the
rest that have no heads.
Costard. Which is the greatest lady, the highest ?
Princess. The thickest and the tallest.
Costard. The thickest and the tallest ! it is so ;
truth is truth.
An your waist, mistress, were as slender as my wit,
One o' these maids' girdles for your waist should
be fit.
Are not you the chief woman ? you are the thickest
here.
Princess. What 's your will, sir ? what 's your will ?
Costard. I have a letter from Monsieur Biron to
one Lady Rosaline.
Princess. O, thy letter, thy letter ! he 's a good
friend of mine :
Stand aside, good bearer. Boyet, you can carve ;
Break up this capon.
Boyet.   I am bound to serve.
This letter is mistook, it importeth none here ;
It is writ to Jaquenetta.
Princess.   We will read it, I swear.
Break the neck of the wax, and every one give ear.
Boyet [*reads*]. ' By heaven, that thou art fair, is
most infallible ; true, that thou art beauteous ;
truth itself, that thou art lovely. More fairer than
fair, beautiful than beauteous, truer than truth itself,
have commiseration on thy heroical vassal ! The
magnanimous and most illustrate king Cophetua
set eye upon the pernicious and indubitate beggar
Zenelophon ; and he it was that might rightly say,
Veni, vidi, vici ; which to annothanize in the vulgar,—
O base and obscure vulgar !—videlicet. He came,
saw, and overcame : he came, one ; saw, two ;
overcame, three. Who came ? the king : why did
he come ? to see : why did he see ? to overcome :
to whom came he ? to the beggar : what saw he ?
the beggar : who overcame he ? the beggar The
conclusion is victory : on whose side ? the king's.
The captive is enriched : on whose side ? the beggar's.
The catastrophe is a nuptial : on whose side ? the
king's : no, on both in one, or one in both I am the
king ; for so stands the comparison : thou the
beggar ; for so witnesseth thy lowliness. Shall I
command thy love ? I may : shall I enforce thy
love ? I could : shall I entreat thy love ? I will.
What shalt thou exchange for rags ? robes ; for
tittles ? titles ; for thyself ? me. Thus, expecting
thy reply, I profane my lips on thy foot, my eyes on

thy picture, and my heart on thy every part. Thine,
in the dearest design of industry,
    DON ADRIANO DE ARMADO.'
Thus dost thou hear the Nemean lion roar
'Gainst thee, thou lamb, that standest as his prey.
Submissive fall his princely feet before,
And he from forage will incline to play :
But if thou strive, poor soul, what art thou then ?
Food for his rage, repasture for his den.
 Princess. What plume of feathers is he that in-
dited this letter ?
What vane ? what weathercock ? did you ever hear
better ?
 Boyet. I am much deceived but I remember the
style.
 Princess. Else your memory is bad, going o'er
it erewhile.
 Boyet. This Armado is a Spaniard, that keeps
here in court ;
A phantasime, a Monarcho, and one that makes
sport
To the prince and his bookmates.
 Princess.   Thou fellow, a word :
Who gave thee this letter ?
 Costard.   I told you ; my lord.
 Princess. To whom shouldst thou give it ?
 Costard.   From my lord to my lady.
 Princess. From which lord to which lady ?
 Costard. From my lord Biron a good master of
mine,
To a lady of France that he call'd Rosaline.
 Princess. Thou hast mistaken his letter. Come,
lords, away.
[*To Rosaline.*] Here, sweet, put up this : 'twill be
thine another day.
      [*Exeunt Princess and train.*
 Boyet. Who is the suitor ? who is the suitor ?
 Rosaline. Shall I teach you to know ?
 Boyet. Ay, my continent of beauty.
 Rosaline. Why, she that bears the bow.
Finely put off !
 Boyet. My lady goes to kill horns ; but, if thou
marry,
Hang me by the neck, if horns that year miscarry.
Finely put on !
 Rosaline. Well, then, I am the shooter.
 Boyet.   And who is your deer ?
 Rosaline. If we chóose by the horns, yourself
come not near.
Finely put on, indeed !
 Maria. You still wrangle with her, Boyet, and
she strikes at the brow.
 Boyet. But she herself is hit lower : have I hit
her now ?
 Rosaline. Shall I come upon thee with an old
saying, that was a man when King Pepin of France
was a little boy as touching the hit it ?
 Boyet. So I may answer thee with one as old,
that was a woman when Queen Guinover of Britain
was a little wench, as touching the hit it.
 Rosaline. Thou canst not hit it, hit it, hit it,
   Thou canst not hit it, my good man.
 Boyet. An I cannot. cannot, cannot,
   An I cannot, another can.
     [*Exeunt Rosaline and Katherine.*
 Costard. By my troth. most pleasant : how both
did fit it !
 Maria. A mark marvellou. well shot, for they
both did hit it.
 Boyet. A mark ! O, mark but that mark ! A
mark, says my lady !

Let the mark have a prick in 't, to mete at, if it
may be.
 Maria. Wide o' the bow hand ! i' faith, your
hand is out.
 Costard. Indeed, a' must shoot nearer, or he 'll
ne'er hit the clout.
 Boyet. An if my hand be out, then belike your
hand is in.
 Costard. Then will she get the upshoot by cleav-
ing the pin.
 Maria. Come, come. you talk greasily ; your
lips grow foul.
 Costard. She 's too hard for you at pricks, sir ;
challenge her to bowl.
 Boyet. I fear too much rubbing. Good night
my good owl. [*Exeunt Boyet and Maria.*
 Costard. By my soul, a swain ! a most simple
clown !
Lord, Lord, how the ladies and I have put him down !
O' my troth. most sweet jests ! most incony vulgar
wit !
When it comes so smoothly off, so obscenely. as it
were, so fit.
Armado o' th' one side,—O, a most dainty man !
To see him walk before a lady and to bear her fan !
To see him kiss his hand ! and how most sweetly
a' will swear !
And his page o' t' other side, that handful of wit !
Ah, heavens, it is a most pathetical nit !
Sola, sola !   [*Shout within.*
       [*Exit Costard running.*

SCENE II. *The same.*

Enter HOLOFERNES, SIR NATHANIEL, *and* DULL.

 Nathaniel. Very reverend sport, truly ; and done
in the testimony of a good conscience.
 Holofernes. The deer was, as you know, sanguis,
in blood ; ripe as the pomewater, who now hangeth
like a jewel in the ear of caelo, the sky, the welkin,
the heaven ; and anon falleth like a crab on the face
of terra, the soil, the land, the earth.
 Nathaniel. Truly, Master Holofernes, the epithets
are sweetly varied, like a scholar at the least : but,
sir, I assure ye it was a buck of the first head.
 Holofernes. Sir Nathaniel, haud credo.
 Dull. 'Twas not a haud credo ; 'twas a pricket.
 Holofernes. Most barbarous intimation ! yet a
kind of insinuation, as it were. in via, in way, of ex-
plication ; facere, as it were, replication, or rather,
ostentare, to show, as it were, his inclination, after
his undressed, unpolished, uneducated, unpruned.
untrained, or rather, unlettered, or ratherest, unconfirmed fashion. to insert again my haud credo for
a deer.
 Dull. I said the deer was not a haud credo :
'twas a pricket.
 Holofernes. Twice-sod simplicity, bis coctus !
O thou monster Ignorance, how deformed dost thou
look !
 Nathaniel Sir, he hath never fed of the dainties
tha are bred in a book ;
he hath not eat paper, as it were ; he hath not drunk
ink : his intellect is not replenished ; he is only
an animal, only sensible in the duller parts :
And such barren plants are set before us, that we
thankful should be,
Which we of taste and feeling are, for those parts
that do fructify in us more than he.
For as it would ill become me to be vain, indiscreet,
or a fool,

So were there a patch set on learning, to see him
  in a school :
But omne bene, say I ; being of an old father's mind,
Many can brook the weather that love not the wind.
  Dull. You two are book-men : can you tell me
    by your wit
What was a month old at Cain's birth, that 's not
  five weeks old as yet ?
  Holofernes. Dictynna, goodman Dull ; Dictynna,
    goodman Dull.
  Dull. What is Dictynna ?
  Nathaniel. A title to Phœbe, to Luna, to the
  moon.
  Holofernes. The moon was a month old when
    Adam was no more,
And raught not to five weeks when he came to
  five-score.
The allusion holds in the exchange.
  Dull. 'Tis true indeed ; the collusion holds in
    the exchange.
  Holofernes. God comfort thy capacity ! I say,
  the allusion holds in the exchange.
  Dull. And I say, the pollusion holds in the ex-
  change ; for the moon is never but a month old :
  and I say beside that, 'twas a pricket that the princess
  killed.
  Holofernes. Sir Nathaniel, will you hear an extemporal epitaph on the death of the deer ? And,
  to humour the ignorant, call I the deer the princess
  killed a pricket.
  Nathaniel. Perge, good Master Holofernes, perge ;
  so it shall please you to abrogate scurrility.
  Holofernes. I will something affect the letter, for
  it argues facility.
The preyful princess pierced and prick'd a pretty
  pleasing pricket ;
Some say a sore ; but not a sore, till now made
  sore with shooting.
The dogs did yell ; put L to sore, then sorel jumps
  from thicket ;
Or pricket sore, or else sorel ; the people fall
  a-hooting.
If sore be sore, then L to sore makes fifty sores one
  sorel.
Of one sore I an hundred make by adding but one
  more L.
  Nathaniel. A rare talent !
  Dull. [*Aside*] If a talent be a claw, look how he
  claws him with a talent.
  Holofernes. This is a gift that I have, simple,
  simple ; a foolish extravagant spirit, full of forms,
  figures, shapes, objects, ideas, apprehensions, motions,
  revolutions : these are begot in the ventricle of
  memory, nourished in the womb of pia mater, and
  delivered upon the mellowing of occasion. But
  the gift is good in those in whom it is acute, and
  I am thankful for it.
  Nathaniel. Sir, I praise the Lord for you : and
  so may my parishioners ; for their sons are well
  tutored by you, and their daughters profit very
  greatly under you : you are a good member of the
  commonwealth.
  Holofernes. Mehercle, if their sons be ingenuous,
  they shall want no instruction ; if their daughters
  be capable, I will put it to them : but vir sapit qui
  pauca loquitur ; a soul feminine saluteth us.

    Enter Jaquenetta *and* Costard.

  Jaquenetta. God give you good morrow, master
  Parson.
  Holofernes. Master Parson, quasi pers-on. An

if one should be pierced, which is the one ?
  Costard. Marry, master schoolmaster, he that is
  likest to a hogshead.
  Holofernes. Piercing a hogshead ! a good lustre
  of conceit in a turf of earth ; fire enough for a flint,
  pearl enough for a swine : 'tis pretty ; it is well.
  Jaquenetta. Good master Parson, be so good as
  read me this letter : it was given me by Costard,
  and sent me from Don Armado : I beseech you,
  read it.
  Holofernes. Fauste, precor gelida quando pecus
  omne sub umbra Ruminat,—and so forth. Ah,
  good old Mantuan ! I may speak of thee as the
  traveller doth of Venice ;
    Venetia, Venetia,
      Chi non ti vede non ti pretia.
Old Mantuan, old Mantuan ! who understandeth
thee not, loves thee not. Ut, re, sol, la, mi, fa. Under
pardon, sir, what are the contents ? or rather, as
Horace says in his—What, my soul, verses ?
  Nathaniel. Ay, sir, and very learned.
  Holofernes. Let me hear a staff, a stanze, a verse ;
lege, domine.
  Nathaniel [*reads*].
If love make me forsworn, how shall I swear to love ?
  Ah, never faith could hold, if not to beauty vow'd !
Though to myself forsworn, to thee I 'll faithful
    prove ;
  Those thoughts to me were oaks, to thee like
    osiers bow'd.
Study his bias leaves and makes his book thine eyes,
  Where all those pleasures live that art would
    comprehend :
If knowledge be the mark, to know thee shall suffice ;
  Well learned is that tongue that well can thee
    commend,
All ignorant that soul that sees thee without wonder ;
  Which is to me some praise that I thy parts admire :
Thy eye Jove's lightning bears, thy voice his dreadful
    thunder,
  Which, not to anger bent, is music and sweet fire.
Celestial as thou art, O, pardon love this wrong,
  That sings heaven's praise with such an earthly
    tongue.
  Holofernes. You find not the apostraphas, and
  so miss the accent : let me supervise the canzonet.
  Here are only numbers ratified ; but, for the ele-
  gancy, facility, and golden cadence of poesy, caret.
  Ovidius Naso was the man : and why, indeed, Naso,
  but for smelling out the odoriferous flowers of fancy,
  the jerks of invention ? Imitari is nothing : so doth
  the hound his master, the ape his keeper, the tired
  horse his rider. But, damosella virgin, was this
  directed to you ?
  Jaquenetta. Ay, sir, from cne Monsieur Biron,
  one of the strange queen's lords.
  Holofernes. I will overglance the superscript :
  ' To the snow-white hand of the most beauteous
  Lady Rosaline.' I will look again on the intellect
  of the letter, for the nomination of the party writing
  to the person written unto : ' Your ladyship's in
  all desired employment, Biron.' Sir Nathaniel, this
  Biron is one of the votaries with the king ; and here
  he hath framed a letter to a sequent of the stranger
  queen's, which accidentally, or by the way of pro-
  gression, hath miscarried. Trip and go, my sweet ;
  deliver this paper into the royal hand of the king :
  it may concern much. Stay not thy compliment ;
  I forgive thy duty : adieu.
  Jaquenetta. Good Costard, go with me. Sir,
  God save your life !

Costard. Have with thee, my girl.
        [Exeunt Costard and Jaquenetta.
  Nathaniel. Sir, you have done this in the fear of God, very religiously : and as a certain father saith,—
  Holofernes. Sir, tell not me of the father ; I do fear colourable colours. But to return to the verses : did they please you, Sir Nathaniel?
  Nathaniel. Marvellous well for the pen.
  Holofernes. I do dine to-day at the father's of a certain pupil of mine ; where, if, before repast, it shall please you to gratify the table with a grace, I will, on my privilege I have with the parents of the foresaid child or pupil, undertake your ben venuto ; where I will prove those verses to be very unlearned, neither savouring of poetry, wit, nor invention : I beseech your society.
  Nathaniel. And thank you too ; for society, saith the text, is the happiness of life.
  Holofernes. And, certes, the text most infallibly concludes it. [*To Dull*] Sir, I do invite you too ; you shall not say me nay : pauca verba. Away ! the gentles are at their game, and we will to our recreation.   *[Exeunt.*

SCENE III. *The same.*

     Enter BIRON, *with a paper.*

  Biron. The king he is hunting the deer ; I am coursing myself : they have pitched a toil ; I am toiling in a pitch,—pitch that defiles : defile ! a foul word. Well, set thee down, sorrow ! for so they say the fool said, and so say I, and I the fool : well proved, wit ! By the Lord, this 'ove is as mad as Ajax : it kills sheep ; it kills me, I a sheep : well proved again o' my side ! I will not love : if I do, hang me ; i' faith, I will not. O, but her eye,— by this light, but for her eye, I would not love her ; yes, for her two eyes. Well, I do nothing in the world but lie, and lie in my throat. By heaven, I do love : and it hath taught me to rhyme and to be melancholy ; and here is part of my rhyme, and here my melancholy. Well, she hath one o' my sonnets already : the clown bore it, the fool sent it, and the lady hath it : sweet clown, sweeter fool, sweetest lady ! By the world, I would not care a pin, if the other three were in. Here comes one with a paper : God give him grace to groan !
          [Stands aside.

     Enter the King, *with a paper.*

  King. Ay me !
  Biron. [*Aside*] Shot, by heaven ! Proceed, sweet Cupid : thou hast thumped him with thy bird-bolt under the left pap. In faith, secrets !
  King [*reads*].
So sweet a kiss the golden sun gives not
  To those fresh morning drops upon the rose,
As thy eye-beams, when their fresh rays have smote
  The night of dew that on my cheeks down flows :
Nor shines the silver moon one half so bright
  Through the transparent bosom of the deep,
As doth thy face through tears of mine give light ;
  Thou shinest in every tear that I do weep ;
No drop but as a coach doth carry thee ;
  So ridest thou triumphing in my woe.
Do but behold the tears that swell in me,
  And they thy glory through my grief will show :
But do not love thyself ; then thou wilt keep
My tears for glasses, and still make me weep.
O queen of queens ! how far dost thou excel,

No thought can think, nor tongue of mortal tell.
How shall she know my griefs ? I 'll drop the paper :
Sweet leaves, shade folly. Who is he comes here ?
          [Steps aside.
What, Longaville ! and reading ! listen, ear.
  Biron. Now, in thy likeness, one more fool appear !

     Enter LONGAVILLE, *with a paper.*

  Longaville. Ay me, I am forsworn !
  Biron. Why, he comes in like a perjure, wearing papers.
  King. In love, I hope : sweet fellowship in shame !
  Biron. One drunkard loves another of the name.
  Longaville. Am I the first that have been perjured so?
  Biron. I could put thee in comfort. Not by two that I know :
Thou makest the triumviry, the corner-cap of society,
The shape of Love's Tyburn that hangs up simplicity,
  Longaville. I fear these stubborn lines lack power to move,
O sweet Maria, empress of my love !
These numbers will I tear, and write in prose.
  Biron. O, rhymes are guards on wanton Cupid's hose :
Disfigure not his slop.
  Longaville. This same shall go. [*Reads.*
Did not the heavenly rhetoric of thine eye,
  Gainst whom the world cannot hold argument,
Persuade my heart to this false perjury ?
  Vows for thee broke deserve not punishment.
A woman I forswore ; but I will prove,
  Thou being a goddess, I forswore not thee :
My vow was earthly, thou a heavenly love ;
  Thy grace being gain'd cures all disgrace in me.
Vows are but breath, and breath a vapour is :
  Then thou, fair sun, which on my earth dost shine,
Exhalest this vapour-vow : in thee it is :
  If broken then, it is no fault of mine :
If by me broke, what fool is not so wise
To lose an oath to win a paradise ?
  Biron. This is the liver-vein, which makes flesh a deity,
A green goose a goddess : pure, pure idolatry.
God amend us, God amend ! we are much out o' the way.
  Longaville. By whom shall I send this ?—Company ! stay.   *[Steps aside.*
  Biron. All hid, all hid ; an old infant play.
Like a demigod here sit I in the sky,
And wretched fools' secrets heedfully o'er-eye.
More sacks to the mill ! O heavens, I have my wish !

     Enter DUMAIN, *with a paper.*
Dumain transform'd ! four woodcocks in a dish !
  Dumain. O most divine Kate !
  Biron. O most profane coxcomb !
  Dumain. By heaven, the wonder in a mortal eye !
  Biron. By earth, she is not, corporal, there you lie.
  Dumain. Her amber hair for foul hath amber quoted.
  Biron. An amber-colour'd raven was well noted.
  Dumain. As upright as the cedar.
  Biron.   Stoop, I say ;
Her shoulder is with child.
  Dumain.   As fair as day.
  Biron. Ay, as some days ; but then no sun must shine.
  Dumain. O that I had my wish !
  Longaville.   And I had mine !
  King. And I mine too, good Lord !

Biron. Amen, so I had mine : is not that a good word ?

Dumain. I would forget her ; but a fever she Reigns in my blood and will remember'd be.

Biron. A fever in your blood ! why, then incision Would let her out in saucers : sweet misprision !

Dumain. Once more I 'll read the ode that I have writ.

Biron. Once more I 'll mark how love can vary wit.

Dumain [*reads*]
On a day—alack the day !—
Love, whose month is ever May,
Spied a blossom passing fair
Playing in the wanton air :
Through the velvet leaves the wind,
All unseen, can passage find ;
That the lover, sick to death,
Wish himself the heaven's breath.
Air, quoth he, thy cheeks may blow ;
Air, would I might triumph so !
But, alack, my hand is sworn
Ne'er to pluck thee from thy thorn ;
Vow, alack, for youth unmeet,
Youth so apt to pluck a sweet !
Do not call it sin in me,
That I am forsworn for thee ;
Thou for whom Jove would swear
Juno but an Ethiope were ;
And deny himself for Jove
Turning mortal for thy love.
This will I send and something else more plain.
That shall express my true love's fasting pain.
O, would the king, Biron, and Longaville,
Were lovers too ! Ill, to example ill,
Would from my forehead wipe a perjured note ;
For none offend where all alike do dote.

Longaville [*advancing*]. Dumain, thy love is far from charity.
That in love's grief desirest society :
You may look pale, but I should blush, I know,
To be o'erheard and taken napping so.

King [*advancing*]. Come, sir, you blush ; as his your case is such ;
You chide at him, offending twice as much ;
You do not love Maria ; Longaville
Did never sonnet for her sake compile,
Nor never lay his wreathed arms athwart
His loving bosom to keep down his heart.
I have been closely shrouded in this bush
And mark'd you both and for you both did blush :
I heard your guilty rhymes, observed your fashion,
Saw sighs reek from you, noted well your passion :
Ay me ! says one ; O Jove ! the other cries ;
One, her hairs were gold, crystal the other's eyes :
[*To Longaville*] You would for paradise break faith and troth ;
[*To Dumain*] And Jove, for your love, would infringe an oath.
What will Biron say when that he shall hear
Faith so infringed, which such zeal did swear ?
How will he scorn ! how will he spend his wit !
How will he triumph, leap and laugh at it !
For all the wealth that ever I did see,
I would not have him know so much by me.

Biron. Now step I forth to whip hypocrisy.
                              [*Advancing.*
Ah, good my liege, I pray thee, pardon me !
Good heart, what grace hast thou, thus to reprove
These worms for loving, that art most in love ?
Your eyes do make no coaches ; in your tears

There is no certain princess that appears ;
You 'll not be perjured, 'tis a hateful thing ;
Tush, none but minstrels like of sonneting !
But are you not ashamed ? nay, are you not,
All three of you, to be thus much o'ershot ?
You found his mote ; the king your mote did see ;
But I a beam do find in each of three.
O, what a scene of foolery have I seen,
Of sighs, of groans, of sorrow and of teen !
O me, with what strict patience have I sat,
To see a king transformed to a gnat !
To see great Hercules whipping a gig,
And profound Solomon to tune a jig,
And Nestor play at push-pin with the boys,
And critic Timon laugh at idle toys !
Where lies thy grief, O, tell me, good Dumain ?
And, gentle Longaville, where lies thy pain ?
And where my liege's ? all about the breast :
A caudle, ho !

King.   Too bitter is thy jest.
Are we betray'd thus to thy over-view ?

Biron. Not you to me, but I betray'd by you :
I, that am honest ; I, that hold it sin
To break the vow I am engaged in ;
I am betray'd, by keeping company
† With men like men of inconstancy.
When shall you see me write a thing in rhyme ?
Or groan for love ? or spend a minute's time
In pruning me ? When shall you hear that I
Will praise a hand, a foot, a face, an eye,
A gait, a state, a brow, a breast, a waist,
A leg, a limb ?

King.   Soft ! whither away so fast ?
A true man or a thief that gallops so ?

Biron. I post from love : good lover, let me go.

Enter JAQUENETTA *and* COSTARD.

Jaquenetta. God bless the king !

King.   What present hast thou there ?

Costard. Some certain treason.

King.   What makes treason here ?

Costard. Nay, it makes nothing, sir.

King.   If it mar nothing neither,
The treason and you go in peace away together.

Jaquenetta. I beseech your grace, let this letter be read :
Our parson misdoubts it ; 'twas treason, he said.

King. Biron read it over.
                          [*Giving him the paper.*
Where hadst thou it ?

Jaquenetta. Of Costard.

King. Where hadst thou it ?

Costard. Of Dun Adramadio, Dun Adramadio.
                          [*Biron tears the letter.*

King. How now ! what is in you ? why dost thou tear it ?

Biron. A toy, my liege, a toy : your grace needs not fear it.

Longaville. It did move him to passion, and therefore let 's hear it.

Dumain. It is Biron's writing, and here is his name.   [*Gathering up the pieces.*

Biron. [*To Costard*]. Ah, you whoreson loggerhead ! you were born to do me shame.
Guilty, my lord, guilty ! I confess, I confess.

King. What ?

Biron. That you three fools lack'd me fool to make up the mess :
He, he, and you, and you, my liege, and I,
Are pick-purses in love, and we deserve to die.
O, dismiss this audience, and I shall tell you more.

Dumain. Now the number is even.

Biron.   True, true ; we are four.
Will these turtles be gone ?

King.   Hence, sirs ; away !

Costard. Walk aside the true folk, and let the
traitors stay.

        [*Exeunt Costard and Jaquenetta.*

Biron. Sweet lords, sweet lovers, O, let us em-
brace !
As true we are as flesh and blood can be :
The sea will ebb and flow, heaven show his face ;
Young blood doth not obey an old decree :
We cannot cross the cause why we were born ;
Therefore of all hands must we be forsworn.

King. What, did these rent lines show some love
of thine ?

Biron. Did they, quoth you ? Who sees the
heavenly Rosaline,
That, like a rude and savage man of Ind,
At the first opening of the gorgeous east,
Bows not his vassal head and strucken blind
Kisses the base ground with obedient breast ?
What peremptory eagle-sighted eye
Dares look upon the heaven of her brow,
That is not blinded by her majesty ?

King. What zeal, what fury hath inspired thee
now ?
My love, her mistress, is a gracious moon ;
She an attending star, scarce seen a light.

Biron. My eyes are then no eyes, nor I Biron :
O, but for my love, day would turn to night !
Of all complexions the cull'd sovereignty
Do meet, as at a fair, in her fair cheek,
Where several worthies make one dignity,
Where nothing wants that want itself doth seek.
Lend me the flourish of all gentle tongues,—
Fie, painted rhetoric ! O, she needs it not :
To things of sale a seller's praise belongs,
She passes praise ; then praise too short doth blot.
A wither'd hermit, five-score winters worn,
Might shake off fifty, looking in her eye :
Beauty doth varnish age, as if new-born,
And gives the crutch the cradle's infancy :
O, 'tis the sun that maketh all things shine.

King. By heaven, thy love is black as ebony.

Biron. Is ebony like her ? O wood divine !
A wife of such wood were felicity.
O, who can give an oath ? where is a book ?
That I may swear beauty doth beauty lack,
If that she learn not of her eye to look :
No face is fair that is not full so black.

King. O paradox ! Black is the badge of hell,
The hue of dungeons and the suit of night ;
And beauty's crest becomes the heavens well.

Biron. Devils soonest tempt, resembling spirits
of light.
O, if in black my lady's brows be deck'd,
It mourns that painting and usurping hair
Should ravish doters with a false aspect ;
And therefore is she born to make black fair.
Her favour turns the fashion of the days,
For native blood is counted painting now ;
And therefore red, that would avoid dispraise,
Paints itself black, to imitate her brow.

Dumain. To look like her are chimney-sweepers
black.

Longaville. And since her time are colliers counted
bright.

King. And Ethiopes of their sweet complexion crack.

Dumain. Dark needs no candles now, for dark is
light.

Biron. Your mistresses dare never come in rain,
For fear their colours should be wash'd away.

King. 'Twere good, yours did ; for, sir, to tell you
plain,
I 'll find a fairer face not wash'd to-day.

Biron. I 'll prove her fair, or talk till doomsday here.

King. No devil will fright thee then so much as she.

Dumain. I never knew man hold vile stuff so dear.

Longaville. Look, here 's thy love : my foot and
her face see.

Biron. O, if the streets were paved with thine eyes,
Her feet were much too dainty for such tread !

Dumain. O vile ! then, as she goes, what upward
lies
The street should see as she walk'd overhead.

King. But what of this ? are we not all in love ?

Biron. Nothing so sure ; and thereby all forsworn.

King. Then leave this chat ; and, good Biron, now
prove
Our loving lawful, and our faith not torn.

Dumain. Ay, marry, there ; some flattery for this
evil.

Longaville. O, some authority how to proceed ;
Some tricks, some quillets, how to cheat the devil.

Dumain. Some salve for perjury.

Biron.   'Tis more than need.
Have at you, then, affection's men at arms.
Consider what you first did swear unto,
To fast, to study, and to see no woman ;
Flat treason 'gainst the kingly state of youth.
Say, can you fast ? your stomachs are too young ;
And abstinence engenders maladies.
And where that you have vow'd to study, lords,
In that each of you have forsworn his book,
Can you still dream and pore and thereon look ?
For when would you, my lord, or you, or you,
Have found the ground of study's excellence
Without the beauty of a woman's face ?
[From women's eyes this doctrine I derive :]
They are the ground, the books, the academes
From whence doth spring the true Promethean fire.]
Why, universal plodding poisons up
The nimble spirits in the arteries,
As motion and long-during action tires
The sinewy vigour of the traveller.
Now, for not looking on a woman's face,
You have in that forsworn the use of eyes
And study too, the causer of your vow ;
For where is any author in the world
Teaches such beauty as a woman's eye ?
Learning is but an adjunct to ourself
And where we are our learning likewise is :
Then when ourselves we see in ladies' eyes,
Do we not likewise see our learning there ?
O, we have made a vow to study, lords,
And in that vow we have forsworn our books.
For when would you, my liege, or you, or you,
In leaden contemplation have found out
Such fiery numbers as the prompting eyes
Of beauty's tutors have enrich'd you with ?
Other slow arts entirely keep the brain ;
And therefore, finding barren practisers,
Scarce show a harvest of their heavy toil :
But love, first learned in a lady's eyes,
Lives not alone immured in the brain ;
But, with the motion of all elements,
Courses as swift as thought in every power,
And gives to every power a double power,
Above their functions and their offices.
It adds a precious seeing to the eye ;

A lover's eyes will gaze an eagle blind ;
A lover's ear will hear the lowest sound,
When the suspicious head of theft is stopp'd :
Love's feeling is more soft and sensible
Than are the tender horns of cockled snails ;
Love's tongue proves dainty Bacchus gross in taste :
For valour, is not Love a Hercules,
Still climbing trees in the Hesperides ?
Subtle as Sphinx ; as sweet and musical
As bright Apollo's lute, strung with his hair ;
And when Love speaks, the voice of all the gods
Make heaven drowsy with the harmony.
Never durst poet touch a pen to write
Until his ink were temper'd with Love's sighs ;
O, then his lines would ravish savage ears
And plant in tyrants mild humility.
From women's eyes this doctrine I derive :
They sparkle still the right Promethean fire ;
They are the books, the arts, the academes,
That show, contain and nourish all the world :
Else none at all in aught proves excellent.
Then fools you were these women to forswear,
Or keeping what is sworn, you will prove fools.
For wisdom's sake, a word that all men love,
Or for love's sake, a word that loves all men,
Or for men's sake, the authors of these women,
Or women's sake, by whom we men are men,
Let us once lose our oaths to find ourselves,
Or else we lose ourselves to keep our oaths,
It is religion to be thus forsworn,
For charity itself fulfils the law,
And who can sever love from charity ?
    King. Saint Cupid, then ! and, soldiers, to the
field !
    Biron. Advance your standards, and upon them,
lords ;
Pell-mell, down with them ! but be first advised,
In conflict that you get the sun of them.
    Longaville. Now to plain-dealing ; lay these
glozes by :
Shall we resolve to woo these girls of France ?
    King. And win them too : therefore let us devise
Some entertainment for them in their tents.
    Biron. First, from the park let us conduct them
thither ;
Then homeward every man attach the hand
Of his fair mistress : in the afternoon
We will with some strange pastime solace them,
Such as the shortness of the time can shape ; .
For revels, dances, masks and merry hours
Forerun fair Love, strewing her way with flowers.
    King. Away, away ! no time shall be omitted
That will betime, and may by us be fitted.
    Biron. Allons ! allons ! Sow'd cockle reap'd no
corn ;
And justice always whirls in equal measure :
Light wenches may prove plagues to men forsworn ;
If so, our copper buys no better treasure.   [*Exeunt.*

ACT V.

SCENE I. *The same.*

Enter HOLOFERNES, SIR NATHANIEL, *and* DULL.

        Holofernes.
S atis quod sufficit.
    Nathaniel. I praise God for you, sir : your reasons
at dinner have been sharp and sententious: pleasant
without scurrility, witty without affection, audacious

without impudency, learned without opinion, and
strange without heresy. I did converse this quondam
day with a companion of the king's, who is intituled,
nominated, or called, Don Adriano de Armado.
    Holofernes. Novi hominem tanquam te : his
humour is lofty, his discourse peromptory, his tongue
filed, his eye ambitious, his gait majestical, and his
general behaviour vain, ridiculous, and thrasonical.
He is too picked, too spruce, too affected, too odd,
as it were, too peregrinate, as I may call it.
    Nathaniel. A most singular and choice epithet.
                                [*Draws out his table-book.*
    Holofernes. He draweth out the thread of his
verbosity finer than the staple of his argument. I
abhor such fanatical phantasimes, such insociable
and point-devise companions ; such rackers of ortho-
graphy, as to speak dout, fine, when he should say
doubt ; det, when he should pronounce debt,—
d, e, b, t, not d, e, t : he clepeth a calf, cauf ; half,
hauf ; neighbour vocatur nebour ; neigh abbreviated
ne. This is abhominable,—which he would call
abbominable : it insinuateth † me of insanie : anne
intelligis, domine ? to make frantic, lunatic.
    Nathaniel. Laus Deo, bene intelligo.
    Holofernes. Bon, bon, fort bon ! Priscian a
little scratched, 'twill serve.
    Nathaniel. Videsne quis venit ?
    Holofernes. Video, et gaudeo.

Enter ARMADO, MOTH, *and* COSTARD.

    Armado. Chirrah !   [*To Moth.*
    Holofernes. Quare chirrah, not sirrah ?
    Armado. Men of peace, well encountered.
    Holofernes. Most military sir, salutation.
    Moth. [*Aside to Costard*] They have been at a
great feast of languages, and stolen the scraps.
    Costard. O, they have lived long on the alms-
basket of words. I marvel thy master hath not
eaten thee for a word ; for thou art not so long by
the head as honorificabilitudinitatibus : thou art
easier swallowed than a flap-dragon.
    Moth. Peace ! the peal begins.
    Armado. [*To Holofernes*]. Monsieur, are you not
lettered ?
    Moth. Yes, yes ; he teaches boys the hornbook.
What is a, b, spelt backward, with the horn on his
head ?
    Holofernes. Ba, pueritia, with a horn added.
    Moth. Ba, most silly sheep with a horn. You
hear his learning.
    Holofernes. Quis, quis, thou consonant ?
    Moth. The third of the five vowels, if you repeat
them ; or the fifth, if I.
    Holofernes. I will repeat them,—a, e, i,—
    Moth. The sheep : the other two concludes it,—
o, u.
    Armado. Now, by the salt wave of the Mediter-
raneum, a sweet touch, a quick venue of wit ! snip,
snap, quick and home ! it rejoiceth my intellect :
true wit !
    Moth. Offered by a child to an old man ; which
is wit-old.
    Holofernes. What is the figure ? what is the
figure ?
    Moth. Horns.
    Holofernes. Thou disputest like an infant : go,
whip thy gig.
    Moth. Lend me your horn to make one, and I
will whip about your infamy circum circa,—a gig
of a cuckold's horn.
    Costard. An I had but one penny in the world,

thou shouldst have it to buy gingerbread : hold,
there is the very remuneration I had of thy master,
thou halfpenny purse of wit, thou pigeon-egg of
discretion. O, an the heavens were so pleased that
thou wert but my bastard, what a joyful father
wouldst thou make me ! Go to ; thou hast it ad
dunghill, at the fingers' ends, as they say.

Holofernes. O, I smell false Latin ; dunghill for
unguem.

Armado. Arts-man, preambulate, we will be sin-
guled from the barbarous. Do you not educate
youth at the charge-house on the top of the mountain ?

Holofernes. Or mons, the hill.

Armado. At your sweet pleasure, for the mountain.

Holofernes. I do, sans question.

Armado. Sir, it is the king's most sweet pleasure
and affection to congratulate the princess at her
pavilion in the posteriors of this day, which the rude
multitude call the afternoon.

Holofernes. The posterior of the day, most
generous sir, is liable, congruent and measurable for
the afternoon : the word is well culled, chose, sweet
and apt, I do assure you, sir, I do assure.

Armado. Sir, the king is a noble gentleman, and
my familiar, I do assure ye, very good friend : for
what is inward between us, let it pass. I do beseech
thee, remember thy courtesy ; I beseech thee, apparel
thy head : and among other important and most
serious designs, and of great import indeed too, but
let that pass : for I must tell thee, it will please his
grace, by the world, sometime to lean upon my poor
shoulder, and with his royal finger, thus, dally with
my excrement, with my mustachio ; but, sweet heart,
let that pass. By the world, I recount no fable :
some certain special honours it pleaseth his greatness
to impart to Armado, a soldier, a man of travel,
that hath seen the world ; but let that pass. The
very all of all is,—but, sweet heart, I do implore
secrecy,—that the king would have me present the
princess, sweet chuck, with some delightful ostentation, or show, or pageant, or antique, or firework.
Now, understanding that the curate and your sweet
self are good at such eruptions and sudden breaking
out of mirth, as it were, I have acquainted you withal,
to the end to crave your assistance.

Holofernes. Sir, you shall present before her the
Nine Worthies. Sir, as concerning some entertainment of time, some show in the posterior of this day
to be rendered by our assistants, at the king's command, and this most gallant, illustrate, and learned
gentleman, before the princess ; I say none so fit
as to present the Nine Worthies.

Nathaniel. Where will you find men worthy
enough to present them ?

Holofernes. † Joshua, yourself ; myself and this
gallant gentleman, Judas Maccabæus ; this swain,
because of his great limb or joint, shall pass Pompey
the Great ; the page, Hercules,—

Armado. Pardon, sir ; error : he is not quantity
enough for that Worthy's thumb : he is not so big
as the end of his club.

Holofernes. Shall I have audience ? he shall
present Hercules in minority : his enter and exit
shall be strangling a snake ; and I will have an
apology for that purpose.

Moth. An excellent device ! so, if any of the
audience hiss, you may cry ' Well done, Hercules !
now thou crushest the snake ! ' that is the way to
make an offence gracious, though few have the
grace to do it.

Armado. For the rest of the Worthies ?—

Holofernes. I will play three myself.

Moth. Thrice-worthy gentleman !

Armado. Shall I tell you a thing ?·

Holofernes. We attend.

Armado. We will have, if this fadge not, an
antique. I beseech you, follow.

Holofernes. Via, goodman Dull ! thou hast
spoken no word all this while.

Dull. Nor understood none neither, sir.

Holofernes. Allons ! we will employ thee.

Dull. I 'll make one in a dance, or so ; or I
will play
On the tabor to the Worthies, and let them dance
the hay.

Holofernes. Most dull, honest Dull ! To our
sport, away ! [*Exeunt.*

SCENE II. *The same.*

Enter the Princess, KATHARINE, ROSALINE, *and*
MARIA.

Princess. Sweet hearts, we shall be rich ere we
depart,
If fairings come thus plentifully in :
A lady wall'd about with diamonds !
Look you what I have from the loving king.

Rosaline. Madame, came nothing else along with
that ?

Princess. Nothing but this ! yes, as much love
in rhyme
As would be cramm'd up in a sheet of paper,
Writ o' both sides the leaf, margent and all,
That he was fain to seal on Cupid's name.

Rosaline. That was the way to make his godhead
wax,
For he hath·been five thousand years a boy.

Katharine. Ay, and a shrewd unhappy gallows
too.

Rosaline. You 'll ne'er be friends with him ; a'
kill'd your sister.

Katharine. He made her melancholy, sad, and
heavy ;
And so she died : had she been light, like you,
Of such a merry, nimble, stirring spirit,
She might ha' been a grandam ere she died :
And so may you ; for a light heart lives long.

Rosaline. What 's your dark meaning, mouse, of
this light word ?

Katharine. A light condition in a beauty dark.

Rosaline. We need more light to find your meaning out.

Katharine. You 'll mar the light by taking it in
snuff ;
Therefore I 'll darkly end the argument.

Rosaline. Look, what you do, you do it still i' the
dark.

Katharine. So do not you, for you are a light
wench.

Rosaline. Indeed I weigh not you, and therefore
light.

Katharine. You weigh me not ? O, that 's you
care not for me.

Rosaline. Great reason ; for 'past cure is still
past care.'

Princess. Well bandied both ; a set of wit well
play'd.
But, Rosaline, you have a favour too :
Who sent it ? and what is it ?

Rosaline.   I would you knew :
An if my face were but as fair as yours,
My favour were as great ; be witness this.

Nay, I have verses too, I thank Biron :
The numbers true ; and, were the numbering too,
I were the fairest goddess on the ground :
I am compared to twenty thousand fairs.
O, he hath drawn my picture in his letter !
Princess. Any thing like ?
Rosaline. Much in the letters ; nothing in the
praise.
Princess. Beauteous as ink ; a good conclusion.
Katharine. Fair as a text B in a copy-book.
Rosaline. 'Ware pencils, ho ! let me not die your
debtor,
My red dominical, my golden letter :
O that your face were not so full of O's !
Katharine. A pox of that jest ! and I beshrew all
shrows.
Princess. But, Katharine, what was sent to you
from fair Dumain ?
Katharine. Madam, this glove.
Princess.   Did he not send you twain ?
Katharine. Yes, madam, and moreover
Some thousand verses of a faithful lover,
A huge translation of hypocrisy,
Vilely compiled, profound simplicity.
Maria. This and these pearls to me sent Lon-
gaville :
The letter is too long by half a mile.
Princess. I think no less. Dost thou not wish
in heart
The chain were longer and the letter short ?
Maria. Ay, or I would these hands might never
part.
Princess. We are wise girls to mock our lovers so.
Rosaline. They are worse fools to purchase
mocking so.
That same Biron I 'll torture ere I go :
O that I knew he were but in by the week !
How I would make him fawn and beg and seek
And wait the season and observe the times
And spend his prodigal wits in bootless rhymes
And shape his service wholly to my hests
And make him proud to make me proud that jests !
† So perttaunt-like would I o'ersway his state
That he should be my fool and I his fate.
Princess. None are so surely caught, when they
are catch'd,
As wit turn'd fool : folly, in wisdom hatch'd,
Hath wisdom's warrant and the help of school
And wit's own grace to grace a learned fool.
Rosaline. The blood of youth burns not with
such excess
As gravity's revolt to wantonness.
Maria. Folly in fools bears not so strong a note
As foolery in the wise, when wit doth dote ;
Since all the power thereof it doth apply
To prove, by wit, worth in simplicity.
Princess. Here comes Boyet, and mirth is in his
face.

Enter BOYET.

Boyet. O, I am stabb'd with laughter !
Where 's her grace ?
Princess. Thy news, Boyet ?
Boyet.   Prepare, madam, prepare !
Arm, wenches, arm ! encounters mounted are
Against your peace : Love doth approach disguised,
Armed in arguments ; you 'll be surprised :
Muster your wits ; stand in your own defence ;
Cr hide your heads like cowards, and fly hence.
Princess. Saint Denis to Saint Cupid ! What
are they

That charge their breath against us ? say, scout,
say.
Boyet. Under the cool shade of a sycamore
I thought to close mine eyes some half an hour ;
When, lo ! to interrupt my purposed rest,
Toward that shade I might behold addrest
The king and his companions : warily
I stole into a neighbour thicket by,
And overheard what you shall overhear ;
That, by and by, disguised they will be here.
Their herald is a pretty knavish page,
That well by heart hath conn'd his embassage :
Action and accent did they teach him there ;
'Thus must thou speak,' and ' thus thy body bear : '
And ever and anon they made a doubt
Presence majestical would put him out ;
' For,' quoth the king, ' an angel shalt thou see ;
Yet fear not thou, but speak audaciously.'
The boy replied, ' An angel is not evil ;
I should have fear'd her had she been a devil.'
With that, all laugh'd and clapp'd him on the shoulder,
Making the bold wag by their praises bolder :
One rubb'd his elbow thus, and fleer'd and swore
A better speech was never spoke before ;
Another, with his finger and his thumb,
Cried, ' Via ! we will do 't, come what will come ; '
The third he caper'd, and cried, ' All goes well ; '
The fourth turn'd on the toe, and down he fell.
With that, they all did tumble on the ground,
With such a zealous laughter, so profound,
That in this spleen ridiculous appears,
To check their folly, passion's solemn tears.
Princess. But what, but what, come they to visit
us ?
Boyet. They do, they do ; and are apparell'd
thus,
Like Muscovites or Russians, as I guess.
Their purpose is to parle, to court and dance ;
And every one his love-feat will advance
Unto his several mistress, which they 'll know
By favours several which they did bestow.
Princess. And will they so ? the gallants shall be
task'd ;
For, ladies, we will every one be mask'd ;
And not a man of them shall have the grace,
Despite of suit, to see a lady's face.
Hold, Rosaline, this favour thou shalt wear,
And then the king will court thee for his dear ;
Hold, take thou this, my sweet, and give me thine,
So shall Biron take me for Rosaline.
And change you favours too ; so shall your loves
Woo contrary, deceived by these removes.
Rosaline. Come on, then ; wear the favours most
in sight.
Katharine. But in this changing what is your
intent ?
Princess. The effect of my intent is to cross theirs :
They do it but in mocking merriment ;
And mock for mock is only my intent.
Their several counsels they unbosom shall
To loves mistook, and so be mock'd withal
Upon the next occasion that we meet,
With visages display'd, to talk and greet.
Rosaline. But shall we dance, if they desire us to 't ?
Princess. No, to the death, we will not move a
foot ;
Nor to their penn'd speech render we no grace,
But while 'tis spoke each turn away her face.
Boyet. Why, that contempt will kill the speaker's
heart,
And quite divorce his memory from his part.

Princess. Therefore I do it ; and I make no doubt
The rest will ne'er come in, if he be out.
There 's no such sport as sport by sport o'erthrown,
To make theirs ours and ours none but our own :
So shall we stay, mocking intended game
And they, well mock'd. depart away with shame.
                                   [*Trumpets sound within.*
Boyet. The trumpet sounds : be mask'd ; the
maskers come.   [*The Ladies mask.*

*Enter Blackamoors with music ; MOTH ; the KING,
BIRON. LONGAVILLE, and DUMAIN, in Russian
habits and masked.*

Moth. All hail, the richest beauties on the
earth !—
Boyet. Beauties no richer than rich taffeta.
Moth. A holy parcel of the fairest dames
                      [*The Ladies turn their backs to him.*
That ever turn'd their—backs— to mortal views !
Biron. [*Aside to Moth*] Their eyes, villain. their
eyes.
Moth. That ever turn'd their eyes to mortal
views !—
Out—
Boyet. True ; out indeed.
Moth. Out of your favours, heavenly spirits,
vouchsafe—
Not to behold—
Biron. [*Aside to Moth*]. Once to behold, rogue.
Moth. Once to behold with your sun-beamed eyes,
——with your sun-beamed eyes—
Boyet. They will not answer to that epithet ;
You were best call it ' daughter-beamed eyes.'
Moth. They do not mark me, and that brings
me out.
Biron. Is this your perfectness ? be gone, you
rogue !   [*Exit Moth.*
Rosaline. What would these strangers ? know
their minds, Boyet :
If they do speak our language, 'tis our will
That some plain man recount their purposes :
Know what they would.
Boyet. What would you with the princess ?
Biron. Nothing but peace and gentle visitation.
Rosaline. What would they, say they ?
Boyet. Nothing but peace and gentle visitation.
Rosaline. Why, that they have ; and bid them
so be gone.
Boyet. She says, you have it, and you may be gone.
King. Say to her, we have measured many miles
To tread a measure with her on this grass.
Boyet. They say that they have measured many
a mile
To tread a measure with you on this grass.
Rosaline. It is not so. Ask them how many
inches
Is in one mile : if they have measured many,
The measure then of one is easily told.
Boyet. If to come hither you have measured miles,
And many miles, the princess bids you tell
How many inches doth fill up one mile.
Biron Tell her, we measure them by weary steps.
Boyet. She hears herself.
Rosaline.   How many weary steps,
Of many weary miles you have o'ergone,
Are number'd in the travel of one mile ?
Biron. We number nothing that we spend for you :
Our duty is so rich, so infinite,
That we may do it still without accompt.
Vouchsafe to show the sunshine of your face,

That we, like savages, may worship it.
Rosaline. My face is but a moon, and clouded too.
King. Blessed are clouds, to do as such clouds too.
Vouchsafe, bright moon, and these thy stars, to shine
Those clouds removed, upon our watery eyne.
Rosaline. O vain petitioner ! beg a greater matter ;
Thou now request'st but moonshine in the water.
King. Then, in our measure do but vouchsafe
one change.
Thou bid'st me beg : this begging is not strange.
Rosaline. Play. music, then ! Nay, you must do
it soon.   [*Music plays.*
Not yet ! no dance ! Thus change I like the moon.
King. Will you not dance ? How come you thus
estranged ?
Rosaline. You took the moon at full, but now
she 's changed.
King. Yet still she is the moon, and I the man.
The music plays ; vouchsafe some motion to it.
Rosaline. Our ears vouchsafe it.
King.   But your legs should do it.
Rosaline. Since you are strangers and come here
by chance.
We 'll not be nice : take hands. We will not dance.
King. Why take we hands, then ?
Rosaline.   Only to part friends :
Curtsy, sweet hearts ; and so the measure ends.
King. More measure of this measure : be not
nice.
Rosaline. We can afford no more at such a price.
King. Prize you yourselves : what buys your
company ?
Rosaline. Your absence only.
King.   That can never be.
Rosaline. Then cannot we be bought : and so,
adieu ;
Twice to your visor, and half once to you.
King. If you deny to dance. let 's hold more chat.
Rosaline. In private. then.
King.   I am best pleased with that.
                                   [*They converse apart.*
Biron. White-handed mistress. one sweet word
with thee.
Princess. Honey, and milk, and sugar ; there is
three.
Biron. Nay then, two treys, and if you grow
so nice,
Metheglin, wort, and malmsey : well run, dice !
There 's half-a-dozen sweets.
Princess.   Seventh sweet, adieu :
Since you can cog, I 'll play no more with you.
Biron: One word in secret.
Princess.   Let it not be sweet.
Biron. Thou grievest my gall.
Princess.   Gall ! bitter.
Biron.   Therefore meet.
                                   [*They converse apart.*
Dumain. Will you vouchsafe with me to change
a word ?
Maria. Name it.
Dumain. Fair lady,—
Maria.   Say you so ? Fair lord,—
Take that for your fair lady.
Dumain.   Please it you,
As much in private, and I 'll bid adieu.
                                   [*They converse apart.*
Katharine. What, was your vizard made without
a tongue ?
Longaville. I know the reason, lady, why you ask.
Katharine. O for your reason ! quickly, sir ; I
long.

Longaville. You have a double tongue within
  your mask,
And would afford my speechless vizard half.
Katharine. Veal, quoth the Dutchman Is not
  veal ' a calf ?
Longaville. A calf, fair lady !
Katharine.   No, a fair lord calf.
Longaville. Let 's part the word.
Katharine.   No, I 'll not be your half :
Take all. and wean it ; it may prove an ox.
Longaville. Look how you butt yourself in these
  sharp mocks !
Will you give horns, chaste lady ? do not so.
Katharine. Then die a calf. before your horns do
  grow.
Longaville. One word in private with you. ere
  I die.
Katharine. Bleat softly then ; the butcher hears
  you cry.   [*They converse apart.*
Boyet The tongues of mocking wenches are as
  keen
As is the razor's edge invisible,
Cutting a smaller hair than may be seen,
  Above the sense of sense ; so sensible
Seemeth their conference ; their conceits have
  wings
Fleeter than arrows, bullets, wind. thought. swifter
  things.
Rosaline. Not one word more, my maids ; break
  off, break off.
Biron. By heaven, all dry-beaten with pure scoff !
King. Farewell, mad wenches : you have simple
  wits.
Princess. Twenty adieus, my frozen Muscovits.
          [*Exeunt King, Lords, and Blackamoors.*
Are these the breed of wits so wonder'd at ?
Boyet. Tapers they are. with your sweet breaths
  puff'd out.
Rosaline. Well-liking wits they have ; gross,
  gross ; fat, fat.
Princess. O poverty in wit, kingly-poor flout !
Will they not, think you, hang themselves to-night ?
Or ever, but in vizards, show their faces ?
This pert Biron was out of countenance quite.
Rosaline. O, they were all in lamentable cases !
The king was weeping-ripe for a good word.
Princess. Biron did swear himself out of all suit.
Maria. Dumain was at my service, and his sword :
No point, quoth I ; my servant straight was mute.
Katharine. Lord Longaville said. I came o'er his
  heart ;
And trow you what he call'd me ?
Princess.   Qualm, perhaps.
Katharine. Yes, in good faith.
Princess.   Go, sickness as thou art !
Rosaline. Well, better wits have worn plain
  statute-caps.
But will you hear ? the king is my love sworn.
Princess. And quick Biron hath plighted faith
  to me.
Katharine. And Longaville was for my service
  born.
Maria. Dumain is mine, as sure as bark on tree.
Boyet. Madam, and pretty mistresses, give ear :
Immediately they will again be here
In their own shapes ; for it can never be
They will digest this harsh indignity.
Princess. Will they return ?
Boyet.   They will, they will, God knows,
And leap for joy, though they are lame with blows :
Therefore change favours ; and, when they repair

Blow like sweet roses in this summer air.
Princess. How blow ? how blow ? speak to be
  understood
Boyet. Fair ladies mask'd are roses in their bud :
Dismask'd. their damask sweet commixture shown.
Are angels vailing clouds or roses blown.
Princess. Avaunt, perplexity ! What shall we do,
If they return in their own shapes to woo ?
Rosaline Good madam if by me you 'll be
  advised.
Let 's mock them still, as well known as disguised :
Let us complain to them what fools were here.
Disguised like Muscovites, in shapeless gear ;
And wonder what they were and to what end
Their shallow shows and prologue vilely penn'd
And their rough carriage so ridiculous,
Should be presented at our tent to us.
Boyet. Ladies. withdraw : the gallants are at
  hand.
Princess. Whip to our tents, as roes run o'er land.
          [*Exeunt Princess, Rosaline. Katharine, and*
                                    Maria

Re-enter the King, Biron, Longaville, *and*
  Dumain, *in their proper habits.*

King. Fair sir. God save you ! Where 's the
  princess ?
Boyet. Gone to her tent. Please it your majesty
Command me any service to her thither ?
King. That she vouchsafe me audience for one
  word.
Boyet. I will : and so will she, I know, my lord.
                                    [*Exit.*
Biron. This fellow pecks up wit as pigeons pease.
And utters it again when God doth please :
He is wit's pedler, and retails his wares
At wakes and wassails, meetings, markets, fairs ;
And we that sell by gross, the Lord doth know,
Have not the grace to grace it with such show.
This gallant pins the wenches on his sleeve ;
Had he been Adam, he had tempted Eve ;
A' can carve too, and lisp : why. this is he
That kiss'd his hand away in courtesy ;
This is the ape of form, monsieur the nice,
That. when he plays at tables, chides the dice
In honourable terms : nay, he can sing
A mean most meanly ; and in ushering
Mend him who can : the ladies call him sweet :
The stairs, as he treads on them, kiss his feet :
This is the flower that smiles on every one,
To show his teeth as white as whale's bone ;
And consciences, that will not die in debt,
Pay him the due of honey-tongued Boyet.
King. A blister on his sweet tongue, with my
  heart,
That put Armado's page out of his part !
Biron. See where it comes ! Behaviour, what
  wert thou
Till this madman show'd thee ? and what art thou
  now ?

Re-enter the Princess, *ushered by* Boyet ; Rosaline,
  Maria, *and* Katharine.

King. All hail, sweet madam, and fair time of
  day !
Princess. ' Fair ' in ' all hail ' is foul, as I conceive.
King. Construe my speeches better, if you may.
Princess. Then wish me better ; I will give you
  leave.
King. We came to visit you, and purpose now
To lead you to our court ; vouchsafe it then.

Princess. This field shall hold me ; and so hold
  your vow :
Nor God, nor I, delights in perjured men.
King. Rebuke me not for that which you provoke :
The virtue of your eye must break my oath.
Princess. You nickname virtue : vice you should
  have spoke ;
For virtue's office never breaks men's troth.
Now by my maiden honour, yet as pure
As the unsullied lily, I protest,
A world of torments though I should endure,
I would not yield to be your house's guest ;
So much I hate a breaking cause to be
Of heavenly oaths, vow'd with integrity.
King. O, you have lived in desolation here,
Unseen, unvisited, much to our shame.
Princess. Not so, my lord ; it is not so, I swear ;
We have had pastimes here and pleasant game :
A mess of Russians left us but of late.
King. How, madam ! Russians !
Princess.   Ay, in truth, my lord ;
Trim gallants, full of courtship and of state.
Rosaline. Madam, speak true. It is not so, my
  lord :
My lady, to the manner of the days,
In courtesy gives undeserving praise,
We four indeed confronted were with four
In Russian habit : here they stay'd an hour,
And talk'd apace ; and in that hour, my lord,
They did not bless us with one happy word.
I dare not call them fools ; but this I think,
When they are thirsty, fools would fain have drink.
Biron. This jest is dry to me. Fair gentle sweet,
Your wit makes wise things foolish : when we greet,
With eyes best seeing, heaven's fiery eye,
By light we lose light : your capacity
Is of that nature that to your huge store
Wise things seem foolish and rich things but poor.
Rosaline. This proves you wise and rich, for in
  my eye,—
Biron. I am a fool, and full of poverty.
Rosaline. But that you take what doth to you
  belong,
It were a fault to snatch words from my tongue.
Biron. O, I am yours, and all that I possess !
Rosaline. All the fool mine ?
Biron.   I cannot give you less.
Rosaline. Which of the vizards was it that you
  wore ?
Biron. Where ? when ? what vizard ? why
  demand you this ?
Rosaline. There, then, that vizard ; that super-
  fluous case
That hid the worse and show'd the better face.
King. We are descried ; they 'll mock us now
  downright.
Dumain. Let us confess and turn it to a jest.
Princess. Amazed, my lord ? why looks your
  highness sad ?
Rosaline. Help, hold his brows ! he 'll swoon !
  Why look you pale ?
Sea-sick, I think, coming from Muscovy.
Biron. Thus pour the stars down plagues for
  perjury.
Can any face of brass hold longer out ?
Here stand I : lady, dart thy skill at me ;
Bruise me with scorn, confound me with a flout ;
Thrust thy sharp wit quite through my ignorance ;
Cut me to pieces with thy keen conceit ;
And I will wish thee never more to dance,
Nor never more in Russian habit wait.

O, never will I trust to speeches penn'd,
Nor to the motion of a schoolboy's tongue,
Nor never come in vizard to my friend,
Nor woo in rhyme, like a blind harper's song !
Taffeta phrases, silken terms precise,
Three-piled hyperboles, spruce affectation,
Figures pedantical ; these summer-flies
Have blown me full of maggot ostentation :
I do forswear them ; and I here protest,
By this white glove,—how white the hand, God
  knows !—
Henceforth my wooing mind shall be express'd
In russet yeas and honest kersey noes :
And, to begin, wench,—so God help me, la !—
My love to thee is sound, sans crack or flaw.
Rosaline. Sans sans, I pray you.
Biron.   Yet I have a trick
Of the old rage : bear with me, I am sick ;
I 'll leave it by degrees. Soft, let us see :
Write, ' Lord have mercy on us ' on those three ;
They are infected ; in their hearts it lies ;
They have the plague, and caught it of your eyes ;
These lords are visited ; you are not free,
For the Lord's tokens on you do I see.
Princess. No, they are free that gave these tokens
  to us.
Biron. Our states are forfeit : seek not to undo us.
Rosaline. It is not so ; for how can this be true,
That you stand forfeit, being those that sue ?
Biron. Peace ! for I will not have to do with you.
Rosaline. Nor shall not, if I do as I intend.
Biron. Speak for yourselves ; my wit is at an
  end.
King. Teach us, sweet madam, for our rude
  transgression
Some fair excuse.
Princess.   The fairest is confession.
Were not you here but even now disguised ?
King. Madam, I was.
Princess.   And were you well advised ?
King. I was, fair madam.
Princess.   When you then were here,
What did you whisper in your lady's ear ?
King. That more than all the world I did respect
  her.
Princess. When she shall challenge this, you will
  reject her.
King. Upon mine honour, no.
Princess.   Peace, peace ! forbear:
Your oath once broke, you force not to forswear.
King. Despise me, when I break this oath of
  mine.
Princess. I will : and therefore keep it. Rosaline,
What did the Russian whisper in your ear ?
Rosaline. Madam, he swore that he did hold me
  dear
As precious eyesight, and did value me
Above this world ; adding thereto moreover
That he would wed me, or else die my lover.
Princess. God give thee joy of him ! the noble
  lord
Most honourably doth uphold his word.
King. What mean you, madam ? by my life,
  my troth,
I never swore this lady such an oath.
Rosaline. By heaven, you did ; and to confirm it
  plain,
You gave me this : but take it, sir, again.
King. My faith and this the princess I did give :
I knew her by this jewel on her sleeve.

Princess. Pardon me, sir, this jewel did she wear ;
And Lord Biron, I thank him is my dear.
What, will you have me, or your pearl again ?
Biron. Neither of either ; I remit both twain.
I see the trick on 't : here was a consent,
Knowing aforehand of our merriment,
To dash it like a Christmas comedy :
Some carry-tale, some please-man, some slight zany,
Some mumble-news, some trencher-knight, some
Dick,
That smiles his cheek in years and knows the trick
To make my lady laugh when she 's disposed,
Told our intents before : which once disclosed,
The ladies did change favours : and then we,
Following the signs, woo'd but the sign of she.
Now, to our perjury to add more terror,
We are again forsworn, in will and error.
Much upon this it is : and might not you
                                                    [*To Boyet.*
Forestall our sport, to make us thus untrue ?
Do not you know my lady's foot by the squier,
    And laugh upon the apple of her eye ?
And stand between her back, sir, and the fire,
    Holding a trencher, jesting merrily ?
You put our page out : go, you are allow'd ;
Die when you will, a smock shall be your shroud.
You leer upon me, do you ? there 's an eye
Wounds like a leaden sword.
Boyet.   Full merrily
Hath this brave manage, this career, been run.
Biron. Lo, he is tilting straight ! Peace ! I have
done.

Enter COSTARD.

Welcome, pure wit ! thou partest a fair fray.
Costard. O Lord, sir, they would know
Whether the three Worthies shall come in or no.
Biron. What, are there but three ?
Costard.   No, sir ; but it is vara fine,
For every one pursents three.
Biron.   And three times thrice is nine.
Costard. Not so, sir ; under correction, sir ; I
hope it is not so.
You cannot beg us, sir, I can assure you, sir ; we
know what we know :
I hope, sir, three times thrice, sir,—
Biron. Is not nine.
Costard. Under correction, sir, we know where-
until it doth amount.
Biron. By Jove I always took three threes for
nine.
Costard. O Lord, sir, it were pity you should get
your living by reckoning, sir.
Biron. How much is it ?
Costard. O Lord, sir, the parties themselves, the
actors, sir, will show whereuntil it doth amount :
for mine own part, I am, as they say but to parfect
one man in one poor man, Pompion the Great, sir.
Biron. Art thou one of the Worthies ?
Costard. It pleased them to think me worthy of
Pompion the Great : for mine own part, I know not
the degree of the Worthy, but I am to stand for him.
Biron. Go, bid them prepare.
Costard. We will turn it finely off, sir ; we will
take some care.   [*Exit.*
King. Biron, they will shame us : let them not
approach.
Biron. We are shame-proof, my lord : and 'tis
some policy,
To have one show worse than the king's and his
company.

King. I say they shall not come.
Princess. Nay, my good lord, let me o'errule
    you now :
That sport best pleases that doth least know how :
† Where zeal strives to content, and the contents
Dies in the zeal of that which it presents :
Their form confounded makes most form in mirth,
When great things labouring perish in their birth.
Biron. A right description of our sport, my lord.

Enter ARMADO.

Armado. Anointed, I implore so much expense
of thy royal sweet breath as will utter a brace of
words.
            [*Converses apart with the King, and
                              delivers him a paper.*
Princess. Doth this man serve God ?
Biron. Why ask you ?
Princess. He speaks not like a man of God's
making.
Armado. That is all one, my fair, sweet, honey
monarch : for, I protest, the schoolmaster is exceed-
ing fantastical ; too too vain, too too vain : but
we will put it, as they say, to fortuna de la guerra.
I wish you the peace of mind, most royal couplement !
                                                    [*Exit.*
King. Here is like to be a good presence of
Worthies. He presents Hector of Troy ; the swain,
Pompey the Great ; the parish curate, Alexander ;
Armado's page Hercules : the pedant, Judas
Maccabæus :
And if these four Worthies in their first show thrive,
These four will change habits, and present the
    other five.
Biron. There is five in the first show.
King. You are deceived ; 'tis not so.
Biron. The pedant, the braggart, the hedge-
priest, the fool and the boy :—
† Abate throw at novum, and the whole world again
Cannot pick out five such, take each one in his vein.
King. The ship is under sail, and here she comes
amain.

Enter COSTARD, *for Pompey.*

Costard. I Pompey am,—
Boyet.   You lie, you are not he.
Costard. I Pompey am,—
Boyet.   With libbard's head on knee.
Biron. Well said, old mocker : I must needs be
friends with thee.
Costard. I Pompey am, Pompey surnamed the
Big,—
Dumain. The Great.
Costard It is, ' Great,' sir :—
                     Pompey surnamed the Great ;
That oft in field, with targe and shield, did make
    my foe to sweat :
And travelling along this coast, I here am come
    by chance,
And lay my arms before the legs of this sweet
    lass of France.
I, your ladyship would say, ' Thanks, Pompey,' I
    had done.
Princess. Great thanks, great Pompey.
Costard. 'Tis not so much worth ; but I hope I
was perfect : I made a little fault in ' Great.'
Biron. My hat to a halfpenny, Pompey proves
the best Worthy.

Enter Sir Nathaniel, *for Alexander.*

Nathaniel. When in the world I lived, I was the world's commander ;
By east, west, north and south, I spread my conquering might :
My scutcheon plain declares that I am Alisander,—
Boyet. Your nose says, no, you are not ; for it stands too right.
Biron. Your nose smells ' no ' in this, most tender-smelling knight.
Princess. The conqueror is dismay'd. Proceed, good Alexander.
Nathaniel. When in the world I lived, I was the world's commander,—
Boyet. Most true, 'tis right ; you were so, Alisander.
Biron. Pompey the Great,— -
Costard. Your servant, and Costard.
Biron. Take away the conqueror, take away Alisander.
Costard. [*To Sir Nathaniel*] O Sir, you have overthrown Alisander the conqueror ! You will be scraped out of the painted cloth for this : your lion, that holds his poll-axe sitting on a close-stool, will be given to Ajax : he will be the ninth Worthy. A conqueror, and afeard to speak ! run away for shame, Alisander. [*Nathaniel retires.*] There, an 't shall please you ; a foolish mild man ; an honest man, look you, and soon dashed. He is a marvellous good neighbour, faith, and a very good bowler : but, for Alisander,—alas, you see how 'tis,—a little o'erparted. But there are Worthies a-coming will speak their mind in some other sort.
Princess. Stand aside, good Pompey.

Enter Holofernes, *for Judas ; and* Moth, *for Hercules.*

Holofernes. Great Hercules is presented by this imp,
Whose club kill'd Cerberus, that three-headed canis ;
And when he was a babe, a child, a shrimp,
Thus did he strangle serpents in his manus.
Quoniam he seemeth in minority,
Ergo I come with this apology.
Keep some state in thy exit, and vanish.
                   [*Moth retires.*
Judas I am,—
Dumain. A Judas !
Holofernes. Not Iscariot, sir.
Judas I am, ycliped Maccabæus.
Dumain. Judas Maccabæus clipt is plain Judas.
Biron. A kissing traitor. How art thou proved Judas ?
Holofernes. Judas I am,—
Dumain. The more shame for you, Judas.
Holofernes. What mean you, sir ?
Boyet. To make Judas hang himself.
Holofernes. Begin, sir ; you are my elder.
Biron. Well followed : Judas was hanged on an elder.
Holofernes. I will not be put out of countenance.
Biron. Because thou hast no face.
Holofernes. What is this ?
Boyet. A cittern-head.
Dumain. The head of a bodkin.
Biron. A Death's face in a ring.
Longaville. The face of an old Roman coin, scarce seen.
Boyet. The pommel of Cæsar's falchion.
Dumain. The carved-bone face on a flask.

Biron. Saint George's half-cheek in a brooch.
Dumain. Ay, and in a brooch of lead.
Biron. Ay, and worn in the cap of a tooth-drawer.
And now forward ; for we have put thee in countenance.
Holofernes. You have put me out of countenance.
Biron. False ; we have given thee faces.
Holofernes. But you have out-faced them all.
Biron. An thou wert a lion, we would do so.
And so adieu, sweet Jude ! nay, why dost thou stay ?
Dumain. For the latter end of his name.
Biron. For the ass to the Jude ; give it him :—Jud-as, away !
Holofernes. This is not generous, not gentle, not humble.
Boyet. A light for Monsieur Judas ! it grows dark, he may stumble.   [*Holofernes retires.*
Princess. Alas, poor Maccabæus, how hath he been baited !

Enter Armado, *for Hector.*

Biron. Hide thy head, Achilles : here comes Hector in arms.
Dumain. Though my mocks come home by me, I will now be merry.
King. Hector was but a Troyan in respect of this.
Boyet. But is this Hector ?
King. I think Hector was notso clean-timbered.
Longaville. His leg is too big for Hector's.
Dumain. More calf, certain.
Boyet. No ; he is best indued in the small.
Biron. This cannot be Hector.
Dumain. He 's a god or a painter ; for he makes faces.
Armado. The armipotent Mars, of lances the almighty,
Gave Hector a gift,—
Dumain. A gilt nutmeg.
Biron. A lemon.
Longaville. Stuck with cloves.
Dumain. No, cloven.
Armado. Peace !—
The armipotent Mars, of lances the almighty,
Gave Hector a gift, the heir of Ilion ;
A man so breathed, that certain he would fight ; yea
From morn till night, out of his pavilion.
I am that flower,—
Dumain.   That mint.
Longaville.   That columbine.
Armado. Sweet Lord Longaville, rein thy tongue.
Longaville. I must rather give it the rein, for it runs against Hector.
Dumain. Ay, and Hector 's a greyhound.
Armado. The sweet war-man is dead and rotten ; sweet chucks, beat not the bones of the buried : when he breathed, he was a man. But I will forward with my device. [*To the Princess*] Sweet royalty, bestow on me the sense of hearing.
Princess. Speak, brave Hector : we are much delighted.
Armado. I do adore thy sweet grace's slipper.
Boyet. [*Aside to Dumain*] Loves her by the foot.
Dumain. [*Aside to Boyet*] He may not by the yard.
Armado. This Hector far surmounted Hannibal,—
Costard. The party is gone, fellow Hector, she is gone ; she is two months on her way.

Armado. What meanest thou ?

Costara. Faith, unless you play the honest Troyan the poor wench is cast away : she 's quick ; the child brags in her belly already : 'tis yours.

Armado. Dost thou infamonize me among potentates ? thou shalt die.

Costard. Then shall Hector be whipped for Jaquenetta that is quick by him and hanged for Pompey that is dead by him.

Dumain. Most rare Pompey !

Boyet. Renowned Pompey !

Biron. Greater than great. great, great, great Pompey ! Pompey the Huge !

Dumain. Hector trembles.

Biron. Pompey is moved. More Ates, more Ates ! stir them on ! stir them on !

Dumain. Hector will challenge him.

Biron. Ay, if a' have no more man's blood in 's belly than will sup a flea.

Armado. By the north pole, I do challenge thee.

Costard. I will not fight with a pole, like a northern man : I 'll slash ; I 'll do it by the sword. I bepray you, let me borrow my arms again.

Dumain. Room for the incensed Worthies !

Costard. I 'll do it in my shirt.

Dumain. Most resolute Pompey !

Moth. Master, let me take you a button-hole lower. Do you not see Pompey is uncasing for the combat ? What mean you ? You will lose your reputation.

Armado. Gentlemen and soldiers, pardon me ; I will not combat in my shirt.

Dumain. You may not deny it : Pompey hath made the challenge.

Armado. Sweet bloods, I both may and will.

Biron. What reason have you for 't ?

Armado. The naked truth of it is, I have no shirt ; I go woolward for penance.

Boyet. True, and it was enjoined him in Rome for want of linen : since when, I 'll be sworn, he wore none but a dishclout of Jaquenetta's, and that a' wears next his heart for a favour.

Enter MERCADE.

Mercade. God save you, madam !

Princess. Welcome, Mercade ;
But that thou interrupt'st our merriment.

Mercade. I am sorry, madam ; for the news I bring
Is heavy in my tongue. The king your father—

Princess. Dead, for my life !

Mercade. Even so ; my tale is told.

Biron. Worthies, away ! the scene begins to cloud.

Armado. For mine own part, I breathe free breath. I have seen the day of wrong through the little hole of discretion. and I will right myself like a soldier.   [*Exeunt Worthies.*

King. How fares your majesty ?

Princess. Boyet, prepare ; I will away to-night.

King. Madam, not so ; I do beseech you, stay.

Princess. Prepare, I say. I thank you, gracious lords,
For all your fair endeavours ; and entreat,
Out of a new-sad soul, that you vouchsafe
In your rich wisdom to excuse or hide
The liberal opposition of our spirits,
If over-boldly we have borne ourselves
In the converse of breath : your gentleness
Was guilty of it. Farewell, worthy lord !
A heavy heart bears not a nimble tongue :

Excuse me so, coming too short of thanks
For my great suit so easily obtain'd.

King. The extreme parts of time extremely forms
All causes to the purpose of his speed,
And often at his very loose decides
That which long process could not arbitrate :
And though the mourning brow of progeny
Forbid the smiling courtesy of love
The holy suit which fain it would convince,
Yet, since love's argument was first on foot,
Let not the cloud of sorrow justle it
From what it purposed ; since to wail friends lost
Is not by much so wholesome-profitable
As to rejoice at friends but newly found.

Princess. I understand you not : my griefs are double.

Biron. Honest plain words best pierce the ear of grief ;
And by these badges understand the king.
For your fair sakes have we neglected time,
Play'd foul play with our oaths : your beauty, ladies,
Hath much deform'd us, fashioning our humours
Even to the opposed end of our intents :
And what in us hath seem'd ridiculous,—
As love is full of unbefitting strains,
All wanton as a child, skipping and vain,
Form'd by the eye and therefore, like the eye,
Full of strange shapes, of habits and of forms,
Varying in subjects as the eye doth roll
To every varied object in his glance :
Which parti-coated presence of loose love
Put on by us, if, in your heavenly eyes,
Have misbecomed our oaths and gravities,
Those heavenly eyes, that look into these faults,
Suggested us to make. Therefore, ladies,
Our love being yours, the error that love makes
Is likewise yours : we to ourselves prove false,
By being once false for ever to be true
To those that make us both,—fair ladies, you :
And even that falsehood, in itself a sin,
Thus purifies itself and turns to grace.

Princess. We have received your letters full of love ;
Your favours, the ambassadors of love ;
And, in our maiden council, rated them
At courtship, pleasant jest and courtesy,
As bombast and as lining to the time :
But more devout than this in our respects
Have we not been ; and therefore met your loves
In their own fashion, like a merriment.

Dumain. Our letters, madam, show'd much more than jest.

Longaville. So did our looks.

Rosaline.   We did not quote them so.

King. Now, at the latest minute of the hour,
Grant us your loves.

Princess.   A time, methinks, too short
To make a world-without-end bargain in.
No, no, my lord, your grace is perjured much,
Full of dear guiltiness ; and therefore this :
If for my love, as there is no such cause,
You will do aught, this shall you do for me :
Your oath I will not trust ; but go with speed
To some forlorn and naked hermitage,
Remote from all the pleasures of the world ;
There stay until the twelve celestial signs
Have brought about the annual reckoning.
If this austere insociable life
Change not your offer made in heat of blood ;
If frosts and fasts, hard lodging and thin weeds

Nip not the gaudy blossoms of your love,
But that it bear this trial and last love ;
Then, at the expiration of the year,
Come challenge me, challenge me by these deserts,
And, by this virgin palm now kissing thine,
I will be thine ; and till that instant shut
My woeful self up in a mourning house,
Raining the tears of lamentation
For the remembrance of my father's death.
If this thou do deny, let our hands part,
Neither intitled in the other's heart.
King. If this, or more than this, I would deny,
To flatter up these powers of mine with rest,
The sudden hand of death close up mine eye !
Hence ever then my heart is in thy breast.
[*Biron.* And what to me, my love ? and what to
   me ?
Rosaline. You must be purged too, your sins are
   rack'd,
You are attaint with faults and perjury :
Therefore if you my favour mean to get,
A twelve month shall you spend, and never rest,
But seek the weary beds of people sick.]
Dumain. But what to me, my love ? but what
   to me ?
A wife ?
Katharine. A beard, fair health, and honesty ;
With three-fold love I wish you all these three.
Dumain. O, shall I say, I thank you, gentle wife ?
Katharine. Not so, my lord ; a twelvemonth and
   a day
I 'll mark no words that smooth-faced wooers say :
Come when the king doth to my lady come ;
Then, if I have much love, I 'll give you some.
Dumain. I 'll serve thee true and faithfully till
   then.
Katharine. Yet swear not, lest ye be forsworn
   again.
Longaville. What says Maria ?
Maria.   At the twelvemonth's end
I 'll change my black gown for a faithful friend.
Longaville. I 'll stay with patience ; but the time
   is long.
Maria. The liker you ; few taller are so young.
Biron. Studies my lady ? mistress, look on me ;
Behold the window of my heart, mine eye,
What humble suit attends thy answer there :
Impose some service on me for thy love.
Rosaline. Oft have I heard of you, my lord Biron,
Before I saw you ; and the world's large tongue
Proclaims you for a man replete with mocks,
Full of comparisons and wounding flouts,
Which you on all estates will execute
That lie within the mercy of your wit.
To weed this wormwood from your fruitful brain,
And therewithal to win me, if you please,
Without the which I am not to be won,
You shall this twelvemonth term from day to day
Visit the speechless sick and still converse
With groaning wretches ; and your task shall be,
With all the fierce endeavour of your wit
To enforce the pained impotent to smile.
Biron. To move wild laughter in the throat of
   death ?
It cannot be ; it is impossible :
Mirth cannot move a soul in agony.
Rosaline. Why, that 's the way to choke a gibing
   spirit,
Whose influence is begot of that loose grace
Which shallow laughing hearers give to fools :
A jest's prosperity lies in the ear

Of him that hears it, never in the tongue
Of him that makes it : then, if sickly ears,
Deaf'd with the clamours of their own dear groans,
Will hear your idle scorns, continue then,
And I will have you and that fault withal ;
But if they will not, throw away that spirit,
And I shall find you empty of that fault,
Right joyful of your reformation.
Biron. A twelvemonth ! well ; befall what will
   befall,
I 'll jest a twelvemonth in an hospital.
Princess. [*To the King*] Ay, sweet my lord ; and
   so I take my leave.
King. No, madam ; we will bring you on your
   way.
Biron. Our wooing doth not end like an old play ;
Jack hath not Jill : these ladies' courtesy
Might well have made our sport a comedy.
King. Come, sir, it wants a twelvemonth and
   a day,
And then 'twill end.
Biron.   That 's too long for a play.

         Re-enter ARMADO.

Armado. Sweet majesty, vouchsafe me,—
Princess. Was not that Hector ?
Dumain. The worthy knight of Troy.
Armado. I will kiss thy royal finger, and take
leave. I am a votary ; I have vowed to Jaquenetta to hold the plough for her sweet love three
years. But, most esteemed greatness, will you hear
the dialogue that the two learned men have compiled
in praise of the owl and the cuckoo ? it should have
followed in the end of our show.
King. Call them forth quickly ; we will do so.
Armado. Holla ! approach.

Re-enter HOLOFERNES, NATHANIEL, MOTH, COSTARD,
       and others.

This side is Hiems, Winter, this Ver, the Spring ;
the one maintained by the owl, the other by the
cuckoo. Ver, begin.

        THE SONG.

        SPRING.

When daisies pied and violets blue
   And lady-smocks all silver-white
And cuckoo-buds of yellow hue
   Do paint the meadows with delight,
The cuckoo then, on every tree,
Mocks married men ; for thus sings he,
          Cuckoo ;
Cuckoo, cuckoo : O word of fear,
Unpleasing to a married ear !
When shepherds pipe on oaten straws
   And merry larks are ploughmen's clocks,
When turtles tread, and rooks, and daws,
   And maidens bleach their summer smocks,
The cuckoo then, on every tree,
Mocks married men ; for thus sings he,
          Cuckoo ;
Cuckoo, cuckoo : O word of fear,
Unpleasing to a married ear !

        WINTER.

When icicles hang by the wall
   And Dick the shepherd blows his nail
And Tom bears logs into the hall

And milk comes frozen home in pail,
When blood is nipp'd and ways be foul,
Then nightly sings the staring owl,
    Tu-whit;
Tu-who, a merry note,
While greasy Joan doth keel the pot.
When all aloud the wind doth blow
 And coughing drowns the parson's saw
And birds sit brooding in the snow

And Marian's nose looks red and raw,
When roasted crabs hiss in the bowl,
Then nightly sings the staring owl,
    Tu-whit;
Tu-who, a merry note,
While greasy Joan doth keel the pot.

Armado. The words of Mercury are harsh after the songs of Apollo. You that way: we this way.

           [Exeunt.

A MIDSUMMER-NIGHT'S DREAM

DRAMATIS PERSONÆ

THESEUS, Duke of Athens.

EGEUS, *father to* Hermia.

LYSANDER,
DEMETRIUS, } *in love with* Hermia.

PHILOSTRATE, *master of the revels to* Theseus.

QUINCE, *a carpenter.*

SNUG, *a joiner.*

BOTTOM, *a weaver.*

FLUTE, *a bellows-mender.*

SNOUT, *a tinker.*

STARVELING, *a tailor.*

HIPPOLYTA, *queen of the* Amazons, *betrothed to* Theseus.

HERMIA, *daughter to* Egeus, *in love with* Lysander.

HELENA, *in love with* Demetrius.

OBERON, *king of the fairies.*

TITANIA, *queen of the fairies.*

PUCK, *or* Robin Goodfellow.

PEASEBLOSSOM,
COBWEB,
MOTH,
MUSTARDSEED, } *fairies.*

Other fairies attending their King *and* Queen. *Attendants on* Theseus *and* Hippolyta.

SCENE : Athens, and a wood near it.

ACT I.

SCENE I. *Athens. The palace of* THESEUS.

Enter THESEUS, HIPPOLYTA, PHILOSTRATE, *and* Attendants.

Theseus.

Now, fair Hippolyta, our nuptial hour
Draws on apace ; four happy days bring in
Another moon : but, O, methinks, how slow
This old moon wanes ! she lingers my desires,
Like to a step-dame or a dowager
Long withering out a young man's revenue.
    Hippolyta. Four days will quickly steep them-
        selves in night ;
Four nights will quickly dream away the time ;
And then the moon, like to a silver bow
New-bent in heaven, shall behold the night
Of our solemnities.
    Theseus.   Go, Philostrate,
Stir up the Athenian youth to merriments ;

Awake the pert and nimble spirit of mirth :
Turn melancholy forth to funerals ;
The pale companion is not for our pomp.
                        [*Exit Philostrate.*
Hippolyta, I woo'd thee with my sword,
And won thy love, doing thee injuries ;
But I will wed thee in another key,
With pomp, with triumph and with revelling.

Enter EGEUS, HERMIA, LYSANDER, *and* DEMETRIUS.

    Egeus. Happy be Theseus, our renowned duke !
    Theseus. Thanks, good Egeus : what 's the news
        with thee ?
    Egeus. Full of vexation come I, with complaint
Against my child, my daughter Hermia.
Stand forth, Demetrius. My noble lord,
This man hath my consent to marry her.
Stand forth, Lysander : and, my gracious duke,
This man hath bewitch'd the bosom of my child :
Thou, thou, Lysander, thou hast given her rhymes
And interchanged love-tokens with my child :
Thou hast by moonlight at her window sung
With feigning voice verses of feigning love,
And stolen the impression of her fantasy
With bracelets of thy hair, rings, gawds, conceits,
Knacks, trifles, nosegays, sweetmeats, messengers
Of strong prevailment in unharden'd youth :
With cunning hast thou filch'd my daughter's heart
Turn'd her obedience, which is due to me,
To stubborn harshness : and, my gracious duke,
Be it so she will not here before your grace
Consent to marry with Demetrius,
I beg the ancient privilege of Athens,
As she is mine, I may dispose of her :
Which shall be either to this gentleman
Or to her death, according to our law
Immediately provided in that case.
    Theseus. What say you, Hermia ? be advised
        fair maid :
To you your father should be as a god ;
One that composed your beauties, yea, and one
To whom you are but as a form in wax
By him imprinted and within his power
To leave the figure or disfigure it.
Demetrius is a worthy gentleman.
    Hermia. So is Lysander.
    Theseus.   In himself he is ;
But in this kind, wanting your father's voice,
The other must be held the worthier.
    Hermia. I would my father look'd but with my
        eyes.
    Theseus. Rather your eyes must with his judge-
        ment look.
    Hermia. I do entreat your grace to pardon me
I know not by what power I am made bold,
Nor how it may concern my modesty,
In such a presence here to plead my thoughts ;
But I beseech your grace that I may know
The worst that may befall me in this case,

If I refuse to wed Demetrius.

Theseus.   Either to die the death or to abjure
For ever the society of men.
Therefore, fair Hermia, question your desires ;
Know of your youth, examine well your blood,
Whether, if you yield not to your father's choice,
You can endure the livery of a nun,
For aye to be in shady cloister mew'd,
To live a barren sister all your life,
Chanting faint hymns to the cold fruitless moon.
Thrice-blessed they that master so their blood,
To undergo such maiden pilgrimage ;
But earthlier happy is the rose distill'd,
Than that which withering on the virgin thorn
Grows, lives and dies in single blessedness.

Hermia.   So will I grow, so live, so die, my lord,
Ere I will yield my virgin patent up
Unto his lordship, whose unwished yoke
My soul consents not to give sovereignty.

Theseus.   Take time to pause ; and, by the next
      new moon—
The sealing-day betwixt my love and me,
For everlasting bond of fellowship—
Upon that day either prepare to die
For disobedience to your father's will,
Or else to wed Demetrius, as he would ;
Or on Diana's altar to protest
For aye austerity and single life.

Demetrius.   Relent, sweet Hermia : and, Lysander,
      yield
Thy crazed title to my certain right.

Lysander.   You have her father's love, Demetrius ;
Let me have Hermia's : do you marry him.

Egeus.   Scornful Lysander ! true, he hath my
      love,
And what is mine my love shall render him.
And she is mine, and all my right of her
I do estate unto Demetrius.

Lysander.   I am, my lord, as well derived as he,
As well possess'd ; my love is more than his ;
My fortunes every way as fairly rank'd
If not with vantage, as Demetrius' ;
And, which is more than all these boasts can be,
I am beloved of beauteous Hermia :
Why should not I then prosecute my right ?
Demetrius, I 'll avouch it to his head,
Made love to Nedar's daughter, Helena,
And won her soul ; and she, sweet lady, dotes,
Devoutly dotes, dotes in idolatry,
Upon this spotted and inconstant man.

Theseus.   I must confess that I have heard so much,
And with Demetrius thought to have spoke thereof ;
But, being over-full of self-affairs,
My mind did lose it. But, Demetrius, come ;
And come, Egeus ; you shall go with me,
I have some private schooling for you both.
For you, fair Hermia, look you arm yourself
To fit your fancies to your father's will ;
Or else the law of Athens yields you up—
Which by no means we may extenuate—
To death, or to a vow of single life.
Come, my Hippolyta : what cheer, my love ?
Demetrius and Egeus, go along :
I must employ you in some business
Against our nuptial and confer with you
Of something nearly that concerns yourselves.

Egeus.   With duty and desire we follow you.
      [*Exeunt all but Lysander and Hermia.*

Lysander.   How now, my love ! why is your cheek
      so pale ?
How chance the roses there do fade so fast ?

Hermia.   Belike for want of rain, which I could
      well
Beteem them from the tempest of my eyes.

Lysander.   Ay me ! for aught that I could ever
      read,
Could ever hear by tale or history,
The course of true love never did run smooth ;
But, either it was different in blood,—

Hermia.   O cross ! too high to be enthrall'd to
      low.

Lysander.   Or else misgraffed in respect of years,—

Hermia.   O spite ! too old to be engaged to young.

Lysander.   Or else it stood upon the choice of
      friends,—

Hermia.   O hell ! to choose love by another's
      eyes.

Lysander.   Or, if there were a sympathy in choice,
War, death, or sickness did lay siege to it,
Making it momentany as a sound,
Swift as a shadow, short as any dream ;
Brief as the lightning in the collied night,
That, in a spleen, unfolds both heaven and earth,
And ere a man hath power to say ' Behold ! '
The jaws of darkness do devour it up :
So quick bright things come to confusion.

Hermia.   If then true lovers have been ever
      cross'd,
It stands as an edict in destiny :
Then let us teach our trial patience,
Because it is a customary cross,
As due to love as thoughts and dreams and sighs,
Wishes and tears, poor fancy's followers.

Lysander.   A good persuasion : therefore, hear
      me, Hermia.
I have a widow aunt, a dowager
Of great revenue, and she hath no child :
From Athens is her house remote seven leagues :
And she respects me as her only son.
There, gentle Hermia, may I marry thee ;
And to that place the sharp Athenian law
Cannot pursue us. If thou lovest me then,
Steal forth thy father's house to-morrow night ;
And in the wood, a league without the town,
Where I did meet thee once with Helena,
To do observance to a morn of May,
There will I stay for thee.

Hermia.   My good Lysander !
I swear to thee, by Cupid's strongest bow,
By his best arrow with the golden head,
By the simplicity of Venus' doves,
By that which knitteth souls and prospers loves,
And by that fire which burn'd the Carthage queen,
When the false Troyan under sail was seen,
By all the vows that ever men have broke,
In number more than ever women spoke,
In that same place thou hast appointed me,
To-morrow truly will I meet with thee.

Lysander.   Keep promise, love. Look, here comes
Helena.

                Enter HELENA.

Hermia.   God speed fair Helena ! whither away ?

Helena.   Call you me fair ? that fair again unsay.
Demetrius loves your fair : O happy fair !
Your eyes are lode-stars ; and your tongue's sweet
      air
More tuneable than lark to shepherd's ear,
When wheat is green, when hawthorn buds appear.
Sickness is catching : O, were favour so,
Yours would I catch fair Hermia, ere I go ;
My ear should catch your voice, my eye your eye,

My tongue should catch your tongue's sweet melody.
Were the world mine, Demetrius being bated,
The rest I 'ld give to be to you translated.
O, teach me how you look, and with what art
You sway the motion of Demetrius' heart.
Hermia. I frown upon him, yet he loves me still.
Helena. O that your frowns would teach my
smiles such skill !
Hermia. I give him curses, yet he gives me love.
Helena. O that my prayers could such affection
move !
Hermia. The more I hate, the more he follows me.
Helena. The more I love, the more he hateth me
Hermia. His folly, Helena, is no fault of mine.
Helena. None, but your beauty : would that
fault were mine !
Hermia. Take comfort : he no more shall see
my face ;
Lysander and myself will fly this place,
Before the time I did Lysander see,
Seem'd Athens as a paradise to me :
O, then, what graces in my love do dwell,
That he hath turn'd a heaven unto a hell !
Lysander. Helen, to you our minds we will unfold:
To-morrow night, when Phœbe doth behold
Her silver visage in the watery glass,
Decking with liquid pearl the bladed grass,
A time that lovers' flights doth still conceal,
Through Athens' gates have we devised to steal.
Hermia. And in the wood, where often you and I
Upon faint primrose-beds were wont to lie,
Emptying our bosoms of their counsel sweet,
There my Lysander and myself shall meet ;
And thence from Athens turn away our eyes,
To seek new friends and stranger companies.
Farewell, sweet playfellow : pray thou for us ;
And good luck grant thee thy Demetrius !
Keep word, Lysander : we must starve our sight
From lovers' food till morrow deep midnight.
Lysander. I will, my Hermia.   [*Exit Hermia.*
Helena, adieu :
As you on him, Demetrius dote on you !   [*Exit.*
Helena. How happy some o'er other some can be !
Through Athens I am thought as fair as she.
But what of that ? Demetrius thinks not so ;
He will not know what all but he do know :
And as he errs, doting on Hermia's eyes,
So I, admiring of his qualities :
Things base and vile, holding no quantity,
Love can transpose to form and dignity :
Love looks not with the eyes, but with the mind ;
And therefore is wing'd Cupid painted blind :
Nor hath Love's mind of any judgement taste ;
Wings and no eyes figure unheedy haste :
And therefore is Love said to be a child,
Because in choice he is so oft beguiled.
As waggish boys in game themselves forswear.
So the boy Love is perjured every where :
For ere Demetrius look'd on Hermia's eyne,
He hail'd down oaths that he was only mine ;
And when this hail some heat from Hermia felt,
So he dissolved, and showers of oaths did melt.
I will go tell him of fair Hermia's flight :
Then to the wood will he to-morrow night
Pursue her ; and for this intelligence
If I have thanks, it is a dear expense :
But herein mean I to enrich my pain,
To have his sight thither and back again.   [*Exit.*

SCENE II.   *Athens.*   QUINCE'S *house.*

Enter QUINCE, SNUG, BOTTOM, FLUTE, SNOUT,
and STARVELING.

Quince. Is all our company here ?
Bottom. You were best to call them generally,
man by man, according to the scrip.
Quince. Here is the scroll of every man's name,
which is thought fit, through all Athens to play in
our interlude before the duke and the duchess, on
his wedding-day at night.
Bottom. First, good Peter Quince, say what the
play treats on, then read the names of the actors,
and so grow to a point.
Quince. Marry, our play is, The most lamentable
comedy, and most cruel death of Pyramus and
Thisby.
Bottom. A very good piece of work, I assure you,
and a merry. Now, good Peter Quince, call forth
your actors by the scroll. Masters, spread yourselves.
Quince. Answer as I call you. Nick Bottom,
the weaver.
Bottom. Ready. Name what part I am for, and
proceed.
Quince. You, Nick Bottom, are set down for
Pyramus.
Bottom. What is Pyramus ? a lover, or a tyrant ?
Quince. A lover, that kills himself most gallant
for love.
Bottom. That will ask some tears in the true
performing of it : if I do it, let the audience look to
their eyes ; I will move storms, I will condole in
some measure. To the rest : yet my chief humour
is for a tyrant : I could play Ercles rarely, or a part
to tear a cat in, to make all split.

> The raging rocks
> And shivering shocks
> Shall break the locks
>   Of prison gates ;
> And Phibbus' car
> Shall shine from far
> And make and mar
>   The foolish Fates.

This was lofty ! Now name the rest of the players.
This is Ercles' vein, a tyrant's vein ; a lover is more
condoling.
Quince. Francis Flute, the bellows-mender.
Flute. Here, Peter Quince.
Quince. Flute, you must take Thisby on you.
Flute. What is Thisby ? a wandering knight ?
Quince. It is the lady that Pyramus must love.
Flute. Nay, faith, let not me play a woman ; I
have a beard coming.
Quince. That 's all one : you shall play it in a
mask, and you may speak as small as you will.
Bottom. An I may hide my face, let me play
Thisby too, I 'll speak in a monstrous little voice,
'Thisne, Thisne ; ' 'Ah Pyramus, my lover dear !
thy Thisby dear, and lady dear ! '
Quince. No, no ; you must play Pyramus : and,
Flute, you Thisby.
Bottom. Well, proceed.
Quince. Robin Starveling, the tailor.
Starveling. Here, Peter Quince.
Quince. Robin Starveling, you must play Thisby's
mother. Tom Snout, the tinker.
Snout. Here, Peter Quince.
Quince. You, Pyramus' father : myself, Thisby's
father. Snug, the joiner ; you, the lion's part : and,
I hope, here is a play fitted.

Snug. Have you the lion's part written? pray you, if it be, give it me, for I am slow of study.

Quince. You may do it extempore, for it is nothing but roaring.

Bottom. Let me play the lion too : I will roar, that I will do any man's heart good to hear me ; I will roar, that I will make the duke say ' Let him roar again, let him roar again.'

Quince. An you should do it too terribly, you would fright the duchess and the ladies, that they would shriek : and that were enough to hang us all.

All. That would hang us, every mother's son.

Bottom. I grant you, friends, if that you should fright the ladies out of their wits, they would have no more discretion but to hang us : but I will aggravate my voice so that I will roar you as gently as any sucking dove ; I will roar you as 'twere any nightingale.

Quince. You can play no part but Pyramus ; for Pyramus is a sweet-faced man ; a proper man, as one shall see in a summer's day ; a most lovely gentleman-like man : therefore you must needs play Pyramus.

Bottom. Well, I will undertake it. What beard were I best to play it in ?

Quince. Why, what you will.

Bottom. I will discharge it in either your straw-colour beard, your orange-tawny beard, your purple-in-grain beard, or your French-crown-colour beard, your perfect yellow.

Quince. Some of your French crowns have no hair at all, and then you will play barefaced. But, masters, here are your parts : and I am to entreat you, request you and desire you, to con them by to-morrow night ; and meet me in the palace wood, a mile without the town, by moonlight ; there will we rehearse, for if we meet in the city, we shall be dogged with company, and our devices known. In the meantime I will draw a bill of properties, such as our play wants. I pray you, fail me not.

Bottom. We will meet ; and there we may rehearse most obscenely and courageously. Take pains ; be perfect : adieu.

Quince. At the duke's oak we meet.

Bottom. Enough ; hold or cut bow-strings.

[*Exeunt.*

ACT II.

SCENE I. *A wood near Athens.*

Enter, from opposite sides, a Fairy, *and* Puck.

Puck.

How now, spirit ! whither wander you?

Fairy.   Over hill, over dale,
  Thorough bush, thorough brier,
Over park, over pale,
  Thorough flood, thorough fire,
I do wander every.where,
Swifter than the moon's sphere ;
And I serve the fairy queen,
To dew her orbs upon the green.
The cowslips tall her pensioners be :
In their gold coats spots you see ;
Those be rubies, fairy favours,
In thoss freckles live their savours :
I must go seek some dewdrops here
And hang a pearl in every cowslip's ear.
Farewell, thou lob of spirits ; I 'll be gone :
Our queen and all her elves come here anon.

Puck. The king doth keep his revels here tonight :
Take heed the queen come not within his sight ;

For Oberon is passing fell and wrath,
Because that she as her attendant hath
A lovely boy, stolen from an Indian king ;
She never had so sweet a changeling ;
And jealous Oberon would have the child
Knight of his train, to trace the forests wild ;
But she perforce withholds the loved boy,
Crowns him with flowers and makes him all her joy :
And now they never meet in grove or green,
By fountain clear, or spangled starlight sheen,
But they do square, that all their elves for fear
Creep into acorn-cups and hide them there.

Fairy. Either I mistake your shape and making quite,
Or else you are that shrewd and knavish sprite
Call'd Robin Goodfellow : are not you he
That frights the maidens of the villagery ;
Skim milk, and sometimes labour in the quern
And bootless make the breathless housewife churn ;
And sometime make the drink to bear no barm ;
Mislead night-wanderers, laughing at their harm ?
Those that Hobgoblin call you and sweet Puck,
You do their work, and they shall have good luck :
Are not you he ?

Puck.   Thou speak'st aright ;
I am that merry wanderer of the night.
I jest to Oberon and make him smile
When I a fat and bean-fed horse beguile,
Neighing in likeness of a filly foal ;
And sometime lurk I in a gossip's bowl,
In very likeness of a roasted crab,
And when she drinks, against her lips I bob
And on her wither'd dewlap pour the ale.
The wisest aunt, telling the saddest tale,
Sometime for three-foot stool mistaketh me ;
Then slip I from her bum, down topples she,
And ' tailor ' cries, and falls into a cough :
And then the whole quire hold their hips and laugh,
And waxen in their mirth and neeze and swear
A merrier hour was never wasted there.
But, room, fairy ! here comes Oberon.

Fairy. And here my mistress. Would that he were gone !

Enter, from one side, Oberon, *with his train ;
  from the other* Titania, *with hers.*

Oberon. Ill met by moonlight, proud Titania.

Titania. What, jealous Oberon ! Fairies, skip hence !
I have forsworn his bed and company.

Oberon. Tarry, rash wanton : am not I thy lord ?

Titania. Then I must be thy lady ; but I know
When thou hast stolen away from fairy land,
And in the shape of Corin sat all day,
Playing on pipes of corn and versing love
To amorous Phillida. Why art thou here,
Come from the farthest steppe of India ?
But that, forsooth, the bouncing Amazon,
Your buskin'd mistress and your warrior love,
To Theseus must be wedded, and you come
To give their bed joy and prosperity.

Oberon. How canst thou thus for shame, Titania,
Glance at my credit with Hippolyta,
Knowing I know thy love to Theseus ?
Didst thou not lead him through the glimmering night
From Perigenia, whom he ravished ?
And make him with fair Ægle break his faith,
With Ariadne and Antiopa ?

Titania. These are the forgeries of jealousy :
And never, since the middle summer's spring,
Met we on hill, in dale, forest or mead,

By paved fountain or by rushy brook,
Or in the beached margent of the sea,
To dance our ringlets to the whistling wind,
But with thy brawls thou hast disturb'd our sport.
Therefore the winds, piping to us in vain,
As in revenge, have suck'd up from the sea
Contagious fogs ; which falling in the land
Have every pelting river made so proud
That they have overborne their continents :
The ox hath therefore stretch'd his yoke in vain,
The ploughman lost his sweat, and the green corn
Hath rotted ere his youth attain'd a beard ;
The fold stands empty in the drowned field,
And crows are fatted with the murrion flock ;
The nine men's morris is fill'd up with mud,
And the quaint mazes in the wanton green
For lack of tread are undistinguishable :
The human mortals want their winter here ;
No night is now with hymn or carol blest :
Therefore the moon, the governess of floods,
Pale in her anger, washes all the air,
That rheumatic diseases do abound :
And thorough this distemperature we see
The seasons alter : hoary-headed frosts
Fall in the fresh lap of the crimson rose,
And on old Hiems' thin and icy crown
An odorous chaplet of sweet summer buds
Is, as in mockery, set : the spring, the summer,
The childing autumn, angry winter, change
Their wonted liveries, and the mazed world,
By their increase, now knows not which is which :
And this same progeny of evils comes
From our debate, from our dissension ;
We are their parents and original.
   Oberon. Do you amend it then ; it lies in you :
Why should Titania cross her Oberon ?
I do but beg a little changeling boy,
To be my henchman.
   Titania.   Set your heart at rest :
The fairy land buys not the child of me.
His mother was a votaress of my order :
And, in the spiced Indian air, by night,
Full often hath she gossip'd by my side,
And sat with me on Neptune's yellow sands,
Marking the embarked traders on the flood,
When we have laugh'd to see the sails conceive
And grow big-bellied with the wanton wind ;
Which she, with pretty and with swimming gait
Following,—her womb then rich with my young
    squire,—
Would imitate, and sail upon the land,
To fetch me trifles, and return again,
As from a voyage, rich with merchandise.
But she, being mortal, of that boy did die ;
And for her sake do I rear up her boy,
And for her sake I will not part with him.
   Oberon. How long within this wood intend you
    stay ?
   Titania. Perchance till after Theseus' wedding-
    day.
If you will patiently dance in our round
And see our moonlight revels, go with us ;
If not, shun me, and I will spare your haunts.
   Oberon. Give me that boy, and I will go with
    thee.
   Titania. Not for thy fairy kingdom. Fairies,
    away !
We shall chide downright, if I longer stay.
                    [*Exit Titania with her train.*
   Oberon. Well, go thy way : thou shalt not from
    this grove

Till I torment thee for this injury.
My gentle Puck, come hither. Thou rememberest
Since once I sat upon a promontory,
And heard a mermaid on a dolphin's back
Uttering such dulcet and harmonious breath
That the rude sea grew civil at her song
And certain stars shot madly from their spheres,
To hear the sea-maid's music.
   Puck.   I remember.
   Oberon. That very time I saw, but thou couldst
    not,
Flying between the cold moon and the earth,
Cupid all arm'd : a certain aim he took
At a fair vestal throned by the west,
And loosed his love-shaft smartly from his bow,
As it should pierce a hundred thousand hearts :
But I might see young Cupid's fiery shaft
Quench'd in the chaste beams of the watery moon,
And the imperial votaress passed on,
In maiden meditation, fancy-free,
Yet mark'd I where the bolt of Cupid fell :
It fell upon a little western flower,
Before milk-white, now purple with love's wound,
And maidens call it love-in-idleness,
Fetch me that flower ; the herb I shew'd thee once :
The juice of it on sleeping eye-lids laid
Will make or man or woman madly dote
Upon the next live creature that it sees,
Fetch me this herb ; and be thou here again
Ere the leviathan can swim a league.
   Puck. I 'll put a girdle round about the earth
In forty minutes.   [*Exit.*
   Oberon.   Having once this juice,
I 'll watch Titania when she is asleep,
And drop the liquor of it in her eyes.
The next thing then she waking looks upon,
Be it on lion, bear, or wolf, or bull,
On meddling monkey, or on busy ape,
She shall pursue it with the soul of love :
And ere I take this charm from off her sight,
As I can take it with another herb,
I 'll make her render up her page to me.
But who comes here ? I am invisible ;
And I will overhear their conference.

      Enter DEMETRIUS, HELENA *following him.*

   Demetrius. I love thee not, therefore pursue me
    not,
Where is Lysander and fair Hermia ?
The one I 'll slay, the other slayeth me.
Thou told'st me they were stolen unto this wood ;
And here am I, and wode within this wood,
Because I cannot meet my Hermia.
Hence, get thee gone, and follow me no more.
   Helena. You draw me, you hard-hearted adamant ;
But yet you draw not iron, for my heart
Is true as steel ; leave you your power to draw,
And I shall have no power to follow you.
   Demetrius. Do I entice you ? do I speak you fair ?
Or, rather, do I not in plainest truth
Tell you, I do not, nor I cannot love you ?
   Helena. And even for that do I love you the more.
I am your spaniel ; and, Demetrius,
The more you beat me, I will fawn on you :
Use me but as your spaniel, spurn me, strike me,
Neglect me, lose me ; only give me leave.
Unworthy as I am, to follow you.
What worser place can I beg in your love,—
And yet a place of high respect with me.—
Than to be used as you use your dog ?

Demetrius. Tempt not too much the hatred of my
    spirit,
For I am sick when I do look on thee.
Helena. And I am sick when I look not on you.
Demetrius. You do impeach your modesty too
    much,
To leave the city and commit yourself
Into the hands of one that loves you not ;
To trust the opportunity of night
And the ill counsel of a desert place
With the rich worth of your virginity.

    Helena. Your virtue is my privilege : for that
It is not night when I do see your face,
Therefore I think I am not in the night ;
Nor doth this wood lack worlds of company,
For you in my respect are all the world :
Then how can it be said I am alone,
When all the world is here to look on me ?

    Demetrius. I 'll run from thee and hide me in the
    brakes,
And leave thee to the mercy of wild beasts.
    Helena. The wildest hath not such a heart as you.
Run when you will, the story shall be changed :
Apollo flies, and Daphne holds the chase ;
The dove pursues the griffin ; the mild hind
Makes speed to catch the tiger ; bootless speed,
When cowardice pursues and valour flies.

    Demetrius. I will not stay thy questions ; let me
    go :
Or, if thou follow me, do not believe
But I shall do thee mischief in the wood.
    Helena. Ay, in the temple, in the town, the field,
You do me mischief. Fie, Demetrius !
Your wrongs do set a scandal on my sex :
We cannot fight for love, as men may do ;
We should be woo'd and were not made to woo.
                       [*Exit Demetrius.*
I 'll follow thee and make a heaven of hell,
To die upon the hand I love so well.   [*Exit.*

    Oberon. Fare thee well, nymph : ere he do leave
    this grove,
Thou shalt fly him and he shall seek thy love.

Re-enter PUCK.

Hast thou the flower there ? Welcome, wanderer.
    Puck. Ay, there it is.
    Oberon.   I pray thee, give it me.
I know a bank where the wild thyme blows,
Where oxlips and the nodding violet grows,
† Quite over-canopied with luscious woodbine,
With sweet musk-roses and with eglantine :
There sleeps Titania sometime of the night,
Lull'd in these flowers with dances and delight ;
And there the snake throws her enamell'd skin,
Weed wide enough to wrap a fairy in :
And with the juice of this I 'll streak her eyes,
And make her full of hateful fantasies.
Take thou some of it, and seek through this grove :
A sweet Athenian lady is in love
With a disdainful youth : anoint his eyes ;
But do it when the next thing he espies
May be the lady : thou shalt know the man
By the Athenian garments he hath on.
Effect it with some care that he may prove
More fond on her than she upon her love :
And look thou meet me ere the first cock crow.
    Puck. Fear not, my lord, your servant shall do
    so.   [*Exeunt.*

SCENE II.   *Another part of the wood.*

Enter TITANIA, *with her train.*

    Titania. Come, now a roundel and a fairy song ;
Then, for the third part of a minute, hence ;
Some to kill cankers in the musk-rose buds,
Some war with rere-mice for their leathern wings,
To make my small elves coats, and some keep back
The clamorous owl that nightly hoots and wonders
At our quaint spirits. Sing me now asleep ;
Then to your offices and let me rest.

The Fairies sing.

You spotted snakes with double tongue,
    Thorny hedgehogs, be not seen ;
Newts and blind-worms, do no wrong,
    Come not near our fairy queen.
    Philomel, with melody
    Sing in our sweet lullaby ;
Lulla, lulla, lullaby, lulla, lulla, lullaby :
    Never harm,
    Nor spell nor charm,
Come our lovely lady nigh ;
So, good night, with lullaby.

Weaving spiders, come not here ;
    Hence, you long-legg'd spinners, hence !
Beetles black, approach not near ;
    Worm nor snail, do no offence.
    Philomel, with melody, &c.

    A Fairy. Hence, away ! now all is well :
    One aloof stand sentinel.
           [*Exeunt Fairies. Titania sleeps.*

Enter OBERON, *and squeezes the flower on
Titania's eyelids.*

    Oberon. What thou seest when thou dost wake,
    Do it for thy true-love take,
    Love and languish for his sake :
    Be it ounce, or cat, or bear,
    Pard, or boar with bristled hair,
    In thy eye that shall appear
    When thou wakest, it is thy dear :
    Wake when some vile thing is near.
                       [*Exit.*

Enter LYSANDER *and* HERMIA.

    Lysander. Fair love, you faint with wandering in
    the wood ;
And to speak troth, I have forgot our way :
We 'll rest us, Hermia, if you think it good,
And tarry for the comfort of the day.
    Hermia. Be it so, Lysander : find you out a bed ;
For I upon this bank will rest my head.
    Lysander. One turf shall serve as pillow for us
    both ;
One heart, one bed, two bosoms and one troth.
    Hermia. Nay, good Lysander ; for my sake, my
    dear,
Lie further off yet, do not lie so near.
    Lysander. O, take the sense, sweet, of my inno-
    cence !
Love takes the meaning in love's conference.
I mean, that my heart unto yours is knit
So that but one heart we can make of it ;
Two bosoms interchained with an oath ;
So then two bosoms and a single troth.
Then by your side no bed-room me deny ;
For lying so, Hermia, I do not lie.
    Hermia. Lysander riddles very prettily :
Now much beshrew my manners and my pride,

If Hermia meant to say Lysander lied.
But, gentle friend, for love and courtesy
Lie further off ; in human modesty,
Such separation as may well be said
Becomes a virtuous bachelor and a maid,
So far be distant ; and, good night, sweet friend :
Thy love ne'er alter till thy sweet life end !
Lysander. Amen, amen, to that fair prayer, say I ;
And then end life when I end loyalty !
Here is my bed ; sleep give thee all his rest !
Hermia. With half that wish the wisher's eyes
be press'd !

[*They sleep.*

Enter PUCK.

Puck. Through the forest have I gone,
But Athenian found I none,
On whose eyes I might approve
This flower's force in stirring love.
Night and silence.—Who is here ?
Weeds of Athens he doth wear ;
This is he, my master said,
Despised the Athenian maid ;
And here the maiden, sleeping sound,
On the dank and dirty ground.
Pretty soul ! she durst not lie
Near this lack-love, this kill-courtesy.
Churl, upon thy eyes I throw
All the power this charm doth owe.
When thou wakest, let love forbid
Sleep his seat on thy eyelid :
So awake when I am gone ;
For I must now to Oberon.   [*Exit.*

Enter DEMETRIUS *and* HELENA, *running.*

Helena. Stay, though thou kill me, sweet Deme-
trius.
Demetrius. I charge thee, hence, and do not haunt
me thus.
Helena. O, wilt thou darkling . leave me ? do
not so.
Demetrius. Stay, on thy peril : I alone will go.
[*Exit.*
Helena. O, I am out of breath in this fond chase !
The more my prayer, the lesser is my grace.
Happy is Hermia, wheresoe'er she lies ;
For she hath blessed and attractive eyes.
How came her eyes so bright ? Not with salt tears :
If so, my eyes are oftener wash'd than hers,
No, no, I am as ugly as a bear ;
For beasts that meet me run away for fear :
Therefore no marvel though Demetrius
Do, as a monster, fly my presence thus.
What wicked and dissembling glass of mine
Made me compare with Hermia's sphery eyne ?
But who is here ? Lysander ! on the ground !
Dead ? or asleep ? I see no blood, no wound.
Lysander, if you live, good sir, awake.
Lysander. [*Awaking*] And run through fire I will
for thy sweet sake.
Transparent Helena ! Nature shows art,
That through thy bosom makes me see thy heart.
Where is Demetrius ? O, how fit a word
Is that vile name to perish on my sword !
Helena. Do not say so, Lysander ; say not so.
What though he love your Hermia ? Lord, what
though ?
Yet Hermia still loves you : then be content.
Lysander. Content with Hermia ! No ; I do
repent

The tedious minutes I with her have spent,
Not Hermia but Helena I love :
Who will not change a raven for a dove ?
The will of man is by his reason sway'd ;
And reason says you are the worthier maid.
Things growing are not ripe until their season :
So I, being young, till now ripe not to reason ;
And touching now the point of human skill,
Reason becomes the marshal to my will
And leads me to your eyes, where I o'erlook
Love's stories written in love's richest book.
Helena. Wherefore was I to this keen mockery
born ?
When at your hands did I deserve this scorn ?
Is 't not enough, is 't not enough, young man,
That I did never, no, nor never can,
Deserve a sweet look from Demetrius' eye,
But you must flout my insufficiency ?
Good troth, you do me wrong, good sooth, you do,
In such disdainful manner me to woo.
But fare you well : perforce I must confess
I thought you lord of more true gentleness.
O, that a lady, of one man refused,
Should of another therefore be abused !   [*Exit.*
Lysander. She sees not Hermia. Hermia, sleep
thou there :
And never mayst thou come Lysander near !
For as a surfeit of the sweetest things
The deepest loathing to the stomach brings,
Or as the heresies that men do leave
Are hated most of those they did deceive,
So thou, my surfeit and my heresy,
Of all be hated, but the most of me !
And, all my powers, address your love and might
To honour Helen and to be her knight !   [*Exit.*
Hermia. [*Awaking*] Help me, Lysander, help me !
do thy best
To pluck this crawling serpent from my breast !
Ay me, for pity ! what a dream was here !
Lysander, look how I do quake with fear :
Methought a serpent eat my heart away,
And you sat smiling at his cruel prey.
Lysander ! what, removed ? Lysander ! lord !
What, out of hearing ? gone ? no sound, no word ?
Alack, where are you ? speak, an if you hear ;
Speak, of all loves ! I swoon almost with fear.
No ? then I well perceive you are not nigh :
Either death or you I 'll find immediately.   [*Exit.*

ACT III.

SCENE I. *The wood. Titania lying asleep.*

Enter QUINCE, SNUG, BOTTOM, FLUTE, SNOUT,
and STARVELING.

Bottom.

A re we all met ?
Quince. Pat, pat ; and here 's a marvellous
convenient place for our rehearsal. This
green plot shall be our stage, this hawthorn-brake
our tiring-house ; and we will do it in action as we
will do it before the duke.
Bottom. Peter Quince,—
Quince. What sayest thou, bully Bottom ?
Bottom. There are things in this comedy of
Pyramus and Thisby that will never please. First,
Pyramus must draw a sword to kill himself ; which
the ladies cannot abide. How answer you that ?
Snout. By'r lakin, a parlous fear.
Starveling. I believe we must leave the killing
out, when all is done.

Bottom. Not a whit : I have a device to make all well. Write me a prologue ; and let the prologue seem to say, we will do no harm with our swords and that Pyramus is not killed indeed ; and, for the more better assurance, tell them that I Pyramus am not Pyramus, but Bottom the weaver : this will put them out of fear.

Quince. Well, we will have such a prologue ; and it shall be written in eight and six.

Bottom. No, make it two more ; let it be written in eight and eight.

Snout. Will not the ladies be afeared of the lion?

Starveling. I fear it, I promise you.

Bottom. Masters, you ought to consider with yourselves : to bring in—God shield us !—a lion among ladies, is a most dreadful thing ; for there is not a more fearful wild-fowl than your lion living ; and we ought to look to 't.

Snout. Therefore another prologue must tell he is not a lion.

Bottom. Nay, you must name his name, and half his face must be seen through the lion's neck : and he himself must speak through, saying thus, or to the same defect,—' Ladies,'—or ' Fair ladies,—I would wish you,'—or ' I would request you,'—or ' I would entreat you,—not to fear, not to tremble : my life for yours. If you think I come hither as a lion, it were pity of my life : no, I am no such thing ; I am a man as other men are ;' and there indeed let him name his name, and tell them plainly he is Snug the joiner.

Quince. Well, it shall be so. But there is two hard things ; that is, to bring the moonlight into a chamber ; for, you know, Pyramus and Thisby meet by moonlight.

Snout. Doth the moon shine that night we play our play?

Bottom. A calendar, a calendar ! look in the almanac ; find out moonshine, find out moonshine.

Quince. Yes, it doth shine that night.

Bottom. Why, then may you leave a casement of the great chamber window, where we play, open, and the moon may shine in at the casement.

Quince. Ay ; or else one must come in with a bush of thorns and a lanthorn, and say he comes to disfigure, or to present, the person of Moonshine. Then, there is another thing ; we must have a wall n the great chamber ; for Pyramus and Thisby, says the story, did talk through the chink of a wall.

Snout. You can never bring in a wall. What say you, Bottom?

Bottom. Some man or other must present Wall : and let him have some plaster, or some loam, or some rough-cast about him, to signify wall ; and let him hold his fingers thus, and through that cranny shall Pyramus and Thisby whisper.

Quince. If that may be, then all is well. Come, sit down, every mother's son, and rehearse your parts. Pyramus, you begin : when you have spoken your speech, enter into that brake : and so every one according to his cue.

Enter PUCK behind.

Puck. What hempen home-spuns have we swaggering here,
So near the cradle of the fairy queen ?
What, a play toward ! I 'll be an auditor ;
An actor too perhaps, if I see cause.

Quince. Speak, Pyramus. Thisby, stand forth.

Bottom. Thisby, the flowers of odious savours sweet,—

Quince. Odours, odours.

Bottom. ——odours savours sweet :
So hath thy breath, my dearest Thisby dear.
But hark, a voice ! stay thou but here awhile,
And by and by I will to thee appear.   [*Exit.*

Puck. A stranger Pyramus than e'er played
here.   [*Exit.*

Flute. Must I speak now ?

Quince. Ay, marry, must you ; for you must understand he goes but to see a noise that he heard, and is to come again.

Flute. Most radiant Pyramus, most lily-white of hue,
Of colour like the red rose on triumphant brier,
Most brisky juvenal and eke most lovely Jew,
As true as truest horse that yet would never tire,
I 'll meet thee, Pyramus, at Ninny's tomb.

Quince. ' Ninus' tomb,' man : why, you must not speak that yet ; that you answer to Pyramus : you speak all your part at once, cues and all. Pyramus enter : your cue is past ; it is, ' never tire.'

Flute. O,—As true as truest horse, that yet would never tire.

Re-enter PUCK, and BOTTOM with an ass's head.

Bottom. If I were fair, Thisby, I were only thine.

Quince. O monstrous ! O strange ! we are haunted. Pray, masters ! fly, masters ! Help !
[*Exeunt Quince, Snug, Flute, Snout, and Starveling.*

Puck. I 'll follow you, I 'll lead you about a round,
Through bog, through bush, through brake,
    through brier :
Sometime a horse I 'll be, sometime a hound,
A hog, a headless bear, sometime a fire ;
And neigh, and bark, and grunt, and roar, and burn,
Like horse, hound, hog, bear, fire, at every turn.
[*Exit.*

Bottom. Why do they run away? this is a knavery of them to make me afeard.

Re-enter SNOUT.

Snout. O Bottom, thou art changed ! what do I see on thee?

Bottom. What do you see? you see an ass-head of your own, do you ?   [*Exit Snout.*

Re-enter QUINCE.

Quince. Bless thee, Bottom ! bless thee ! thou art translated.   [*Exit.*

Bottom. I see their knavery : this is to make an ass of me ; to fright me, if they could. But I will not stir from this place, do what they can : I will walk up and down here, and I will sing, that they shall hear I am not afraid.   [*Sings.*

The ousel cock so black of hue,
    With orange-tawny bill,
The throstle with his note so true,
    The wren with little quill,—

Titania. [*Awaking*] What angel wakes me from my flowery bed ?

Bottom. [*Sings*]
The finch, the sparrow and the lark,
    The plain-song cuckoo gray,
Whose note full many a man doth mark,
    And dares not answer nay ;—

for, indeed, who would set his wit to so foolish a bird? who would give a bird the lie, though he cry ' cuckoo ' never so ?

Titania. I pray thee, gentle mortal, sing again :
Mine ear is much enamour'd of thy note ;
So is mine eye enthralled to thy shape ;
And thy fair virtue's force perforce doth move me
On the first view to say, to swear, I love thee.
    Bottom. Methinks, mistress, you should have
little reason for that : and yet, to say the truth,
reason and love keep little company together now-
a-days ; the more the pity that some honest neigh-
bours will not make them friends. Nay, I can gleek
upon occasion.
    Titania. Thou art as wise as thou art beautiful.
    Bottom. Not so, neither : but if I had wit enough
to get out of this wood, I have enough to serve
mine own turn.
    Titania. Out of this wood do not desire to go :
Thou shalt remain here, whether thou wilt or no.
I am a spirit of no common rate :
The summer still doth tend upon my state ;
And I do love thee : therefore, go with me ;
I 'll give thee fairies to attend on thee,
And they shall fetch thee jewels from the deep,
And sing while thou on pressed flowers dost sleep :
And I will purge thy mortal grossness so
That thou shalt like an airy spirit go.
Peaseblossom ! Cobweb ! Moth ! and Mustard-
    seed !

Enter PEASEBLOSSOM, COBWEB, MOTH, *and*
        MUSTARDSEED.

    Peaseblossom. Ready.
    Cobweb.   And I.
    Moth.   And I.
    Mustardseed.   And I.
    All.   Where shall we go ?
    Titania. Be kind and courteous to this gentleman ;
Hop in his walks and gambol in his eyes ;
Feed him with apricocks and dewberries,
With purple grapes, green figs, and mulberries ;
The honey-bags steal from the humble-bees,
And for night-tapers crop their waxen thighs
And light them at the fiery glow-worm's eyes,
To have my love to bed and to arise ;
And pluck the wings from painted butterflies
To fan the moonbeams from his sleeping eyes :
Nod to him, elves, and do him courtesies.
    Peaseblossom. Hail, mortal !
    Cobweb. Hail !
    Moth. Hail !
    Mustardseed. Hail !
    Bottom. I cry your worships mercy, heartily : I
beseech your worship's name.
    Cobweb. Cobweb.
    Bottom. I shall desire you of more acquaintance,
good Master Cobweb : if I cut my finger, I shall
make bold with you. Your name, honest gentleman ?
    Peaseblossom. Peaseblossom.
    Bottom. I pray you, commend me to Mistress
Squash, your mother, and to Master Peascod, your
father. Good Master Peaseblossom, I shall desire
you of more acquaintance too. Your name, I
beseech you, sir ?
    Mustardseed. Mustardseed.
    Bottom. Good Master Mustardseed, I know your
patience well : that same cowardly, giant-like ox-
beef hath devoured many a gentleman of your house :
I promise you your kindred hath made my eyes
water ere now. I desire your more acquaintance,
good Master Mustardseed.

Titania. Come, wait upon him ; lead him to my
        bower.
The moon methinks looks with a watery eye ;
And when she weeps, weeps every little flower,
Lamenting some enforced chastity.
Tie up my love's tongue, bring him silently.
                                        [*Exeunt.*

SCENE II.   *Another part of the wood.*

            Enter OBERON.

    Oberon. I wonder if Titania be awaked ;
Then, what it was that next came in her eye,
Which she must dote on in extremity.

            Enter PUCK.

Here comes my messenger.
                        How now, mad spirit !
What night-rule now about this haunted grove ?
    Puck. My mistress with a monster is in love.
Near to her close and consecrated bower,
While she was in her dull and sleeping hour,
A crew of patches, rude mechanicals,
That work for bread upon Athenian stalls,
Were met together to rehearse a play
Intended for great Theseus' nuptial-day.
The shallowest thick-skin of that barren sort,
Who Pyramus presented, in their sport
Forsook his scene and enter'd in a brake :
When I did him at this advantage take,
An ass's nole I fixed on his head :
Anon his Thisbe must be answered,
And forth my mimic comes. When they him spy,
As wild geese that the creeping fowler eye,
Or russet-pated choughs, many in sort,
Rising and cawing at the gun's report,
Sever themselves and madly sweep the sky,
So, at his sight, away his fellows fly ;
And, at our stamp, here o'er and o'er one falls ;
He murder cries and help from Athens calls.
Their sense thus weak, lost with their fears thus strong,
Made senseless things begin to do them wrong ;
For briers and thorns at their apparel snatch ;
Some sleeves, some hats, from yielders all things
    catch.
I led them on in this distracted fear,
And left sweet Pyramus translated there :
When in that moment, so it came to pass,
Titania waked and straightway loved an ass.
    Oberon. This falls out better than I could devise.
But hast thou yet latch'd the Athenian's eyes
With the love-juice, as I did bid thee do ?
    Puck. I took him sleeping,—that is finish'd
    too,—
And the Athenian woman by his side ;
That, when he waked, of force she must be eyed.

        Enter HERMIA *and* DEMETRIUS.

    Oberon. Stand close : this is the same Athenian.
    Puck. This is the woman, but not this the man.
    Demetrius. O, why rebuke you him that loves
        you so ?
Lay breath so bitter on your bitter foe.
    Hermia. Now I but chide ; but I should use thee
        worse,
For thou, I fear, hast given me cause to curse.
If thou hast slain Lysander in his sleep,
Being o'er shoes in blood, plunge in the deep,

And kill me too.
The sun was not so true unto the day
As he to me : would he have stolen away
From sleeping Hermia ? I 'll believe as soon
This whole earth may be bored and that the moon
May through the centre creep and so displease
Her brother's noontide with the Antipodes.
It cannot be but thou hast murder'd him ;
So should a murderer look, so dead, so grim.

Demetrius. So should the murder'd look, and so
   should I,
Pierced through the heart with your stern cruelty :
Yet you, the murderer, look as bright, as clear,
As yonder Venus in her glimmering sphere.

Hermia. What 's this to my Lysander ? where
   is he ?
Ah, good Demetrius, wilt thou give him me ?

Demetrius. I had rather give his carcass to my
   hounds.

Hermia. Out, dog ! out, cur ! thou drivest me
   past the bounds
Of maiden's patience. Hast thou slain him, then ?
Henceforth be never number'd among men !
O, once tell true, tell true, even for my sake !
Durst thou have look'd upon him being awake,
And hast thou kill'd him sleeping ? O brave touch !
Could not a worm, an adder, do so much ?
An adder did it ; for with doubler tongue
Than thine, thou serpent, never adder stung.

Demetrius. You spend your passion on a misprised
   mood :
I am not guilty of Lysander's blood ;
Nor is he dead, for aught that I can tell.

Hermia. I pray thee, tell me then that he is well.

Demetrius. An if I could. what should I get
   therefore ?

Hermia. A privilege never to see me more.
And from thy hated presence part I so :
See me no more, whether he be dead or no.
                                      [*Exit.*

Demetrius. There is no following her in this fierce
   vein :
Here therefore for a while I will remain.
So sorrow's heaviness doth heavier grow
For debt that bankrupt sleep doth sorrow owe ;
Which now in some slight measure it will pay,
If for his tender here I make some stay.
                        [*Lies down and sleeps.*

Oberon. What hast thou done ? thou hast mis-
   taken quite
And laid the love-juice on some true-love's sight :
Of thy misprision must perforce ensue
Some true love turn'd and not a false turn'd true.

Puck. Then fate o'er-rules, that, one man holding
   troth,
A million fail, confounding oath on oath.

Oberon. About the wood go swifter than the
   wind,
And Helena of Athens look thou find ;
All fancy-sick she is and pale of cheer,
With sighs of love, that costs the fresh blood dear :
By some illusion see thou bring her here :
I 'll charm his eyes against she do appear.

Puck. I go. I go ; look how I go,
Swifter than arrow from the Tartar's bow.   [*Exit.*

Oberon. Flower of this purple dye,
   Hit with Cupid's archery,
   Sink in apple of his eye.
   When his love he doth espy,
   Let her shine as gloriously
   As the Venus of the sky.

When thou wakest, if she be by,
Beg of her for remedy.

Re-enter Puck.

Puck. Captain of our fairy band,
Helena is here at hand ;
And the youth, mistook by me,
Pleading for a lover's fee.
Shall we their fond pageant see ?
Lord, what fools these mortals be !

Oberon. Stand aside : the noise they make
Will cause Demetrius to awake.

Puck. Then will two at once woo one ;
That must needs be sport alone ;
And those things do best please me
That befal preposterously.

Enter Lysander *and* Helena.

Lysander. Why should you think that I should woo
   in scorn ?
Scorn and derision never come in tears :
Look, when I vow, I weep ; and vows so born,
In their nativity all truth appears.
How can these things in me seem scorn to you,
Bearing the badge of faith, to prove them true ?

Helena. You do advance your cunning more and
   more.
When truth kills truth, O devilish-holy fray !
These vows are Hermia's : will you give her o'er ?
Weigh oath with oath. and you will nothing
   weigh :
Your vows to her and me, put in two scales,
Will even weigh, and both as light as tales.

Lysander. I had no judgement when to her I
   swore.

Helena. Nor none. in my mind, now you give
   her o'er.

Lysander. Demetrius loves her, and he loves not
   you.

Demetrius. [*Awaking*] O Helen, goddess, nymph,
   perfect, divine !
To what, my love. shall I compare thine eyne ?
Crystal is muddy. O, how ripe in show
Thy lips, those kissing cherries, tempting grow !
That pure congealed white, high Taurus' snow,
Fann'd with the eastern wind, turns to a crow
When thou hold'st up thy hand : O, let me kiss
This princess of pure white, this seal of bliss !

Helena. O spite ! O hell ! I see you all are bent
To set against me for your merriment :
If you were civil and knew courtesy,
You would not do me thus much injury.
Can you not hate me, as I know you do,
But you must join in souls to mock me too ?
If you were men, as men you are in show,
You would not use a gentle lady so :
To vow, and swear, and superpraise my parts,
When I am sure you hate me with your hearts.
You both are rivals, and love Hermia ;
And now both rivals, to mock Helena :
A trim exploit, a manly enterprise,
To conjure tears up in a poor maid's eyes
With your derision ! none of noble sort
Would so offend a virgin and extort
A poor soul's patience, all to make you sport.

Lysander. You are unkind, Demetrius ; be not so;
For you love Hermia ; this you know I know :
And here, with all good will, with all my heart,
In Hermia's love I yield you up my part :

And yours of Helena to me bequeath,
Whom I do love and will do till my death.
Helena. Never did mockers waste more idle
breath.
Demetrius. Lysander, keep thy Hermia ; I will
none :
If e'er I loved her, all that love is gone.
My heart to her but as guest-wise sojourn'd,
And now to Helen is it home return'd,
There to remain.
Lysander. Helen, it is not so.
Demetrius. Disparage not the faith thou dost not
know,
Lest, to thy peril, thou aby it dear.
Look, where thy love comes ; yonder is thy dear.

Re-enter HERMIA.

Hermia. Dark night, that from the eye his
function takes,
The ear more quick of apprehension makes ;
Wherein it doth impair the seeing sense,
It pays the hearing double recompense.
Thou art not by mine eye, Lysander, found ;
Mine ear, I thank it, brought me to thy sound.
But why unkindly didst thou leave me so ?
Lysander. Why should he stay, whom love doth
press to go ?
Hermia. What love could press Lysander from
my side ?
Lysander. Lysander's love, that would not let
him bide,
Fair Helena, who more engilds the night
Than all yon fiery oes and eyes of light.
Why seek'st thou me ? could not this make thee
know,
The hate I bear thee made me leave thee so ?
Hermia. You speak not as you think : it cannot
be.
Helena. Lo, she is one of this confederacy !
Now I perceive they have conjoin'd all three
To fashion this false sport, in spite of me,
Injurious Hermia ! most ungrateful maid !
Have you conspired, have you with these contrived
To bait me with this foul derision ?
Is all the counsel that we two have shared,
The sisters' vows, the hours that we have spent,
When we have chid the hasty-footed time
For parting us,—O, is it all forgot ?
All school-days' friendship, childhood innocence ?
We, Hermia, like two artificial gods,
Have with our needles created both one flower,
Both on one sampler, sitting on one cushion,
Both warbling of one song, both in one key,
As if our hands, our sides, voices and minds,
Had been incorporate. So we grew together,
Like to a double cherry, seeming parted,
But yet an union in partition :
Two lovely berries moulded on one stem ;
So, with two seeming bodies, but one heart ;
Two of the first, like coats in heraldry,
Due but to one and crowned with one crest,
And will you rent our ancient love asunder,
To join with men in scorning your poor friend ?
It is not friendly, 'tis not maidenly :
Our sex, as well as I, may chide you for it,
Though I alone do feel the injury.
Hermia. I am amazed at your passionate words.
I scorn you not : it seems that you scorn me.
Helena. Have you not set Lysander, as in scorn,
To follow me and praise my eyes and face ?

And made your other love, Demetrius,
Who even but now did spurn me with his foot,
To call me goddess, nymph, divine and rare,
Precious, celestial ? Wherefore speaks he this
To her he hates ? and wherefore doth Lysander
Deny your love, so rich within his soul,
And tender me, forsooth, affection,
But by your setting on, by your consent ?
What though I be not so in grace as you,
So hung upon with love, so fortunate,
But miserable most, to love unloved ?
This you should pity rather than despise.
Hermia. I understand not what you mean by this.
Helena. Ay, do, persever, counterfeit sad looks,
Make mouths upon me when I turn my back ;
Wink each at other ; hold the sweet jest up :
This sport, well carried, shall be chronicled.
If you have any pity, grace, or manners,
You would not make me such an argument.
But fare ye well : 'tis partly my own fault ;
Which death or absence soon shall remedy.
Lysander. Stay, gentle Helena ; hear my excuse :
My love, my life, my soul, fair Helena !
Helena. O excellent !
Hermia. Sweet, do not scorn her so.
Demetrius. If she cannot entreat, I can compel.
Lysander. Thou canst compel no more than she
entreat :
Thy threats have no more strength than her weak
prayers.
Helen, I love thee ; by my life I do :
I swear by that which I will lose for thee,
To prove him false that says I love thee not.
Demetrius. I say I love thee more than he can do.
Lysander. If thou say so, withdraw, and prove
it too.
Demetrius. Quick, come !
Hermia. Lysander, whereto tends all this ?
Lysander. Away, you Ethiope !
Demetrius. †No, no ; he 'll . . .
Seem to break loose ; take on as you would follow,
But yet come not : you are a tame man, go !
Lysander. Hang off, thou cat, thou burr ! vile
thing, let loose,
Or I will shake thee from me like a serpent !
Hermia. Why are you grown so rude ? what
change is this ?
Sweet love,—
Lysander. Thy love ! out, tawny Tartar, out !
Out, loathed medicine ! hated potion, hence !
Hermia. Do you not jest ?
Helena. Yes, sooth ; and so do you.
Lysander. Demetrius, I will keep my word with
thee.
Demetrius. I would I had your bond, for I perceive
A weak bond holds you : I 'll not trust your word.
Lysander. What, should I hurt her, strike her,
kill her dead ?
Although I hate her, I 'll not harm her so.
Hermia. What, can you do me greater harm than
hate ?
Hate me ! wherefore ? O me ! what news, my
love !
Am not I Hermia ? are not you Lysander ?
I am as fair now as I was erewhile.
Since night you loved me : yet since night you
left me :
Why, then you left me—O, the gods forbid !—
In earnest, shall I say ?
Lysander. Ay, by my life ;
And never did desire to see thee more.

Therefore be out of hope, of question, of doubt ;
Be certain, nothing truer ; 'tis no jest
That I do hate thee and love Helena.
Hermia. O me ! you juggler ! you canker-
blossom !
You thief of love ! what, have you come by night
And stolen my love's heart from him ?
Helena.   Fine, i' faith !
Have you no modesty, no maiden shame,
No touch of bashfulness ? What, will you tear
Impatient answers from my gentle tongue ?
Fie, fie ! you counterfeit, you puppet, you !
Hermia. Puppet ? why so ? ay, that way goes
the game.
Now I perceive that she hath made compare
Between our statures ; she hath urged her height ;
And with her personage, her tall personage,
Her height, forsooth, she hath prevail'd with him.
And are you grown so high in his esteem,
Because I am so dwarfish and so low ?
How low am I, thou painted maypole ? speak ;
How low am I ! I am not yet so low
But that my nails can reach unto thine eyes.
Helena. I pray you, though you mock me,
gentlemen,
Let her not hurt me : I was never curst ;
I have no gift at all in shrewishness ;
I am a right maid for my cowardice :
Let her not strike me. You perhaps may think,
Because she is something lower than myself,
That I can match her.
Hermia.   Lower ! hark, again.
Helena. Good Hermia, do not be so bitter with
me,
I evermore did love you, Hermia,
Did ever keep your counsels, never wrong'd you ;
Save that, in love unto Demetrius,
I told him of your stealth unto this wood.
He follow'd you ; for love I follow'd him ;
But he hath chid me hence and threaten'd me
To strike me, spurn me, nay, to kill me too :
And now, so you will let me quiet go,
To Athens will I bear my folly back
And follow you no further : let me go :
You see how simple and how fond I am.
Hermia. Why, get you gone : who is 't that
hinders you ?
Helena. A foolish heart, that I leave here behind.
Hermia. What, with Lysander ?
Helena.   With Demetrius.
Lysander. Be not afraid ; she shall not harm thee,
Helena.
Demetrius. No, sir, she shall not, though you
take her part.
Helena. O, when she 's angry, she is keen and
shrewd !
She was a vixen when she went to school ;
And though she be but little, she is fierce.
Hermia. ' Little ' again ! nothing but ' low ' and
' little ' !
Why will you suffer her to flout me thus ?
Let me come to her.
Lysander.   Get you gone, you dwarf ;
You minimus, of hindering knot-grass made ;
You bead, you acorn.
Demetrius.   You are too officious
In her behalf that scorns your services.
Let her alone : speak not of Helena ;
Take not her part ; for, if thou dost intend
Never so little show of love to her,
Thou shalt aby it.

Lysander.   Now she holds me not ;
Now follow, if thou darest, to try whose right,
Of thine or mine, is most in Helena.
Demetrius. Follow ! nay, I 'll go with thee,
cheek by jole. [*Exeunt Lysander and Demetrius.*
Hermia. You, mistress, all this coil is 'long of you:
Nay, go not back.
Helena.   I will not trust you, I,
Nor longer stay in your curst company.
Your hands than mine are quicker for a fray,
My legs are longer though, to run away.   [*Exit.*
Hermia. I am amazed, and know not what to
say.   [*Exit.*
Oberon. This is thy negligence : still thou mis-
takest,
Or else committ'st thy knaveries wilfully.
Puck. Believe me, king of shadows, I mistook.
Did not you tell me I should know the man
By the Athenian garments he had on ?
And so far blameless proves my enterprise,
That I have 'nointed an Athenian's eyes ;
And so far am I glad it so did sort
As this their jangling I esteem a sport.
Oberon. Thou see'st these lovers seek a place to
fight :
Hie therefore, Robin, overcast the night :
The starry welkin cover thou anon
With drooping fog as black as Acheron,
And lead these testy rivals so astray
As one come not within another's way.
Like to Lysander sometime frame thy tongue,
Then stir Demetrius up with bitter wrong ;
And sometime rail thou like Demetrius ;
And from each other look thou lead them thus,
Till o'er their brows death-counterfeiting sleep
With leaden legs and batty wings doth creep :
Then crush this herb into Lysander's eye ;
Whose liquor hath this virtuous property,
To take from thence all error with his might,
And make his eyeballs roll with wonted sight.
When they next wake, all this derision
Shall seem a dream and fruitless vision,
And back to Athens shall the lovers wend,
With league whose date till death shall never end,
Whiles I in this affair do thee employ
I 'll to my queen and beg her Indian boy ;
And then I will her charmed eye release
From monster's view, and all things shall be peace.
Puck. My fairy lord, this must be done with haste,
For night's swift dragons cut the clouds full fast,
And yonder shines Aurora's harbinger ;
At whose approach, ghosts, wandering here and there,
Troop home to churchyards : damned spirits all,
That in crossways and floods have burial,
Already to their wormy beds are gone ;
For fear lest day should look their shames upon,
They wilfully themselves exile from light
And must for aye consort with black-brow'd night.
Oberon. But we are spirits of another sort :
I with the morning's love have oft made sport,
And, like a forester, the groves may tread,
Even till the eastern gate, all fiery-red,
Opening on Neptune with fair blessed beams,
Turns into yellow gold his salt green streams.
But, notwithstanding, haste ; make no delay :
We may effect this business yet ere day.   [*Exit.*
Puck. Up and down, up and down,
I will lead them up and down :
I am fear'd in field and town :
Goblin, lead them up and down.
Here comes one.

Re-enter Lysander.

Lysander. Where art thou, proud Demetrius?
 speak thou now.
Puck. Here, villain ; drawn and ready. Where
 art thou?
Lysander. I will be with thee straight.
Puck.   Follow me, then,
To plainer ground.
 [*Exit Lysander, as following the voice.*

Re-enter Demetrius.

Demetrius.   Lysander ! speak again :
Thou runaway, thou coward, art thou fled?
Speak ! In some bush? Where dost thou hide thy
 head?
 Puck. Thou coward, art thou bragging to the
 stars,
Telling the bushes that thou look'st for wars,
And wilt not come? Come, recreant ; come, thou
 child,
I 'll whip thee with a rod : he is defiled
That draws a sword on thee.
Demetrius.   Yea, art thou there?
Puck. Follow my voice : we 'll try no manhood
 here.   [*Exeunt.*

Re-enter Lysander.

Lysander. He goes before me and still dares me on :
When I come where he calls, then he is gone.
The villain is much lighter-heel'd than I :
I follow'd fast, but faster he did fly ;
That fallen am I in dark uneven way,
And here will rest me. [*Lies down.*] Come, thou
 gentle day !
For if but once thou show me thy grey light,
I 'll find Demetrius and revenge this spite.
                                   [*Sleeps.*

Re-enter Puck *and* Demetrius.

Puck. Ho, ho, ho ! Coward, why comest thou
 not?
Demetrius. Abide me, if thou darest ; for well
 I wot
Thou runn'st before me, shifting every place,
And darest not stand, nor look me in the face.
Where art thou now?
Puck.   Come hither : I am here.
Demetrius. Nay, then, thou mock'st me. Thou
 shalt buy this dear,
If ever I thy face by daylight see :
Now, go thy way. Faintness constraineth me
To measure out my length on this cold bed.
By day's approach look to be visited.
                      [*Lies down and sleeps.*

Re-enter Helena.

Helena. O weary night, O long and tedious night,
 Abate thy hours ! Shine comforts from the east,
That I may back to Athens by daylight,
 From these that my poor company detest :
And sleep, that sometimes shuts up sorrow's eye,
Steal me awhile from mine own company.
                       [*Lies down and sleeps.*
Puck. Yet but three? come one more ;
 Two of both kinds makes up four.
 Here she comes, curst and sad :

 Cupid is a knavish lad,
 Thus to make poor females mad.

Re-enter Hermia.

Hermia. Never so weary, never so in woe,
 Bedabbled with the dew and torn with briers,
I can no further crawl, no further go ;
 My legs can keep no pace with my desires :
Here will I rest me till the break of day,
Heavens shield Lysander, if they mean a fray !
                       [*Lies down and sleeps.*
Puck.   On the ground
                 Sleep sound :
                 I 'll apply
                 To your eye,
             Gentle lover, remedy.
       [*Squeezing the juice on Lysander's eyes.*
                 When thou wakest,
                 Thou takest
                 True delight
                 In the sight
             Of thy former lady's eye :
             And the country proverb known,
             That every man should take his own,
             In your waking shall be shown :
                 Jack shall have Jill ;
                 Nought shall go ill ;
 The man shall have his mare again, and all shall
 be well.   [*Exit.*

ACT IV.

SCENE I. *The same.* Lysander, Demetrius,
 Helena, *and* Hermia *lying asleep.*

Enter Titania *and* Bottom ; Peaseblossom, Cobweb,
 Moth, Mustardseed, *and other Fairies attending;*
 Oberon *behind unseen.*

Titania.

Come sit thee down upon this flowery bed,
 While I thy amiable cheeks do coy,
 And stick musk-roses in thy sleek smooth
 head,
 And kiss thy fair large ears, my gentle joy.
Bottom. Where 's Peaseblossom?
Peaseblossom. Ready.
Bottom. Scratch my head, Peaseblossom. Where 's
Mounsier Cobweb?
Cobweb. Ready.
Bottom. Mounsier Cobweb, good mounsier,
get you your weapons in your hand, and kill me a
red-hipped humble-bee on the top of a thistle ; and,
good mounsier, bring me the honey-bag. Do not
fret yourself too much in the action, mounsieur ;
and, good mounsieur, have a care the honey-bag
break not ; I would be loath to have you overflown
with a honey-bag, signior. Where 's Mounsier
Mustardseed?
Mustardseed. Ready.
Bottom. Give me your neaf, Mounsier Mustardseed. Pray you, leave your courtesy, good mounsier.
Mustardseed. What 's your will?
Bottom. Nothing, good mounsier, but to help
Cavalero Cobweb to scratch. I must to the barber's,
mounsieur ; for methinks I am marvellous hairy
about the face ; and I am such a tender ass, if my
hair do but tickle me, I must scratch.
Titania. What, wilt thou hear some music, my
 sweet love?

Bottom. I have a reasonable good ear in music.
Let 's have the tongs and the bones.

Titania. Or say sweet love, what thou desirest
to eat.

Bottom. Truly, a peck of provender : I could
munch your good dry oats. Methinks I have a
great desire to a bottle of hay : good hay, sweet
hay, hath no fellow.

Titania. I have a venturous fairy- that shall seek
The squirrel's hoard, and fetch thee new nuts.

Bottom. I had rather have a handful or two of
dried peas. But, I pray you, let none of your people
stir me : I have an exposition of sleep come upon
me.

Titania. Sleep thou, and I will wind thee in my
   arms,
Fairies, be gone, and be all ways away.
                        [*Exeunt fairies.*
So doth the woodbine the sweet honeysuckle
Gentle entwist ; the female ivy so
Enrings the barky fingers of the elm.
O, how I love thee ! how I dote on thee !
                        [*They sleep.*

            Enter PUCK.

Oberon. [*Advancing*] Welcome, good Robin.
   See'st thou this sweet sight ?
Her dotage now I do begin to pity :
For, meeting her of late behind the wood,
Seeking sweet favours for this hateful fool,
I did upbraid her and fall out with her ;
For she his hairy temples then had rounded
With coronet of fresh and fragrant flowers ;
And that same dew, which sometime on the buds
Was wont to swell like round and orient pearls,
Stood now within the pretty flowerets' eyes
Like tears that did their own disgrace bewail.
When I had at my pleasure taunted her
And she in mild terms begg'd my patience,
I then did ask of her her changeling child ;
Which straight she gave me, and her fairy sent
To bear him to my bower in fairy land.
And now I have the boy, I will undo
This hateful imperfection of her eyes :
And, gentle Puck, take this transformed scalp
From off the head of this Athenian swain ;
That, he awaking when the other do,
May all to Athens back again repair
And think no more of this night's accidents
But as the fierce vexation of a dream.
But first I will release the fairy queen.
   Be as thou wast wont to be ;
   See as thou wast wont to see :
   Dian's bud o'er Cupid's flower
   Hath such force and blessed power.
Now, my Titania ; wake you, my sweet queen.

Titania. My Oberon ! what visions have I seen !
Methought I was enamour'd of an ass.

Oberon. There lies your love.

Titania.   How came these things to pass ?
O, how mine eyes do loathe his visage now !

Oberon. Silence awhile. Robin, take off this head.
Titania, music call ; and strike more dead
Than common sleep of all these five the sense.

Titania. Music, ho ! music, such as charmeth
   sleep !   [*Music, still.*

Puck. Now, when thou wakest, with thine own
   fool's eyes peep.

Oberon. Sound, music ! Come, my queen, take
   hands with me,

And rock the ground whereon these sleepers be.
Now thou and I are new in amity
And will to-morrow midnight solemnly
Dance in Duke Theseus' house triumphantly
And bless it to all fair prosperity :
There shall the pairs of faithful lovers be
Wedded, with Theseus, all in jollity.

Puck. Fairy king, attend, and mark :
   I do hear the morning lark.

Oberon. Then, my queen, in silence sad,
   Trip we after night's shade :
   We the globe can compass soon,
   Swifter than the wandering moon.

Titania. Come, my lord, and in our flight
   Tell me how it came this night
   That I sleeping here was found
   With these mortals on the ground.
                           [*Exeunt.*
                  [*Horns winded within.*

Enter THESEUS, HIPPOLYTA, EGEUS, *and train.*

Theseus. Go, one of you, find out the forester ;
For now our observation is perform'd ;
And since we have the vaward of the day,
My love shall hear the music of my hounds.
Uncouple in the western valley ; let them go :
Dispatch. I say. and find the forester.
                       [*Exit an Attendant.*
We will, fair queen, up to the mountain's top
And mark the musical confusion
Of hounds and echo in conjunction.

Hippolyta. I was with Hercules and Cadmus once
When in a wood of Crete they bay'd the bear
With hounds of Sparta : never did I hear
Such gallant chiding ; for, besides the groves,
The skies. the fountains, every region near
Seem'd all one mutual cry : I never heard
So musical a discord, such sweet thunder.

Theseus. My hounds are bred out of the Spartan
   kind,
So flew'd, so sanded, and their heads are hung
With ears that sweep away the morning dew ;
Crook-knee'd, and dew-lapp'd like Thessalian bulls ;
Slow in pursuit, but match'd in mouth like bells,
Each under each. A cry more tuneable
Was never holla'd to, nor cheer'd with horn,
In Crete, in Sparta, nor in Thessaly :
Judge when you hear. But, soft ! what nymphs
   are these ?

Egeus. My lord, this is my daughter here asleep ;
And this, Lysander ; this Demetrius is ;
This Helena, old Nedar's Helena :
I wonder of their being here together.

Theseus. No doubt they rose up early to observe
The rite of May, and, hearing our intent,
Came here in grace of our solemnity.
But speak, Egeus ; is not this the day
That Hermia should give answer of her choice ?

Egeus. It is, my lord.

Theseus. Go, bid the huntsmen wake them with
   their horns. [*Horns and shout within. Lysander,
Demetrius, Helena, and Hermia, wake and start up.*
Good morrow, friends, Saint Valentine is past :
Begin these wood-birds but to couple now ?

Lysander. Pardon, my lord.

Theseus.   I pray you all, stand up.
I know you two are rival enemies :
How comes this gentle concord in the world,
That hatred is so far from jealousy
To sleep by hate, and fear no enmity ?

Lysander.   My lord, I shall reply amazedly,
Half sleep, half waking ; but as yet, I swear,
I cannot truly say how I came here ;
But, as I think,—for truly would I speak,
And now I do bethink me, so it is,—
I came with Hermia hither : our intent
Was to be gone from Athens, where we might,
Without the peril of the Athenian law.
Egeus.   Enough, enough, my lord ; you have
    enough :
I beg the law, the law, upon his head.
They would have stolen away ; they would,
    Demetrius,
Thereby to have defeated you and me,
You of your wife and me of my consent,
Of my consent that she should be your wife.
Demetrius.   My lord, fair Helen told me of their
    stealth,
Of this their purpose hither to this wood ;
And I in fury hither follow'd them,
Fair Helena in fancy following me.
But, my good lord, I wot not by what power,—
But by some power it is,—my love to Hermia,
Melted as the snow, seems to me now
As the remembrance of an idle gawd
Which in my childhood I did dote upon ;
And all the faith, the virtue of my heart,
The object and the pleasure of mine eye,
Is only Helena.   To her, my lord,
Was I betroth'd ere I saw Hermia :
But, like in sickness, did I loathe this food ;
But, as in health, come to my natural taste,
Now I do wish it, love it, long for it,
And will for evermore be true to it.
Theseus.   Fair lovers, you are fortunately met :
Of this discourse we more will hear anon.
Egeus, I will overbear your will ;
For in the temple, by and by, with us
These couples shall eternally be knit :
And, for the morning now is something worn,
Our purposed hunting shall be set aside.
Away with us to Athens ; three and three,
We 'll hold a feast in great solemnity.
Come Hippolyta.
          [*Exeunt Theseus, Hippolyta, Egeus and train.*
Demetrius.   These things seem small and undis-
    tinguishable,
Like far-off mountains turned into clouds.
Hermia.   Methinks I see these things with parted
    eye,
When every thing seems double.
Helena.   So methinks :
And I have found Demetrius like a jewel,
Mine own, and not mine own.
Demetrius.   Are you sure
That we are awake ?   It seems to me
That yet we sleep, we dream.   Do not you think
The duke was here, and bid us follow him ?
Hermia.   Yea ; and my father.
Helena.   And Hippolyta.
Lysander.   And he did bid us follow to the temple.
Demetrius.   Why, then, we are awake : let 's
    follow him ;
And by the way let us recount our dreams.
                                    [*Exeunt.*
Bottom. [*Awaking*] When my cue comes, call
me, and I will answer : my next is ' Most fair Pyra-
mus.'   Heigh-ho ! Peter Quince ! Flute, the bellows-
mender ! Snout, the tinker ! Starveling ! God 's
my life, stolen hence, and left me asleep ! I have
had a most rare vision.   I have had a dream, past

the wit of man to say what dream it was : man is
but an ass, if he go about to expound this dream.
Methought I was—there is no man can tell what.
Methought I was,—and methought I had,—but
man is but a patched fool, if he will offer to say
what methought I had.   The eye of man hath not
heard, the ear of man hath not seen, man's hand is
not able to taste, his tongue to conceive, nor his
heart to report, what my dream was.   I will get
Peter Quince to write a ballad of this dream : it
shall be called Bottom's Dream, because it hath
no bottom ; and I will sing it in the latter end of a
play, before the duke : peradventure, to make it
the more gracious, † I shall sing it at her death.   [*Exit.*

SCENE II.   *Athens.*   QUINCE'S *house.*

Enter QUINCE, FLUTE, SNOUT, *and* STARVELING.

Quince.   Have you sent to Bottom's house ? is
he come home yet ?
Starveling.   He cannot be heard of.   Out of doubt
he is transported.
Flute.   If he come not, then the play is marred :
it goes not forward, doth it ?
Quince. · It is not possible : you have not a man
in all Athens able to discharge Pyramus but he.
Flute.   No, he hath simply the best wit of any
handicraft man in Athens.
Quince.   Yea, and the best person too ; and he
is a very paramour for a sweet voice.
Flute.   You must say ' paragon : ' a paramour
is, God bless us, a thing of naught.

Enter SNUG.

Snug.   Masters, the duke is coming from the
temple, and there is two or three lords and ladies
more married : if our sport had gone forward, we
had all been made men.
Flute.   O sweet bully Bottom ! Thus hath he
lost sixpence a day during his life ; he could not
have 'scaped sixpence a day : an the duke had not
given him sixpence a day for playing Pyramus, I 'll
be hanged ; he would have deserved it : sixpence a
day in Pyramus. or nothing.

Enter BOTTOM.

Bottom.   Where are these lads ? where are these
hearts ?
Quince.   Bottom ! O most courageous day ! O
most happy hour !
Bottom.   Masters, I am to discourse wonders :
but ask me not what ; for if I tell you, I am no true
Athenian.   I will tell you everything, right as it
fell out.
Quince.   Let us hear, sweet Bottom.
Bottom.   Not a word of me.   All that I will tell
you is, that the duke hath dined.   Get your apparel
together, good strings to your beards, new ribbons
to your pumps ; meet presently at the palace ;
every man look o'er his part ; for the short and the
long is, our play is preferred.   In any case, let Thisby
have clean linen ; and let not him that plays the
lion pare his nails, for they shall hang out for the
lion's claws.   And, most dear actors, eat no onions
nor garlic, for we are to utter sweet breath ; and I
do not doubt but to hear them say, it is a sweet
comedy.   No more words : away ! go, away !
                                    [*Exeunt.*

ACT V.

SCENE I. *Athens. The palace of* THESEUS.

Enter THESEUS, HIPPOLYTA, PHILOSTRATE, Lords,
and Attendants.

Hippolyta.

'T is strange, my Theseus, that these lovers
   speak of.
   Theseus. More strange than true : I never
may believe
These antique fables, nor these fairy toys,
Lovers and madmen have such seething brains,
Such shaping fantasies, that apprehend
More than cool reason ever comprehends.
The lunatic, the lover and the poet
Are of imagination all compact :
One sees more devils than vast hell can hold,
That is, the madman : the lover, all as frantic,
Sees Helen's beauty in a brow of Egypt :
The poet's eye, in a fine frenzy rolling,
Doth glance from heaven to earth, from earth to
   heaven ;
And as imagination bodies forth
The forms of things unknown, the poet's pen
Turns them to shapes and gives to airy nothing
A local habitation and a name.
Such tricks hath strong imagination,
That, if it would but apprehend some joy,
It comprehends some bringer of that joy ;
Or in the night, imagining some fear,
How easy is a bush supposed a bear !
   Hippolyta. But all the story of the night told over,
And all their minds transfigured so together,
More witnesseth than fancy's images
And grows to something of great constancy ;
But, howsoever, strange and admirable.
   Theseus. Here come the lovers, full of joy and
   mirth.

Enter LYSANDER, DEMETRIUS, HERMIA, *and* HELENA.

Joy, gentle friends ! joy and fresh days of love
Accompany your hearts !
   Lysander.   More than to us
Wait in your royal walks, your board, your bed !
   Theseus. Come now ; what masques, what dances
shall we have,
To wear away this long age of three hours
Between our after-supper and bed-time ?
Where is our usual manager of mirth ?
What revels are in hand ? Is there no play,
To ease the anguish of a torturing hour ?
Call Philostrate.
   Philostrate. Here, mighty Theseus.
   Theseus. Say, what abridgement have you for
this evening ?
What masque ? what music ? How shall we beguile
The lazy time, if not with some delight ?
   Philostrate. There is a brief how many sports are
ripe :
Make choice of which your highness will see first.
                          [Giving a paper.
   Theseus. [*Reads*] ' The battle with the Centaurs,
to be sung
By an Athenian eunuch to the harp.'
We 'll none of that : that have I told my love,
In glory of my kinsman Hercules.
[*Reads*] ' The riot of the tipsy Bacchanals,
Tearing the Thracian singer in their rage '
That is an old device ; and it was play'd

When I from Thebes came last a conqueror.
[*Reads*] ' The thrice three Muses mourning for the
   death
Of Learning, late deceased in beggary.'
That is some satire, keen and critical,
Not sorting with a nuptial ceremony.
[*Reads*] 'A tedious brief scene of young Pyramus
And his love Thisbe ; very tragical mirth.'
Merry and tragical ! tedious and brief !
   That is, hot ice and wondrous strange snow.
How shall we find the concord of this discord ?
   Philostrate. A play there is, my lord, some ten
   words long,
Which is as brief as I have known a play ;
But by ten words, my lords, it is too long,
Which makes it tedious ; for in all the play
There is not one word apt, one player fitted :
And tragical, my noble lord, it is ;
For Pyramus therein doth kill himself,
Which, when I saw rehearsed, I must confess,
Made mine eyes water ; but more merry tears
The passion of loud laughter never shed.
   Theseus. What are they that do play it ?
   Philostrate. Hard-handed men that work in Athens
   here,
Which never labour'd in their minds till now
And now have toil'd their unbreathed memories
With this same play, against your nuptial.
   Theseus. And we will hear it.
   Philostrate.   No, my noble lord ;
It is not for you : I have heard it over,
And it is nothing, nothing in the world ;
Unless you can find sport in their intents,
Extremely stretch'd and conn'd with cruel pain,
To do you service.
   Theseus.   I will hear that play ;
For never anything can be amiss,
When simpleness and duty tender it.
Go, bring them in : and take your places, ladies.
                         [Exit Philostrate.
   Hippolyta. I love not to see wretchedness o'er-
   charged
And duty in his service perishing.
   Theseus. Why, gentle sweet, you shall see no
   such thing.
   Hippolyta. He says they can do nothing in this
   kind.
   Theseus. The kinder we, to give them thanks for
   nothing.
Our sport shall be to take what they mistake :
And what poor duty cannot do, noble respect
†Takes it in might, not merit.
Where I have come, great clerks have purposed
To greet me with premeditated welcomes ;
Where I have seen them shiver and look pale,
Make periods in the midst of sentences,
Throttle their practised accent in their fears
And in conclusion dumbly have broke off,
Not paying me a welcome. Trust me, sweet,
Out of this silence yet I pick'd a welcome ;
And in the modesty of fearful duty
I read as much as from the rattling tongue
Of saucy and audacious eloquence,
Love, therefore, and tongue-tied simplicity
In least speak most, to my capacity.

         Re-enter PHILOSTRATE.

   Philostrate. So please your grace, the Prologue is
   address'd.
   Theseus. Let him approach.
                        [Flourish of trumpets.

Enter QUINCE *for the* Prologue.

Prologue. If we offend, it is with our good will,
That you should think, we come not to offend,
But with good will.   To show our simple skill,
That is the true beginning of our end.
Consider then we come but in despite,
   We do not come as minding to content you,
Our true intent is.   All for your delight
   We are not here.   That you should here repent
   you,
The actors are at hand, and by their show
You shall know all that you are like to know.
Theseus. This fellow doth not stand upon points.
Lysander. He hath rid his prologue like a rough
colt ; he knows not the stop.   A good moral, my
lord : it is not enough to speak, but to speak true.
Hippolyta. Indeed he hath played on his prologue
like a child on a recorder ; a sound, but not in
government.
Theseus. His speech was like a tangled chain ;
nothing impaired, but all disordered. Who is
next ?

Enter PYRAMUS *and* THISBE, WALL, MOONSHINE,
and LION.

Prologue. Gentles, perchance you wonder at this
show ;
But wonder on, till truth make all things plain.
This man is Pyramus, if you would know ;
   This beauteous lady Thisby is certain.
This man, with lime and rough-cast, doth present
   Wall, that vile Wall which did these lovers sunder ;
And through Wall's chink. poor souls, they are
   content
To whisper.   At the which let no man wonder.
This man, with lanthorn, dog, and bush of thorn
   Presenteth Moonshine ; for, if you will know,
By moonshine did these lovers think no scorn
   To meet at Ninus' tomb, there, there to woo.
This grisly beast, which Lion hight by name,
   The trusty Thisby, coming first by night,
Did scare away, or rather did affright ;
And, as she fled, her mantle she did fall,
   Which Lion vile with bloody mouth did stain.
Anon comes Pyramus, sweet youth and tall,
   And finds his trusty Thisby's mantle slain ;
Whereat with blade, with bloody blameful blade,
   He bravely broach'd his boiling bloody breast ;
And Thisby, tarrying in mulberry shade,
   His dagger drew, and died.   For all the rest,
Let Lion, Moonshine, Wall and lovers twain
At large discourse, while here they do remain.
      [*Exeunt Prologue, Pyramus, Thisbe, Lion, and
                                 Moonshine.*
Theseus. I wonder if the lion be to speak.
Demetrius. No wonder, my lord : one lion may,
when many asses do.
Wall. In this same interlude it doth befall
That I, one Snout by name, present a wall ;
And such a wall, as I would have you think,
That had in it a crannied hole or chink,
Through which the lovers, Pyramus and Thisby,
Did whisper often very secretly.
This loam, this rough-cast and this stone doth show
That I am that same wall ; the truth is so :
And this the cranny is, right and sinister,
Through which the fearful lovers are to whisper.
   Theseus. Would you desire lime and hair to speak
better ?

Demetrius. It is the wittiest partition that ever I
heard discourse, my lord.

Re-enter PYRAMUS.

Theseus. Pyramus draws near the wall : silence !
Pyramus. O grim-look'd night ! O night with hue
   so black !
O night, which ever art when day is not !
O night, O night ! alack, alack, alack.
I fear my Thisby's promise is forgot !
And thou, O wall, O sweet, O lovely wall,
   That stand'st between her father's ground and
   mine !
Thou wall, O wall, O sweet and lovely wall,
   Show me thy chink, to blink through with mine
   eyne !   [*Wall holds up his fingers.*
Thanks, courteous wall : Jove shield thee well for
   this !
But what see I ? No Thisby do I see.
O wicked wall, through whom I see no bliss !
   Cursed be thy stones for thus deceiving me !
Theseus. The wall, methinks, being sensible,
should curse again.
Pyramus. No, in truth, sir, he should not. 'De-
ceiving me ' is Thisby's cue : she is to enter now, and
I am to spy her through the wall.   You shall see,
it will fall pat as I told you.   Yonder she comes.

Re-enter THISBE

Thisbe. O wall, full often hast thou heard my
   moans,
For parting my fair Pyramus and me !
My cherry lips have often kiss'd thy stones,
   Thy stones with lime and hair knit up in thee.
Pyramus. I see a voice : now will I to the chink,
To spy an I can hear my Thisby's face.
Thisby !
   Thisby. My love thou art, my love I think.
Pyramus. Think what thou wilt, I am thy lover's
   grace :
And, like Limander, am I trusty still.
   Thisby. And I like Helen, till the Fates me kill.
Pyramus. Not Shafalus to Procrus was so true.
   Thisby. As Shafalus to Procrus, I to you.
Pyramus. O, kiss me through the hole of this vile
   wall !
   Thisby. I kiss the wall's hole, not your lips at all.
Pyramus. Wilt thou at Ninny's tomb meet me
   straightway ?
   Thisby. 'Tide life, 'tide death, I come without
   delay.   [*Exeunt Pyramus and Thisbe.*
Wall. Thus have I, Wall, my part discharged so ;
And, being done, thus Wall away doth go.   [*Exit.*
Theseus. Now is the mural down between the
two neighbours.
Demetrius. No remedy, my lord, when walls are
so wilful to hear without warning.
Hippolyta. This is the silliest stuff that ever I
heard.
Theseus. The best in this kind are but shadows ;
and the worst are no worse, if imagination amend
them.
Hippolyta. It must be your imagination then, and
not theirs.
Theseus. If we imagine no worse of them than
they of themselves, they may pass for excellent men
Here come two noble beasts in, a man and a lion.

Re-enter Lion *and* Moonshine

Lion. You, ladies, you, whose gentle hearts do fear
  The smallest monstrous mouse that creeps on floor,
May now perchance both quake and tremble here,
  When lion rough in wildest rage doth roar.
Then know that I, one Snug the joiner, am
A lion-fell, nor else no lion's dam ;
For, if I should as lion come in strife
Into this place, 'twere pity on my life.
Theseus. A very gentle beast, and of a good
conscience.
Demetrius. The very best at a beast, my lord,
that e'er I saw.
Lysander. This lion is a very fox for his valour.
Theseus. True ; and a goose for his discretion.
Demetrius. Not so, my lord ; for his valour
cannot carry his discretion ; and the fox carries the
goose.
Theseus. His discretion, I am sure, cannot carry
his valour ; for the goose carries not the fox. It
is well : leave it to his discretion, and let us listen
to the moon.
Moonshine. This lanthorn doth the horned moon
present ;—
Demetrius. He should have worn the horns on
his head.
Theseus. He is no crescent, and his horns are
invisible within the circumference.
Moonshine. This lanthorn doth the horned moon
present ;
Myself the man i' the moon do seem to be.
Theseus. This is the greatest error of all the rest :
the man should be put into the lanthorn. How is it
else the man i' the moon ?
Demetrius. He dares not come there for the
candle ; for, you see, it is already in snuff.
Hippolyta. I am aweary of this moon : would he
would change !
Theseus. It appears, by his small light of discretion, that he is in the wane ; but yet, in courtesy,
in all reason, we must stay the time.
Lysander. Proceed, Moon.
Moonshine. All that I have to say is, to tell you
that the lanthorn is the moon ; I, the man in the
moon ; this thorn-bush, my thorn-bush : and this
dog, my dog.
Demetrius. Why, all these should be in the lanthorn : for all these are in the moon. But, silence !
here comes Thisbe.

Re-enter Thisbe.

Thisbe. This is old Ninny's tomb. Where is
my love ?
Lion. [*Roaring*] Oh—   [*Thisbe runs off.*
Demetrius. Well roared, Lion.
Theseus. Well run, Thisbe.
Hippolyta. Well shone, Moon. Truly, the moon
shines with a good grace.
    [*The Lion shakes Thisbe's mantle, and exit.*
Theseus. Well moused, Lion.
Lysander. And so the lion vanished.
Demetrius. And then came Pyramus.

Re-enter Pyramus.

Pyramus. Sweet Moon, I thank thee for thy sunny
  beams ;
I thank thee, Moon, for shining now so bright ;
For, by thy gracious, golden, glittering gleams,
  I trust to take of truest Thisby sight.

But stay, O spite !
But mark, poor knight,
What dreadful dole is here ?
Eyes, do you see ?
How can it be ?
O dainty duck ! O dear !
Thy mantle good,
What, stain'd with blood !
Approach, ye Furies fell !
O Fates, come, come,
Cut thread and thrum ;
Quail, crush, conclude, and quell !
Theseus. This passion, and the death of a dear
friend, would go near to make a man look sad.
Hippolyta. Beshrew my heart, but I pity the man.
Pyramus. O wherefore, Nature, didst thou lions
frame ?
Since lion vile hath here deflower'd my dear :
Which is—no. no—which was the fairest dame
That lived, that loved, that liked, that look'd
  with cheer.
Come, tears, confound ;
Out, sword, and wound
The pap of Pyramus ;
Ay, that left pap,
Where heart doth hop :   [*Stabs himself.*
Thus die I, thus, thus, thus.
Now am I dead,
Now am I fled ;
My soul is in the sky :
Tongue, lose thy light ;
Moon, take thy flight :   [*Exit Moonshine.*
Now die, die, die, die, die.   [*Dies.*
Demetrius. No die, but an ace, for him ; for he
is but one.
Lysander. Less than an ace, man ; for he is
dead ; he is nothing.
Theseus. With the help of a surgeon he might
yet recover, and prove an ass.
Hippolyta. How chance Moonshine is gone before
Thisbe comes back and finds her lover ?
Theseus. She will find him by starlight. Here
she comes ; and her passion ends the play.

Re-enter Thisbe.

Hippolyta. Methinks she should not use a long
one for such a Pyramus : I hope she will be brief.
Demetrius. A mote will turn the balance, which
Pyramus, which Thisbe, is the better ; he for a man,
God warrant us ; she for a woman, God bless us.
Lysander. She hath spied him already with those
sweet eyes.
Demetrius. And thus she means, videlicet :—
Thisbe. Asleep, my love ?
What, dead, my dove ?
O Pyramus, arise !
Speak, speak. Quite dumb ?
Dead, dead ? A tomb
Must cover thy sweet eyes.
These lily lips,
This cherry nose,
These yellow cowslip cheeks,
Are gone, are gone :
Lovers, make moan :
His eyes were green as leeks.
O Sisters Three,
Come, come to me,
With hands as pale as milk ;
Lay them in gore,
Since you have shore

With shears his thread of silk.
   Tongue, not a word :
   Come, trusty sword ;
   Come, blade. my breast imbrue :
                              [*Stabs herself.*
   And, farewell, friends :
   Thus Thisby ends :
   Adieu, adieu, adieu.   [*Dies.*
Theseus. Moonshine and Lion are left to bury
the dead.
Demetrius. Ay, and Wall too.
Bottom. [*Starting up*] No, I assure you ; the
wall is down that parted their fathers. Will it please
you to see the epilogue, or to hear a Bergomask
dance between two of our company ?
Theseus. No epilogue, I pray you : for your play
needs no excuse. Never excuse ; for when the
players are all dead, there need none to be blamed.
Marry, if he that writ it had played Pyramus and
hanged himself in Thisbe's garter, it would have
been a fine tragedy : and so it is, truly ; and very
notably discharged. But. come, your Bergomask :
let your epilogue alone.   [*A dance.*
The iron tongue of midnight hath told twelve :
Lovers, to bed ; 'tis almost fairy time.
I fear we shall out-sleep the coming morn
As much as we this night have overwatch'd.
This palpable gross play hath well beguiled
The heavy gait of night. Sweet friends, to bed.
A fortnight hold we this solemnity
In nightly revels and new jollity.   [*Exeunt.*

                    Enter PUCK.

Puck. Now the hungry lion roars,
   And the wolf behowls the moon :
Whilst the heavy ploughman snores,
   All with weary task fordone.
Now the wasted brands do glow,
   Whilst the screech-owl, screeching loud.
Puts the wretch that lies in woe
   In remembrance of a shroud.
Now it is the time of night
   That the graves all gaping wide,
Every one lets forth his sprite,
   In the church-way paths to glide :
And we fairies. that do run
   By the triple Hecate's team,
From the presence of the sun,
   Following darkness like a dream.
Now are frolic : not a mouse
Shall disturb this hallow'd house :
I am sent with broom before,
To sweep the dust behind the door.

Enter OBERON *and* TITANIA *with their train.*

Oberon. Through the house give glimmering
      light,
   By the dead and drowsy fire :
Every elf and fairy sprite
   Hop as light as bird from brier ;
And this ditty, after me,
Sing. and dance it trippingly.
Titania First, rehearse your song by rote,
   To each word a warbling note :
Hand in hand, with fairy grace,
Will we sing. and bless this place.
                         [*Song and dance.*

Oberon. Now, until the break of day,
Through this house each fairy stray,
To the best bride-bed will we,
Which by us shall blessed be ;
And the issue there create
Ever shall be fortunate.
So shall all the couples three
Ever true in loving be ;
And the blots of Nature's hand
Shall not in their issue stand ;
Never mole, hare lip, nor scar,
Nor mark prodigious such as are
Despised in nativity
Shall upon their children be.
With this field-dew consecrate,
Every fairy take his gait ;
And each several chamber bless,
Through this palace with sweet peace ;
And the owner of it blest
Ever shall in safety rest.
Trip away ; make no stay :
Meet me all by break of day.
         [*Exeunt Oberon. Titania, and train.*

Puck. If we shadows have offended,
Think but this, and all is mended.
That you have but slumber'd here
While these visions did appear.
And this weak and idle theme,
No more yielding but a dream.
Gentles, do not reprehend :
If you pardon, we will mend :
And, as I am an honest Puck.
If we have unearned luck
Now to 'scape the serpent's tongue,
We will make amends ere long ;
Else the Puck a liar call :
So, good night unto you all.
Give me your hands, if we be friends,
And Robin shall restore amends.   [*Exit.*

THE

MERCHANT OF VENICE

DRAMATIS PERSONÆ

The DUKE OF VENICE.
The PRINCE OF MOROCCO, } suitors to Portia.
The PRINCE OF ARRAGON,
ANTONIO, a merchant of Venice.
BASSANIO, his friend, suitor likewise to Portia.
SALANIO,
SALARINO, } friends to Antonio and Bassanio.
GRATIANO,
SALERIO,
LORENZO, in love with Jessica.
SHYLOCK, a rich Jew.
TUBAL, a Jew, his friend.
LAUNCELOT GOBBO, the clown, servant to Shylock.
OLD GOBBO, father to Launcelot.
LEONARDO, servant to Bassanio.
BALTHASAR, } servants to Portia.
STEPHANO,

PORTIA, a rich heiress.
NERISSA, her waiting-maid.
JESSICA daughter to Shylock.

Magnificoes of Venice, Officers of the Court of
Justice, Gaoler, Servants to Portia, and other
Attendants.

SCENE : Partly at Venice, and partly at Belmont,
the seat of Portia, on the Continent.

ACT I.

SCENE I. *Venice. A street.*

Enter ANTONIO, SALARINO, *and* SALANIO.

Antonio.
In sooth, I know not why I am so sad :
    It wearies me ; you say it wearies you ;
    But how I caught it, found it, or came by it,
What stuff 'tis made of, whereof it is born,
I am to learn ;
And such a want-wit sadness makes of me,
That I have much ado to know myself.
    Salarino. Your mind is tossing on the ocean ;
There, where your argosies with portly sail,
Like signiors and rich burghers on the flood,
Or, as it were, the pageants of the sea,
Do overpeer the petty traffickers,
That curtsy to them, do them reverence,
As they fly by them with their woven wings.
    Salanio. Believe me, sir, had I such venture forth,
The better part of my affections would

Be with my hopes abroad. I should be still
Plucking the grass, to know where sits the wind,
Peering in maps for ports and piers and roads ;
And every object that might make me fear
Misfortune to my ventures, out of doubt
Would make me sad.
    Salarino. My wind cooling my broth
Would blow me to an ague, when I thought
What harm a wind too great at sea might do.
I should not see the sandy hour-glass run,
But I should think of shallows and of flats,
And see my wealthy Andrew dock'd in sand,
Vailing her high-top lower than her ribs
To kiss her burial. Should I go to church
And see the holy edifice of stone,
And not bethink me straight of dangerous rocks,
Which touching but my gentle vessel's side,
Would scatter all her spices on the stream,
Enrobe the roaring waters with my silks,
And, in a word, but even now worth this,
And now worth nothing ? Shall I have the thought
To think on this, and shall I lack the thought
That such a thing bechanced would make me sad ?
But tell not me ; I know, Antonio
Is sad to think upon his merchandise.
    Antonio. Believe me. no : I thank my fortune
    for it,
My ventures are not in one bottom trusted,
Nor to one place ; nor is my whole estate
Upon the fortune of this present year :
Therefore my merchandise makes me not sad.
    Salarino. Why, then you are in love.
    Antonio. Fie, fie !
    Salarino. Not in love neither ? Then let us say
    you are sad,
Because you are not merry : and 'twere as easy
For you to laugh and leap and say you are merry,
Because you are not sad. Now, by two-headed
    Janus,
Nature hath framed strange fellows in her time :
Some that will evermore peep through their eyes
And laugh like parrots at a bag-piper,
And other of such vinegar aspect
That they 'll not show their teeth in way of smile,
Though Nestor swear the jest be laughable.

Enter BASSANIO, LORENZO, *and* GRATIANO.

    Salanio. Here comes Bassanio, your most noble
    kinsman,
Gratiano and Lorenzo. Fare ye well :
We leave you now with better company.
    Salarino. I would have stay'd till I had made
    you merry,
If worthier friends had not prevented me.
    Antonio. Your worth is very dear in my regard.
I take it, your own business calls on you
And you embrace the occasion to depart.
    Salarino. Good morrow. my good lords.

Bassanio. Good signiors both, when shall we laugh ? say, when ?
You grow exceeding strange : must it be so ?
Salarino. We 'll make our leisures to attend on yours. [*Exeunt Salarino and Salanio.*
Lorenzo. My Lord Bassanio, since you have found Antonio,
We two will leave you : but at dinner-time,
I pray you, have in mind where we must meet.
Bassanio. I will not fail you.
Gratiano. You look not well, Signior Antonio ;
You have too much respect upon the world :
They lose it that do buy it with much care :
Believe me, you are marvellously changed.
Antonio. I hold the world but as the world, Gratiano ;
A stage where every man must play a part,
And mine a sad one.
Gratiano.   Let me play the fool :
With mirth and laughter let old wrinkles come,
And let my liver rather heat with wine
Than my heart cool with mortifying groans.
Why should a man, whose blood is warm within,
Sit like his grandsire cut in alabaster ?
Sleep when he wakes and creep into the jaundice
By being peevish ? I tell thee what, Antonio—
I love thee, and it is my love that speaks—
There are a sort of men whose visages
Do cream and mantle like a standing pond,
And do a wilful stillness entertain,
With purpose to be dress'd in an opinion
Of wisdom, gravity, profound conceit,
As who should say ' I am Sir Oracle,
And when I ope my lips let no dog bark ! '
O my Antonio, I do know of these
That therefore only are reputed wise
For saying nothing, when, I am very sure,
If they should speak, would almost damn those ears
Which, hearing them, would call their brothers fools.
I 'll tell thee more of this another time :
But fish not, with this melancholy bait,
For this fool gudgeon, this opinion.
Come, good Lorenzo. Fare ye well awhile :
I 'll end my exhortation after dinner.
Lorenzo. Well, we will leave you then till dinner-time :
I must be one of these same dumb wise men,
For Gratiano never lets me speak.
Gratiano. Well, keep me company but two years moe,
Thou shalt not know the sound of thine own tongue.
Antonio. Farewell : I 'll grow a talker for this gear.
Gratiano. Thanks, i' faith, for silence is only commendable
In a neat's tongue dried and a maid not vendible.
          [*Exeunt Gratiano and Lorenzo.*
Antonio. Is that any thing now ?
Bassanio. Gratiano speaks an infinite deal of nothing, more than any man in all Venice. His reasons are as two grains of wheat hid in two bushels of chaff : you shall seek all day ere you find them, and when you have them, they are not worth the search.
Antonio. Well, tell me now what lady is the same
To whom you swore a secret pilgrimage,
That you to-day promised to tell me of ?
Bassanio. 'Tis not unknown to you, Antonio,
How much I have disabled mine estate,
By something showing a more swelling port
Than my faint means would grant continuance

Nor do I now make moan to be abridged
From such a noble rate ; but my chief care
Is to come fairly off from the great debts
Wherein my time something too prodigal
Hath left me gaged. To you, Antonio,
I owe the most, in money and in love,
And from your love I have a warranty
To unburden all my plots and purposes
How to get clear of all the debts I owe.
Antonio. I pray you. good Bassanio, let me know it ;
And if it stand, as you yourself still do,
Within the eye of honour, be assured,
My purse, my person, my extremest means,
Lie all unlock'd to your occasions.
Bassanio. In my school-days, when I had lost one shaft,
I shot his fellow of the self-same flight
The self-same way with more advised watch,
To find the other forth, and by adventuring both
I oft found both : I urge this childhood proof,
Because what follows is pure innocence.
I owe you much, and, like a wilful youth,
That which I owe is lost ; but if you please
To shoot another arrow that self way
Which you did shoot the first, I do not doubt,
As I will watch the aim, or to find both
Or bring your latter hazard back again
And thankfully rest debtor for the first.
Antonio. You know me well. and herein spend but time
To wind about my love with circumstance ;
And out of doubt you do me now more wrong
In making question of my uttermost
Than if you had made waste of all I have :
Then do but say to me what I should do
That in your knowledge may by me be done,
And I am prest unto it : therefore, speak.
Bassanio. In Belmont is a lady richly left ;
And she is fair and, fairer than that word,
Of wondrous virtues : sometimes from her eyes
I did receive fair speechless messages :
Her name is Portia, nothing undervalued
To Cato's daughter, Brutus' Portia :
Nor is the wide world ignorant of her worth,
For the four winds blow in from every coast
Renowned suitors, and her sunny locks
Hang on her temples like a golden fleece ;
Which makes her seat of Belmont Colchos' strand.
And many Jasons come in quest of her.
O my Antonio, had I but the means
To hold a rival place with one of them,
I have a mind presages me such thrift,
That I should questionless be fortunate !
Antonio. Thou know'st that all my fortunes are at sea ;
Neither have I money nor commodity
To raise a present sum : therefore go forth ;
Try what my credit can in Venice do :
That shall be rack'd, even to the uttermost,
To furnish thee to Belmont, to fair Portia.
Go presently inquire, and so will I,
Where money is, and I no question make
To have it of my trust or for my sake.   [*Exeunt.*

SCENE II. *Belmont. A room in* PORTIA'S *house.*

Enter PORTIA *and* NERISSA.

Portia. By my troth, Nerissa, my little body is aweary of this great world.

Nerissa. You would be, sweet madam, if your miseries were in the same abundance as your good fortunes are : and yet, for aught I see, they are as sick that surfeit with too much as they that starve with nothing. It is no mean happiness therefore, to be seated in the mean : superfluity comes sooner by white hairs, but competency lives longer.

Portia. Good sentences and well pronounced.

Nerissa. They would be better, if well followed.

Portia. If to do were as easy as to know what were good to do, chapels had been churches and poor men's cottages princes' palaces. It is a good divine that follows his own instructions : I can easier teach twenty what were good to be done, than be one of the twenty to follow mine own teaching. The brain may devise laws for the blood, but a hot temper leaps o'er a cold decree : such a hare is madness the youth, to skip o'er the meshes of good counsel the cripple. But this reasoning is not in the fashion to choose me a husband. O me, the word ' choose ! ' I may neither choose whom I would nor refuse whom I dislike ; so is the will of a living daughter curbed by the will of a dead father. Is it not hard, Nerissa, that I cannot choose one nor refuse none ?

Nerissa. Your father was ever virtuous ; and holy men at their death have good inspirations : therefore the lottery, that he hath devised in these three chests of gold, silver and lead, whereof who chooses his meaning chooses you, will, no doubt, never be chosen by any rightly but one who shall rightly love. But what warmth is there in your affection towards any of these princely suitors that are already come ?

Portia. I pray thee, over-name them ; and as thou namest them, I will describe them ; and, according to my description, level at my affection.

Nerissa. First, there is the Neapolitan prince.

Portia. Ay, that 's a colt indeed, for he doth nothing but talk of his horse ; and he makes it a great appropriation to his own good parts, that he can shoe him himself. I am much afeard my lady his mother played false with a smith.

Nerissa. Then there is the County Palatine.

Portia. He doth nothing but frown, as who should say ' If you will not have me, choose : ' he hears merry tales and smiles not : I fear he will prove the weeping philosopher when he grows old, being so full of unmannerly sadness in his youth. I had rather be married to a death's-head with a bone in his mouth than to either of these. God defend me from these two !

Nerissa. How say you by the French lord, Monsieur Le Bon ?

Portia. God made him, and therefore let him pass for a man. In truth, I know it is a sin to be a mocker : but, he ! why, he hath a horse better than the Neapolitan's, a better bad habit of frowning than the Count Palatine ; he is every man in no man ; if a throstle sing, he falls straight a capering : he will fence with his own shadow : if I should marry him, I should marry twenty husbands. If he would despise me, I would forgive him, for if he love me to madness, I shall never requite him.

Nerissa. What say you, then, to Falconbridge, the young baron of England ?

Portia. You know I say nothing to him, for he understands not me, nor I him : he hath neither Latin, French, nor Italian, and you will come into the court and swear that I have a poor pennyworth in the English. He is a proper man's picture, but, alas, who can converse with a dumb-show ? How oddly he is suited ! I think he bought his doublet in Italy, his round hose in France, his bonnet in Germany and his behaviour every where.

Nerissa. What think you of the Scottish lord, his neighbour ?

Portia. That he hath a neighbourly charity in him, for he borrowed a box of the ear of the Englishman and swore he would pay him again when he was able : I think the Frenchman became his surety and sealed under for another.

Nerissa. How like you the young German, the Duke of Saxony's nephew ?

Portia. Very vilely in the morning, when he is sober, and most vilely in the afternoon, when he is drunk : when he is best, he is a little worse than a man, and when he is worst, he is little better than a beast : an the worst fall that ever fell, I hope I shall make shift to go without him.

Nerissa. If he should offer to choose, and choose the right casket, you should refuse to perform your father's will, if you should refuse to accept him.

Portia. Therefore, for fear of the worst, I pray thee, set a deep glass of rhenish wine on the contrary casket, for if the devil be within and that temptation without, I know he will choose it. I will do any thing, Nerissa, ere I 'll be married to a sponge.

Nerissa. You need not fear, lady, the having any of these lords : they have acquainted me with their determinations ; which is, indeed, to return to their home and to trouble you with no more suit, unless you may be won by some other sort than your father's imposition depending on the caskets.

Portia. If I live to be as old as Sibylla, I will die as chaste as Diana, unless I be obtained by the manner of my father's will. I am glad this parcel of wooers are so reasonable, for there is not one among them but I dote on his very absence, and I pray God grant them a fair departure.

Nerissa. Do you not remember, lady, in your father's time, a Venetian, a scholar and a soldier, that came hither in company of the Marquis of Montferrat ?

Portia. Yes, yes, it was Bassanio ; as I think, he was so called.

Nerissa. True, madam : he, of all the men that ever my foolish eyes looked upon, was the best deserving a fair lady.

Portia. I remember him well, and I remember him worthy of thy praise.

Enter a Serving-man.

How now ! what news ?

Serving-man. The four strangers seek for you, madam, to take their leave : and there is a forerunner come from a fifth, the Prince of Morocco, who brings word the prince his master will be here to-night.

Portia. If I could bid the fifth welcome with so good a heart as I can bid the other four farewell, I should be glad of his approach : if he have the condition of a saint and the complexion of a devil, I had rather he should shrive me than wive me. Come, Nerissa. Sirrah, go before. Whiles we shut the gates upon one wooer, another knocks at the door.   [*Exeunt.*

SCENE III. *Venice. A public place.*

Enter BASSANIO *and* SHYLOCK.

Shylock. Three thousand ducats ; well.

Bassanio. Ay, sir, for three months.

Shylock. For three months ; well.

Bassanio. For the which, as I told you, Antonio shall be bound.

Shylock. Antonio shall become bound ; well.

Bassanio. May you stead me ? will you pleasure me ? shall I know your answer ?

Shylock. Three thousand ducats for three months and Antonio bound.

Bassanio. Your answer to that.

Shylock. Antonio is a good man.

Bassanio. Have you heard any imputation to the contrary ?

Shylock. Oh, no, no, no, no : my meaning in saying he is a good man is to have you understand me that he is sufficient. Yet his means are in supposition : he hath an argosy bound to Tripolis, another to the Indies ; I understand, moreover, upon the Rialto, he hath a third at Mexico, a fourth for England, and other ventures he hath, squandered abroad. But ships are but boards, sailors but men : there be land-rats and water-rats, water-thieves and land-thieves, I mean pirates, and then there is the peril of waters, winds, and rocks. The man is, notwithstanding, sufficient. Three thousand ducats ; I think I may take his bond.

Bassanio. Be assured you may.

Shylock. I will be assured I may ; and, that I may be assured, I will bethink me. May I speak with Antonio ?

Bassanio. If it please you to dine with us.

Shylock. Yes, to smell pork ; to eat of the habitation which your prophet the Nazarite conjured the devil into. I will buy with you, sell with you, talk with you, walk with you, and so following, but I will not eat with you, drink with you, nor pray with you. What news on the Rialto ? Who is he comes here ?

Enter ANTONIO.

Bassanio. This is Signior Antonio.

Shylock. [*Aside*] How like a fawning publican he looks !
I hate him for he is a Christian,
But more for that in low simplicity
He lends out money gratis and brings down
The rate of usance here with us in Venice.
If I can catch him once upon the hip,
I will feed fat the ancient grudge I bear him.
He hates our sacred nation, and he rails,
Even there where merchants most do congregate,
On me, my bargains and my well-won thrift,
Which he calls interest. Cursed be my tribe,
If I forgive him !

Bassanio. Shylock, do you hear ?

Shylock. I am debating of my present store,
And, by the near guess of my memory,
I cannot instantly raise up the gross
Of full three thousand ducats. What of that ?
Tubal, a wealthy Hebrew of my tribe,
Will furnish me. But soft ! how many months
Do you desire ? [*To Antonio*] Rest you fair, good signior ;
Your worship was the last man in our mouths.

Antonio. Shylock, although I neither lend nor borrow
By taking nor by giving of excess,
Yet, to supply the ripe wants of my friend,
I 'll break a custom. Is he yet possess'd
How much ye would ?

Shylock.   Ay, ay, three thousand ducats.

Antonio. And for three months.

Shylock. I had forgot ; three months ; you told me so.
Well then, your bond ; and let me see ; but hear you ;
Methought you said you neither lend nor borrow
Upon advantage.

Antonio.   I do never use it.

Shylock. When Jacob grazed his uncle Laban's sheep—
This Jacob from our holy Abram was,
As his wise mother wrought in his behalf,
The third possessor ; ay, he was the third—

Antonio. And what of him ? did he take interest ?

Shylock. No, not take interest, not, as you would say,
Directly interest : mark what Jacob did.
When Laban and himself were compromised
That all the eanlings which were streak'd and pied
Should fall as Jacob's hire, the ewes, being rank,
In the end of autumn turned to the rams,
And, when the work of generation was
Between these woolly breeders in the act,
The skilful shepherd peel'd me certain wands
And, in the doing of the deed of kind,
He stuck them up before the fulsome ewes,
Who then conceiving did in eaning time
Fall parti-colour'd lambs, and those were Jacob's.
This was a way to thrive, and he was blest :
And thrift is blessing, if men steal it not.

Antonio. This was a venture, sir, that Jacob served for ;
A thing not in his power to bring to pass,
But sway'd and fashion'd by the hand of heaven.
Was this inserted to make interest good ?
Or is your gold and silver ewes and rams ?

Shylock. I cannot tell ; I make it breed as fast :
But note me, signior.

Antonio.   Mark you this, Bassanio,
The devil can cite Scripture for his purpose.
An evil soul producing holy witness
Is like a villain with a smiling cheek,
A goodly apple rotten at the heart :
O, what a goodly outside falsehood hath !

Shylock. Three thousand ducats ; 'tis a good round sum.
Three months from twelve ; then, let me see ; the rate—

Antonio. Well, Shylock, shall we be beholding to you ?

Shylock. Signior Antonio, many a time and oft
In the Rialto you have rated me
About my moneys and my usances :
Still have I borne it with a patient shrug.
For sufferance is the badge of all our tribe.
You call me misbeliever, cut-throat dog,
And spit upon my Jewish gaberdine,
And all for use of that which is mine own.
Well then, it now appears you need my help :
Go to, then ; you come to me, and you say
' Shylock, we would have moneys : ' you say so ;
You, that did void your rheum upon my beard
And foot me as you spurn a stranger cur
Over your threshold : moneys is your suit.
What should I say to you ? Should I not say
' Hath a dog money ? is it possible
A cur can lend three thousand ducats ?' Or
Shall I bend low and in a bondman's key,
With bated breath and whispering humbleness,
Say this ;

' Fair sir, you spit on me on Wednesday last ;
You spurn'd me such a day ; another time
You call'd me dog ; and for these courtesies
I 'll lend you thus much moneys ' ?

Antonio. I am as like to call thee so again,
To spit on thee again, to spurn thee too.
If thou wilt lend this money, lend it not
As to thy friends ; for when did friendship take
A breed for barren metal of his friend ?
But lend it rather to thine enèmy,
Who, if he break, thou mayst with better face
Exact the penalty.

Shylock.   Why, look you, how you storm !
I would be friends with you and have your love,
Forget the shames that you have stain'd me with,
Supply your present wants and take no doit
Of usance for my moneys, and you 'll not hear me :
This is kind I offer.

Bassanio. This were kindness.

Shylock.   This kindness will I show.
Go with me to a notary, seal me there
Your single bond ; and, in a merry sport,
If you repay me not on such a day,
In such a place, such sum or sums as are
Express'd in the condition, let the forfeit
Be nominated for an equal pound
Of your fair flesh, to be cut off and taken
In what part of your body pleaseth me.

Antonio. Content, i' faith : I 'll seal to such a
bond
And say there is much kindness in the Jew.

Bassanio, You shall not seal to such a bond for
me :
I 'll rather dwell in my necessity.

Antonio. Why, fear not, man ; I will not forfeit
it :
Within these two months, that 's a month before
This bond expires, I do expect return
Of thrice three times the value of this bond.

Shylock. O father Abram, what these Christians
are,
Whose own hard dealings teaches them suspect
The thoughts of others ! Pray you, tell me this ;
If he should break his day, what should I gain
By the exaction of the forfeiture ?
A pound of man's flesh taken from a man
Is not so estimable, profitable neither,
As flesh of muttons, beefs, or goats. I say,
To buy his favour, I extend this friendship :
If he will take it, so ; if not, adieu ;
And, for my love, I pray you wrong me not.

Antonio. Yes, Shylock, I will seal unto this bond.

Shylock. Then meet me forthwith at the notary's ;
Give him direction for this merry bond,
And I will go and purse the ducats straight,
See to my house, left in the fearful guard
Of an unthrifty knave, and presently
I will be with you.

Antonio. Hie thee, gentle Jew. [*Exit Shylock.*
The Hebrew will turn Christian : he grows kind.

Bassanio. I like not fair terms and a villain's
mind.

Antonio. Come on : in this there can be no dismay ;
My ships come home a month before the day.

                                        [*Exeunt.*

ACT II.

SCENE I. *Belmont. A room in* PORTIA'S *house.*

Flourish of Cornets. Enter the PRINCE OF MOROCCO
and his train ; PORTIA, NERISSA, *and others
attending.*

Morocco.

Mislike me not for my complexion,
The shadow'd livery of the burnish'd sun,
To whom I am a neighbour and near bred.
Bring me the fairest creature northward born,
Where Phœbus' fire scarce thaws the icicles,
And let us make incision for your love,
To prove whose blood is reddest, his or mine.
I tell thee, lady, this aspect of mine
Hath fear'd the valiant : by my love, I swear
The best-regarded virgins of our clime
Have loved it too : I would not change this hue,
Except to steal your thoughts, my gentle queen.

Portia. In terms of choice I am not solely led
By nice direction of a maiden's eyes ,
Besides, the lottery of my destiny
Bars me the right of voluntary choosing :
But if my father had not scanted me
And hedged me by his wit, to yield myself
His wife who wins me by that means I told you,
Yourself, renowned prince, then stood as fair
As any comer I have look'd on yet
For my affection.

Morocco.   Even for that I thank you :
Therefore, I pray you, lead me to the caskets
To try my fortune. By this scimitar
That slew the Sophy and a Persian prince
That won three fields of Sultan Solyman,
I would outstare the sternest eyes that look,
Outbrave the heart most daring on the earth,
Pluck the young sucking cubs from the she-bear,
Yea, mock the lion when he roars for prey,
To win thee, lady. But, alas the while !
If Hercules and Lichas play at dice
Which is the better man, the greater throw
May turn by fortune from the weaker hand :
So is Alcides beaten by his page ;
And so may I, blind fortune leading me,
Miss that which one unworthier may attain,
And die with grieving.

Portia.   You must take your chance,
And either not attempt to choose at all
Or swear before you choose, if you choose wrong
Never to speak to lady afterward
In way of marriage : therefore be advised.

Morocco. Nor will not. Come, bring me unto
my chance.

Portia. First, forward to the temple : after
dinner
Your hazard shall be made.

Morocco.   Good fortune then !
To make me blest or cursed'st among men.

                          [*Cornets, and exeunt.*

SCENE II. *Venice. A street.*

Enter LAUNCELOT.

Launcelot. Certainly my conscience will serve me
to run from this Jew my master. The fiend is at
mine elbow and tempts me saying to me ' Gobbo,
Launcelot, Gobbo, good Launcelot,' or ' good
Gobbo,' or ' good Launcelot Gobbo, use your legs,
take the start, run away.' My conscience says

'No ; take heed, honest Launcelot ; take heed, honest Gobbo,' or, as aforesaid, 'honest Launcelot Gobbo ; do not run ; scorn running with thy heels.' Well, the most courageous fiend bids me pack : 'Via !' says the fiend ; 'away !' says the fiend ; 'for the heavens, rouse up a brave mind,' says the fiend, 'and run.' Well, my conscience, hanging about the neck of my heart, says very wisely to me 'My honest friend Launcelot, being an honest man's son,' or rather an honest woman's son ; for, indeed, my father did something smack, something grow to, he had a kind of taste ; well, my conscience says 'Launcelot, budge not.' 'Budge,' says the fiend. 'Budge not,' says my conscience. 'Conscience,' say I, 'you counsel well ;' 'Fiend,' say I, 'you counsel well :' to be ruled by my conscience, I should stay with the Jew my master, who, God bless the mark, is a kind of devil ; and, to run away from the Jew, I should be ruled by the fiend, who, saving your reverence, is the devil himself. Certainly the Jew is the very devil incarnal ; and, in my conscience, my conscience is but a kind of hard conscience, to offer to counsel me to stay with the Jew. The fiend gives the more friendly counsel : I will run, fiend ; my heels are at your command : I will run.

Enter Old Gobbo, *with a basket.*

Gobbo. Master young man, you, I pray you, which is the way to master Jew's ?

Launcelot. [*Aside*] O heavens, this is my true-begotten father ! who, being more than sand-blind, high-gravel blind, knows me not : I will try confusions with him.

Gobbo. Master young gentleman, I pray you, which is the way to master Jew's ?

Launcelot. Turn up on your right hand at the next turning, but, at the next turning of all, on your left ; marry, at the very next turning, turn of no hand, but turn down indirectly to the Jew's house.

Gobbo. By God's sonties, 'twill be a hard way to hit. Can you tell me whether one Launcelot, that dwells with him, dwell with him or no ?

Launcelot. Talk you of young Master Launcelot ? [*Aside*] Mark me now ; now will I raise the waters. Talk you of young Master Launcelot ?

Gobbo. No master, sir, but a poor man's son : his father, though I say it, is an honest exceeding poor man and, God be thanked, well to live.

Launcelot. Well, let his father be what a' will, we talk of young Master Launcelot.

Gobbo. Your worship's friend and Launcelot, sir.

Launcelot. But I pray you, ergo, old man, ergo, I beseech you, talk you of young Master Launcelot ?

Gobbo. Of Launcelot, an 't please your mastership.

Launcelot. Ergo, Master Launcelot. Talk not of Master Launcelot, father ; for the young gentleman, according to Fates and Destinies and such odd sayings, the Sisters Three and such branches of learning, is indeed deceased, or, as you would say in plain terms, gone to heaven.

Gobbo. Marry, God forbid ! the boy was the very staff of my age, my very prop.

Launcelot. Do I look like a cudgel or a hovel-post, a staff or a prop ? Do you know me, father ?

Gobbo. Alack the day, I know you not, young gentleman : but, I pray you, tell me, is my boy, God rest his soul, alive or dead ?

Launcelot. Do you not know me, father ?

Gobbo. Alack, sir, I am sand-blind ; I know

you not.

Launcelot. Nay, indeed, if you had your eyes, you might fail of the knowing me : it is a wise father that knows his own child. Well, old man, I will tell you news of your son : give me your blessing : truth will come to light ; murder cannot be hid long ; a man's son may, but at the length truth will out.

Gobbo. Pray you, sir, stand up : I am sure you are not Launcelot, my boy.

Launcelot. Pray you, let 's have no more fooling about it, but give me your blessing : I am Launcelot, your boy that was. your son that is, your child that shall be.

Gobbo. I cannot think you are my son.

Launcelot. I know not what I shall think of that : but I am Launcelot, the Jew's man, and I am sure Margery your wife is my mother.

Gobbo. Her name is Margery, indeed : I 'll be sworn, if thou be Launcelot, thou art mine own flesh and blood. Lord worshipped might he be ! what a beard hast thou got ! thou hast got more hair on thy chin than Dobbin my fill-horse has on his tail.

Launcelot. It should seem, then, that Dobbin's tail grows backward : I am sure he had more hair of his tail than I have of my face when I last saw him.

Gobbo. Lord, how art thou changed ! How dost thou and thy master agree ? I have brought him a present. How 'gree you now ?

Launcelot. Well, well : but, for mine own part, as I have set up my rest to run away, so I will not rest till I have run some ground. My master's a very Jew : give him a present ! give him a halter : I am famished in his service ; you may tell every finger I have with my ribs. Father, I am glad you are come : give me your present to one Master Bassanio, who, indeed, gives rare new liveries : if I serve not him, I will run as far as God has any ground. O rare fortune ! here comes the man : to him, father ; for I am a Jew, if I serve the Jew any longer.

Enter Bassanio, *with* Leonardo *and other followers.*

Bassanio. You may do so ; but let it be so hasted that supper be ready at the farthest by five of the clock. See these letters delivered ; put the liveries to making, and desire Gratiano to come anon to my lodging. [*Exit a Servant.*

Launcelot. To him, father.

Gobbo. God bless your worship !

Bassanio. Gramercy ! wouldst thou aught with me ?

Gobbo. Here 's my son, sir, a poor boy,—

Launcelot. Not a poor boy, sir, but the rich Jew's man ; that would, sir, as my father shall specify—

Gobbo. He hath a great infection, sir, as one would say, to serve,—

Launcelot. Indeed, the short and the long is, I serve the Jew, and have a desire, as my father shall specify—

Gobbo. His master and he, saving your worship's reverence, are scarce cater-cousins—

Launcelot. To be brief, the very truth is that the Jew, having done me wrong, doth cause me, as my father being I hope, an old man, shall frutify unto you—

Gobbo. I have here a dish of doves that I would

bestow upon your worship, and my suit is—

Launcelot. In very brief, the suit is impertinent to myself, as your worship shall know by this honest old man ; and, though I say it, though old man, yet poor man, my father.

Bassanio.. One speak for both. What would you ?

Launcelot. Serve you, sir.

Gobbo. That is the very defect of the matter, sir.

Bassanio. I know thee well : thou hast obtain'd thy suit :

Shylock thy master spoke with me this day,
And hath preferr'd thee, if it be preferment
To leave a rich Jew's service, to become
The follower of so poor a gentleman.

Launcelot. The old proverb is very well parted between my master Shylock and you, sir : you have the grace of God, sir, and he hath enough.

Bassanio. Thou speak'st it well. Go, father, with thy son.

Take leave of thy old master and inquire
My lodging out. Give him a livery
More guarded than his fellows' : see it done.

Launcelot. Father, in. I cannot get a service, no ; I have ne'er a tongue in my head. Well, if any man in Italy have a fairer table which doth offer to swear upon a book, I shall have good fortune. Go to, here 's a simple line of life : here 's a small trifle of wives : alas, fifteen wives is nothing ! eleven widows and nine maids is a simple coming-in for one man : and then to 'scape drowning thrice, and to be in peril of my life with the edge of a feather-bed ; here are simple scapes. Well, if Fortune be a woman, she 's a good wench for this gear. Father, come ; I 'll take my leave of the Jew in the twinkling of an eye.

[*Exeunt Launcelot and Old Gobbo.*

Bassanio. I pray thee, good Leonardo, think on this :
These things being bought and orderly bestow'd,
Return in haste, for I do feast to-night
My best-esteem'd acquaintance : hie thee, go.

Leonardo. My best endeavours shall be done herein.

Enter GRATIANO.

Gratiano. Where is your master ?

Leonardo. Yonder, sir, he walks. [*Exit.*

Gratiano. Signior Bassanio !

Bassanio. Gratiano !

Gratiano. I have a suit to you.

Bassanio. You have obtain'd it.

Gratiano. You must not deny me : I must go with you to Belmont.

Bassanio. Why, then you must. But hear thee, Gratiano ;
Thou art too wild, too rude and bold of voice :
Parts that become thee happily enough
And in such eyes as ours appear not faults ;
But where thou art not known, why, there they show
Something too liberal. Pray thee, take pain
To allay with some cold drops of modesty
Thy skipping spirit, lest through thy wild behaviour
I be misconstrued in the place I go to
And lose my hopes.

Gratiano. Signior Bassanio, hear me :
If I do not put on a sober habit,
Talk with respect and swear but now and then,
Wear prayer-books in my pocket, look demurely,
Nay more, while grace is saying hood mine eyes

Thus with my hat, and sigh and say ' amen,'
Use all the observance of civility,
Like one well studied in a sad ostent
To please his grandam, never trust me more.

Bassanio. Well, we shall see your bearing.

Gratiano. Nay, but I bar to-night : you shall not gauge me
By what we do to-night.

Bassanio. No, that were pity :
I would entreat you rather to put on
Your boldest suit of mirth, for we have friends
That purpose merriment. But fare you well :
I have some business.

Gratiano. And I must to Lorenzo and the rest :
But we will visit you at supper-time. [*Exeunt.*

SCENE III. *The same. A room in* SHYLOCK'S *house.*

Enter JESSICA and LAUNCELOT.

Jessica. I am sorry thou wilt leave my father so :
Our house is hell, and thou, a merry devil,
Didst rob it of some taste of tediousness.
But fare thee well, there is a ducat for thee :
And, Launcelot, soon at supper shalt thou see
Lorenzo, who is thy new master's guest :
Give him this letter ; do it secretly ;
And so farewell : I would not have my father
See me talk with thee.

Launcelot. Adieu ! tears exhibit my tongue.
Most beautiful pagan, most sweet Jew ! if a Christian
did not play the knave and get thee, I am much
deceived. But, adieu : these foolish drops do
something drown my manly spirit : adieu.

Jessica. Farewell, good Launcelot.

[*Exit Launcelot.*

Alack, what heinous sin is it in me
To be ashamed to be my father's child !
But though I am a daughter to his blood,
I am not to his manners. O Lorenzo,
If thou keep promise, I shall end this strife,
Become a Christian and thy loving wife. [*Exit.*

SCENE IV. *The same. A street.*

Enter GRATIANO, LORENZO, SALARINO and SALANIO.

Lorenzo. Nay, we will slink away in supper-time,
Disguise us at my lodging and return,
All in an hour.

Gratiano. We have not made good preparation.

Salarino. We have not spoke us yet of torch-bearers.

Salanio. 'Tis vile, unless it may be quaintly order'd,
And better in my mind not undertook.

Lorenzo. 'Tis now but four o'clock : we have two hours
To furnish us.

Enter LAUNCELOT, *with a letter.*

Friend Launcelot, what 's the news ?

Launcelot. An it shall please you to break up this, it shall seem to signify.

Lorenzo. I know the hand : in faith, 'tis a fair hand ;
And whiter than the paper it writ on
Is the fair hand that writ.

Gratiano.   Love-news, in faith.
Launcelot. By your leave, sir.
Lorenzo. Whither goest thou?
Launcelot. Marry, sir, to bid my old master the
Jew to sup to-night with my new master the Christian.
Lorenzo. Hold here, take this : tell gentle Jessica
I will not fail her ; speak it privately.
Go, gentlemen,   [*Exit Launcelot.*
Will you prepare you for this masque to-night?
I am provided of a torch-bearer.
Salarino. Ay, marry, I 'll be gone about it straight.
Salanio. And so will I.
Lorenzo.   Meet me and Gratiano
At Gratiano's lodging some hour hence.
Salarino. 'Tis good we do so.
                    [*Exeunt Salarino and Salanio.*
Gratiano. Was not that letter from fair Jessica?
Lorenzo. I must needs tell thee all. She hath
directed
How I shall take her from her father's house,
What gold and jewels she is furnish'd with,
What page's suit she hath in readiness.
If e'er the Jew her father come to heaven,
It will be for his gentle daughter's sake :
And never dare misfortune cross her foot,
Unless she do it under this excuse.
That she is issue to a faithless Jew.
Come, go with me ; peruse this as thou goest :
Fair Jessica shall be my torch-bearer.   [*Exeunt.*

SCENE V.   *The same.   Before* SHYLOCK'S *house.*

Enter SHYLOCK *and* LAUNCELOT.

Shylock. Well, thou shalt see, thy eyes shall be
thy judge,
The difference of old Shylock and Bassanio :—
What, Jessica !—thou shalt not gormandise,
As thou hast done with me :—What, Jessica !—
And sleep and snore, and rend apparel out ;—
Why, Jessica, I say !
Launcelot.   Why, Jessica !
Shylock. Who bids thee call? I do not bid thee
call.
Launcelot. Your worship was wont to tell me
that I could do nothing without bidding.

Enter JESSICA.

Jessica. Call you? what is your will?
Shylock. I am bid forth to supper, Jessica :
There are my keys. But wherefore should I go?
I am not bid for love ; they flatter me :
But yet I 'll go in hate, to feed upon
The prodigal Christian. Jessica, my girl,
Look to my house. I am right loath to go :
There is some ill a-brewing towards my rest,
For I did dream of money-bags to-night.
Launcelot. I beseech you, sir, go : my young
master doth expect your reproach.
Shylock. So do I his.
Launcelot. And they have conspired together, I
will not say you shall see a masque ; but if you do,
then it was not for nothing that my nose fell a-bleed-
ing on Black-Monday last at six o'clock i' the morning
falling out that year on Ash-Wednesday was four
year, in the afternoon.
Shylock. What, are there masques? Hear you
me, Jessica :
Lock up my doors : and when you hear the drum
And the vile squealing of the wry-neck'd fife,

Clamber not you up to the casements then,
Nor thrust your head into the public street
To gaze on Christian fools with varnish'd faces,
But stop my house's ears, I mean my casements :
Let not the sound of shallow foppery enter
My sober house. By Jacob's staff, I swear,
I have no mind of feasting forth to-night :
But I will go. Go you before me, sirrah ;
Say I will come.
Launcelot. I will go before, sir. Mistress, look
out at window, for all this ;
                    There will come a Christian by,
                    Will be worth a Jewess' eye.   [*Exit.*
Shylock. What says that fool of Hagar's offspring,
ha?
Jessica. His words were ' Farewell, mistress ;
nothing else.
Shylock. The patch is kind enough, but a huge
feeder ;
Snail-slow in profit, and he sleeps by day
More than the wild-cat : drones hive not with me ;
Therefore I part with him, and part with him
To one that I would have him help to waste
His borrow'd purse. Well, Jessica, go in :
Perhaps I will return immediately :
Do as I bid you ; shut doors after you :
Fast bind, fast find ;
A proverb never stale in thrifty mind.   [*Exit.*
Jessica. Farewell ; and if my fortune be not crost,
I have a father, you a daughter, lost.   [*Exit.*

SCENE VI.   *The same.*

Enter GRATIANO *and* SALARINO, *masqued.*

Gratiano. This is the pent-house under which
Lorenzo
Desired us to make stand.
Salarino.   His hour is almost past.
Gratiano. And it is marvel he out-dwells his hour,
For lovers ever run before the clock.
Salarino. O, ten times faster Venus' pigeons fly
To seal love's bonds new-made, than they are wont
To keep obliged faith unforfeited !
Gratiano. That ever holds : who riseth from a feast
With that keen appetite that he sits down?
Where is the horse that doth untread again
His tedious measures with the unbated fire
That he did pace them first? All things that are,
Are with more spirit chased than enjoy'd.
How like a younker or a prodigal
The scarfed bark puts from her native bay,
Hugg'd and embraced by the strumpet wind !
How like the prodigal doth she return,
With over-weather'd ribs and ragged sails,
Lean, rent and beggar'd by the strumpet wind !
Salarino. Here comes Lorenzo : more of this
hereafter.

Enter LORENZO.

Lorenzo. Sweet friends, your patience for my
long abode ;
Not I, but my affairs, have made you wait :
When you shall please to play the thieves for wives,
I 'll watch as long for you then. Approach ;
Here dwells my father Jew. Ho ! who's within?

Enter JESSICA, *above, in boy's clothes.*

Jessica. Who are you? Tell me, for more certainty.

Albeit I 'll swear that I do know your tongue.
Lorenzo. Lorenzo, and thy love.
Jessica. Lorenzo, certain, and my love indeed,
For who love I so much ? And now who knows
But you, Lorenzo, whether I am yours ?
Lorenzo. Heaven and thy thoughts are witness
    that thou art.
Jessica. Here, catch this casket ; it is worth the
    pains.
I am glad 'tis night, you do not look on me,
For I am much ashamed of my exchange :
But love is blind and lovers cannot see
The pretty follies that themselves commit ;
For if they could, Cupid himself would blush
To see me thus transformed to a boy.
Lorenzo. Descend. for you must be my torch-
    bearer
Jessica. What, must I hold a candle to my
    shames ?
They in themselves, good sooth, are too too light,
Why, 'tis an office of discovery, love ;
And I should be obscured.
Lorenzo.   So are you, sweet,
Even in the lovely garnish of a boy.
But come at once ;
For the close night doth play the runaway,
And we are stay'd for at Bassanio's feast.
Jessica. I will make fast the doors, and gild
    myself
With some more ducats, and be with you straight.
                                    [*Exit above.*
Gratiano. Now, by my hood, a Gentile and no
    Jew.
Lorenzo. Beshrew me but I love her heartily ;
For she is wise, if I can judge of her,
And fair she is, if that mine eyes be true,
And true she is, as she hath proved herself,
And therefore, like herself, wise, fair and true.
Shall she be placed in my constant soul.

        Enter JESSICA, *below.*

What, art thou come ? Oh, gentlemen ; away !
Our masquing mates by this time for us stay.
                [*Exit with Jessica and Salarino.*

        Enter ANTONIO.

Antonio. Who 's there ?
Gratiano. Signior Antonio !
Antonio. Fie, fie, Gratiano ! where are all the
    rest ?
'Tis nine o'clock : our friends all stay for you.
No masque to-night : the wind is come about :
Bassanio presently will go aboard ;
I have sent twenty out to seek for you.
Gratiano. I am glad on 't : I desire no more
    delight
Than to be under sail and gone to-night.
                                    [*Exeunt.*

SCENE VII. *Belmont. A room in* PORTIA'S *house.*

Flourish of cornets. Enter PORTIA, *with the* PRINCE
    OF MOROÇCO, *and their trains.*

Portia. Go draw aside the curtains and discover
The several caskets to this noble prince.
Now make your choice.
Morocco. The first, of gold, who this inscription
    bears,
'Who chooseth me shall gain what many men
    desire ; '
The second, silver, which this promise carries,

'Who chooseth me shall get as much as he
    deserves ;'
This third, dull lead, with warning all as blunt,
'Who chooseth me must give and hazard all he
    hath.'
How shall I know if I do choose the right ?
Portia. The one of them contains my picture,
    prince :
If you choose that, then I am yours withal.
Morocco. Some god direct my judgement ! Let
    me see ;
I will survey the inscriptions back again.
What says this leaden casket ?
'Who chooseth me must give and hazard all he
    hath.'
Must give : for what ? for lead ? hazard for lead ?
This casket threatens. Men that hazard all
Do it in hope of fair advantages :
A golden mind stoops not to shows of dross ;
I 'll then nor give nor hazard aught for lead.
What says the silver with her virgin hue ?
'Who chooseth me shall get as much as he deserves.'
As much as he deserves ! Pause there, Morocco,
And weigh thy value with an even hand :
If thou be'st rated by thy estimation,
Thou dost deserve enough ; and yet enough
May not extend so far as to the lady :
And yet to be afeard of my deserving
Were but a weak disabling of myself.
As much as I deserve ! Why, that 's the lady :
I do in birth deserve her, and in fortunes,
In graces and in qualities of breeding ;
But more than these, in love I do deserve.
What if I stray'd no further, but chose here ?
Let 's see once more this saying graved in gold ;
'Who chooseth me shall gain what many men
    desire.'
Why, that 's the lady ; all the world desires her ;
From the four corners of the earth they come,
To kiss this shrine, this mortal-breathing saint :
The Hyrcanian deserts and the vasty wilds
Of wide Arabia are as throughfares now
For princes to come view fair Portia :
The watery kingdom, whose ambitious head
Spits in the face of heaven, is no bar
To stop the foreign spirits, but they come,
As o'er a brook, to see fair Portia.
One of these three contains her heavenly picture.
Is 't like that lead contains her ? 'Twere damnation
To think so base a thought : it were too gross
To rib her cerecloth in the obscure grave.
Or shall I think in silver she 's immured,
Being ten times undervalued to tried gold ?
O sinful thought ! Never so rich a gem
Was set in worse than gold. They have in England
A coin that bears the figure of an angel
Stamped in gold, but that 's insculp'd upon ;
But here an angel in a golden bed
Lies all within. Deliver me the key :
Here do I choose, and thrive I as I may !
Portia. There, take it, prince ; and if my form
    lie there,
Then I am yours. [*He unlocks the golden casket.*
Morocco.   O hell ! what have we here ?
A carrion Death, within whose empty eye
There is a written scroll ! I 'll read the writing.
[*Reads*] All that glisters is not gold ;
        Often have you heard that told :
        Many a man his life hath sold
        But my outside to behold :
        Gilded tombs do worms infold.

Had you been as wise as bold,
Young in limbs, in judgement old,
Your answer had not been inscroll'd :
Fare you well ; your suit is cold.

Cold, indeed ; and labour lost :
Then, farewell, heat, and welcome, frost !
Portia, adieu. I have too grieved a heart
To take a tedious leave : thus losers part.
         [*Exit with his train. Flourish of cornets.*
Portia. A gentle riddance. Draw the curtains,
go.
Let all of his complexion choose me so.   [*Exeunt.*

SCENE VIII.   *Venice. A street.*

Enter SALARINO *and* SALANIO.

    Salarino. Why, man, I saw Bassanio under sail :
With him is Gratiano gone along ;
And in their ship I am sure Lorenzo is not.
    Salanio. The villain Jew with outcries raised the
duke,
Who went with him to search Bassanio's ship.
    Salarino. He came too late, the ship was under
sail :
But there the duke was given to understand
That in a gondola were seen together
Lorenzo and his amorous Jessica :
Besides, Antonio certified the duke
They were not with Bassanio in his ship.
    Salanio. I never heard a passion so confused,
So strange, outrageous, and so variable,
As the dog Jew did utter in the streets :
' My daughter ! O my ducats ! O my daughter !
Fled with a Christian ! O my Christian ducats !
Justice ! the law ! my ducats, and my daughter !
A sealed bag, two sealed bags of ducats,
Of double ducats, stolen from me by my daughter !
And jewels, two stones, two rich and precious stones,
Stolen by my daughter ! Justice ! find the girl ;
She hath the stones upon her, and the ducats.'
    Salarino. Why, all the boys in Venice follow him,
Crying, his stones, his daughter, and his ducats.
    Salanio. Let good Antonio look he keep his day,
Or he shall pay for this.
    Salarino.   Marry, well remember'd.
I reason'd with a Frenchman yesterday,
Who told me, in the narrow seas that part
The French and English, there miscarried
A vessel of our country richly fraught :
I thought upon Antonio when he told me ;
And wish'd in silence that it were not his.
    Salanio. You were best to tell Antonio what you
hear ;
Yet do not suddenly, for it may grieve him.
    Salarino. A kinder gentleman treads not the
earth.
I saw Bassanio and Antonio part :
Bassanio told him he would make some speed
Of his return : he answer'd, ' Do not so ;
Slubber not business for my sake, Bassanio,
But stay the very riping of the time ;
And for the Jew's bond which he hath of me,
Let it not enter in your mind of love :
Be merry, and employ your chiefest thoughts
To courtship and such fair ostents of love
As shall conveniently become you there :'
And even there, his eye being big with tears,
Turning his face, he put his hand behind him,
And with affection wondrous sensible
He wrung Bassanio's hand ; and so they parted.

    Salanio. I think he only loves the world for him.
I pray thee, let us go and find him out
And quicken his embraced heaviness
With some delight or other.
    Salarino.   Do we so.   [*Exeunt.*

SCENE IX.   *Belmont. A room in* PORTIA'S *house.*

Enter NERISSA *with a Servitor.*

    Nerissa. Quick, quick, I pray thee ; draw the
curtain straight :
The Prince of Arragon hath ta'en his oath,
And comes to his election presently.

Flourish of cornets. Enter the PRINCE OF ARRAGON,
PORTIA, *and their trains.*

    Portia. Behold, there stand the caskets, noble
prince :
If you choose that wherein I am contain'd,
Straight shall our nuptial rites be solemnized :
But if you fail, without more speech, my lord,
You must be gone from hence immediately.
    Arragon. I am enjoin'd by oath to observe three
things :
First, never to unfold to any one
Which casket 'twas I chose ; next, if I fail
Of the right casket, never in my life
To woo a maid in way of marriage :
Lastly,
If I do fail in fortune of my choice,
Immediately to leave you and be gone.
    Portia. To these injunctions every one doth
swear
That comes to hazard for my worthless self.
    Arragon. And so have I address'd me. Fortune
now
To my heart's hope ! Gold ; silver ; and base
lead.
' Who chooseth me must give and hazard all he
hath.'
You shall look fairer, ere I give or hazard.
What says the golden chest ? ha ! let me see :
' Who chooseth me shall gain what many men
desire.'
What many men desire ! that ' many ' may be meant
By the fool multitude, that choose by show,
Not learning more than the fond eye doth teach ;
Which pries not to the interior, but, like the martlet,
Builds in the weather on the outward wall,
Even in the force and road of casualty.
I will not choose what many men desire,
Because I will not jump with common spirits
And rank me with the barbarous multitudes.
Why, then to thee, thou silver treasure-house ;
Tell me once more what title thou dost bear :
' Who chooseth me shall get as much as he deserves :'
And well said too ; for who shall go about
To cozen fortune and be honourable
Without the stamp of merit ? Let none presume
To wear an undeserved dignity.
O, that estates, degrees and offices
Were not derived corruptly, and that clear honour
Were purchased by the merit of the wearer !
How many then should cover that stand bare !
How many be commanded that command !
How much low peasantry would then be glean'd
From the true seed of honour ! and how much
honour
Pick'd from the chaff and ruin of the times

To be new-varnish'd ! Well, but to my choice :
' Who chooseth me shall get as much as he deserves.'
I will assume desert. Give me a key for this.
And instantly unlock my fortunes here.

[He opens the silver casket.

Portia. Too long a pause for that which you
find there.

Arragon. What 's here ? the portrait of a blinking
idiot,
Presenting me a schedule ! I will read it.
How much unlike art thou to Portia !
How much unlike my hopes and my deservings !
' Who chooseth me shall have as much as he de-
serves.'
Did I deserve no more than a fool's head ?
Is that my prize ? are my deserts no better ?

Portia. To offend, and judge, are distinct offices
And of opposed natures.

Arragon.   What is here ?

[Reads]   The fire seven times tried this :
Seven times tried that judgement is,
That did never choose amiss.
Some there be that shadows kiss ;
Such have but a shadow's bliss :
There be fools alive, I wis,
Silver'd o'er ; and so was this,
Take what wife you will to bed,
I will ever be your head :
So be gone : you are sped.

Still more fool I shall appear
By the time I linger here :
With one fool's head I came to woo,
But I go away with two.
Sweet, adieu. I 'll keep my oath,
Patiently to bear my wroth.

[Exeunt Arragon and train.

Portia. Thus hath the candle singed the moth.
O, these deliberate fools ! when they do choose,
They have the wisdom by their wit to lose.

Nerissa. The ancient saying is no heresy,
Hanging and wiving goes by destiny.

Portia. Come, draw the curtain, Nerissa.

Enter a Servant.

Servant. Where is my lady ?

Portia.   Here : what would my lord ?

Servant. Madam, there is alighted at your gate
A young Venetian, one that comes before
To signify the approaching of his lord ;
From whom he bringeth sensible regreets,
To wit, besides commends and courteous breath,
Gifts of rich value. Yet I have not seen
So likely an ambassador of love :
A day in April never came so sweet,
To show how costly summer was at hand,
As this fore-spurrer comes before his lord.

Portia. No more, I pray thee : I am half afeard
Thou wilt say anon he is some kin to thee,
Thou spend'st such high-day wit in praising him.
Come, come, Nerissa ; for I long to see
Quick Cupid's post that comes so mannerly.

Nerissa. Bassanio, lord Love, if thy will it be !

[Exeunt.

ACT III.

SCENE I.   *Venice. A street.*

Enter SALANIO *and* SALARINO.

Salanio.

Now, what news on the Rialto ?
Salarino. Why, yet it lives there unchecked
that Antonio hath a ship of rich lading
wrecked on the narrow seas ; the Goodwins, I think
they call the place ; a very dangerous flat and fatal,
where the carcases of many a tall ship lie buried, as
they say, if my gossip Report be an honest woman
of her word.

Salanio. I would she were as lying a gossip in
that as ever knapped ginger or made her neighbours
believe she wept for the death of a third husband.
But it is true, without any slips of prolixity or crossing the plain highway of talk, that the good Antonio,
the honest Antonio,——O that I had a title good
enough to keep his name company !—

Salarino. Come, the full stop.

Salanio. Ha ! what sayest thou ? Why, the end
is, he hath lost a ship.

Salarino. I would it might prove the end of his
losses.

Salanio. Let me say ' amen ' betimes, lest the
devil cross my prayer, for here he comes in the
likeness of a Jew.

Enter SHYLOCK.

How now, Shylock ! what news among the merchants ?

Shylock. You knew, none so well, none so well
as you, of my daughter's flight.

Salarino. That 's certain : I, for my part, knew
the tailor that made the wings she flew withal.

Salanio. And Shylock, for his own part, knew
the bird was fledged ; and then it is the complexion
of them all to leave the dam.

Shylock. She is damned for it.

Salarino. That 's certain, if the devil may be her
judge.

Shylock. My own flesh and blood to rebel !

Salanio. Out upon it, old carrion ! rebels it at
these years ?

Shylock. I say, my daughter is my flesh and
blood.

Salarino. There is more difference between thy
flesh and hers than between jet and ivory ; more
between your bloods than there is between red wine
and rhenish. But tell us, do you hear whether
Antonio have had any loss at sea or no ?

Shylock. There I have another bad match : a
bankrupt, a prodigal, who dare scarce show his
head on the Rialto ; a beggar, that was used to come
so smug upon the mart ; let him look to his bond :
he was wont to call me usurer ; let him look to his
bond : he was wont to lend money for a Christian
courtesy ; let him look to his bond.

Salarino. Why, I am sure, if he forfeit, thou wilt
not take his flesh : what 's that good for ?

Shylock. To bait fish withal : if it will feed nothing else, it will feed my revenge. He hath disgraced
me, and hindered me half a million ; laughed at
my losses, mocked at my gains, scorned my nation,
thwarted my bargains, cooled my friends, heated
mine enemies ; and what 's his reason ? I am a Jew.
Hath not a Jew eyes ? hath not a Jew hands, organs,

dimensions, senses, affections, passions ? fed with the same food, hurt with the same weapons, subject to the same diseases, healed by the same means, warmed and cooled by the same winter and summer, as a Christian is ? If you prick us, do we not bleed ? if you tickle us, do we not laugh ? if you poison us, do we not die ? and if you wrong us, shall we not revenge ? If we are like you in the rest, we will resemble you in that. If a Jew wrong a Christian, what is his humility ? Revenge. If a Christian wrong a Jew, what should his sufferance be by Christian example ? Why, revenge. The villany you teach me, I will execute, and it shall go hard but I will better the instruction.

Enter a Servant.

Servant. Gentlemen, my master Antonio is at his house and desires to speak with you both.
Salarino. We have been up and down to seek him.

Enter TUBAL.

Salanio. Here comes another of the tribe : a third cannot be matched, unless the devil himself turn Jew.

　　　　　[*Exeunt Salanio, Salarino and Servant.*
Shylock. How now, Tubal ! what news from Genoa ? hast thou found my daughter ?
Tubal. I often came where I did hear of her, but cannot find her.
Shylock. Why, there, there, there, there ! a diamond gone, cost me two thousand ducats in Frankfort ! The curse never fell upon our nation till now ; I never felt it till now : two thousand ducats in that ; and other precious, precious jewels. I would my daughter were dead at my foot, and the jewels in her ear ! would she were hearsed at my foot, and the ducats in her coffin ! No news of them ? Why so : and I know not what 's spent in the search: why, thou loss upon loss ! the thief gone with so much. and so much to find the thief ; and no satisfaction, no revenge : nor no ill luck stirring but what lights on my shoulders ; no sighs but of my breathing ; no tears but of my shedding.
Tubal. Yes, other men have ill luck too : Antonio, as I heard in Genoa,—
Shylock. What, what, what ? ill luck, ill luck ?
Tubal. Hath an argosy cast away, coming from Tripolis.
Shylock. I thank God, I thank God. Is 't true, is 't true ?
Tubal. I spoke with some of the sailors that escaped the wreck.
Shylock. I thank thee, good Tubal : good news, good news ! ha, ha ! where ? in Genoa ?
Tubal. Your daughter spent in Genoa, as I heard, in one night fourscore ducats.
Shylock. Thou stickest a dagger in me : I shall never see my gold again : fourscore ducats at a sitting ! fourscore ducats !
Tubal. There came divers of Antonio's creditors in my company to Venice, that swear he cannot choose but break.
Shylock. I am very glad of it : I 'll plague him : I 'll torture him : I am glad of it.
Tubal. One of them showed me a ring that he had of your daughter for a monkey.
Shylock. Out upon her ! Thou torturest me, Tubal : it was my turquoise ; I had it of Leah when

I was a bachelor : I would not have given it for a wilderness of monkeys.
Tubal. But Antonio is certainly undone.
Shylock. Nay, that 's true, that 's very true. Go, Tubal, fee me an officer ; bespeak him a fortnight before. I will have the heart of him, if he forfeit ; for, were he out of Venice, I can make what merchandise I will. Go, go, Tubal, and meet me at our synagogue ; go. good Tubal ; at our synagogue.
Tubal.　　　　　　　　　　　　　[*Exeunt.*

SCENE II.　*Belmont.　A room in* PORTIA'S *house.*

Enter BASSANIO, PORTIA, GRATIANO. NERISSA, *and* Attendants.

Portia. I pray you, tarry : pause a day or two
Before you hazard ; for, in choosing wrong,
I lose your company : therefore forbear awhile.
There 's something tells me, but it is not love,
I would not lose you ; and you know yourself,
Hate counsels not in such a quality.
But lest you should not understand me well,—
And yet a maiden hath no tongue but thought,—
I would detain you here some month or two
Before you venture for me. I could teach you
How to choose right, but I am then forsworn ;
So will I never be : so may you miss me ;
But if you do, you 'll make me wish a sin,
That I had been forsworn. Beshrew your eyes,
They have o'erlook'd me and divided me ;
One half of me is yours, the other half yours,
Mine own, I would say ; but if mine, then yours.
And so all yours. O, these naughty times
Put bars between the owners and their rights !
And so, though yours, not yours. Prove it so,
Let fortune go to hell for it, not I.
I speak too long ; but 'tis to peize the time,
To eke it and to draw it out in length,
To stay you from election
Bassanio.　　　　　　　　Let me choose ;
For as I am, I live upon the rack.
Portia. Upon the rack, Bassanio ! then confess
What treason there is mingled with your love.
Bassanio. None but that ugly treason of mistrust,
Which makes me fear the enjoying of my love :
There may as well be amity and life
'Tween snow and fire, as treason and my love.
Portia. Ay, but I fear you speak upon the rack,
Where men enforced do speak anything.
Bassanio. Promise me life, and I 'll confess the truth.
Portia. Well then, confess and live.
Bassanio.　　　　　　　　' Confess ' and ' love '
Had been the very sum of my confession :
O happy torment, when my torturer
Doth teach me answers for deliverance !
But let me to my fortune and the caskets.
Portia. Away. then ! I am lock'd in one of them :
If you do love me, you will find me out.
Nerissa and the rest, stand all aloof
Let music sound while he doth make his choice ;
Then, if he lose, he makes a swan-like end,
Fading in music : that the comparison
May stand more proper, my eye shall be the stream
And watery death-bed for him. He may win ;
And what is music then ? Then music is
Even as the flourish when true subjects bow
To a new-crowned monarch : such it is
As are those dulcet sounds in break of day
That creep into the dreaming bridegroom's ear

And summon him to marriage. Now he goes,
With no less presence, but with much more love,
Than young Alcides, when he did redeem
The virgin tribute paid by howling Troy
To the sea-monster : I stand for sacrifice ;
The rest aloof are the Dardanian wives,
With bleared visages, come forth to view
The issue of the exploit. Go, Hercules !
Live thou, I live : with much much more dismay
I view the fight than thou that makest the fray.

Music, whilst BASSANIO *comments on the
caskets to himself.*

SONG.

Tell me where is fancy bred,
Or in the heart or in the head ?
How begot, how nourished ?
  Reply, reply.
It is engender'd in the eyes,
With gazing fed ; and fancy dies
In the cradle where it lies.   '
  Let us all ring fancy's knell :
  I 'll begin it,—Ding, dong, bell.
All. Ding, dong, bell.
Bassanio. So may the outward shows be least
    themselves :
The world is still deceived with ornament.
In law, what plea so tainted and corrupt
But, being season'd with a gracious voice,
Obscures the show of evil ? In religion,
What damned error, but some sober brow
Will bless it and approve it with a text,
Hiding the grossness with fair ornament ?
There is no vice so simple but assumes
Some mark of virtue on his outward parts :
How many cowards, whose hearts are all as false
As stairs of sand, wear yet upon their chins
The beards of Hercules and frowning Mars,
Who, inward search'd, have livers white as milk ;
And these assume but valour's excrement
To render them redoubted ! Look on beauty,
And you shall see 'tis purchased by the weight ;
Which therein works a miracle in nature,
Making them lightest that wear most of it :
So are those crisped snaky golden locks
Which make such wanton gambols with the wind,
Upon supposed fairness, often known
To be the dowry of a second head,
The skull that bred them in the sepulchre.
Thus ornament is but the guiled shore
To a most dangerous sea ; the beauteous scarf
†Veiling an Indian beauty ; in a word,
The seeming truth which cunning times put on
To entrap the wisest. Therefore, thou gaudy
    gold,
Hard food for Midas, I will none of thee ;
Nor none of thee, thou pale and common drudge
'Tween man and man : but thou, thou meagre lead,
Which rather threatenest than dost promise aught,
Thy paleness moves me more than eloquence ;
And here choose I : joy be the consequence !
Portia. [*Aside*] How all the other passions fleet
    to air,
As doubtful thoughts, and rash-embraced despair,
And shuddering fear, and green-eyed jealousy !
O love,
Be moderate ; allay thy ecstasy ; scant this excess.
I feel too much thy blessing : make it less,

For fear I surfeit.
  Bassanio.   What find I here ?
                    [*Opening the leaden casket.*
Fair Portia's counterfeit ! What demi-god
Hath come so near creation ? Move these eyes ?
Or whether, riding on the balls of mine,
Seem they in motion ? Here are sever'd lips,
Parted with sugar breath : so sweet a bar
Should sunder such sweet friends. Here in her hairs
The painter plays the spider and hath woven
A golden mesh to entrap the hearts of men
Faster than gnats in cobwebs : but her eyes,—
How could he see to do them ? having made one,
Methinks it should have power to steal both his
And leave itself unfurnish'd. Yet look, how far
The substance of my praise doth wrong this shadow
In underprizing it, so far this shadow
Doth limp behind the substance. Here 's the
    scroll,
The continent and summary of my fortune.
  [*Reads*] You that choose not by the view,
    Chance as fair and choose as true !
    Since this fortune falls to you,
    Be content and seek no new.
    If you be well pleased with this
    And hold your fortune for your bliss,
    Turn you where your lady is
    And claim her with a loving kiss.
A gentle scroll. Fair lady, by your leave ;
I come by note, to give and to receive.
Like one of two contending in a prize,
That thinks he hath done well in people's eyes,
Hearing applause and universal shout,
Giddy in spirit, still gazing in a doubt
Whether those peals of praise be his or no ;
So, thrice-fair lady, stand I, even so ;
As doubtful whether what I see be true,
Until confirm'd, sign'd, ratified by you.
Portia. You see me, Lord Bassanio, where I
    stand,
Such as I am : though for myself alone
I would not be ambitious in my wish,
To wish myself much better ; yet, for you
I would be trebled twenty times myself ;
A thousand times more fair, ten thousand times
More rich ;
That only to stand high in your account,
I might in virtues, beauties, livings, friends,
Exceed account ; but the full sum of me
†Is sum of something, which, to term in gross,
Is an unlesson'd girl, unschool'd, unpractised ;
Happy in this, she is not yet so old
†But she may learn ; happier than this,
She is not bred so dull, but she can learn ;
Happiest of all is that her gentle spirit
Commits itself to yours to be directed,
As from her lord, her governor, her king.
Myself and what is mine to you and yours
Is now converted : but now I was the lord
Of this fair mansion, master of my servants,
Queen o'er myself ; and even now, but now,
·This house, these servants and this same myself
Are yours, my lord : I give them with this ring ;
Which when you part from, lose, or give away,
Let it presage the ruin of your love
And be my vantage to exclaim on you.
  Bassanio. Madam, you have bereft me of all
    words,
Only my blood speaks to you in my veins ;
And there is such confusion in my powers,
As, after some oration fairly spoke

By a beloved prince, there doth appear
Among the buzzing pleased multitude ;
Where every something, being blent together,
Turns to a wild of nothing, save of joy,
Express'd and not express'd. But when this ring
Parts from this finger, then parts life from hence :
O, then be bold to say Bassanio's dead !
 Nerissa. My lord and lady, it is now our time,
That have stood by and seen our wishes prosper,
To cry, good joy : good joy, my lord and lady !
 Gratiano. My lord Bassanio and my gentle lady,
I wish you all the joy that you can wish ;
For I am sure you can wish none from me :
And when your honours mean to solemnize
The bargain of your faith, I do beseech you,
Even at that time I may be married too.
 Bassanio. With all my heart, so thou canst get
a wife.
 Gratiano. I thank your lordship, you have got
me one.
My eyes, my lord, can look as swift as yours :
You saw the mistress, I beheld the maid ;
You loved, I loved for intermission.
No more pertains to me, my lord, than you.
Your fortune stood upon the casket there,
And so did mine too, as the matter falls ;
For wooing here until I sweat again,
And swearing till my very roof was dry
With oaths of love, at last, if promise last,
I got a promise of this fair one here
To have her love, provided that your fortune
Achieved her mistress.
 Portia.   Is this true, Nerissa ?
 Nerissa. Madam, it is, so you stand pleased
withal.
 Bassanio. And do you, Gratiano, mean good
faith ?
 Gratiano. Yes, faith, my lord.
 Bassanio. Our feast shall be much honour'd in
your marriage.
 Gratiano. We 'll play with them the first boy for
a thousand ducats.
 Nerissa. What, and stake down ?
 Gratiano. No ; we shall ne'er win at that sport,
and stake down.
But who comes here ? Lorenzo and his infidel ?
What, and my old Venetian friend Salerio ?

  Enter LORENZO, JESSICA, *and* SALERIO,
   A Messenger from Venice.

 Bassanio. Lorenzo and Salerio, welcome hither ;
If that the youth of my new interest here
Have power to bid you welcome. By your leave,
I bid my very friends and countrymen,
Sweet Portia, welcome.
 Portia.   So do I, my lord :
They are entirely welcome.
 Lorenzo. I thank your honour. For my part,
my lord,
My purpose was not to have seen you here ;
But meeting with Salerio by the way,
He did intreat me, past all saying nay,
To come with him along.
 Salerio.   I did, my lord ;
And I have reason for it. Signior Antonio
Commends him to you.
     [*Gives Bassanio a letter.*
 Bassanio. Ere I ope his letter,
I pray you, tell me how my good friend doth.

 Salerio. Not sick, my lord, unless it be in mind ;
Nor well, unless in mind : his letter there
Will show you his estate.
 Gratiano. Nerissa, cheer yon stranger ; bid her
welcome.
Your hand, Salerio : what 's the news from Venice ?
How doth that royal merchant, good Antonio ?
I know he will be glad of our success ;
We are the Jasons, we have won the fleece.
 Salerio. I would you had won the fleece that he
hath lost.
 Portia. There are some shrewd contents in yon
same paper,
That steals the colour from Bassanio's cheek :
Some dear friend dead ; else nothing in the world
Could turn so much the constitution
Of any constant man. What, worse and worse !
With leave, Bassanio ; I am half yourself,
And I must freely have the half of anything
That this same paper brings you.
 Bassanio.   O sweet Portia,
Here are a few of the unpleasant'st words
That ever blotted paper ! Gentle lady,
When I did first impart my love to you,
I freely told you, all the wealth I had
Ran in my veins, I was a gentleman ;
And then I told you true : and yet, dear lady,
Rating myself at nothing, you shall see
How much I was a braggart. When I told you
My state was nothing, I should then have told you
That I was worse than nothing ; for, indeed,
I have engaged myself to a dear friend,
Engaged my friend to his mere enemy,
To feed my means. Here is a letter, lady ;
The paper as the body of my friend,
And every word in it a gaping wound,
Issuing life-blood. But is it true, Salerio ?
Have all his ventures fail'd ? What, not one hit ?
From Tripolis, from Mexico and England,
From Lisbon, Barbary and India ?
And not one vessel 'scape the dreadful touch
Of merchant-marring rocks ?
 Salerio.   Not one, my lord.
Besides, it should appear, that if he had
The present money to discharge the Jew,
He would not take it. Never did I know
A creature, that did bear the shape of man,
So keen and greedy to confound a man ;
He plies the duke at morning and at night,
And doth impeach the freedom of the state,
If they deny him justice : twenty merchants,
The duke himself, and the magnificoes
Of greatest port, have all persuaded with him ;
But none can drive him from the envious plea
Of forfeiture, of justice and his bond.
 Jessica. When I was with him I have heard him
swear
To Tubal and to Chus, his countrymen,
That he would rather have Antonio's flesh
Than twenty times the value of the sum
That he did owe him : and I know, my lord,
If law, authority and power deny not,
It will go hard with poor Antonio.
 Portia. Is it your dear friend that is thus in trouble ?
 Bassanio. The dearest friend to me, the kindest man,
The best-condition'd and unwearied spirit
In doing courtesies, and one in whom
The ancient Roman honour more appears
Than any that draws breath in Italy.
 Portia. What sum owes he the Jew ?
 Bassanio. For me three thousand ducats.

Portia.   What, no more?
Pay him six thousand, and deface the bond ;
Double six thousand, and then treble that,
Before a friend of this description
Shall lose a hair through Bassanio's fault.
First go with me to church and call me wife,
And then away to Venice to your friend ;
For never shall you lie by Portia's side
With an unquiet soul.   You shall have gold
To pay the petty debt twenty times over :
When it is paid, bring your true friend along.
My maid Nerissa and myself meantime
Will live as maids and widows.   Come, away !
For you shall hence upon your wedding-day :
Bid your friends welcome, show a merry cheer :
Since you are dear bought, I will love you dear.
But let me hear the letter of your friend.
    Bassanio. [*Reads*] Sweet Bassanio, my ships have
all miscarried, my creditors grow cruel, my estate
is very low, my bond to the Jew is forfeit ; and since
in paying it, it is impossible I should live, all debts
are cleared between you and I, if I might but see
you at my death. Notwithstanding, use your
pleasure : if your love do not persuade you to come,
let not my letter.
    Portia. O love, dispatch all business, and be
gone !
    Bassanio. Since I have your good leave to go
away,
I 'll make haste : but, till I come again,
No bed shall e'er be guilty of my stay,
    No rest be interposer 'twixt us twain.
                                        [*Exeunt.*

SCENE III.   *Venice.   A street.*

Enter SHYLOCK, SALARINO, ANTONIO, *and* Gaoler.

    Shylock. Gaoler, look to him : tell not me of
mercy ;
This is the fool that lent out money gratis :
Gaoler, look to him.
    Antonio.   Hear me yet, good Shylock.
    Shylock. I 'll have my bond ; speak not against
my bond :
I have sworn an oath that I will have my bond.
Thou call'dst me dog before thou hadst a cause ;
But, since I am a dog, beware my fangs :
The duke shall grant me justice.   I do wonder,
Thou naughty gaoler, that thou art so fond
To come abroad with him at his request.
    Antonio. I pray thee, hear me speak.
    Shylock. I 'll have my bond : I will not hear thee
speak :
I 'll have my bond ; and therefore speak no more.
I 'll not be made a soft and dull-eyed fool,
To shake the head, relent, and sigh, and yield
To Christian intercessors.   Follow not ;
I 'll have no speaking : I will have my bond.
                                        [*Exit.*
    Salarino. It is the most impenetrable cur
That ever kept with men.
    Antonio.   Let him alone :
I 'll follow him no more with bootless prayers.
He seeks my life : his reason well I know :
I oft deliver'd from his forfeitures
Many that have at times made moan to me ;
Therefore he hates me.
    Salarino.   I am sure the duke
Will never grant this forfeiture to hold.
    Antonio. The duke cannot deny the course of law :

For the commodity that strangers have
With us in Venice, if it be denied,
Will much impeach the justice of his state ;
Since that the trade and profit of the city
Consisteth of all nations.   Therefore, go :
These griefs and losses have so bated me,
That I shall hardly spare a pound of flesh
To-morrow to my bloody creditor.
Well, gaoler, on.   Pray God, Bassanio come
To see me pay his debt, and then I care not !   [*Exeunt.*

SCENE IV.   *Belmont.   A room in* PORTIA'S *house.*

Enter PORTIA, NERISSA, LORENZO, JESSICA, *and*
                    BALTHASAR.

    Lorenzo. Madam, although I speak it in your
presence,
You have a noble and a true conceit
Of god-like amity ; which appears most strongly
In bearing thus the absence of your lord.
But if you knew to whom you show this honour,
How true a gentleman you send relief,
How dear a lover of my lord your husband,
I know you would be prouder of the work
Than customary bounty can enforce you.
    Portia. I never did repent for doing good,
Nor shall not now : for in companions
That do converse and waste the time together,
Whose souls do bear an equal yoke of love,
There must be needs a like proportion
Of lineaments, of manners and of spirit ;
Which makes me think that this Antonio,
Being the bosom lover of my lord,
Must needs be like my lord.   If it be so,
How little is the cost I have bestow'd
In purchasing the semblance of my soul
From out the state of hellish misery !
This comes too near the praising of myself ;
Therefore no more of it : hear other things.
Lorenzo, I commit into your hands
The husbandry and manage of my house
Until my lord's return : for mine own part,
I have toward heaven breathed a secret vow
To live in prayer and contemplation,
Only attended by Nerissa here,
Until her husband and my lord's return :
There is a monastery two miles off ;
And there will we abide   I do desire you
Not to deny this imposition ;
The which my love and some necessity
Now lays upon you.
    Lorenzo.   Madam, with all my heart ;
I shall obey you in all fair commands.
    Portia. My people do already know my mind,
And will acknowledge you and Jessica
In place of Lord Bassanio and myself.
And so farewell, till we shall meet again.
    Lorenzo. Fair thoughts and happy hours attend
on you !
    Jessica. I wish your ladyship all heart's content.
    Portia. I thank you for your wish, and am well
pleased
To wish it back on you : fare you well, Jessica.
                    [*Exeunt Jessica and Lorenzo.*
Now, Balthasar,
As I have ever found thee honest-true,
So let me find thee still.   Take this same letter,
And use thou all the endeavour of a man
In speed to Padua : see thou render this
Into my cousin's hand, Doctor Bellario ;

And, look, what notes and garments he doth give
thee,
Bring them, I pray thee, with imagined speed
Unto the tranect, to the common ferry
Which trades to Venice. Waste no time in words,
But get thee gone : I shall be there before thee.
Balthasar.   Madam, I go with all convenient
speed.   [*Exit.*
Portia.   Come on, Nerissa ; I have work in hand
That you yet know not of : we 'll see our husbands
Before they think of us.
Nerissa.   Shall they see us ?
Portia.   They shall, Nerissa ; but in such a habit,
That they shall think we are accomplished
With that we lack. I 'll hold thee any wager,
When we are both accoutred like young men,
I 'll prove the prettier fellow of the two,
And wear my dagger with the braver grace,
And speak between the change of man and boy
With a reed voice, and turn two mincing steps
Into a manly stride, and speak of frays
Like a fine bragging youth, and tell quaint lies,
How honourable ladies sought my love,
Which I denying, they fell sick and died ;
I could not do withal ; then I 'll repent,
And wish, for all that, that I had not kill'd them ;
And twenty of these puny lies I 'll tell,
That men shall swear I have discontinued school
Above a twelvemonth. I have within my mind
A thousand raw tricks of these bragging Jacks,
Which I will practise.
Nerissa.   Why, shall we turn to men ?
Portia.   Fie, what a question 's that,
If thou wert near a lewd interpreter !
But come, I 'll tell thee all my whole device
When I am in my coach, which stays for us
At the park gate ; and therefore haste away,
For we must measure twenty miles to-day.
                                          [*Exeunt.*

SCENE V. *The same. A garden.*

Enter LAUNCELOT *and* JESSICA.

Launcelot.   Yes, truly ; for, look you, the sins of
the father are to be laid upon the children : therefore, I promise ye, I fear you. I was always plain
with you, and so now I speak my agitation of the
matter : therefore be of good cheer, for truly I think
you are damned. There is but one hope in it that
can do you any good ; and that is but a kind of
bastard hope neither.
Jessica.   And what hope is that, I pray thee ?
Launcelot.   Marry, you may partly hope that
your father got you not, that you are not the Jew's
daughter.
Jessica.   That were a kind of bastard hope,
indeed : so the sins of my mother should be visited
upon me.
Launcelot.   Truly then I fear you are damned
both by father and mother : thus when I shun
Scylla, your father, I fall into Charybdis, your
mother : well, you are gone both ways.
Jessica.   I shall be saved by my husband ; he
hath made me a Christian.
Launcelot.   Truly, the more to blame he : we were
Christians enow before ; e'en as many as could
well live, one by another. This making of Christians
will raise the price of hogs : if we grow all to be
pork-eaters, we shall not shortly have a rasher on
the coals for money.

Enter LORENZO.

Jessica.   I 'll tell my husband, Launcelot, what
you say : here he comes.
Lorenzo.   I, shall grow jealous of you shortly,
Launcelot, if you thus get my wife into corners.
Jessica.   Nay, you need not fear us, Lorenzo :
Launcelot and I are out. He tells me flatly there
is no mercy for me in heaven, because I am a Jew's
daughter : and he says, you are no good member
of the commonwealth, for in converting Jews to
Christians, you raise the price of pork.
Lorenzo.   I shall answer that better to the commonwealth than you can the getting up of the negro's
belly : the Moor is with child by you, Launcelot.
Launcelot.   It is much that the Moor should be
more than reason : but if she be less than an honest
woman, she is indeed more than I took her for.
Lorenzo.   How every fool can play upon the word !
I think the best grace of wit will shortly turn into
silence, and discourse grow commendable in none
only but parrots. Go in, sirrah ; bid them prepare
for dinner.
Launcelot.   That is done, sir ; they have all
stomachs.
Lorenzo.   Goodly Lord, what a wit-snapper are
you ! then bid them prepare dinner.
Launcelot.   That is done too, sir ; only ' cover '
is the word.
Lorenzo.   Will you cover then, sir ?
Launcelot.   Not so, sir, neither ; I know my
duty.
Lorenzo.   Yet more quarrelling with occasion !
Wilt thou show the whole wealth of thy wit in an
instant ? I pray thee, understand a plain man in
his plain meaning : go to thy fellows ; bid them cover
the table, serve in the meat, and we will come in
to dinner.
Launcelot.   For the table, sir, it shall be served
in ; for the meat, sir, it shall be covered ; for your
coming in to dinner, sir, why, let it be as humours
and conceits shall govern.   [*Exit.*
Lorenzo.   O dear discretion, how his words are
suited !
The fool hath planted in his memory
An army of good words ; and I do know
A many fools, that stand in better place,
Garnish'd like him, that for a tricksy word
Defy the matter. How cheer'st thou, Jessica ?
And now, good sweet, say thy opinion,
How dost thou like the Lord Bassanio's wife ?
Jessica.   Past all expressing. It is very meet
The Lord Bassanio live an upright life ;
For, having such a blessing in his lady,
He finds the joys of heaven here on earth ;
† And if on earth he do not mean it, then
In reason he should never come to heaven.
Why, if two gods should play some heavenly match
And on the wager lay two earthly women,
And Portia one, there must be something else
Pawn'd with the other, for the poor rude world
Hath not her fellow.
Lorenzo.   Even such a husband
Hast thou of me as she is for a wife.
Jessica.   Nay, but ask my opinion too of that.
Lorenzo.   I will anon : first, let us go to dinner.
Jessica.   Nay, let me praise you while I have a
stomach.
Lorenzo.   No, pray thee, let it serve for table-talk ;
Then, howsoe'er thou speak'st, 'mong other things
I shall digest it.

Jessica.   Well, I 'll set you forth.   [*Exeunt.*

ACT IV.

SCENE I.   *Venice.   A court of justice.*

Enter the DUKE, *the* Magnificoes, ANTONIO,
BASSANIO, GRATIANO, SALERIO, *and others.*

Duke.

What, is Antonio here?
     Antonio.   Ready, so please your grace.
     Duke.   I am sorry for thee : thou art
come to answer
A stony adversary, an inhuman wretch
Uncapable of pity, void and empty
From any dram of mercy.
     Antonio.   I have heard
Your grace hath ta'en great pains to qualify
His rigorous course ; but since he stands obdurate
And that no lawful means can carry me
Out of his envy's reach, I do oppose
My patience to his fury, and am arm'd
To suffer, with a quietness of spirit,
The very tyranny and rage of his.
     Duke.   Go one, and call the Jew into the court.
     Salerio.   He is ready at the door : he comes,
my lord.

Enter SHYLOCK.

     Duke.   Make room, and let him stand before
our face.
Shylock, the world thinks, and I think so too,
That thou but lead'st this fashion of thy malice
To the last hour of act ; and then 'tis thought
Thou 'lt show thy mercy and remorse more strange
Than is thy strange apparent cruelty ;
And where thou now exact'st the penalty,
Which is a pound of this poor merchant's flesh,
Thou wilt not only loose the forfeiture,
But, touch'd with human gentleness and love,
Forgive a moiety of the principal ;
Glancing an eye of pity on his losses,
That have of late so huddled on his back,
Enow to press a royal merchant down
And pluck commiseration of his state
From brassy bosoms and rough hearts of flint,
From stubborn Turks and Tartars, never train'd
To offices of tender courtesy.
We all expect a gentle answer, Jew.
     Shylock.   I have possess'd your grace of what I
purpose ;
And by our holy Sabbath, have I sworn
To have the due and forfeit of my bond :
If you deny it, let the danger light
Upon your charter and your city's freedom.
You 'll ask me, why I rather choose to have
A weight of carrion flesh than to receive
Three thousand ducats : I 'll not answer that :
But, say, it is my humour : is it answer'd ?
What if my house be troubled with a rat
And I be pleased to give ten thousand ducats
To have it baned ? What, are you answer'd yet ?
Some men there are love not a gaping pig ;
Some, that are mad if they behold a cat ;
And others, when the bagpipe sings i' the nose,
Cannot contain their urine : for affection,
Mistress of passion, sways it to the mood
Of what it likes or loathes. Now, for your answer :
As there is no firm reason to be render'd,

Why he cannot abide a gaping pig ;
Why he, a harmless necessary cat ;
† Why he, a woollen bag-pipe ; but of force
Must yield to such inevitable shame
As to offend, himself being offended ;
So can I give no reason, nor I will not,
More than a lodged hate and a certain loathing
I bear Antonio, that I follow thus
A losing suit against him. Are you answer'd ?
     Bassanio.   This is no answer, thou unfeeling man,
To excuse the current of thy cruelty.
     Shylock.   I am not bound to please thee with my
answers.
     Bassanio.   Do all men kill the things they do not
love ?
     Shylock.   Hates any man the thing he would not
kill ?
     Bassanio.   Every offence is not a hate at first.
     Shylock.   What, wouldst thou have a serpent
sting thee twice ?
     Antonio.   I pray you, think you question with
the Jew :
You may as well go stand upon the beach
And bid the main flood bate his usual height ;
You may as well use question with the wolf
Why he hath made the ewe bleat for the lamb ;
You may as well forbid the mountain pines
To wag their high tops and to make no noise,
When they are fretten with the gusts of heaven ;
You may as well do any thing most hard,
As seek to soften that—than which what 's harder ?—
His Jewish heart : therefore, I do beseech you,
Make no more offers, use no farther means,
But with all brief and plain conveniency
Let me have judgement and the Jew his will.
     Bassanio.   For thy three thousand ducats here is
six.
     Shylock.   If every ducat in six thousand ducats
Were in six parts and every part a ducat,
I would not draw them ; I would have my bond.
     Duke.   How shalt thou hope for mercy, rendering
none ?
     Shylock.   What judgement shall I dread, doing
no wrong ?
You have among you many a purchased slave,
Which, like your asses and your dogs and mules,
You use in abject and in slavish parts,
Because you bought them : shall I say to you,
Let them be free, marry them to your heirs ?
Why sweat they under burthens ? let their beds
Be made as soft as yours and let their palates
Be season'd with such viands ? You will answer
' The slaves are ours : ' so do I answer you :
The pound of flesh, which I demand of him,
Is dearly bought ; 'tis mine and I will have it.
If you deny me, fie upon your law !
There is no force in the decrees of Venice.
I stand for judgement : answer ; shall I have it ?
     Duke.   Upon my power I may dismiss this court,
Unless Bellario, a learned doctor,
Whom I have sent for to determine this,
Come here to-day.
     Salerio.   My lord, here stays without
A messenger with letters from the doctor,
New come from Padua.
     Duke.   Bring us the letters ; call the messenger.
     Bassanio.   Good cheer, Antonio ! What, man,
courage yet !
The Jew shall have my flesh, blood, bones and all,
Ere thou shalt loose for me one drop of blood.

Antonio. I am a tainted wether of the flock,
Meetest for death : the weakest kind of fruit
Drops earliest to the ground ; and so let me :
You cannot better be employ'd, Bassanio,
Than to live still and write mine epitaph.

Enter NERISSA, *dressed like a lawyer's clerk.*

Duke. Came you from Padua, from Bellario ?
Nerissa. From both, my lord. Bellario greets
  your grace.   [*Presenting a letter.*
Bassanio. Why dost thou whet thy knife so
  earnestly ?
Shylock. To cut the forfeiture from that bankrupt
  there.
Gratiano. Not on thy sole, but on thy soul, harsh
  Jew,
Thou makest thy knife keen ; but no metal can,
No, not the hangman's axe, bear half the keenness
Of thy sharp envy. Can no prayers pierce thee ?
Shylock. No, none that thou hast wit enough to
  make.
Gratiano. O, be thou damn'd, inexecrable dog !
And for thy life let justice be accused.
Thou almost makest me waver in my faith
To hold opinion with Pythagoras,
That souls of animals infuse themselves
Into the trunks of men : thy currish spirit
Govern'd a wolf, who, hang'd for human slaughter,
Even from the gallows did his fell soul fleet,
And, whilst thou lay'st in thy unhallow'd dam,
Infused itself in thee ; for thy desires
Are wolvish, bloody, starved and ravenous.
Shylock. Till thou canst rail the seal from off my
  bond,
Thou but offend'st thy lungs to speak so loud :
Repair thy wit, good youth, or it will fall
To cureless ruin. I stand here for law.
Duke. This letter from Bellario doth commend
A young and learned doctor to our court.
Where is he ?
Nerissa. He attendeth here hard by,
To know your answer, whether you 'll admit him.
Duke. With all my heart. Some three or four of
  you
Go give him courteous conduct to this place.
Meantime the court shall hear Bellario's letter.
Clerk. [*Reads*] Your grace shall understand
that at the receipt of your letter I am very sick : but
in the instant that your messenger came, in loving
visitation was with me a young doctor of Rome ; his
name is Balthasar. I acquainted him with the cause
in controversy between the Jew and Antonio the
merchant : we turned o'er many books together : he
is furnished with my opinion ; which, bettered with
his own learning, the greatness whereof I cannot
enough commend, comes with him, at my impor-
tunity, to fill up your grace's request in my stead. I
beseech you, let his lack of years be no impediment
to let him lack a reverend estimation ; for I never
knew so young a body with so old a head. I leave
him to your gracious acceptance whose trial shall
better publish his commendation.
Duke. You hear the learn'd Bellario, what he
  writes :
And here, I take it, is the doctor come.

Enter PORTIA, *dressed like a doctor of laws.*

Give me your hand. Come you from old Bellario ?
Portia. I did, my lord.

Duke. You are welcome : take your place.
Are you acquainted with the difference
That holds this present question in the court ?
Portia. I am informed throughly of the cause.
Which is the merchant here, and which the Jew ?
Duke. Antonio and Shylock, both stand forth.
Portia. Is your name Shylock ?
Shylock.   Shylock is my name
Portia. Of a strange nature is the suit you follow
Yet in such rule that the Venetian law
Cannot impugn you as you do proceed.
You stand within his danger do you not ?
Antonio. Ay, so he says.
Portia.   Do you confess the bond ?
Antonio. I do.
Portia.   Then must the Jew be merciful.
Shylock. On what compulsion must I ? tell me
  that.
Portia. The quality of mercy is not strain'd,
It droppeth as the gentle rain from heaven
Upon the place beneath : it is twice blest ;
It blesseth him that gives and him that takes :
'Tis mightiest in the mightiest : it becomes
The throned monarch better than his crown ;
His sceptre shows the force of temporal power,
The attribute to awe and majesty,
Wherein doth sit the dread and fear of kings ;
But mercy is above this sceptred sway ;
It is enthroned in the hearts of kings.
It is an attribute to God himself ;
And earthly power doth then show likest God's
When mercy seasons justice. Therefore, Jew,
Though justice be thy plea, consider this,
That, in the course of justice, none of us
Should see salvation : we do pray for mercy ;
And that same prayer doth teach us all to render
The deeds of mercy. I have spoken thus much
To mitigate the justice of thy plea ;
Which if thou follow, this strict court of Venice
Must needs give sentence 'gainst the merchant there.
Shylock. My deeds upon my head ! I crave the
  law,
The penalty and forfeit of my bond.
Portia. Is he not able to discharge the money ?
Bassanio. Yes, here I tender it for him in the
  court ;
Yea, twice the sum : if that will not suffice,
I will be bound to pay it ten times o'er,
On forfeit of my hands, my head, my heart :
If this will not suffice, it must appear
That malice bears down truth. And I beseech you,
Wrest once the law to your authority :
To do a great right, do a little wrong,
And curb this cruel devil of his will.
Portia. It must not be ; there is no power in
  Venice
Can alter a decree established :
'Twill be recorded for a precedent,
And many an error by the same example
Will rush into the state : it cannot be.
Shylock. A Daniel come to judgement ! yea, a
  Daniel !
O wise young judge, how I do honour thee !
Portia. I pray you, let me look upon the bond.
Shylock. Here 'tis, most reverend doctor, here
  it is.
Portia. Shylock, there 's thrice thy money offer'd
  thee.
Shylock. An oath, an oath, I have an oath in
  heaven :
Shall I lay perjury upon my soul ?

No, not for Venice.

Portia.   Why, this bond is forfeit ;
And lawfully by this the Jew may claim
A pound of flesh, to be by him cut off
Nearest the merchant's heart.   Be merciful :
Take thrice thy money ; bid me tear the bond.

Shylock.   When it is paid according to the tenour.
It doth appear you are a worthy judge ;
You know the law, your exposition
Hath been most sound : I charge you by the law,
Whereof you are a well-deserving pillar,
Proceed to judgement : by my soul I swear
There is no power in the tongue of man
To alter me : I stay here on my bond.

Antonio.   Most heartily I do beseech the court
To give the judgement.

Portia.   Why then, thus it is :
You must prepare your bosom for his knife.

Shylock.   O noble judge ! O excellent young
   man !

Portia.   For the intent and purpose of the law
Hath full relation to the penalty,
Which here appeareth due upon the bond.

Shylock.   'Tis very true : O wise and upright
   judge !
How much more elder art thou than thy looks !

Portia.   Therefore lay bare your bosom.

Shylock.   Ay, his breast :
So says the bond : doth it not, noble judge ?
'Nearest his heart : ' those are the very words.

Portia.   It is so.   Are there balance here to weigh
The flesh ?

Shylock.   I have them ready.

Portia.   Have by some surgeon, Shylock, on
   your charge,
To stop his wounds, lest he do bleed to death.

Shylock.   Is it so nominated in the bond ?

Portia.   It is not so express'd : but what of that ?
'Twere good you do so much for charity.

Shylock.   I cannot find it ; 'tis not in the bond.

Portia.   You, merchant, have you any thing to
   say ?

Antonio.   But little : I am arm'd and well prepared.
Give me your hand, Bassanio : fare you well !
Grieve not that I am fallen to this for you ;
For herein Fortune shows herself more kind
Than is her custom : it is still her use
To let the wretched man outlive his wealth,
To view with hollow eye and wrinkled brow
An age of poverty ; from which lingering penance
Of such misery doth she cut me off.
Commend me to your honourable wife :
Tell her the process of Antonio's end ;
Say how I loved you, speak me fair in death ;
And, when the tale is told, bid her be judge
Whether Bassanio had not once a love.
Repent but you that you shall lose your friend,
And he repents not that he pays your debt ;
For if the Jew do cut but deep enough,
I 'll pay it presently, with all my heart.

Bassanio.   Antonio, I am married to a wife
Which is as dear to me as life itself ;
But life itself, my wife, and all the world,
Are not with me esteem'd above thy life :
I would lose all, ay, sacrifice them all
Here to this devil, to deliver you.

Portia.   Your wife would give you little thanks
   for that,
If she were by, to hear you make the offer.

Gratiano.   I have a wife, whom, I protest, I love :
I would she were in heaven, so she could

Entreat some power to change this currish Jew.

Nerissa.   'Tis well you offer it behind her back ;
The wish would make else an unquiet house.

Shylock.   These be the Christian husbands.   I
   have a daughter ;
Would any of the stock of Barrabas
Had been her husband rather than a Christian !
                                        [*Aside.*
We trifle time : I pray thee, pursue sentence.

Portia.   A pound of that same merchant's flesh
   is thine :
The court awards it, and the law doth give it.

Shylock.   Most rightful judge !

Portia.   And you must cut this flesh from off his
   breast :
The law allows it, and the court awards it.

Shylock.   Most learned judge ! A sentence !
   Come, prepare !

Portia.   Tarry a little ; there is something else.
This bond doth give thee here no jot of blood ;
The words expressly are ' a pound of flesh : '
Take then thy bond, take thou thy pound of flesh ;
But, in the cutting it, if thou dost shed
One drop of Christian blood, thy lands and goods
Are, by the laws of Venice, confiscate
Unto the state of Venice.

Gratiano.   O upright judge ! Mark, Jew : O
   learned judge !

Shylock.   Is that the law ?

Portia.   Thyself shalt see the act :
For, as thou urgest justice, be assured
Thou shalt have justice, more than thou desirest.

Gratiano.   O learned judge ! Mark, Jew : a
   learned judge !

Shylock.   I take this offer, then ; pay the bond
   thrice
And let the Christian go.

Bassanio.   Here is the money.

Portia.   Soft !
The Jew shall have all justice ; soft ! no haste :
He shall have nothing but the penalty.

Gratiano.   O Jew ! an upright judge, a learned
   judge !

Portia.   Therefore prepare thee to cut off the flesh.
Shed thou no blood, nor cut thou less nor more
But just a pound of flesh : if thou cut'st more
Or less than a just pound, be it but so much
As makes it light or heavy in the substance,
Or the division of the twentieth part
Of one poor scruple, nay, if the scale do turn
But in the estimation of a hair,
Thou diest and all thy goods are confiscate.

Gratiano.   A second Daniel, a Daniel, Jew !
Now, infidel, I have you on the hip.

Portia.   Why doth the Jew pause ? take thy
   forfeiture.

Shylock.   Give me my principal, and let me go.

Bassanio.   I have it ready for thee ; here it is.

Portia.   He hath refused it in the open court :
He shall have merely justice and his bond.

Gratiano.   A Daniel, still say I, a second Daniel !
I thank thee, Jew, for teaching me that word.

Shylock.   Shall I not have barely my principal ?

Portia.   Thou shalt have nothing but the forfeiture,
To be so taken at thy peril, Jew.

Shylock.   Why, then the devil give him good of it !
I 'll stay no longer question.

Portia.   Tarry, Jew :
The law hath yet another hold on you.
It is enacted in the laws of Venice,
If it be proved against an alien

That by direct or indirect attempts
He seek the life of any citizén,
The party 'gainst the which he doth contrive
Shall seize one half his goods ; the other half
Comes to the privy coffer of the state ;
And the offender's life lies in the mercy
Of the duke only, 'gainst all other voice.
In which predicament, I say, thou stand'st ;
For it appears, by manifest proceeding,
That indirectly and directly too
Thou hast contrived against the very life
Of the defendant ; and thou hast incurr'd
The danger formerly by me rehearsed.
Down therefore and beg mercy of the duke.
Gratiano. Beg that thou mayst have leave to
hang thyself :
And yet, thy wealth being forfeit to the state,
Thou hast not left the value of a cord ;
Therefore thou must be hang'd at the state's charge.
Duke. That thou shalt see the difference of our
spirits,
I pardon thee thy life before thou ask it :
For half thy wealth, it is Antonio's ;
The other half comes to the general state,
Which humbleness may drive unto a fine.
Portia. Ay, for the state, not for Antonio.
Shylock. Nay, take my life and all : pardon not
that :
You take my house when you do take the prop
That doth sustain my house ; you take my life
When you do take the means whereby I live.
Portia. What mercy can you render him, Antonio ?
Gratiano. A halter gratis ; nothing else, for God's
sake.
Antonio. So please my lord the duke and all the
court
To quit the fine for one half of his goods,
I am content ; so he will let me have
The other half in use, to render it,
Upon his death, unto the gentleman
That lately stole his daughter :
Two things provided more, that, for this favour,
He presently become a Christian ;
The other, that he do record a gift,
Here in the court, of all he dies possess'd,
Unto his son Lorenzo and his daughter.
Duke. He shall do this, or else I do recant
The pardon that I late pronounced here.
Portia. Art thou contented, Jew ? what dost
thou say ?
Shylock. I am content.
Portia. Clerk, draw a deed of gift.
Shylock. I pray you, give me leave to go from
hence ;
I am not well : send the deed after me,
And I will sign it.
Duke. Get thee gone, but do it.
Gratiano. In christening shalt thou have two
godfathers :
Had I been judge, thou shouldst have had ten more,
To bring thee to the gallows, not the font.
                                    [*Exit Shylock.*
Duke. Sir, I entreat you home with me to dinner.
Portia. I humbly do desire your grace of pardon :
I must away this night towards Padua,
And it is meet I presently set forth.
Duke. I am sorry that your leisure serves you not.
Antonio, gratify this gentleman,
For, in my mind, you are much bound to him.
                           [*Exeunt Duke and his train.*
Bassanio. Most worthy gentleman, I and my friend

Have by your wisdom been this day acquitted
Of grievous penalties ; in lieu whereof,
Three thousand ducats, due unto the Jew,
We freely cope your courteous pains withal.
Antonio. And stand indebted, over and above,
In love and service to you evermore.
Portia. He is well paid that is well satisfied ;
And I, delivering you, am satisfied
And therein do account myself well paid :
My mind was never yet more mercenary.
I pray you, know me when we meet again :
I wish you well, and so I take my leave.
Bassanio. Dear sir, of force I must attempt you
further :
Take some remembrance of us, as a tribute,
Not as a fee ; grant me two things I pray you,
Not to deny me, and to pardon me.
Portia. You press me far, and therefore I will
yield.
[*To Antonio*] Give me your gloves, I 'll wear them
for your sake ;
[*To Bassanio*] And, for your love, I 'll take this
ring from you :
Do not draw back your hand ; I 'll take no more :
And you in love shall not deny me this.
Bassanio. This ring, good sir, alas, it is a trifle !
I will not shame myself to give you this.
Portia. I will have nothing else but only this ;
And now methinks I have a mind to it.
Bassanio. There 's more depends on this than on
the value.
The dearest ring in Venice will I give you,
And find it out by proclamation :
Only for this, I pray you, pardon me.
Portia. I see, sir, you are liberal in offers :
You taught me first to beg ; and now methinks
You teach me how a beggar should be answer'd.
Bassanio. Good sir, this ring was given me by
my wife ;
And when she put it on, she made me vow
That I should neither sell nor give nor lose it.
Portia. That 'scuse serves many men to save
their gifts.
An if your wife be not a mad-woman,
And know how well I have deserved the ring,
She would not hold out enemy for ever,
For giving it to me. Well, peace be with you !
                              [*Exeunt Portia and Nerissa.*
Antonio. My Lord Bassanio, let him have the
ring :
Let his deservings and my love withal
Be valued 'gainst your wife's commandment.
Bassanio. Go, Gratiano, run and overtake him ;
Give him the ring, and bring him, if thou canst,
Unto Antonio's house : away ! make haste.
                                             [*Exit Gratiano.*
Come, you and I will thither presently ;
And in the morning early will we both
Fly toward Belmont ; come, Antonio.   [*Exeunt.*

SCENE II.   *The same.   A street.*

Enter PORTIA *and* NERISSA.

Portia. Inquire the Jew's house out, give him
this deed
And let him sign it : we 'll away to-night
And be a day before our husbands home :
This deed will be well welcome to Lorenzo.

Enter GRATIANO.

Gratiano. Fair sir, you are well o'erta'en :
My Lord Bassanio upon more advice
Hath sent you here this ring, and doth entreat
Your company at dinner. .
    Portia.   That cannot be :
His ring I do accept most thankfully :
And so, I pray you, tell him : furthermore,
I pray you, show my youth old Shylock's house.
    Gratiano. That will I do.
    Nerissa.   Sir, I would speak with you.
[*Aside to Portia*] I 'll see if I can get my husband's
                                                ring,
Which I did make him swear to keep for ever.
    Portia. [*Aside to Nerissa*] Thou mayst, I warrant.
We shall have old swearing
That they did give the rings away to men ;
But we 'll outface them, and outswear them too.
[*Aloud*] Away ! make haste : thou know'st where
        I will tarry.
    Nerissa. Come, good sir, will you show me to
        this house ?   [*Exeunt.*

ACT. V.

SCENE I. *Belmont. Avenue to* PORTIA'S *house.*

Enter LORENZO *and* JESSICA.

Lorenzo.

T̲he moon shines bright : in such a night
        as this,
        When the sweet wind did gently kiss the trees
And they did make no noise, in such a night
Troilus methinks mounted the Troyan walls
And sigh'd his soul toward the Grecian tents,
Where Cressid lay that night.
    Jessica.   In such a night
Did Thisbe fearfully o'ertrip the dew
And saw the lion's shadow ere himself
And ran dismay'd away.
    Lorenzo.   In such a night
Stood Dido with a willow in her hand
Upon the wild sea banks and waft her love
To come again to Carthage.
    Jessica.   In such a night
Medea gather'd the enchanted herbs
That did renew old Æson.
    Lorenzo.   In such a night
Did Jessica steal from the wealthy Jew
And with an unthrift love did run from Venice
As far as Belmont.
    Jessica.   In such a night
Did young Lorenzo swear he loved her well,
Stealing her soul with many vows of faith
And ne'er a true one.
    Lorenzo.   In such a night
Did pretty Jessica, like a little shrew,
Slander her love, and he forgave it her.
    Jessica. I would out-night you, did no body
        come ;
But, hark, I hear the footing of a man.

Enter STEPHANO.

Lorenzo. Who comes so fast in silence of the
        night ?
Stephano. A friend.
Lorenzo. A friend ! what friend ? your name, I
        pray you, friend ?

Stephano. Stephano is my name ; and I bring
        word
My mistress will before the break of day
Be here at Belmont : she doth stray about
By holy crosses, where she kneels and prays
For happy wedlock hours.
    Lorenzo.   Who comes with her ?
Stephano. None but a holy hermit and her maid.
I pray you, is my master yet return'd ?
Lorenzo. He is not, nor we have not heard from
        him.
But go we in, I pray thee, Jessica,
And ceremoniously let us prepare
Some welcome for the mistress of the house.

Enter LAUNCELOT.

Launcelot. Sola, sola ! wo ha, ho ! sola, sola !
Lorenzo. Who calls ?
Launcelot. Sola ! did you see Master Lorenzo ?
Master Lorenzo, sola, sola !
Lorenzo. Leave hollaing, man : here.
Launcelot. Sola ! where ? where ?
Lorenzo. Here.
Launcelot. Tell him there 's a post come from
my master, with his horn full of good news : my
master will be here ere morning.   [*Exit.*
Lorenzo. Sweet soul, let 's in, and there expect
        their coming.
And yet no matter : why should we go in ?
My friend Stephano, signify, I pray you,
Within the house, your mistress is at hand ;
And bring your music forth into the air.
                                        [*Exit Stephano.*
How sweet the moonlight sleeps upon this bank !
Here will we sit and let the sounds of music
Creep in our ears ; soft stillness and the night
Become the touches of sweet harmony.
Sit, Jessica. Look how the floor of heaven
Is thick inlaid with patines of bright gold :
There 's not the smallest orb which thou behold'st
But in his motion like an angel sings,
Still quiring to the young-eyed cherubins ;
Such harmony is in immortal souls ;
But whilst this muddy vesture of decay
Doth grossly close it in, we cannot hear it.

Enter Musicians.

Come, ho and wake Diana with a hymn :
With sweetest touches pierce your mistress' ear
And draw her home with music.   [*Music.*
    Jessica. I am never merry when I hear sweet
        music.
    Lorenzo. The reason is, your spirits are atten-
        tive :
For do but note a wild and wanton herd,
Or race of youthful and unhandled colts,
Fetching mad bounds, bellowing and neighing
        loud,
Which is the hot condition of their blood ;
If they but hear perchance a trumpet sound,
Or any air of music touch their ears,
You shall perceive them make a mutual stand,
Their savage eyes turn'd to a modest gaze
By the sweet power of music : therefore the poet
Did feign that Orpheus drew trees, stones and
        floods ;
Since nought so stockish, hard and full of rage,
But music for the time doth change his nature.
The man that hath no music in himself,

Nor is not moved with concord of sweet sounds,
Is fit for treasons, stratagems and spoils ;
The motions of his spirit are dull as night
And his affections dark as Erebus :
Let no such man be trusted.   Mark the music.

Enter PORTIA *and* NERISSA.

Portia.   That light we see is burning in my hall,
How far that little candle throws his beams !
So shines a good deed in a naughty world.
Nerissa.   When the moon shone, we did not see
  the candle.
Portia.   So doth the greater glory dim the less :
A substitute shines brightly as a king
Until a king be by, and then his state
Empties itself, as doth an inland brook
Into the main of waters.   Music ! hark !
Nerissa.   It is your music, madam, of the house.
Portia.   Nothing is good, I see, without respect :
Methinks it sounds much sweeter than by day.
Nerissa.   Silence bestows that virtue on it,
  madam.
Portia.   The crow doth sing as sweetly as the lark
When neither is attended, and I think
The nightingale, if she should sing by day,
When every goose is cackling, would be thought
No better a musician than the wren.
How many things by season season'd are
To their right praise and true perfection !
Peace, ho !   the moon sleeps with Endymion
And would not be awaked.   [*Music ceases.*
Lorenzo.   That is the voice,
Or I am much deceived, of Portia.
Portia.   He knows me as the blind man knows
  the cuckoo,
By the bad voice.
Lorenzo.   Dear lady, welcome home.
Portia.   We have been praying for our husbands'
  healths,
Which speed, we hope, the better for our words.
Are they return'd ?
Lorenzo.   Madam, they are not yet ;
But there is come a messenger before,
To signify their coming.
Portia.   Go in, Nerissa ;
Give order to my servants that they take
No note at all of our being absent hence ;
Nor you, Lorenzo ;   Jessica, nor you.
                            [*A tucket sounds.*
Lorenzo.   Your husband is at hand ;   I hear his
  trumpet :
We are no tell-tales, madam ;   fear you not.
Portia.   This night methinks is but the daylight
  sick ;
It looks a little paler : 'tis a day,
Such as the day is when the sun is hid.

Enter BASSANIO, ANTONIO, GRATIANO, *and their
          followers.*

Bassanio.   We should hold day with the Anti-
  podes,
If you would walk in absence of the sun.
Portia.   Let me give light, but let me not be light ;
For a light wife doth make a heavy husband,
And never be Bassanio so for me :
But God sort all !   You are welcome home, my lord.
Bassanio.   I thank you, madam.   Give welcome
  to my friend.
This is the man, this is Antonio,

To whom I am so infinitely bound.
Portia.   You should in all sense be much bound
  to him,
For, as I hear, he was much bound for you.
Antonio.   No more than I am well acquitted of.
Portia.   Sir, you are very welcome to our house :
It must appear in other ways than words,
Therefore I scant this breathing courtesy.
Gratiano.   [*To Nerissa*] By yonder moon I swear
  you do me wrong ;
In faith, I gave it to the judge's clerk :
Would he were gelt that had it, for my part,
Since you do take it, love, so much at heart.
Portia.   A quarrel, ho, already !   what 's the
  matter ?
Gratiano.   About a hoop of gold, a paltry ring
That she did give me, whose posy was
For all the world like cutler's poetry
Upon a knife, ' Love me, and leave me not.'
Nerissa.   What talk you of the posy or the value ?
You swore to me, when I did give it you,
That you would wear it till your hour of death
And that it should lie with you in your grave :
Though not for me, yet for your vehement oaths,
You should have been respective and have kept it.
Gave it a judge's clerk !   no, God 's my judge,
The clerk will ne'er wear hair on 's face that had it.
Gratiano.   He will, an if he live to be a man.
Nerissa.   Ay, if a woman live to be a man.
Gratiano.   Now, by this hand, I gave it to a youth,
A kind of boy, a little scrubbed boy,
No higher than thyself, the judge's clerk,
A prating boy, that begg'd it as a fee :
I could not for my heart deny it him.
Portia.   You were to blame, I must be plain with
  you,
To part so slightly with your wife's first gift ;
A thing stuck on with oaths upon your finger
And so riveted with faith unto your flesh.
I gave my love a ring and made him swear
Never to part with it ;   and here he stands ;
I dare be sworn for him he would not leave it
Nor pluck it from his finger, for the wealth
That the world masters.   Now, in faith, Gratiano,
You give your wife too unkind a cause of grief :
An 'twere to me, I should be mad at it.
Bassanio. [*Aside*] Why, I were best to cut my left
  hand off
And swear I lost the ring defending it.
Gratiano.   My Lord Bassanio gave his ring away
Unto the judge that begg'd it and indeed
Deserved it too ;   and then the boy, his clerk,
That took some pains in writing, he begg'd mine ;
And neither man nor master would take aught
But the two rings.
Portia.   What ring gave you, my lord ?
Not that, I hope, which you received of me.
Bassanio.   If I could add a lie unto a fault,
I would deny it ;   but you see my finger
Hath not the ring upon it ;   it is gone.
Portia.   Even so void is your false heart of truth.
By heaven, I will ne'er come in your bed
Until I see the ring.
Nerissa.   Nor I in yours
Till I again see mine.
Bassanio.   Sweet Portia,
If you did know to whom I gave the ring,
If you did know for whom I gave the ring
And would conceive for what I gave the ring
And how unwillingly I left the ring,
When nought would be accepted but the ring,

You would abate the strength of your displeasure.

Portia. If you had known the virtue of the ring,
Or half her worthiness that gave the ring,
Or your own honour to contain the ring,
You would not then have parted with the ring.
What man is there so much unreasonable.
If you had pleased to have defended it
With any terms of zeal, wanted the modesty
To urge the thing held as a ceremony ?
Nerissa teaches me what to believe :
I 'll die for 't but some woman had the ring.

Bassanio. No, by my honour, madam, by my
    soul,
No woman had it, but a civil doctor,
Which did refuse three thousand ducats of me
And begg'd the ring ; the which I did deny him
And suffer'd him to go displeased away ;
Even he that did uphold the very life
Of my dear friend. What should I say, sweet lady ?
I was enforced to send it after him ;
I was beset with shame and courtesy ;
My honour would not let ingratitude
So much besmear it. Pardon me, good lady ;
For, by these blessed candles of the night,
Had you been there, I think you would have been.
The ring of me to give the worthy doctor.

Portia. Let not that doctor e'er come near my
    house ;
Since he hath got the jewel that I loved,
And that which you did swear to keep for me,
I will become as liberal as you ;
I 'll not deny him any thing I have,
No, not my body nor my husband's bed :
Know him I shall, I am well sure of it :
Lie not a night from home ; watch me like Argus :
If you do not, if I be left alone,
Now, by mine honour, which is yet mine own,
I 'll have that doctor for my bedfellow.

Nerissa. And I his clerk ; therefore be well
    advised
How you do leave me to mine own protection.

Gratiano. Well, do you so : let not me take him,
    then ;
For if I do, I 'll mar the young clerk's pen.

Antonio. I am the unhappy subject of these
    quarrels.

Portia. Sir, grieve not you ; you are welcome
    notwithstanding.

Bassanio. Portia, forgive me this enforced wrong ;
And, in the hearing of these many friends
I swear to thee, even by thine own fair eyes,
Wherein I see myself—

Portia.   Mark you but that !
In both my eyes he doubly sees himself ;
In each eye, one : swear by your double self,
And there 's an oath of credit.

Bassanio.   Nay, but hear me :
Pardon this fault, and by my soul I swear
I never more will break an oath with thee.

Antonio. I once did lend my body for his wealth
Which, but for him that had your husband's ring,
Had quite miscarried : I dare be bound again,
My soul upon the forfeit, that your lord
Will never more break faith advisedly.

Portia. Then you shall be his surety. Give him
this

And bid him keep it better than the other.

Antonio. Here, Lord Bassanio ; swear to keep
    this ring.

Bassanio. By heaven, it is the same I gave the
    doctor !

Portia. I had it of him : pardon me, Bassanio ;
For, by this ring, the doctor lay with me.

Nerissa. And pardon me, my gentle Gratiano ;
For that same scrubbed boy, the doctor's clerk,
In lieu of this last night did lie with me.

Gratiano. Why, this is like the mending of high-
    ways
In summer, where the ways are fair enough :
What, are we cuckolds ere we have deserved it ?

Portia. Speak not so grossly. You are all
    amazed :
Here is a letter ; read it at your leisure ;
It comes from Padua, from Bellario ;
There you shall find that Portia was the doctor,
Nerissa there her clerk : Lorenzo here
Shall witness I set forth as soon as you
And even but now return'd ; I have not yet
Enter'd my house. Antonio, you are welcome ;
And I have better news in store for you
Than you expect : unseal this letter soon ;
There you shall find three of your argosies
Are richly come to harbour suddenly :
You shall not know by what strange accident
I chanced on this letter.

Antonio.   I am dumb.

Bassanio. Were you the doctor and I knew you
    not ?

Gratiano. Were you the clerk that is to make me
    cuckold ?

Nerissa. Ay, but the clerk that never means to
    do it,
Unless he live until he be a man.

Bassanio. Sweet doctor, you shall be my bed-
    fellow :
When I am absent, then lie with my wife.

Antonio. Sweet lady, you have given me life and
    living ;
For here I read for certain that my ships
Are safely come to road.

Portia.   How now, Lorenzo !
My clerk hath some good comforts too for you.

Nerissa. Ay, and I 'll give them him without a
    fee.
There do I give to you and Jessica,
From the rich Jew, a special deed of gift,
After his death, of all he dies possess'd of.

Lorenzo. Fair ladies, you drop manna in the way
Of starved people.

Portia.   It is almost morning,
And yet I am sure you are not satisfied
Of these events at full. Let us go in ;
And charge us there upon inter'gatories,
And we will answer all things faithfully.

Gratiano. Let it be so : the first inter'gatory
That my Nerissa shall be sworn on is,
Whether till the next night she had rather stay
Or go to bed now, being two hours to day :
But were the day come, I should wish it dark,
That I were couching with the doctor's clerk.
Well, while I live I 'll fear no other thing
So sore as keeping safe Nerissa's ring. [*Exeunt.*

AS YOU LIKE IT

DRAMATIS PERSONÆ

DUKE, *living in banishment.*

FREDERICK, *his brother, and usurper of his dominions.*

AMIENS,
JAQUES, } *lords attending on the banished duke.*

LE BEAU, *a courtier attending upon* Frederick.

CHARLES, *wrestler to* Frederick.

OLIVER,
JAQUES, } *sons of* Sir Rowland de Boys.
ORLANDO,

ADAM,
DENNIS, } *servants to* Oliver.

TOUCHSTONE, *a clown.*

SIR OLIVER MARTEXT, *a vicar.*

CORIN,
SILVIUS, } *shepherds.*

WILLIAM, *a country fellow, in love with* Audrey.

A person representing Hymen.

ROSALIND, *daughter to the banished* Duke.

CELIA, *daughter to* Frederick.

PHEBE, *a shepherdess.*

AUDREY, *a country wench.*

Lords, pages, *and* attendants, &c.

SCENE : Oliver's house ; Duke Frederick's court ;
and the Forest of Arden.

ACT I.

SCENE I. *Orchard of* OLIVER'S *house.*

Enter ORLANDO *and* ADAM.

Orlando.

As I remember, Adam, it was upon this fashion; bequeathed me by will but poor a thousand crowns, and, as thou sayest, charged my brother, on his blessing, to breed me well : and there begins my sadness. My brother Jaques he keeps at school, and report speaks goldenly of his profit : for my part, he keeps me rustically at home, or, to speak more properly, stays me here at home unkept ; for call you that keeping for a gentleman of my birth, that differs not from the stalling of an ox ? His horses are bred better ; for, besides that they are fair with their feeding, they are taught their manage, and to that end riders dearly hired : but I, his brother, gain nothing under him but growth ; for the which his animals on his dunghills are as much bound to him as I. Besides this nothing that he so plentifully gives me, the something that nature gave me his countenance seems to take from me : he lets me feed with his hinds, bars me the place of a brother, and, as much as in him lies, mines my gentility with my education. This is it, Adam, that grieves me ; and the spirit of my father, which I think is within me, begins to mutiny against this servitude : I will no longer endure it, though yet I know no wise remedy how to avoid it.

Adam. Yonder comes my master, your brother.

Orlando. Go apart, Adam, and thou shalt hear how he will shake me up.

Enter OLIVER.

Oliver. Now, sir ! what make you here ?

Orlando. Nothing : I am not taught to make anything.

Oliver. What mar you then, sir ?

Orlando. Marry, sir, I am helping you to mar that which God made, a poor unworthy brother of yours, with idleness.

Oliver. Marry, sir, be better employed, and be naught awhile.

Orlando. Shall I keep your hogs and eat husks with them ? What prodigal portion have I spent, that I should come to such penury ?

Oliver. Know you where you are, sir ?

Orlando. O, sir, very well : here in your orchard.

Oliver. Know you before whom, sir ?

Orlando. Ay, better than him I am before knows me. I know you are my eldest brother ; and, in the gentle condition of blood, you should so know me. The courtesy of nations allows you my better, in that you are the first-born ; but the same tradition takes not away my blood, were there twenty brothers betwixt us : I have as much of my father in me as you ; albeit, I confess, your coming before me is nearer to his reverence.

Oliver. What, boy !

Orlando. Come, come, elder brother, you are too young in this.

Oliver. Wilt thou lay hands on me, villain ?

Orlando. I am no villain ; I am the youngest son of Sir Rowland de Boys ; he was my father, and he is thrice a villain that says such a father begot villains. Wert thou not my brother, I would not take this hand from thy throat till this other had pulled out thy tongue for saying so : thou hast railed on thyself.

Adam. Sweet masters, be patient : for your father's remembrance, be at accord.

Oliver. Let me go, I say.

Orlando. I will not, till I please : you shall hear me. My father charged you in his will to give me good education : you have trained me like a peasant, obscuring and hiding from me all gentleman-like qualities. The spirit of my father grows strong in me, and I will no longer endure it : therefore allow me such exercises as may become a gentleman, or give me the poor allottery my father left me by testament ; with that I will go buy my fortunes.

Oliver. And what wilt thou do ? beg, when that is spent ? Well, sir, get you in : I will not long be troubled with you ; you shall have some part of your will : I pray you, leave me.

Orlando. I will no further offend you than becomes me for my good.

Oliver. Get you with him, you old dog.

Adam. Is ' old dog ' my reward ? Most true, I have lost my teeth in your service. God be with my old master ! he would not have spoke such a word. [*Exeunt Orlando and Adam.*

Oliver. Is it even so ? begin you to grow upon me ? I will physic your rankness, and yet give no thousand crowns neither. Holla, Dennis !

Enter DENNIS.

Dennis. Calls your worship ?

Oliver. Was not Charles, the duke's wrestler, here to speak with me ?

Dennis. So please you, he is here at the door and importunes access to you.

Oliver. Call him in. [*Exit Dennis.*] 'Twill be a good way ; and to-morrow the wrestling is.

Enter CHARLES.

Charles. Good morrow to your worship.

Oliver. Good Monsieur Charles, what 's the new news at the new court ?

Charles. There 's no news at the court, sir, but the old news : that is, the old duke is banished by his younger brother the new duke ; and three or four loving lords have put themselves into voluntary exile with him, whose lands and revenues enrich the new duke ; therefore he gives them good leave to wander.

Oliver. Can you tell if Rosalind, the duke's daughter, be banished with her father ?

Charles. O, no ; for the duke's daughter, her cousin, so loves her, being ever from their cradles bred together, that she would have followed her exile, or have died to stay behind her. She is at the court, and no less beloved of her uncle than his own daughter ; and never two ladies loved as they do.

Oliver. Where will the old duke live ?

Charles. They say he is already in the forest of Arden, and a many merry men with him ; and there they live like the old Robin Hood of England : they say many young gentlemen flock to him every day, and fleet the time carelessly, as they did in the golden world.

Oliver. What, you wrestle to-morrow before the new duke ?

Charles. Marry, do I, sir ; and I came to acquaint you with a matter. I am given, sir, secretly to understand that your younger brother Orlando hath a disposition to come in disguised against me to try a fall. To-morrow, sir, I wrestle for my credit ; and he that escapes me without some broken limb shall acquit him well. Your brother is but young and tender ; and, for your love, I would be loath to foil him, as I must, for my own honour, if he come in : therefore, out of my love to you, I came hither to acquaint you withal, that either you might stay him from his intendment or brook such disgrace well as he shall run into, in that it is a thing of his own search and altogether against my will.

Oliver. Charles, I thank thee for thy love to me, which thou shalt find I will most kindly requite. I had myself notice of my brother's purpose herein and have by underhand means laboured to dissuade him from it, but he is resolute. I 'll tell thee, Charles : it is the stubbornest young fellow of France, full of ambition, an envious emulator of every man's good parts, a secret and villanous contriver against me his natural brother : therefore use thy discretion ; I had as lief thou didst break his neck as his finger. And thou wert best look to 't ; for if thou dost him any slight disgrace or if he do not mightily grace himself on thee, he will practise against thee by poison, entrap thee by some treacherous device and never leave thee till he hath ta'en thy life by some indirect means or other ; for, I assure thee, and almost with tears I speak it, there is not one so young and so villanous this day living. I speak but brotherly of him ; but should I anatomize him to thee as he is, I must blush and weep and thou must look pale and wonder.

Charles. I am heartily glad I came hither to you. If he come to-morrow, I 'll give him his payment : if ever he go alone again, I 'll never wrestle for prize more : and so God keep your worship !

Oliver. Farewell, good Charles. [*Exit Charles.*] Now will I stir this gamester : I hope I shall see an end of him ; for my soul, yet I know not why, hates nothing more than he. Yet he 's gentle, never schooled and yet learned, full of noble device, of all sorts enchantingly beloved, and indeed so much in the heart of the world, and especially of my own people, who best know him, that I am altogether misprised : but it shall not be so long ; this wrestler shall clear all : nothing remains but that I kindle the boy thither ; which now I 'll go about. [*Exit.*

SCENE II. *Lawn before the DUKE's palace.*

Enter CELIA and ROSALIND.

Celia. I pray thee, Rosalind, sweet my coz, be merry.

Rosalind. Dear Celia, I show more mirth than I am mistress of ; and would you yet I were merrier ? Unless you could teach me to forget a banished father, you must not learn me how to remember any extraordinary pleasure.

Celia. Herein I see thou lovest me not with the full weight that I love thee. If my uncle, thy banished father, had banished thy uncle, the duke my father, so thou hadst been still with me, I could have taught my love to take thy father for mine : so wouldst thou, if the truth of thy love to me were so righteously tempered as mine is to thee.

Rosalind. Well, I will forget the condition of my estate, to rejoice in yours.

Celia. You know my father hath no child but I, nor none is like to have : and, truly, when he dies, thou shalt be his heir, for what he hath taken away from thy father perforce, I will render thee again in affection ; by mine honour, I will ; and when I break that oath, let me turn monster : therefore, my sweet Rose, my dear Rose, be merry.

Rosalind. From henceforth I will, coz, and devise sports. Let me see ; what think you of falling in love ?

Celia. Marry, I prithee, do, to make sport withal : but love no man in good earnest ; nor no further in sport neither than with safety of a pure blush thou mayst in honour come off again.

Rosalind. What shall be our sport, then ?

Celia. Let us sit and mock the good housewife Fortune from her wheel that her gifts may henceforth be bestowed equally.

Rosalind. I would we could do so, for her benefits are mightily misplaced, and the bountiful blind woman doth most mistake in her gifts to women.

Celia. 'Tis true ; for those that she makes fair she scarce makes honest, and those that she makes honest she makes very ill-favouredly.

Rosalind. Nay, now thou goest from Fortune's office to Nature's : Fortune reigns in gifts of the world, not in the lineaments of Nature.

Enter TOUCHSTONE.

Celia. No ? when Nature hath made a fair creature, may she not by Fortune fall into the fire ? Though Nature hath given us wit to flout at Fortune, hath not Fortune sent in this fool to cut off the argument ?

Rosalind. Indeed, there is Fortune too hard for Nature, when Fortune makes Nature's natural the cutter-off of Nature's wit.

Celia. Peradventure this is not Fortune's work neither, but Nature's : who perceiveth our natural wits too dull to reason of such goddesses and hath sent this natural for our whetstone ; for always the dulness of the fool is the whetstone of the wits. How now, wit ! whither wander you ?

Touchstone. Mistress, you must come away to your father.

Celia. Were you made the messenger ?

Touchstone. No, by mine honour, but I was bid to come for you.

Rosalind. Where learned you that oath, fool ?

Touchstone. Of a certain knight that swore by his honour they were good pancakes and swore by his honour the mustard was naught : now I 'll stand to it, the pancakes were naught and the mustard was good and yet was not the knight forsworn.

Celia. How prove you that, in the great heap of your knowledge ?

Rosalind. Ay, marry, now unmuzzle your wisdom.

Touchstone. Stand you both forth now : stroke your chins, and swear by your beards that I am a knave.

Celia. By our beards, if we had them, thou art.

Touchstone. By my knavery, if I had it, then I were ; but if you swear by that that is not, you are not forsworn : no more was this knight, swearing by his honour, for he never had any : or if he had, he had sworn it away before ever he saw those pancakes or that mustard.

Celia. Prithee, who is 't that thou meanest ?

Touchstone. One that old Frederick, your father, loves.

Celia. My father's love is enough to honour him : enough ! speak no more of him ; you 'll be whipped for taxation one of these days.

Touchstone. The more pity that fools may not speak wisely what wise men do foolishly.

Celia. By my troth, thou sayest true ; for since the little wit that fools have was silenced, the little foolery that wise men have makes a great show. Here comes Monsieur Le Beau.

Rosalind. With his mouth full of news.

Celia. Which he will put on us, as pigeons feed their young.

Rosalind. Then shall we be news-crammed.

Celia. All the better ; we shall be the more marketable.

Enter LE BEAU.

Bon jour, Monsieur Le Beau : what 's the news ?

Le Beau. Fair princess, you have lost much good sport.

Celia. Sport ! of what colour ?

Le Beau. What colour, madam ! how shall I answer you ?

Rosalind. As wit and fortune will.

Touchstone. Or as the Destinies decree.

Celia. Well said : that was laid on with a trowel.

Touchstone. Nay, if I keep not my rank.—

Rosalind. Thou losest thy old smell.

Le Beau. You amaze me, ladies : I would have told you of good wrestling, which you have lost the sight of.

Rosalind. Yet tell us the manner of the wrestling.

Le Beau. I will tell you the beginning and, if it please your ladyships, you may see the end ; for the best is yet to do ; and here, where you are, they are coming to perform it.

Celia. Well, the beginning that is dead and buried.

Le Beau. There comes an old man and his three sons,—

Celia. I could match this beginning with an old tale.

Le Beau. Three proper young men, of excellent growth and presence.

Rosalind. With bills on their necks, ' Be it known unto all men by these presents.'

Le Beau. The eldest of the three wrestled with Charles, the duke's wrestler; which Charles in a moment threw him and broke three of his ribs, that there is little hope of life in him : so he served the second, and so the third. Yonder they lie . the poor old man, their father, making such pitiful dole over them that all the beholders take his part with weeping.

Rosalind. Alas !

Touchstone. But what is the sport, monsieur, that the ladies have lost ?

Le Beau. Why, this that I speak of.

Touchstone. Thus men may grow wiser every day : it is the first time that ever I heard breaking of ribs was sport for ladies.

Celia. Or I, I promise thee.

Rosalind. But is there any else longs to see this broken music in his sides ? is there yet another dotes upon rib-breaking ? Shall we see this wrestling, cousin ?

Le Beau. You must, if you stay here : for here is the place appointed for the wrestling, and they are ready to perform it.

Celia. Yonder, sure, they are coming : let us now stay and see it.

Flourish. Enter DUKE FREDERICK, Lords. ORLANDO, CHARLES, *and* Attendants.

Duke Frederick. Come on : since the youth will not be entreated, his own peril on his forwardness.

Rosalind. Is yonder the man ?

Le Beau. Even he, madam.

Celia. Alas, he is too young ! yet he looks successfully.

Duke Frederick. How now, daughter and cousin !

are you crept hither to see the wrestling?

Rosalind. Ay, my liege, so please you give us leave.

Duke Frederick. You will take little delight in it, I can tell you ; there is such odds in the man. In pity of the challenger's youth I would fain dissuade him, but he will not be entreated. Speak to him, ladies ; see if you can move him.

Celia. Call him hither, good Monsieur Le Beau.

Duke Frederick. Do so : I 'll not be by.

Le Beau. Monsieur the challenger, the princesses call for you.

Orlando. I attend them with all respect and duty.

Rosalind. Young man, have you challenged Charles the wrestler ?

Orlando. No, fair princess ; he is the general challenger : I come but in, as others do, to try with him the strength of my youth.

Celia. Young gentleman, your spirits are too bold for your years. You have seen cruel proof of this man's strength : if you saw yourself with your eyes or knew yourself with your judgement, the fear of your adventure would counsel you to a more equal enterprise. We pray you, for your own sake, to embrace your own safety and give over this attempt.

Rosalind. Do, young sir ; your reputation shall not therefore be misprised : we will make it our suit to the duke that the wrestling might not go forward.

Orlando. I beseech you, punish me not with your hard thoughts ; wherein I confess me much guilty, to deny so fair and excellent ladies any thing. But let your fair eyes and gentle wishes go with me to my trial : wherein if I be foiled, there is but one shamed that was never gracious ; if killed, but one dead that is willing to be so : I shall do my friends no wrong, for I have none to lament me, the world no injury, for in it I have nothing ; only in the world I fill up a place, which may be better supplied when I have made it empty.

Rosalind. The little strength that I have, I would it were with you.

Celia. And mine, to eke out hers.

Rosalind. Fare you well : pray heaven I be deceived in you !

Celia. Your heart's desires be with you !

Charles. Come, where is this young gallant that is so desirous to lie with his mother earth ?

Orlando. Ready, sir ; but his will hath in it a more modest working.

Duke Frederick. You shall try but one fall.

Charles. No, I warrant your grace, you shall not entreat him to a second, that have so mightily persuaded him from a first.

Orlando. An you mean to mock me after, you should not have mocked me before : but come your ways.

Rosalind. Now Hercules be thy speed, young man !

Celia. I would I were invisible, to catch the strong fellow by the leg. [*They wrestle.*

Rosalind. O excellent young man !

Celia. If I had a thunderbolt in mine eye, I can tell who should down.

[*Shout. Charles is thrown.*

Duke Frederick. No more, no more.

Orlando. Yes, I beseech your grace : I am not yet well breathed.

Duke Frederick. How dost thou, Charles ?

Le Beau. He cannot speak, my lord.

Duke Frederick. Bear him away. What is thy name, young man?

Orlando. Orlando, my liege ; the youngest son of Sir Rowland de Boys.

Duke Frederick. I would thou hadst been son to some man else :
The world esteem'd thy father honourable,
But I did find him still mine enemy :
Thou shouldst have better pleased me with this deed,
Hadst thou descended from another house.
But fare thee well ; thou art a gallant youth :
I would thou hadst told me of another father.

[*Exeunt Duke Frederick, train and Le Beau.*

Celia. Were I my father, coz, would I do this ?

Orlando. I am more proud to be Sir Rowland's son,
His youngest son ; and would not change that calling,
To be adopted heir to Frederick.

Rosalind. My father loved Sir Rowland as his soul,
And all the world was of my father's mind :
Had I before known this young man his son,
I should have given him tears unto entreaties,
Ere he should thus have ventured.

Celia.   Gentle cousin,
Let us go thank him and encourage him :
My father's rough and envious disposition
Sticks me at heart. Sir, you have well deserved :
If you do keep your promises in love
But justly, as you have exceeded all promise,
Your mistress shall be happy.

Rosalind.   Gentleman,

[*Giving him a chain from her neck.*

Wear this for me, one out of suits with fortune,
That could give more, but that her hand lacks means.
Shall we go, coz ?

Celia.   Ay. Fare you well, fair gentleman.

Orlando. Can I not say, I thank you ? My better parts
Are all thrown down, and that which here stands up
Is but a quintain, a mere lifeless block.

Rosalind. He calls us back : my pride fell with my fortunes ;
I 'll ask him what he would. Did you call, sir ?
Sir, you have wrestled well and overthrown
More than your enemies.

Celia.   Will you go, coz ?

Rosalind. Have with you. Fare you well.

[*Exeunt Rosalind and Celia.*

Orlando. What passion hangs these weights upon my tongue ?
I cannot speak to her, yet she urged conference.
O poor Orlando, thou art overthrown !
Or Charles or something weaker masters thee.

Re-enter LE BEAU.

Le Beau. Good sir, I do in friendship counsel you
To leave this place. Albeit you have deserved
High commendation, true applause and love,
Yet such is now the duke's condition
That he misconstrues all that you have done.
The duke is humorous : what he is indeed,
More suits you to conceive than I to speak of.

Orlando. I thank you, sir : and, pray you, tell me this ;
Which of the two was daughter of the duke
That here was at the wrestling ?

Le Beau. Neither his daughter, if we judge by manners ;

But yet indeed the lesser is his daughter :
The other is daughter to the banish'd duke,
And here detain'd by her usurping uncle, -
To keep his daughter company ; whose loves
Are dearer than the natural bond of sisters. ~affection~
But I can tell you that of late this duke
Hath ta'en displeasure 'gainst his gentle niece,
Grounded upon no other argument
But that the people praise her for her virtues
And pity her for her good father's sake ;
And, on my life, his malice 'gainst the lady
Will suddenly break forth. Sir, fare you well :
Hereafter, in a better world than this,
I shall desire more love and knowledge of you.

Orlando. I rest much bounden to you : fare you
well. [*Exit Le Beau.*
Thus must I from the smoke into the smother ;
From tyrant duke unto a tyrant brother :
But heavenly Rosalind ! [*Exit.*

ORLANDO WANTS ROSALIND!

SCENE III. *A room in the palace.*

Enter CELIA *and* ROSALIND.

Celia. Why, cousin ! why, Rosalind ! Cupid
have mercy ! not a word ?

Rosalind. Not one to throw at a dog.

Celia. No, thy words are too precious to be cast
away upon curs ; throw some of them at me ; come,
lame me with reasons.

Rosalind. Then there were two cousins laid up ;
when the one should be lamed with reasons and the
other mad without any.

Celia. But is all this for your father ?

Rosalind. No, some of it is for my child's father.
O, how full of briers is this working-day world !

Celia. They are but burs, cousin, thrown upon
thee in holiday foolery : if we walk not in the trodden
paths, our very petticoats will catch them.

Rosalind. I could shake them off my coat : these
burs are in my heart.

Celia. Hem them away.

Rosalind. I would try, if I could cry ' hem ' and
have him.

Celia. Come, come, wrestle with thy affections.

Rosalind. O, they take the part of a better wrestler
than myself !

Celia. O, a good wish upon you ! you will try
in time, in despite of a fall. But, turning these jests
out of service, let us talk in good earnest : is it
possible, on such a sudden, you should fall into so
strong a liking with old Sir Rowland's youngest
son ?

Rosalind. The duke my father loved his father
dearly.

Celia. Doth it therefore ensue that you should
love his son dearly ? By this kind of chase, I should
hate him, for my father hated his father dearly ;
yet I hate not Orlando.

Rosalind. No, faith, hate him not, for my sake.

Celia. Why should I not ? doth he not deserve
well ?

Rosalind. Let me love him for that, and do you
love him because I do. Look, here comes the
duke.

Celia. With his eyes full of anger.

Enter DUKE FREDERICK, *with* Lords.

Duke Frederick. Mistress, dispatch you with
your safest haste
And get you from our court.

Rosalind. Me, uncle ?

Duke Frederick. You, cousin :
Within these ten days if that thou be'st found
So near our public court as twenty miles,
Thou diest for it.

Rosalind. I do beseech your grace,
Let me the knowledge of my fault bear with me :
If with myself I hold intelligence
Or have acquaintance with mine own desires,
If that I do not dream or be not frantic,—
As I do trust I am not—then, dear uncle,
Never so much as in a thought unborn
Did I offend your highness.

Duke Frederick. Thus do all traitors :
If their purgation did consist in words,
They are as innocent as grace itself :
Let it suffice thee that I trust thee not.

Rosalind. Yet your mistrust cannot make me a
traitor :
Tell me whereon the likelihood depends.

Duke Frederick. Thou art thy father's daughter ;
there 's enough. ~banished becau~

Rosalind. So was I when your highness took his
dukedom ; D
So was I when your highness banish'd him :
Treason is not inherited, my lord ;
Or, if we did derive it from our friends,
What 's that to me ? my father was no traitor :
Then, good my liege, mistake me not so much
To think my poverty is treacherous.

Celia. Dear sovereign, hear me speak.

Duke Frederick. Ay, Celia ; we stay'd her for
your sake,
Else had she with her father ranged along.

Celia. I did not then entreat to have her stay ;
It was your pleasure and your own remorse :
I was too young that time to value her ;
But now I know her : if she be a traitor,
Why so am I ; we still have slept together,
Rose at an instant, learn'd, play'd, eat together,
And wheresoe'er we went, like Juno's swans,
Still we went coupled and inseparable.

Duke Frederick. She is too subtle for thee ; and
her smoothness,
Her very silence and her patience
Speak to the people, and they pity her.
Thou art a fool : she robs thee of thy name ;
And thou wilt show more bright and seem more
virtuous
When she is gone. Then open not thy lips :
Firm and irrevocable is my doom
Which I have pass'd upon her ; she is banish'd.

Celia. Pronounce that sentence then on me,
my liege :
I cannot live out of her company.

Duke Frederick. You are a fool. You, niece,
provide yourself :
If you outstay the time, upon mine honour,
And in the greatness of my word, you die.
[*Exeunt Duke Frederick and Lords.*

Celia. O my poor Rosalind, whither wilt thou
go ?
Wilt thou change fathers ? I will give thee mine.
I charge thee, be not thou more grieved than I am.

Rosalind. I have more cause.

Celia. Thou hast not, cousin ;

Feminists → Gone to find banished duke.

Prithee, be cheerful : know'st thou not, the duke
Hath banish'd me, his daughter ?
  Rosalind.   That he hath not.
  Celia.   No, hath not ? Rosalind lacks then the love
Which teacheth thee that thou and I am one :
Shall we be sunder'd ? shall we part, sweet girl ?
No : let my father seek another heir.
Therefore devise with me how we may fly,
Whither to go and what to bear with us ;
And do not seek to take your change upon you,
To bear your griefs yourself and leave me out ;
For, by this heaven, now at our sorrows pale,
Say what thou canst, I 'll go along with thee.
  Rosalind.   Why, whither shall we go ?
  Celia.   To seek my uncle in the forest of Arden.
  Rosalind.   Alas, what danger will it be to us,
Maids as we are, to travel forth so far !
Beauty provoketh thieves sooner than gold.
  Celia.   I 'll put myself in poor and mean attire
And with a kind of umber smirch my face ;
The like do you : so shall we pass along
And never stir assailants.
  Rosalind.   Were it not better,
Because that I am more than common tall,
That I did suit me all points like a man ?
A gallant curtle-axe upon my thigh,
A boar-spear in my hand ; and—in my heart
Lie there what hidden woman's fear there will—
We 'll have a swashing and a martial outside,
As many other mannish cowards have
That do outface it with their semblances.
  Celia.   What shall I call thee when thou art a man ?
  Rosalind.   I 'll have no worse a name than Jove's own page ;
And therefore look you call me Ganymede.
But what will you be call'd ?
  Celia.   Something that hath a reference to my state ;
No longer Celia, but Aliena.
  Rosalind.   But, cousin, what if we assay'd to steal
The clownish fool out of your father's court ?
Would he not be a comfort to our travel ?
  Celia.   He 'll go along o'er the wide world with me ;
Leave me alone to woo him. Let 's away,
And get our jewels and our wealth together,
Devise the fittest time and safest way
To hide us from pursuit that will be made
After my flight. Now go we in content
To liberty and not to banishment.   [*Exeunt.*

ACT II.

SCENE I. *The forest of Arden.*

  Enter DUKE senior, AMIENS, *and two or three
Lords, like foresters.*

    Duke Senior.

Now, my co-mates and brothers in exile,
Hath not old custom made this life more sweet
Than that of painted pomp ? Are not these woods
More free from peril than the envious court ?
Here feel we but the penalty of Adam,
The seasons' difference, as the icy fang
And churlish chiding of the winter's wind,
Which, when it bites and blows upon my body,
Even till I shrink with cold, I smile and say

' This is no flattery : these are counsellors
That feelingly persuade me what I am.'
Sweet are the uses of adversity,
Which, like the toad, ugly and venomous,
Wears yet a precious jewel in his head ;
And this our life exempt from public haunt
Finds tongues in trees, books in the running brooks,
Sermons in stones and good in every thing.
I would not change it.
  Amiens.   Happy is your grace,
That can translate the stubbornness of fortune
Into so quiet and so sweet a style.
  Duke Senior.   Come, shall we go and kill us venison ?
And yet it irks me the poor dappled fools,
Being native burghers of this desert city,
Should in their own confines with forked heads
Have their round haunches gored.
  First Lord.   Indeed, my lord,
The melancholy Jaques grieves at that,
And, in that kind, swears you do more usurp
Than doth your brother, that hath banish'd you.
To-day my Lord of Amiens and myself
Did steal behind him as he lay along
Under an oak whose antique root peeps out
Upon the brook that brawls along this wood :
To the which place a poor sequester'd stag,
That from the hunter's aim had ta'en a hurt,
Did come to languish, and indeed, my lord,
The wretched animal heaved forth such groans
That their discharge did stretch his leathern coat
Almost to bursting, and the big round tears
Coursed one another down his innocent nose
In piteous chase ; and thus the hairy fool,
Much marked of the melancholy Jaques,
Stood on the extremest verge of the swift brook,
Augmenting it with tears.
  Duke Senior.   But what said Jaques ?
Did he not moralize this spectacle ?
  First Lord.   O, yes, into a thousand similes.
First, for his weeping into the needless stream ;
' Poor deer,' quoth he, ' thou makest a testament
As worldlings do, giving thy sum of more
To that which had too much :' then, being there alone,
Left and abandon'd of his velvet friends,
' 'Tis right,' quoth he ; ' thus misery doth part
The flux of company :' anon a careless herd,
Full of the pasture, jumps along by him
And never stays to greet him ; ' Ay,' quoth Jaques,
' Sweep on, you fat and greasy citizens ;
'Tis just the fashion : wherefore do you look
Upon that poor and broken bankrupt there ? '
Thus most invectively he pierceth through
The body of the country, city, court,
Yea, and of this our life, swearing that we
Are mere usurpers, tyrants and what 's worse,
To fright the animals and to kill them up
In their assign'd and native dwelling-place.
  Duke Senior.   And did you leave him in this contemplation ?
  Second Lord.   We did, my lord, weeping and commenting
Upon the sobbing deer.
  Duke Senior.   Show me the place :
I love to cope him in these sullen fits,
For then he 's full of matter.
  First Lord.   I 'll bring you to him straight.
                      [*Exeunt.*

SCENE II. *A room in the palace.*

Enter DUKE FREDERICK, *with* Lords.

Duke Frederick. Can it be possible that no man
saw them ?
It cannot be : some villains of my court
Are of consent and sufferance in this.
   First Lord. I cannot hear of any that did see her.
The ladies, her attendants of her chamber,
Saw her a-bed, and in the morning early
They found the bed untreasured. of their mistress.
   Second Lord. My lord, the roynish clown, at
      whom so oft
Your grace was wont to laugh, is also missing.
Hisperia, the princess' gentlewoman,
Confesses that she secretly o'erheard
Your daughter and her cousin much commend
The parts and graces of the wrestler
That did but lately foil the sinewy Charles ;
And she believes, wherever they are gone,
That youth is surely in their company.
   Duke Frederick. Send to his brother ; fetch that
      gallant hither ;
If he be absent, bring his brother to me ;
I 'll make him find him : do this suddenly,
And let not search and inquisition quail
To bring again these foolish runaways.   [*Exeunt.*

SCENE III. *Before* OLIVER'S *house.*

Enter ORLANDO *and* ADAM, *meeting.*

Orlando. Who 's there ?
Adam. What, my young master ? O my gentle
master !
O my sweet master ! O you memory
Of old Sir Rowland ! why, what make you here ?
Why are you virtuous ? why do people love you ?
And wherefore are you gentle, strong and valiant ?
Why would you be so fond to overcome
The bonny priser of the humorous duke ?
Your praise is come too swiftly home before you.
Know you not, master, to some kind of men
Their graces serve them but as enemies ?
No more do yours : your virtues, gentle master,
Are sanctified and holy traitors to you.
O; what a world is this, when what is comely
Envenoms him that bears it !
   Orlando. Why, what 's the matter ?
   Adam.   O unhappy youth !
Come not within these doors ; within this roof
The enemy of all your graces lives :
Your brother—no, no brother ; yet the son—
Yet not the son, I will not call him son
Of him I was about to call his father—
Hath heard your praises, and. this night he means
To burn the lodging where you use to lie
And you within it : if he fail of that,
He will have other means to cut you off.
I overheard him and his practices.
This is no place ; this house is but a butchery:
Abhor it, fear it, do not enter it.
   Orlando. Why, whither, Adam, wouldst thou
      have me go ?
   Adam. No matter whither, so you come not
here.
   Orlando. What, wouldst thou have me go and
      beg my food ?
Or with a base and boisterous sword enforce
A thievish living on the common road ?

This I must do, or know not what to do :
Yet this I will not do, do how I can ;
I rather will subject me to the malice
Of a diverted blood and bloody brother.
   Adam. But do not so. I have five hundred
      crowns,
The thrifty hire I saved under your father,
Which I did store to be my foster-nurse
When service should in my old limbs lie lame
And unregarded age in corners thrown :
Take that, and He that doth the ravens feed,
Yea, providently caters for the sparrow,
Be comfort to my age ! Here is the gold ;
All this I give you. Let me be your servant :
Though I look old, yet I am strong and lusty ;
For in my youth I never did apply
Hot and rebellious liquors in my blood,
Nor did not with unbashful forehead woo
The means of weakness and debility ;
Therefore my age is as a lusty winter,
Frosty, but kindly : let me go with you ;
I 'll do the service of a younger man
In all your business and necessities.
   Orlando. O good old man, how well in thee
      appears
The constant service of the antique world,
When service sweat for duty, not for meed !
Thou art not for the fashion of these times,
Where none will sweat but for promotion,
And having that, do choke their service up
Even with the having : it is not so with thee.
But, poor old man, thou prunest a rotten tree,
That cannot so much as a blossom yield
In lieu of all thy pains and husbandry.
But come thy ways ; we 'll go along together.
And ere we have thy youthful wages spent,
We 'll light upon some settled low content.
   Adam. Master, go on, and I will follow thee,
To the last gasp, with truth and loyalty.
From seventeen years till now almost fourscore
Here lived I, but now live here no more.
At seventeen years many their fortunes seek :
But at fourscore it is too late a week :
Yet fortune cannot recompense me better
Than to die well and not my master's debtor.
                                    [*Exeunt.*

SCENE IV. *The Forest of Arden.*

Enter ROSALIND *for* GANYMEDE, CELIA *for* ALIENA,
and TOUCHSTONE.

Rosalind. O Jupiter, how weary are my spirits !
Touchstone. I care not for my spirits, if my legs
were not weary.
Rosalind. I could find in my heart to disgrace my
man's apparel and to cry like a woman ; but I must
comfort the weaker vessel, as doublet and hose
ought to show itself courageous to petticoat : therefore courage, good Aliena !
Celia. I pray you, bear with me ; I cannot go
no further.
Touchstone. For my part, I had rather bear with
you than bear you ; yet, I should bear no cross if
I did bear you, for I think you have no money in
your purse.
Rosalind. Well, this is the forest of Arden.
Touchstone. Ay, now am I in Arden ; the more
fool I ; when I was at home, I was in a better place :
but travellers must be content.
Rosalind. Ay, be so, good Touchstone.

Enter Corin *and* Silvius.

Look you, who comes here ; a young man and an old in solemn talk.

Corin.   That is the way to make her scorn you still.

Silvius.   O Corin, that thou knew'st how I do love her !

Corin.   I partly guess ; for I have loved ere now.

Silvius.   No, Corin, being old, thou canst not guess,
Though in thy youth thou wast as true a lover
As ever sigh'd upon a midnight pillow :
But if thy love were ever like to mine—
As sure I think did never man love so—
How many actions most ridiculous
Hast thou been drawn to by thy fantasy ?

Corin.   Into a thousand that I have forgotten.

Silvius.   O, thou didst then ne'er love so heartily !
If thou remember'st not the slightest folly
That ever love did make thee run into,
Thou hast not loved :
Or if thou hast not sat as I do now,
Wearying thy hearer in thy mistress' praise,
Thou hast not loved :
Or if thou hast not broke from company
Abruptly, as my passion now makes me,
Thou hast not loved.
O Phebe, Phebe, Phebe !   [*Exit.*

Rosalind.   Alas, poor shepherd ! searching of thy wound,
I have by hard adventure found mine own.

Touchstone.   And I mine. I remember, when I was in love I broke my sword upon a stone and bid him take that for coming a-night to Jane Smile ; and I remember the kissing of her batlet and the cow's dugs that her pretty chopt hands had milked ; and I remember the wooing of a peascod instead of her, from whom I took two cods and, giving her them again, said with weeping tears ' Wear these for my sake.' We that are true lovers run into strange capers ; but as all is mortal in nature, so is all nature in love mortal in folly.

Rosalind.   Thou speakest wiser than thou art ware of.

Touchstone.   Nay, I shall ne'er be ware of mine own wit till I break my shins against it.

Rosalind.   Jove, Jove ! this shepherd's passion Is much upon my fashion.

Touchstone.   And mine ; but it grows something stale with me.

Celia.   I pray you, one of you question yond man If he for gold will give us any food :
I faint almost to death.

Touchstone.   Holla, you clown !

Rosalind.   Peace, fool : he 's not thy kinsman.

Corin.   Who calls ?

Touchstone.   Your betters, sir.

Corin.   Else are they very wretched.

Rosalind.   Peace, I say.   Good even to you, friend.

Corin.   And to you, gentle sir, and to you all.

Rosalind.   I prithee, shepherd, if that love or gold
Can in this desert place buy entertainment,
Bring us where we may rest ourselves and feed :
Here 's a young maid with travel much oppress'd
And faints for succour.

Corin.   Fair sir, I pity her
And wish, for her sake more than for mine own,
My fortunes were more able to relieve her ;
But I am shepherd to another man
And do not shear the fleeces that I graze :

My master is of churlish disposition
And little recks to find the way to heaven
By doing deeds of hospitality :
Besides, his cote, his flocks and bounds of feed
Are now on sale, and at our sheepcote now,
By reason of his absence, there is nothing
That you will feed on ; but what is, come see,
And in my voice most welcome shall you be.

Rosalind.   What is he that shall buy his flock and pasture ?

Corin.   That young swain that you saw here but erewhile,
That little cares for buying any thing.

Rosalind.   I pray thee, if it stand with honesty,
Buy thou the cottage, pasture and the flock,
And thou shalt have to pay for it of us.

Celia.   And we will mend thy wages.   I like this place,
And willingly could waste my time in it.

Corin.   Assuredly the thing is to be sold :
Go with me : if you like upon report
The soil, the profit and this kind of life,
I will your very faithful feeder be
And buy it with your gold right suddenly.
                                        [*Exeunt.*

SCENE V.   *The forest.*

Enter Amiens, Jaques, *and others.*

SONG.

Amiens.   Under the greenwood tree
          Who loves to lie with me,
          And turn his merry note
          Unto the sweet bird's throat,
     Come hither, come hither, come hither :
          Here shall he see
          No enemy
     But winter and rough weather.

Jaques.   More, more, I prithee, more.

Amiens.   It will make you melancholy, Monsieur Jaques.

Jaques.   I thank it.   More, I prithee, more.   I can suck melancholy out of a song, as a weasel sucks eggs.   More, I prithee, more.

Amiens.   My voice is ragged : I know I cannot please you.

Jaques.   I do not desire you to please me ; I do desire you to sing.   Come, more ; another stanzo : call you 'em stanzos ?

Amiens.   What you will, Monsieur Jaques.

Jaques.   Nay, I care not for their names ; they owe me nothing.   Will you sing ?

Amiens.   More at your request than to please myself.

Jaques.   Well then, if ever I thank any man, I 'll thank you ; but that they call compliment is like the encounter of two dog-apes, and when a man thanks me heartily, methinks I have given him a penny and he renders me the beggarly thanks.   Come, sing ; and you that will not, hold your tongues.

Amiens.   Well, I 'll end the song.   Sirs, cover the while ; the duke will drink under this tree.   He hath been all this day to look you.

Jaques.   And I have been all this day to avoid him.   He is too disputable for my company : I think of as many matters as he, but I give heaven thanks and make no boast of them.   Come, warble, come.

SONG

Who doth ambition shun   [*All together here.*
And loves to live i' the sun,
Seeking the food he eats
And pleased with what he gets,
Come hither, come hither, come hither :
 Here shall he see
 No enemy
But winter and rough weather.

Jaques. I 'll give you a verse to this note that I
made yesterday in despite of my invention.
Amiens. And I 'll sing it.
Jaques. Thus it goes :—

 If it do come to pass
 That any man turn ass,
 Leaving his wealth and ease,
 A stubborn will to please,
Ducdame, ducdame, ducdame :
 Here shall he see
 Gross fools as he,
An if he will come to me.

Amiens. What 's that ' ducdame ' ?
Jaques. 'Tis a Greek invocation, to call fools
into a circle. I 'll go sleep, if I can ; if I cannot,
I 'll rail against all the first-born of Egypt.
Amiens. And I 'll go seek the duke : his banquet
is prepared.   [*Exeunt severally.*

SCENE VI. *The forest.*

Enter ORLANDO *and* ADAM.

Adam. Dear master, I can go no further : O,
I die for food ! Here lie I down, and measure out
my grave. Farewell, kind master.
Orlando. Why, how now, Adam ! no greater
heart in thee ? Live a little ; comfort a little ; cheer
thyself a little. If this uncouth forest yield anything
savage, I will either be food for it or bring it for
food to thee. Thy conceit is nearer death than thy
powers. For my sake be comfortable ; hold death
awhile at the arm's end : I will here be with thee
presently ; and if I bring thee not something to eat,
I will give thee leave to die : but if thou diest before
I come, thou art a mocker of my labour. Well said !
thou lookest cheerly, and I 'll be with thee quickly.
Yet thou liest in the bleak air : come, I will bear thee
to some shelter ; and thou shalt not die for lack of
a dinner, if there live any thing in this desert. Cheerly,
good Adam !   [*Exeunt.*

SCENE VII. *The forest.*

A table set out. Enter DUKE senior, AMIENS,
and Lords like outlaws.

Duke Senior. I think he be transform'd into a
beast ;
For I can no where find him like a man.
First Lord. My Lord, he is but even now gone
hence :
Here was he merry, hearing of a song.
Duke Senior. If he compact of jars, grow musical,
We shall have shortly discord in the spheres.
Go, seek him : tell him I would speak with him.

Enter JAQUES.

First Lord. He saves my labour by his own
approach.
Duke Senior. Why, how now, monsieur ! what
a life is this,
That your poor friends must woo your company ?
What, you look merrily !
Jaques. A fool, a fool ! I met a fool i' the forest,
A motley fool ; a miserable world !
As I do live by food, I met a fool ;
Who laid him down and bask'd him in the sun,
And rail'd on Lady Fortune in good terms,
In good set terms and yet a motley fool.
' Good morrow, fool,' quoth I. ' No, sir,' quoth
he,
' Call me not fool till heaven hath sent me fortune : '
And then he drew a dial from his poke,
And, looking on it with lack-lustre eye,
Says very wisely, ' It is ten o'clock :
Thus we may see,' quoth he, ' how the world wags :
'Tis but an hour ago since it was nine,
And after one hour more 'twill be eleven ;
And so, from hour to hour, we ripe and ripe,
And then, from hour to hour, we rot and rot ;
And thereby hangs a tale.' When I did hear
The motley fool thus moral on the time,
My lungs began to crow like chanticleer,
That fools should be so deep-contemplative,
And I did laugh sans intermission
An hour by his dial. O noble fool !
A worthy fool ! Motley 's the only wear.
Duke Senior. What fool is this ?
Jaques. O worthy fool ! One that hath been a
courtier,
And says, if ladies be but young and fair,
They have the gift to know it : and in his brain,
Which is as dry as the remainder biscuit
After a voyage, he hath strange places cramm'd
With observation, the which he vents
In mangled forms. O that I were a fool !
I am ambitious for a motley coat.
Duke Senior. Thou shalt have one.
Jaques.   It is my only suit ;
Provided that you weed your better judgements
Of all opinion that grows rank in them
That I am wise. I must have liberty
Withal, as large a charter as the wind,
To blow on whom I please ; for so fools have ;
And they that are most galled with my folly,
They most must laugh. And why, sir, must they
so ?
The ' why ' is plain as way to parish church :
He that a fool doth very wisely hit
Doth very foolishly, although he smart,
Not to seem senseless of the bob : if not,
The wise man's folly is anatomized
Even by the squandering glances of the fool.
Invest me in my motley ; give me leave
To speak my mind, and I will through and through
Cleanse the foul body of the infected world,
If they will patiently receive my medicine.
Duke Senior. Fie on thee ! I can tell what thou
wouldst do.
Jaques. What, for a counter, would I do but
good ?
Duke Senior. Most mischievous foul sin, in
chiding sin :
For thou thyself hast been a libertine,
As sensual as the brutish sting itself ;
And all the embossed sores and headed evils,

That thou with license of free foot hast caught,
Wouldst thou disgorge into the general world.
Jaques. Why, who cries out on pride,
That can therein tax any private party?
Doth it not flow as hugely as the sea,
† Till that the weary very means do ebb?
What woman in the city do I name,
When that I say the city-woman bears
The cost of princes on unworthy shoulders?
Who can come in and say that I mean her,
When such a one as she such is her neighbour?
Or what is he of basest function
That says his bravery is not on my cost,
Thinking that I mean him, but therein suits
His folly to the mettle of my speech?
There then; how then? what then? Let me see
 wherein
My tongue hath wrong'd him: if it do him right,
Then he hath wrong'd himself; if he be free,
Why then my taxing like a wild-goose flies,
Unclaim'd of any man. But who comes here?

Enter ORLANDO, *with his sword drawn.*

Orlando. Forbear, and eat no more.
Jaques. Why, I have eat none yet.
Orlando. Nor shalt not, till necessity be served.
Jaques. Of what kind should this cock come of?
Duke Senior. Art thou thus bolden'd, man, by
 thy distress,
Or else a rude despiser of good manners,
That in civility thou seem'st so empty?
Orlando. You touch'd my vein at first: the thorny
 point
Of bare distress hath ta'en from me the show
Of smooth civility: yet am I inland bred
And know some nurture. But forbear, I say:
He dies that touches any of this fruit
Till I and my affairs are answered.
Jaques. An you will not be answered with reason,
I must die.
Duke Senior. What would you have? Your
 gentleness shall force
More than your force move us to gentleness.
Orlando. I almost die for food; and let me have it.
Duke Senior. Sit down and feed, and welcome to
 our table.
Orlando. Speak you so gently? Pardon me, I
 pray you:
I thought that all things had been savage here;
And therefore put I on the countenance
Of stern commandment. But whate'er you are
That in this desert inaccessible,
Under the shade of melancholy boughs,
Lose and neglect the creeping hours of time;
If ever you have look'd on better days,
If ever been where bells have knoll'd to church,
If ever sat at any good man's feast,
If ever from your eyelids wiped a tear
And know what 'tis to pity and be pitied,
Let gentleness my strong enforcement be:
In the which hope I blush and hide my sword.
Duke Senior. True is it that we have seen better
 days,
And have with holy bell been knoll'd to church
And sat at good men's feasts and wiped our eyes
Of drops that sacred pity hath engender'd:
And therefore sit you down in gentleness
And take upon command what help we have
That to your wanting may be minister'd.

Orlando. Then but forbear your food a little
 while,
Whiles, like a doe, I go to find my fawn
And give it food. There is an old poor man,
Who after me hath many a weary step
Limp'd in pure love: till he be first sufficed,
Oppress'd with two weak evils, age and hunger,
I will not touch a bit.
Duke Senior. Go find him out,
And we will nothing waste till you return.
Orlando. I thank ye; and be blest for your good
 comfort!   [*Exit.*
Duke Senior. Thou seest we are not all alone
 unhappy:
This wide and universal theatre
Presents more woeful pageants than the scene
Wherein we play in.
Jaques. All the world's a stage,
And all the men and women merely players:
They have their exits and their entrances;
And one man in his time plays many parts,
His acts being seven ages. At first the infant,
Mewling and puking in the nurse's arms.
And then the whining school-boy, with his satchel
And shining morning face, creeping like snail
Unwillingly to school. And then the lover,
Sighing like furnace, with a woeful ballad
Made to his mistress' eyebrow. Then a soldier,
Full of strange oaths and bearded like the pard,
Jealous in honour, sudden and quick in quarrel,
Seeking the bubble reputation
Even in the cannon's mouth. And then the justice,
In fair round belly with good capon lined,
With eyes severe and beard of formal cut,
Full of wise saws and modern instances;
And so he plays his part. The sixth age shifts
Into the lean and slipper'd pantaloon,
With spectacles on nose and pouch on side,
His youthful hose, well saved, a world too wide
For his shrunk shank; and his big manly voice
Turning again toward childish treble, pipes
And whistles in his sound. Last scene of all,
That ends this strange eventful history,
Is second childishness and mere oblivion,
Sans teeth, sans eyes, sans taste, sans everything.

Re-enter ORLANDO, *with* ADAM.

Duke Senior. Welcome. Set down your venerable
 burden
And let him feed.
Orlando. I thank you most for him.
Adam. So had you need:
I scarce can speak to thank you for myself.
Duke Senior. Welcome; fall to: I will not
 trouble you
As yet, to question you about your fortunes.
Give us some music; and, good cousin, sing.

SONG.

Amiens. Blow, blow, thou winter wind,
 Thou art not so unkind'
  As man's ingratitude;
 Thy tooth is not so keen,
 Because thou art not seen,
  Although thy breath be rude.
Heigh-ho! sing, heigh-ho! unto the green holly:
Most friendship is feigning, most loving mere folly:
 Then, heigh-ho, the holly!
  This life is most jolly.

Freeze, freeze, thou bitter sky,
That dost not bite so nigh
    As benefits forgot :
Though thou the waters warp,
Thy sting is not so sharp
    As friend remember'd not.
Heigh-ho ! sing. &c.

Duke Senior. If that you were the good Sir Row-
    land's son,
As you have whisper'd faithfully you were,
And as mine eye doth his effigies witness
Most truly limn'd and living in your face,
Be truly welcome hither : I am the duke
That loved your father : the residue of your fortune,
Go to my cave and tell me. Good old man,
Thou art right welcome as thy master is.
Support him by the arm. Give me your hand,
And let me all your fortunes understand.
                                    [*Exeunt.*

ACT III.

SCENE I. *A room in the palace.*

Enter DUKE FREDERICK, *Lords, and* OLIVER.

Duke Frederick.

Not seen him since ! Sir, sir, that cannot be :
    But were I not the better part made mercy,
    I should not seek an absent argument
Of my revenge, thou present. But look to it :
Find out thy brother, wheresoe'er he is ;
Seek him with candle ; bring him dead or living
Within this twelvemonth, or turn thou no more
To seek a living in our territory.
Thy lands and all things that thou dost call thine
Worth seizure do we seize into our hands,
Till thou canst quit thee by thy brother's mouth
Of what we think against thee.
    Oliver. O that your highness knew my heart
    in this !
I never loved my brother in my life.
    Duke Frederick. More villain thou. Well, push
    him out of doors ;
And let my officers of such a nature
Make an extent upon his house and lands :
Do this expediently and turn him going.
                                    [*Exeunt.*

SCENE II. *The forest.*

Enter ORLANDO, *with a paper.*

Orlando. Hang there, my verse, in witness of my
    love :
And thou, thrice-crowned queen of night, survey
With thy chaste eye, from thy pale sphere above,
Thy huntress' name that my full life doth sway.
O Rosalind ! these trees shall be my books
    And in their barks my thoughts I 'll character ;
That every eye which in this forest looks
    Shall see thy virtue witness'd every where.
Run, run, Orlando ; carve on every tree
The fair, the chaste and unexpressive she. [*Exit.*

Enter CORIN *and* TOUCHSTONE.

Corin. And how like you this shepherd's life,
Master Touchstone ?
Touchstone. Truly, shepherd, in respect of itself,
it is a good life ; but in respect that it is a shepherd's
life, it is naught. In respect that it is solitary, I
like it very well ; but in respect that it is private,
it is a very vile life. Now, in respect it is in the
fields, it pleaseth me well ; but in respect it is not
in the court, it is tedious. As it is a spare life, look
you, it fits my humour well : but as there is no more
plenty in it, it goes much against my stomach.
Hast any philosophy in thee, shepherd ?
Corin. No more but that I know the more one
sickens the worse at ease he is ; and that he that
wants money, means and content is without three
good friends ; that the property of rain is to wet and
fire to burn ; that good pasture makes fat sheep,
and that a great cause of the night is lack of the sun ;
that he that hath learned no wit by nature nor art
may complain of good breeding or comes of a very
dull kindred.
Touchstone. Such a one is a natural philosopher.
Wast ever in court, shepherd ?
Corin. No, truly.
Touchstone. Then thou art damned.
Corin. Nay, I hope.
Touchstone. Truly, thou art damned, like an ill-
roasted egg all on one side.
Corin. For not being at court ? Your reason.
Touchstone. Why, if thou never wast at court,
thou never sawest good manners ; if thou never
sawest good manners, then thy manners must be
wicked ; and wickedness is sin, and sin is damnation.
Thou art in a parlous state, shepherd.
Corin. Not a whit, Touchstone : those that
are good manners at the court are as ridiculous in
the country as the behaviour of the country is most
mockable at the court. You told me you salute
not at the court, but you kiss your hands : that
courtesy would be uncleanly, if courtiers were
shepherds.
Touchstone. Instance, briefly ; come, instance.
Corin. Why, we are still handling our ewes,
and their fells, you know, are greasy.
Touchstone. Why, do not your courtier's hands
sweat ? and is not the grease of a mutton as wholesome as the sweat of a man ? Shallow, shallow.
A better instance, I say ; come.
Corin. Besides, our hands are hard.
Touchstone. Your lips will feel them the sooner.
Shallow again. A more sounder instance, come.
Corin. And they are often tarred over with the
surgery of our sheep ; and would you have us kiss
tar ? The courtier's hands are perfumed with civet.
Touchstone. Most shallow man ! thou worms-
meat, in respect of a good piece of flesh indeed !
Learn of the wise, and perpend : civet is of a baser
birth than tar, the very uncleanly flux of a cat.
Mend the instance, shepherd.
Corin. You have too courtly a wit for me :
I 'll rest.
Touchstone. Wilt thou rest damned ? God help
thee, shallow man ! God make incision in thee !
thou art raw.
Corin. Sir, I am a true labourer : I earn that
I eat, get that I wear, owe no man hate, envy no
man's happiness, glad of other men's good, content
with my harm, and the greatest of my pride is to
see my ewes graze and my lambs suck.
Touchstone. That is another simple sin in you,
to bring the ewes and the rams together and to
offer to get your living by the copulation of cattle ;
to be bawd to a bell-wether, and to betray a she-
lamb of a twelvemonth to a crooked-pated, old,

cuckoldly ram, out of all reasonable match. If
thou beest not damned for this, the devil himself
will have no shepherds ; I cannot see else how thou
shouldst 'scape.

Corin. Here comes young Master Ganymede,
my new mistress's brother.

Enter ROSALIND, *with a paper, reading.*

Rosalind. From the east to western Ind,
No jewel is like Rosalind.
Her worth, being mounted on the wind,
Through all the world bears Rosalind.
All the pictures fairest lined
Are but black to Rosalind.
Let no fair be kept in mind
But the fair of Rosalind.

Touchstone. I 'll rhyme you so eight years together, dinners and suppers and sleeping-hours
excepted : it is the right butter-women's rank to
market.

Rosalind. Out, fool !

Touchstone. For a taste :
If a hart do lack a hind,
Let him seek out Rosalind.
If the cat will after kind,
So be sure will Rosalind.
Winter garments must be lined,
So must slender Rosalind.
They that reap must sheaf and bind ;
Then to cart with Rosalind.
Sweetest nut hath sourest rind,
Such a nut is Rosalind.
He that sweetest rose will find
Must find love's prick and Rosalind.
This is the very false gallop of verses : why do you
infect yourself with them ?

Rosalind. Peace you dull fool ! I found them
on a tree.

Touchstone. Truly, the tree yields bad fruit.

Rosalind. I 'll graff it with you, and then I shall
graff it with a medlar : then it will be the earliest
fruit i' the country ; for you 'll be rotten ere you
be half ripe, and that 's the right virtue of the medlar.

Touchstone. You have said : but whether wisely
or no, let the forest judge.

Enter CELIA, *with a writing.*

Rosalind. Peace !
Here comes my sister, reading : stand aside.

Celia. ⌈*Reads*⌉
Why should this a desert be ?
For it is unpeopled ? No ;
Tongues I 'll hang on every tree,
That shall civil sayings show :
Some, how brief the life of man
Runs his erring pilgrimage,
That the stretching of a span
Buckles in his sum of age ;
Some, of violated vows
'Twixt the souls of friend and friend :
But upon the fairest boughs,
Or at every sentence end,
Will I Rosalinda write,
Teaching all that read to know
The quintessence of every sprite
Heaven would in little show.
Therefore Heaven Nature charged
That one body should be fill'd
With all graces wide-enlarged :

Nature presently distill'd
Helen's cheek, but not her heart,
Cleopatra's majesty,
Atalanta's better part,
Sad Lucretia's modesty.
Thus Rosalind of many parts
By heavenly synod was devised,
Of many faces, eyes and hearts,
To have the touches dearest prized.
Heaven would that she these gifts should have,
And I to live and die her slave.

Rosalind. O most gentle pulpiter ! what tedious
homily of love have you wearied your parishioners
withal, and never cried ' Have patience, good people' !

Celia. How now ! back, friends ! Shepherd,
go off a little. Go with him, sirrah.

Touchstone. Come, shepherd, let us make an
honourable retreat ; though not with bag and
baggage. yet with scrip and scrippage.

       ⌈*Exeunt Corin and Touchstone.*

Celia. Didst thou hear these verses ?

Rosalind. O, yes, I heard them all, and more too ;
for some of them had in them more feet than the
verses would bear.

Celia. That 's no matter : the feet might bear
the verses.

Rosalind. Ay, but the feet were lame and could
not bear themselves without the verse and therefore
stood lamely in the verse.

Celia. But didst thou hear without wondering
how thy name should be hanged and carved upon
these trees ?

Rosalind. I was seven of the nine days out of
the wonder before you came ; for look here what
I found on a palm-tree. I was never so berhymed
since Pythagoras' time, that I was an Irish rat, which
I can hardly remember.

Celia. Trow you who hath done this ?

Rosalind. Is it a man ?

Celia. And a chain, that you once wore, about
his neck. Change you colour ?

Rosalind. I prithee, who ?

Celia. O Lord, Lord ! it is a hard matter for
friends to meet ; but mountains may be removed
with earthquakes and so encounter.

Rosalind. Nay, but who is it ?

Celia. Is it possible ?

Rosalind. Nay, I prithee now with most petitio-
nary vehemence, tell me who it is.

Celia. O wonderful, wonderful, and most wonderful wonderful ! and yet again wonderful, and
after that out of all hooping !

Rosalind. Good my complexion ! dost thou think,
though I am caparisoned like a man, I have a doublet
and hose in my disposition ? One inch of delay
more is a South-sea of discovery ; I prithee, tell me
who is it quickly, and speak apace. I would thou
couldst stammer, that thou mightst pour this concealed man out of thy mouth, as wine comes out
of a narrow-mouthed bottle, either too much at
once, or none at all. I prithee, take the cork out
of thy mouth that I may drink thy tidings.

Celia. So you may put a man in your belly.

Rosalind. Is he of God's making ? What manner
of man ? Is his head worth a hat, or his chin worth
a beard ?

Celia. Nay, he hath but a little beard.

Rosalind. Why, God will send more, if the man
will be thankful : let me stay the growth of his
beard, if thou delay me not the knowledge of his chin.

Celia. It is young Orlando, that tripped up the

wrestler's heels and your heart both in an instant.

Rosalind. Nay, but the devil take mocking: speak, sad brow and true maid.

Celia. I' faith, coz, 'tis he.

Rosalind. Orlando?

Celia. Orlando.

Rosalind. Alas the day ! what shall I do with my doublet and hose? What did he when thou sawest him? What said he? How looked he? Wherein went he? What makes he here? Did he ask for me? Where remains he? How parted he with thee? and when shalt thou see him again? Answer me in one word.

Celia. You must borrow me Gargantua's mouth first : 'tis a word too great for any mouth of this age's size. To say ay and no to these particulars is more than to answer in a catechism.

Rosalind. But doth he know that I am in this forest and in man's apparel? Looks he as freshly as he did the day he wrestled?

Celia. It is as easy to count atomies as to resolve the propositions of a lover ; but take a taste of my finding him, and relish it with good observance. I found him under a tree, like a dropped acorn.

Rosalind. It may well be called Jove's tree, when it drops forth such fruit.

Celia. Give me audience, good madam.

Rosalind. Proceed.

Celia. There lay he, stretched along, like a wounded knight.

Rosalind. Though it be pity to see such a sight, it well becomes the ground.

Celia. Cry ' holla ' to thy tongue, I prithee ; it curvets unseasonably. He was furnished like a hunter.

Rosalind. O, ominous ! he comes to kill my heart.

Celia. I would sing my song without a burden : thou bringest me out of tune.

Rosalind. Do you not know I am a woman? when I think, I must speak. Sweet, say on.

Celia. You bring me out. Soft ! comes he not here?

Enter ORLANDO *and* JAQUES.

Rosalind. 'Tis he : slink by, and note him.

Jaques. I thank you for your company ; but, good faith, I had as lief have been myself alone.

Orlando. And so had I ; but yet, for fashion sake, I thank you too for your society.

Jaques. God be wi' you : let 's meet as little as we can.

Orlando. I do desire we may be better strangers.

Jaques. I pray you, mar no more trees with writing love-songs in their barks.

Orlando. I pray you, mar no moe of my verses with reading them ill-favouredly.

Jaques. Rosalind is your love's name?

Orlando. Yes, just.

Jaques. I do not like her name.

Orlando. There was no thought of pleasing you when she was christened.

Jaques. What stature is she of?

Orlando. Just as high as my heart.

Jaques. You are full of pretty answers. Have you not been acquainted with goldsmiths' wives, and conned them out of rings?

Orlando. Not so ; but I answer you right painted cloth, from whence you have studied your questions.

Jaques. You have a nimble wit : I think 'twas made of Atalanta's heels. Will you sit down with me? and we two will rail against our mistress the world and all our misery.

Orlando. I will chide no breather in the world but myself, against whom I know most faults.

Jaques. The worst fault you have is to be in love.

Orlando. 'Tis a fault I will not change for your best virtue. I am weary of you.

Jaques. By my troth, I was seeking for a fool when I found you.

Orlando. He is drowned in the brook : look but in, and you shall see him.

Jaques. There I shall see mine own figure.

Orlando. Which I take to be either a fool or a cipher.

Jaques. I 'll tarry no longer with you : farewell, good Signior Love.

Orlando. I am glad of your departure : adieu, good Monsieur Melancholy.   [*Exit Jaques.*

Rosalind. [*Aside to Celia*] I will speak to him like a saucy lackey and under that habit play the knave with him. Do you hear, forester?

Orlando. Very well ; what would you?

Rosalind. I pray you, what is 't o'clock?

Orlando. You should ask me what time o' day ; there 's no clock in the forest.

Rosalind. Then there is no true lover in the forest ; else sighing every minute and groaning every hour would detect the lazy foot of Time as well as a clock.

Orlando. And why not the swift foot of Time ? had not that been as proper?

Rosalind. By no means, sir : Time travels in divers paces with divers persons. I 'll tell you who Time ambles withal, who Time trots withal, who Time gallops withal and who he stands still withal.

Orlando. I prithee, who doth he trot withal ?

Rosalind. Marry, he trots hard with a young maid between the contract of her marriage and the day it is solemnized : if the interim be but a se'nnight, Time's pace is so hard that it seems the length of seven year.

Orlando. Who ambles Time withal ?

Rosalind. With a priest that lacks Latin and a rich man that hath not the gout, for the one sleeps easily because he cannot study and the other lives merrily because he feels no pain, the one lacking the burden of lean and wasteful learning, the other knowing no burden of heavy tedious penury ; these Time ambles withal.

Orlando. Who doth he gallop withal ?

Rosalind. With a thief to the gallows, for though he go as softly as foot can fall, he thinks himself too soon there.

Orlando. Who stays it still withal ?

Rosalind. With lawyers in the vacation ; for they sleep between term and term and then they perceive not how Time moves.

Orlando. Where dwell you, pretty youth ?

Rosalind. With this shepherdess, my sister ; here in the skirts of the forest, like fringe upon a petticoat.

Orlando. Are you native of this place ?

Rosalind. As the cony that you see dwell where she is kindled.

Orlando. Your accent is something finer than you could purchase in so removed a dwelling.

Rosalind. I have been told so of many : but indeed an old religious uncle of mine taught me to speak, who was in his youth an inland man ; one that knew courtship too well, for there he fell in love. I have heard him read many lectures against it, and I thank God I am not a woman, to be touched with so many giddy offences as he hath generally taxed their whole sex withal.

Orlando. Can you remember any of the principal evils that he laid to the charge of women ?

Rosalind. There were none principal : they were all like one another as half-pence are, every one fault seeming monstrous till his fellow-fault came to match it.

Orlando. I prithee, recount some of them.

Rosalind. No, I will not cast away my physic but on those that are sick. There is a man haunts the forest, that abuses our young plants with carving ' Rosalind ' on their barks ; hangs odes upon hawthorns and elegies on brambles, all, forsooth, deifying the name of Rosalind : if I could meet that fancy-monger, I would give him some good counsel, for he seems to have the quotidian of love upon him.

Orlando. I am he that is so love-shaked : I pray you, tell me your remedy.

Rosalind. There is none of my uncle's marks upon you · he taught me how to know a man in love ; in which cage of rushes I am sure you are not prisoner.

Orlando. What were his marks .

Rosalind. A lean cheek, which you have not, a blue eye and sunken, which you have not, an unquestionable spirit, which you have not, a beard neglected, which you have not ; but I pardon you for that, for simply your having in beard is a younger brother's revenue : then your hose should be ungartered, your bonnet unbanded, your sleeve unbuttoned, your shoe untied and every thing about you demonstrating a careless desolation ; but you are no such man ; you are rather point-device in your accoutrements as loving yourself than seeming the lover of any other.

Orlando. Fair youth, I would I could make thee believe I love.

Rosalind. Me believe it ! you may as soon make her that you love believe it ; which, I warrant, she is apter to do than to confess she does : that is one of the points in the which women still give the lie to their consciences. But, in good sooth, are you he that hangs the verses on the trees, wherein Rosalind is so admired ?

Orlando. I swear to thee, youth, by the white hand of Rosalind, I am that he, that unfortunate he.

Rosalind. But are you so much in love as your rhymes speak ?

Orlando. Neither rhyme nor reason can express how much.

Rosalind. Love is merely a madness, and, I tell you, deserves as well a dark house and a whip as madmen do : and the reason why they are not so punished and cured is, that the lunacy is so ordinary that the whippers are in love too. Yet I profess curing it by counsel.

Orlando. Did you ever cure any so ?

Rosalind. Yes, one, and in this manner. He was to imagine me his love, his mistress ; and I set him every day to woo me : at which time would I, being but a moonish youth, grieve, be effeminate, changeable, longing and liking, proud, fantastical, apish, shallow, inconstant, full of tears, full of smiles, for every passion something and for no passion truly any thing, as boys and women are for the most part cattle of this colour ; would now like him now loathe him ; then entertain him, then forswear him ; now weep for him, then spit at him ; that I drave my suitor from his mad humour of love to

a living humour of madness ; which was, to forswear the full stream of the world and to live in a nook merely monastic. And thus I cured him ; and this way will I take upon me to wash your liver as clean as a sound sheep's heart, that there shall not be one spot of love in it.

Orlando. I would not be cured, youth.

Rosalind. I would cure you, if you would but call me Rosalind and come every day to my cote and woo me.

Orlando. Now, by the faith of my love. I will : tell me where it is.

Rosalind. Go with me to it and I 'll show it you : and by the way you shall tell me where in the forest you live. Will you go ?

Orlando. With all my heart, good youth.

Rosalind. Nay, you must call me Rosalind. Come, sister, will you go ?   [*Exeunt.*

SCENE III.   *The forest.*

Enter TOUCHSTONE *and* AUDREY ; JAQUES *behind.*

Touchstone. Come apace, good Audrey : will fetch up your goats. Audrey. And how, Audrey ? am I the man yet ? doth my simple feature content you ?

Audrey. Your features ! Lord warrant us ! what features ?

Touchstone. I am here with thee and thy goats, as the most capricious poet, honest Ovid, was among the Goths.

Jaques. [*Aside*] O knowledge ill-inhabited, worse than Jove in a thatched house !

Touchstone. When a man's verses cannot be understood, nor a man's good wit seconded with the forward child Understanding, it strikes a man more dead than a great reckoning in a little room. Truly, I would the gods had made thee poetical.

Audrey. I do not know what ' poetical ' is : is it honest in deed and word ? is it a true thing ?

Touchstone. No, truly ; for the truest poetry is the most feigning ; and lovers are given to poetry, and what they swear in poetry may be said as lovers they do feign.

Audrey. Do you wish then that the gods had made me poetical ?

Touchstone. I do, truly ; for thou swearest to me thou art honest : now, if thou wert a poet, I might have some hope thou didst feign.

Audrey. Would you not have me honest ?

Touchstone. No, truly, unless thou wert hard-favoured ; for honesty coupled to beauty is to have honey a sauce to sugar.

Jaques. [*Aside*] A material fool !

Audrey. Well, I am not fair ; and therefore I pray the gods make me honest.

Touchstone. Truly, and to cast away honesty upon a foul slut were to put good meat into an unclean dish.

Audrey. I am not a slut, though I thank the gods I am foul.

Touchstone. Well, praised be the gods for thy foulness ! sluttishness may come hereafter. But be it as it may be, I will marry thee, and to that end I have been with Sir Oliver Martext, the vicar of the next village, who hath promised to meet me in this place of the forest and to couple us.

Jaques. [*Aside*] I would fain see this meeting.

Audrey. Well, the gods give us joy !

Touchstone. Amen. A man may, if he were of a fearful heart, stagger in this attempt ; for here we have no temple but the wood, no assembly but hornbeasts. But what though ? Courage ! As horns are odious, they are necessary. It is said, ' many a man knows no end of his goods : ' right ; many a man has good horns, and knows no end of them. Well, that is the dowry of his wife ; 'tis none of his own getting. Horns ? Even so. Poor men alone ? No, no ; the noblest deer hath them as huge as the rascal. Is the single man therefore blessed ? No : as a walled town is more worthier than a village, so is the forehead of a married man more honourable than the bare brow of a bachelor ; and by how much defence is better than no skill, by so much is a horn more precious than to want. Here comes Sir Oliver.

Enter SIR OLIVER MARTEXT.

Sir Oliver Martext, you are well met : will you dispatch us here under this tree, or shall we go with you to your chapel ?

Sir Oliver. Is there none here to give the woman ?

Touchstone. I will not take her on gift of any man.

Sir Oliver. Truly, she must be given, or the marriage is not lawful.

Jaques. [*Advancing*] Proceed, proceed : I 'll give her.

Touchstone. Good even, good Master What-ye-call 't : how do you, sir ? You are very well met : God 'ild you for your last company : I am very glad to see you : even a toy in hand here. sir : nay, pray be covered.

Jaques. Will you be married, motley ?

Touchstone. As the ox hath his bow, sir, the horse his curb and the falcon her bells, so man hath his desires ; and as pigeons bill, so wedlock would be nibbling.

Jaques. And will you, being a man of your breeding, be married under a bush like a beggar ? Get you to church, and have a good priest that can tell you what marriage is : this fellow will but join you together as they join wainscot ; then one of you will prove a shrunk panel and, like green timber, warp, warp.

Touchstone. [*Aside*] I am not in the mind but I were better to be married of him than of another : for he is not like to marry me well ; and not being well married, it will be a good excuse for me hereafter to leave my wife.

Jaques. Go thou with me, and let me counsel thee.

Touchstone. Come, sweet Audrey :
We must be married, or we must live in bawdry.
Farewell, good Master Oliver : not,—

O sweet Oliver,
O brave Oliver,
Leave me not behind thee :

but,—

Wind away,
Begone, I say,
I will not to wedding with thee.
[*Exeunt Jaques. Touchstone and Audrey*

Sir Oliver. 'Tis no matter : ne'er a fantastical knave of them all shall flout me out of my calling.
[*Exit.*

SCENE IV. *The forest.*

Enter ROSALIND *and* CELIA.

Rosalind. Never talk to me ; I will weep.

Celia. Do, I prithee ; but yet have the grace to consider that tears do not become a man.

Rosalind. But have I not cause to weep ?

Celia. As good cause as one would desire ; therefore weep.

Rosalind. His very hair is of the dissembling colour.

Celia. Something browner than Judas's : marry, his kisses are Judas's own children.

Rosalind. I' faith, his hair is of a good colour.

Celia. An excellent colour : your chestnut was ever the only colour.

Rosalind. And his kissing is as full of sanctity as the touch of holy bread.

Celia. He hath bought a pair of cast lips of Diana : a nun of winter's sisterhood kisses not more religiously ; the very ice of chastity is in them.

Rosalind. But why did he swear he would come this morning, and comes not ?

Celia. Nay, certainly, there is no truth in him.

Rosalind. Do you think so ?

Celia. Yes ; I think he is not a pick-purse nor a horse-stealer, but for his verity in love, I do think him as concave as a covered goblet or a worm-eaten nut.

Rosalind. Not true in love ?

Celia. Yes, when he is in ; but I think he is not in.

Rosalind. You have heard him swear downright he was.

Celia. ' Was ' is not ' is :' besides, the oath of a lover is no stronger than the word of a tapster ; they are both the confirmer of false reckonings. He attends here in the forest on the duke your father.

Rosalind. I met the duke yesterday and had much question with him : he asked me of what parentage I was ; I told him, of as good as he ; so he laughed and let me go. But what talk we of fathers. when there is such a man as Orlando ?

Celia. O, that 's a brave man ! he writes brave verses, speaks brave words, swears brave oaths and breaks them bravely, quite traverse, athwart the heart of his lover ; as a puisny tilter, that spurs his horse but on one side, breaks his staff like a noble goose : but all 's brave that youth mounts and folly guides. Who comes here ?

Enter CORIN.

Corin. Mistress and master, you have oft inquired
After the shepherd that complain'd of love,
Who you saw sitting by me on the turf,
Praising the proud disdainful shepherdess
That was his mistress.

Celia. Well, and what of him ?

Corin. If you will see a pageant truly play'd,
Between the pale complexion of true love
And the red glow of scorn and proud disdain,
Go hence a little and I shall conduct you,
If you will mark it.

Rosalind. O, come, let us remove :
The sight of lovers feedeth those in love.
Bring us to this sight, and you shall say
I 'll prove a busy actor in their play. [*Exeunt*

SCENE V. *Another part of the forest.*

Enter Silvius *and* Phebe.

Silvius.   Sweet Phebe, do not scorn me ; do not, Phebe ;
Say that you love me not, but say not so
In bitterness.   The common executioner,
Whose heart the accustom'd sight of death makes hard,
Falls not the axe upon the humbled neck
But first begs pardon : will you sterner be
†Than he that dies and lives by bloody drops ?

Enter Rosalind, Celia, *and* Corin, *behind.*

Phebe.   I would not be thy executioner :
I fly thee, for I would not injure thee.
Thou tell'st me there is murder in mine eye :
'Tis pretty, sure, and very probable,
That eyes, that are the frail'st and softest things,
Who shut their coward gates on atomies,
Should be call'd tyrants, butchers, murderers !
Now I do frown on thee with all my heart ;
And if mine eyes can wound, now let them kill thee :
Now counterfeit to swoon ; why now fall down ;
Or if thou canst not, O, for shame, for shame,
Lie not, to say mine eyes are murderers !
Now show the wound mine eye hath made in thee :
Scratch thee but with a pin, and there remains
Some scar of it ; lean but upon a rush,
The cicatrice and capable impressure
Thy palm some moment keeps ; but now mine eyes,
Which I have darted at thee, hurt thee not,
Nor, I am sure, there is no force in eyes
That can do hurt.
Silvius.   O dear Phebe,
If ever,—as that ever may be near,—
You meet in some fresh cheek the power of fancy,
Then shall you know the wounds invisible
That love's keen arrows make.
Phebe.   But till that time
Come not thou near me : and when that time comes,
Afflict me with thy mocks, pity me not ;
As till that time I shall not pity thee.
Rosalind.   And why, I pray you ? Who might be your mother,
That you insult, exult, and all at once,
Over the wretched ?   What though you have no beauty,—
As, by my faith, I see no more in you
Than without candle may go dark to bed—
Must you be therefore proud and pitiless ?
Why, what means this ?   Why do you look on me ?
I see no more in you than in the ordinary
Of nature's sale-work.   'Od's my little life,
I think she means to tangle my eyes too !
No, faith, proud mistress, hope not after it :
'Tis not your inky brows, your black silk hair,
Your bugle eyeballs, nor your cheek of cream,
That can entame my spirits to your worship.
You foolish shepherd, wherefore do you follow her,
Like foggy south puffing with wind and rain ?
You are a thousand times a properer man
Than she a woman : 'tis such fools as you
That makes the world full of ill-favour'd children :
'Tis not her glass, but you, that flatters her ;
And out of you she sees herself more proper
Than any of her lineaments can show her.
But, mistress, know yourself : down on your knees,
And thank heaven, fasting, for a good man's love :

For I must tell you friendly in your ear,
Sell when you can : you are not for all markets :
Cry the man mercy ; love him ; take his offer :
Foul is most foul, being foul to be a scoffer.
So take her to thee, shepherd : fare you well.
Phebe.   Sweet youth, I pray you, chide a year together :
I had rather hear you chide than this man woo.
Rosalind.   He 's fallen in love with your foulness
and she 'll fall in love with my anger.   If it be so,
as fast as she answers thee with frowning looks,
I 'll sauce her with bitter words.   Why look you so upon me ?
Phebe.   For no ill will I bear you.
Rosalind.   I pray you, do not fall in love with me,
For I am falser than vows made in wine :
Besides, I like you not.   If you will know my house,
'Tis at the tuft of olives here hard by.
Will you go, sister ? Shepherd, ply her hard.
Come, sister.   Shepherdess, look on him better,
And be not proud : though all the world could see,
None could be so abused in sight as he.
Come, to our flock.
                              [*Exeunt Rosalind, Celia and Corin.*
Phebe.   Dead shepherd, now I find thy saw of might,
' Who ever loved that loved not at first sight ? '
Silvius.   Sweet Phebe,—
Phebe.   Ha, what say'st thou, Silvius ?
Silvius.   Sweet Phebe, pity me.
Phebe.   Why, I am sorry for thee, gentle Silvius.
Silvius.   Wherever sorrow is, relief would be :
If you do sorrow at my grief in love,
By giving love your sorrow and my grief
Were both extermined.
Phebe.   Thou hast my love : is not that neighbourly ?
Silvius.   I would have you.
Phebe.   Why, that were covetousness.
Silvius, the time was that I hated thee,
And yet it is not that I bear thee love ;
But since that thou canst talk of love so well,
Thy company, which erst was irksome to me,
I will endure, and I 'll employ thee too :
But do not look for further recompense
Than thine own gladness that thou art employ'd.
Silvius.   So holy and so perfect is my love,
And I in such a poverty of grace,
That I shall think it a most plenteous crop
To glean the broken ears after the man
That the main harvest reaps : loose now and then
A scatter'd smile, and that I 'll live upon.
Phebe.   Know'st thou the youth that spoke to me erewhile ?
Silvius.   Not very well, but I have met him oft ;
And he hath bought the cottage and the bounds
That the old carlot once was master of.
Phebe.   Think not I love him, though I ask for him ;
'Tis but a peevish boy ; yet he talks well ;
But what care I for words ? yet words do well
When he that speaks them pleases those that hear.
It is a pretty youth : not very pretty :
But, sure, he 's proud, and yet his pride becomes him :
He 'll make a proper man : the best thing in him
Is his complexion : and faster than his tongue
Did make offence his eye did heal it up.
He is not very tall ; yet for his years he 's tall :
His leg is but so so ; and yet 'tis well :

There was a pretty redness in his lip,
A little riper and more lusty red
Than that mix'd in his cheek ; 'twas just the difference
Betwixt the constant red and mingled damask.
There be some women, Silvius, had they mark'd him
In parcels as I did, would have gone near
To fall in love with him ; but, for my part,
I love him not nor hate him not ; and yet
I have more cause to hate him than to love him :
For what had he to do to chide at me ?
He said mine eyes were black and my hair black ;
And, now I am remember'd, scorn'd at me :
I marvel why I answer'd not again :
But that 's all one ; omittance is no quittance.
I 'll write to him a very taunting letter,
And thou shalt bear it : wilt thou, Silvius ?

Silvius. Phebe, with all my heart.

Phebe. I 'll write it straight ;
The matter 's in my head and in my heart :
I will be bitter with him and passing short.
Go with me, Silvius. [*Exeunt.*

ACT IV.

SCENE I. *The forest.*

Enter ROSALIND, CELIA, *and* JAQUES.

Jaques.
I prithee, pretty youth, let me be better acquainted with thee.

Rosalind. They say you are a melancholy fellow.

Jaques. I am so ; I do love it better than laughing.

Rosalind. Those that are in extremity of either are abominable fellows and betray themselves to every modern censure worse than drunkards.

Jaques. Why, 'tis good to be sad and say nothing.

Rosalind. Why then, 'tis good to be a post.

Jaques. I have neither the scholar's melancholy, which is emulation, nor the musician's, which is fantastical, nor the courtier's, which is proud, nor the soldier's, which is ambitious, nor the lawyer's, which is politic, nor the lady's, which is nice, nor the lover's, which is all these : but it is a melancholy of mine own, compounded of many simples, extracted from many objects, and indeed the sundry contemplation of my travels, in which my often rumination wraps me in a most humorous sadness.

Rosalind. A traveller ! By my faith, you have great reason to be sad : I fear you have sold your own lands to see other men's ; then, to have seen much and so have nothing, is to have rich eyes and poor hands.

Jaques. Yes, I have gained my experience.

Rosalind. And your experience makes you sad : I had rather have a fool to make me merry than experience to make me sad ; and to travel for it too !

Enter ORLANDO.

Orlando. Good day and happiness, dear Rosalind !

Jaques. Nay, then God be wi' you, an you talk in blank verse. [*Exit.*

Rosalind. Farewell, Monsieur Traveller : look you lisp and wear strange suits, disable all the benefits of your own country, be out of love with your nativity and almost chide God for making you that countenance you are, or I will scarce think you have swam in a gondola. Why, how now, Orlando !

where have you been all this while ? You a lover ! An you serve me such another trick, never come in my sight more.

Orlando. My fair Rosalind, I come within an hour of my promise.

Rosalind. Break an hour's promise in love ! He that will divide a minute into a thousand parts and break but a part of the thousandth part of a minute in the affairs of love, it may be said of him that Cupid hath clapped him o' the shoulder, but I 'll warrant him heart-whole.

Orlando. Pardon me, dear Rosalind.

Rosalind. Nay, an you be so tardy, come no more in my sight : I had as lief be wooed of a snail.

Orlando. Of a snail ?

Rosalind. Ay, of a snail ; for though he comes slowly, he carries his house on his head ; a better jointure, I think, than you make a woman : besides, he brings his destiny with him.

Orlando. What 's that ?

Rosalind. Why, horns, which such as you are fain to be beholding to your wives for : but he comes armed in his fortune and prevents the slander of his wife.

Orlando. Virtue is no horn-maker ; and my Rosalind is virtuous.

Rosalind. And I am your Rosalind.

Celia. It pleases him to call you so ; but he hath a Rosalind of a better leer than you.

Rosalind. Come, woo me, woo me, for now I am in a holiday humour and like enough to consent. What would you say to me now. an I were your very very Rosalind ?

Orlando. I would kiss before I spoke.

Rosalind. Nay, you were better speak first, and when you were gravelled for lack of matter, you might take occasion to kiss. Very good orators, when they are out, they will spit ; and for lovers lacking—God warn us !—matter. the cleanliest shift is to kiss.

Orlando. How if the kiss be denied ?

Rosalind. Then she puts you to entreaty, and there begins new matter.

Orlando. Who could be out, being before his beloved mistress ?

Rosalind. Marry, that should you, if I were your mistress, or I should think my honesty ranker than my wit.

Orlando. What, of my suit ?

Rosalind. Not out of your apparel, and yet out of your suit. Am not I your Rosalind ?

Orlando. I take some joy to say you are, because I would be talking of her.

Rosalind. Well. in her person, I say I will not have you.

Orlando. Then in mine own person I die.

Rosalind. No, faith, die by attorney. The poor world is almost six thousand years old, and in all this time there was not any man died in his own person, videlicet, in a love-cause. Troilus had his brains dashed out with a Grecian club ; yet he did what he could to die before, and he is one of the patterns of love. Leander, he would have lived many a fair year, though Hero had turned nun, if it had not been for a hot midsummer night ; for, good youth, he went but forth to wash him in the Hellespont and being taken with the cramp was drowned : and the foolish chroniclers of that age found it was ' Hero of Sestos.' But these are all lies ; men have died from time to time and worms have eaten them, but not for love.

Orlando. I would not have my right Rosalind of this mind, for, I protest, her frown might kill me.

Rosalind. By this hand, it will not kill a fly. But come, now I will be your Rosalind in a more coming-on disposition, and ask me what you will, I will grant it.

Orlando. Then love me, Rosalind.

Rosalind. Yes, faith, will I, Fridays and Saturdays and all.

Orlando. And wilt thou have me ?

Rosalind. Ay, and twenty such.

Orlando. What sayest thou ?

Rosalind. Are you not good ?

Orlando. I hope so.

Rosalind. Why then, can one desire too much of a good thing ? Come, sister, you shall be the priest and marry us. Give me your hand, Orlando. What do you say, sister ?

Orlando. Pray thee, marry us.

Celia. I cannot say the words.

Rosalind. You must begin, ' Will you, Orlando—'

Celia. Go to. Will you, Orlando, have to wife this Rosalind ?

Orlando. I will.

Rosalind. Ay, but when ?

Orlando. Why now ; as fast as she can marry us.

Rosalind. Then you must say ' I take thee, Rosalind, for wife.'

Orlando. I take thee, Rosalind, for wife.

Rosalind. I might ask you for your commission ; but I do take thee, Orlando, for my husband : there 's a girl goes before the priest ; and certainly a woman's thought runs before her actions.

Orlando. So do all thoughts ; they are winged.

Rosalind. Now tell me how long you would have her after you have possessed her.

Orlando. For ever and a day.

Rosalind. Say ' a day ' without the ' ever.' No, no, Orlando ; men are April when they woo, December when they wed : maids are May when they are maids, but the sky changes when they are wives. I will be more jealous of thee than a Barbary cock-pigeon over his hen, more clamorous than a parrot against rain, more new-fangled than an ape, more giddy in my desires than a monkey : I will weep for nothing, like Diana in the fountain, and I will do that when you are disposed to be merry ; I will laugh like a hyen, and that when thou art inclined to sleep.

Orlando. But will my Rosalind do so ?

Rosalind. By my life, she will do as I do.

Orlando. O, but she is wise.

Rosalind. Or else she could not have the wit to do this : the wiser, the waywarder : make the doors upon a woman's wit and it will out at the casement ; shut that and 'twill out at the key-hole ; stop that, 'twill fly with the smoke out at the chimney.

Orlando. A man that had a wife with such a wit, he might say ' Wit, whither wilt ? '

Rosalind. Nay, you might keep that check for it till you met your wife's wit going to your neighbour's bed.

Orlando. And what wit could wit have to excuse that ?

Rosalind. Marry, to say she came to seek you there. You shall never take her without her answer, unless you take her without her tongue. O, that woman that cannot make her fault her husband's occasion, let her never nurse her child herself, for she will breed it like a fool !

Orlando. For these two hours, Rosalind, I will leave thee.

Rosalind. Alas ! dear love, I cannot lack thee two hours.

Orlando. I must attend the duke at dinner : by two o'clock I will be with thee again.

Rosalind. Ay, go your ways, go your ways ; I knew what you would prove : my friends told me as much, and I thought no less : that flattering tongue of yours won me : 'tis but one cast away, and so, come, death ! Two o'clock is your hour ?

Orlando. Ay, sweet Rosalind.

Rosalind. By my troth, and in good earnest, and so God mend me, and by all pretty oaths that are not dangerous, if you break one jot of your promise or come one minute behind your hour, I will think you the most pathetical break-promise and the most hollow lover and the most unworthy of her you call Rosalind that may be chosen out of the gross band of the unfaithful : therefore beware my censure and keep your promise.

Orlando. With no less religion than if thou wert indeed my Rosalind : so adieu.

Rosalind. Well, Time is the old justice that examines all such offenders, and let Time try : adieu.   [*Exit Orlando.*

Celia. You have simply misused our sex in your love-prate : we must have your doublet and hose plucked over your head, and show the world what the bird hath done to her own nest.

Rosalind. O coz, coz, coz, my pretty little coz, that thou didst know how many fathom deep I am in love ! But it cannot be sounded : my affection hath an unknown bottom, like the bay of Portugal.

Celia. Or rather, bottomless, that as fast as your pour affection in, it runs out.

Rosalind. No, that same wicked bastard of Venus that was begot of thought, conceived of spleen and born of madness, that blind rascally boy that abuses every one's eyes because his own are out, let him be judge how deep I am in love. I 'll tell thee, Aliena, I cannot be out of the sight of Orlando : I 'll go find a shadow and sigh till he come.

Celia. And I 'll sleep.   [*Exeunt.*

SCENE II. *The forest.*

Enter JAQUES, *Lords, and* Foresters.

Jaques. Which is he that killed the deer ?

A Lord. Sir, it was I.

Jaques. Let 's present him to the duke, like a Roman conqueror ; and it would do well to set the deer's horns upon his head, for a branch of victory. Have you no song, forester, for this purpose ?

Forester. Yes, sir.

Jaques. Sing it : 'tis no matter how it be in tune, so it make noise enough.

SONG.

Forester. What shall he have that kill'd the deer ?
     His leather skin and horns to wear.
       Then sing him home ;
       [*The rest shall bear this burden.*
Take thou no scorn to wear the horn ;
It was a crest ere thou wast born :
     Thy father's father wore it,
     And thy father bore it :
The horn, the horn, the lusty horn

Is not a thing to laugh to scorn.
                                    [*Exeunt.*

SCENE III. *The forest.*

Enter ROSALIND *and* CELIA.

Rosalind. How say you now? Is it not past two
o'clock? and here much Orlando!
Celia. I warrant you, with pure love and troubled
brain, he hath ta'en his bow and arrows and is gone
forth to sleep. Look, who comes here.

Enter SILVIUS.

Silvius. My errand is to you, fair youth;
My gentle Phebe bid me give you this:
I know not the contents; but, as I guess
By the stern brow and waspish action
Which she did use as she was writing of it,
It bears an angry tenour: pardon me;
I am but as a guiltless messenger.
Rosalind. Patience herself would startle at this
letter
And play the swaggerer; bear this, bear all:
She says I am not fair, that I lack manners;
She calls me proud, and that she could not love me,
Were man as rare as phœnix. 'Od's my will!
Her love is not the hare that I do hunt:
Why writes she so to me? Well, shepherd, well,
This is a letter of your own device.
Silvius. No, I protest, I know not the contents:
Phebe did write it.
Rosalind.   Come, come, you are a fool
And turn'd into the extremity of love.
I saw her hand: she has a leathern hand,
A freestone-colour'd hand; I verily did think
That her old gloves were on, but 'twas her hands:
She has a huswife's hand; but that 's no matter:
I say she never did invent this letter;
This is a man's invention and his hand.
Silvius. Sure, it is hers.
Rosalind. Why, 'tis a boisterous and a cruel style,
A style for challengers; why, she defies me,
Like Turk to Christian: women's gentle brain
Could not drop forth such giant-rude invention,
Such Ethiope words, blacker in their effect
Than in their countenance. Will you hear the letter?
Silvius. So please you, for I never heard it yet;
Yet heard too much of Phebe's cruelty.
Rosalind. She Phebes me: mark how the tyrant
writes.   [*Reads.*
     Art thou god to shepherd turn'd,
     That a maiden's heart hath burn'd?
Can a woman rail thus?
Silvius. Call you this railing?
Rosalind. [*Reads*]
     Why, thy godhead laid apart,
     Warr'st thou with a woman's heart?
Did you ever hear such railing?
     Whiles the eye of man did woo me,
     That could do no vengeance to me.
Meaning me a beast.
     If the scorn of your bright eyne
     Have power to raise such love in mine,
     Alack, in me what strange effect
     Would they work in mild aspect!
     Whiles you chid me, I did love;
     How then might your prayers move!
     He that brings this love to thee
     Little knows this love in me:

And by him seal up thy mind;
Whether that thy youth and kind
Will the faithful offer take
Of me and all that I can make;
Or else by him my love deny,
And then I 'll study how to die.
Silvius. Call you this chiding?
Celia. Alas, poor shepherd!
Rosalind. Do you pity him? no, he deserves no
pity. Wilt thou love such a woman? What, to
make thee an instrument and play false strains
upon thee! not to be endured! Well, go your
way to her, for I see love hath made thee a tame
snake, and say this to her: that if she love me, I
charge her to love thee; if she will not, I will never
have her unless thou entreat for her. If you be a
true lover, hence, and not a word; for here comes
more company.   [*Exit Silvius.*

Enter OLIVER.

Oliver. Good morrow, fair ones: pray you, if
you know,
Where in the purlieus of this forest stands
A sheep-cote fenced about with olive trees?
Celia. West of this place, down in the neigh-
bour bottom:
The rank of osiers by the murmuring stream
Left on your right hand brings you to the place,
But at this hour the house doth keep itself;
There 's none within.
Oliver. If that an eye may profit by a tongue,
Then should I know you by description;
Such garments and such years: 'The boy is fair,
Of female favour, and bestows himself
Like a ripe sister: the woman low
And browner than her brother.' Are not you
The owner of the house I did enquire for?
Celia. It is no boast, being ask'd, to say we are.
Oliver. Orlando doth commend him to you both,
And to that youth he calls his Rosalind
He sends this bloody napkin. Are you he?
Rosalind. I am: what must we understand by
this?
Oliver. Some of my shame; if you will know
of me
What man I am, and how, and why, and where
This handkercher was stain'd.
Celia.   I pray you, tell it.
Oliver. When last the young Orlando parted
from you
He left a promise to return again
Within an hour, and pacing through the forest,
Chewing the food of sweet and bitter fancy,
Lo, what befel! he threw his eye aside,
And mark what object did present itself:
Under an oak, whose boughs were moss'd with age
And high top bald with dry antiquity,
A wretched ragged man, o'ergrown with hair,
Lay sleeping on his back: about his neck
A green and gilded snake had wreathed itself,
Who with her head nimble in threats approach'd
The opening of his mouth; but suddenly,
Seeing Orlando, it unlink'd itself,
And with indented glides did slip away
Into a bush: under which bush's shade
A lioness, with udders all drawn dry,
Lay couching, head on ground, with catlike watch,
When that the sleeping man should stir; for 'tis
The royal disposition of that beast
To prey on nothing that doth seem as dead:

This seen, Orlando did approach the man
And found it was his brother, his elder brother.
  Celia. O, I have heard him speak of that same
    brother ;
And he did render him the most unnatural
That lived amongst men.
  Oliver.   And well he might so do,
For well I know he was unnatural.
  Rosalind. But, to Orlando : did he leave him
    there,
Food to the suck'd and hungry lioness ?
  Oliver. Twice did he turn his back and pur-
    posed so ;
But kindness, nobler ever than revenge,
And nature, stronger than his just occasion,
Made him give battle to the lioness,
Who quickly fell before him : in which hurtling
From miserable slumber I awaked.
  Celia. Are you his brother ?
  Rosalind.   Was 't you he rescued ?
  Celia. Was 't you that did so oft contrive to kill
    him ?
  Oliver. 'Twas I ; but 'tis not I : I do not shame
To tell you what I was, since my conversion
So sweetly tastes, being the thing I am.
  Rosalind. But, for the bloody napkin ?
  Oliver.   By and by.
When from the first to last betwixt us two
Tears our recountments had most kindly bathed,
As how I came into that desert place :—
In brief, he led me to the gentle duke,
Who gave me fresh array and entertainment,
Committing me unto my brother's love ;
Who led me instantly unto his cave,
There stripp'd himself, and here upon his arm
The lioness had torn some flesh away,
Which all this while had bled ; and now he fainted
And cried, in fainting, upon Rosalind.
Brief, I recover'd him, bound up his wound ;
And, after some small space, being strong at heart,
He sent me hither, stranger as I am,
To tell this story, that you might excuse
His broken promise, and to give this napkin
Dyed in his blood unto the shepherd youth
That he in sport doth call his Rosalind.
                          [*Rosalind swoons.*
  Celia. Why, how now, Ganymede ! sweet
    Ganymede !
  Oliver. Many will swoon when they do look on
    blood.
  Celia. There is more in it. Cousin Ganymede !
  Oliver. Look, he recovers.
  Rosalind. I would I were at home.
  Celia.   We 'll lead you thither.
I pray you, will you take him by the arm ?
  Oliver. Be of good cheer. youth : you a man !
you lack a man's heart.
  Rosalind. I do so, I confess it. Ah, sirrah, a
body would think this was well counterfeited ! I
pray you, tell your brother how well I counterfeited.
Heigh-ho !
  Oliver. This was not counterfeit : there is too
great testimony in your complexion that it was a
passion of earnest.
  Rosalind. Counterfeit, I assure you.
  Oliver. Well then, take a good heart and counterfeit to be a man.
  Rosalind. So I do : but, i' faith. I should have
been a woman by right.
  Celia. Come, you look paler and paler : pray
you, draw homewards. Good sir, go with us.

  Oliver. That will I, for I must bear answer
    back
How you excuse my brother, Rosalind.
  Rosalind. I shall devise something : but, I pray
you, commend my counterfeiting to him. Will
you go ?   [*Exeunt.*

ACT V.

SCENE I. *The forest.*

Enter TOUCHSTONE *and* AUDREY.

          Touchstone.

W E shall find a time, Audrey ; patience,
     gentle Audrey.
  Audrey. Faith, the priest was good enough,
for all the old gentleman's saying.
  Touchstone. A most wicked Sir Oliver, Audrey,
a most vile Martext. But, Audrey, there is a youth
here in the forest, lays claim to you.
  Audrey. Ay, I know who 'tis ; he hath no interest
in me in the world : here comes the man you mean.
  Touchstone. It is meat and drink to me to see a
clown : by my troth, we that have good wits have
much to answer for ; we shall be flouting ; we
cannot hold.

Enter WILLIAM.

  William. Good even, Audrey.
  Audrey. God ye good even, William.
  William. And good even to you, sir.
  Touchstone. Good even, gentle friend. Cover
thy head, cover thy head ; nay. prithee, be covered.
How old are you, friend ?
  William. Five and twenty, sir.
  Touchstone. A ripe age. Is thy name William ?
  William. William, sir.
  Touchstone. A fair name. Wast born i' the forest
here ?
  William. Ay, sir, I thank God.
  Touchstone. 'Thank God ;' a good answer.
Art rich ?
  William. Faith, sir, so so.
  Touchstone. 'So so' is good, very good, very
excellent good ; and yet it is not ; it is but so so.
Art thou wise ?
  William. Ay, sir, I have a pretty wit.
  Touchstone. Why, thou sayest well. I do now
remember a saying, ' The fool doth think he is wise,
but the wise man knows himself to be a fool.' The
heathen philosopher, when he had a desire to eat a
grape, would open his lips when he put it into his
mouth ; meaning thereby that grapes were made to
eat and lips to open. You do love this maid ?
  William. I do, sir.
  Touchstone. Give me your hand. Art thou
learned ?
  William. No, sir.
  Touchstone. Then learn this of me : to have, is
to have ; for it is a figure in rhetoric that drink,
being poured out of a cup into a glass, by filling the
one doth empty the other ; for all your writers do
consent that ipse is he : now. you are not ipse,
for I am he.
  William. Which he, sir ?
  Touchstone. He, sir, that must marry this woman.
Therefore, you clown, abandon,—which is in the
vulgar leave,—the society,—which in the boorish
is company,—of this female,—which in the common

is woman ; which together is, abandon the society of this female, or, clown, thou perishest ; or, to thy better understanding, diest ; or, to wit, I kill thee, make thee away, translate thy life into death. thy liberty into bondage : I will deal in poison with thee, or in bastinado, or in steel ; I will bandy with thee in faction ; I will o'er-run thee with policy ; I will kill thee a hundred and fifty ways : therefore tremble, and depart.

Audrey. Do, good William.

William. God rest you merry, sir.   [*Exit.*

Enter CORIN.

Corin. Our master and mistress seeks you ; come, away, away !

Touchstone. Trip. Audrey ! trip, Audrey ! I attend, I attend.   [*Exeunt.*

SCENE II. *The forest.*

Enter ORLANDO *and* OLIVER.

Orlando. Is 't possible that on so little acquaintance you should like her ? that but seeing you should love her ? and loving woo ? and, wooing, she should grant ? and will you persever to enjoy her ?⁻

Oliver. Neither call the giddiness of it in question, the poverty of her, the small acquaintance, my sudden wooing, nor her sudden consenting ; but say with me, I love Aliena ; say with her that she loves me ; consent with both that we may enjoy each other : it shall be to your good ; for my father's house and all the revenue that was old Sir Rowland's will I estate upon you. and here live and die a shepherd.

Orlando. You have my consent. Let your wedding be to-morrow : thither will I invite the duke and all 's contented followers. Go you and prepare Aliena : for look you, here comes my Rosalind.

Enter ROSALIND.

Rosalind. God save you, brother.

Oliver. And you, fair sister.   [*Exit.*

Rosalind. O, my dear Orlando, how it grieves me to see thee wear thy heart in a scarf !

Orlando. It is my arm.

Rosalind. I thought thy heart had been wounded with the claws of a lion.

Orlando. Wounded it is, but with the eyes of a lady.

Rosalind. Did your brother tell you how I counterfeited to swoon when he showed me your handkercher ?

Orlando. Ay, and greater wonders than that.

Rosalind. O, I know where you are : nay, 'tis true : there was never any thing so sudden but the fight of two rams and Cæsar's thrasonical brag of ' I came, saw, and overcame : ' for your brother and my sister no sooner met but they looked, no sooner looked but they loved, no sooner loved but they sighed, no sooner sighed but they asked one another the reason, no sooner knew the reason but they sought the remedy ; and in these degrees have they made a pair of stairs to marriage which they will climb incontinent, or else be incontinent before marriage : they are in the very wrath of love and they will together ; clubs cannot part them.

Orlando. They shall be married to-morrow, and

I will bid the duke to the nuptial. But, O, how bitter a thing it is to look into happiness through another man's eyes ! By so much the more shall I to-morrow be at the height of heart-heaviness, by how much I shall think my brother happy in having what he wishes for.

Rosalind. Why then, to-morrow I cannot serve your turn for Rosalind ?

Orlando. I can live no longer by thinking.

Rosalind. I will weary you then no longer with idle talking. Know of me then, for now I speak to some purpose, that I know you are a gentleman of good conceit : I speak not this that you should bear a good opinion of my knowledge, insomuch I say I know you are ; neither do I labour for a greater esteem than may in some little measure draw a belief from you, to do yourself good and not to grace me. Believe then, if you please, that I can do strange things : I have, since I was three year old, conversed with a magician, most profound in his art and yet not damnable. If you do love Rosalind so near the heart as your gesture cries it out, when your brother marries Aliena, shall you marry her : I know into what straits of fortune she is driven ; and it is not impossible to me, if it appear not inconvenient to you, to set her before your eyes to-morrow human as she is and without any danger.

Orlando. Speakest thou in sober meanings ?

Rosalind. By my life, I do ; which I tender dearly, though I say I am a magician. Therefore, put you in your best array ; bid your friends ; for if you will be married to-morrow, you shall, and to Rosalind, if you will.

Enter SILVIUS *and* PHEBE.

Look, here comes a lover of mine and a lover of hers.

Phebe. Youth, you have done me much ungentleness,
To show the letter that I writ to you.

Rosalind. I care not if I have : it is my study
To seem despiteful and ungentle to you :
You are there followed by a faithful shepherd ;
Look upon him, love him ; he worships you.

Phebe. Good shepherd, tell this youth what 'tis to love.

Silvius. It is to be all made of sighs and tears ;
And so am I for Phebe.

Phebe. And I for Ganymede.

Orlando. And I for Rosalind.

Rosalind. And I for no woman.

Silvius. It is to be all made of faith and service ;
And so am I for Phebe.

Phebe. And I for Ganymede.

Orlando. And I for Rosalind.

Rosalind. And I for no woman.

Silvius. It is to be all made of fantasy,
All made of passion and all made of wishes,
All adoration, duty, and observance,
All humbleness, all patience and impatience,
† All purity, all trial, all observance ;
And so am I for Phebe.

Phebe. And so am I for Ganymede.

Orlando. And so am I for Rosalind.

Rosalind. And so am I for no woman.

Phebe. If this be so, why blame you me to love you ?

Silvius. If this be so, why blame you me to love you ?

Orlando. If this be so, why blame you me to love you?

Rosalind. Who do you speak to, 'Why blame you me to love you?'

Orlando. To her that is not here, nor doth not hear.

Rosalind. Pray you, no more of this; 'tis like the howling of Irish wolves against the moon. [*To Silvius*] I will help you, if I can : [*To Phebe*] I would love you, if I could. To-morrow meet me all together. [*To Phebe*] I will marry you, if ever I marry woman, and I 'll be married to-morrow : [*To Orlando*] I will satisfy you, if ever I satisfied man, and you shall be married to-morrow : [*To Silvius*] I will content you, if what pleases you contents you, and you shall be married to-morrow. [*To Orlando*] As you love Rosalind, meet : [*To Silvius*] as you love Phebe, meet : and as I love no woman, I 'll meet. So fare you well : I have left you commands.

Silvius. I 'll not fail, if I live.

Phebe. Nor I.

Orlando. Nor I.   [*Exeunt.*

SCENE III. *The forest.*

Enter TOUCHSTONE *and* AUDREY.

Touchstone. To-morrow is the joyful day, Audrey ; to-morrow will we be married.

Audrey. I do desire it with all my heart ; and I hope it is no dishonest desire to desire to be a woman of the world. Here come two of the banished duke's pages.

Enter *two* Pages.

First Page. Well met, honest gentleman.

Touchstone. By my troth, well met. Come, sit, sit, and a song.

Second Page. We are for you : sit i' the middle.

First Page. Shall we clap into 't roundly, without hawking or spitting or saying we are hoarse, which are the only prologues to a bad voice?

Second Page. I' faith, i' faith ; and both in a tune, like two gipsies on a horse.

SONG.

It was a lover and his lass,
  With a hey, and a ho, and a hey nonino,
That o'er the green corn-field did pass
In the spring time, the only pretty ring time,
When birds do sing, hey ding a ding, ding :
Sweet lovers love the spring.

Between the acres of the rye,
  With a hey, and a ho, and a hey nonino,
These pretty country folks would lie,
  In spring time, &c.

This caro they began that hour,
  With a hey, and a ho, and a hey nonino,
How that a life was but a flower
  In spring time, &c.

And therefore take the present time,
  With a hey, and a ho, and a hey nonino ;
For love is crowned with the prime
  In spring time, &c.

Touchstone. Truly, young gentlemen, though there was no great matter in the ditty, yet the note was very untuneable.

First Page. You are deceived, sir : we kept time, we lost not our time.

Touchstone. By my troth, yes ; I count it but time lost to hear such a foolish song. God be wi' you ; and God mend your voices! Come, Audrey.
                                              [*Exeunt.*

SCENE IV. *The forest.*

Enter DUKE senior, AMIENS, JAQUES, ORLANDO,
    OLIVER, *and* CELIA.

Duke Senior. Dost thou believe, Orlando, that the boy
Can do all this that he hath promised?

Orlando. I sometimes do believe, and sometimes do not ;
† As those that fear they hope, and know they fear.

Enter ROSALIND, SILVIUS, *and* PHEBE.

Rosalind. Patience once more, whiles our compact is urged :
You say, if I bring in your Rosalind,
You will bestow her on Orlando here?

Duke Senior. That would I, had I kingdoms to give with her.

Rosalind. And you say, you will have her, when I bring her?

Orlando. That would I, were I of all kingdoms king.

Rosalind. You say, you 'll marry me, if I be willing?

Phebe. That will I, should I die the hour after.

Rosalind. But if you do refuse to marry me,
You 'll give yourself to this most faithful shepherd?

Phebe. So is the bargain.

Rosalind. You say, that you 'll have Phebe, if she will?

Silvius. Though to have her and death were both one thing.

Rosalind. I have promised to make all this matter even.
Keep you your word, O duke, to give your daughter ;
You yours, Orlando, to receive his daughter :
Keep your word, Phebe, that you 'll marry me,
Or else refusing me, to wed this shepherd :
Keep your word, Silvius, that you 'll marry her,
If she refuse me : and from hence I go,
To make these doubts all even.
                          [*Exeunt Rosalind and Celia.*

Duke Senior. I do remember in this shepherd boy
Some lively touches of my daughter's favour.

Orlando. My lord, the first time that I ever saw him
Methought he was a brother to your daughter :
But, my good lord, this boy is forest-born,
And hath been tutor'd in the rudiments
Of many desperate studies by his uncle,
Whom he reports to be a great magician,
Obscured in the circle of this forest.

Enter TOUCHSTONE *and* AUDREY.

Jaques. There is, sure, another flood toward, and these couples are coming to the ark. Here comes a pair of very strange beasts, which in all tongues are called fools.

Touchstone. Salutations and greeting to you all !

Jaques. Good my lord, bid him welcome : this is the motley-minded gentleman that I have so often met in the forest : he hath been a courtier, he swears.

Touchstone. If any man doubt that, let him put me to my purgation. I have trod a measure ; I have flattered a lady ; I have been politic with my friend, smooth with mine enemy ; I have undone three tailors ; I have had four quarrels, and like to have fought one.

Jaques. And how was that ta'en up ?

Touchstone. Faith, we met, and found the quarrel was upon the seventh cause.

Jaques. How seventh cause ? Good my lord, like this fellow.

Duke Senior. I like him very well.

Touchstone. God 'ild you, sir ; I desire you of the like. I press in here, sir, amongst the rest of the country copulatives, to swear and to forswear ; according as marriage binds and blood breaks : a poor virgin, sir, an ill-favoured thing, sir, but mine own ; a poor humour of mine, sir, to take that that no man else will : rich honesty dwells like a miser, sir, in a poor house ; as your pearl in your foul oyster.

Duke Senior. By my faith, he is very swift and sententious.

Touchstone. According to the fool's bolt, sir, and such dulcet diseases.

Jaques. But, for the seventh cause ; how did you find the quarrel on the seventh cause ?

Touchstone. Upon a lie seven times removed :— bear your body more seeming, Audrey :—as thus, sir. I did dislike the cut of a certain courtier's beard : he sent me word, if I said his beard was not cut well, he was in the mind it was : this is called the Retort Courteous. If I sent him word again, ' it was not well cut,' he would send me word, he cut it to please himself : this is called the Quip Modest. If again ' it was not well cut,' he disabled my judgement : this is called the Reply Churlish. If again ' it was not well cut,' he would answer, I spake not true : this is called the Reproof Valiant. If again ' it was not well cut,' he would say, I lied : this is called the Countercheck Quarrelsome : and so to the Lie Circumstantial and the Lie Direct.

Jaques. And how oft did you say his beard was not well cut ?

Touchstone. I durst go no further than the Lie Circumstantial, nor he durst not give me the Lie Direct ; and so we measured swords and parted.

Jaques. Can you nominate in order now the degrees of the lie ?

Touchstone. O sir, we quarrel in print, by the book ; as you have books for good manners : I will name you the degrees. The first, the Retort Courteous ; the second, the Quip Modest ; the third, the Reply Churlish ; the fourth, the Reproof Valiant ; the fifth, the Countercheck Quarrelsome ; the sixth, the Lie with Circumstance ; the seventh, the Lie Direct. All these you may avoid but the Lie Direct ; and you may avoid that too, with an If. I knew when seven justices could not take up a quarrel, but when the parties were met themselves, one of them thought but of an If, as, ' If you said so, then I said so ; ' and they shook hands and swore brothers. Your If is the only peace-maker ; much virtue in If.

Jaques. Is not this a rare fellow, my lord ? he 's as good at any thing and yet a fool.

Duke Senior. He uses his folly like a stalking-horse and under the presentation of that he shoots his wit.

Enter Hymen, Rosalind, *and* Celia.

Still Music.

Hymen. Then is there mirth in heaven,
  When earthly things made even
   Atone together.
 Good duke, receive thy daughter :
 Hymen from heaven brought her,
  Yea, brought her hither,
 That thou mightst join her hand with his
 Whose heart within his bosom is.

Rosalind. [*To Duke*] To you I give myself, for I am yours.
[*To Orlando*] To you I give myself, for I am yours.

Duke Senior. If there be truth in sight, you are my daughter.

Orlando. If there be truth in sight, you are my Rosalind.

Phebe. If sight and shape be true,
Why then, my love adieu !

Rosalind. I 'll have no father, if you be not he :
I 'll have no husband, if you be not he :
Nor ne'er wed woman, if you be not she.

Hymen. Peace, ho ! I bar confusion :
 'Tis I must make conclusion
 Of these most strange events :
 Here 's eight that must take hands
 To join in Hymen's bands,
  If truth holds true contents.
 You and you no cross shall part :
 You and you are heart in heart :
 You to his love must accord,
 Or have a woman to your lord :
 You and you are sure together,
 As the winter to foul weather.
 Whiles a wedlock-hymn we sing,
 Feed yourselves with questioning ;
 That reason wonder may diminish,
 How thus we met, and these things finish.

Song.

Wedding is great Juno's crown :
 A blessed bond of board and bed !
'Tis Hymen peoples every town ;
 High wedlock then be honoured :
Honour, high honour and renown,
To Hymen, god of every town !

Duke Senior. O my dear niece, welcome thou art to me !
Even daughter, welcome, in no less degree.

Phebe. I will not eat my word, now thou art mine ;
Thy faith my fancy to thee doth combine.

Enter Jaques de Boys.

Jaques de Boys. Let me have audience for a word or two :
I am the second son of old Sir Rowland,
That bring these tidings to this fair assembly.
Duke Frederick, hearing how that every day
Men of great worth resorted to this forest,
Address'd a mighty power ; which were on foot,
In his own conduct, purposely to take
His brother here and put him to the sword :
And to the skirts of this wild wood he came ;
Where meeting with an old religious man,
After some question with him, was converted

Both from his enterprise and from the world,
His crown bequeathing to his banish'd brother,
And all their lands restored to them again
That were with him exiled. This to be true,
I do engage my life.
   Duke Senior.   Welcome, young man ;
Thou offer'st fairly to thy brothers' wedding :
To one his lands withheld, and to the other
A land itself at large, a potent dukedom.
First, in this forest let us do those ends
That here were well begun and well begot :
And after, every of this happy number
That have endured shrewd days and nights with us
Shall share the good of our returned fortune,
According to the measure of their states.
Meantime, forget this new-fall'n dignity
And fall into our rustic revelry.
Play, music ! And you, brides and bridegrooms all
With measure heap'd in joy, to the measures fall.
   Jaques.   Sir, by your patience. If I heard you
rightly,
The duke hath put on a religious life
And thrown into neglect the pompous court ?
   Jaques de Boys.   He hath.
   Jaques.   To him will I : out of these convertites
there is much matter to be heard and learn'd.
[*To Duke*] You to your former honour I bequeath ;
Your patience and your virtue well deserves it :
[*To Orlando*] You to a love that your true faith doth
   merit :
[*To Oliver*] You to your land and love and great
   allies ;
[*To Silvius*] You to a long and well-deserved bed :
[*To Touchstone*] And you to wrangling ; for thy
   loving voyage
Is but for two months victuall'd. So, to your pleasures :

I am for other than for dancing measures.
   Duke Senior. Stay, Jaques, stay.
   Jaques. To see no pastime I : what you would
   have
I 'll stay to know at your abandon'd cave.   [*Exit.*
   Duke Senior. Proceed, proceed : we will begin
   these rites,
As we do trust they 'll end, in true delights.
                           [*A dance.*

EPILOGUE.

   Rosalind. It is not the fashion to see the lady the
epilogue ; but it is no more unhandsome than to
see the lord the prologue. If it be true that good
wine needs no bush, 'tis true that a good play needs
no epilogue ; yet to good wine they do use good
bushes, and good plays prove the better by the help
of good epilogues. What a case am I in then, that
am neither a good epilogue nor cannot insinuate
with you in the behalf of a good play ! I am not
furnished like a beggar, therefore to beg will not
become me : my way is to conjure you ; and I 'll
begin with the women. I charge you, O women,
for the love you bear to men, to like as much of this
play as please you : and I charge you, O men, for
the love you bear to women—as I perceive by your
simpering, none of you hates them—that between
you and the women the play may please. If I were
a woman I would kiss as many of you as had beards
that pleased me, complexions that liked me and
breaths that I defied not : and, I am sure, as many as
have good beards or good faces or sweet breaths
will, for my kind offer, when I make curtsy, bid me
farewell.   [*Exeunt.*

THE

TAMING OF THE SHREW

DRAMATIS PERSONÆ

A Lord.
CHRISTOPHER SLY, *a tinker,* ⎫ Persons in the
Hostess, Page, Players, Hunts-⎬ Induction.
men, and Servants. ⎭

BAPTISTA, *a rich gentleman of Padua.*
VINCENTIO, *an old gentleman of Pisa.*
LUCENTIO, *son of Vincentio, in love with* Bianca.
PETRUCHIO, *a gentleman of Verona, a suitor to*
Katharina.

GREMIO, ⎫ *suitors to* Bianca.
HORTENSIO, ⎭

TRANIO, ⎫ *servants to* Lucentio.
BIONDELLO, ⎭

GRUMIO, ⎫ *servants to* Petruchio.
CURTIS, ⎭

A Pedant.

KATHARINA, *the shrew,* ⎫ *daughters to* Baptista.
BIANCA, ⎭
Widow.

Tailor, Haberdasher, *and* Servants *attending on*
Baptista *and* Petruchio.

SCENE : Padua, and Petruchio's country house.

INDUCTION

SCENE I. *Before an alehouse on a heath.*

Enter HOSTESS *and* SLY.

Sly.

I 'll pheeze you, in faith.
Hostess. A pair of stocks, you rogue !
Sly. Ye are a baggage : the Slys are no rogues ;
look in the chronicles ; we came in with Richard
Conqueror. Therefore *paucas pallabris* ; let the world
slide : *sessa* !
Hostess. You will not pay for the glasses you
have burst ?
Sly. No, not a denier. Go by, Jeronimy : go
to thy cold bed, and warm thee.
Hostess. I know my remedy ; I must go fetch
the third-borough. [*Exit.*
Sly. Third, or fourth, or fifth borough, I 'll
answer him by law : I 'll not budge an inch, boy :
let him come, and kindly. [*Falls asleep.*

Horns winded. Enter a Lord, *from hunting,*
with his train.

Lord. Huntsman, I charge thee, tender well my
hounds :
† Brach Merriman, the poor cur is emboss'd :
And couple Clowder with the deep-mouth'd brach.
Saw'st thou not, boy, how Silver made it good
At the hedge-corner, in the coldest fault ?
I would not lose the dog for twenty pound.
First Huntsman. Why, Belman is as good as he,
my lord ;
He cried upon it at the merest loss
And twice to-day pick'd out the dullest scent :
Trust me, I take him for the better dog.
Lord. Thou art a fool : if Echo were as fleet,
I would esteem him worth a dozen such,
But sup them well and look unto them all :
To-morrow I intend to hunt again.
First Huntsman. I will, my lord.
Lord. What 's here ? one dead, or drunk ? See,
doth he breathe ?
Second Huntsman. He breathes, my lord. Were
he not warm'd with ale,
This were a bed but cold to sleep so soundly.
Lord. A monstrous beast ! how like a swine
he lies !
Grim death, how foul and loathsome is thine image !
Sirs, I will practise on this drunken man.
What think you, if he were convey'd to bed,
Wrapp'd in sweet clothes, rings put upon his fingers,
A most delicious banquet by his bed,
And brave attendants near him when he wakes,
Would not the beggar then forget himself ?
First Huntsman. Believe me, lord, I think he
cannot choose.
Second Huntsman. It would seem strange unto him
when he waked.
Lord. Even as a flattering dream or worthless
fancy.
Then take him up and manage well the jest :
Carry him gently to my fairest chamber
And hang it round with all my wanton pictures :
Balm his foul head in warm distilled waters
And burn sweet wood to make the lodging sweet :
Procure me music ready when he wakes,
To make a dulcet and a heavenly sound ;
And if he chance to speak, be ready straight
And with a low submissive reverence
Say ' What is it your honour will command ?'
Let one attend him with a silver basin
Full of rose-water and bestrew'd with flowers ;
Another bear the ewer, the third a diaper,
And say ' Will 't please your lordship cool your
hands ?'
Some one be ready with a costly suit
And ask him what apparel he will wear ;

Another tell him of his hounds and horse,
And that his lady mourns at his disease :
Persuade him that he hath been lunatic ;
† And when he says he is, say that he dreams,
For he is nothing but a mighty lord.
This do and do it kindly, gentle sirs :
It will be pastime passing excellent,
If it be husbanded with modesty.
First Huntsman.   My lord, I warrant you we will
   play our part,
As he shall think by our true diligence
He is no less than what we say he is.
Lord.   Take him up gently and to bed with him ;
And each one to his office when he wakes.
   [*Some bear out Sly. A trumpet sounds.*
Sirrah, go see what trumpet 'tis that sounds :
   [*Exit Servingman.*
Belike, some noble gentleman that means,
Travelling some journey, to repose him here.

Re-enter Servingman.

How now ! who is it ?
Servingman.   An 't please your honour, players
That offer service to your lordship.
Lord.   Bid them come near.

Enter Players.

   Now, fellows, you are welcome.
Players.   We thank your honour.
Lord.   Do you intend to stay with me to-night ?
A Player.   So please your lordship to accept
   our duty.
Lord.   With all my heart.   This fellow I remember
Since once he play'd a farmer's eldest son :
'Twas where you woo'd the gentlewoman so well :
I have forgot your name ; but, sure, that part
Was aptly fitted and naturally perform'd.
A Player.   I think 'twas Soto that your honour
means.
Lord.   'Tis very true : thou didst it excellent.
Well, you are come to me in happy time ;
The rather for I have some sport in hand
Wherein your cunning can assist me much.
There is a lord will hear you play to-night :
But I am doubtful of your modesties ;
Lest over-eyeing of his odd behaviour,—
For yet his honour never heard a play—
You break into some merry passion
And so offend him ; for I tell you, sirs,
If you should smile he grows impatient.
A Player.   Fear not, my lord : we can contain
   ourselves,
Were he the veriest antic in the world.
Lord.   Go, sirrah, take them to the buttery,
And give them friendly welcome every one :
Let them want nothing that my house affords.
   [*Exit one with the Players.*
Sirrah, go you to Barthol'mew my page,
And see him dress'd in all suits like a lady :
That done, conduct him to the drunkard's chamber ;
And call him ' madam,' do him obeisance.
Tell him from me, as he will win my love,
He bear himself with honourable action,
Such as he hath observed in noble ladies
Unto their lords, by them accomplished :
Such duty to the drunkard let him do
With soft low tongue and lowly courtesy,

And say ' What is 't your honour will command,
Wherein your lady and your humble wife
May show her duty and make known her love ? '
And then with kind embracements, tempting kisses,
And with declining head into his bosom,
Bid him shed tears, as being overjoy'd
To see her noble lord restored to health,
Who for this seven years hath esteemed him
No better than a poor and loathsome beggar :
And if the boy have not a woman's gift
To rain a shower of commanded tears,
An onion will do well for such a shift,
Which in a napkin being close convey'd
Shall in despite enforce a watery eye.
See this dispatch'd with all the haste thou canst :
Anon I 'll give thee more instructions.
   [*Exit a Servingman.*
I know the boy will well usurp the grace,
Voice, gait and action of a gentlewoman :
I long to hear him call the drunkard husband,
And how my men will stay themselves from laughter
When they do homage to this simple peasant.
I 'll in to counsel them ; haply my presence
May well abate the over-merry spleen,
Which otherwise would grow into extremes.
   [*Exeunt.*

SCENE II.   *A bed-chamber in the Lord's house.*

Enter aloft Sly, *with* Attendants ; *some with
   apparel, others with basin and ewer and other
   appurtenances ; and* Lord.

Sly.   For God's sake, a pot of small ale.
First Servingman.   Will 't please your lordship
   drink a cup of sack ?
Second Servingman.   Will 't please your honour
   taste of these conserves ?
Third Servingman.   What raiment will your honour
   wear to-day ?
Sly.   I am Christophero Sly ; call not me ' honour '
nor ' lordship : ' I ne'er drank sack in my life ;
and if you give me any conserves, give me conserves
of beef : ne'er ask me what raiment I 'll wear ; for
I have no more doublets than backs, no more stockings than legs, nor no more shoes than feet ; nay,
sometime more feet than shoes, or such shoes as
my toes look through the over-leather.
Lord.   Heaven cease this idle humour in your
   honour !
O, that a mighty man of such descent,
Of such possessions and so high esteem,
Should be infused with so foul a spirit !
Sly.   What, would you make me mad ?   Am not
I Christopher Sly, old Sly's son of Burton-heath,
by birth a pedlar, by education a cardmaker, by
transmutation a bear-herd, and now by present
profession a tinker ?   Ask Marian Hacket, the fat
ale-wife of Wincot, if she know me not : if she say
I am not fourteen pence on the score for sheer ale,
score me up for the lyingest knave in Christendom.
What !   I am not bestraught : here 's—
Third Servingman.   O, this it is that makes your
   lady mourn !
Second Servingman.   O, this it is that makes your
   servants droop !
Lord.   Hence comes it that your kindred shuns
   your house,
As beaten hence by your strange lunacy.
O noble lord, bethink thee of thy birth,
Call home thy ancient thoughts from banishment

And banish hence these abject lowly dreams.
Look how thy servants do attend on thee,
Each in his office ready at thy beck.
Wilt thou have music ? hark ! Apollo plays
                             [*Music.*
And twenty caged nightingales do sing :
Or wilt thou sleep ? we 'll have thee to a couch
Softer and sweeter than the lustful bed
On purpose trimm'd up for Semiramis.
Say thou wilt walk ; we will bestrew the ground :
Or wilt thou ride ? thy horses shall be trapp'd,
Their harness studded all with gold and pearl.
Dost thou love hawking ? thou hast hawks will soar
Above the morning lark : or wilt thou hunt ?
Thy hounds shall make the welkin answer them
And fetch shrill echoes from the hollow earth.
    First Servingman. Say thou wilt course ; thy
      greyhounds are as swift
As breathed stags, ay, fleeter than the roe.
    Second Servingman. Dost thou love pictures ? we
      will fetch thee straight
Adonis painted by a running brook,
And Cytherea all in sedges hid,
Which seem to move and wanton with her breath,
Even as the waving sedges play with wind.
    Lord. We 'll show thee Io as she was a maid,
And how she was beguiled and surprised,
As lively painted as the deed was done.
    Third Servingman. Or Daphne roaming through a
      thorny wood,
Scratching her legs that one shall swear she bleeds,
And at that sight shall sad Apollo weep,
So workmanly the blood and tears are drawn.
    Lord. Thou art a lord and nothing but a lord :
Thou hast a lady far more beautiful
Than any woman in this waning age.
    First Servingman. And till the tears that she hath
    shed for thee
Like envious floods o'er-run her lovely face,
She was the fairest creature in the world ;
And yet she is inferior to none.
    Sly. Am I a lord ? and have I such a lady ?
Or do I dream ? or have I dream'd till now ?
I do not sleep : I see, I hear, I speak ;
I smell sweet savours and I feel soft things :
Upon my life, I am a lord indeed
And not a tinker nor Christopher Sly.
Well, bring our lady hither to our sight ;
And once again, a pot o' the smallest ale.
    Second Servingman. Will 't please your mightiness
      to wash your hands ?
O, how we joy to see your wit restored !
O, that once more you knew but what you are !
These fifteen years you have been in a dream ;
Or when you waked, so waked as if you slept.
    Sly. These fifteen years ! by my fay, a goodly
    nap.
But did I never speak of all that time ?
    First Servingman. O, yes, my lord, but very idle
      words :
For though you lay here in this goodly chamber,
Yet would you say ye were beaten out of door ;
And rail upon the hostess of the house ;
And say you would present her at the leet,
Because she brought stone jugs and no seal'd
    quarts :
Sometimes you would call out for Cicely Hacket.
    Sly. Ay, the woman's maid of the house.
    Third Servingman. Why, sir, you know no house
      nor no such maid,
Nor no such men as you have reckon'd up,

As Stephen Sly, and old John Naps of Greece
And Peter Turph and Henry Pimpernell
And twenty more such names and men as these
Which never were nor no man ever saw.
    Sly. Now Lord be thanked for my good amends !
    All. Amen.
    Sly. I thank thee : thou shalt not lose by it.

Enter the Page *as a lady, with attendants.*

    Page. How fares my noble lord ?
    Sly. Marry, I fare well ; for here is cheer enough.
Where is my wife ?
    Page. Here, noble lord : what is thy will with
    her :
    Sly. Are you my wife and will not call me hus-
    band ?
My men should call me ' lord : ' I am your goodman.
    Page. My husband and my lord, my lord and
    husband ;
I am your wife in all obedience.
    Sly. I know it well. What must I call her ?
    Lord. Madam.
    Sly. Al'ce madam, or Joan madam ?
    Lord. ' Madam,' and nothing else : so lords
    call ladies.
    Sly. Madam wife, they say that I have dream'd
And slept above some fifteen year or more.
    Page. Ay, and the time seems thirty unto me,
Being all this time abandon'd from your bed.
    Sly. 'Tis much. Servants, leave me and her
alone.
Madam, undress you and come now to bed.
    Page. Thrice-noble lord, let me entreat of you
To pardon me yet for a night or two,
Or, if not so, until the sun be set :
For your physicians have expressly charged,
In peril to incur your former malady,
That I should yet absent me from your bed :
I hope this reason stands for my excuse.
    Sly. Ay, it stands so that I may hardly tarry so
long. But I would be loath to fall into my dreams
again : I will therefore tarry in despite of the flesh
and the blood.

Enter a Messenger.

    Messenger. Your honour's players, hearing your
    amendment,
Are come to play a pleasant comedy ;
For so your doctors hold it very meet,
Seeing too much sadness hath congeal'd your blood,
And melancholy is the nurse of frenzy :
Therefore they thought it good you hear a play
And frame your mind to mirth and merriment.
Which bars a thousand harms and lengthens life.
    Sly. Marry, I will, let them play it. Is not a
comonty a Christmas gambold or a tumbling-trick ?
    Page. No, my good lord ; it is more pleasing
    stuff.
    Sly. What, household stuff ?
    Page. It is a kind of history.
    Sly. Well, we 'll see 't. Come, madam wife,
sit by my side and let the world slip : we shall ne'er
be younger.

                      Flourish.

ACT I.

SCENE I. *Padua. A public place.*

Enter LUCENTIO *and his man* TRANIO.

Lucentio.

Tranio, since for the great desire I had
    To see fair Padua, nursery of arts,
    I am arrived for fruitful Lombardy,
The pleasant garden of great Italy ;
And by my father's love and leave am arm'd
With his good will and thy good company,
My trusty servant, well approved in all,
Here let us breathe and haply institute
A course of learning and ingenious studies.
Pisa renown'd for grave citizens
Gave me my being and my father first,
A merchant of great traffic through the world,
Vincentio, come of the Bentivolii.
Vincentio's son brought up in Florence
It shall become to serve all hopes conceived,
To deck his fortune with his virtuous deeds :
And therefore, Tranio, for the time I study,
Virtue and that part of philosophy
Will I apply that treats of happiness
By virtue specially to be achieved.
Tell me thy mind ; for I have Pisa left
And am to Padua come, as he that leaves
A shallow plash to plunge him in the deep
And with satiety seeks to quench his thirst.
    Tranio. Mi perdonato, gentle master mine,
I am in all affected as yourself ;
Glad that you thus continue your resolve
To suck the sweets of sweet philosophy.
Only, good master, while we do admire
This virtue and this moral discipline,
Let 's be no stoics nor no stocks, I pray ;
Or so devote to Aristotle's checks
As Ovid be an outcast quite abjured :
Balk logic with acquaintance that you have
And practise rhetoric in your common talk ;
Music and poesy use to quicken you ;
The mathematics and the metaphysics,
Fall to them as you find your stomach serves you ;
No profit grows where is no pleasure ta'en :
In brief, sir, study what you most affect.
    Lucentio. Gramercies, Tranio, well dost thou
advise,
If, Biondello, thou wert come ashore,
We could at once put us in readiness,
And take a lodging fit to entertain
Such friends as time in Padua shall beget.
But stay a while : what company is this ?
    Tranio. Master, some show to welcome us to
town.

Enter BAPTISTA, KATHARINA, BIANCA, GREMIO,
and HORTENSIO. LUCENTIO *and* TRANIO
stand by.

    Baptista. Gentlemen, importune me no farther,
For how I firmly am resolved you know ;
That is, not to bestow my youngest daughter
Before I have a husband for the elder :
If either of you both love Katharina,
Because I know you well and love you well,
Leave shall you have to court her at your pleasure.
    Gremio. [*Aside*] To cart her rather : she 's too
rough for me.
There, there, Hortensio, will you any wife ?

    Katharina. I pray you, sir, is it your will
To make a stale of me amongst these mates ?
    Hortensio. Mates, maid ! how mean you that ?
    no mates for you,
Unless you were of gentler, milder mould.
    Katharina. I' faith, sir, you shall never need to
    fear :
I wis it is not half way to her heart ;
But if it were, doubt not her care should be
To comb your noddle with a three-legg'd stool
And paint your face and use you like a fool.
    Hortensio. From all such devils, good Lord de-
liver us !
    Gremio. And me too, good Lord !
    Tranio. Hush, master ! here 's some good
pastime toward :
That wench is stark mad or wonderful froward.
    Lucentio. But in the other's silence do I see
Maid's mild behaviour and sobriety.
Peace, Tranio !
    Tranio. Well said, master ; mum ! and gaze
your fill.
    Baptista. Gentlemen, that I may soon make good
What I have said, Bianca, get you in :
And let it not displease thee, good Bianca,
For I will love thee ne'er the less, my girl.
    Katharina. A pretty peat ! it is best
Put finger in the eye, an she knew why.
    Bianca. Sister, content you in my discontent.
Sir, to your pleasure humbly I subscribe :
My books and instruments shall be my company,
On them to look and practise by myself.
    Lucentio. Hark, Tranio ! thou may'st hear Min-
erva speak.
    Hortensio. Signior Baptista, will you be so
strange ?
Sorry am I that our good will effects
Bianca's grief.
    Gremio. Why will you mew her up,
Signior Baptista, for this fiend of hell,
And make her bear the penance of her tongue ?
    Baptista. Gentlemen, content ye ; I am resolved :
Go in, Bianca :   [*Exit Bianca.*
And for I know she taketh most delight
In music, instruments and poetry,
Schoolmasters will I keep within my house,
Fit to instruct her youth. If you, Hortensio,
Or Signior Gremio, you, know any such,
Prefer them hither ; for to cunning men
I will be very kind, and liberal
To mine own children in good bringing up :
And so farewell. Katharina, you may stay ;
For I have more to commune with Bianca.
    [*Exit.*
    Katharina. Why, and I trust I may go too, may
I not ? What, shall I be appointed hours ; as though,
belike, I knew not what to take, and what to leave,
ha ?   [*Exit.*
    Gremio. You may go to the devil's dam : your
gifts are so good, here 's none will hold you. Their
love is not so great, Hortensio, but we may blow
our nails together, and fast it fairly out : our cake 's
dough on both sides. Farewell : yet, for the love
I bear my sweet Bianca, if I can by any means light
on a fit man to teach her that wherein she delights,
I will wish him to her father.
    Hortensio. So will I, Signior Gremio : but a
word, I pray. Though the nature of our quarrel yet
never brooked parle, know now, upon advice, it
toucheth us both, that we may yet again have access
to our fair mistress and be happy rivals in Bianca's

love, to labour and effect one thing specially.

Gremio. What 's that, I pray ?

Hortensio. Marry, sir, to get a husband for her sister.

Gremio. A husband ! a devil.

Hortensio. I say, a husband.

Gremio. I say, a devil. Thinkest thou, Hortensio, though her father be very rich, any man is so very a fool to be married to hell ?

Hortensio. Tush, Gremio, though it pass your patience and mine to endure her loud alarums, why, man, there be good fellows in the world, an a man could light on them, would take her with all faults, and money enough.

Gremio. I cannot tell ; but I had as lief take her dowry with this condition, to be whipped at the high cross every morning.

Hortensio. Faith, as you say, there 's small choice in rotten apples. But come ; since this bar in law makes us friends, it shall be so far forth friendly maintained till by helping Baptista's eldest daughter to a husband we set his youngest free for a husband, and then have to 't afresh. Sweet Bianca ! Happy man be his dole ! He that runs fastest gets the ring. How say you, Signior Gremio ?

Gremio. I am agreed ; and would I had given him the best horse in Padua to begin his wooing that would thoroughly woo her, wed her and bed her and rid the house of her ! Come on.

[*Exeunt Gremio and Hortensio.*

Tranio. I pray, sir, tell me, is it possible
That love should of a sudden take such hold ?

Lucentio. O Tranio, till I found it to be true,
I never thought it possible or likely ;
But see, while idly I stood looking on,
I found the effect of love in idleness :
And now in plainness do confess to thee,
That art to me as secret and as dear
As Anna to the queen of Carthage was,
Tranio, I burn, I pine, I perish, Tranio,
If I achieve not this young modest girl.
Counsel me, Tranio, for I know thou canst ;
Assist me, Tranio, for I know thou wilt.

Tranio. Master, it is no time to chide you now ;
Affection is not rated from the heart :
If love have touch'd you, nought remains but so,
' Redime te captum quam queas minimo.'

Lucentio. Gramercies, lad, go forward ; this contents :
The rest will comfort, for thy counsel 's sound.

Tranio. Master, you look'd so longly on the maid,
Perhaps you mark'd not what 's the pith of all.

Lucentio. O yes, I saw sweet beauty in her face,
Such as the daughter of Agenor had,
That made great Jove to humble him to her hand,
When with his knees he kiss'd the Cretan strand.

Tranio. Saw you no more ? mark'd you not how her sister
Began to scold and raise up such a storm
That mortal ears might hardly endure the din ?

Lucentio. Tranio, I saw her coral lips to move
And with her breath she did perfume the air :
Sacred and sweet was all I saw in her.

Tranio. Nay, then, 'tis time to stir him from his trance.
I pray, awake, sir : if you love the maid,
Bend thoughts and wits to achieve her. Thus it stands :
Her elder sister is so curst and shrewd
That till the father rid his hands of her,

Master, your love must live a maid at home ;
And therefore has he closely mew'd her up,
Because she will not be annoy'd with suitors.

Lucentio. Ah, Tranio, what a cruel father's he !
But art thou not advised, he took some care
To get her cunning schoolmasters to instruct her ?

Tranio. Ay, marry, am I, sir ; and now 'tis plotted.

Lucentio. I have it, Tranio.

Tranio.   Master, for my hand,
Both our inventions meet and jump in one.

Lucentio. Tell me thine first.

Tranio.   You will be schoolmaster
And undertake the teaching of the maid :
That 's your device.

Lucentio.   It is : may it be done ?

Tranio. Not possible ; for who shall bear your part,
And be in Padua here Vincentio's son,
Keep house and ply his book, welcome his friends,
Visit his countrymen and banquet them ?

Lucentio. Basta ; content thee, for I have it full.
We have not yet been seen in any house,
Nor can we be distinguish'd by our faces
For man or master ; then it follows thus ;
Thou shalt be master, Tranio, in my stead,
Keep house and port and servants, as I should :
I will some other be, some Florentine,
Some Neapolitan, or meaner man of Pisa.
'Tis hatch'd and shall be so : Tranio, at once
Uncase thee ; take my colour'd hat and cloak :
When Biondello comes, he waits on thee ;
But I will charm him first to keep his tongue.

Tranio. So had you need.
In brief, sir, sith it your pleasure is,
And I am tied to be obedient ;
For so your father charged me at our parting,
' Be serviceable to my son,' quoth he,
Although I think 'twas in another sense ;
I am content to be Lucentio,
Because so well I love Lucentio.

Lucentio. Tranio, be so, because Lucentio loves
And let me be a slave, to achieve that maid
Whose sudden sight hath thrall'd my wounded eye.
Here comes the rogue.

Enter BIONDELLO.

                    Sirrah, where have you been ?

Biondello. Where have I been ! Nay, how now ! where are you ? Master, has my fellow Tranio stolen your clothes ? Or you stolen his ? or both ? pray, what 's the news ?

Lucentio. Sirrah, come hither : 'tis no time to jest,
And therefore frame your manners to the time.
Your fellow Tranio here, to save my life,
Puts my apparel and my countenance on,
And I for my escape have put on his ;
For in a quarrel since I came ashore
I kill'd a man and fear I was descried :
Wait you on him, I charge you, as becomes,
While I make way from hence to save my life :
You understand me ?

Biondello. I, sir ! ne'er a whit.

Lucentio. And not a jot of Tranio in your mouth :
Tranio is changed into Lucentio.

Biondello. The better for him : would I were so too !

Tranio. So could I, faith, boy, to have the next wish after,

That Lucentio indeed had Baptista's youngest
  daughter.
But, sirrah, not for my sake, but your master's,
  I advise
You use your manners discreetly in all kinds of
  companies :
When I am alone, why, then I am Tranio ;
But in all places else your master Lucentio.
  Lucentio. Tranio, let 's go : one thing more
rests, that thyself execute, to make one among these
wooers : if thou ask me why, sufficeth, my reasons
are both good and weighty.   [*Exeunt.*

The presenters above speak.

  First Servingman. My lord, you nod ; you do
  not mind the play.
  Sly. Yes, by Saint Anne, do I. A good matter,
surely : comes there any more of it ?
  Page. My lord, 'tis but begun.
  Sly. 'Tis a very excellent piece of work, madam
lady : would 'twere done !
                              [*They sit and mark.*

SCENE II. *Padua. Before* HORTENSIO'S *house.*

Enter PETRUCHIO *and his man* GRUMIO.

  Petruchio. Verona, for a while I take my leave,
To see my friends in Padua, but of all
My best beloved and approved friend,
Hortensio ; and I trow this is his house.
Here, sirrah Grumio ; knock, I say.
  Grumio. Knock, sir ! whom should I knock ?
is there any man has rebused your worship ?
  Petruchio. Villain, I say, knock me here soundly.
  Grumio. Knock you here, sir ! why, sir, what
am I, sir, that I should knock you here, sir ?
  Petruchio. Villain, I say, knock me at this gate
And rap me well, or I 'll knock your knave's pate.
  Grumio. My master is grown quarrelsome. I
should knock you first,
And then I know after who comes by the worst.
  Petruchio. Will it not be ?
Faith, sirrah, an you 'll not knock, I 'll ring it ;
I 'll try how you can sol, fa, and sing it.
                       [*He wrings him by the ears.*
  Grumio. Help, masters, help ! my master is mad.
  Petruchio. Now, knock when I bid you, sirrah
villain !

Enter HORTENSIO.

  Hortensio. How now ! what 's the matter ? My
old friend Grumio ! and my good friend Petruchio !
How do you all at Verona ?
  Petruchio. Signior Hortensio, come you to part
the fray ?
' Con tutto il cuore, ben trovato,' may I say.
  Hortensio. ' Alla nostra casa ben venuto, molto
honorato signor mio Petruchio.'
Rise, Grumio, rise : we will compound this quarrel.
  Grumio. Nay, 'tis no matter, sir, what he 'leges
in Latin. If this be not a lawful cause for me to
leave his service, look you, sir, he bid me knock
him and rap him soundly, sir : well, was it fit for a
servant to use his master so, being perhaps, for aught
I see, two and thirty, a pip out ?
Whom would to God I had well knock'd at first,
Then had not Grumio come by the worst.
  Petruchio. A senseless villain ! Good Hortensio,

I bade the rascal knock upon your gate
And could not get him for my heart to do it.
  Grumio. Knock at the gate ! O heavens ! Spake
you not these words plain, ' Sirrah, knock me here,
rap me here, knock me well, and knock me soundly' ?
And come you now with, ' knocking at the gate ' ?
  Petruchio. Sirrah, be gone, or talk not, I advise you.
  Hortensio. Petruchio, patience : I am Grumio's
pledge :
Why, this 's a heavy chance 'twixt him and you,
Your ancient, trusty, pleasant servant Grumio.
And tell me now, sweet friend, what happy gale
Blows you to Padua here from old Verona ?
  Petruchio. Such wind as scatters young men
through the world
To seek their fortunes farther than at home
Where small experience grows. But in a few,
Signior Hortensio, thus it stands with me :
Antonio, my father, is deceased ;
And I have thrust myself into this maze,
Haply to wive and thrive as best I may :
Crowns in my purse I have and goods at home,
And so am come abroad to see the world.
  Hortensio. Petruchio, shall I then come roundly
to thee
And wish thee to a shrewd ill-favour'd wife ?
Thou 'ldst thank me but a little for my counsel :
And yet I 'll promise thee she shall be rich
And very rich : but thou 'rt too much my friend,
And I 'll not wish thee to her.
  Petruchio. Signior Hortensio, 'twixt such friends
as we
Few words suffice ; and therefore, if thou know
One rich enough to be Petruchio's wife,
As wealth is burden of my wooing dance,
Be she as foul as was Florentius' love,
As old as Sibyl and as curst and shrewd
As Socrates' Xanthippe, or a worse,
She moves me not, or not removes, at least,
Affection's edge in me, were she as rough
As are the swelling Adriatic seas :
I come to wive it wealthily in Padua ;
If wealthily, then happily in Padua.
  Grumio. Nay, look you, sir, he tells you flatly
what his mind is : why, give him gold enough and
marry him to a puppet or an aglet-baby ; or an old
trot with ne'er a tooth in her head, though she have
as many diseases as two and fifty horses : why,
nothing comes amiss, so money comes withal.
  Hortensio. Petruchio, since we are stepp'd thus
far in,
I will continue that I broach'd in jest.
I can, Petruchio, help thee to a wife
With wealth enough and young and beauteous,
Brought up as best becomes a gentlewoman :
Her only fault, and that is faults enough,
Is that she is intolerable curst
And shrewd and froward, so beyond all measure
That, were my state far worser than it is,
I would not wed her for a mine of gold.
  Petruchio. Hortensio, peace ! thou know'st not
gold's effect :
Tell me her father's name and 'tis enough ;
For I will board her, though she chide as loud
As thunder when the clouds in autumn crack.
  Hortensio. Her father is Baptista Minola,
An affable and courteous gentleman :
Her name is Katharina Minola,
Renown'd in Padua for her scolding tongue.
  Petruchio. I know her father, though I know not
her ;

And he knew my deceased father well.
I will not sleep, Hortensio, till I see her ;
And therefore let me be thus bold with you
To give you over at this first encounter,
Unless you will accompany me thither.
   Grumio. I pray you, sir, let him go while the
humour lasts. O' my word, an she knew him as
well as I do, she would think scolding would do
little good upon him : she may perhaps call him
half a score knaves or so : why, that 's nothing ;
an he begin once, he 'll rail in his rope-tricks. I 'll
tell you what, sir, an she stand him but a little, he
will throw a figure in her face and so disfigure her
with it that she shall have no more eyes to see withal
than a cat. You know him not, sir.
   Hortensio. Tarry, Petruchio, I must go with thee,
For in Baptista's keep my treasure is :
He hath the jewel of my life in hold,
His youngest daughter, beautiful Bianca,
And her withholds from me and other more,
Suitors to her and rivals in my love,
Supposing it a thing impossible,
For those defects I have before rehearsed,
That ever Katharina will be woo'd :
Therefore this order hath Baptista ta'en,
That none shall have access unto Bianca
Till Katharine the curst have got a husband.
   Grumio. Katharine the curst !
A title for a maid of all titles the worst.
   Hortensio. Now shall my friend Petruchio do me
   grace,
And offer me disguised in sober robes
To old Baptista as a schoolmaster
Well seen in music, to instruct Bianca ;
That so I may, by this device, at least
Have leave and leisure to make love to her
And unsuspected court her by herself.
   Grumio. Here 's no knavery ! See, to beguile
the old folks, how the young folks lay their heads
together !

     Enter GREMIO, *and* LUCENTIO *disguised.*

Master, master, look about you : who goes there,
   ha ?
   Hortensio. Peace, Grumio ! it is the rival of
my love.
Petruchio, stand by a while.
   Grumio. A proper stripling and an amorous !
   Gremio. O, very well ; I have perused the note.
Hark you, sir ; I 'll have them very fairly bound :
All books of love, see that at any hand ;
And see you read no other lectures to her :
You understand me : over and beside
Signior Baptista's liberality,
I 'll mend it with a largess. Take your paper too,
And let me have them very well perfumed :
For she is sweeter than perfume itself
To whom they go to. What will you read to her ?
   Lucentio. Whate'er I read to her, I 'll plead for
   you
As for my patron, stand you so assured,
As firmly as yourself were still in place :
Yea, and perhaps with more successful words
Than you, unless you were a scholar, sir.
   Gremio. O this learning, what a thing it is !
   Grumio. O this woodcock, what an ass it is !
   Petruchio. Peace, sirrah !
   Hortensio. Grumio, mum ! God save you,
Signior Gremio.
   Gremio. And you are well met, Signior Hortensio.

Trow you whither I am going? To Baptista Minola.
I promised to inquire carefully
About a schoolmaster for the fair Bianca :
And by good fortune I have lighted well
On this young man, for learning and behaviour
Fit for her turn, well read in poetry
And other books, good ones, I warrant ye.
   Hortensio. 'Tis well ; and I have met a gentleman
Hath promised me to help me to another,
A fine musician to instruct our mistress ;
So shall I no whit be behind in duty
To fair Bianca, so beloved of me.
   Gremio. Beloved of me ; and that my deeds
   shall prove.
   Grumio. And that his bags shall prove.
   Hortensio. Gremio, 'tis now no time to vent our
   love :
Listen to me, and if you speak me fair,
I 'll tell you news indifferent good for either.
Here is a gentleman whom by chance I met,
Upon agreement from us to his liking,
Will undertake to woo curst Katharine,
Yea, and to marry her, if her dowry please.
   Gremio. So said, so done, is well.
Hortensio, have you told him all her faults ?
   Petruchio. I know she is an irksome brawling
   scold :
If that be all, masters, I hear no harm.
   Gremio. No, say'st me so, friend ? What coun-
   tryman ?
   Petruchio. Born in Verona, old Antonio's son :
My father dead, my fortune lives for me ;
And I do hope good days and long to see.
   Gremio. O sir, such a life, with such a wife, were
strange !
But if you have a stomach, to 't i' God's name :
You shall have me assisting you in all.
But will you woo this wild-cat ?
   Petruchio.   Will I live ?
   Grumio. Will he woo her ? ay, or I 'll hang her.
   Petruchio. Why came I hither but to that intent ?
Think you a little din can daunt mine ears ?
Have I not in my time heard lions roar ?
Have I not heard the sea puff'd up with winds
Rage like an angry boar chafed with sweat ?
Have I not heard great ordnance in the field,
And heaven's artillery thunder in the skies ?
Have I not in a pitched battle heard
Loud 'larums, neighing steeds, and trumpets' clang ?
And do you tell me of a woman's tongue,
That gives not half so great a blow to hear
As will a chestnut in a farmer's fire ?
Tush, tush ! fear boys with bugs.
   Grumio.   For he fears none.
   Gremio. Hortensio, hark :
This gentleman is happily arrived,
My mind presumes, for his own good and ours.
   Hortensio. I promised we would be contributors
And bear his charge of wooing, whatsoe'er.
   Gremio. And so we will, provided that he win her.
   Grumio. I would I were as sure of a good dinner.

     Enter TRANIO, *brave, and* BIONDELLO.

   Tranio. Gentlemen, God save you. If I may
   be bold,
Tell me, I beseech you, which is the readiest way
To the house of Signior Baptista Minola ?
   Biondello. He that has the two fair daughters :
is 't he you mean ?
   Tranio. Even he, Biondello.

Gremio. Hark you, sir ; you mean not her to—
Tranio. Perhaps, him and her, sir : what have
you to do ?
Petruchio. Not her that chides, sir, at any hand,
I pray.
Tranio. I love no chiders, sir. Biondello, let 's
away.
Lucentio. Well begun, Tranio.
Hortensio.   Sir, a word ere you go ;
Are you a suitor to the maid you talk of, yea or
no ?
Tranio. And if I be, sir, is it any offence ?
Gremio. No ; if without more words you will
get you hence.
Tranio. Why, sir, I pray, are not the streets as free
For me as for you ?
Gremio.   But so is not she.
Tranio. For what reason, I beseech you ?
Gremio.   For this reason, if you 'll know,
That she 's the choice love of Signior Gremio.
Hortensio.   That she 's the chosen of Signior
Hortensio.
Tranio. Softly, my masters ! if you be gentlemen,
Do me this right ; hear me with patience.
Baptista is a noble gentleman,
To whom my father is not all unknown ;
And were his daughter fairer than she is,
She may more suitors have and me for one.
Fair Leda's daughter had a thousand wooers ;
Then well one more may fair Bianca have :
And so she shall ; Lucentio shall make one,
Though Paris came in hope to speed alone.
Gremio. What ! this gentleman will out-talk us
all.
Lucentio. Sir, give him head : I know he 'll prove
a jade.
Petruchio. Hortensio, to what end are all these
words ?
Hortensio. Sir, let me be so bold as ask you,
Did you yet ever see Baptista's daughter ?
Tranio. No, sir ; but hear I do that he hath two,
The one as famous for a scolding tongue
As is the other for beauteous modesty.
Petruchio. Sir, sir, the first 's for me ; let her
go by.
Gremio. Yea, leave that labour to great Hercules ;
And let it be more than Alcides' twelve.
Petruchio. Sir, understand you this of me in
sooth :
The youngest daughter whom you hearken for
Her father keeps from all access of suitors,
And will not promise her to any man
Until the elder sister first be wed :
The younger then is free and not before.
Tranio. If it be so, sir, that you are the man
Must stead us all and me amongst the rest,
And if you break the ice and do this feat,
Achieve the elder, set the younger free
For our access, whose hap shall be to have her
Will not so graceless be to be ingrate.
Hortensio. Sir, you say well and well you do
conceive ;
And since you do profess to be a suitor,
You must, as we do, gratify this gentleman,
To whom we all rest generally beholding.
Tranio. Sir, I shall not be slack : in sign whereof,
Please ye we may contrive this afternoon,
And quaff carouses to our mistress' health,
And do as adversaries do in law,
Strive mightily, but eat and drink as friends.
Grumio, Biondello. O excellent motion ! Fellows,

let 's be gone.
Hortensio. The motion 's good indeed and be
it so,
Petruchio, I shall be your ben venuto.   [*Exeunt.*

ACT II.

SCENE I.   *Padua.   A room in* BAPTISTA'S *house.*

Enter KATHARINA *and* BIANCA.

Bianca.

Good sister, wrong me not, nor wrong yourself,
     To make a bondmaid and a slave of me ;
     That I disdain : but for these other gawds,
Unbind my hands, I 'll pull them off myself,
Yea, all my raiment, to my petticoat ;
Or what you will command me will I do,
So well I know my duty to my elders.
Katharina. Of all thy suitors, here I charge thee,
tell
Whom thou lovest best : see thou dissemble not.
Bianca. Believe me, sister, of all the men alive
I never yet beheld that special face
Which I could fancy more than any other.
Katharina. Minion, thou liest. Is 't not Hor-
tensio ?
Bianca. If you affect him, sister, here I swear
I 'll plead for you myself, but you shall have him.
Katharina. O then, belike, you fancy riches more :
You will have Gremio to keep you fair.
Bianca. Is it for him you do envy me so ?
Nay then you jest, and now I well perceive
You have but jested with me all this while :
I prithee, sister Kate, untie my hands.
Katharina. If that be jest, then all the rest was so.
                                          [*Strikes her.*

Enter BAPTISTA.

Baptista. Why, how now, dame ! whence grows
this insolence ?
Bianca, stand aside. Poor girl ! she weeps.
Go ply thy needle ; meddle not with her.
For shame, thou hilding of a devilish spirit,
Why dost thou wrong her that did ne'er wrong thee ?
When did she cross thee with a bitter word ?
Katharina. Her silence flouts me, and I 'll be
revenged.   [*Flies after Bianca.*
Baptista. What, in my sight ? Bianca, get thee in.
                                          [*Exit Bianca.*
Katharina. What, will you not suffer me ? Nay,
now I see
She is your treasure, she must have a husband ;
I must dance bare-foot on her wedding day
And for your love to her lead apes in hell.
Talk not to me : I will go sit and weep
Till I can find occasion of revenge.   [*Exit.*
Baptista. Was ever gentleman thus grieved as I ?
But who comes here ?

Enter GREMIO, LUCENTIO *in the habit of a mean
     man ;* PETRUCHIO, *with* HORTENSIO *as a
     musician ;* and TRANIO, *with* BIONDELLO
     bearing a lute and books.

Gremio. Good morrow, neighbour Baptista.
Baptista. Good morrow, neighbour Gremio.
God save you, gentlemen !
Petruchio. And you, good sir ! Pray, have you
not a daughter

Call'd Katharina, fair and virtuous ?

Baptista. I have a daughter, sir, called Katharina.

Gremio. You are too blunt : go to it orderly.

Petruchio. You wrong me, Signior Gremio : give
me leave.

I am a gentleman of Verona, sir,
That, hearing of her beauty and her wit,
Her affability and bashful modesty,
Her wondrous qualities and mild behaviour,
Am bold to show myself a forward guest
Within your house, to make mine eye the witness
Of that report which I so oft have heard.
And, for an entrance to my entertainment,
I do present you with a man of mine,

[*Presenting Hortensio.*

Cunning in music and the mathematics,
To instruct her fully in those sciences,
Whereof I know she is not ignorant :
Accept of him, or else you do me wrong :
His name is Licio, born in Mantua.

Baptista. You 're welcome, sir ; and he, for your
good sake.

But for my daughter Katharine, this I know,
She is not for your turn, the more my grief.

Petruchio. I see you do not mean to part with her,
Or else you like not of my company.

Baptista. Mistake me not ; I speak but as I find.
Whence are you, sir ? what may I call your name ?

Petruchio. Petruchio is my name ; Antonio's son,
A man well known throughout all Italy.

Baptista. I know him well : you are welcome for
his sake.

Gremio. Saving your tale, Petruchio, I pray,
Let us, that are poor petitioners, speak too :
Baccare ! you are marvellous forward.

Petruchio. O, pardon me, Signior Gremio ; I
would fain be doing.

Gremio. I doubt it not, sir ; but you will curse
your wooing.

Neighbour, this is a gift very grateful, I am sure of
it. To express the like kindness, myself, that have
been more kindly beholding to you than any, freely
give unto you this young scholar [*presenting Lucentio*],
that hath been long studying at Rheims ; as cunning
in Greek, Latin, and other languages, as the other
in music and mathematics : his name is Cambio ;
pray, accept his service.

Baptista. A thousand thanks, Signior Gremio.
Welcome, good Cambio. [*To Tranio*] But, gentle
sir, methinks you walk like a stranger : may I be
so bold to know the cause of your coming ?

Tranio. Pardon me, sir, the boldness is mine own,
That, being a stranger in this city here,
Do make myself a suitor to your daughter,
Unto Bianca, fair and virtuous.
Nor is your firm resolve unknown to me,
In the preferment of the eldest sister.
This liberty is all that I request,
That, upon knowledge of my parentage,
I may have welcome 'mongst the rest that woo
And free access and favour as the rest :
And, toward the education of your daughters,
I here bestow a simple instrument,
And this small packet of Greek and Latin books :
If you accept them, then their worth is great.

Baptista. Lucentio is your name : of whence, I
pray ?

Tranio. Of Pisa, sir ; son to Vincentio.

Baptista. A mighty man of Pisa ; by report
I know him well : you are very welcome, sir.
Take you the lute, and you the set of books ;

You shall go see your pupils presently.
Holla, within !

Enter a Servant.

Sirrah, lead these gentlemen
To my daughters ; and tell them both,
These are their tutors : bid them use them well.

[*Exit Servant, with Lucentio and Hortensio,
Biondello following.*

We will go walk a little in the orchard,
And then to dinner. You are passing welcome,
And so I pray you all to think yourselves.

Petruchio. Signior Baptista, my business asketh
haste,

And every day I cannot come to woo.
You knew my father well, and in him me,
Left solely heir to all his lands and goods,
Which I have better'd rather than decreased :
Then tell me, if I get your daughter's love,
What dowry shall I have with her to wife ?

Baptista. After my death the one half of my
lands,

And in possession twenty thousand crowns.

Petruchio. And, for that dowry, I 'll assure her of
Her widowhood, be it that she survive me,
In all my lands and leases whatsoever :
Let specialties be therefore drawn between us,
That covenants may be kept on either hand.

Baptista. Ay, when the special thing is well
obtain'd,

That is, her love ; for that is all in all.

Petruchio. Why, that is nothing ; for I tell you,
father,

I am as peremptory as she proud-minded ;
And where two raging fires meet together
They do consume the thing that feeds their fury :
Though little fire grows great with little wind,
Yet extreme gusts will blow out fire and all :
So I to her and so she yields to me ;
For I am rough and woo not like a babe.

Baptista. Well mayst thou woo, and happy be
thy speed !

But be thou arm'd for some unhappy words.

Petruchio. Ay, to the proof ; as mountains are
for winds,

That shake not, though they blow perpetually.

Re-enter HORTENSIO, *with his head broke.*

Baptista. How now, my friend ! why dost thou
look so pale ?

Hortensio. For fear, I promise you, if I look pale.

Baptista. What, will my daughter prove a good
musician ?

Hortensio. I think she 'll sooner prove a soldier :
Iron may hold with her, but never lutes.

Baptista. Why, then thou canst not break her to
the lute ?

Hortensio. Why, no ; for she hath broke the lute
to me.

I did but tell her she mistook her frets,
And bow'd her hand to teach her fingering ;
When, with a most impatient devilish spirit,
' Frets, call you these ? ' quoth she ; ' I 'll fume
with them : '
And, with that word, she struck me on the head,
And through the instrument my pate made way ;
And there I stood amazed for a while,
As on a pillory, looking through the lute ;
While she did call me rascal fiddler

And twangling Jack ; with twenty such vile terms,
As had she studied to misuse me so.
Petruchio. Now, by the world, it is a lusty wench ;
I love her ten times more than e'er I did :
O, how I long to have some chat with her !
Baptista. Well, go with me and be not so dis-
comfited :
Proceed in practice with my younger daughter ;
She 's apt to learn and thankful for good turns.
Signior Petruchio, will you go with us,
Or shall I send my daughter Kate to you ?
Petruchio. I pray you do. [*Exeunt all but Petru-
chio.*] I will attend her here,
And woo her with some spirit when she comes.
Say that she rail ; why then I 'll tell her plain
She sings as sweetly as a nightingale :
Say that she frown ; I 'll say she looks as clear
As morning roses newly wash'd with dew :
Say she be mute and will not speak a word :
Then I 'll commend her volubility,
And say she uttereth piercing eloquence :
If she do bid me pack, I 'll give her thanks,
As though she bid me stay by her a week :
If she deny to wed, I 'll crave the day
When I shall ask the banns and when be married.
But here she comes ; and now, Petruchio, speak.

Enter KATHARINA.

Good morrow, Kate ; for that 's your name, I hear.
Katharina. Well have you heard, but something
hard of hearing :
They call me Katharina that do talk of me.
Petruchio. You lie, in faith ; for you are call'd
plain Kate,
And bonny Kate and sometimes Kate the curst ;
But Kate, the prettiest Kate in Christendom,
Kate of Kate Hall, my super-dainty Kate,
For dainties are all Kates, and therefore, Kate,
Take this of me, Kate of my consolation ;
Hearing thy mildness praised in every town,
Thy virtues spoke of, and thy beauty sounded,
Yet not so deeply as to thee belongs,
Myself am moved to woo thee for my wife.
Katharina. Moved ! in good time let him that
moved you hither
Remove you hence : I knew you at the first
You were a moveable.
Petruchio.   Why, what 's a moveable ?
Katharina. A join'd-stool.
Petruchio.   Thou hast hit it : come, sit on me.
Katharina. Asses are made to bear, and so are
you.
Petruchio. Women are made to bear, and so are
you.
Katharina. No such jade as you, if me you mean.
Petruchio. Alas ! good Kate, I will not burden
thee ;
For, knowing thee to be but young and light—
Katharina. Too light for such a swain as you to
catch ;
And yet as heavy as my weight should be.
Petruchio. Should be ! should—buzz !
Katharina.   Well ta'en, and like a buzzard.
Petruchio. O slow-wing'd turtle ! shall a buzzard
take thee ?
Katharina. Ay, for a turtle, as he takes a buzzard.
Petruchio. Come, come, you wasp ; i' faith, you
are too angry.
Katharina. If I be waspish, best beware my sting.
Petruchio. My remedy is then, to pluck it out.

Katharina. Ay, if the fool could find it where it
lies.
Petruchio. Who knows not where a wasp does
wear his sting ? In his tail.
Katharina. In his tongue.
Petruchio. Whose tongue ?
Katharina. Yours, if you talk of tails : and so
farewell.
Petruchio. What, with my tongue in your tail ?
nay, come again,
Good Kate ; I am a gentleman.
Katharina. That I 'll try. [*She strikes him.*
Petruchio. I swear I 'll cuff you, if you strike
again.
Katharina. So may you lose your arms :
If you strike me, you are no gentleman ;
And if no gentleman, why then no arms.
Petruchio. A herald, Kate ? O, put me in thy
books !
Katharina. What is your crest ? a coxcomb ?
Petruchio. A combless cock, so Kate will be my
hen.
Katharina. No cock of mine : you crow too like
a craven.
Petruchio. Nay, come, Kate, come ; you must not
look so sour.
Katharina. It is my fashion, when I see a crab.
Petruchio. Why, here 's no crab ; and therefore
look not sour.
Katharina. There is, there is.
Petruchio. Then show it me.
Katharina. Had I a glass, I would.
Petruchio. What, you mean my face ?
Katharina. Well aim'd of such a young one.
Petruchio. Now, by Saint George, I am too young
for you.
Katharina. Yet you are wither'd.
Petruchio. 'Tis with cares.
Katharina. I care not.
Petruchio. Nay, hear you, Kate ; in sooth you
scape not so.
Katharina. I chafe you, if I tarry : let me go.
Petruchio. No, not a whit : I find you passing
gentle.
'Twas told me you were rough and coy and sullen,
And now I find report a very liar :
For thou art pleasant, gamesome, passing courteous,
But slow in speech, yet sweet as spring-time flowers :
Thou canst not frown, thou canst not look askance,
Nor bite the lip, as angry wenches will,
Nor hast thou pleasure to be cross in talk,
But thou with mildness entertain'st thy wooers,
With gentle conference, soft and affable.
Why does the world report that Kate doth limp ?
O slanderous world ! Kate like the hazel-twig
Is straight and slender and as brown in hue
As hazel nuts and sweeter than the kernels.
O, let me see thee walk : thou dost not halt.
Katharina. Go, fool, and whom thou keep'st
command.
Petruchio. Did ever Dian so become a grove
As Kate this chamber with her princely gait ?
O, be thou Dian, and let her be Kate ;
And then let Kate be chaste and Dian sportful !
Katharina. Where did you study all this goodly
speech ?
Petruchio. It is extempore, from my mother-wit.
Katharina. A witty mother ! witless else her son.
Petruchio. Am I not wise ?
Katharina. Yes ; keep you warm.
Petruchio. Marry, so I mean, sweet Katharine, in

thy bed :
And therefore, setting all this chat aside,
Thus in plain terms : your father hath consented
That you shall be my wife ; your dowry 'greed on ;
And, will you, nill you, I will marry you.
Now, Kate, I am a husband for your turn ;
For, by this light, whereby I see thy beauty,
Thy beauty, that doth make me like thee well,
Thou must be married to no man but me ;
For I am he am born to tame you, Kate,
And bring you from a wild Kate to a Kate
Conformable as other household Kates.
Here comes your father : never make denial ;
I must and will have Katharine to my wife.

Re-enter BAPTISTA, GREMIO, *and* TRANIO.

Baptista. Now, Signior Petruchio, how speed you
  with my daughter ?
Petruchio. How but well, sir ? how but well ?
It were impossible I should speed amiss.
Baptista. Why, how now, daughter Katharine !
  in your dumps ?
Katharina. Call you me daughter ? now, I promise
  you,
You have show'd a tender fatherly regard,
To wish me wed to one half lunatic ;
A mad-cap ruffian and a swearing Jack,
That thinks with oaths to face the matter out.
Petruchio. Father, 'tis thus : yourself and all the
  world,
That talk'd of her, have talk'd amiss of her :
If she be curst, it is for policy,
For she 's not froward, but modest as the dove ;
She is not hot, but temperate as the morn ;
For patience she will prove a second Grissel,
And Roman Lucrece for her chastity :
And to conclude, we have 'greed so well together,
That upon Sunday is the wedding-day.
Katharina. I 'll see thee hang'd on Sunday first.
Gremio. Hark, Petruchio ; she says she 'll see
  thee hang'd first.
Tranio. Is this your speeding ? nay, then, good
  night our part !
Petruchio. Be patient, gentlemen ; I choose her
  for myself :
If she and I be pleased, what 's that to you ?
'Tis bargain'd 'twixt us twain, being alone,
That she shall still be curst in company.
I tell you, 'tis incredible to believe
How much she loves me : O, the kindest Kate
She hung about my neck ; and kiss on kiss
She vied so fast, protesting oath on oath,
That in a twink she won me to her love.
O, you are novices ! 'tis a world to see,
How tame, when men and women are alone,
A meacock wretch can make the curstest shrew.
Give me thy hand, Kate : I will unto Venice,
To buy apparel 'gainst the wedding-day.
Provide the feast, father, and bid the guests ;
I will be sure my Katharine shall be fine.
Baptista. I know not what to say : but give me
  your hands ;
God send you joy, Petruchio ! 'tis a match.
Gremio, Tranio. Amen, say we : we will be
  witnesses.
Petruchio. Father, and wife, and gentlemen,
  adieu ;
I will to Venice ; Sunday comes apace :
We will have rings and things and fine array ;
And kiss me, Kate, we will be married o' Sunday.

                [*Exeunt Petruchio and Katharina severally.*
Gremio. Was ever match clapp'd up so suddenly ?
Baptista. Faith, gentlemen, now I play a mer-
  chant's part,
And venture madly on a desperate mart.
Tranio. 'Twas a commodity lay fretting by you :
'Twill bring you gain, or perish on the seas.
Baptista. The gain I seek is, quiet in the match.
Gremio. No doubt but he hath got a quiet catch.
But now, Baptista, to your younger daughter :
Now is the day we long have looked for :
I am your neighbour, and was suitor first.
Tranio. And I am one that love Bianca more
Than words can witness, or your thoughts can guess.
Gremio. Youngling, thou canst not love so dear
  as I.
Tranio. Greybeard, thy love doth freeze.
Gremio.   But thine doth fry.
Skipper, stand back : 'tis age that nourisheth.
Tranio. But youth in ladies' eyes that flourisheth.
Baptista. Content you, gentlemen : I will com-
  pound this strife :
'Tis deeds must win the prize ; and he of both
That can assure my daughter greatest dower
Shall have my Bianca's love.
Say, Signior Gremio, what can you assure her ?
Gremio. First, as you know, my house within
  the city
Is richly furnished with plate and gold ;
Basins and ewers to lave her dainty hands ;
My hangings all of Tyrian tapestry ;
In ivory coffers I have stuff'd my crowns ;
In cypress chests my arras counterpoints,
Costly apparel, tents and canopies,
Fine linen, Turkey cushions boss'd with pearl,
Valance of Venice gold in needlework,
Pewter and brass and all things that belong
To house or housekeeping : then, at my farm
I have a hundred milch-kine to the pail,
Sixscore fat oxen standing in my stalls,
And all things answerable to this portion.
Myself am struck in years, I must confess ;
And if I die to-morrow, this is hers,
If whilst I live she will be only mine.
Tranio. That ' only ' came well in. Sir, list
  to me :
I am my father's heir and only son :
If I may have your daughter to my wife,
I 'll leave her houses three or four as good,
Within rich Pisa walls, as any one
Old Signior Gremio has in Padua ;
Besides two thousand ducats by the year
Of fruitful land, all which shall be her jointure.
What, have I pinch'd you, Signior Gremio ?
Gremio. Two thousand ducats by the year of
  land !
My land amounts not to so much in all :
That she shall have ; besides an argosy
That now is lying in Marseilles' road.
What, have I choked you with an argosy ?
Tranio. Gremio, 'tis known my father hath no
  less
Than three great argosies ; besides two galliases,
And twelve tight galleys : these I will assure her,
And twice as much, whate'er thou offer'st next.
Gremio. Nay, I have offer'd all, I have no more ;
And she can have no more than all I have :
If you like me, she shall have me and mine.
Tranio. Why, then the maid is mine from all the
  world,
By your firm promise : Gremio is out-vied.

Baptista. I must confess your offer is the best ;
And, let your father make her the assurance,
She is your own ; else, you must pardon me,
If you should die before him, where 's her dower ?
Tranio. That 's but a cavil : he is old, I young.
Gremio. And may not young men die, as well as
old ?
Baptista. Well, gentlemen,
I am thus resolved : on Sunday next you know
My daughter Katharine is to be married :
Now, on the Sunday following, shall Bianca
Be bride to you, if you make this assurance ;
If not, to Signior Gremio :
And so, I take my leave, and thank you both.
Gremio. Adieu, good 'neighbour. [*Exit Baptista.*
                    Now I fear thee not :
Sirrah young gamester, your father were a fool
To give thee all, and in his waning age
Set foot under thy table : tut, a toy !
An old Italian fox is not so kind, my boy.
                                    [*Exit.*
Tranio. A vengeance on your crafty wither'd
hide !
Yet I have faced it with a card of ten.
'Tis in my head to do my master good :
I see no reason but supposed Lucentio
Must get a father, call'd ' supposed Vincentio ;
And that 's a wonder : fathers commonly
Do get their children ; but in this case of wooing,
A child shall get a sire, if I fail not of my cunning.
                                    [*Exit.*

ACT III.

SCENE I. *Padua.* BAPTISTA'S *house.*

Enter LUCENTIO, HORTENSIO, *and* BIANCA.

Lucentio.

Fiddler, forbear ; you grow too forward, sir :
Have you so soon forgot the entertainment
Her sister Katharine welcomed you withal ?
Hortensio. But, wrangling pedant, this is
The patroness of heavenly harmony :
Then give me leave to have my prerogative ;
And when in music we have spent an hour,
Your lecture shall have leisure for as much.
Lucentio. Preposterous ass, that never read so far
To know the cause why music was ordain'd !
Was it not to refresh the mind of man
After his studies or his usual pain ?
Then give me leave to read philosophy,
And while I pause, serve in your harmony.
Hortensio. Sirrah, I will not bear these braves of
thine.
Bianca. Why, gentlemen, you do me double
wrong,
To strive for that which resteth in my choice :
I am no breeching scholar in the schools ;
I 'll not be tied to hours nor 'pointed times,
But learn my lessons as I please myself.
And, to cut off all strife, here sit we down :
Take you your instrument, play you the whiles ;
His lecture will be done ere you have tuned.
Hortensio. You 'll leave his lecture when I am in
tune ?
Lucentio. That will be never ; tune your instru-
ment.
Bianca. Where left we last ?
Lucentio. Here, madam :
' Hic ibat Simois ; hic est Sigeia tellus ;

Hic steterat Priami regia celsa senis.'
Bianca. Construe them.
Lucentio. ' Hic ibat,' as I told you before, ' Simo-
is,' I am Lucentio, ' hic est,' son unto Vincentio of
Pisa, ' Sigeia tellus,' disguised thus to get your love ;
' Hic steterat,' and that Lucentio that comes a-
wooing, ' Priami,' is my man Tranio, ' regia,'
bearing my port, ' celsa senis,' that we might beguile
the old pantaloon.
Hortensio. Madam, my instrument 's in tune.
Bianca. Let 's hear. O fie ! the treble jars.
Lucentio. Spit in the hole, man, and tune again.
Bianca. Now let me see if I can construe it :
' Hic ibat Simois,' I know you not, ' hic est Sigeia
tellus,' I trust you not ; ' Hic steterat Priami,' take
heed he hear us not, ' regia,' presume not, ' celsa
senis,' despair not.
Hortensio. Madam, 'tis now in tune.
Lucentio.   All but the base.
Hortensio. The base is right ; 'tis the base knave
that jars.
[*Aside*] How fiery and forward our pedant is !
Now, for my life, the knave doth court my love :
Pedascule, I 'll watch you better yet.
Bianca. In time I may believe, yet I mistrust.
Lucentio. Mistrust it not ; for, sure, Æacides
Was Ajax, call'd so from his grandfather.
Bianca. I must believe my master ; else, I pro-
mise you,
I should be arguing still upon that doubt :
But let it rest. Now, Licio, to you :
Good masters, take it not unkindly, pray,
That I have been thus pleasant with you both.
Hortensio. You may go walk, and give me leave
a while :
My lessons make no music in three parts.
Lucentio. Are you so formal, sir ? well, I must
wait,
[*Aside*] And watch withal ; for, but I be deceived,
Our fine musician groweth amorous.
Hortensio. Madam, before you touch the instru-
ment,
To learn the order of my fingering,
I must begin with rudiments of art ;
To teach you gamut in a briefer sort,
More pleasant, pithy and effectual,
Than hath been taught by any of my trade :
And there it is in writing, fairly drawn.
Bianca. Why, I am past my gamut long ago.
Hortensio. Yet read the gamut of Hortensio.
Bianca. [*Reads*] " ' Gamut ' I am, the ground of
all accord,
    ' A re,' to plead Hortensio's passion ;
    ' B mi,' Bianca, take him for thy lord,
    ' C fa ut,' that loves with all affection :
    ' D sol re,' one clef, two notes have I :
    ' E la mi,' show pity, or I die."
Call you this gamut ? tut, I like it not :
Old fashions please me best ; I am not so nice,
To change true rules for old inventions.

Enter a Servant.

Servant. Mistress, your father prays you leave
your books
And help to dress your sister's chamber up :
You know to-morrow is the wedding-day.
Bianca. Farewell, sweet masters both ; I must
be gone.   [*Exeunt Bianca and Servant.*
Lucentio. Faith, mistress, then I have no cause
to stay.   [*Exit.*

Hortensio. But I have cause to pry into this
pedant :
Methinks he looks as though he were in love :
Yet if thy thoughts, Bianca, be so humble
To cast thy wandering eyes on every stale,
Seize thee that list : if once I find thee ranging,
Hortensio will be quit with thee by changing.
[*Exit.*

SCENE II.   *Padua.   Before* BAPTISTA'S *house.*

Enter BAPTISTA, GREMIO, TRANIO, KATHARINA,
BIANCA, LUCENTIO, *and* others, attendants.

Baptista.   [*To Tranio*] Signior Lucentio, this is
the 'pointed day
That Katharine and Petruchio should be married,
And yet we hear not of our son-in-law.
What will be said ? what mockery will it be,
To want the bridegroom when the priest attends
To speak the ceremonial rites of marriage !
What says Lucentio to this shame of ours ?
Katherina.   No shame but mine : I must, forsooth,
be forced
To give my hand opposed against my heart
Unto a mad-brain rudesby full of spleen ;
Who woo'd in haste and means to wed at leisure.
I told you, I, he was a frantic fool,
Hiding his bitter jests in blunt behaviour :
And, to be noted for a merry man,
He 'll woo a thousand, 'point the day of marriage,
Make feasts, invite friends, and proclaim the banns ;
Yet never means to wed where he hath woo'd.
Now must the world point at poor Katharine,
And say, ' Lo, there is mad Petruchio's wife,
If it would please him come and marry her ! '
Tranio.   Patience, good Katharine, and Baptista
too.
Upon my life, Petruchio means but well,
Whatever fortune stays him from his word :
Though he be blunt, I know him passing wise ;
Though he be merry, yet withal he 's honest.
Katharina.   Would Katherine had never seen him
though !
[*Exit weeping, followed by Bianca and others.*
Baptista.   Go, girl ; I cannot blame thee now to
weep ;
For such an injury would vex a very saint,
Much more a shrew of thy impatient humour.

Enter BIONDELLO.

Biondello.   Master, master ! news, old news, and
such news as you never heard of !
Baptista.   Is it new and old too ? how may that
be ?
Biondello.   Why, is it not news, to hear of Petru-
chio's coming ?
Baptista.   Is he come ?
Biondello.   Why, no, sir.
Baptista.   What then ?
Biondello.   He is coming.
Baptista.   · When will he be here ?
Biondello.   When he stands where I am and sees
you there.
Tranio.   But say, what to thine old news ?
Biondello.   Why, Petruchio is coming in a new
hat and an old jerkin, a pair of old breeches thrice
turned, a pair of boots that have been candle-cases,
one buckled, another laced, an old rusty sword
ta'en out of the town-armoury, with a broken hilt,
and chapeless ; with two broken points ; his horse
hipped with an old mothy saddle and stirrups of no
kindred ; besides, possessed with the glanders and
like to mose in the chine ; troubled with the lampass,
infected with the fashions, full of windgalls, sped
with spavins, rayed with the yellows, past cure of
the fives, stark spoiled with the staggers, begnawn
with the bots, swayed in the back and shoulder-
shotten ; near-legged before and with a half-cheeked
bit and a head-stall of sheep's leather which, being
restrained to keep him from stumbling, hath been
often burst and now repaired with knots ; one
girth six times pieced and a woman's crupper of
velure, which hath two letters for her name fairly
set down in studs, and here and: here pieced with
pack-thread.
Baptista.   Who comes with him ?
Biondello.   O, sir, his lackey, for all the world
caparisoned like the horse ; with a linen stock on
one leg and a kersey boot-hose on the other, gartered
with a red and blue list ; an old hat and ' the humour
of forty fancies ' pricked in 't for a feather : a
monster, a very monster in apparel, and not like a
Christian footboy or a gentleman's lackey.
Tranio.   'Tis some odd humour pricks him to
this fashion ;
Yet oftentimes he goes but mean-apparell'd.
Baptista.   I am glad he 's come, howsoe'er he
comes.
Biondello.   Why, sir, he comes not.
Baptista.   Didst thou not say he comes ?
Biondello.   Who ? that Petruchio came ?
Baptista.   Ay, that Petruchio came.
Biondello.   No, sir ; I say his horse comes, with
him on his back.
Baptista.   Why, that 's all one.
Biondello.   Nay, by Saint Jamy,
I hold you a penny,
A horse and a man
Is more than one,
And yet not many.

Enter PETRUCHIO *and* GRUMIO.

Petruchio.   Come, where be these gallants ? who 's
at home ?
Baptista.   You are welcome, sir.
Petruchio.   And yet I come not well.
Baptista.   And yet you halt not.
Tranio.   Not so well apparell'd
As I wish you were.
Petruchio.   Were it better, I should rush in thus.
But where is Kate ? where is my lovely bride ?
How does my father ? Gentles, methinks you frown :
And wherefore gaze this goodly company,
As if they saw some wondrous monument,
Some comet or unusual prodigy ?
Baptista.   Why, sir, you know this is your wed-
ding-day :
First were we sad, fearing you would not come ;
Now sadder, that you come so unprovided.
Fie, doff this habit, shame to your estate,
An eye-sore to our solemn festival !
Tranio.   And tell us, what occasion of import
Hath all so long detain'd you from your wife,
And sent you hither so unlike yourself ?
Petruchio.   Tedious it were to tell, and harsh to
hear :
Sufficeth, I am come to keep my word,
Though in some part enforced to digress ;
Which, at more leisure, I will so excuse

As you shall well be satisfied withal.
But where is Kate ? I stay too long from her :
The morning wears, 'tis time we were at church.
  Tranio. See not your bride in these unreverent robes :
Go to my chamber ; put on clothes of mine.
  Petruchio. Not I, believe me : thus I 'll visit her.
  Baptista. But thus, I trust, you will not marry her.
  Petruchio. Good sooth, even thus ; therefore ha' done with words :
To me she 's married, not unto my clothes :
Could I repair what she will wear in me,
As I can change these poor accoutrements,
'Twere well for Kate and better for myself.
But what a fool am I to chat with you,
When I should bid good morrow to my bride,
And seal the title with a lovely kiss !
                   [Exeunt Petruchio and Grumio.
  Tranio. He hath some meaning in his mad attire :
We will persuade him, be it possible,
To put on better ere he go to church.
  Baptista. I 'll after him, and see the event of this.
         [Exeunt Baptista, Gremio, and attendants.
  Tranio. But to her love concerneth us to add
Her father's liking : which to bring to pass,
As I before imparted to your worship,
I am to get a man,—whate'er he be,
It skills not much, we 'll fit him to our turn,—
And he shall be Vincentio of Pisa ;
And make assurance here in Padua
Of greater sums than I have promised.
So shall you quietly enjoy your hope,
And marry sweet Bianca with consent.
  Lucentio. Were it not that my fellow-schoolmaster
Doth watch Bianca's steps so narrowly,
'Twere good, methinks, to steal our marriage ;
Which once perform'd, let all the world say no,
I 'll keep mine own, despite of all the world.
  Tranio. That by degrees we mean to look into,
And watch our vantage in this business :
We 'll over-reach the greybeard, Gremio,
The narrow-prying father, Minola,
The quaint musician, amorous Licio ;
All for my master's sake, Lucentio.

            Re-enter GREMIO.

Signior Gremio, came you from the church ?
  Gremio. As willingly as e'er I came from school.
  Tranio. And is the bride and bridegroom coming home ?
  Gremio. A bridegroom say you ? 'tis a groom indeed,
A grumbling groom, and that the girl shall find.
  Tranio. Curster than she ? why, 'tis impossible.
  Gremio. Why, he 's a devil, a devil, a very fiend.
  Tranio. Why, she 's a devil, a devil, the devil's dam.
  Gremio. Tut, she 's a lamb, a dove, a fool to him !
I 'll tell you, Sir Lucentio : when the priest
Should ask, if Katharine should be his wife,
' Ay, by gogs-wouns,' quoth he ; and swore so loud,
That, all-amazed, the priest let fall the book ;
And, as he stoop'd again to take it up,
This mad-brain'd bridegroom took him such a cuff
That down fell priest and book and book and priest :
'Now take them up,' quoth he, ' if any list.'
  Tranio. What said the wench when he rose again ?

  Gremio. Trembled and shook ; for why, he stamp'd and swore,
As if the vicar meant to cozen him.
But after many ceremonies done,
He calls for wine : ' A health ! ' quoth he, as if
He had been aboard, carousing to his mates
After a storm ; quaff'd off the muscadel
And threw the sops all in the sexton's face ;
Having no other reason
But that his beard grew thin and hungerly
And seem'd to ask him sops as he was drinking.
This done, he took the bride about the neck
And kiss'd her lips with such a clamorous smack
That at the parting all the church did echo :
And I seeing this came thence for very shame ;
And after me, I know, the rout is coming.
Such a mad marriage never was before :
Hark, hark ! I hear the minstrels play.   *[Music.*

Re-enter PETRUCHIO, KATHARINA, BIANCA, BAPTISTA, HORTENSIO, GRUMIO, *and Train.*

  Petruchio. Gentlemen and friends, I thank you for your pains :
I know you think to dine with me to-day,
And have prepared great store of wedding cheer ;
But so it is, my haste doth call me hence,
And therefore here I mean to take my leave.
  Baptista. Is 't possible you will away to-night ?
  Petruchio. I must away to-day, before night come :
Make it no wonder ; if you knew my business,
You would entreat me rather go than stay.
And, honest company, I thank you all,
That have beheld me give away myself
To this most patient, sweet and virtuous wife :
Dine with my father, drink a health to me ;
For I must hence ; and farewell to you all.
  Tranio. Let us entreat you stay till after dinner.
  Petruchio. It may not be.
  Gremio.   Let me entreat you.
  Petruchio. It cannot be.
  Katharina.   Let me entreat you.
  Petruchio. I am content.
  Katharina.   Are you content to stay ?
  Petruchio. I am content you shall entreat me stay :
But yet not stay, entreat me how you can.
  Katharina. Now, if you love me, stay.
  Petruchio.   Grumio, my horse.
  Grumio. Ay, sir, they be ready : the oats have eaten the horses.
  Katharina. Nay, then,
Do what thou canst, I will not go to-day ;
No, nor to-morrow, not till I please myself.
The door is open, sir ; there lies your way ;
You may be jogging whiles your boots are green ;
For me, I 'll not be gone till I please myself :
'Tis like you 'll prove a jolly surly groom,
That take it on you at the first so roundly.
  Petruchio. O Kate, content thee ; prithee, be not angry.
  Katharina. I will be angry : what hast thou to do ?
Father, be quiet : he shall stay my leisure.
  Gremio. Ay, marry, sir, now it begins to work.
  Katharina. Gentlemen, forward to the bridal dinner :
I see a woman may be made a fool,
If she had not a spirit to resist.
  Petruchio. They shall go forward, Kate, at thy command.
Obey the bride, you that attend on her ;
Go to the feast, revel and domineer,

Carouse full measure to her maidenhead,
Be mad and merry, or go hang yourselves :
But for my bonny Kate, she must with me.
Nay, look not big, nor stamp, nor stare, nor fret ;
I will be master of what is mine own :
She is my goods, my chattels ; she is my house,
My household stuff, my field, my barn,
My horse, my ox, my ass, my any thing ;
And here she stands, touch her whoever dare ;
I 'll bring mine action on the proudest he
That stops my way in Padua. Grumio,
Draw forth thy weapon, we are beset with thieves ;
Rescue thy mistress, if thou be a man.
Fear not, sweet wench, they shall not touch thee,
Kate :
I 'll buckler thee against a million.

[*Exeunt Petruchio, Katharina, and Grumio.*
Baptista. Nay, let them go, a couple of quiet
ones.
Gremio. Went they not quickly, I should die
with laughing.
Tranio. Of all mad matches never was the like.
Lucentio. Mistress, what 's your opinion of your
sister ?
Bianca. That, being mad herself, she 's madly
mated.
Gremio. I warrant him Petruchio is Kated.
Baptista. Neighbours and friends, though bride
and bridegroom wants
For to supply the places at the table,
You know there wants no junkets at the feast.
Lucentio, you shall supply the bridegroom's place ;
And let Bianca take her sister's room.
Tranio. Shall sweet Bianca practise how to
bride it ?
Baptista. She shall, Lucentio. Come, gentlemen,
let 's go. [*Exeunt.*

ACT IV.

SCENE I. PETRUCHIO's *country house.*

Enter GRUMIO.

Grumio.

Fie, fie on all tired jades, on all mad masters,
and all foul ways ! was ever man so beaten ?
was ever man so rayed ? was ever man so
weary ? I am sent before to make a fire, and they are
coming after to warm them. Now, were not I a
little pot and soon hot, my very lips might freeze to
my teeth, my tongue to the roof of my mouth, my
heart in my belly, ere I should come by a fire to thaw
me : but I, with blowing the fire, shall warm myself ;
for, considering the weather, a taller man than I
will take cold. Holla, ho ! Curtis.

Enter CURTIS.

Curtis. Who is that calls so coldly ?
Grumio. A piece of ice : if thou doubt it, thou
mayst slide from my shoulder to my heel with no
greater a run but my head and my neck. A fire,
good Curtis.
Curtis. Is my master and his wife coming, Grumio ?
Grumio. O, ay, Curtis, ay : and therefore fire,
fire ; cast on no water.
Curtis. Is she so hot a shrew as she 's reported ?
Grumio. She was, good Curtis, before this frost :
but, thou knowest, winter tames man, woman and
beast ; for it hath tamed my old master and my

new mistress and myself, fellow Curtis.
Curtis. Away, you three-inch fool ! I am no
beast.
Grumio. Am I but three inches ? why, thy horn
is a foot ; and so long am I at the least. But wilt
thou make a fire, or shall I complain on thee to our
mistress, whose hand, she being now at hand, thou
shalt soon feel, to thy cold comfort, for being slow
in thy hot office ?
Curtis. I prithee, good Grumio. tell me, how
goes the world ?
Grumio. A cold world, Curtis, in every office
but thine : and therefore fire : do thy duty, and
have thy duty ; for my master and mistress are
almost frozen to death.
Curtis. There 's fire ready ; and therefore, good
Grumio, the news.
Grumio. Why, ' Jack, boy ! ho ! boy ! ' and as
much news as will thaw.
Curtis. Come, you are so full of cony-catching !
Grumio. Why, therefore fire ; for I have caught
extreme cold. Where 's the cook ? is supper ready,
the house trimmed, rushes strewed, cobwebs swept ;
the serving-men in their new fustian, their white
stockings, and every officer his wedding-garment on ?
Be the jacks fair within, the jills fair without, the
carpets laid, and every thing in order ?
Curtis. All ready ; and therefore, I pray thee,
news.
Grumio. First, know, my horse is tired ; my
master and mistress fallen out.
Curtis. How ?
Grumio. Out of their saddles into the dirt ; and
thereby hangs a tale.
Curtis. Let 's ha 't, good Grumio.
Grumio. Lend thine ear.
Curtis. Here.
Grumio. There. [*Strikes him.*
Curtis. This is to feel a tale, not to hear a tale.
Grumio. And therefore 'tis called a sensible tale :
and this cuff was but to knock at your ear, and
beseech listening. Now I begin : Imprimis, we
came down a foul hill, my master riding behind my
mistress,—
Curtis. Both of one horse ?
Grumio. What 's that to thee ?
Curtis. Why, a horse.
Grumio. Tell thou the tale : but hadst thou not
crossed me, thou shouldst have heard how her horse
fell and she under her horse ; thou shouldst have
heard in how miry a place, how she was bemoiled,
how he left her with the horse upon her, how he
beat me because her horse stumbled, how she waded
through the dirt to pluck him off me, how he swore,
how she prayed, that never prayed before, how I
cried, how the horses ran away, how her bridle was
burst, how I lost my crupper, with many things of
worthy memory, which now shall die in oblivion
and thou return unexperienced to thy grave.
Curtis. By this reckoning he is more shrew
than she.
Grumio. Ay ; and that thou and the proudest
of you all shall find when he comes home. But
what talk I of this ? Call forth Nathaniel, Joseph,
Nicholas, Philip, Walter, Sugarsop and the rest :
let their heads be sleekly combed, their blue coats
brushed and their garters of an indifferent knit :
let them curtsy with their left legs and not presume
to touch a hair of my master's horse-tail till they
kiss their hands. Are they all ready ?
Curtis. They are.

Grumio. Call them forth.

Curtis. Do you hear, ho? you must meet my master to countenance my mistress.

Grumio. Why, she hath a face of her own.

Curtis. Who knows not that?

Grumio. Thou, it seems, that calls for company to countenance her.

Curtis. I call them forth to credit her.

Grumio. Why, she comes to borrow nothing of them.

Enter four or five Serving-men.

Nathaniel. Welcome home, Grumio!

Philip. How now, Grumio!

Joseph. What, Grumio!

Nicholas. Fellow Grumio!

Nathaniel. How now, old lad?

Grumio. Welcome, you;—how now, you;— what, you;—fellow, you;—and thus much for greeting. Now, my spruce companions, is all ready and all things neat?

Nathaniel. All things is ready. How near is our master?

Grumio. E'en at hand, alighted by this; and therefore be not—Cock's passion, silence! I hear my master.

Enter PETRUCHIO *and* KATHARINA.

Petruchio. Where be these knaves? What, no man at door
To hold my stirrup nor to take my horse!
Where is Nathaniel, Gregory, Philip?

All Servants. Here, here, sir! here, sir.

Petruchio. Here, sir! here, sir! here, sir! here, sir!
You logger-headed and unpolish'd grooms!
What, no attendance? no regard? no duty?
Where is the foolish knave I sent before?

Grumio. Here, sir; as foolish as I was before.

Petruchio. You peasant swain! you whoreson malt-horse drudge!
Did I not bid thee meet me in the park,
And bring along these rascal knaves with thee?

Grumio. Nathaniel's coat, sir, was not fully made,
And Gabriel's pumps were all unpink'd i' the heel;
There was no link to colour Peter's hat,
And Walter's dagger was not come from sheathing:
There were none fine but Adam, Ralph, and Gregory;
The rest were ragged, old, and beggarly;
Yet, as they are, here are they come to meet you.

Petruchio. Go, rascals, go, and fetch my supper in.
                                    [*Exeunt Servants.*

[*Singing*] Where is the life that late I led—
Where are those—Sit down, Kate, and welcome.—
Soud, soud, soud, soud!

Re-enter Servants *with supper.*

Why, when, I say? Nay, good sweet Kate, be merry.
Off with my boots, you rogues! you villains, when?
[*Sings*] It was the friar of orders grey,
    As he forth walked on his way:—
Out, you rogue! you pluck my foot awry:
Take that, and mend the plucking off the other.
                                    [*Strikes him.*
Be merry, Kate. Some water, here; what, ho!
Where 's my spaniel Troilus? Sirrah, get you hence,
And bid my cousin Ferdinand come hither:

One, Kate, that you must kiss, and be acquainted with.
Where are my slippers? Shall I have some water?

Enter one with water.

Come, Kate, and wash, and welcome heartily.
You whoreson villain! will you let it fall?
                                    [*Strikes him*

Katharina. Patience, I pray you; 'twas a fault unwilling.

Petruchio. A whoreson beetle-headed, flap-ear'd knave!
Come, Kate, sit down; I know you have a stomach.
Will you give thanks, sweet Kate; or else shall I?
What 's this? mutton?

First Servant.   Ay.

Petruchio.   Who brought it?

Peter.   I.

Petruchio. 'Tis burnt; and so is all the meat.
What dogs are these! Where is the rascal cook?
How durst you, villains, bring it from the dresser,
And serve it thus to me that love it not?
There, take it to you, trenchers, cups, and all:
                    [*Throws the meat, &c. about the stage.*
You heedless joltheads and unmanner'd slaves!
What, do you grumble? I 'll be with you straight.

Katharina. I pray you, husband, be not so disquiet:
The meat was well, if you were so contented.

Petruchio. I tell thee, Kate, 'twas burnt and dried away;
And I expressly am forbid to touch it,
For it engenders choler, planteth anger;
And better 'twere that both of us did fast,
Since, of ourselves, ourselves are choleric,
Than feed it with such over-roasted flesh.
Be patient; to-morrow 't shall be mended,
And, for this night, we 'll fast for company:
Come, I will bring thee to thy bridal chamber.
                                    [*Exeunt.*

Re-enter Servants *severally.*

Nathaniel. Peter, didst ever see the like?

Peter. He kills her in her own humour.

Re-enter CURTIS.

Grumio. Where is he?

Curtis. In her chamber, making a sermon of continency to her;
And rails, and swears, and rates, that she, poor soul,
Knows not which way to stand, to look, to speak,
And sits as one new-risen from a dream.
Away, away! for he is coming hither.   [*Exeunt.*

Re-enter PETRUCHIO.

Petruchio. Thus have I politicly begun my reign,
And 'tis my hope to end successfully.
My falcon now is sharp and passing empty;
And till she stoop she must not be full-gorged,
For then she never looks upon her lure.
Another way I have to man my haggard,
To make her come and know her keeper's call,
That is, to watch her, as we watch these kites
That bate and beat and will not be obedient.
She eat no meat to-day, nor none shall eat;
Last night she slept not, nor to-night she shall not;
As with the meat, some undeserved fault
I 'll find about the making of the bed;

And here I 'll fling the pillow, there the bolster,
This way the coverlet, another way the sheets :
Ay, and amid this hurly I intend
That all is done in reverend care of her ;
And in conclusion she shall watch all night :
And if she chance to nod I 'll rail and brawl
And with the clamour keep her still awake.
This is a way to kill a wife with kindness ;
And thus I 'll curb her mad and headstrong humour.
He that knows better how to tame a shrew,
Now let him speak : 'tis charity to show.   [*Exit.*

SCENE II. *Padua. Before* BAPTISTA'S *house.*

Enter TRANIO *and* HORTENSIO.

Tranio. Is 't possible, friend Licio, that Mistress
    Bianca
Doth fancy any other but Lucentio ?
I tell you, sir, she bears me fair in hand.
Hortensio. Sir, to satisfy you in what I have said,
Stand by and mark the manner of his teaching.

Enter BIANCA *and* LUCENTIO.

Lucentio. Now, mistress, profit you in what you
    read ?
Bianca. What, master, read you ? first resolve
    me that.
Lucentio. I read that I profess, the Art to Love.
Bianca. And may you prove, sir, master of
    your art !
Lucentio. While you, sweet dear, prove mistress
    of my heart !
Hortensio. Quick proceeders, marry ! Now, tell
    me, I pray,
You that durst swear that your mistress Bianca
Loved none in the world so well as Lucentio.
Tranio. O despiteful love ! unconstant woman-
    kind !
I tell thee, Licio, this is wonderful.
Hortensio. Mistake no more : I am not Licio,
Nor a musician, as I seem to be ;
But one that scorn to live in this disguise,
For such a one as leaves a gentleman,
And makes a god of such a cullion :
Know, sir, that I am call'd Hortensio.
Tranio. Signior Hortensio, I have often heard
Of your entire affection to Bianca ;
And since mine eyes are witness of her lightness,
I will with you, if you be so contented,
Forswear Bianca and her love for ever.
Hortensio. See, how they kiss and court ! Signior
    Lucentio,
Here is my hand, and here I firmly vow
Never to woo her more, but do forswear her,
As one unworthy all the former favours
That I have fondly flatter'd her withal.
Tranio. And here I take the like unfeigned oath,
Never to marry with her though she would entreat :
Fie on her ! see, how beastly she doth court him !
Hortensio. Would all the world but he had quite
    forsworn !
For me, that I may surely keep mine oath,
I will be married to a wealthy widow,
Ere three days pass, which hath as long loved me
As I have loved this proud disdainful haggard.
And so farewell, Signior Lucentio.
Kindness in women, not their beauteous looks,
Shall win my love : and so I take my leave,
In resolution as I swore before.   [*Exit.*

Tranio. Mistress Bianca, bless you with such grace
As 'longeth to a lover's blessed case !
Nay, I have ta'en you napping, gentle love,
And have forsworn you with Hortensio.
Bianca. Tranio, you jest : but have you both
    forsworn me ?
Tranio. Mistress, we have.
Lucentio.   Then we are rid of Licio.
Tranio. I' faith, he 'll have a lusty widow now,
That shall be woo'd and wedded in a day.
Bianca. God give him joy !
Tranio. Ay, and he 'll tame her.
Bianca.   He says so, Tranio.
Tranio. Faith, he is gone unto the taming-school.
Bianca. The taming-school ! what, is there such
    a place ?
Tranio. Ay, mistress, and Petruchio is the master ;
That teacheth tricks eleven and twenty long,
To tame a shrew and charm her chattering tongue.

Enter BIONDELLO.

Biondello. O master, master, I have watch'd so
    long
That I am dog-weary : but at last I spied
† An ancient angel coming down the hill,
Will serve the turn.
Tranio.   What is he, Biondello ?
Biondello. Master, a mercatante, or a pedant,
I know not what ; but formal in apparel,
In gait and countenance surely like a father.
Lucentio. And what of him, Tranio ?
Tranio. If he be credulous and trust my tale,
I 'll make him glad to seem Vincentio,
And give assurance to Baptista Minola,
As if he were the right Vincentio.
Take in your love, and then let me alone.
                    [*Exeunt Lucentio and Bianca.*

Enter a Pedant.

Pedant. God save you, sir !
Tranio.   And you, sir ! you are welcome.
Travel you far on, or are you at the farthest ?
Pedant. Sir, at the farthest for a week or two :
But then up farther, and as far as Rome ;
And so to Tripoli, if God lend me life.
Tranio. What countryman, I pray ?
Pedant.   Of Mantua.
Tranio. Of Mantua, sir ? marry, God forbid !
And come to Padua, careless of your life ?
Pedant. My life, sir ! how, I pray ? for that goes
    hard.
Tranio. 'Tis death for any one in Mantua
To come to Padua. Know you not the cause ?
Your ships are stay'd at Venice, and the duke,
For private quarrel 'twixt your grace and him,
Hath publish'd and proclaim'd it openly :
'Tis marvel, but that you are but newly come,
You might have heard it else proclaim'd about.
Pedant. Alas ! sir, it is worse for me than so :
For I have bills for money by exchange
From Florence and must here deliver them.
Tranio. Well, sir, to do you courtesy,
This will I do, and this I will advise you :
First, tell me, have you ever been at Pisa ?
Pedant. Ay, sir, in Pisa have I often been,
Pisa renowned for grave citizens.
Tranio. Among them know you one Vincentio ?
Pedant. I know him not, but I have heard of
    him ;

A merchant of incomparable wealth.
   Tranio. He is my father, sir ; and, sooth to say,
In countenance somewhat doth resemble you.
   Biondello. [*Aside*] As much as an apple doth an
    oyster and all one.
   Tranio. To save your life in this extremity,
This favour will I do you for his sake ;
And think it not the worst of all your fortunes
That you are like to Sir Vincentio.
His name and credit shall you undertake,
And in my house you shall be friendly lodged :
Look that you take upon you as you should ;
You understand me, sir : so shall you stay
Till you have done your business in the city :
If this be courtesy, sir, accept of it.
   Pedant. O sir, I do ; and will repute you ever
The patron of my life and liberty.
   Tranio. Then go with me to make the matter
    good.
This, by the way, I let you understand ;
My father is here look'd for every day,
To pass assurance of a dower in marriage
'Twixt me and one Baptista's daughter here :
In all these circumstances I 'll instruct you :
Go with me to clothe you as becomes you.
                      Exeunt.

SCENE III.   *A room in* Petruchio's *house.*

Enter Katharina *and* Grumio.

   Grumio. No, no, forsooth ; I dare not for my
    life.
   Katharina. The more my wrong, the more his
    spite appears :
What, did he marry me to famish me ?
Beggars, that come unto my father's door
Upon entreaty have a present alms ;
If not, elsewhere they meet with charity :
But I, who never knew how to entreat,
Nor never needed that I should entreat,
Am starved for meat, giddy for lack of sleep,
With oaths kept waking and with brawling fed :
And that which spites me more than all these wants,
He does it under name of perfect love ;
As who should say, if I should sleep or eat,
'Twere deadly sickness or else present death.
I prithee go and get me some repast ;
I care not what, so it be wholesome food.
   Grumio. What say you to a neat's foot ?
   Katharina. 'Tis passing good : I prithee let me
    have it.
   Grumio. I fear it is too choleric a meat.
How say you to a fat tripe finely broil'd ?
   Katharina. I like it well : good Grumio, fetch
    it me.
   Grumio. I cannot tell ; I fear 'tis choleric.
What say you to a piece of beef and mustard ?
   Katharina. A dish that I do love to feed upon.
   Grumio. Ay, but the mustard is too hot a little.
   Katharina. Why then, the beef, and let the
    mustard rest.
   Grumio. Nay then, I will not : you shall have
    the mustard,
Or else you get no beef of Grumio.
   Katharina. Then both, or one, or any thing thou
    wilt.
   Grumio. Why then, the mustard without the
    beef.
   Katharina. Go, get thee gone, thou false deluding
    slave,   [*Beats him.*

That feed'st me with the very name of meat :
Sorrow on thee and all the pack of you,
That triumph thus upon my misery !
Go, get thee gone, I say.

Enter Petruchio *and* Hortensio, *with meat.*

   Petruchio. How fares my Kate ? What, sweeting,
    all amort ?
   Hortensio. Mistress, what cheer ?
   Katharina.   Faith, as cold as can be.
   Petruchio. Pluck up thy spirits ; look cheerfully
    upon me.
Here, love ; thou see'st how diligent I am
To dress thy meat myself and bring it thee :
I am sure, sweet Kate, this kindness merits thanks.
What, not a word ? Nay, then thou lovest it not ;
And all my pains is sorted to no proof.
Here, take away this dish.
   Katharina.   I pray you, let it stand.
   Petruchio. The poorest service is repaid with
    thanks ;
And so shall mine, before you touch the meat.
   Katharina. I thank you, sir.
   Hortensio. Signior Petruchio, fie ! you are to
    blame.
Come, Mistress Kate, I 'll bear you company.
   Petruchio. [*Aside*] Eat it up all, Hortensio, if
    thou lovest me.
Much good do it unto thy gentle heart !
Kate, eat apace : and now, my honey love,
Will we return unto thy father's house
And revel it as bravely as the best,
With silken coats and caps and golden rings,
With ruffs and cuffs and fardingales and things ;
With scarfs and fans and double change of bravery,
With amber bracelets, beads and all this knavery.
What, hast thou dined ? The tailor stays thy leisure,
To deck thy body with his ruffling treasure.

Enter Tailor.

Come, tailor, let us see these ornaments :
Lay forth the gown.

Enter Haberdasher.

           What news with you, sir ?
   Haberdasher. Here is the cap your worship did
    bespeak.
   Petruchio. Why, this was moulded on a porringer ;
A velvet dish : fie, fie ! 'tis lewd and filthy :
Why, 'tis a cockle or a walnut-shell,
A knack, a toy, a trick, a baby's cap :
Away with it ! come, let me have a bigger.
   Katharina. I 'll have no bigger : this doth fit the
    time,
And gentlewomen wear such caps as these.
   Petruchio. When you are gentle, you shall have
    one too,
And not till then.
   Hortensio. [*Aside*] That will not be in haste.
   Katharina. Why, sir, I trust I may have leave to
    speak ;
And speak I will ; I am no child, no babe :
Your betters have endured me say my mind,
And if you cannot, best you stop your ears.
My tongue will tell the anger of my heart,
Or else my heart concealing it will break,
And rather than it shall, I will be free
Even to the uttermost, as I please, in words.
   Petruchio. Why, thou say'st true ; it is a paltry
    cap,

A custard-coffin, a bauble, a silken pie :
I love thee well, in that thou likest it not.
Katharina. Love me, or love me not, I like the
  cap ;
And it I will have, or I will have none.
                              [Exit Haberdasher.
Petruchio. Thy gown ? why, ay : come, tailor,
  let us see 't.
O mercy, God ! what masquing stuff is here ?
What 's this ? a sleeve ? 'tis like a demi-cannon :
What, up and down, carved like an apple-tart ?
Here 's snip and nip and cut and slish and slash,
Like to a censer in a barber's shop :
Why, what, i' devil's name, tailor, call'st thou this ?
Hortensio. [Aside] I see she 's like to have neither
  cap nor gown.
Tailor. You bid me make it orderly and well,
According to the fashion and the time.
Petruchio. Marry, and did ; but if you be remem-
  ber'd,
I did not bid you mar it to the time.
Go, hop me over every kennel home,
For you shall hop without my custom, sir :
I 'll none of it : hence ! make your best of it.
Katharina. I never saw a better-fashion'd gown,
More quaint, more pleasing, nor more commendable :
Belike you mean to make a puppet of me.
Petruchio. Why, true ; he means to make a
  puppet of thee.
Tailor. She says your worship means to make a
puppet of her.
Petruchio. O monstrous arrogance ! Thou liest,
thou thread, thou thimble,
Thou yard, three-quarters, half-yard, quarter, nail !
Thou flea, thou nit, thou winter-cricket thou !
Braved in mine own house with a skein of thread ?
Away, thou rag, thou quantity, thou remnant ;
Or I shall so be-mete thee with thy yard
As thou shalt think on prating whilst thou livest !
I tell thee, I, that thou hast marr'd her gown.
Tailor. Your worship is deceived ; the gown is
  made
Just as my master had direction :
Grumio gave order how it should be done.
Grumio. I gave him no order ; I gave him the
  stuff.
Tailor. But how did you desire it should be
made ?
Grumio. Marry, sir, with needle and thread.
Tailor. But did you not request to have it cut ?
Grumio. Thou hast faced many things.
Tailor. I have.
Grumio. Face not me : thou hast braved many
men ; brave not me ; I will neither be faced nor
braved. I say unto thee, I bid thy master cut out
the gown ; but I did not bid him cut it to pieces :
ergo, thou liest.
Tailor. Why, here is the note of the fashion to
testify.
Petruchio. Read it.
Grumio. The note lies in 's throat, if he say I
said so.
Tailor. [Reads] ' Imprimis, a loose-bodied gown : '
Grumio. Master, if ever I said loose-bodied gown,
sew me in the skirts of it, and beat me to death
with a bottom of brown thread : . I said a gown.
Petruchio. Proceed.
Tailor. [Reads] ' With a small compassed cape : '
Grumio. I confess the cape.
Tailor. [Reads] ' With a trunk sleeve : '

Grumio. I confess two sleeves.
Tailor. [Reads] ' The sleeves curiously cut.'
Petruchio. Ay, there 's the villany.
Grumio. Error i' the bill, sir ; error i' the bill. I
commanded the sleeves should be cut out and sewed
up again ; and that I 'll prove upon thee, though
thy little finger be armed in a thimble.
Tailor. This is true that I say : an I had thee in
place where, thou shouldst know it.
Grumio. I am for thee straight : take thou the
bill, give me thy mete-yard, and spare not me.
Hortensio. God-a-mercy, Grumio ! then he shall
have no odds.
Petruchio. Well, sir, in brief, the gown is not for
me.
Grumio. You are i' the right, sir : 'tis for my
mistress.
Petruchio. Go, take it up unto thy master's use.
Grumio. Villain, not for thy life : take up my
mistress' gown for thy master's use !
Petruchio. Why, sir, what 's your conceit in that ?
Grumio. O, sir, the conceit is deeper than you
think for :
Take up my mistress' gown to his master's use ! -
O, fie, fie, fie !
Petruchio. [Aside] Hortensio, say thou wilt see
  the tailor paid.
Go take it hence ; be gone, and say no more.
Hortensio. Tailor, I 'll pay thee for thy gown
to-morrow :
Take no unkindness of his hasty words :
Away ! I say : commend me to thy master.
                                      [Exit Tailor.
Petruchio. Well, come, my Kate ; we will unto
  your father's
Even in these honest mean habiliments :
Our purses shall be proud, our garments poor ;
For 'tis the mind that makes the body rich ;
And as the sun breaks through the darkest clouds,
So honour peereth in the meanest habit.
What is the jay more precious than the lark,
Because his feathers are more beautiful ?
Or is the adder better than the eel,
Because his painted skin contents the eye ?
O, no, good Kate ; neither art thou the worse
For this poor furniture and mean array.
If thou account'st it shame, lay it on me ;
And therefore frolic : we will hence forthwith,
To feast and sport us at thy father's house.
Go, call my men, and let us straight to him ;
And bring our horses unto Long-lane end ;
There will we mount, and thither walk on foot.
Let 's see ; I think 'tis now some seven o'clock,
And well we may come there by dinner-time.
Katharina. I dare assure you, sir, 'tis almost two ;
And 'twill be supper-time ere you come there.
Petruchio. It shall be seven ere I go to horse :
Look, what I speak, or do, or think to do,
You are still crossing it. Sirs, let 't alone :
I will not go to-day ; and ere I do,
It shall be what o'clock I say it is.
Hortensio. [Aside] Why, so this gallant will com-
          mand the sun.   [Exeunt.

SCENE IV. Padua. Before BAPTISTA'S house.

Enter TRANIO, and the Pedant, dressed like
          VINCENTIO.

Tranio. Sir, this is the house : please it you that
I call ?

Pedant. Ay, what else ? and but I be deceived
Signior Baptista may remember me,
Near twenty years ago, in Genoa,
Where we were lodgers at the Pegasus.
Tranio. 'Tis well ; and hold your own, in any case,
With such austerity as 'longeth to a father.
Pedant. I warrant you.

Enter BIONDELLO.

But, sir, here comes your boy ;
'Twere good he were school'd.
Tranio. Fear you not him. Sirrah Biondello,
Now do your duty throughly, I advise you :
Imagine 'twere the right Vincentio.
Biondello. Tut, fear not me.
Tranio. But hast thou done thy errand to Baptista ?
Biondello. I told him that your father was at Venice,
And that you look'd for him this day in Padua.
Tranio. Thou 'rt a tall fellow : hold thee that to drink.
Here comes Baptista : set your countenance, sir.

Enter BAPTISTA *and* LUCENTIO.

Signior Baptista, you are happily met.
[*To the Pedant*] Sir, this is the gentleman I told you of :
I pray you, stand good father to me now,
Give me Bianca for my patrimony.
Pedant. Soft, son !
Sir, by your leave : having come to Padua
To gather in some debts, my son Lucentio
Made me acquainted with a weighty cause
Of love between your daughter and himself :
And, for the good report I hear of you
And for the love he beareth to your daughter
And she to him, to stay him not too long,
I am content, in a good father's care,
To have him match'd ; and if you please to like
No worse than I, upon some agreement
Me shall you find ready and willing
With one consent to have her so bestow'd ;
For curious I cannot be with you,
Signior Baptista, of whom I hear so well.
Baptista. Sir, pardon me in what I have to say :
Your plainness and your shortness please me well.
Right true it is, your son Lucentio here
Doth love my daughter and she loveth him,
Or doth dissemble deeply their affections :
And therefore, if you say no more than this,
That like a father you will deal with him
And pass my daughter a sufficient dower,
The match is made, and all is done :
Your son shall have my daughter with consent.
Tranio. I thank you, sir. Where then do you know best
We be affied and such assurance ta'en
As shall with either part's agreement stand ?
Baptista. Not in my house, Lucentio ; for, you know,
Pitchers have ears, and I have many servants :
Besides, old Gremio is hearkening still ;
And happily we might be interrupted.
Tranio. Then at my lodging, an it like you :
There doth my father lie ; and there, this night,
We 'll pass the business privately and well.
Send for your daughter by your servant here ;
My boy shall fetch the scrivener presently.

The worst is this, that, at so slender warning,
You are like to have a thin and slender pittance.
Baptista. It likes me well. Biondello, hie you home,
And bid Bianca make her ready straight ;
And, if you will, tell what hath happened,
Lucentio's father is arrived in Padua,
And how she 's like to be Lucentio's wife.
Biondello. I pray the gods she may with all my heart !
Tranio. Dally not with the gods, but get thee gone.   [*Exit Biondello.*
Signior Baptista, shall I lead the way ?
Welcome ! one mess is like to be your cheer :
Come, sir ; we will better it in Pisa.
Baptista. I follow you.
                    [*Exeunt Tranio, Pedant, and Baptista.*

Re-enter BIONDELLO.

Biondello. Cambio !
Lucentio. What sayest thou, Biondello ?
Biondello. You saw my master wink and laugh upon you ?
Lucentio. Biondello, what of that ?
Biondello. Faith, nothing ; but has left me here behind, to expound the meaning or moral of his signs and tokens.
Lucentio. I pray thee, moralize them.
Biondello. Then thus. Baptista is safe, talking with the deceiving father of a deceitful son.
Lucentio. And what of him ?
Biondello. His daughter is to be brought by you to the supper.
Lucentio. And then ?
Biondello. The old priest of Saint Luke's church is at your command at all hours.
Lucentio. And what of all this ?
Biondello. I cannot tell ; expect they are busied about a counterfeit assurance : take you assurance of her, ' cum privilegio ad imprimendum solum : ' to the church ; take the priest, clerk, and some sufficient honest witnesses :
If this be not that you look for, I have no more to say,
But bid Bianca farewell for ever and a day.
Lucentio. Hearest thou, Biondello ?
Biondello. I cannot tarry : I knew a wench married in an afternoon as she went to the garden for parsley to stuff a rabbit ; and so may you, sir : and so, adieu, sir. My master hath appointed me to go to Saint Luke's, to bid the priest be ready to come against you come with your appendix.   [*Exit.*
Lucentio. I may, and will, if she be so contented :
She will be pleased ; then wherefore should I doubt ?
Hap what hap may, I 'll roundly go about her :
It shall go hard if Cambio go without her. [*Exit.*

SCENE V. *A public road.*

Enter PETRUCHIO, KATHARINA, HORTENSIO,
and Servants.

Petruchio. Come on, i' God's name ; once more toward our father's.
Good Lord, how bright and goodly shines the moon !
Katharina. The moon ! the sun : it is not moonlight now.
Petruchio. I say it is the moon that shines so bright.
Katharina. I know it is the sun that shines so bright.

Petruchio. Now, by my mother's son, and that 's myself,
It shall be moon, or star, or what I list,
Or ere I journey to your father's house.
Go on, and fetch our horses back again.
Evermore cross'd and cross'd ; nothing but cross'd !
Hortensio. Say as he says, or we shall never go.
Katharina. Forward, I pray, since we have come so far,
And be it moon, or sun, or what you please :
An if you please to call it a rush-candle,
Henceforth I vow it shall be so for me.
Petruchio. I say it is the moon.
Katharina. I know it is the moon.
Petruchio. Nay, then you lie : it is the blessed sun.
Katharina. Then, God be bless'd, it is the blessed sun :
But sun it is not, when you say it is not ;
And the moon changes even as your mind.
What you will have it named, even that it is ;
And so it shall be so for Katherine.
Hortensio. Petruchio, go thy ways ; the field is won.
Petruchio. Well, forward, forward ! thus the bowl should run,
And not unluckily against the bias.
But, soft ! company is coming here.

Enter VINCENTIO.

[*To Vincentio*] Good morrow, gentle mistress : where away ?
Tell me, sweet Kate, and tell me truly too,
Hast thou beheld a fresher gentlewoman ?
Such war of white and red within her cheeks !
What stars do spangle heaven with such beauty,
As those two eyes become that heavenly face ?
Fair lovely maid, once more good day to thee.
Sweet Kate, embrace her for her beauty's sake.
Hortensio. A' will make the man mad, to make a woman of him.
Katharina. Young budding virgin, fair and fresh and sweet,
Whither away, or where is thy abode ?
Happy the parents of so fair a child ;
Happier the man, whom favourable stars
Allot thee for his lovely bed-fellow !
Petruchio. Why, how now, Kate ! I hope thou art not mad :
This is a man, old, wrinkled, faded, wither'd,
And not a maiden, as thou say'st he is.
Katharina. Pardon, old father, my mistaking eyes,
That have been so bedazzled with the sun
That everything I look on seemeth green :
Now I perceive thou art a reverend father ;
Pardon, I pray thee, for my mad mistaking.
Petruchio. Do, good old grandsire ; and withal make known
Which way thou travellest : if along with us,
We shall be joyful of thy company.
Vincentio. Fair sir, and you my merry mistress,
That with your strange encounter much amazed me,
My name is call'd Vincentio ; my dwelling Pisa ;
And bound I am to Padua ; there to visit
A son of mine, which long I have not seen.
Petruchio. What is his name ?
Vincentio. Lucentio, gentle sir.
Petruchio. Happily met ; the happier for thy son,
And now by law, as well as reverend age,
I may entitle thee my loving father :

The sister to my wife, this gentlewoman,
Thy son by this hath married. Wonder not,
Nor be not grieved : she is of good esteem,
Her dowry wealthy, and of worthy birth ;
Beside, so qualified as may beseem
The spouse of any noble gentleman.
Let me embrace with old Vincentio,
And wander we to see thy honest son,
Who will of thy arrival be full joyous.
Vincentio. But is this true ? or is it else your pleasure,
Like pleasant travellers, to break a jest
Upon the company you overtake ?
Hortensio. I do assure thee, father, so it is.
Petruchio. Come, go along, and see the truth hereof ;
For our first merriment hath made thee jealous.
[*Exeunt all but Hortensio.*
Hortensio. Well, Petruchio, this has put me in heart.
Have to my widow ! and if she be froward,
Then hast thou taught Hortensio to be untoward.
[*Exit.*

ACT V.

SCENE I. *Padua. Before* LUCENTIO'S *house.*

GREMIO *discovered. Enter behind* BIONDELLO,
LUCENTIO, *and* BIANCA.

Biondello. Softly and swiftly, sir ; for the priest is ready.
Lucentio. I fly, Biondello : but they may chance to need thee at home; therefore leave us.
Biondello. Nay, faith, I 'll see the church o' your back ; and then come back to my master's as soon as I can.
[*Exeunt Lucentio, Bianca, and Biondello.*
Gremio. I marvel Cambio comes not all this while.

Enter PETRUCHIO, KATHARINA, VINCENTIO, GRUMIO,
with Attendants.

Petruchio. Sir, here 's the door, this is Lucentio's house :
My father's bears more toward the market-place ;
Thither must I, and here I leave you, sir.
Vincentio. You shall not choose but drink before you go :
I think I shall command your welcome here,
And, by all likelihood, some cheer is toward.
[*Knocks.*
Gremio. They 're busy within ; you were best knock louder.

Pedant *looks out of the window.*

Pedant. What 's he that knocks as he would beat down the gate ?
Vincentio. Is Signior Lucentio within, sir ?
Pedant. He 's within, sir, but not to be spoken withal.
Vincentio. What if a man bring him a hundred pound or two, to make merry withal ?
Pedant. Keep your hundred pounds to yourself : he shall need none, so long as I live.
Petruchio. Nay, I told you your son was well beloved in Padua. Do you hear, sir ? To leave frivolous circumstances, I pray you, tell Signior Lucentio that his father is come from Pisa and is

here at the door to speak with him.

Pedant. Thou liest : his father is come from Padua and here looking out at the window.

Vincentio. Art thou his father ?

Pedant. Ay, sir ; so his mother says, if I may believe her.

Petruchio. [*To Vincentio*] Why, how now, gentleman ! why, this is flat knavery, to take upon you another man's name.

Pedant. Lay hands on the villain : I believe a' means to cozen somebody in this city under my countenance.

Re-enter BIONDELLO.

Biondello. I have seen them in the church together : God send 'em good shipping ! But who is here ? mine old master Vincentio ! now we are undone and brought to nothing.

Vincentio. [*Seeing Biondello*] Come hither, crackhemp.

Biondello. I hope I may choose, sir.

Vincentio. Come hither, you rogue. What, have you forgot me ?

Biondello. Forgot you ! no, sir : I could not forget you, for I never saw you before in all my life.

Vincentio. What, you notorious villain, didst thou never see thy master's father, Vincentio ?

Biondello. What, my old worshipful old master ? yes, marry, sir : see where he looks out of the window.

Vincentio. Is 't so, indeed ?   [*Beats Biondello.*

Biondello. Help, help, help ! here 's a madman will murder me.   [*Exit.*

Pedant. Help, son ! help, Signior Baptista !
          [*Exit from above.*

Petruchio. Prithee, Kate, let 's stand aside and see the end of this controversy.   [*They retire.*

Re-enter Pedant below ; TRANIO, BAPTISTA, and Servants.

Tranio. Sir, what are you that offer to beat my servant ?

Vincentio. What am I, sir ! nay, what are you, sir ? O immortal gods ! O fine villain ! A silken doublet ! a velvet hose ! a scarlet cloak ! and a copatain hat ! O, I am undone ! I am undone ! while I play the good husband at home, my son and my servant spend at the university.

Tranio. How now ! what 's the matter ?

Baptista. What, is the man lunatic ?

Tranio. Sir, you seem a sober ancient gentleman by your habit, but your words show you a madman. Why, sir, what 'cerns it you if I wear pearl and gold ? I thank my good father, I am able to maintain it.

Vincentio. Thy father ! O villain ! he is a sailmaker in Bergamo.

Baptista. You mistake, sir, you mistake, sir. Pray, what do you think is his name ?

Vincentio. His name ! as if I knew not his name : I have brought him up ever since he was three years old, and his name is Tranio.

Pedant. Away, away, mad ass ! his name is Lucentio ; and he is mine only son, and heir to the lands of me, Signior Vincentio.

Vincentio. Lucentio ! O, he hath murdered his master ! Lay hold on him, I charge you, in the duke's name. O, my son, my son ! Tell me, thou villain, where is my son Lucentio ?

Tranio. Call forth an officer.

Enter one with an officer.

Carry this mad knave to the gaol. Father Baptista, I charge you see that he be forthcoming.

Vincentio. Carry me to the gaol !

Gremio. Stay, officer : he shall not go to prison.

Baptista. Talk not, Signior Gremio : I say he shall go to prison.

Gremio. Take heed, Signior Gremio, lest you be cony-catched in this business : I dare swear this is the right Vincentio.

Pedant. Swear, if thou darest.

Gremio. Nay, I dare not swear it.

Tranio. Then thou wert best say that I am not Lucentio.

Gremio. Yes, I know thee to be Signior Lucentio.

Baptista. Away with the dotard ! to the gaol with him !

Vincentio. Thus strangers may be haled and abused : O monstrous villain !

Re-enter BIONDELLO, with LUCENTIO and BIANCA.

Biondello. O ! we are spoiled and—yonder he is : deny him, forswear him, or else we are all undone.

Lucentio. [*Kneeling*] Pardon, sweet father.

Vincentio.   Lives my sweet son ?
          [*Exeunt Biondello, Tranio, and Pedant, as fast as may be.*

Bianca. Pardon, dear father.

Baptista.   How hast thou offended ? Where is Lucentio ?

Lucentio.   Here 's Lucentio, Right son to the right Vincentio ;
That have by marriage made thy daughter mine, While counterfeit supposes blear'd thine eyne.

Gremio. Here 's packing, with a witness, to deceive us all !

Vincentio. Where is that damned villain Tranio, That faced and braved me in this matter so ?

Baptista. Why, tell me, is not this my Cambio ?

Bianca. Cambio is changed into Lucentio.

Lucentio. Love wrought these miracles. Bianca's love
Made me exchange my state with Tranio, While he did bear my countenance in the town ;
And happily I have arrived at the last Unto the wished haven of my bliss.
What Tranio did, myself enforced him to ;
Then pardon him, sweet father, for my sake.

Vincentio. I 'll slit the villain's nose, that would have sent me to the gaol.

Baptista. But do you hear, sir ? have you married my daughter without asking my good will ?

Vincentio. Fear not, Baptista ; we will content you, go to : but I will in, to be revenged for this villany.   [*Exit.*

Baptista. And I, to sound the depth of this knavery.   [*Exit.*

Lucentio. Look not pale, Bianca ; thy father will not frown.   [*Exeunt Lucentio and Bianca.*

Gremio. My cake is dough ; but I 'll in among the rest,
Out of hope of all, but my share of the feast.
          [*Exit.*

Katharina. Husband, let 's follow, to see the end of this ado.

Petruchio. First kiss me, Kate, and we will.

Katharina. What, in the midst of the street ?

Petruchio. What, art thou ashamed of me ?

Katharina. No, sir, God forbid ; but ashamed to kiss.

Petruchio. Why, then let 's home again. Come,
    sirrah, let 's away.
Katharina. Nay, I will give thee a kiss : now
    pray thee, love, stay.
Petruchio. Is not this well? Come, my sweet
    Kate :
Better once than never, for never too late.
                    [*Exeunt.*

SCENE II.   *Padua.* LUCENTIO'S *house.*

Enter BAPTISTA, VINCENTIO, GREMIO, *the* Pedant,
    LUCENTIO, BIANCA, PETRUCHIO, KATHARINA,
    HORTENSIO, *and* Widow, TRANIO, BIONDELLO,
    and GRUMIO : *the Serving-men with* Tranio
    bringing in a banquet.

Lucentio. At last, though long, our jarring notes
    agree :
And time it is, when raging war is done,
To smile at scapes and perils overblown.
My fair Bianca, bid my father welcome,
While I with self-same kindness welcome thine.
Brother Petruchio, sister Katharina,
And thou, Hortensio, with thy loving widow,
Feast with the best, and welcome to my house :
My banquet is to close our stomachs up,
After our great good cheer. Pray you, sit down ;
For now we sit to chat as well as eat.
Petruchio. Nothing but sit and sit, and eat and
    eat !
Baptista. Padua affords this kindness, son Pet-
    ruchio.
Petruchio. Padua affords nothing but what is kind.
Hortensio. For both our sakes, I would that
    word were true.
Petruchio. Now, for my life, Hortensio fears his
    widow.
Widow. Then never trust me, if I be afeard.
Petruchio. You are very sensible, and yet you miss
    my sense :
I mean, Hortensio is afeard of you.
Widow. He that is giddy thinks the world turns
    round.
Petruchio. Roundly replied.
Katharina.   Mistress, how mean you that?
Widow. Thus I conceive by him.
Petruchio. Conceives by me ! How likes Hor-
    tensio that ?
Hortensio. My widow says, thus she conceives
    her tale.
Petruchio. Very well mended. Kiss him for that,
    good widow.
Katharina. ' He that is giddy thinks the world
    turns round : '
I pray you, tell me what you meant by that.
Widow. Your husband, being troubled with a
    shrew,
Measures my husband's sorrow by his woe :
And now you know my meaning.
Katharina. A very mean meaning.
Widow.   Right, I mean you.
Katharina. And I am mean indeed, respecting
    you.
Petruchio. To her, Kate !
Hortensio. To her, widow !
Petruchio. A hundred marks, my Kate does put
    her down.
Hortensio. That 's my office.
Petruchio. Spoke like an officer : ha' to thee, lad !
                  [*Drinks to Hortensio.*

Baptista. How likes Gremio these quick-witted
    folks ?
Gremio. Believe me, sir, they butt together well.
Bianca. Head, and butt ! an hasty-witted body
Would say your head and butt were head and horn.
Vincentio. Ay, mistress bride, hath that awaken'd
    you ?
Bianca. Ay, but not frighted me ; therefore
    I 'll sleep again.
Petruchio. Nay, that you shall not : since you
    have begun,
Have at you for a bitter jest or two !
Bianca. Am I your bird ? I mean to shift my
    bush ;
And then pursue me as you draw your bow.
You are welcome all.
    [*Exeunt Bianca, Katharina, and Widow.*
Petruchio. She hath prevented me. Here, Signior
    Tranio,
This bird you aim'd at, though you hit her not ;
Therefore a health to all that shot and miss'd.
Tranio. O, sir, Lucentio slipp'd me like his
    greyhound,
Which runs himself and catches for his master.
Petruchio. A good swift simile, but something
    currish.
Tranio. 'Tis well, sir, that you hunted for your-
    self :
'Tis thought your deer does hold you at a bay.
Baptista. O ho, Petruchio ! Tranio hits you now.
Lucentio. I thank thee for that gird, good Tranio.
Hortensio. Confess, confess, hath he not hit you
    here ?
Petruchio. A' has a little gall'd me, I confess ;
And, as the jest did glance away from me,
'Tis ten to one it maim'd you two outright.
Baptista. Now, in good sadness, son Petruchio,
I think thou hast the veriest shrew of all.
Petruchio. Well, I say no : and therefore for
    assurance
Let 's each one send unto his wife ;
And he whose wife is most obedient
To come at first when he doth send for her,
Shall win the wager which we will propose.
Hortensio. Content. What is the wager ?
Lucentio.   Twenty crowns.
Petruchio. Twenty crowns !
I 'll venture so much of my hawk or hound,
But twenty times so much upon my wife.
Lucentio. A hundred then.
Hortensio.   Content.
Petruchio.   A match ! 'tis done.
Hortensio. Who shall begin ?
Lucentio.   That will I.
Go, Biondello, bid your mistress come to me.
Biondello. I go.   [*Exit.*
Baptista. Son, I 'll be your half, Bianca comes.
Lucentio. I 'll have no halves ; I 'll bear it all
    myself.

Re-enter BIONDELLO.

How now ! what news ?
Biondello. Sir, my mistress sends you word
That she is busy and she cannot come.
Petruchio. How ! she is busy and she cannot
    come !
Is that an answer ?
Gremio. Ay, and a kind one too :
Pray God, sir, your wife send you not a worse.
Petruchio. I hope, better.

Hortensio. Sirrah Biondello, go and entreat my wife
To come to me forthwith.   [Exit Biondello.
Petruchio.   O, ho ! entreat her !
Nay, then she must needs come.
Hortensio.   I am afraid, sir,
Do what you can, yours will not be entreated.

Re-enter BIONDELLO.

Now, where 's my wife ?
Biondello. She says you have some goodly jest in hand :
She will not come ; she bids you come to her.
Petruchio. Worse and worse ; she will not come ! O vile,
Intolerable, not to be endured !
Sirrah Grumio, go to your mistress ;
Say, I command her come to me.
                    [Exit Grumio.
Hortensio. I know her answer.
Petruchio.   What ?
Hortensio.   She will not.
Petruchio. The fouler fortune mine, and there an end.
Baptista. Now, by my holidame, here comes Katharina !

Re-enter KATHARINA.

Katharina. What is your will, sir, that you send for me ?
Petruchio. Where is your sister, and Hortensio's wife ?
Katharina. They sit conferring by the parlour fire.
Petruchio. Go, fetch them hither : if they deny to come,
Swinge me them soundly forth unto their husbands :
Away, I say, and bring them hither straight.
                    [Exit Katharina.
Lucentio. Here is a wonder, if you talk of a wonder.
Hortensio. And so it is : I wonder what it bodes.
Petruchio. Marry, peace it bodes, and love and quiet life,
And awful rule and right supremacy ;
And, to be short, what not, that 's sweet and happy ?
Baptista. Now, fair befal thee, good Petruchio !
The wager thou hast won ; and I will add
Unto their losses twenty thousand crowns ;
Another dowry to another daughter,
For she is changed, as she had never been.
Petruchio. Nay, I will win my wager better yet
And show more sign of her obedience.
Her new-built virtue and obedience.
See where she comes and brings your froward wives
As prisoners to her womanly persuasion.

Re-enter KATHARINA, with BIANCA and Widow.

Katharine, that cap of yours becomes you not :
Off with that bauble, throw it under-foot.
Widow. Lord, let me never have a cause to sigh,
Till I be brought to such a silly pass !
Bianca. Fie ! what a foolish duty call you this ?
Lucentio. I would your duty were as foolish too :
The wisdom of your duty, fair Bianca,
Hath cost me an hundred crowns since supper-time.
Bianca. The more fool you, for laying on my duty.
Petruchio. Katharine, I charge thee, tell these headstrong women

What duty they do owe their lords and husbands.
Widow. Come, come, you 're mocking : we will have no telling.
Petruchio. Come on, I say ; and first begin with her.
Widow. She shall not.
Petruchio. I say she shall : and first begin with her.
Katharina. Fie, fie ! unknit that threatening unkind brow,
And dart not scornful glances from those eyes,
To wound thy lord, thy king, thy governor :
It blots thy beauty as frosts do bite the meads,
Confounds thy fame as whirlwinds shake fair buds,
And in no sense is meet or amiable.
A woman moved is like a fountain troubled,
Muddy, ill-seeming, thick, bereft of beauty ;
And while it is so, none so dry or thirsty
Will deign to sip or touch one drop of it.
Thy husband is thy lord, thy life, thy keeper,
Thy head, thy sovereign ; one that cares for thee,
And for thy maintenance commits his body
To painful labour both by sea and land,
To watch the night in storms, the day in cold,
Whilst thou liest warm at home, secure and safe ;
And craves no other tribute at thy hands
But love, fair looks and true obedience ;
Too little payment for so great a debt.
Such duty as the subject owes the prince
Even such a woman oweth to her husband ;
And when she is froward, peevish, sullen, sour,
And not obedient to his honest will,
What is she but a foul contending rebel
And graceless traitor to her loving lord ?
I am ashamed that women are so simple
To offer war where they should kneel for peace,
Or seek for rule, supremacy and sway,
When they are bound to serve, love and obey.
Why are our bodies soft and weak and smooth,
Unapt to toil and trouble in the world,
But that our soft conditions and our hearts
Should well agree with our external parts ?
Come, come, you froward and unable worms !
My mind hath been as big as one of yours,
My heart as great, my reason haply more,
To bandy word for word and frown for frown ;
But now I see our lances are but straws,
Our strength as weak, our weakness past compare,
That seeming to be most which we indeed least are.
Then vail your stomachs, for it is no boot,
And place your hands below your husband's foot :
In token of which duty, if he please,
My hand is ready ; may it do him ease.
Petruchio. Why, there 's a wench ! Come on, and kiss me, Kate.
Lucentio. Well, go thy ways, old lad ; for thou shalt ha 't.
Vincentio. 'Tis a good hearing when children are toward.
Lucentio. But a harsh hearing when women are froward.
Petruchio. Come, Kate, we 'll to bed.
We three are married, but you two are sped.
[To Lucentio] 'Twas I won the wager, though you hit the white ;
And, being a winner, God give you good night !
                    [Exeunt Petruchio and Katharina.
Hortensio. Now, go thy ways ; thou hast tamed a curst shrew.
Lucentio. 'Tis a wonder, by your leave, she will be tamed so.
                    [Exeunt.

ALL'S WELL THAT ENDS WELL

DRAMATIS PERSONÆ

KING OF FRANCE.
DUKE OF FLORENCE.
BERTRAM, Count of Rousillon.
LAFEU, *an old lord.*
PAROLLES, *a follower of* Bertram.
Steward, } *servants to the* Countess of
Clown, } Rousillon.
A Page.

COUNTESS OF ROUSILLON, *mother to* Bertram.
HELENA, *a gentlewoman protected by the* Countess.
An old Widow of Florence.
DIANA, *daughter to the* Widow.
VIOLENTA, } *neighbours and friends to the*
MARIANA, } Widow.

Lords, Officers, Soldiers, &c., French *and*
Florentine.

SCENE : Rousillon ; Paris ; Florence ; Marseilles.

ACT I.

SCENE I. *Rousillon. The* COUNT'S *palace.*

Enter BERTRAM, *the* COUNTESS OF ROUSILLON,
HELENA, *and* LAFEU, *all in black.*

Countess.

In delivering my son from me, I bury a second
husband.

Bertram. And I in going, madam, weep o'er my
father's death anew : but I must attend his majesty's
command, to whom I am now in ward, evermore
in subjection.

Lafeu. You shall find of the king a husband,
madam ; you, sir, a father : he that so generally
is at all times good must of necessity hold his virtue
to you ; whose worthiness would stir it up where
it wanted rather than lack it where there is such
abundance.

Countess. What hope is there of his majesty's
amendment ?

Lafeu. He hath abandoned his physicians, madam ; under whose practices he hath persecuted
time with hope, and finds no other advantage in
the process but only the losing of hope by time.

Countess. This young gentlewoman had a father,
—O, that ' had ' ! how sad a passage 'tis !—whose
skill was almost as great as his honesty ; had it
stretched so far, would have made nature immortal,

and death should have play for lack of work. Would,
for the king's sake, he were living ! I think it would
be the death of the king's disease.

Lafeu. How called you the man you speak of,
madam ?

Countess. He was famous, sir, in his profession,
and it was his great right to be so : Gerard de
Narbon.

Lafeu. He was excellent indeed, madam : the
king very lately spoke of him admiringly and mourn-
ingly : he was skilful enough to have lived still, if
knowledge could be set up against mortality.

Bertram. What is it, my good lord, the king
languishes of ?

Lafeu. A fistula, my lord.

Bertram. I heard not of it before.

Lafeu. I would it were not notorious. Was
this gentlewoman the daughter of Gerard de Narbon?

Countess. His sole child, my lord, and bequeathed
to my overlooking. I have those hopes of her good
that her education promises ; her dispositions she
inherits, which makes fair gifts fairer ; for where
an unclean mind carries virtuous qualities, there
commendations go with pity ; they are virtues and
traitors too : in her they are the better for their
simpleness ; she derives her honesty and achieves
her goodness.

Lafeu. Your commendations, madam, get from
her tears.

Countess. 'Tis the best brine a maiden can season her praise in. The remembrance of her father
never approaches her heart but the tyranny of her
sorrows takes all livelihood from her cheek. No
more of this, Helena ; go to, no more ; lest it be
rather thought you affect a sorrow than have it.

Helena. I do affect a sorrow indeed, but I have
it too.

Lafeu. Moderate lamentation is the right of the
dead, excessive grief the enemy to the living.

Countess. If the living be enemy to the grief,
the excess makes it soon mortal.

Bertram. Madam, I desire your holy wishes.

Lafeu. How understand we that ?

Countess. Be thou blest, Bertram, and succeed
    thy father
In manners, as in shape ! thy blood and virtue
Contend for empire in thee, and thy goodness
Share with thy birthright ! Love all, trust a few,
Do wrong to none : be able for thine enemy
Rather in power than use, and keep thy friend
Under thy own life's key : be check'd for silence,
But never tax'd for speech. What heaven more will,
That thee may furnish and my prayers pluck down,
Fall on thy head ! Farewell, my lord ;
'Tis an unseason'd courtier ; good my lord,
Advise him.

Lafeu. He cannot want the best
That shall attend his love.

Countess. Heaven bless him ! Farewell, Bertram.
                                                [Exit.

Bertram. [*To Helena*] The best wishes that can be forged in your thoughts be servants to you ! Be comfortable to my mother, your mistress, and make much of her.

Lafeu. Farewell, pretty lady : you must hold the credit of your father.

[*Exeunt Bertram and Lafeu.*

Helena. O, were that all ! I think not on my father ;
And these great tears grace his remembrance more
Than those I shed for him. What was he like ?
I have forgot him : my imagination
Carries no favour in 't but Bertram's.
I am undone : there is no living, none,
If Bertram be away. 'Twere all one
That I should love a bright particular star
And think to wed it, he is so above me :
In his bright radiance and collateral light
Must I be comforted, not in his sphere.
The ambition in my love thus plagues itself :
The hind that would be mated by the lion
Must die for love. 'Twas pretty, though a plague,
To see him every hour ; to sit and draw
His arched brows, his hawking eye, his curls,
In our heart's table ; heart too capable
Of every line and trick of his sweet favour :
But now he's gone, and my idolatrous fancy
Must sanctify his reliques. Who comes here ?

Enter PAROLLES.

[*Aside*] One that goes with him : I love him for his sake ;
And yet I know him a notorious liar,
Think him a great way fool, solely a coward ;
Yet these fix'd evils sit so fit in him,
That they take place, when virtue's steely bones
† Look bleak i' the cold wind : withal, full oft we see
Cold wisdom waiting on superfluous folly.

Parolles. Save you, fair queen !

Helena. And you. monarch !

Parolles. No.

Helena. And no.

Parolles. Are you meditating on virginity ?

Helena. Ay. You have some stain of soldier in you : let me ask you a question. Man is enemy to virginity ; how may we barricado it against him ?

Parolles. Keep him out.

Helena. But he assails ; and our virginity, though valiant, in the defence yet is weak : unfold to us some warlike resistance.

Parolles. There is none : man, sitting down before you, will undermine you and blow you up.

Helena. Bless our poor virginity from underminers and blowers up ! Is there no military policy, how virgins might blow up men ?

Parolles. Virginity being blown down, man will quicklier be blown up : marry, in blowing him down again, with the breach yourselves made, you lose your city. It is not politic in the commonwealth of nature to preserve virginity. Loss of virginity is rational increase and there was never virgin got till virginity was first lost. That you were made of is metal to make virgins. Virginity by being once lost may be ten times found ; by being ever kept, it is ever lost : 'tis too cold a companion ; away with 't !

Helena. I will stand for 't a little, though therefore I die a virgin.

Parolles. There's little can be said in 't ; 'tis against the rule of nature. To speak on the part of virginity, is to accuse your mothers ; which is most infallible disobedience. He that hangs himself is a virgin : virginity murders itself ; and should be buried in highways out of all sanctified limit, as a desperate offendress against nature. Virginity breeds mites, much like a cheese ; consumes itself to the very paring, and so dies with feeding his own stomach. Besides, virginity is peevish, proud, idle, made of self-love, which is the most inhibited sin in the canon. Keep it not ; you cannot choose but lose by 't : out with 't ! within ten year it will make itself ten, which is a goodly increase ; and the principal tself not much the worse : away with 't !

Helena. How might one do, sir, to lose it to her own liking ?

Parolles. Let me see : marry, ill, to like him that ne'er it likes. 'Tis a commodity will lose the gloss with lying ; the longer kept, the less worth : off with 't while 'tis vendible ; answer the time of request. Virginity, like an old courtier, wears her cap out of fashion : richly suited, but unsuitable just like the brooch and the tooth-pick, which wear not now. Your date is better in your pie and your porridge than in your cheek : and your virginity, your old virginity, is like one of our French withered pears, it looks ill, it eats drily ; marry, 'tis a withered pear ; it was formerly better ; marry, yet 'tis a withered pear : will you any thing with it ?

Helena. † Not my virginity yet......
There shall your master have a thousand loves,
A mother and a mistress and a friend,
A phœnix, captain and an enemy,
A guide, a goddess, and a sovereign,
A counsellor, a traitress, and a dear ;
His humble ambition, proud humility,
His jarring concord, and his discord dulcet,
His faith, his sweet disaster ; with a world
Of pretty, fond, adoptious christendoms,
That blinking Cupid gossips. Now shall he—
I know not what he shall. God send him well !
The court 's a learning place, and he is one—

Parolles. What one, i' faith ?

Helena. That I wish well. 'Tis pity—

Parolles. What's pity ?

Helena. That wishing well had not a body in 't, Which might be felt ; that we, the poorer born, Whose baser stars do shut us up in wishes, Might with effects of them follow our friends, And show what we alone must think, which never Returns us thanks.

Enter Page.

Page. Monsieur Parolles, my lord calls for you.
[*Exit.*

Parolles. Little Helen, farewell : if I can remember thee, I will think of thee at court.

Helena. Monsieur Parolles, you were born under a charitable star.

Parolles. Under Mars, I.

Helena. I especially think, under Mars.

Parolles. Why under Mars ?

Helena. The wars have so kept you under that you must needs be born under Mars.

Parolles. When he was predominant.

Helena. When he was retrograde. I think, rather.

Parolles. Why think you so ?

Helena. You go so much backward when you fight.

Parolles. That's for advantage.

Helena. So is running away, when fear proposes the safety : but the composition that your valour

and fear makes in you is a virtue of a good wing,
and I like the wear well.

Parolles. I am so full of businesses, I cannot
answer thee acutely. I will return perfect courtier ;
in the which, my instruction shall serve to naturalize
thee, so thou wilt be capable of a courtier's counsel
and understand what advice shall thrust upon thee ;
else thou diest in thine unthankfulness, and thine
ignorance makes thee away : farewell. When thou
hast leisure, say thy prayers ; when thou hast none,
remember thy friends : get thee a good husband,
and use him as he uses thee : so, farewell.
                     [*Exit.*

Helena. Our remedies oft in ourselves do lie,
Which we ascribe to heaven : the fated sky
Gives us free scope, only doth backward pull
Our slow designs when we ourselves are dull.
What power is it which mounts my love so high,
That makes me see, and cannot feed mine eye ?
The mightiest space in fortune nature brings
To join like likes and kiss like native things.
Impossible be strange attempts to those
That weigh their pains in sense and do suppose
What hath been cannot be : who ever strove
To show her merit, that did miss her love ?
The king's disease—my project may deceive me,
But my intents are fix'd and will not leave me.
                     [*Exit.*

SCENE II. *Paris. The* KING'S *palace.*

Flourish of cornets. Enter the KING OF FRANCE,
with letters, and divers Attendants.

King. The Florentines and Senoys are by the ears ;
Have fought with equal fortune and continue
A braving war.

First Lord. So 'tis reported, sir.

King. Nay, 'tis most credible ; we here receive it
A certainty, vouch'd from our cousin Austria,
With caution that the Florentine will move us
For speedy aid ; wherein our dearest friend
Prejudices the business and would seem
To have us make denial.

First Lord. His love and wisdom,
Approved so to your majesty, may plead
For amplest credence.

King. He hath arm'd our answer,
And Florence is denied before he comes :
Yet, for our gentlemen that mean to see
The Tuscan service, freely have they leave
To stand on either part.

Second Lord. It well may serve
A nursery to our gentry, who are sick
For breathing and exploit.

King. What 's he comes here ?

Enter BERTRAM, LAFEU, *and* PAROLLES.

First Lord. It is the Count Rousillon, my good
lord,
Young Bertram.

King. Youth, thou bear'st thy father's face ;
Frank nature, rather curious than in haste,
Hath well composed thee. Thy father's moral parts
Mayst thou inherit too ! Welcome to Paris.

Bertram. My thanks and duty are your majesty's.

King. I would I had that corporal soundness now,
As when thy father and myself in friendship
First tried our soldiership ! He did look far
Into the service of the time and was
Discipled of the bravest : he lasted long ;

But on us both did haggish age steal on
And wore us out of act. It much repairs me
To talk of your good father. In his youth
He had the wit which I can well observe
To-day in our young lords ; but they may jest
Till their own scorn return to them unnoted
Ere they can hide their levity in honour :
† So like a courtier, contempt nor bitterness
Were in his pride or sharpness ; if they were,
His equal had awaked them, and his honour,
Clock to itself, knew the true minute when
Exception bid him speak, and at this time
His tongue obey'd his hand : who were below him
He used as creatures of another place
And bow'd his eminent top to their low ranks,
Making them proud of his humility,
† In their poor praise he humbled. Such a man
Might be a copy to these younger times ;
Which, follow'd well, would demonstrate them now
But goers backward.

Bertram. His good remembrance, sir,
Lies richer in your thoughts than on his tomb ;
So in approof lives not his epitaph
As in your royal speech.

King. Would I were with him ! He would
     always say—
Methinks I hear him now ; his plausive words
He scatter'd not in ears, but grafted them,
To grow there and to bear,—' Let me not live,'—
This his good melancholy oft began,
On the catastrophe and heel of pastime,
When it was out,—' Let me not live,' quoth he,
' After my flame lacks oil, to be the snuff
Of younger spirits, whose apprehensive senses
All but new things disdain ; whose judgements
     are
Mere fathers of their garments ; whose constancies
Expire before their fashions.' This he wish'd :
I after him do after him wish too,
Since I nor wax nor honey can bring home,
I quickly were dissolved from my hive,
To give some labourers room.

Second Lord. You are loved, sir ;
They that least lend it you shall lack you first.

King. I fill a place, I know 't. How long is 't,
     count,
Since the physician at your father's died ?
He was much famed.

Bertram. Some six months since, my lord.

King. If he were living, I would try him yet.
Lend me an arm ; the rest have worn me out
With several applications : nature and sickness
Debate it at their leisure. Welcome, count ;
My son 's no dearer.

Bertram. Thank your majesty.
                     [*Exeunt. Flourish.*

SCENE III. *Rousillon. The* COUNT'S *palace.*

Enter COUNTESS, *Steward, and* Clown.

Countess. I will now hear ; what say you of this
gentlewoman ?

Steward. Madam, the care I have had to even
your content, I wish might be found in the calendar
of my past endeavours ; for then we wound our
modesty and make foul the clearness of our deservings, when of ourselves we publish them.

Countess. What does this knave here ? Get you
gone, sirrah : the complaints I have heard of you
I do not all believe : 'tis my slowness that I do not ;
for I know you lack not folly to commit them, and

have ability enough to make such knaveries yours.

Clown. 'Tis not unknown to you, madam, I am a poor fellow.

Countess. Well, sir.

Clown. No, madam, 'tis not so well that I am poor, though many of the rich are damned : but, if I may have your ladyship's good will to go to the world, Isbel the woman and I will do as we may.

Countess. Wilt thou needs be a beggar ?

Clown. I do beg your good will in this case.

Countess. In what case ?

Clown. In Isbel's case and mine own. Service is no heritage : and I think I shall never have the blessing of God till I have issue o' my body ; for they say barnes are blessings.

Countess. Tell me thy reason why thou wilt marry.

Clown. My poor body, madam, requires it : I am driven on by the flesh ; and he must needs go that the devil drives.

Countess. Is this all your worship's reason ?

Clown. Faith, madam, I have other holy reasons, such as they are.

Countess. May the world know them ?

Clown. I have been, madam, a wicked creature, as you and all flesh and blood are ; and, indeed, I do marry that I may repent.

Countess. Thy marriage, sooner than thy wickedness.

Clown. I am out o' friends, madam ; and I hope to have friends for my wife's sake.

Countess. Such friends are thine enemies, knave.

Clown. You 're shallow, madam, in great friends ; for the knaves come to do that for me which I am aweary of. He that ears my land spares my team and gives me leave to in the crop ; if I be his cuckold, he 's my drudge : he that comforts my wife is the cherisher of my flesh and blood ; he that cherishes my flesh and blood loves my flesh and blood ; he that loves my flesh and blood is my friend : ergo, he that kisses my wife is my friend. If men could be contented to be what they are, there were no fear in marriage ; for young Charbon the puritan and old Poysam the papist, howsome'er their hearts are severed in religion, their heads are both one ; they may joul horns together, like any deer i' the herd.

Countess. Wilt thou ever be a foul-mouthed and calumnious knave ?

Clown. A prophet I, madam ; and I speak the truth the next way :

For I the ballad will repeat,
   Which men full true shall find ;
Your marriage comes by destiny,
   Your cuckoo sings by kind.

Countess. Get you gone, sir ; I 'll talk with you more anon.

Steward. May it please you, madam, that he bid Helen come to you : of her I am to speak.

Countess. Sirrah, tell my gentlewoman I would speak with her ; Helen, I mean.

Clown. Was this fair face the cause, quoth she,
Why the Grecians sacked Troy ?
   Fond done, done fond,
Was this King Priam's joy ?
With that she sighed as she stood,
With that she sighed as she stood,
   And gave this sentence then ;
Among nine bad if one be good,
Among nine bad if one be good,
   There 's yet one good in ten.

Countess. What, one good in ten ? you corrupt the song, sirrah.

Clown. One good woman in ten, madam ; which is a purifying o' the song : would God would serve the world so all the year ! we 'ld find no fault with the tithe-woman, if I were the parson. One in ten, quoth a' ! An we might have a good woman born but one every blazing star, or at an earthquake, 'twould mend the lottery well : a man may draw his heart out, ere a' pluck one.

Countess. You 'll be gone, sir knave, and do as I command you.

Clown. That man should be at woman's command, and yet no hurt done ! Though honesty be no puritan, yet it will do no hurt ; it will wear the surplice of humility over the black gown of a big heart. I am going, forsooth : the business is for Helen to come hither.   [*Exit.*

Countess. Well, now.

Steward. I know, madam, you love your gentlewoman entirely.

Countess. Faith, I do : her father bequeathed her to me ; and she herself, without other advantage, may lawfully make title to as much love as she finds : there is more owing her than is paid ; and more shall be paid her than she 'll demand.

Steward. Madam, I was very late more near her than I think she wished me : alone she was, and did communicate to herself her own words to her own ears ; she thought, I dare vow for her, they touched not any stranger sense. Her matter was, she loved your son : Fortune, she said, was no goddess, that had put such difference betwixt their two estates ; Love no god, that would not extend his might, only where qualities were level ; Dian no queen of virgins, that would suffer her poor knight surprised, without rescue in the first assault or ransom afterward. This she delivered in the most bitter touch of sorrow that e'er I heard virgin exclaim in : which I held my duty speedily to acquaint you withal ; sithence, in the loss that may happen, it concerns you something to know it.

Countess. You have discharged this honestly ; keep it to yourself : many likelihoods informed me of this before, which bring so tottering in the balance that I could neither believe nor misdoubt. Pray you, leave me : stall this in your bosom ; and I thank you for your honest care : I will speak with you further anon.   [*Exit Steward.*

Enter Helena.

Even so it was with me when I was young :
If ever we are nature's, these are ours ; this thorn
Doth to our rose of youth rightly belong ;
  Our blood to us, this to our blood is born ;
It is the show and seal of nature's truth,
Where love's strong passion is impress'd in youth :
By our remembrances of days foregone,
† Such were our faults, or then we thought them none.
Her eye is sick on 't : I observe her now.

Helena. What is your pleasure, madam ?

Countess.   'You know, Helen,
I am a mother to you.

Helena. Mine honourable mistress.

Countess.   Nay, a mother :
Why not a mother ? When I said ' a mother,'
Methought you saw a serpent : what 's in ' mother,'
That you start at it ? I say, I am your mother ;
And put you in the catalogue of those
That were enwombed mine : 'tis often seen
Adoption strives with nature and choice breeds
A native slip to us from foreign seeds :

You ne'er oppress'd me with a mother's groan,
Yet I express to you a mother's care :
God's mercy, maiden ! does it curd thy blood
To say I am thy mother ? What 's the matter,
That this distemper'd messenger of wet,
The many-colour'd Iris, rounds thine eye ?
Why ? that you are my daughter ?
 Helena.   That I am not.
 Countess. I say, I am your mother.
 Helena.   Pardon, madam ;
The Count Rousillon cannot be my brother :
I am from humble, he from honour'd name ;
No note upon my parents, his all noble :
My master, my dear lord he is ; and I
His servant live, and will his vassal die :
He must not be my brother.
 Countess.   Nor I your mother ?
 Helena. You are my mother, madam ; would you
  were,—
So that my lord your son were not my brother,—
Indeed my mother ! or were you both our mothers,
I care no more for than I do for heaven,
So I were not his sister. Can 't no other,
But, I your daughter, he must be my brother ?
 Countess. Yes, Helen, you might be my daughter-
  in-law :
God shield you mean it not ! daughter and mother
So strive upon your pulse. What, pale again ?
My fear hath catch'd your fondness : now I see
The mystery of your loneliness, and find
Your salt tears' head : now to all sense 'tis gross
You love my son ; invention is ashamed,
Against the proclamation of thy passion,
To say thou dost not : therefore tell me true ;
But tell me then, 'tis so ; for, look, thy cheeks
Confess it, th' one to th' other ; and thine eyes
See it so grossly shown in thy behaviours
That in their kind they speak it : only sin
And hellish obstinacy tie thy tongue,
That truth should be suspected. Speak, is 't so ?
If it be so, you have wound a goodly clew ;
If it be not, forswear 't : howe'er, I charge thee,
As heaven shall work in me for thine avail,
To tell me truly.
 Helena.   Good madam, pardon me !
 Countess. Do you love my son ?
 Helena.   Your pardon, noble mistress !
 Countess. Love you my son ?
 Helena.   Do not you love him, madam ?
 Countess. Go not about ; my love hath in 't a
  bond,
Whereof the world takes note : come, come, disclose
The state of your affection ; for your passions
Have to the full appeach'd.
 Helena.   Then, I confess,
Here on my knee, before high heaven and you,
That before you, and next unto high heaven,
I love your son.
My friends were poor, but honest ; so 's my love :
Be not offended ; for it hurts not him
That he is loved of me : I follow him not
By any token of presumptuous suit ;
Nor would I have him till I do deserve him ;
Yet never know how that desert should be.
I know I love in vain, strive against hope ;
Yet in this captious and intenible sieve
I still pour in the waters of my love
And lack not to lose still : thus, Indian-like,
Religious in mine error, I adore
The sun, that looks upon his worshipper,

But knows of him no more. My dearest madam,
Let not your hate encounter with my love
For loving where you do : but if yourself,
Whose aged honour cites a virtuous youth,
Did ever in so true a flame of liking
Wish chastely and love dearly, that your Dian
Was both herself and love ; O, then, give pity
To her, whose state is such that cannot choose
But lend and give where she is sure to lose ;
That seeks not to find that her search implies,
But riddle-like lives sweetly where she dies !
 Countess. Had you not lately an intent,—speak
  truly,—
To go to Paris ?
 Helena. Madam, I had.
 Countess.   Wherefore ? tell true.
 Helena. I will tell truth ; by grace itself I swear.
You know my father left me some prescriptions
Of rare and proved such effects, as his reading
And manifest experience had collected
For general sovereignty ; and that he will'd me
In heedfull'st reservation to bestow them,
As notes whose faculties inclusive were
More than they were in note : amongst the rest
There is a remedy, approved, set down,
To cure the desperate languishings whereof
The king is render'd lost.
 Countess.   This was your motive
For Paris, was it ? speak.
 Helena. My lord your son made me to think of
  this ;
Else Paris and the medicine and the king
Had from the conversation of my thoughts
Haply been absent then.
 Countess.   But think you, Helen,
If you should tender your supposed aid,
He would receive it ? he and his physicians
Are of a mind ; he, that they cannot help him,
They, that they cannot help : how shall they credit
A poor unlearned virgin, when the schools,
Embowell'd of their doctrine, have left off
The danger to itself ?
 Helena.   There 's something in 't,
More than my father's skill, which was the greatest
Of his profession, that his good receipt
Shall for my legacy be sanctified
By the luckiest stars in heaven : and, would your
  honour
But give me leave to try success, I 'ld venture
The well-lost life of mine on his grace's cure
By such a day and hour.
 Countess.   Dost thou believe 't ?
 Helena. Ay, madam, knowingly.
 Countess. Why, Helen, thou shalt have my leave
  and love,
Means and attendants and my loving greetings
To those of mine in court : I 'll stay at home
And pray God's blessing into thy attempt :
Be gone to-morrow ; and be sure of this,
What I can help thee to thou shalt not miss.
             [Exeunt.

ACT II.

SCENE I. *Paris. The* KING'S *palace.*

Flourish of cornets. Enter the KING, *attended
 with divers young* Lords *taking leave for the
 Florentine war ;* BERTRAM *and* PAROLLES.

King.

Farewell, young lords ; these warlike principles
Do not throw from you : and you, my lords,
  farewell :
Share the advice betwixt you ; if both gain, all
The gift doth stretch itself as 'tis received,
And is enough for both.
First Lord.   'Tis our hope, sir,
After well enter'd soldiers, to return
And find your grace in health.
King.   No, no, it cannot be ; and yet my heart
Will not confess he owes the malady
That doth my life besiege.   Farewell, young lords ;
Whether I live or die, be you the sons
Of worthy Frenchmen : let higher Italy,—
† Those bated that inherit but the fall
Of the last monarchy,—see that you come
Not to woo honour, but to wed it ; when
The bravest questant shrinks, find what you seek,
That fame may cry you loud ; I say, farewell.
Second Lord.   Health, at your bidding, serve your
  majesty !
King.   Those girls of Italy, take heed of them :
They say, our French lack language to deny,
If they demand : beware of being captives,
Before you serve.
Both.   Our hearts receive your warnings.
King.   Farewell.   Come hither to me.
                            [*Exit, attended.*
First Lord.   O my sweet lord, that you will stay
  behind us !
Parolles.   'Tis not his fault, the spark.
Second Lord.   O, 'tis brave wars !
Parolles.   Most admirable : I have seen those wars.
Bertram.   I am commanded here, and kept a coil
  with
' Too young ' and ' the next year ' and ' 'tis too
  early.'
Parolles.   An thy mind stand to 't boy, steal away
  bravely.
Bertram.   I shall stay here the forehorse to a
  smock,
Creaking my shoes on the plain masonry,
Till honour be bought up and no sword worn
But one to dance with !   By heaven, I 'll steal away.
First Lord.   There 's honour in the theft.
Parolles.   Commit it, count.
Second Lord.   I am your accessary ; and so,
  farewell.
Bertram.   I grow to you, and our parting is a
tortured body.
First Lord.   Farewell, captain.
Second Lord.   Sweet Monsieur Parolles !
Parolles.   Noble heroes, my sword and yours are
kin.   Good sparks and lustrous, a word, good
metals : you shall find in the regiment of the Spinii
one Captain Spurio, with his cicatrice, an emblem
of war, here on his sinister cheek ; it was this very
sword entrenched it : say to him, I live ; and observe
his reports for me.
First Lord.   We shall, noble captain.
                            [*Exeunt Lords.*
Parolles.   Mars dote on you for his novices !   what
will ye do ?
Bertram.   Stay : the king.

Re-enter KING.   BERTRAM *and* PAROLLES *retire.*

Parolles.   [*To Bertram*] Use a more spacious ceremony to the noble lords ;   you have restrained
yourself within the list of too cold an adieu : be

more expressive to them : for they wear themselves
in the cap of the time, there do muster true gait,
eat, speak, and move under the influence of the most
received star ; and though the devil lead the measure,
such are to be followed : after them, and take a more
dilated farewell.
Bertram.   And I will do so.
Parolles.   Worthy fellows ; and like to prove most
sinewy sword-men.
                    [*Exeunt Bertram and Parolles.*

Enter LAFEU.

Lafeu. [*Kneeling*] Pardon, my lord, for me and
  for my tidings.
King.   I 'll fee thee to stand up.
Lafeu.   Then here 's a man stands, that has
  brought his pardon.
I would you had kneel'd, my lord, to ask me mercy,
And that at my bidding you could so stand up.
King.   I would I had ;   so I had broke thy pate,
And ask'd thee mercy for 't.
Lafeu.   Good faith, across : but, my good lord,
  'tis thus ;
Will you be cured of your infirmity ?
King.   No.
Lafeu.   O, will you eat no grapes, my royal fox ?
Yes, but you will my noble grapes, an if
My royal fox could reach them : I have seen a
  medicine
That 's able to breathe life into a stone,
Quicken a rock, and make you dance canary
With spritely fire and motion ; whose simple touch
Is powerful to araise King Pepin, nay,
To give great Charlemain a pen in 's hand
And write to her a love-line.
King.   What ' her ' is this ?
Lafeu.   Why, Doctor She : my lord, there 's one
  arrived,
If you will see her : now, by my faith and honour,
If seriously I may convey my thoughts
In this my light deliverance, I have spoke
With one that, in her sex, her years, profession,
Wisdom and constancy, hath amazed me more
Than I dare blame my weakness : will you see her,
For that is her demand, and know her business ?
That done, laugh well at me.
King.   Now, good Lafeu,
Bring in the admiration ; that we with thee
May spend our wonder too, or take off thine
By wondering how thou took'st it.
Lafeu.   Nay, I 'll fit you,
And not be all day neither.   [*Exit.*
King.   Thus he his special nothing ever prologues.

Re-enter LAFEU, *with* HELENA.

Lafeu.   Nay, come your ways.
King.   This haste hath wings indeed.
Lafeu.   Nay, come your ways ;
This is his majesty ; say your mind to him :
A traitor you do look like ; but such traitors
His majesty seldom fears : I am Cressid's uncle,
That dare leave two together ; fare you well.
                            [*Exit.*
King.   Now, fair one, does your business follow
  us ?
Helena.   Ay, my good lord,
Gerard de Narbon was my father ;
In what he did profess, well found.
King.   I knew him.

Helena. The rather will I spare my praises to-
wards him ;
Knowing him is enough. On 's bed of death
Many receipts he gave me ; chiefly one,
Which, as the dearest issue of his practice,
And of his old experience the only darling,
He bade me store up, as a triple eye,
Safer than mine own two, more dear ; I have so ;
And, hearing your high majesty is touch'd
With that malignant cause wherein the honour
Of my dear father's gift stands chief in power,
I come to tender it and my appliance
With all bound humbleness.
  King.   We thank you, maiden ;
But may not be so credulous of cure,
When our most learned doctors leave us and
The congregated college have concluded
That labouring art can never ransom nature
From her inaidible estate ; I say we must not
So stain our judgement, or corrupt our hope,
To prostitute our past-cure malady
To empirics, or to dissever so
Our great self and our credit, to esteem
A senseless help when help past sense we deem.
  Helena. My duty then shall pay me for my pains :
I will no more enforce mine office on you ;
Humbly entreating from your royal thoughts
A modest one, to bear me back again.
  King. I cannot give thee less, to be call'd grateful :
Thou thought'st to help me ; and such thanks I give
As one near death to those that wish him live :
But what at full I know, thou know'st no part,
I knowing all my peril, thou no art.
  Helena. What I can do can do no hurt to try,
Since you set up your rest 'gainst remedy.
He that of greatest works is finisher
Oft does them by the weakest minister :
So holy writ in babes hath judgement shown,
When judges have been babes ; great floods have
  flown
From simple sources, and great seas have dried
When miracles have by the greatest been denied.
Oft expectation fails and most oft there
Where most it promises, and oft it hits
Where hope is coldest and despair most fits.
  King. I must not hear thee ; fare thee well,
  kind maid :
Thy pains not used must by thyself be paid :
Proffers not took reap thanks for their reward.
  Helena. Inspired merit so by breath is barr'd :
It is not so with Him that all things knows
As 'tis with us that square our guess by shows ;
But most it is presumption in us when
The help of heaven we count the act of men.
Dear sir, to my endeavours give consent ;
Of heaven, not me, make an experiment.
I am not an impostor that proclaim
Myself against the level of mine aim ;
But know I think and think I know most sure
My art is not past power nor you past cure.
  King. Art thou so confident ? within what space
Hopest thou my cure ?
  Helena.   The great'st grace lending grace,
Ere twice the horses of the sun shall bring
Their fiery torcher his diurnal ring,
Ere twice in murk and occidental damp
Moist Hesperus hath quench'd his sleepy lamp,
Or four and twenty times the pilot's glass
Hath told the thievish minutes how they pass,
What is infirm from your sound parts shall fly,
Health shall live free and sickness freely die.

  King. Upon thy certainty and confidence
What darest thou venture ?
  Helena.   Tax of impudence,
A strumpet's boldness, a divulged shame
Traduced by odious ballads : my maiden's name
Sear'd otherwise ; nay, worse—if worse—extended
With vilest torture let my life be ended.
  King. Methinks in thee some blessed spirit doth
  speak
His powerful sound within an organ weak :
And what impossibility would slay
In common sense, sense saves another way.
Thy life is dear ; for all that life can rate
Worth name of life in thee hath estimate,
Youth, beauty, wisdom, courage, all
That happiness and prime can happy call :
Thou this to hazard needs must intimate
Skill infinite or monstrous desperate.
Sweet practiser, thy physic I will try,
That ministers thine own death if I die.
  Helena. If I break time, or flinch in property
Of what I spoke, unpitied let me die,
And well deserved : not helping, death 's my fee ;
But, if I help, what do you promise me ?
  King. Make thy demand.
  Helena.   But will you make it even ?
  King. Ay, by my sceptre and my hopes of heaven.
  Helena. Then shalt thou give me with thy kingly
  hand
What husband in thy power I will command :
Exempted be from me the arrogance
To choose from forth the royal blood of France,
My low and humble name to propagate
With any branch or image of thy state ;
But such a one, thy vassal, whom I know
Is free for me to ask, thee to bestow.
  King. Here is my hand ; the premises observed,
Thy will by my performance shall be served :
So make the choice of thy own time, for I,
Thy resolved patient, on thee still rely.
More should I question thee, and more I must,
Though more to know could not be more to trust,
From whence thou camest, how tended on : but
  rest
Unquestion'd welcome and undoubted blest.
Give me some help here, ho ! If thou proceed
As high as word, my deed shall match thy meed.
          [*Flourish. Exeunt.*

SCENE II.   *Rousillon.   The* COUNT'S *palace.*

          Enter COUNTESS *and* CLOWN.

  Countess. Come on, sir ; I shall now put you to
the height of your breeding.
  Clown. I will show myself highly fed and lowly
taught : I know my business is but to the court.
  Countess. To the court ! why, what place make
you special, when you put off that with such contempt ? But to the court !
  Clown. Truly, madam, if God have lent a man
any manners, he may easily put it off at court : he
that cannot make a leg, put off 's cap, kiss his hand
and say nothing, has neither leg, hands, lip, nor cap ;
and indeed such a fellow, to say precisely, were not
for the court ; but for me, I have an answer will
serve all men.
  Countess. Marry, that 's a bountiful answer that
fits all questions.
  Clown. It is like a barber's chair that fits all
buttocks, the pin-buttock, the quatch-buttock, the

brawn buttock, or any buttock.

Countess. Will your answer serve fit to all questions?

Clown. As fit as ten groats is for the hand of an attorney, as your French crown for your taffeta punk, as Tib's rush for Tom's forefinger, as a pancake for Shrove Tuesday, a morris for May-day, as the nail to his hole, the cuckold to his horn, as a scolding quean to a wrangling knave, as the nun's lip to the friar's mouth, nay, as the pudding to his skin.

Countess. Have you, I say, an answer of such fitness for all questions?

Clown. From below your duke to beneath your constable, it will fit any question.

Countess. It must be an answer of most monstrous size that must fit all demands.

Clown. But a trifle neither, in good faith, if the learned should speak truth of it : here it is, and all that belongs to 't. Ask me if I am a courtier : it shall do you no harm to learn.

Countess. To be young again, if we could : I will be a fool in question, hoping to be the wiser by your answer. I pray you, sir, are you a courtier?

Clown. O Lord, sir ! There 's a simple putting off. More, more, a hundred of them.

Countess. Sir, I am a poor friend of yours, that loves you.

Clown. O Lord, sir ! Thick, thick, spare not me.

Countess. I think, sir, you can eat none of this homely meat.

Clown. O Lord, sir ! Nay, put me to 't, I warrant you.

Countess. You were lately whipped, sir, as I think.

Clown. O Lord, sir ! spare not me.

Countess. Do you cry, ' O Lord, sir ! ' at your whipping, and ' spare not me ' ? Indeed your ' O Lord, sir ! ' is very sequent to your whipping : you would answer very well to a whipping, if you were but bound to 't.

Clown. I ne'er had worse luck in my life in my ' O Lord, sir ! ' I see things may serve long, but not serve ever.

Countess. I play the noble housewife with the time,
To entertain 't so merrily with a fool.

Clown. O Lord, sir ! why, there 't serves well again.

Countess. An end, sir ; to your business. Give Helen this,
And urge her to a present answer back :
Commend me to my kinsmen and my son :
This is not much.

Clown. Not much commendation to them.

Countess. Not much employment for you : you understand me?

Clown. Most fruitfully : I am there before my legs.

Countess. Haste you again.   [*Exeunt severally.*

SCENE III.   *Paris.   The* King's *palace.*

Enter Bertram, Lafeu, *and* Parolles.

Lafeu. They say miracles are past ; and we have our philosophical persons, to make modern and familiar, things supernatural and causeless. Hence is it that we make trifles of terrors, ensconcing ourselves into seeming knowledge, when we should submit ourselves to an unknown fear.

Parolles. Why, 'tis the rarest argument of wonder that hath shot out in our latter times.

Bertram. And so 'tis.

Lafeu. To be relinquished of the artists,—

Parolles. So I say.

Lafeu. Both of Galen and Paracelsus.

Parolles. So I say.

Lafeu. Of all the learned and authentic fellows,—

Parolles. Right ; so I say.

Lafeu. That gave him out incurable,—

Parolles. Why, there 'tis ; so say I too.

Lafeu. Not to be helped,—

Parolles. Right : as 'twere, a man assured of a—

Lafeu. Uncertain life, and sure death.

Parolles. Just, you say well ; so would I have said.

Lafeu. I may truly say, it is a novelty to the world.

Parolles. It is, indeed : if you will have it in showing, you shall read it in—what do ye call there ?

Lafeu. A showing of a heavenly effect in an earthly actor.

Parolles. That 's it ; I would have said the very same.

Lafeu. Why, your dolphin is not lustier : 'fore me, I speak in respect—

Parolles. Nay, 'tis strange, 'tis very strange, that is the brief and the tedious of it ; and he 's of a most facinerious spirit that will not acknowledge it to be the—

Lafeu. Very hand of heaven.

Parolles. Ay, so I say.

Lafeu. In a most weak—[*pausing*] and debile minister, great power, great transcendence : which should, indeed, give us a further use to be made than alone the recovery of the king, as to be— [*pausing*] generally thankful.

Parolles. I would have said it ; you say well. Here comes the king.

Enter King, Helena, *and* Attendants.
Lafeu *and* Parolles *retire.*

Lafeu. Lustig, as the Dutchman says : I 'll like a maid the better, whilst I have a tooth in my head : why, he 's able to lead her a coranto.

Parolles. Mort du vinaigre ! is not this Helen ?

Lafeu. 'Fore God, I think so.

King. Go, call before me all the lords in court.
Sit, my preserver, by thy patient's side ;
And with this healthful hand, whose banish'd sense
Thou hast repeal'd, a second time receive
The confirmation of my promised gift,
Which but attends thy naming.

Enter three or four Lords.

Fair maid, send forth thine eye ; this youthful parcel
Of noble bachelors stand at my bestowing,
O'er whom both sovereign power and father's voice
I have to use : thy frank election make ;
Thou hast power to choose, and they none to forsake.

Helena. To each of you one fair and virtuous mistress
Fall, when Love please ! marry, to each, but one !

Lafeu. I 'ld give bay Curtal and his furniture,
My mouth no more were broken than these boys',
And writ as little beard.

King.   Peruse them well :
Not one of those but had a noble father.

Helena. Gentlemen,
Heaven hath through me restored the king to health.

All. We understand it, and thank heaven for you.

Helena. I am a simple maid, and therein wealthiest,

That I protest I simply am a maid.

Please it your majesty, I have done already :

The blushes in my cheeks thus whisper me,

' We blush that thou shouldst choose ; but, be refused,

Let the white death sit on thy cheek for ever ;

We 'll ne'er come there again.'

King.   Make choice ; and see,

Who shuns thy love shuns all his love in me.

Helena. Now, Dian, from thy altar do I fly,

And to imperial Love, that god most high,

Do my sighs stream. Sir, will you hear my suit ?

First Lord. And grant it.

Helena.   Thanks, sir ; all the rest is mute.

Lafeu. I had rather be in this choice than throw ames-ace for my life.

Helena. The honour, sir, that flames in your fair eyes,

Before I speak, too threateningly replies :

Love make your fortunes twenty times above

Her that so wishes and her humble love !

Second Lord. No better. if you please.

Helena.   My wish receive,

Which great Love grant ! and so, I take my leave.

Lafeu. Do all they deny her ? An they were sons of mine, I 'd have them whipped ; or I would send them to the Turk, to make eunuchs of.

Helena. Be not afraid that I your hand should take ;

I 'll never do you wrong for your own sake :

Blessing upon your vows ! and in your bed

Find fairer fortune, if you ever wed !

Lafeu. These boys are boys of ice, they 'll none have her : sure, they are bastards to the English ; the French ne'er got 'em.

Helena. You are too young, too happy, and too good,

To make yourself a son out of my blood.

Fourth Lord. Fair one, I think not so.

Lafeu. There 's one grape yet ; I am sure thy father drunk wine : but if thou be'st not an ass, I am a youth of fourteen ; I have known thee already.

Helena. [*To Bertram*] I dare not say I take you ; but I give

Me and my service, ever whilst I live,

Into your guiding power. This is the man.

King. Why, then, young Bertram, take her ; she 's thy wife.

Bertram. My wife, my liege ! I shall beseech your highness,

In such a business give me leave to use

The help of mine own eyes.

King.   Know'st thou not, Bertram,

What she has done for me ?

Bertram.   Yes, my good lord ;

But never hope to know why I should marry her.

King. Thou know'st she has raised me from my sickly bed.

Bertram. But follows it, my lord, to bring me down

Must answer for your raising ? I know her well :

She had her breeding at my father's charge.

A poor physician's daughter my wife ! Disdain

Rather corrupt me ever !

King. 'Tis only title thou disdain'st in her, the which

I can build up. Strange is it that our bloods,

Of colour, weight, and heat, pour'd all together,

Would quite confound distinction, yet stand off

In differences so mighty. If she be

All that is virtuous save what thou dislikest,

A poor physician's daughter, thou dislikest

Of virtue for the name : but do not so :

From lowest place when virtuous things proceed

The place is dignified by the doer's deed :

Where great additions swell's, and virtue none

It is a dropsied honour. Good alone

Is good without a name. Vileness is so :

The property by what it is should go,

Not by the title. She is young, wise, fair ;

In these to nature she 's immediate heir,

And these breed honour : that is honour's scorn,

Which challenges itself as honour's born

And is not like the sire : honours thrive,

When rather from our acts we them derive

Than our foregoers : the mere word 's a slave

Debosh'd on every tomb, on every grave

A lying trophy, and as oft is dumb

Where dust and damn'd oblivion is the tomb

Of honour'd bones indeed. What should be said ?

If thou canst like this creature as a maid,

I can create the rest : virtue and she

Is her own dower : honour and wealth from me.

Bertram. I cannot love her, nor will strive to do 't.

King. Thou wrong'st thyself, if thou shouldst strive to choose.

Helena. That you are well restored, my lord, I 'm glad :

Let the rest go.

King. My honour 's at the stake ; which to defeat,

I must produce my power. Here, take her hand,

Proud scornful boy, unworthy this good gift ;

That dost in vile misprision shackle up

My love and her desert ; that canst not dream.

We, poising us in her defective scale,

Shall weigh thee to the beam ; that wilt not know,

It is in us to plant thine honour where

We please to have it grow. Check thy contempt :

Obey our will, which travails in thy good :

Believe not thy disdain, but presently

Do thine own fortunes that obedient right

Which both thy duty owes and our power claims ;

Or I will throw thee from my care for ever

Into the staggers and the careless lapse

Of youth and ignorance ; both my revenge and hate

Loosing upon thee, in the name of justice,

Without all terms of pity. Speak ; thine answer.

Bertram. Pardon, my gracious lord ; for I submit

My fancy to your eyes : when I consider

What great creation and what dole of honour

Flies where you bid it, I find that she, which late

Was in my nobler thoughts most base, is now

The praised of the king ; who, so ennobled,

Is as 'twere born so.

King.   Take her by the hand,

And tell her she is thine : to whom I promise

A counterpoise, if not to thy estate

A balance more replete.

Bertram.   I take her hand.

King. Good fortune and the favour of the king

Smile upon this contract ; whose ceremony

Shall seem expedient on the now-born brief,

And be perform'd to-night : the solemn feast

Shall more attend upon the coming space,

Expecting absent friends. As thou lovest her,

Thy love 's to me religious ; else, does err.

                    [*Exeunt all but Lafeu and Parolles.*

Lafeu. [*Advancing*] Do you hear, monsieur? a word with you.

Parolles. Your pleasure, sir?

Lafeu. Your lord and master did well to make his recantation.

Parolles. Recantation ! My lord ! my master !

Lafeu.. Ay ; is it not a language I speak ?

Parolles. A most harsh one, and not to be understood without bloody succeeding. My master !

Lafeu. Are you companion to the Count Rousillon ?

Parolles. To any count, to all counts, to what is man.

Lafeu. To what is count's man : count's master is of another style.

Parolles. You are too old, sir ; let it satisfy you, you are too old.

Lafeu. I must tell thee, sirrah, I write man ; to which title age cannot bring thee.

Parolles. What I dare too well do, I dare not do.

Lafeu. I did think thee, for two ordinaries, to be a pretty wise fellow ; thou didst make tolerable vent of thy travel ; it might pass : yet the scarfs and the bannerets about thee did manifoldly dissuade me from believing thee a vessel of too great a burthen. I have now found thee ; when I lose thee again, I care not : yet art thou good for nothing but taking up ; and that thou 'rt scarce worth.

Parolles. Hadst thou not the privilege of antiquity upon thee,—

Lafeu. Do not plunge thyself too far in anger, lest thou hasten thy trial ; which if—Lord have mercy on thee for a hen ! So, my good window of lattice, fare thee well : thy casement I need not open, for I look through thee. Give me thy hand.

Parolles. My lord, you give me most egregious indignity.

Lafeu. Ay, with all my heart ; and thou art worthy of it.

Parolles. I have not, my lord, deserved it.

Lafeu. Yes, good faith, every dram of it ; and I will not bate thee a scruple.

Parolles. Well, I shall be wiser.

Lafeu. Even as soon as thou canst, for thou hast to pull at a smack o' the contrary. If ever thou be'st bound in thy scarf and beaten, thou shalt find what it is to be proud of thy bondage. I have a desire to hold my acquaintance with thee, or rather my knowledge, that I may say in the default, he is a man I know.

Parolles. My lord, you do me most insupportable vexation.

Lafeu. I would it were hell-pains for thy sake, and my poor doing eternal : for doing I am past ; as I will by thee, in what motion age will give me leave.   [*Exit.*

Parolles. Well, thou hast a son shall take this disgrace off me ; scurvy, old, filthy, scurvy lord ! Well, I must be patient ; there is no fettering of authority. I 'll beat him, by my life, if I can meet him with any convenience, an he were double and double a lord. I 'll have no more pity of his age than I would have of—I 'll beat him, an if I could but meet him again.

Re-enter LAFEU.

Lafeu. Sirrah, your lord and master 's married ; there 's news for you ; you have a new mistress.

Parolles. I must unfeignedly beseech your lordship to make some reservation of your wrongs : he is my good lord : whom I serve above is my master.

Lafeu. Who ? God ?

Parolles. Ay, sir.

Lafeu. The devil it is that 's thy master. Why dost thou garter up thy arms o' this fashion ? dost make hose of thy sleeves ? do other servants so ? Thou wert best set thy lower part where thy nose stands. By mine honour, if I were but two hours younger, I 'ld beat thee : methinks, thou art a general offence, and every man should beat thee : I think thou wast created for men to breathe themselves upon thee.

Parolles. This is hard and undeserved measure, my lord.

Lafeu. Go to, sir ; you were beaten in Italy for picking a kernel out of a pomegranate ; you are a vagabond, and no true traveller : you are more saucy with lords and honourable personages than the commission of your birth and virtue gives you heraldry. You are not worth another word, else I 'ld call you knave. I leave you.   [*Exit.*

Parolles. Good, very good : it is so then : good, very good, let it be concealed awhile.

Re-enter BERTRAM.

Bertram. Undone, and forfeited to cares for ever !

Parolles. What 's the matter, sweet-heart ?

Bertram. Although before the solemn priest I have sworn,
I will not bed her.

Parolles. What, what, sweet-heart ?

Bertram. O my Parolles, they have married me !
I 'll to the Tuscan wars, and never bed her.

Parolles. France is a dog-hole, and it no more merits
The tread of a man's foot : to the wars !

Bertram. There 's letters from my mother : what the import is, I know not yet.

Parolles. Ay, that would be known. To the wars, my boy, to the wars !
He wears his honour in a box unseen,
That hugs his kicky-wicky here at home,
Spending his manly marrow in her arms,
Which should sustain the bound and high curvet
Of Mars's fiery steed. To other regions
France is a stable ; we that dwell in 't jades ;
Therefore, to the war !

Bertram. It shall be so : I 'll send her to my house,
Acquaint my mother with my hate to her,
And wherefore I am fled ; write to the king
That which I durst not speak : his present gift
Shall furnish me to those Italian fields,
Where noble fellows strike : war is no strife
To the dark house and the detested wife.

Parolles. Will this capriccio hold in thee ? art sure ?

Bertram. Go with me to my chamber, and advise me.
I 'll send her straight away : to-morrow
I 'll to the wars, she to her single sorrow.

Parolles. Why, these balls bound ; there 's noise in it. 'Tis hard
A young man married is a man that 's marr'd :
Therefore away, and leave her bravely ; go :
The king has done you wrong : but, hush, 'tis so.

[*Exeunt.*

SCENE IV. *Paris. The* KING's *palace.*

Enter HELENA *and* CLOWN.

Helena. My mother greets me kindly : is she well ?

Clown. She is not well ; but yet she has her health : she 's very merry ; but yet she is not well : but thanks be given, she 's very well and wants nothing i' the world ; but yet she is not well.

Helena. If she be very well, what does she ail, that she 's not very well ?

Clown. Truly, she 's very well indeed, but for two things.

Helena. What two things ?

Clown. One, that she 's not in heaven, whither God send her quickly ! the other, that she 's in earth, from whence God send her quickly !

Enter PAROLLES.

Parolles. Bless you, my fortunate lady !

Helena. I hope, sir, I have your good will to have mine own good fortunes.

Parolles. You had my prayers to lead them on ; and to keep them on, have them still. O, my knave, how does my old lady ?

Clown. So that you had her wrinkles and I her money, I would she did as you say.

Parolles. Why, I say nothing.

Clown. Marry, you are the wiser man ; for many a man's tongue shakes out his master's undoing : to say nothing, to do nothing, to know nothing, and to have nothing, is to be a great part of your title ; which is within a very little of nothing.

Parolles. Away ! thou 'rt a knave.

Clown. You should have said, sir, before a knave thou 'rt a knave ; that 's, before me thou 'rt a knave : this had been truth, sir.

Parolles. Go to, thou art a witty fool ; I have found thee.

Clown. Did you find me in yourself, sir ? or were you taught to find me ? The search, sir, was profitable ; and much fool may you find in you, even to the world's pleasure and the increase of laughter.

Parolles. A good knave, i' faith, and well fed. Madam, my lord will go away to-night ; A very serious business calls on him. The great prerogative and rite of love, Which, as your due, time claims, he does acknowledge ; But puts it off to a compell'd restraint ; Whose want, and whose delay, is strew'd with sweets, Which they distil now in the curbed time, To make the coming hour o'erflow with joy And pleasure drown the brim.

Helena. What 's his will else ?

Parolles. That you will take your instant leave o' the king, And make this haste as your own good proceeding, Strengthen'd with what apology you think May make it probable need.

Helena. What more commands he ?

Parolles. That, having this obtain'd, you presently Attend his further pleasure.

Helena. In every thing I wait upon his will.

Parolles. I shall report it so.

Helena. I pray you. [*Exit Parolles.*]

Come, sirrah. [*Exeunt.*

SCENE V. *Paris. The* KING's *palace.*

Enter LAFEU *and* BERTRAM.

Lafeu. But I hope your lordship thinks not him a soldier.

Bertram. Yes, my lord, and of very valiant approof.

Lafeu. You have it from his own deliverance.

Bertram. And by other warranted testimony.

Lafeu. Then my dial goes not true : I took this lark for a bunting.

Bertram. I do assure you, my lord, he is very great in knowledge and accordingly valiant.

Lafeu. I have then sinned against his experience and transgressed against his valour ; and my state that way is dangerous, since I cannot yet find in my heart to repent. Here he comes : I pray you, make us friends ; I will pursue the amity.

Enter PAROLLES.

Parolles. [*To Bertram*] These things shall be done, sir.

Lafeu. Pray you, sir, who 's his tailor ?

Parolles. Sir ?

Lafeu. O, I know him well, I, sir ; he, sir, 's a good workman, a very good tailor.

Bertram. [*Aside to Parolles*] Is she gone to the king ?

Parolles. She is.

Bertram. Will she away to-night ?

Parolles. As you 'll have her.

Bertram. I have writ my letters, casketed my treasure, Given orders for our horses ; and to-night, When I should take possession of the bride, End ere I do begin.

Lafeu. A good traveller is something at the latter end of a dinner ; but one that lies three thirds and uses a known truth to pass a thousand nothings with, should be once heard and thrice beaten. God save you, captain.

Bertram. Is there any unkindness between my lord and you, monsieur ?

Parolles. I know not how I have deserved to run into my lord's displeasure.

Lafeu. You have made shift to run into 't, boots and spurs and all, like him that leaped into the custard ; and out of it you 'll run again, rather than suffer question for your residence.

Bertram. It may be you have mistaken him, my lord.

Lafeu. And shall do so ever, though I took him at 's prayers. Fare you well, my lord ; and believe this of me, there can be no kernel in this light nut : the soul of this man is his clothes. Trust him not in matter of heavy consequence ; I have kept of them tame, and know their natures. Farewell, monsieur ; I have spoken better of you † than you have or will to deserve at my hand ; but we must do good against evil. [*Exit.*

Parolles. An idle lord, I swear.

Bertram. I think so.

Parolles. Why, do you not know him ?

Bertram. Yes, I do know him well, and common speech Gives him a worthy pass. Here comes my clog.

Enter HELENA.

Helena. I have, sir, as I was commanded from
you,
Spoke with the king and have procured his leave
For present parting ; only he desires
Some private speech with you.
Bertram.   I shall obey his will.
You must not marvel, Helen, at my course,
Which holds not colour with the time, nor does
The ministration and required office
On my particular. Prepared I was not
For such a business ; therefore am I found
So much unsettled : this drives me to entreat you
That presently you take your way for home ;
And rather muse than ask why I entreat you,
For my respects are better than they seem
And my appointments have in them a need
Greater than shows itself at the first view
To you that know them not. This to my mother :
                              [*Giving a letter.*
'Twill be two days ere I shall see you, so
I leave you to your wisdom.
Helena.   Sir, I can nothing say,
But that I am your most obedient servant.
Bertram. Come, come, no more of that.
Helena.   And ever shall
With true observance seek to eke out that
Wherein toward me my homely stars have fail'd
To equal my great fortune.
Bertram.   Let that go ;
My haste is very great : farewell ; hie home.
Helena. Pray, sir, your pardon.
Bertram.   Well, what would you say ?
Helena. I am not worthy of the wealth I owe,
Nor dare I say 'tis mine, and yet it is ;
But, like a timorous thief, most fain would steal
What law does vouch mine own.
Bertram.   What would you have ?
Helena. Something ; and scarce so much : no-
thing, indeed.
I would not tell you what I would, my lord :
Faith, yes ;
Strangers and foes do sunder, and not kiss.
Bertram. I pray you, stay not, but in haste to
horse.
Helena. I shall not break your bidding, good
my lord.
Bertram. Where are my other men, monsieur ?
Farewell.   [*Exit Helena.*
Go thou toward home ; where I will never come
Whilst I can shake my sword or hear the drum.
Away, and for our flight.
Parolles.   Bravely, coragio !
                              [*Exeunt.*

ACT III.

SCENE I. *Florence. The* DUKE'S *palace.*

Flourish. Enter the DUKE *of Florence, attended ;
the two Frenchmen, with a troop of soldiers.*

Duke.

So that from point to point now have you
    heard
The fundamental reasons of this war,
Whose great decision hath much blood let forth
And more thirsts after.
First Lord.   Holy seems the quarrel
Upon your grace's part ; black and fearful

On the opposer.
Duke. Therefore we marvel much our cousin
    France
Would in so just a business shut his bosom
Against our borrowing prayers.
Second Lord.   Good my lord,
The reasons of our state I cannot yield,
But like a common and an outward man,
That the great figure of a council frames
By self-unable motion : therefore dare not
Say what I think of it, since I have found
Myself in my incertain grounds to fail
As often as I guess'd.
Duke.   Be it his pleasure.
First Lord. But I am sure the younger of our
    nature,
That surfeit on their ease, will day by day
Come here for physic.
Duke.   Welcome shall they be ;
And all the honours that can fly from us
Shall on them settle. You know your places well ;
When better fall, for your avails they fell :
To-morrow to the field.   [*Flourish. Exeunt.*

SCENE II. *Rousillon. The* COUNT'S *palace.*

Enter COUNTESS *and* CLOWN.

Countess. It hath happened all as I would have
had it, save that he comes not along with her.
Clown. By my troth, I take my young lord to be
a very melancholy man.
Countess. By what observance, I pray you ?
Clown. Why, he will look upon his boot and
sing ; mend the ruff and sing ; ask questions and
sing ; pick his teeth and sing. I know a man that
had this trick of melancholy sold a goodly manor
for a song.
Countess. Let me see what he writes, and when
he means to come.   [*Opening a letter.*
Clown. I have no mind to Isbel since I was at
court : our old ling and our Isbels o' the country
are nothing like your old ling and your Isbels o'
the court : the brains of my Cupid 's knocked out,
and I begin to love, as an old man loves money,
with no stomach.
Countess. What have we here ?
Clown. E'en that you have there.   [*Exit.*
Countess. [*Reads*] I have sent you a daughter-
in-law : she hath recovered the king, and undone
me. I have wedded her, not bedded her ; and
sworn to make the ' not ' eternal. You shall hear
I am run away : know it before the report come.
If there be breadth enough in the world, I will hold a
long distance. My duty to you.
                    Your unfortunate son,
                                        BERTRAM.
This is not well, rash and unbridled boy,
To fly the favours of so good a king ;
To pluck his indignation on thy head
By the misprising of a maid too virtuous
For the contempt of empire.

Re-enter CLOWN.

Clown. O madam, yonder 'is heavy news within
between two soldiers and my young lady !
Countess. What is the matter ?
Clown. Nay, there is some comfort in the news,
some comfort ; your son will not be killed so soon
as I thought he would.

Countess. Why should he be killed ?

Clown. So say I, madam, if he run away, as I hear he does : the danger is in standing to 't ; that 's the loss of men, though it be the getting of children. Here they come will tell you more : for my part, I only hear your son was run away.   [*Exit.*

Enter HELENA *and two* Gentlemen.

First Gentleman. Save you, good madam.

Helen. Madam, my lord is gone, for ever gone.

Second Gentleman. Do not say so.

Countess. Think upon patience. Pray you, gentlemen,
I have felt so many quirks of joy and grief,
That the first face of neither, on the start,
Can woman me unto 't : where is my son, I pray you ?

Second Gentleman. Madam, he 's gone to serve the duke of Florence :
We met him thitherward ; for thence we came,
And, after some dispatch in hand at court,
Thither we bend again.

Helena. Look on his letter, madam ; here 's my passport.
[*Reads*]   When thou canst get the ring upon my finger which never shall come off, and show me a child begotten of thy body that I am father to, then call me husband : but in such a ' then ' I write a ' never.'
This is a dreadful sentence.

Countess. Brought you this letter, gentlemen ?

First Gentleman.   Ay, madam ;
And for the contents' sake are sorry for our pains.

Countess. I prithee, lady, have a better cheer ;
If thou engrossest all the griefs are thine,
Thou robb'st me of a moiety : he was my son ;
But I do wash his name out of my blood,
And thou art all my child. Towards Florence is he ?

Second Gentleman. Ay, madam.

Countess.   And to be a soldier ?

Second Gentleman. Such is his noble purpose ; and, believe 't,
The duke will lay upon him all the honour
That good convenience claims.

Countess.   Return you thither ?

First Gentleman. Ay, madam, with the swiftest wing of speed.

Helena. [*Reads*] Till I have no wife, I have nothing in France.
'Tis bitter.

Countess. Find you that there ?

Helena.   Ay, madam.

First Gentleman. 'Tis but the boldness of his hand, haply, which his heart was not consenting to.

Countess. Nothing in France, until he have no wife !
There 's nothing here that is too good for him
But only she ; and she deserves a lord
That twenty such rude boys might tend upon
And call her hourly mistress. Who was with him ?

First Gentleman. A servant only, and a gentleman Which I have sometime known.

Countess. Parolles, was it not ?

First Gentleman. Ay, my good lady, he.

Countess. A very tainted fellow, and full of wickedness.
My son corrupts a well-derived nature
With his inducement.

First Gentleman. Indeed, good lady,
The fellow has a deal of that too much,

Which holds him much to have.

Countess. You 're welcome, gentlemen.
I will entreat you, when you see my son,
To tell him that his sword can never win
The honour that he loses : more I 'll entreat you
Written to bear along.

Second Gentleman. We serve you, madam,
In that and all your worthiest affairs.

Countess. Not so, but as we change our courtesies.
Will you draw near ?
                    [*Exeunt Countess and Gentlemen.*

Helena. 'Till I have no wife, I have nothing in France.'
Nothing in France, until he has no wife !
Thou shalt have none, Rousillon, none in France ;
Then hast thou all again.   Poor lord ! is 't I
That chase thee from thy country and expose
Those tender limbs of thine to the event
Of the none-sparing war ? and is it I
That drive thee from the sportive court, where thou
Wast shot at with fair eyes, to be the mark
Of smoky muskets ? O you leaden messengers,
That ride upon the violent speed of fire,
† Fly with false aim ; move the still-peering air,
That sings with piercing ; do not touch my lord.
Whoever shoots at him, I set him there ;
Whoever charges on his forward breast,
I am the caitiff that do hold him to 't ;
And, though I kill him not, I am the cause
His death was so effected : better 'twere
I met the ravin lion when he roar'd
With sharp constraint of hunger ; better 'twere
That all the miseries which nature owes
Were mine at once. No, come thou home, Rousillon,
Whence honour but of danger wins a scar,
As oft it loses all : I will be gone ;
My being here it is that holds thee hence :
Shall I stay here to do 't ? no, no, although
The air of paradise did fan the house
And angels officed all : I will be gone,
That pitiful rumour may report my flight,
To consolate thine ear. Come, night ; end, day !
For with the dark, poor thief, I 'll steal away.
                                          [*Exit.*

SCENE III. *Florence. Before the* DUKE'S *palace.*

Flourish. Enter the DUKE *of Florence,* BERTRAM, PAROLLES, *Soldiers, Drum, and Trumpets.*

Duke. The general of our horse thou art ; and we,
Great in our hope, lay our best love and credence
Upon thy promising fortune.

Bertram.   Sir, it is
A charge too heavy for my strength, but yet
We 'll strive to bear it for your worthy sake
To the extreme edge of hazard.

Duke.   Then go thou forth ;
And fortune play upon thy prosperous helm,
As thy auspicious mistress !

Bertram.   This very day,
Great Mars, I put myself into thy file :
Make me but like my thoughts, and I shall prove
A lover of thy drum, hater of love.   [*Exeunt.*

SCENE IV. *Rousillon. The* COUNT'S *palace.*

Enter COUNTESS *and Steward.*

Countess. Alas ! and would you take the letter of her ?

Might you not know she would do as she has done,
By sending me a letter ? Read it again.

    Steward. [*Reads*]
I am Saint Jaques' pilgrim, thither gone :
    Ambitious love hath so in me offended,
That barefoot plod I the cold ground upon,
    With sainted vow my faults to have amended.
Write, write, that from the bloody course of war
    My dearest master, your dear son, may hie :
Bless him at home in peace, whilst I from far
    His name with zealous fervour sanctify :
His taken labours bid him me forgive ;
    I, his despiteful Juno, sent him forth
From courtly friends, with camping foes to live,
    Where death and danger dogs the heels of worth :
He is too good and fair for death and me ;
    Whom I myself embrace, to set him free.

    Countess. Ah, what sharp stings are in her mildest
words !
Rinaldo, you did never lack advice so much,
As letting her pass so : had I spoke with her,
I could have well diverted her intents,
Which thus she hath prevented.

    Steward.   Pardon me, madam :
If I had given you this at over-night,
She might have been o'erta'en ; and yet she writes,
Pursuit would be but vain.

    Countess.   What angel shall
Bless this unworthy husband ? he cannot thrive,
Unless her prayers, whom heaven delights to hear
And loves to grant, reprieve him from the wrath
Of greatest justice. Write, write, Rinaldo,
To this unworthy husband of his wife ;
Let every word weigh heavy of her worth
That he does weigh too light : my greatest grief,
Though little he do feel it, set down sharply.
Dispatch the most convenient messenger :
When haply he shall hear that she is gone,
He will return ; and hope I may that she,
Hearing so much, will speed her foot again,
Led hither by pure love : which of them both
Is dearest to me, I have no skill in sense
To make distinction : provide this messenger :
My heart is heavy and mine age is weak ;
Grief would have tears, and sorrow bids me speak.
                                        [*Exeunt.*

SCENE V. *Florence. Without the walls. A*
        tucket afar off.

Enter an old Widow *of Florence,* DIANA, VIOLENTA,
    and MARIANA, *with other* Citizens.

    Widow. Nay, come ; for if they do approach the
city, we shall lose all the sight.
    Diana. They say the French count has done
most honourable service.
    Widow. It is reported that he has taken their
greatest commander ; and that with his own hand
he slew the duke's brother. [*Tucket.*] We have lost
our labour ; they are gone a contrary way : hark !
you may know by their trumpets.
    Mariana. Come, let 's return again, and suffice
ourselves with the report of it. Well, Diana, take
heed of this French earl : the honour of a maid is
her name ; and no legacy is so rich as honesty.
    Widow. I have told my neighbour how you
have been solicited by a gentleman his companion.
    Mariana. I know that knave ; hang him ! one
Parolles : a filthy officer he is in those suggestions

for the young earl. Beware of them, Diana ; their
promises, enticements, oaths, tokens, and all these
engines of lust, are no the things they go under :
many a maid hath been seduced by them ; and the
misery is, example, that so terrible shows in the
wreck of maidenhood, cannot for all that dissuade
succession, but that they are limed with the twigs
that threaten them. I hope I need not to advise
you further ; but I hope your own grace will keep
you where you are, though there were no further
danger known but the modesty which is so lost.
    Diana. You shall not need to fear me.
    Widow. I hope so.

    Enter HELENA, *disguised like a Pilgrim.*

Look, here comes a pilgrim : I know she will
lie at my house ; thither they send one another :
I 'll question her. God save you, pilgrim ! whither
are you bound ?
    Helena. To Saint Jaques le Grand.
Where do the palmers lodge, I do beseech you ?
    Widow. At the Saint Francis here beside the port.
    Helena. Is this the way ?
    Widow. Ay, marry, is 't.   [*A march afar.*]
Hark you ! they come this way.
If you will tarry, holy pilgrim,
But till the troops come by,
I will conduct you where you shall be lodged ;
The rather, for I think I know your hostess
As ample as myself.
    Helena.   Is it yourself ?
    Widow. If you shall please so, pilgrim.
    Helena. I thank you, and will stay upon your
leisure.
    Widow. You came, I think, from France ?
    Helena.   I did so.
    Widow. Here you shall see a countryman of
yours
That has done worthy service.
    Helena.   His name, I pray you.
    Diana. The Count Rousillon : know you such
a one ?
    Helena. But by the ear, that hears most nobly
of him :
His face I know not.
    Diana.   Whatsome'er he is,
He 's bravely taken here. He stole from France,
As 'tis reported, for the king had married him
Against his liking : think you it is so ?
    Helena. Ay, surely, mere the truth : I know his
lady.
    Diana. There is a gentleman that serves the
count
Reports but coarsely of her.
    Helena.   What 's his name ?
    Diana. Monsieur Parolles.
    Helena.   O, I believe with him,
In argument of praise, or to the worth
Of the great count himself, she is too mean
To have her name repeated : all her deserving
Is a reserved honesty, and that
I have not heard examined.
    Diana.   Alas, poor lady !
'Tis a hard bondage to become the wife
Of a detesting lord.
    Widow. I warrant, good creature, wheresoe'er
she is,
Her heart weighs sadly : this young maid might
do her
A shrewd turn, if she pleased.
    Helena.   How do you mean ?

May be the amorous count solicits her
In the unlawful purpose.
Widow.   He does indeed ;
And brokes with all that can in such a suit
Corrupt the tender honour of a maid :
But she is arm'd for him and keeps her guard
In honestest defence.
Mariana.   The gods forbid else !
Widow. So, now they come :

Drums and Colours.

Enter BERTRAM, PAROLLES, *and the whole army.*

That is Antonio, the duke's eldest son ;
That, Escalus.
Helena.   Which is the Frenchman ?
Diana.   He ;
That with the plume : 'tis a most gallant fellow.
I would he loved his wife : if he were honester
He were much goodlier : is 't not a handsome
        gentleman ?
Helena. I like him well.
Diana. 'Tis pity he is not honest : yond 's that
        same knave
That leads him to these places : were I his lady,
I would poison that vile rascal.
Helena.   Which is he ?
Diana. That jack-an-apes with scarfs : why is
he melancholy ?
Helena. Perchance he 's hurt i' the battle.
Parolles. Lose our drum ! well.
Mariana. He 's shrewdly vexed at something :
look, he has spied us.
Widow. Marry, hang you !
Mariana. And your courtesy, for a ring-carrier !
                [*Exeunt Bertram, Parolles, and army.*
Widow. The troop is past. Come, pilgrim, I
will bring you
Where you shall host : of enjoin'd penitents
There 's four or five, to great Saint Jaques bound,
Already at my house.
Helena.   I humbly thank you :
Please it this matron and this gentle maid
To eat with us to-night, the charge and thanking
Shall be for me ; and, to requite you further,
I will bestow some precepts of this virgin
Worthy the note.
Both.   We 'll take your offer kindly.
                                        [*Exeunt.*

SCENE VI. *Camp before Florence.*

Enter BERTRAM *and the two French* Lords.

Second Lord. Nay, good my lord, put him to 't ;
let him have his way.
First Lord. If your lordship find him not a
hilding, hold me no more in your respect.
Second Lord. On my life, my lord, a bubble.
Bertram. Do you think I am so far deceived in
him ?
Second Lord. Believe it, my lord, in mine own
direct knowledge, without any malice, but to speak
of him as my kinsman, he 's a most notable coward,
an infinite and endless liar, an hourly promise-
breaker, the owner of no one good quality worthy
your lordship's entertainment.
First Lord. It were fit you knew him ; lest,
reposing too far in his virtue, which he hath not,
he might at some great and trusty business in a main

danger fail you.
Bertram. I would I knew in what particular
action to try him.
First Lord. None better than to let him fetch
off his drum, which you hear him so confidently
undertake to do.
Second Lord. I, with a troop of Florentines, will
suddenly surprise him ; such I will have, whom
I am sure he knows not from the enemy : we will
bind and hoodwink him so, that he shall suppose
no other but that he is carried into the leaguer of
the adversaries, when we bring him to our own tents.
Be but your lordship present at his examination :
if he do not, for the promise of his life and in the
highest compulsion of base fear, offer to betray you
and deliver all the intelligence in his power against
you, and that with the divine forfeit of his soul upon
oath, never trust my judgement in any thing.
First Lord. O, for the love of laughter, let him
fetch his drum : he says he was a stratagem for 't :
when your lordship sees the bottom of his success
in 't, and to what metal this counterfeit lump of ore
will be melted, if you give him not John Drum's
entertainment, your inclining cannot be removed.
Here he comes.

Enter PAROLLES.

Second Lord. [*Aside to Bertram*] O, for the love
of laughter, hinder not the honour of his design :
let him fetch off his drum in any hand.
Bertram. How now, monsieur ! this drum sticks
sorely in your disposition.
First Lord. A pox on 't, let it go ; 'tis but a
drum.
Parolles. ' But a drum '! is 't ' but a drum ' ? A
drum so lost ! There was excellent command,—
to charge in with our horse upon our own wings,
and to rend our own soldiers !
First Lord. That was not to be blamed in the
command of the service : it was a disaster of war
that Cæsar himself could not have prevented, if he
had been there to command.
Bertram. Well, we cannot greatly condemn our
success : some dishonour we had in the loss of that
drum ; but it is not to be recovered.
Parolles. It might have been recovered.
Bertram. It might ; but it is not now.
Parolles. It is to be recovered : but that the merit
of service is seldom attributed to the true and exact
performer, I would have that drum or another, or
' hic jacet.'
Bertram. Why, if you have a stomach, to 't, monsieur : if you think your mystery in stratagem can
bring this instrument of honour again into his native
quarter, be magnanimous in the enterprise and go
on : I will grace the attempt for a worthy exploit :
if you speed well in it, the duke shall both speak of
it, and extend to you what further becomes his
greatness, even to the utmost syllable of your worthiness.
Parolles. By the hand of a soldier, I will undertake it.
Bertram. But you must not now slumber in it.
Parolles. I 'll about it this evening : and I will
presently pen down my dilemmas, encourage myself
in my certainty, put myself into my mortal preparation ; and by midnight look to hear further
from me.
Bertram. May I be bold to acquaint his grace

you are gone about it ?

Parolles. I know not what the success will be, my lord ; but the attempt I vow.

Bertram. I know thou 'rt valiant ; and, to the possibility of thy soldiership, will subscribe for thee. Farewell.

Parolles. I love not many words.   [*Exit.*

Second Lord. No more than a fish loves water. Is not this a strange fellow, my lord, that so confidently seems to undertake this business, which he knows is not to be done ; damns himself to do and dares better be damned than to do 't ?

First Lord. You do not know him, my lord, as we do : certain it is, that he will steal himself into a man's favour and for a week escape a great deal of discoveries ; but when you find him out, you have him ever after.

Bertram. Why, do you think he will make no deed at all of this that so seriously he does address himself unto ?

Second Lord. None in the world ; but return with an invention and clap upon you two or three probable lies : but we have almost embossed him ; you shall see his fall to-night ; for indeed he is not for your lordship's respect.

First Lord. We 'll make you some sport with the fox ere we case him. He was first smoked by the old lord Lafeu : when his disguise and he is parted, tell me what a sprat you shall find him ; which you shall see this very night.

Second Lord. I must go look my twigs : he shall be caught.

Bertram. Your brother he shall go along with me.

Second Lord. As 't please your lordship ; I 'll leave you.   [*Exit.*

Bertram. Now will I lead you to the house, and show you
The lass I spoke of.

First Lord.   But you say she 's honest.

Bertram. That 's all the fault : I spoke with her but once
And found her wondrous cold ; but I sent to her,
By this same coxcomb that we have i' the wind,
Tokens and letters which she did re-send ;
And this is all I have done. She 's a fair creature :
Will you go see her ?

First Lord.   With all my heart, my lord.

[*Exeunt.*

SCENE VII.   *Florence.   The* Widow's *house.*

Enter Helena *and* Widow.

Helena. If you misdoubt me that I am not she,
I know not how I shall assure you further,
But I shall lose the grounds I work upon.

Widow. Though my estate be fallen, I was well born,
Nothing acquainted with these businesses ;
And would not put my reputation now
In any staining act.

Helena.   Nor would I wish you.
First, give me trust, the count he is my husband,
And what to your sworn counsel I have spoken
Is so from word to word ; and then you cannot,
By the good aid that I of you shall borrow,
Err in bestowing it.

Widow.   I should believe you ;
For you have show'd me that which well approves
You 're great in fortune.

Helena.   Take this purse of gold,
And let me buy your friendly help thus far,
Which I will over-pay and pay again
When I have found it. The count he wooes your daughter,
Lays down his wanton siege before her beauty,
Resolved to carry her : let her in fine consent,
As we 'll direct her how 'tis best to bear it.
Now his important blood will nought deny
That she 'll demand : a ring the county wears,
That downward hath succeeded in his house
From son to son, some four or five descents
Since the first father wore it : this ring he holds
In most rich choice ; yet in his idle fire,
To buy his will, it would not seem too dear,
Howe'er repented after.

Widow.   Now I see
The bottom of your purpose.

Helena. You see it lawful, then : it is no more,
But that your daughter, ere she seems as won,
Desires this ring ; appoints him an encounter ;
In fine, delivers me to fill the time,
Herself most chastely absent : after this,
To marry her, I 'll add three thousand crowns
To what is past already.

Widow.   I have yielded :
Instruct my daughter how she shall persever,
That time and place with this deceit so lawful
May prove coherent. Every night he comes
With musics of all sorts and songs composed
To her unworthiness : it nothing steads us
To chide him from our eaves ; for he persists
As if his life lay on 't.

Helena.   Why then to-night
Let us assay our plot ; which, if it speed,
Is wicked meaning in a lawful deed
And lawful meaning in a lawful act,
Where both not sin, and yet a sinful fact :
But let 's about it.   [*Exeunt.*

ACT IV.

SCENE I.   *Without the Florentine camp.*

Enter Second French Lord, *with five or six other* Soldiers *in ambush.*

Second Lord.

He can come no other way but by this hedge-corner. When you sally upon him, speak what terrible language you will : though you understand it not yourselves, no matter ; for we must not seem to understand him, unless some one among us whom we must produce for an interpreter.

First Soldier. Good captain, let me be the interpreter.

Second Lord. Art not acquainted with him ? knows he not thy voice ?

First Soldier. No, sir, I warrant you.

Second Lord. But what linsey-woolsey hast thou to speak to us again ?

First Soldier. E'en such as you speak to me.

Second Lord. He must think us some band of strangers i' the adversary's entertainment. Now he hath a smack of all neighbouring languages ; therefore we must every one be a man of his own fancy, not to know what we speak one to another ; so we seem to know, is to know straight our purpose : choughs' language, gabble enough, and good enough. As for you, interpreter, you must seem very politic. But couch, ho ! here he comes, to beguile two

hours in a sleep, and then to return and swear the
lies he forges.

Enter PAROLLES.

Parolles. Ten o'clock : within these three hours
'twill be time enough to go home. What shall I
say I have done ? It must be a very plausive invention
that carries it : they begin to smoke me ; and
disgraces have of late knocked too often at my door.
I find my tongue is too foolhardy ; but my heart
hath the fear of Mars before it and of his creatures,
not daring the reports of my tongue.
Second Lord. This is the first truth that e'er
thine own tongue was guilty of.
Parolles. What the devil should move me to
undertake the recovery of this drum, being not
ignorant of the impossibility, and knowing.I had no
such purpose ? I must give myself some hurts, and
say I got them in exploit : yet slight ones will not
carry it ; they will say, ' Came you off with so
little ? ' and great ones I dare not give. Wherefore,
what 's the instance ? Tongue, I must put you into
a butter-woman's mouth and buy myself another
of Bajazet's mule, if you prattle me into these perils.
Second Lord. Is it possible he should know what
he is, and be that he is ?
Parolles. I would the cutting of my garments
would serve the turn, or the breaking of my Spanish
sword.
Second Lord. We cannot afford you so.
Parolles. Or the baring of my beard ; and to say
it was in stratagem.
Second Lord. 'Twould not do.
Parolles. Or to drown my clothes, and say I was
stripped.
Second Lord. Hardly serve.
Parolles. Though I swore I leaped from the
window of the citadel—
Second Lord. How deep ?
Parolles. Thirty fathom.
Second Lord. Three great oaths would scarce
make that be believed.
Parolles. I would I had any drum of the enemy's :
I would swear I recovered it.
Second Lord. You shall hear one anon.
Parolles. A drum now of the enemy's,—
                              [*Alarum within.*
Second Lord. Throca movousus, cargo, cargo,
cargo.
All. Cargo, cargo, cargo, villianda par corbo,
cargo.
Parolles. O, ransom, ransom ! do not hide mine
eyes.   [*They seize and blindfold him.*
First Soldier. Boskos thromuldo boskos.
Parolles. I know you are the Muskos' regiment :
And I shall lose my life for want of language : If
there be here German, or Dane, low Dutch, Italian,
or French, let him speak to me ; I 'll discover
that which shall undo the Florentine.
First Soldier. Boskos vauvado : I understand
thee, and can speak thy tongue. Kerelybonto, sir,
betake thee to thy faith, for seventeen poniards
are at thy bosom.
Parolles. O !
First Soldier. O, pray, pray, pray ! Manka
revania dulche.
Second Lord. Oscorbidulchos volivorco.
First Soldier. The general is content to spare
thee yet ;
And, hoodwink'd as thou art, will lead thee on

To gather from thee : haply thou mayst inform
Something to save thy life.
Parolles.   O, let me live !
And all the secrets of our camp I 'll show,
Their force, their purposes ; nay, I 'll speak that
Which you will wonder at.
First Soldier.   But wilt thou faithfully ?
Parolles. If I do not, damn me.
First Soldier. Acordo linta.
Come on ; thou art granted space.
              [*Exit, with Parolles guarded. A short
                                alarum within.*
Second Lord. Go, tell the Count Rousillon, and
my brother,
We have caught the woodcock, and will keep him
muffled
Till we do hear from them.
Second Soldier.   Captain, I will.
Second Lord. A' will betray us all unto ourselves :
Inform on that.
Second Soldier. So I will, sir.
Second Lord. Till then I 'll keep him dark and
safely lock'd.   [*Exeunt.*

SCENE II.   *Florence.   The* Widow's *house.*

Enter BERTRAM *and* DIANA.

Bertram. They told me that your name was
Fontibell.
Diana. No, my good lord, Diana.
Bertram.   Titled goddess ;
And worth it, with addition ! But, fair soul,
In your fine frame hath love no quality ?
If the quick fire of youth light not your mind,
You are no maiden, but a monument ·
When you are dead, you should be such a one
As you are now, for you are cold and stern ;
And now you should be as your mother was
When your sweet self was got.
Diana. She then was honest.
Bertram.   So should you be.
Diana.   No :
My mother did but duty ; such, my lord,
As you owe to your wife.
Bertram.   No more o' that ;
I prithee, do not strive against my vows :
I was compell'd to her ; but I love thee
By love's own sweet constraint, and will for ever
Do thee all rights of service.
Diana.   Ay, so you serve us
Till we serve you ; but when you have our roses,
You barely leave our thorns to prick ourselves
And mock us with our bareness.
Bertram.   How have I sworn !
Diana. 'Tis not the many oaths that makes the
truth,
But the plain single vow that is vow'd true.
What is not holy, that we swear not by
But take the High'st to witness : then, pray you,
tell me,
If I should swear by God's great attributes,
I loved you dearly, would you believe my oaths,
When I did love you ill ? This has no holding,
To swear by him whom I protest to love,
That I will work against him : therefore your oaths
Are words and poor conditions, but unseal'd,
At least in my opinion.
Bertram.   Change it, change it ;
Be not so holy-cruel : love is holy ;
And my integrity ne'er knew the crafts

That you do charge men with. Stand no more off,
But give thyself unto my sick desires,
Who then recover : say thou art mine, and ever
My love as it begins shall so persever.
  Diana. † I see that men make ropes in such a
    scarre
That we 'll forsake ourselves. Give me that ring.
  Bertram. I 'll lend it thee, my dear ; but have no
    power
To give it from me.
  Diana.   Will you not, my lord ?
  Bertram. It is an honour 'longing to our house,
Bequeathed down from many ancestors ;
Which were the greatest obloquy i' the world
In me to lose.
  Diana.   Mine honour's such a ring :
My chastity 's the jewel of our house,
Bequeathed down from many ancestors ;
Which were the greatest obloquy i' the world
In me to lose : thus your own proper wisdom
Brings in the champion Honour on my part,
Against your vain assault.
  Bertram.   Here, take my ring :
My house, mine honour, yea, my life, be thine,
And I 'll be bid by thee.
  Diana. When midnight comes, knock at my
    chamber-window :
I 'll order take my mother shall not hear.
Now will I charge you in the band of truth,
When you have conquer'd my yet maiden bed,
Remain there but an hour, nor speak to me :
My reasons are most strong ; and you shall know
    them
When back again this ring shall be deliver'd :
And on your finger in the night I 'll put
Another ring, that what in time proceeds
May token to the future our past deeds.
Adieu, till then ; then, fail not. You have won
A wife of me, though there my hope be done.
  Bertram. A heaven on earth I have won by wooing
thee.   [*Exit.*
  Diana. For which live long to thank both heaven
    and me !
You may so in the end.
My mother told me just how he would woo,
As if she sat in 's heart ; she says all men
Have the like oaths : he had sworn to marry me
When his wife 's dead ; therefore I 'll lie with him
When I am buried. Since Frenchmen are so braid,
Marry that will, I live and die a maid :
Only in this disguise I think 't no sin
To cozen him that would unjustly win.   [*Exit.*

SCENE III. *The Florentine camp.*

*Enter the two French Lords and some two or
three Soldiers.*

  First Lord. You have not given him his mother's
letter ?
  Second Lord. I have delivered it an hour since :
there is something in 't that stings his nature ;
for on the reading it he changed almost into another
man.
  First Lord. He has much worthy blame laid
upon him for shaking off so good a wife and so
sweet a lady.
  Second Lord. Especially he hath incurred the
everlasting displeasure of the king, who had even
tuned his bounty to sing happiness to him. I will
tell you a thing, but you shall let it dwell darkly

with you.
  First Lord. When you have spoken it, 'tis dead,
and I am the grave of it.
  Second Lord. He hath perverted a young gentlewoman here in Florence, of a most chaste renown ;
and this night he fleshes his will in the spoil of her
honour : he hath given her his monumenta' ring,
and thinks himself made in the unchaste composition.
  First Lord. Now, God delay our rebellion !
as we are ourselves, what things are we !
  Second Lord. Merely our own traitors. And as
in the common course of all reasons, we stil see them
reveal themselves, till they attain to their abhorred
ends, so he that in this action contrives against his
own nobility, in his proper stream o'erflows himself.
  First Lord. Is it not meant damnable in us,
to be trumpeters of our unlawful intents ? We shall
not then have his company to-night ?
  Second Lord. Not till after midnight ; for he is
dieted to his hour.
  First Lord. That approaches apace ; I would
gladly have him see his company anatomized, that
he might take a measure of his own judgement,
wherein so curiously he had set this counterfeit.
  Second Lord. We will not meddle with him till
he come ; for his presence must be the whip of the
other.
  First Lord. In the mean time, what hear you
of these wars ?
  Second Lord. I hear there is an overture of peace.
  First Lord. Nay, I assure you, a peace concluded.
  Second Lord. What will Count Rousillon do
then ? will he travel higher, or return again into
France ?
  First Lord. I perceive, by this demand, you are
not altogether of his council.
  Second Lord. Let it be forbid, sir ; so should I
be a great deal of his act.
  First Lord. Sir, his wife some two months since
fled from his house : her pretence is a pilgrimage
to Saint Jaques le Grand ; which holy undertaking
with most austere sanctimony she accomplished ;
and, there residing, the tenderness of her nature
became as a prey to her grief ; in fine, made a groan
of her last breath, and now she sings in heaven.
  Second Lord. How is this justified ?
  First Lord. The stronger part of it by her own
letters, which makes her story true, even to the
point of her death : her death itself, which could
not be her office to say is come, was faithfully confirmed by the rector of the place.
  Second Lord. Hath the count all this intelligence ?
  First Lord. Ay, and the particular confirma-
tions, point from point, to the full arming of the
verity.
  Second Lord. I am heartily sorry that he 'll be
glad of this.
  First Lord. How mightily sometimes we make
us comforts of our losses !
  Second Lord. And how mightily some other
times we drown our gain in tears ! The great dignity
that his valour hath here acquired for him shall
at home be encountered with a shame as ample.
  First Lord. The web of our life is of a mingled
yarn, good and ill together : our virtues would be
proud, if our faults whipped them not ; and our
crimes would despair, if they were not cherished
by our virtues.

Enter a Messenger.

How now ! where 's your master ?

Servant. He met the duke in the street, sir, of whom he hath taken a solemn leave : his lordship will next morning for France. The duke hath offered him letters of commendations to the king.

Second Lord. They shall be no more than needful there, if they were more than they can commend.

First Lord. They cannot be too sweet for the king's tartness. Here 's his lordship now.

Enter BERTRAM.

How now, my lord ! is 't not after midnight ?

Bertram. I have to-night dispatched sixteen businesses, a month's length a-piece, by an abstract of success : I have congied with the duke, done my adieu with my nearest ; buried a wife, mourned for her ; writ to my lady mother I am returning ; entertained my convoy ; and between these main parcels of dispatch effected many nicer needs : the last was the greatest, but that I have not ended yet.

Second Lord. If the business be of any difficulty, and this morning your departure hence, it requires haste of your lordship.

Bertram. I mean, the business is not ended, as fearing to hear of it hereafter. But shall we have this dialogue between the fool and the soldier ? Come, bring forth this counterfeit module, has deceived me, like a double-meaning prophesier.

Second Lord. Bring him forth : has sat i' the stocks all night, poor gallant knave.

Bertram. No matter ; his heels have deserved it, in usurping his spurs so long. How does he carry himself ?

Second Lord. I have told your lordship already, the stocks carry him. But to answer you as you would be understood ; he weeps like a wench that had shed her milk : he hath confessed himself to Morgan, whom he supposes to be a friar, from the time of his remembrance to this very instant disaster of his setting i' the stocks : and what think you he hath confessed ?

Bertram. Nothing of me, has a' ?

Second Lord. His confession is taken, and it shall be read to his face : if your lordship be in 't, as I believe you are, you must have the patience to hear it.

Enter PAROLLES *guarded, and* First Soldier.

Bertram. A plague upon him ! muffled ! he can say nothing of me : hush, hush !

First Lord. Hoodman comes ! Portotartarosa.

First Soldier. He calls for the tortures : what will you say without 'em ?

Parolles. I will confess what I know without constraint : if ye pinch me like a pasty, I can say no more.

First Soldier. Bosko chimurcho.

First Soldier. Boblibindo chicurmurco.

First Soldier. You are a merciful general. Our general bids you answer to what I shall ask you out of a note.

Parolles. And truly, as I hope to live.

First Soldier. [*Reads*] ' First demand of him how many horse the duke is strong.' What say you to that ?

Parolles. Five or six thousand ; but very weak and unserviceable : the troops are all scattered,

and the commanders very poor rogues, upon my reputation and credit and as I hope to live.

First Soldier. Shall I set down your answer so ?

Parolles. Do : I 'll take the sacrament on 't, how and which way you will.

Bertram. All 's one to him. What a past-saving slave is this !

First Lord. You 're deceived, my lord : this is Monsieur Parolles, the gallant militarist,—that was his own phrase,—that had the whole theoric of war in the knot of his scarf, and the practice in the chape of his dagger.

Second Lord. I will never trust a man again for keeping his sword clean, nor believe he can have every thing in him by wearing his apparel neatly.

First Soldier. Well, that 's set down.

Parolles. Fix or six thousand horse, I said,—I will say true,—or thereabouts, set down, for I 'll speak truth.

First Lord. He 's very near the truth in this.

Bertram. But I con him no thanks for 't, in the nature he delivers it.

Parolles. Poor rogues, I pray you, say.

First Soldier. Well, that 's set down.

Parolles. I humbly thank you, sir : a truth 's a truth, the rogues are marvellous poor.

First Soldier. [*Reads*] ' Demand of him, of what strength they are a-foot.' What say you to that ?

Parolles. By my troth, sir, if I were to live this present hour, I will tell true. Let me see : Spurio, a hundred and fifty ; Sebastian, so many ; Corambus, so many ; Jaques, so many ; Guiltian, Cosmo, Lodowick, and Gratii, two hundred and fifty each ; mine own company, Chitopher, Vaumond, Bentii, two hundred and fifty each : so that the muster-file, rotten and sound, upon my life, amounts not to fifteen thousand poll ; half of the which dare not shake the snow from off their cassocks, lest they shake themselves to pieces.

Bertram. What shall be done to him ?

First Lord. Nothing, but let him have thanks. Demand of him my condition, and what credit I have with the duke.

First Soldier. Well, that 's set down. [*Reads*] ' You shall demand of him, whether one Captain Dumain be i'. the camp, a Frenchman ; what his reputation is with the duke ; what his valour, honesty and expertness in wars ; or whether he thinks it were not possible, with well-weighing sums of gold, to corrupt him to a revolt.' What say you to this ? what do you know of it ?

Parolles. I beseech you, let me answer to the particular of the inter'gatories : demand them singly.

First Soldier. Do you know this Captain Dumain ?

Parolles. I know him : a' was a botcher's 'prentice in Paris, from whence he was whipped for getting the shrieve's fool with child,—a dumb innocent, that could not say him nay.

Bertram. Nay, by your leave, hold your hands ; though I know his brains are forfeit to the next tile that falls.

First Soldier. Well, is this captain in the duke of Florence's camp ?

Parolles. Upon my knowledge, he is, and lousy.

First Lord. Nay, look not so upon me ; we shall hear of your lordship anon.

First Soldier. What is his reputation with the duke ?

Parolles. The duke knows him for no other but a poor officer of mine ; and writ to me this other day to turn him out o' the band : I think I have his letter in my pocket.

First Soldier. Marry, we'll search.

Parolles. In good sadness, I do not know ; either it is there, or it is upon a file with the duke's other letters in my tent.

First Soldier. Here 'tis : here's a paper : shall I read it to you ?

Parolles. I do not know if it be it or no.

Bertram. Our interpreter does it well.

First Lord. Excellently.

First Soldier. [*Reads*] ' Dian, the count's a fool, and full of gold,'—

Parolles. That is not the duke's letter, sir ; that is an advertisement to a proper maid in Florence, one Diana, to take heed of the allurement of one Count Rousillon, a foolish idle boy, but for all that very ruttish : I pray you, sir, put it up again.

First Soldier. Nay, I'll read it first, by your favour.

Parolles. My meaning in't, I protest, was very honest in the behalf of the maid ; for I knew the young count to be a dangerous and lascivious boy, who is a whale to virginity and devours up all the fry it finds.

Bertram. Damnable both-sides rogue !

First Soldier. [*Reads*] ' When he swears oaths, bid him drop gold, and take it ; After he scores, he never pays the score : Half won is match well made ; match, and well make it ; He ne'er pays after-debts, take it before ; And say a soldier, Dian, told thee this, Men are to mell with, boys are not to kiss : For count of this, the count's a fool, I know it, Who pays before, but not when he does owe it. Thine, as he vowed to thee in thine ear, PAROLLES.'

Bertram. He shall be whipped through the army with this rhyme in's forehead.

Second Lord. This is your devoted friend, sir, the manifold linguist and the armipotent soldier.

Bertram. I could endure any thing before but a cat, and now he's a cat to me.

First Soldier. I perceive, sir, by the general's looks, we shall be fain to hang you.

Parolles. My life, sir, in any case : not that I am afraid to die ; but that, my offences being many, I would repent out the remainder of nature : let me live, sir, in a dungeon, i' the stocks, or any where, so I may live.

First Soldier. We'll see what may be done, so you confess freely ; therefore, once more to this Captain Dumain : you have answered to his reputation with the duke and to his valour : what is his honesty ?

Parolles. He will steal, sir, an egg out of a cloister : for rapes and ravishments he parallels Nessus : he professes not keeping of oaths ; in breaking 'em he is stronger than Hercules : he will lie, sir, with such volubility, that you would think truth were a fool : drunkenness is his best virtue, for he will be swine-drunk ; and in his sleep he does little harm, save to his bed-clothes about him ; but they know his conditions and lay him in straw. I have but little more to say, sir, of his honesty : he has every thing that an honest man should not have ; what an honest man should have, he has nothing.

First Lord. I begin to love him for this.

Bertram. For this description of thine honesty ? A pox upon him for me, he's more and more a cat.

First Soldier. What say you to his expertness in war ?

Parolles. Faith, sir, has led the drum before the English tragedians ; to belie him, I will not, and more of his soldiership I know not ; except, in that country he had the honour to be the officer at a place there called Mile-end, to instruct for the doubling of files : I would do the man what honour I can, but of this I am not certain.

First Lord. He hath out-villained villany so far, that the rarity redeems him.

Bertram. A pox on him, he's a cat still.

First Soldier. His qualities being at this poor price, I need not to ask you if gold will corrupt him to revolt.

Parolles. Sir, for a quart d'ecu, he will sell the fee-simple of his salvation, the inheritance of it ; and cut the entail from all remainders, and a perpetual succession for it perpetually.

First Soldier. What's his brother, the other Captain Dumain ?

Second Lord. Why does he ask him of me ?

First Soldier. What's he ?

Parolles. E'en a crow o' the same nest ; not altogether so great as the first in goodness, but greater a great deal in evil : he excels his brother for a coward, yet his brother is reputed one of the best that is : in a retreat he outruns any lackey ; marry, in coming on he has the cramp.

First Soldier. If your life be saved, will you undertake to betray the Florentine ?

Parolles. Ay, and the captain of his horse, Count Rousillon.

First Soldier. I'll whisper with the general, and know his pleasure.

Parolles. [*Aside*] I'll no more drumming ; a plague of all drums ! Only to seem to deserve well and to beguile the supposition of that lascivious young boy the count, have I run into this danger. Yet who would have suspected an ambush where I was taken ?

First Soldier. There is no remedy, sir, but you must die : the general says, you that have so traitorously discovered the secrets of your army and made such pestiferous reports of men very nobly held, can serve the world for no honest use ; therefore you must die. Come, headsman, off with his head.

Parolles. O Lord, sir, let me live, or let me see my death !

First Soldier. That shall you, and take your leave of all your friends.   [*Unblinding him.* So, look about you ; know you any here ?

Bertram. Good morrow, noble captain.

Second Lord. God bless you, Captain Parolles.

First Lord. God save you, noble captain.

Second Lord. Captain, what greeting will you to my Lord Lafeu ? I am for France.

First Lord. Good captain, will you give me a copy of the sonnet you writ to Diana in behalf of the Count Rousillon ? an I were not a very coward, I'ld compel it of you : but fare you well.

[*Exeunt Bertram and Lords.*

First Soldier. You are undone, captain, all but your scarf ; that has a knot on't yet.

Parolles. Who cannot be crushed with a plot ?

First Soldier. If you could find out a country where but women were that had received so much shame, you might begin an impudent nation. Fare ye well, sir ; I am for France too : we shall speak of you there.

[*Exit, with Soldiers.*

Parolles.   Yet am I thankful : if my heart were
great,
'Twould burst at this. Captain I 'll be no more ;
But I will eat and drink, and sleep as soft
As captain shall : simply the thing I am
Shall make me live. Who knows himself a brag-
gart,
Let him fear this, for it will come to pass
That every braggart shall be found an ass.
Rust, sword ! cool, blushes ! and, Parolles, live
Safest in shame ! being fool'd, by foolery thrive !
There 's place and means for every man alive.
I 'll after them.   [*Exit.*

SCENE IV. *Florence. The* Widow's *house.*

Enter HELENA, Widow, *and* DIANA.

Helena.   That you may well perceive I have not
wrong'd you,
One of the greatest in the Christian world
Shall be my surety ; 'fore whose throne 'tis needful,
Ere I can perfect mine intents, to kneel :
Time was, I did him a desired office,
Dear almost as his life ; which gratitude
Through flinty Tartar's bosom would peep forth,
And answer, thanks : I duly am inform'd
His grace is at Marseilles ; to which place
We have convenient convoy. You must know,
I am supposed dead : the army breaking,
My husband hies him home ; where, heaven aiding,
And by the leave of my good lord the king,
We 'll be before our welcome.

Widow.   Gentle madam,
You never had a servant to whose trust
Your business was more welcome.

Helena.   Nor you, mistress,
Ever a friend whose thoughts more truly labour
To recompense your love : doubt not but heaven
Hath brought me up to be your daughter's dower,
As it hath fated her to be my motive
And helper to a husband. But, O strange men !
That can such sweet use make of what they hate,
When saucy trusting of the cozen'd thoughts
Defiles the pitchy night : so lust doth play
With what it loathes for that which is away.
But more of this hereafter. You, Diana,
Under my poor instructions yet must suffer
Something in my behalf.

Diana.   Let death and honesty
Go with your impositions, I am yours
Upon your will to suffer.

Helena.   Yet, I pray you :
But with the word the time will bring on summer,
When briers shall have leaves as well as thorns,
And be as sweet as sharp. We must away ;
Our waggon is prepared, and time revives us :
ALL 'S WELL THAT ENDS WELL : still the fine 's the
crown ;
Whate'er the course, the end is the renown.
                                  [*Exeunt.*

SCENE V. *Rousillon. The* COUNT's *palace.*

Enter COUNTESS, LAFEU, *and* CLOWN.

Lafeu. No, no, no, your son was misled with a
snipt-taffeta fellow there, whose villanous saffron
would have made all the unbaked and doughy youth
of a nation in his colour : your daughter-in-law
had been alive at this hour, and your son here at
home, more advanced by the king than by that
red-tailed humble-bee I speak of.

Countess. I would I had not known him ; it was
the death of the most virtuous gentlewoman that ever
nature had praise for creating. If she had partaken
of my flesh, and cost me the dearest groans of
mother, I could not have owed her a more rooted lov .

Lafeu. 'Twas a good lady, 'twas a good lady :
We may pick a thousand salads ere we light on
such another herb.

Clown. Indeed, sir, she was the sweet-marjoram
of the salad, or rather, the herb of grace.

Lafeu. They are not herbs, you knave ; they
are nose-herbs.

Clown. I am no great Nebuchadnezzar, sir ; I
have not much skill in grass.

Lafeu. Whether dost thou profess thyself, a
knave or a fool ?

Clown. A fool, sir, at a woman's service, and a
knave at a man's.

Lafeu. Your distinction ?

Clown. I would cozen the man of his wife and
do his service.

Lafeu. So you were a knave at his service indeed.

Clown. And I would give his wife my bauble, sir,
to do her service.

Lafeu. I will subscribe for thee, thou art both
knave and fool.

Clown. At your service.

Lafeu. No, no, no.

Clown. Why, sir, if I cannot serve you, I can
serve as great a prince as you are.

Lafeu. Who 's that ? a Frenchman ?

Clown. Faith, sir, a' has an English name ; but
his fisnomy is more hotter in France than there.

Lafeu. What prince is that ?

Clown. The black prince, sir ; alias, the prince
of darkness ; alias, the devil.

Lafeu. Hold thee, there 's my purse : I give thee
not this to suggest thee from thy master thou talkest
of ; serve him still.

Clown. I am a woodland fellow, sir, that always
loved a great fire ; and the master I speak of ever
keeps a good fire. But, sure, he is the prince of the
world ; let his nobility remain in 's court. I am for
the house with the narrow gate, which I take to be
too little for pomp to enter : some that humble
themselves may ; but the many will be too chill
and tender, and they 'll be for the flowery way that
leads to the broad gate and the great fire.

Lafeu. Go thy ways, I begin to be aweary of
thee ; and I tell thee so before, because I would not
fall out with thee. Go thy ways : let my horses
be well looked to, without any tricks.

Clown. If I put any tricks upon 'em, sir, they
shall be jades' tricks ; which are their own right
by the law of nature.   [*Exit.*

Lafeu. A shrewd knave and an unhappy.

Countess. So he is. My lord that 's gone made
himself much sport out of him : by his authority
he remains here, which he thinks is a patent for his
sauciness ; and, indeed, he has no pace, but runs
where he will.

Lafeu. I like him well ; 'tis not amiss. And I
was about to tell you, since I heard of the good
lady's death and that my lord your son was upon his
return home, I moved the king my master to speak
in the behalf of my daughter ; which, in the minority
of them both, his majesty, out of a self-gracious
remembrance, did first propose : his highness hath
promised me to do it : and, to stop up the displeasure

he hath conceived against your son, there is no fitter matter. How does your ladyship like it ?

Countess. With very much content, my lord ; and I wish it happily effected.

Lafeu. His highness comes post from Marseilles, of as able body as when he numbered thirty : he will be here to-morrow, or I am deceived by him that in such intelligence hath seldom failed.

Countess. It rejoices me, that I hope I shall see him ere I die. I have letters that my son will be here to-night : I shall beseech your lordship to remain with me till they meet together.

Lafeu. Madam, I was thinking with what manners I might safely be admitted.

Countess. You need but plead your honourable privilege.

Lafeu. Lady, of that I have made a bold charter ; but I thank my God it holds yet.

Re-enter CLOWN.

Clown. O madam, yonder 's my lord your son with a patch of velvet on 's face : whether there be a scar under 't or no, the velvet knows ; but 'tis a goodly patch of velvet : his left cheek is a cheek of two pile and a half, but his right cheek is worn bare.

Lafeu. A scar nobly got, or a noble scar, is a good livery of honour ; so belike is that.

Clown. But it is your carbonadoed face.

Lafeu. Let us go see your son, I pray you : I long to talk with the young noble soldier.

Clown. Faith, there 's a dozen of 'em, with delicate fine hats and most courteous feathers, which bow the head and nod at every man.   [*Exeunt.*

ACT V.

SCENE I. *Marseilles. . A street.*

Enter HELENA, Widow, *and* DIANA, *with two Attendants.*

Helena.

B ut this exceeding posting day and night
Must wear your spirits low ; we cannot help it :
But since you have made the days and nights as one,
To wear your gentle limbs in my affairs,
Be bold you do so grow in my requital
As nothing can unroot you. In happy time ;

Enter a Gentleman.

This man may help me to his majesty's ear,
If he would spend his power. God save you, sir.

Gentleman. And you.

Helena. Sir, I have seen you in the court of France.

Gentleman. I have been sometimes there.

Helena. I do presume, sir, that you are not fallen From the report that goes upon your goodness ;
And therefore, goaded with most sharp occasions,
Which lay nice manners by, I put you to
The use of your own virtues, for the which
I shall continue thankful.

Gentleman.   What 's your will ?

Helena. That it will please you
To give this poor petition to the king,
And aid me with that store of power you have
To come into his presence.

Gentleman. The king 's not here.

Helena.   Not here, sir !

Gentleman.   Not, indeed :
He hence removed last night and with more haste Than is his use.

Widow. Lord, how we lose our pains !

Helena. ALL 'S WELL THAT ENDS WELL yet,
Though time seem so adverse and means unfit.
I do beseech you, whither is he gone ?

Gentleman. Marry, as I take it, to Rousillon ; Whither I am going.

Helena.   I do beseech you, sir,
Since you are like to see the king before me,
Commend the paper to his gracious hand,
Which I presume shall render you no blame
But rather make you thank your pains for it.
I will come after you with what good speed
Our means will make us means.

Gentleman.   This I 'll do for you.

Helena. And you shall find yourself to be well thank'd,
Whate'er falls more. We must to horse again.
Go, go, provide.   [*Exeunt.*

SCENE II. *Rousillon. Before the* COUNT'S *palace.*

Enter CLOWN, *and* PAROLLES, *following.*

Parolles. Good Monsieur Lavache, give my Lord Lafeu this letter : I have ere now, sir, been better known to you, when I have held familiarity with fresher clothes ; but I am now, sir, muddied in fortune's mood, and smell somewhat strong of her strong displeasure.

Clown. Truly, fortune's displeasure is but sluttish, if it smell so strongly as thou speakest of : I will henceforth eat no fish of fortune's buttering. Prithee, allow the wind.

Parolles. Nay, you need not to stop your nose, sir ; I spake but by a metaphor.

Clown. Indeed, sir, if your metaphor stink, I will stop my nose ; or against any man's metaphor. Prithee, get thee further.

Parolles. Pray you, sir, deliver me this paper.

Clown. Foh ! prithee, stand away : a paper from fortune's close-stool to give to a nobleman ! Look, here he comes himself.

Enter LAFEU.

Here is a purr of fortune's, sir, or of fortune's cat,— but not a musk-cat,—that has fallen into the unclean fishpond of her displeasure, and, as he says, is muddied withal : pray you, sir, use the carp as you may ; for he looks like a poor, decayed, ingenious, foolish, rascally knave. I do pity his distress in my similes of comfort and leave him to your lordship.   [*Exit.*

Parolles. My lord, I am a man whom fortune hath cruelly scratched.

Lafeu. And what would you have me to do ? 'Tis too late to pare her nails now. Wherein have you played the knave with fortune, that she should scratch you, who of herself is a good lady and would not have knaves thrive long under her ? There 's a quart d'ecu for you : let the justices make you and fortune friends : I am for other business.

Parolles. I beseech your honour to hear me one single word.

Lafeu. You beg a single penny more : come, you shall ha 't ; save your word.

Parolles. My name, my good lord, is Parolles.

Lafeu. You beg more than ' word ' then. Cox my passion ! give me your hand. How does your drum ?

Parolles. O my good lord, you were the first that found me !

Lafeu. Was I, in sooth ? and I was the first that lost thee.

Parolles. It lies in you, my lord, to bring me in some grace, for you did bring me out.

Lafeu. Out upon thee, knave ! dost thou put upon me at once both the office of God and the devil ? one brings thee in grace and the other brings thee out. [*Trumpets sound.*] The king 's coming ; I know by his trumpets. Sirrah, inquire further after me ; I had talk of you last night : though you are a fool and a knave, you shall eat ; go to, follow.

Parolles. I praise God for you. [*Exeunt.*

SCENE III. *Rousillon. The* COUNT'S *palace.*

Flourish. Enter KING, COUNTESS, LAFEU, *the two French Lords, with* Attendants.

King. We lost a jewel of her ; and our esteem
Was made much poorer by it : but your son,
As mad in folly, lack'd the sense to know
Her estimation home.
Countess.   'Tis past, my liege ;
And I beseech your majesty to make it
Natural rebellion, done i' the blaze of youth ;
When oil and fire, too strong for reason's force,
O'erbears it and burns on.
King.   My honour'd lady,
I have forgiven and forgotten all ;
Though my revenges were high bent upon him,
And watch'd the time to shoot.
Lafeu.   This I must say,
But first I beg my pardon, the young lord
Did to his majesty, his mother and his lady
Offence of mighty note ; but to himself
The greatest wrong of all. He lost a wife
Whose beauty did astonish the survey
Of richest eyes, whose words all ears took captive,
Whose dear perfection hearts that scorn'd to serve
Humbly call'd mistress.
King.   Praising what is lost
Makes the remembrance dear. Well, call him hither ;
We are reconciled, and the first view shall kill
All repetition : let him not ask our pardon ;
The nature of his great offence is dead,
And deeper than oblivion we do bury
The incensing relics of it : let him approach,
A stranger, no offender ; and inform him
So 'tis our will he should.
Gentleman. I shall, my liege. [*Exit.*
King. What says he to your daughter ? have you spoke ?
Lafeu. All that he is hath reference to your highness.
King. Then shall we have a match. I have letters sent me
That set him high in fame.

    Enter BERTRAM.

Lafeu.   He looks well on 't.
King. I am not a day of season,
For thou mayst see a sunshine and a hail
In me at once : but to the brightest beams

Distracted clouds give way ; so stand thou forth ;
The time is fair again.
Bertram. My high-repented blames,
Dear sovereign, pardon to me.
King.   All is whole ;
Not one word more of the consumed time.
Let 's take the instant by the forward top ;
For we are old, and on our quick'st decrees
The inaudible and noiseless foot of Time
Steals ere we can effect them. You remember
The daughter of this lord ?
Bertram. Admiringly, my liege, at first
I stuck my choice upon her, ere my heart
Durst make too bold a herald of my tongue :
Where the impression of mine eye infixing,
Contempt his scornful perspective·did lend me,
Which warp'd the line of every other favour ;
Scorn'd a fair colour, or express'd it stolen ;
Extended or contracted all proportions
To a most hideous object : thence it came
That she whom all men praised and whom myself,
Since I have lost, have loved, was in mine eye
The dust that did offend it.
King.   Well excused :
That thou didst love her, strikes some scores away
From the great compt : but love that comes too late,
Like a remorseful pardon slowly carried,
To the great sender turns a sour offence,
Crying, ' That 's good that 's gone.' Our rash faults
Make trivial price of serious things we have,
Not knowing them until we know their grave :
Oft our displeasures, to ourselves unjust,
Destroy our friends and after weep their dust :
† Our own love waking cries to see what 's done,
While shame full late sleeps out the afternoon.
Be this sweet Helen's knell, and now forget her.
Send forth your amorous token for fair Maudlin :
The main consents are had ; and here we 'll stay
To see our widower's second marriage-day.
Countess. Which better than the first, O dear heaven, bless !
Or, ere they meet, in me, O nature, cesse !
Lafeu. Come on, my son, in whom my house's name
Must be digested, give a favour from you
To sparkle in the spirits of my daughter,
That she may quickly come. [*Bertram gives a ring.*]
    By my old beard,
And every hair that 's on 't, Helen, that 's dead,
Was a sweet creature : such a ring as this,
The last that e'er I took her leave at court,
I saw upon her finger.
Bertram. Hers it was not.
King. Now, pray you, let me see it ; for mine eye,
While I was speaking, oft was fasten'd to 't.
This ring was mine ; and, when I gave it Helen,
I bade her, if her fortunes ever stood
Necessitied to help, that by this token
I would relieve her. Had you that craft, to reave her
Of what should stead her most ?
Bertram. My gracious sovereign,
Howe'er it pleases you to take it so,
The ring was never hers.
Countess. Son, on my life,
I have seen her wear it ; and she reckon'd it
At her life's rate.
Lafeu. I am sure I saw her wear it.
Bertram. You are deceived, my lord ; she never saw it :
In Florence was it from a casement thrown me,

Wrapp'd in a paper, which contain'd the name
Of her that threw it : noble she was, and thought
I stood engaged : but when I had subscribed
To mine own fortune and inform'd her fully
I could not answer in that course of honour
As she had made the overture, she ceased
In heavy satisfaction and would never
Receive the ring again.
   King.   Plutus himself,
That knows the tinct and multiplying medicine,
Hath not in nature's mystery more science
Than I have in this ring : 'twas mine, 'twas Helen's,
Whoever gave it you.   Then, if you know
That you are well acquainted with yourself,
Confess 'twas hers, and by what rough enforcement
You got it from her : she call'd the saints to surety
That she would never put it from her finger,
Unless she gave it to yourself in bed,
Where you have never come, or sent it us
Upon her great disaster.
   Bertram.   She never saw 't.
   King.   Thou speak'st it falsely, as I love mine
honour ;
And makest conjectural fears to come into me,
Which I would fain shut out.   If it should prove
That thou art so inhuman,—'twill not prove so ;—
And yet I know not : thou didst hate her deadly,
And she is dead ; which nothing, but to close
Her eyes myself, could win me to believe,
More than to see this ring.   Take him away.
                  [*Guards seize Bertram.*
My fore-past proofs, howe'er the matter fall,
Shall tax my fears of little vanity,
Having vainly fear'd too little.   Away with him !
We 'll sift this matter further.
   Bertram.   If you shall prove
This ring was ever hers, you shall as easy
Prove that I husbanded her bed in Florence,
Where yet she never was.   [*Exit, guarded.*
   King.   I am wrapp'd in dismal thinkings.

          Enter a Gentleman.

   Gentleman.   Gracious sovereign,
Whether I have been to blame or no, I know not :
Here 's a petition from a Florentine,
Who hath for four or five removes come short
To tender it herself.   I undertook it,
Vanquish'd thereto by the fair grace and speech
Of the poor suppliant, who by this I know
Is here attending : her business looks in her
With an importing visage ; and she told me,
In a sweet verbal brief, it did concern
Your highness with herself.
   King. [*Reads*] Upon his many protestations to
marry me when his wife was dead, I blush to say it,
he won me.   Now is the Count Rousillon a widower :
his vows are forfeited to me, and my honour's paid
to him.   He stole from Florence, taking no leave,
and I follow him to his country for justice : grant
it me, O king ! in you it best lies ; otherwise a
seducer flourishes, and a poor maid is undone.
                       DIANA CAPILET.
   Lafeu.   I will buy me a son-in-law in a fair, and
toll for this : I 'll none of him.
   King.   The heavens have thought well on thee,
Lafeu,
To bring forth this discovery.   Seek these suitors :
Go speedily and bring again the count,
I am afeard the life of Helen, lady,
Was foully snatch'd.

   Countess.   Now, justice on the doers !

      Re-enter BERTRAM, *guarded.*

   King.   I wonder, sir, sith wives are monsters to
   you,
And that you fly them as you swear them lordship,
Yet you desire to marry.

      Enter Widow, *and* DIANA.

                What woman 's that ?
   Diana.   I am, my lord, a wretched Florentine,
Derived from the ancient Capilet :
My suit, as I do understand, you know,
And therefore know how far I may be pitied.
   Widow.   I am her mother, sir, whose age and
honour
Both suffer under this complaint we bring,
And both shall cease, without your remedy.
   King.   Come hither, count ; do you know these
women ?
   Bertram.   My lord, I neither can nor will deny
But that I know them : do they charge me further ?
   Diana.   Why do you look so strange upon your
wife ?
   Bertram.   She 's none of mine, my lord.
   Diana.   If you shall marry,
You give away this hand, and that is mine ;
You give away heaven's vows, and those are mine ;
You give away myself, which is known mine ;
For I by vow am so embodied yours,
That she which marries you must marry me,
Either both or none.
   Lafeu.   Your reputation comes too short for my
daughter ; you are no husband for her.
   Bertram.   My lord, this is a fond and desperate
creature,
Whom sometime I have laugh'd with : let your
highness
Lay a more noble thought upon mine honour
Than for to think that I would sink it here.
   King.   Sir, for my thoughts, you have them ill
to friend
Till your deeds gain them : fairer prove your honour
Than in my thought it lies.
   Diana.   Good my lord,
Ask him upon his oath, if he does think
He had not my virginity.
   King.   What say'st thou to her ?
   Bertram.   She 's impudent, my lord,
And was a common gamester to the camp.
   Diana.   He does me wrong, my lord ; if I were so,
He might have bought me at a common price ;
Do not believe him.   O, behold this ring,
Whose high respect and rich validity
Did lack a parallel ; yet for all that
He gave it to a commoner o' the camp,
If I be one.
   Countess.   He blushes and 'tis it :
Of six preceding ancestors, that gem,
Conferr'd by testament to the sequent issue,
Hath it been owed and worn.   This is his wife ;
That ring 's a thousand proofs.
   King.   Methought you said
You saw one here in court could witness it.
   Diana.   I did, my lord, but loath am to produce
So bad an instrument : his name 's Parolles.
   Lafeu.   I saw the man to-day, if man he be.
   King.   Find him, and bring him hither.
                   [*Exit an Attendant.*

Bertram.   What of him ?
He 's quoted for a most perfidious slave,
With all the spots o' the world tax'd and debosh'd ;
Whose nature sickens but to speak a truth.
Am I or that or this for what he 'll utter,
That will speak any thing ?
King.   She hath that ring of yours.
Bertram. I think she has : certain it is I liked her,
And boarded her i' the wanton way of youth :
She knew her distance and did angle for me,
Madding my eagerness with her restraint,
As all impediments in fancy's course
Are motives of more fancy ; and, in fine,
Her infinite cunning, with her modern grace,
Subdued me to her rate : she got the ring ;
And I had that which any inferior might
At market-price have bought.
Diana.   I must be patient :
You, that have turn'd off a first so noble wife,
May justly diet me. I pray you yet ;
Since you lack virtue, I will lose a husband ;
Send for your ring, I will return it home,
And give me mine again.
Bertram.   I have it not.
King. What ring was yours, I pray you ?
Diana.   Sir, much like
The same upon your finger.
King. Know you this ring ? this ring was his
of late.
Diana. And this was it I gave him, being abed.
King. The story then goes false, you threw it him
Out of a casement.
Diana.   I have spoke the truth.

Enter PAROLLES.

Bertram. My lord, I do confess the ring was hers.
King. You boggle shrewdly, every feather starts
you.
Is this the man you speak of ?
Diana.   Ay, my lord.
King. Tell me, sirrah, but tell me true, I charge
you,
Not fearing the displeasure of your master,
Which on your just proceeding I 'll keep off,
By him and by this woman here what know you ?
Parolles. So please your majesty, my master hath
been an honourable gentleman : tricks he hath had
in him, which gentlemen have.
King. Come, come, to the purpose : did he
love this woman ?
Parolles. Faith, sir, he did love her ; but how ?
King. How, I pray you ?
Parolles. He did love her, sir, as a gentleman
loves a woman.
King. How is that ?
Parolles. He loved her, sir, and loved her not.
King. As thou art a knave, and no knave. What
an equivocal companion is this !
Parolles. I am a poor man, and at your majesty's
command.
Lafeu. He 's a good drum, my lord, but a naughty
orator.
Diana. Do you know he promised me marriage ?
Parolles. Faith, I know more than I 'll speak.
King. But wilt thou not speak all thou knowest ?
Parolles. Yes, so please your majesty. I did go
between them, as I said ; but more than that he
loved her : for indeed he was mad for her, and
talked of Satan and of Limbo and of Furies and I know
not what : yet I was in that credit with them at that

time that I knew of their going to bed, and of other
motions, as promising her marriage, and things
which would derive me ill will to speak of ; therefore
I will not speak what I know.
King. Thou hast spoken all already, unless thou
canst say they are married : but thou art too fine in
thy evidence ; therefore stand aside. This ring,
you say, was yours ?
Diana.   Ay, my good lord.
King. Where did you buy it ? or who gave it you ?
Diana. It was not given me, nor I did not buy it.
King. Who lent it you ?
Diana.   It was not lent me neither.
King. Where did you find it, then ?
Diana.   I found it not.
King. If it were yours by none of all these ways,
How could you give it him ?
Diana.   I never gave it him.
Lafeu. This woman 's an easy glove, my lord ;
she goes off and on at pleasure.
King. This ring was mine ; I gave it his first
wife.
Diana. It might be yours or hers, for aught I
know.
King. Take her away ; I do not like her now ;
To prison with her : and away with him.
Unless thou tell'st me where thou hadst this ring,
Thou diest within this hour.
Diana.   I 'll never tell you.
King. Take her away.
Diana.   I 'll put in bail, my liege.
King. I think thee now some common customer.
Diana. By Jove, if ever I knew man, 'twas you.
King. Wherefore hast thou accused him all this
while ?
Diana.   Because he 's guilty, and he is not
guilty :
He knows I am no maid, and he 'll swear to 't ;
I 'll swear I am a maid, and he knows not.
Great King, I am no strumpet, by my life ;
I am either maid, or else this old man's wife.
King. She does abuse our ears : to prison with
her.
Diana. Good mother, fetch my bail. Stay, royal
sir :   [*Exit* Widow.
The jeweller that owes the ring is sent for,
And he shall surety me. But for this lord,
Who hath abused me, as he knows himself,
Though yet he never harm'd me, here I quit him :
He knows himself my bed he hath defiled ;
And at that time he got his wife with child :
Dead though she be, she feels her young one kick :
So there 's my riddle : one that 's dead is quick :
And now behold the meaning.

Re-enter Widow, *with* HELENA.

King.   Is there no exorcist
Beguiles the truer office of mine eyes ?
Is 't real that I see ?
Helena.   No, my good lord ;
'Tis but the shadow of a wife you see,
The name and not the thing.
Bertram.   Both, both. O, pardon !
Helena. O my good lord, when I was like this
maid,
I found you wondrous kind. There is your ring ;
And, look you, here 's your letter : this it says :
' When from my finger you can get this ring
And are by me with child,' &c. This is done :
Will you be mine, now you are doubly won ?

Bertram. If she, my liege, can make me know
  this clearly,
I 'll love her dearly, ever, ever dearly.
  Helena. If it appear not plain and prove untrue,
Deadly divorce step between me and you !
O my dear mother, do I see you living ?
  Lafeu. Mine eyes smell onions ; I shall weep
  anon :
[*To Parolles*] Good Tom Drum, lend me a hand-
  kercher : so,
I thank thee : wait on me home, I 'll make sport
  with thee :
Let thy courtesies alone, they are scurvy ones.
  King. Let us from point to point this story know,
To make the even truth in pleasure flow.
[*To Diana*] If thou be'st yet a fresh uncropped
  flower,
Choose thou thy husband, and I 'll pay thy dower ;

For I can guess that by thy honest aid
Thou kept'st a wife herself, thyself a maid.
Of that and all the progress, more and less,
Resolvedly more leisure shall express :
All yet seems well ; and if it end so meet,
The bitter past, more welcome is the sweet.

  [Flourish.

EPILOGUE.

  King. The king's a beggar, now the play is done :
All is well ended, if this suit be won,
That you express content ; which we will pay,
With strife to please you, day exceeding day :
Ours be your patience then, and yours our parts ;
Your gentle hands lend us, and take our hearts.

  [Exeunt.

TWELFTH NIGHT; OR, WHAT YOU WILL

DRAMATIS PERSONÆ

ORSINO, Duke of Illyria.
SEBASTIAN, *brother to* Viola.
ANTONIO, a sea captain, *friend to* Sebastian.
A Sea Captain, *friend to* Viola.
VALENTINE, } *gentlemen attending on the*
CURIO, } Duke.
SIR TOBY BELCH, *uncle to* Olivia.
SIR ANDREW AGUECHEEK.
MALVOLIO, *steward to* Olivia.
FABIAN, } *servants to* Olivia.
FESTE, a Clown, }

OLIVIA.
VIOLA.
MARIA, Olivia's woman.

Lords, Priests, Sailors, Officers, Musicians, *and other*
Attendants.

SCENE : A city in Illyria, and the sea-coast near it.

ACT I.

SCENE I. *The* DUKE'S *palace.*

Enter DUKE, CURIO, *and other* Lords ; Musicians
attending.

Duke.

If music be the food of love, play on ;
Give me excess of it, that, surfeiting,
The appetite may sicken, and so die.
That strain again ! it had a dying fall :
O, it came o'er my ear like the sweet sound,
That breathes upon a bank of violets,
Stealing and giving odour ! no more :
'Tis not so sweet now as it was before.
O spirit of love ! how quick and fresh art thou,
That, notwithstanding thy capacity
Receiveth as the sea, nought enters there,
Of what validity and pitch soe'er,
But falls into abatement and low price,
Even in a minute : so full of shapes is fancy
That it alone is high fantastical.
    Curio. Will you go hunt, my lord ?
    Duke.   What, Curio ?
    Curio. The hart.
    Duke. Why, so I do, the noblest that I have :
O, when mine eyes did see Olivia first,
Methought she purged the air of pestilence !

That instant was I turn'd into a hart ;
And my desires, like fell and cruel hounds,
E'er since pursue me.

Enter VALENTINE.

              How now! what news from her ?
    Valentine. So please my lord, I might not be
    admitted ;
But from her handmaid do return this answer :
The element itself, till seven years' heat,
Shall not behold her face at ample view ;
But, like a cloistress, she will veiled walk
And water once a day her chamber round
With eye-offending brine : all this to season
A brother's dead love, which she would keep fresh
And lasting in her sad remembrance.
    Duke. O, she that hath a heart of that fine frame
To pay this debt of love but to a brother,
How will she love, when the rich golden shaft
Hath kill'd the flock of all affections else
That live in her ; when liver, brain and heart,
These sovereign thrones, are all supplied, and fill'd
Her sweet perfections with one self king !
Away before me to sweet beds of flowers :
Love-thoughts lie rich when canopied with bowers.
                            [Exeunt.

SCENE II. *The sea-coast.*

Enter VIOLA, *a* Captain, *and* Sailors.

    Viola. What country, friends, is this ?
    Captain. This is Illyria, lady.
    Viola. And what should I do in Illyria ?
My brother he is in Elysium.
Perchance he is not drown'd : what think you,
    sailors ?
    Captain. It is perchance that you yourself were
    saved.
    Viola. O my poor brother ! and so perchance
    may he be.
    Captain. True, madam : and, to comfort you
    with chance,
Assure yourself, after our ship did split,
When you and those poor number saved with you
Hung on our driving boat, I saw your brother,
Most provident in peril, bind himself,
Courage and hope both teaching him the practice,
To a strong mast that lived upon the sea ;
Where, like Arion on the dolphin's back,
I saw him hold acquaintance with the waves
So long as I could see.
    Viola. For saying so, there 's gold :
Mine own escape unfoldeth to my hope,
Whereto thy speech serves for authority,
The like of him. Know'st thou this country ?

Captain. Ay, madam, well ; for I was bred and
born
Not three hours' travel from this very place.
Viola. Who governs here ?
Captain. A noble duke, in nature as in name.
Viola. What is his name ?
Captain. Orsino.
Viola. Orsino ! I have heard my father name
him :
He was a bachelor then.
Captain. And so is now, or was so very late ;
For but a month ago I went from hence,
And then 'twas fresh in murmur,—as, you know,
What great ones do the less will prattle of,—
That he did seek the love of fair Olivia.
Viola. What 's she ?
Captain. A virtuous maid, the daughter of a
count
That died some twelvemonth since, then leaving her
In the protection of his son, her brother,
Who shortly also died : for whose dear love,
They say, she hath abjured the company
And sight of men.
Viola.   O, that I served that lady
And might not be delivered to the world,
Till I had made mine own occasion mellow,
What my estate is !
Captain.   That were hard to compass ;
Because she will admit no kind of suit,
No, not the duke's.
Viola. There is a fair behaviour in thee, captain ;
And though that nature with a beauteous wall
Doth oft close in pollution, yet of thee
I will believe thou hast a mind that suits
With this thy fair and outward character.
I prithee, and I 'll pay thee bounteously,
Conceal me what I am, and be my aid
For such disguise as haply shall become
The form of my intent. I 'll serve this duke :
Thou shalt present me as an eunuch to him :
It may be worth thy pains ; for I can sing
And speak to him in many sorts of music
That will allow me very worth his service.
What else may hap to time I will commit ;
Only shape thou thy silence to my wit.
Captain. Be you his eunuch, and your mute
I 'll be :
When my tongue blabs, then let mine eyes not see.
Viola. I thank thee : lead me on.   [*Exeunt.*

SCENE III.   OLIVIA'S *house.*

Enter SIR TOBY BELCH *and* MARIA.

Sir Toby. What a plague means my niece, to
take the death of her brother thus ? I am sure care 's
an enemy to life.
Maria. By my troth, Sir Toby, you must come
in earlier o' nights : your cousin, my lady, takes
great exceptions to your ill hours.
Sir Toby. Why, let her except, before excepted.
Maria. Ay, but you must confine yourself within
the modest limits of order.
Sir Toby. Confine ! I 'll confine myself no finer
than I am : these clothes are good enough to drink
in ; and so be these boots too : an they be not,
let them hang themselves in their own straps.
Maria. That quaffing and drinking will undo
you : I heard my lady talk of it yesterday ; and of a
foolish knight that you brought in one night here
to be her wooer.
Sir Toby. Who, Sir Andrew Aguecheek ?

Maria. Ay, he.
Sir Toby. He 's as tall a man as any 's in Illyria.
Maria. What 's that to the purpose ?
Sir Toby. Why, he has three thousand ducats
a year.
Maria. Ay, but he 'll have but a year in all these
ducats : he 's a very fool and a prodigal.
Sir Toby. Fie, that you 'll say so ! he plays o'
the viol-de-gamboys, and speaks three or four
languages word for word without book, and hath
all the good gifts of nature.
Maria. He hath indeed, almost natural : for
besides that he 's a fool, he 's a great quarreller ;
and but that he hath the gift of a coward to allay
the gust he hath in quarrelling, 'tis thought among
the prudent he would quickly have the gift of a
grave.
Sir Toby. By this hand, they are scoundrels and
substractors that say so of him. Who are they ?
Maria. They that add, moreover, he 's drunk
nightly in your company.
Sir Toby. With drinking healths to my niece :
I 'll drink to her as long as there is a passage in my
throat and drink in Illyria : he 's a coward and a
coystrill that will not drink to my niece till his brains
turn o' the toe like a parish-top. What, wench !
Castiliano vulgo ! for here comes Sir Andrew
Agueface.

Enter SIR ANDREW AGUECHEEK.

Sir Andrew. Sir Toby Belch ! how now, Sir
Toby Belch !
Sir Toby. Sweet Sir Andrew !
Sir Andrew. Bless you, fair shrew.
Maria. And you too, sir.
Sir Toby. Accost, Sir Andrew, accost.
Sir Andrew. What 's that ?
Sir Toby. My niece's chambermaid.
Sir Andrew. Good Mistress Accost, I desire
better acquaintance.
Maria. My name is Mary, sir.
Sir Andrew. Good Mistress Mary Accost,—
Sir Toby. You mistake, knight : ' accost ' is
front her, board her, woo her, assail her.
Sir Andrew. By my troth, I would not undertake
her in this company. Is that the meaning of ' accost '?
Maria. Fare you well, gentlemen.
Sir Toby. An thou let part so, Sir Andrew,
would thou mightst never draw sword again.
Sir Andrew. An you part so, mistress, I would I
might never draw sword again. Fair lady, do you
think you have fools in hand ?
Maria. Sir, I have not you by the hand.
Sir Andrew. Marry, but you shall have ; and
here 's my hand.
Maria. Now, sir, ' thought is free :' I pray you,
bring your hand to the buttery-bar and let it drink.
Sir Andrew. Wherefore, sweet-heart ? what 's
your metaphor ?
Maria. It 's dry, sir.
Sir Andrew. Why, I think so : I am not such an
ass but I can keep my hand dry. But what 's your
jest ?
Maria. A dry jest, sir.
Sir Andrew. Are you full of them ?
Maria. Ay, sir, I have them at my fingers' ends :
marry, now I let go your hand, I am barren. [*Exit.*
Sir Toby. O knight, thou lackest a cup of canary :
when did I see thee so put down ?
Sir Andrew. Never in your life, I think ; unless

you see canary put me down. Methinks sometimes I have no more wit than a Christian or an ordinary man has : but I am a great eater of beef and I believe that does harm to my wit.

Sir Toby. No question.

Sir Andrew. An I thought that, I 'ld forswear it. I 'll ride home to-morrow, Sir Toby.

Sir Toby. Pourquoi, my dear knight ?

Sir Andrew. What is ' pourquoi ' ? do or not do ? I would I had bestowed that time in the tongues that I have in fencing, dancing and bear-baiting : O, had I but followed the arts !

Sir Toby. Then hadst thou had an excellent head of hair.

Sir Andrew. Why, would that have mended my hair ?

Sir Toby. Past question ; for thou seest it will not curl by nature.

Sir Andrew. But it becomes me well enough, does 't not ?

Sir Toby. Excellent ; it hangs like flax on a distaff ; and I hope to see a housewife take thee between her legs and spin it off.

Sir Andrew. Faith, I 'll home to-morrow, Sir Toby : your niece will not be seen ; or if she be, it 's four to one she 'll none of me : the count himself here hard by woos her.

Sir Toby. She 'll none o' the count : she 'll not match above her degree, neither in estate, years, nor wit ; I have heard her swear 't. Tut, there 's life in 't, man.

Sir Andrew. I 'll stay a month longer. I am a fellow o' the strangest mind i' the world ; I delight in masques and revels sometimes altogether.

Sir Toby. Art thou good at these kickshawses, knight ?

Sir Andrew. As any man in Illyria, whatsoever he be, under the degree of my betters ; and yet I will not compare with an old man.

Sir Toby. What is thy excellence in a galliard, knight ?

Sir Andrew. Faith, I can cut a caper.

Sir Toby. And I can cut the mutton to 't.

Sir Andrew. And I think I have the back-trick simply as strong as any man in Illyria.

Sir Toby. Wherefore are these things hid ? wherefore have these gifts a curtain before 'em ? are they like to take dust, like Mistress Mall's picture ? why dost thou not go to church in a galliard and come home in a coranto ? My very walk should be a jig ; I would not so much as make water but in a sink-a-pace. What dost thou mean ? Is it a world to hide virtues in ? I did think, by the excellent constitution of thy leg, it was formed under the star of a galliard.

Sir Andrew. Ay, 'tis strong, and it does indifferent well in a flame-coloured stock. Shall we set about some revels ?

Sir Toby. What shall we do else ? were we not born under Taurus ?

Sir Andrew. Taurus ! That 's sides and heart.

Sir Toby. No, sir ; it is legs and. thighs. Let me see thee caper : ha ! higher : ha, ha ! excellent !   [*Exeunt.*

SCENE IV. *The* DUKE's *palace.*

Enter VALENTINE, *and* VIOLA *in man's attire.*

Valentine. If the duke continue these favours towards you, Cesario, you are like to be much advanced:

he hath known you but three days, and already you are no stranger.

Viola. You either fear his humour or my negligence, that you call in question the continuance of his love : is he inconstant, sir, in his favours ?

Valentine. No, believe me.

Viola. I thank you. Here comes the count.

Enter DUKE, CURIO, *and* Attendants.

Duke. Who saw Cesario, ho ?

Viola. On your attendance, my lord ; here.

Duke. Stand you a while aloof. Cesario, Thou know'st no less but all ; I have unclasp'd To thee the book even of my secret soul : Therefore, good youth, address thy gait unto her ; Be not denied access, stand at her doors, And tell them, there thy fixed foot shall grow Till thou have audience.

Viola.   Sure, my noble lord, If she be so abandon'd to her sorrow As it is spoke, she never will admit me.

Duke. Be clamorous and leap all civil bounds Rather than make unprofited return.

Viola. Say I do speak with her, my lord, what then ?

Duke. O, then unfold the passion of my love, Surprise her with discourse of my dear faith : It shall become thee well to act my woes ; She will attend it better in thy youth Than in a nuncio's of more grave aspect.

Viola. I think not so, my lord.

Duke.   Dear lad, believe it ; For they shall yet belie thy happy years, That say thou art a man : Diana's lip Is not more smooth and rubious ; thy small pipe Is as the maiden's organ, shrill and sound, And all is semblative a woman's part. I know thy constellation is right apt For this affair. Some four or five attend him ; All, if you will ; for I myself am best When least in company. Prosper well in this, And thou shalt live as freely as thy lord, To call his fortunes thine.

Viola.   I 'll do my best To woo your lady : [*Aside*] yet, a barful strife ! Whoe'er I woo, myself would be his wife.

[*Exeunt.*

SCENE V. OLIVIA'S *house.*

Enter MARIA *and* CLOWN.

Maria. Nay, either tell me where thou hast been, or I will not open my lips so wide as a bristle may enter in way of thy excuse : my lady will hang thee for thy absence.

Clown. Let her hang me : he that is well hanged in this world needs to fear no colours.

Maria. Make that good.

Clown. He shall see none to fear.

Maria. A good lenten answer : I can tell thee where that saying was born, of ' I fear no colours.'

Clown. Where, good Mistress Mary ?

Maria. In the wars ; and that may you be bold to say in your foolery.

Clown. Well, God give them wisdom that have it ; and those that are fools, let them use their talents.

Maria. Yet you will be hanged for being so long absent ; or to be turned away, is not that as good as a hanging to you?

Clown. Many a good hanging prevents a bad marriage ; and, for turning away, let summer bear it out.

Maria. You are resolute, then?

Clown. Not so, neither ; but I am resolved on two points.

Maria. That if one break the other will hold ; or, if both break, your gaskins fall.

Clown. Apt, in good faith ; very apt. Well, go thy way ; if Sir Toby would leave drinking, thou wert as witty a piece of Eve's flesh as any in Illyria.

Maria. Peace, you rogue, no more o' that. Here comes my lady : make your excuse wisely, you were best.   [*Exit.*

Clown. Wit, an 't be thy will, put me into good fooling ! Those wits, that think they have thee, do very oft prove fools ; and I, that am sure I lack thee, may pass for a wise man : for what says Quinapalus ? ' Better a witty fool than a foolish wit.'

Enter Lady OLIVIA *with* MALVOLIO.

God bless thee, lady !

Olivia. Take the fool away.

Clown. Do you not hear, fellows ? Take away the lady.

Olivia. Go to, you 're a dry fool ; I 'll no more of you : besides, you grow dishonest.

Clown. Two faults, madonna, that drink and good counsel will amend : for give the dry fool drink, then is the fool not dry : bid the dishonest man mend himself ; if he mend, he is no longer dishonest : if he cannot let the botcher mend him. Any thing that 's mended is but patched : virtue that transgresses is but patched with sin ; and sin that amends is but patched with virtue. If that this simple syllogism will serve, so ; if it will not, what remedy ? As there is no true cuckold but calamity, so beauty 's a flower. The lady bade take away the fool ; therefore, I say again, take her away.

Olivia. Sir, I bade them take away the fool.

Clown. Misprision in the highest degree! Lady, cucullus non facit monachum ; that 's as much to say as I wear not motley in my brain. Good madonna, give me leave to prove you a fool.

Olivia. Can you do it ?

Clown. Dexteriously, good madonna.

Olivia. Make your proof.

Clown. I must catechize you for it, madonna : good my mouse of virtue, answer me.

Olivia. Well, sir, for want of other dleness, I 'll bide your proof.

Clown. Good madonna, why mournest thou ?

Olivia. Good fool, for my brother's death.

Clown. I think his soul is in hell, madonna.

Olivia. I know his soul is in heaven, fool.

Clown. The more fool, madonna, to mourn for your brother's soul being in heaven. Take away the fool, gentlemen.

Olivia. What think you of this fool, Malvolio ? doth he not mend ?

Malvolio. Yes, and shall do till the pangs of death shake him : infirmity, that decays the wise, doth ever make the better fool.

Clown. God send you, sir, a speedy infirmity, for the better increasing your folly ! Sir Toby wil be sworn that I am no fox ; but he will not pass his word for two pence that you are no fool.

Olivia. How say you to that, Malvolio ?

Malvolio. I marvel your ladyship takes delight in such a barren rascal : I saw him put down the other day with an ordinary fool that has no more brain than a stone. Look you now, he 's out of his guard already ; unless you laugh and minister occasion to him, he is gagged. I protest, I take these wise men, that crow so at these set kind of fools, no better than the fools' zanies.

Olivia. O, you are sick of self-love, Malvolio, and taste with a distempered appetite. To be generous, guiltless and of free disposition, is to take those things for bird-bolts that you deem cannon-bullets : there is no slander in an allowed fool, though he do nothing but rail ; nor no railing in a known discreet man, though he do nothing but reprove.

Clown. Now Mercury endue thee with leasing, for thou speakest well of fools !

Re-enter MARIA.

Maria. Madam, there is at the gate a young gentleman much desires to speak with you.

Olivia. From the Count Orsino is it ?

Maria. know not, madam : 'tis a fair young man, and well attended.

Olivia. Who of my people hold him in delay ?

Maria. Sir Toby, madam, your kinsman.

Olivia. Fetch him off, I pray you ; he speaks nothing but madman : fie on him ! [*Exit Maria.*] Go you, Malvolio, if it be a suit from the count, I am sick, or not at home ; what you will, to dismiss it. [*Exit Malvolio.*] Now you see, sir, how your fooling grows old, and people dislike it.

Clown. Thou hast spoke for us, madonna, as if thy eldest son should be a fool ; whose skull Jove cram with brains ! for,—here he comes,—one of thy kin has a most weak pia mater.

Enter SIR TOBY.

Olivia. By mine honour, half drunk. What is he at the gate, cousin ?

Sir Toby. A gentleman.

Olivia. A gentleman ! what gentleman ?

Sir Toby. 'Tis a gentleman here—a plague o' these pickle-herring ! How now, sot !

Clown. Good Sir Toby !

Olivia. Cousin, cousin, how have you come so early by this lethargy ?

Sir Toby. Lechery ! I defy lechery. There 's one at the gate.

Olivia. Ay, marry, what is he ?

Sir Toby. Let him be the devil, an he will, I care not : give me faith, say I. Well, it 's all one.
                                      [*Exit.*

Olivia. What 's a drunken man like, fool ?

Clown. Like a drowned man, a fool and a mad man : one draught above heat makes him a fool ; the second mads him ; and a third drowns him.

Olivia. Go thou and seek the crowner, and let him sit o' my coz ; for he 's in the third degree of drink, he 's drowned : go, look after him.

Clown. He is but mad yet, madonna ; and the fool shall look to the madman.   [*Exit.*

Re-enter MALVOLIO.

Malvolio. Madam, yond young fellow swears he will speak with you. I told him you were sick ; he takes on him to understand so much, and therefore comes to speak with you. I told him you were asleep ; he seems to have a foreknowledge of that too, and therefore comes to speak with you. What is to be said to him, lady ? he 's fortified against any denial.

Olivia. Tell him he shall not speak with me.

Malvolio. Has been told so ; and he says, he 'll stand at your door like a sheriff's post, and be the supporter to a bench, but he 'll speak with you.

Olivia. What kind o' man is he ?

Malvolio. Why, of mankind.

Olivia. What manner of man ?

Malvolio. Of very ill manner ; he 'll speak with you, will you or no.

Olivia. Of what personage and years is he ?

Malvolio. Not yet old enough for a man, nor young enough for a boy ; as a squash is before 'tis a peascod, or a codling when 'tis almost an apple : 'tis with him in standing water, between boy and man. He is very well-favoured and he speaks very shrewishly ; one would think his mother's milk were scarce out of him.

Olivia. Let him approach : call in my gentlewoman.

Malvolio. Gentlewoman, my lady calls.　　[*Exit.*

Re-enter Maria.

Olivia. Give me my veil : come, throw it o'er my face.
We 'll once more hear Orsino's embassy.

Enter Viola, *and* Attendants.

Viola. The honourable lady of the house, which is she ?

Olivia. Speak to me ; I shall answer for her. Your will ?

Viola. Most radiant, exquisite and unmatchable beauty,—I pray you, tell me if this be the lady of the house, for I never saw her : I would be loath to cast away my speech, for besides that it is excellently well penned, I have taken great pains to con it. Good beauties, let me sustain no scorn ; I am very comptible, even to the least sinister usage.

Olivia. Whence came you, sir ?

Viola. I can say little more than I have studied, and that question 's out of my part. Good gentle one, give me modest assurance if you be the lady of the house, that I may proceed in my speech.

Olivia. Are you a comedian ?

Viola. No, my profound heart : and yet, by the very fangs of malice I swear, I am not that I play. Are you the lady of the house ?

Olivia. If I do not usurp myself, I am.

Viola. Most certain, if you are she, you do usurp yourself ; for what is yours to bestow is not yours to reserve. But this is from my commission : I will on with my speech in your praise, and then show you the heart of my message.

Olivia. Come to what is important in 't : I forgive you the praise.

Viola. Alas, I took great pains to study it, and 'tis poetical.

Olivia. It is the more like to be feigned : I pray you, keep it in. I heard you were saucy at my gates, and allowed your approach rather to wonder at you than to hear you. If you be not mad, be gone ; if you have reason, be brief : 'tis not that time of moon with me to make one in so skipping a dialogue.

Maria. Will you hoist sail, sir ? here lies your way.

Viola. No, good swabber ; I am to hull here a little longer. Some mollification for your giant, sweet lady. Tell me your mind : I am a messenger.

Olivia. Sure, you have some hideous matter to deliver, when the courtesy of it is so fearful. Speak your office.

Viola. It alone concerns your ear. I bring no overture of war, no taxation of homage : I hold the olive in my hand ; my words are as full of peace as matter.

Olivia. Yet you began rudely. What are you ? what would you ?

Viola. The rudeness that hath appeared in me have I learned from my entertainment. What I am, and what I would, are as secret as maidenhead; to your ears, divinity, to any other's, profanation.

Olivia. Give us the place alone ; we will hear this divinity. [*Exeunt Maria and Attendants.*] Now, sir, what is your text ?

Viola. Most sweet lady,—

Olivia. A comfortable doctrine, and much may be said of it. Where lies your text ?

Viola. In Orsino's bosom.

Olivia. In his bosom ! In what chapter of his bosom ?

Viola. To answer by the method, in the first of his heart.

Olivia. O, I have read it : it is heresy. Have you no more to say ?

Viola. Good madam, let me see your face.

Olivia. Have you any commission from your lord to negotiate with my face ? You are now out of your text : but we will draw the curtain and show you the picture. Look you, sir, such a one I was this present : is 't not well done ?　　[*Unveiling.*

Viola. Excellently done, if God did all.

Olivia. 'Tis in grain, sir ; 'twill endure wind and weather.

Viola. 'Tis beauty truly blent, whose red and white
Nature's own sweet and cunning hand laid on :
Lady, you are the cruell'st she alive,
If you will lead these graces to the grave
And leave the world no copy.

Olivia. O, sir, I will not be so hard-hearted ; I will give out divers schedules of my beauty : it shall be inventoried, and every particle and utensil labelled to my will : as, item, two lips, indifferent red ; item, two grey eyes, with lids to them ; item, one neck, one chin, and so forth. Were you sent hither to praise me ?

Viola. I see you what you are, you are too proud ;
But, if you were the devil, you are fair.
My lord and master loves you : O, such love
Could be but recompensed, though you were crown'd
The nonpareil of beauty !

Olivia.　　　　　　　How does he love me ?

Viola. With adorations, fertile tears,
With groans that thunder love, with sighs of fire.

Olivia. Your lord does know my mind ; I cannot love him :
Yet I suppose him virtuous, know him noble,
Of great estate, of fresh and stainless youth ;
In voices well divulged, free, learn'd and valiant ;
And in dimension and the shape of nature
A gracious person : but yet I cannot love him ;
He might have took his answer long ago.

Viola. If I did love you in my master's flame,
With such a suffering, such a deadly life,
In your denial I would find no sense ;
I would not understand it.
Olivia.   Why, what would you ?
Viola. Make me a willow cabin at your gate,
And call upon my soul within the house ;
Write loyal cantons of contemned love
And sing them loud even in the dead of night ;
Halloo your name to the reverberate hills
And make the babbling gossip of the air
Cry out ' Olivia ! ' O, you should not rest
Between the elements of air and earth,
But you should pity me !
Olivia.   You might do much.
What is your parentage ?
Viola. Above my fortunes, yet my state is well :
I am a gentleman.
Olivia.   Get you to your lord ;
I cannot love him : let him send no more ;
Unless, perchance, you come to me again,
To tell me how he takes it. Fare you well ;
I thank you for your pains : spend this for me.
Viola. I am no fee'd post, lady ; keep your purse :
My master, not myself, lacks recompense.
Love make his heart of flint that you shall love ;
And let your fervour, like my master's, be
Placed in contempt ! Farewell, fair cruelty.
                                          [*Exit.*

Olivia. ' What is your parentage ?
Above my fortunes, yet my state is well :
I am a gentleman.' I 'll be sworn thou art ;
Thy tongue, thy face, thy limbs, actions and spirit,
Do give thee five-fold blazon : not too fast ; soft,
    soft !
Unless the master were the man. How now !
Even so quickly may one catch the plague ?
Methinks I feel this youth's perfections
With an invisible and subtle stealth
To creep in at mine eyes. Well, let it be.
What ho, Malvolio !

Re-enter MALVOLIO.

Malvolio.   Here, madam, at your service.
Olivia. Run after that same peevish messenger,
The county's man : he left this ring behind him,
Would I or not : tell him I 'll none of it.
Desire him not to flatter with his lord,
Nor hold him up with hopes ; I am not for him :
If that the youth will come this way to-morrow,
I 'll give him reasons for 't : hie thee. Malvolio.
Malvolio. Madam, I will.   [*Exit.*
Olivia. I do I know not what, and fear to find
Mine eye too great a flatterer for my mind.
Fate, show thy force : ourselves we do not owe ;
What is decreed must be. and be this so.   [*Exit.*

ACT II.

SCENE I.   *The sea-coast.*

Enter ANTONIO and SEBASTIAN.

Antonio.

Will you stay no longer ? nor will you not
    that I go with you ?
    Sebastian. By your patience, no. My stars
shine darkly over me : the malignancy of my fate might
perhaps distemper yours ; therefore I shall crave

of you your leave that I may bear my evils alone :
it were a bad recompense for your love, to lay any
of them on you.
Antonio. Let me yet know of you whither you
are bound.
Sebastian. No, sooth, sir : my determinate voyage
is mere extravagancy. But I perceive in you so
excellent a touch of modesty, that you will not
extort from me what I am willing to keep in ; therefore it charges me in manners the rather to express
myself. You must know of me then, Antonio, my
name is Sebastian, which I called Roderigo. My
father was that Sebastian of Messaline, whom I
know you have heard of. He left behind him myself
and a sister, both born in an hour : if the heavens
had been pleased, would we had so ended ! but you,
sir, altered that ; for some hour before you took
me from the breach of the sea was my sister drowned.
Antonio. Alas the day !
Sebastian. A lady, sir, though it was said she much
resembled me, was yet of many accounted beautiful : but, though I could not with such estimable
wonder overfar believe that, yet thus far I will boldly
publish her ; she bore a mind that envy could not
but call fair. She is drowned already, sir, with salt
water, though I seem to drown her remembrance
again with more.
Antonio. Pardon me, sir, your bad entertainment.
Sebastian. O good Antonio, forgive me your
trouble.
Antonio. If you will not murder me for my love,
let me be your servant.
Sebastian. If you will not undo what you have
done, that is, kill him whom you have recovered,
desire it not. Fare ye well at once : my bosom is
full of kindness, and I am yet so near the manners
of my mother, that upon the least occasion more
mine eyes will tell tales of me. I am bound to the
Count Orsino's court : farewell.   [*Exit.*
Antonio. The gentleness of all the gods go with
    thee !
I have many enemies in Orsino's court,
Else would I very shortly see thee there.
But, come what may, I do adore thee so,
That danger shall seem sport, and I will go.
                                          [*Exit.*

SCENE II.   *A street.*

Enter VIOLA, MALVOLIO *following.*

Malvolio. Were not you even now with the
Countess Olivia ?
Viola. Even now, sir ; on a moderate pace I
have since arrived but hither.
Malvolio. She returns this ring to you, sir : you
might have saved me my pains, to have taken it
away yourself. She adds, moreover, that you
should put your lord into a desperate assurance she
will none of him : and one thing more, that you be
never so hardy to come again in his affairs, unless
it be to report your lord's taking of this. Receive
it so.
Viola. She took the ring of me : I 'll none of it.
Malvolio. Come, sir, you peevishly threw it to
her ; and her will is, it should be so returned : if
it be worth stooping for, there it lies in your eye ;
if not, be it his that finds it.   [*Exit.*
Viola. I left no ring with her : what means
    this lady ?

Fortune forbid my outside have not charm'd her !
She made good view of me ; indeed, so much,
That sure methought her eyes had lost her tongue,
For she did speak in starts distractedly.
She loves me, sure ; the cunning of her passion
Invites me in this churlish messenger.
None of my lord's ring ! why, he sent her none.
I am the man : if it be so, as 'tis,
Poor lady, she were better love a dream.
Disguise, I see, thou art a wickedness,
Wherein the pregnant enemy does much.
How easy is it for the proper-false
In women's waxen hearts to set their forms !
Alas, our frailty is the cause, not we !
For such as we are made of, such we be.
How will this fadge ? my master loves her dearly ;
And I, poor monster, fond as much on him ;
And she, mistaken, seems to dote on me.
What will become of this ? As I am man,
My state is desperate for my master's love ;
As I am woman,—now alas the day !—
What thriftless sighs shall poor Olivia breathe !
O time ! thou must untangle this, not I ;
It is too hard a knot for me to untie !   [*Exit.*

SCENE III. OLIVIA'S *house.*

Enter SIR TOBY *and* SIR ANDREW.

Sir Toby. Approach, Sir Andrew : not to be
abed after midnight is to be up betimes ; and ' dilu-
culo surgere,' thou know'st,—
Sir Andrew. Nay, by my troth, I know not ;
but I know, to be up late is to be up late.
Sir Toby. A false conclusion : I hate it as an
unfilled can. To be up after midnight and to go
to bed then, is early : so that to go to bed after
midnight is to go to bed betimes. Does not our life
consist of the four elements ?
Sir Andrew. Faith, so they say ; but I think it
rather consists of eating and drinking.
Sir Toby. Thou 'rt a scholar ; let us therefore
eat and drink. Marian, I say ! a stoup of wine !

Enter CLOWN.

Sir Andrew. Here comes the fool, i' faith.
Clown. How now, my hearts ! did you never
see the picture of ' we three ' ?
Sir Toby. Welcome, ass. Now let 's have a
catch.
Sir Andrew. By my troth, the fool has an excellent breast. I had rather than forty shillings I
had such a leg, and so sweet a breath to sing, as the
fool has. In sooth, thou wast in very gracious fooling last night, when thou spokest of Pigrogromitus,
of the Vapians passing the equinoctial of Queubus :
'twas very good, i' faith. I sent thee sixpence for
thy leman : hadst it ?
Clown. I did impeticos thy gratillity ; for Malvolio's nose is no whipstock : my lady has a white
hand, and the Myrmidons are no bottle-ale houses.
Sir Andrew. Excellent ! why, this is the best
fooling, when all is done. Now, a song.
Sir Toby. Come on ; there is sixpence for you :
let 's have a song.
Sir Andrew. There 's a testril of me too : if one
knight give a—
Clown. Would you have a love-song, or a song
of good life ?
Sir Toby. A love-song, a love-song.

Sir Andrew. Ay, ay : I care not for good life.
Clown. [*Sings*]
O mistress mine, where are you roaming ?
O, stay and hear ; your true love 's coming,
    That can sing both high and low :
Trip no further, pretty sweeting ;
Journeys end in lovers meeting,
    Every wise man's son doth know.
Sir Andrew. Excellent good, i' faith.
Sir Toby. Good, good.
Clown. [*Sings*]
What is love ? 'tis not hereafter ;
Present mirth hath present laughter ;
    What 's to come is still unsure :
In delay there lies no plenty ;
Then come kiss me, sweet and twenty,
    Youth 's a stuff will not endure.
Sir Andrew. A mellifluous voice, as I am true
knight.
Sir Toby. A contagious breath.
Sir Andrew. Very sweet and contagious, i' faith.
Sir Toby. To hear by the nose, it is dulcet in
contagion. But shall we make the welkin dance
indeed ? shall we rouse the night-owl in a catch
that will draw three souls out of one weaver ? shall
we do that ?
Sir Andrew. An you love me, let 's do 't : I am
dog at a catch.
Clown. By 'r lady, sir, and some dogs will catch
well.
Sir Andrew. Most certain. Let our catch be,
' Thou knave.'
Clown. ' Hold thy peace, thou knave,' knight ?
I shall be constrained in 't to call thee knave, knight.
Sir Andrew. 'Tis not the first time I have con-
strained one to call me knave. Begin, fool : it
begins ' Hold thy peace.'
Clown. I shall never begin if I hold my peace.
Sir Andrew. Good, i' faith. Come, begin.
                                        [*Catch sung.*

Enter MARIA.

Maria. What a caterwauling do you keep here !
If my lady have not called up her steward Malvolio
and bid him turn you out of doors, never trust me.
Sir Toby. My lady 's a Cataian, we are politi-
cians, Malvolio 's a Peg-a-Ramsey, and ' Three
merry men be we.' Am not I consanguineous ? am
I not of her blood ? Tillyvally. Lady ! [*Sings*]
' There dwelt a man in Babylon, lady, lady ! '
Clown. Beshrew me, the knight 's in admirable
fooling.
Sir Andrew. Ay, he does well enough if he be
disposed, and so do I too : he does it with a better
grace, but I do it more natural.
Sir Toby. [*Sings*] ' O, the twelfth day of Dec-
ember,'—
Maria. For the love o' God, peace !

Enter MALVOLIO.

Malvolio. My masters, are you mad ? or what
are you ? Have you no wit, manners, nor honesty,
but to gabble like tinkers at this time of night ?
Do ye make an alehouse of my lady's house, that
ye squeak out your coziers' catches without any
mitigation or remorse of voice ? Is there no respect
of place, persons, nor time in you ?
Sir Toby. We did keep time, sir, in our catches.
Sneck up !

Malvolio. Sir Toby, I must be round with you. My lady bade me tell you, that, though she harbours you as her kinsman, she's nothing allied to your disorders. If you can separate yourself and your misdemeanours, you are welcome to the house ; if not, an it would please you to take leave of her, she is very willing to bid you farewell.

Sir Toby. 'Farewell, dear heart, since I must needs be gone.'

Maria. Nay, good Sir Toby.

Clown. 'His eyes do show his days are almost done.'

Malvolio. Is 't even so ?

Sir Toby. 'But I will never die.'

Clown. Sir Toby, there you lie.

Malvolio. This is much credit to you.

Sir Toby. 'Shall I bid him go ?'

Clown. 'What an if you do ? '

Sir Toby. 'Shall I bid him go, and spare not ? '

Clown. 'O no, no, no, no, you dare not.'

Sir Toby. Out o' tune, sir : ye lie. Art any more than a steward ? Dost thou think, because thou art virtuous, there shall be no more cakes and ale ?

Clown. Yes, by Saint Anne, and ginger shall be hot i' the mouth too.

Sir Toby. Thou 'rt i' the right. Go, sir, rub your chain with crums. A stoup of wine, Maria !

Malvolio. Mistress Mary, if you prized my lady's favour at any thing more than contempt, you would not give means for this uncivil rule : she shall know of it, by this hand.   [*Exit.*

Maria. Go shake your ears.

Sir Andrew. 'Twere as good a deed as to drink when a man 's a-hungry, to challenge him the field, and then to break promise with him and make a fool of him.

Sir Toby. Do 't, knight, I 'll write thee a challenge ; or I 'll deliver thy indignation to him by word of mouth.

Maria. Sweet Sir Toby, be patient for to-night : since the youth of the count's was to-day with my lady, she is much out of quiet. For Monsieur Malvolio, let me alone with him : if I do not gull him into a nayword, and make him a common recreation, do not think I have wit enough to lie straight in my bed : I know I can do it.

Sir Toby. Possess us, possess us ; tell us something of him.

Maria. Marry, sir, sometimes he is a kind of puritan.

Sir Andrew. O, if I thought that, I 'ld beat him like a dog !

Sir Toby. What, for being a puritan ? thy exquisite reason, dear knight ?

Sir Andrew. I have no exquisite reason for 't, but I have reason good enough.

Maria. The devil a puritan that he is, or any thing constantly, but a time-pleaser ; an affectioned ass, that cons state without book and utters it by great swarths : the best persuaded of himself, so crammed, as he thinks, with excellencies, that it is his grounds of faith that all that look on him love him ; and on that vice in him will my revenge find notable cause to work.

Sir Toby. What wilt thou do ?

Maria. I will drop in his way some obscure epistles of love ; wherein, by the colour of his beard, the shape of his leg, the manner of his gait, the expressure of his eye, forehead, and complexion,

he shall find himself most feelingly personated. I can write very like my lady your niece : on a forgotten matter we can hardly make distinction of our hands.

Sir Toby. Excellent ! I smell a device.

Sir Andrew. I have 't in my nose too.

Sir Toby. He shall think, by the letters that thou wilt drop, that they come from my niece, and that she 's in love with him.

Maria. My purpose is, indeed, a horse of that colour.

Sir Andrew. And your horse now would make him an ass.

Maria. Ass, I doubt not.

Sir Andrew. O, 'twill be admirable !

Maria. Sport royal, I warrant you : I know my physic will work with him. I will plant you two, and let the fool make a third, where he shall find the letter ; observe his construction of it. For this night, to bed, and dream on the event. Farewell.   [*Exit.*

Sir Toby. Good night, Penthesilea.

Sir Andrew. Before me, she 's a good wench.

Sir Toby. She 's a beagle, true-bred, and one that adores me : what o' that ?

Sir Andrew. I was adored once too.

Sir Toby. Let 's to bed, knight. Thou hadst need send for more money.

Sir Andrew. If I cannot recover your niece, I am a foul way out.

Sir Toby. Send for money, knight : if thou hast her not i' the end, call me cut.

Sir Andrew. If I do not, never trust me, take it how you will.

Sir Toby. Come, come, I 'll go burn some sack ; 'tis too late to go to bed now : come, knight ; come, knight.   [*Exeunt*

SCENE IV.   *The* Duke's *palace.*

Enter Duke, Viola, Curio, *and others.*

Duke. Give me some music. Now, good morrow, friends.
Now, good Cesario, but that piece of song,
That old and antique song we heard last night :
Methought it did relieve my passion much,
More than light airs and recollected terms
Of these most brisk and giddy-paced times :
Come, but one verse.

Curio. He is not here, so please your lordship, that should sing it.

Duke. Who was it ?

Curio. Feste, the jester, my lord ; a fool that the lady Olivia's father took much delight in. He is about the house.

Duke. Seek him out, and play the tune the while.   [*Exit Curio. Music plays.*
Come hither, boy : if ever thou shalt love,
In the sweet pangs of it remember me ;
For such as I am all true lovers are,
Unstaid and skittish in all motions else,
Save in the constant image of the creature
That is beloved. How dost thou like this tune ?

Viola. It gives a very echo to the seat
Where Love is throned.

Duke. Thou dost speak masterly :
My life upon 't, young though thou art, thine eye
Hath stay'd upon some favour that it loves :
Hath it not, boy ?

Viola.   A little, by your favour.
Duke.   What kind of woman is 't ?
Viola.·   Of your complexion.
Duke.   She is not worth thee, then. What years,
i' faith ?
Viola.   About your years, my lord.
Duke.   Too old, by heaven : let still the woman
take
An elder than herself ; so wears she to him,
So sways she level in her husband's heart :
For, boy, however we do praise ourselves,
Our fancies are more giddy and unfirm,
More longing, wavering, sooner lost and worn,
Than women's are.
Viola.   I think it well, my lord.
Duke.   Then let thy love be younger than thyself,
Or thy affection cannot hold the bent ;
For women are as roses, whose fair flower
Being once display'd, doth fall that very hour.
Viola.   And so they are : alas, that they are so ;
To die, even when they to perfection grow !

Re-enter CURIO *and* CLOWN.

Duke.   O, fellow, come, the song we had last night.
Mark it, Cesario, it is old and plain ;
The spinsters and the knitters in the sun
And the free maids that weave their thread with
bones
Do use to chant it : it is silly sooth,
And dallies with the innocence of love,
Like the old age.
Clown.   Are you ready, sir ?
Duke.   Ay ; prithee, sing.   [*Music.*

SONG.

Clown. Come away, come away, death,
      And in sad cypress let me be laid ;
Fly away, fly away, breath ;
      I am slain by a fair cruel maid.
My shroud of white, stuck all with yew,
      O, prepare it !
My part of death, no one so true
      Did share it.

Not a flower, not a flower sweet,
      On my black coffin let there be strown ;
Not a friend, not a friend greet
      My poor corpse, where my bones shall
      be thrown :
A thousand thousand sighs to save,
      Lay me, O, where
Sad true lover never find my grave,
      To weep there !

Duke.   There 's for thy pains.
Clown.   No pains, sir ; I take pleasure in singing,
sir.
Duke.   I 'll pay thy pleasure then.
Clown.   Truly, sir, and pleasure will be paid,
one time or another.
Duke.   Give me now leave to leave thee.
Clown.   Now, the melancholy god protect thee ;
and the tailor make thy doublet of changeable
taffeta, for thy mind is a very opal. I would have
men of such constancy put to sea, that their business
might be every thing and their intent every where ;
for that 's it that always makes a good voyage of
nothing. Farewell.   [*Exit.*

Duke.   Let all the rest give place.

[*Curio and Attendants retire.*
                    Once more, Cesario,
Get thee to yond same sovereign cruelty :
Tell her, my love, more noble than the world,
Prizes not quantity of dirty lands ;
The parts that fortune hath bestow'd upon her,
Tell her, I hold as giddily as fortune ;
But 'tis that miracle and queen of gems
That nature pranks her in attracts my soul.
Viola.   But if she cannot love you. sir ?
Duke.   I cannot be so answer'd.
Viola.   Sooth, but you must.
Say that some lady, as perhaps there is,
Hath for your love as great a pang of heart
As you have for Olivia : you cannot love her ;
You tell her so ; must she not then be answer'd ?
Duke.   There is no woman's sides
Can bide the beating of so strong a passion
As love doth give my heart ; no woman's heart
So big, to hold so much ; they lack retention.
Alas, their love may be call'd appetite,
No motion of the liver, but the palate,
That suffer surfeit, cloyment and revolt ;
But mine is all as hungry as the sea,
And can digest as much : make no compare
Between that love a woman can bear me
And that I owe Olivia.
Viola.   Ay, but I know—
Duke.   What dost thou know ?
Viola.   Too well what love women to men may
   owe :
In faith, they are as true of heart as we.
My father had a daughter loved a man,
As it might be, perhaps, were I a woman,
I should your lordship.
Duke.   And what 's her history ?
Viola.   A blank, my lord. She never told her
   love,
But let concealment, like a worm i' the bud,
Feed on her damask cheek : she pined in thought,
And with a green and yellow melancholy
She sat like patience on a monument,
Smiling at grief.   Was not this love indeed ?
We men may say more, swear more : but indeed
Our shows are more than will ; for still we prove
Much in our vows, but little in our love.
Duke.   But died thy sister of her love, my boy ?
Viola.   I am all the daughters of my father's
   house,
And all the brothers too : and yet I know not.
Sir, shall I to this lady ?
Duke.   Ay, that 's the theme.
To her in haste ; give her this jewel ; say,
My love can give no place, bide no denay.
                    [*Exeunt.*

SCENE V. OLIVIA'S *garden.*

Enter SIR TOBY, SIR ANDREW, *and* FABIAN.

Sir Toby.   Come thy ways, Signior Fabian.
Fabian.   Nay, I 'll come : if I lose a scruple of
this sport, let me be boiled to death with melancholy.
Sir Toby.   Wouldst thou not be glad to have
the niggardly rascally sheep-biter come by some
notable shame ?
Fabian.   I would exult, man : you know, he
brought me out o' favour with my lady about a
bear-baiting here.
Sir Toby.   To anger him we 'll have the bear
again ; and we will fool him black and blue : shall

we not, Sir Andrew ?

Sir Andrew. An we do not, it is pity of our lives.

Sir Toby. Here comes the little villain.

Enter MARIA.

How now, my metal of India !

Maria. Get ye all three into the box-tree : Malvolio 's coming down this walk : he has been yonder i' the sun practising behaviour to his own shadow this half hour : observe him, for the love of mockery ; for I know this letter will make a contemplative idiot of him. Close, in the name of jesting ! Lie thou there [*throws down a letter*] ; for here comes the trout that must be caught with tickling. [*Exit.*

Enter MALVOLIO.

Malvolio. 'Tis but fortune ; all is fortune. Maria once told me she did affect me : and I have heard herself come thus near, that, should she fancy, it should be one of my complexion. Besides, she uses me with a more exalted respect than any one else that follows her. What should I think on 't ?

Sir Toby. Here 's an overweening rogue !

Fabian. O, peace ! Contemplation makes a rare turkey-cock of him : how he jets under his advanced plumes !

Sir Andrew. 'Slight, I could so beat the rogue !

Sir Toby. Peace, I say.

Malvolio. To be Count Malvolio !

Sir Toby. Ah, rogue !

Sir Andrew. Pistol him, pistol him.

Sir Toby. Peace, peace !

Malvolio. There is example for 't ; the lady of the Strachy married the yeoman of the wardrobe.

Sir Andrew. Fie on him, Jezebel !

Fabian. O, peace ! now he 's deeply in : look how imagination blows him.

Malvolio. Having been three months married to her, sitting in my state,—

Sir Toby. O, for a stone-bow, to hit him in the eye !

Malvolio. Calling my officers about me, in my branched velvet gown ; having come from a day-bed, where I have left Olivia sleeping,—

Sir Toby. Fire and brimstone !

Fabian. O, peace, peace !

Malvolio. And then to have the humour of state ; and after a demure travel of regard, telling them I know my place as I would they should do theirs, to ask for my kinsman Toby,—

Sir Toby. Bolts and shackles !

Fabian. O peace, peace, peace ! now, now.

Malvolio. Seven of my people, with an obedient start, make out for him : I frown the while ; and perchance wind up my watch, or play with my—some rich jewel. Toby approaches ; courtesies there to me,—

Sir Toby. Shall this fellow live ?

Fabian. Though our silence be drawn from us with cars, yet peace.

Malvolio. I extend my hand to him thus, quenching my familiar smile with an austere regard of control,—

Sir Toby. And does not Toby take you a blow o' the lips then ?

Malvolio. Saying, Cousin Toby, my fortunes having cast me on your niece give me this prerogative of speech,'—

Sir Toby. What, what ?

Malvolio. ' You must amend your drunkenness.'

Sir Toby. Out, scab !

Fabian. Nay, patience, or we break the sinews of our plot.

Malvolio. ' Besides, you waste the treasure of your time with a foolish knight,'—

Sir Andrew. That 's me, I warrant you.

Malvolio. ' One Sir Andrew,'—

Sir Andrew. I knew 'twas I ; for many do call me fool.

Malvolio. What employment have we here ?

[*Taking up the letter.*

Fabian. Now is the woodcock near the gin.

Sir Toby. O, peace ! and the spirit of humours intimate reading aloud to him !

Malvolio. By my life, this is my lady's hand : these be her very C's, her U's and her T's ; and thus makes she her great P's. It is, in contempt of question, her hand.

Sir Andrew. Her C's, her U's and her T's : why that ?

Malvolio. [*Reads*] ' To the unknown beloved, this, and my good wishes :'— her very phrases ! By your leave, wax. Soft ! and the impressure her Lucrece, with which she uses to seal : 'tis my lady. To whom should·this be ?

Fabian. This wins him, liver and all.

Malvolio. [*Reads*]
　　Jove knows I love :
　　　　But who ?
　　Lips, do not move ;
　　　　No man must know.
' No man must know.' What follows ? the numbers altered ! ' No man must know :' if this should be thee, Malvolio ?

Sir Toby. Marry, hang thee, brock !

Malvolio. [*Reads*]
　　I may command where I adore ;
　　　　But silence, like a Lucrece knife,
　　With bloodless stroke my heart doth gore
　　　　M, O, A, I, doth sway my life.

Fabian. A fustian riddle !

Sir Toby. Excellent wench, say I.

Malvolio. ' M, O, A, I, doth sway my life.' Nay but first, let me see, let me see, let me see.

Fabian. What dish o' poison has she dressed him !

Sir Toby. And with what wing the staniel checks at it !

Malvolio. ' I may command where I adore. Why, she may command me : I serve her ; she is my lady. Why, this is evident to any formal capacity ; there is no obstruction in this : and the end,—what should that alphabetical position portend ? If I could make that resemble something in me,—Softly ! M, O, A, I,—

Sir Toby. O, ay, make up that : he is now at a cold scent.

Fabian. Sowter will cry upon 't for all this, though it be as rank as a fox.

Malvolio. M,—Malvolio ; M,—why, that begins my name.

Fabian. Did not I say he would work it out ? the cur is excellent at faults.

Malvolio. M,—but then there is no consonancy in the sequel ; that suffers under probation : A should follow, but O does.

Fabian. And O shall end, I hope.

Sir Toby. Ay, or I 'll cudgel him, and make him cry O !

Malvolio. And then I comes behind.

Fabian. Ay, an you had any eye behind you, you might see more detraction at your heels than fortunes before you.

Malvolio. M, O, A, I ; this simulation is not as the former : and yet, to crush this a little, it would bow to me, for every one of these letters are in my name. Soft ! here follows prose. [*Reads*] ' If this fall into thy hand, revolve. In my stars I am above thee ; but be not afraid of greatness : some are born great, some achieve greatness and some have greatness thrust upon 'em. Thy Fates open their hands ; let thy blood and spirit embrace them ; and, to inure thyself to what thou art like to be, cast thy humble slough and appear fresh. Be opposite with a kinsman, surly with servants ; let thy tongue tang arguments of state ; put thyself into the trick of singularity ; she thus advises thee that sighs for thee. Remember who commended thy yellow stockings, and wished to see thee ever cross-gartered : I say, remember. Go to, thou art made, if thou desirest to be so ; if not, let me see thee a steward still, the fellow of servants, and not worthy to touch Fortune's fingers. Farewell. She that would alter services with thee, THE FORTUNATE-UNHAPPY.' Daylight and champain discovers not more : this is open. I will be proud, I will read politic authors, I will baffle Sir Toby, I will wash off gross acquaintance, I will be point-devise the very man. I do not now fool myself, to let imagination jade me ; for every reason excites to this, that my lady loves me, She did commend my yellow stockings of late, she did praise my leg being cross-gartered ; and in this she manifests herself to my love, and with a kind of injunction drives me to these habits of her liking. I thank my stars I am happy. I will be strange, stout, in yellow stockings, and cross-gartered, even with the swiftness of putting on. Jove and my stars be praised ! Here is yet a postscript. [*Reads*] ' Thou canst not choose but know who I am. If thou entertainest my love, let it appear in thy smiling ; thy smiles become thee well ; therefore in my presence still smile, dear my sweet, I prithee.' Jove, I thank thee : I will smile ; I will do everything that thou wilt have me.   [*Exit.*

Fabian. I will not give my part of this sport for a pension of thousands to be paid from the Sophy.

Sir Toby. I could marry this wench for this device.

Sir Andrew. So could I too.

Sir Toby. And ask no other dowry with her but such another jest.

Sir Andrew. Nor I neither.

Fabian. Here comes my noble gull-catcher.

Re-enter MARIA.

Sir Toby. Wilt thou set thy foot o' my neck ?

Sir Andrew. Or o' mine either ?

Sir Toby. Shall I play my freedom at tray-tip, and become thy bond-slave ?

Sir Andrew. I' faith, or I either ?

Sir Toby. Why, thou hast put him in such a dream, that when the image of it leaves him he must run mad.

Maria. Nay, but say true ; does it work upon him ?

Sir Toby. Like aqua-vitæ with a midwife.

Maria. If you will then see the fruits of the sport, mark his first approach before my lady : he will come to her in yellow stockings and 'tis a colour she abhors, and cross-gartered, a fashion she detests ; and he will smile upon her, which will now be so unsuitable to her disposition, being addicted to a melancholy as she is, that it cannot but turn him into a notable contempt. If you will see it, follow me.

Sir Toby. To the gates of Tartar, thou most excellent devil of wit !

Sir Andrew. I 'll make one too.   [*Exeunt.*

ACT III.

SCENE I. OLIVIA'S *garden.*

Enter VIOLA, *and* CLOWN *with a tabor.*

Viola.

Save thee, friend, and thy music : dost thou live by thy tabor ?

Clown. No, sir, I live by the church.

Viola. Art thou a churchman ?

Clown. No such matter, sir : I do live by the church ; for I do live at my house, and my house doth stand by the church.

Viola. So thou mayst say, the king lies by a beggar, if a beggar dwell near him ; or, the church stands by thy tabor, if thy tabor stand by the church.

Clown. You have said, sir. To see this age ! A sentence is but a cheveril glove to a good wit : how quickly the wrong side may be turned outward !

Viola. Nay, that 's certain ; they that dally nicely with words may quickly make them wanton.

Clown. I would, therefore, my sister had had no name, sir.

Viola. Why, man ?

Clown. Why, sir, her name 's a word ; and to dally with that word might make my sister wanton. But indeed words are very rascals since bonds disgraced them.

Viola. Thy reason, man ?

Clown. Troth, sir, I can yield you none without words ; and words are grown so false, I am loath to prove reason with them.

Viola. I warrant thou art a merry fellow and carest for nothing.

Clown. Not so, sir, I do care for something ; but in my conscience, sir, I do not care for you : if that be to care for nothing, sir, I would it would make you invisible.

Viola. Art not thou the Lady Olivia's fool ?

Clown. No, indeed, sir ; the Lady Olivia has no folly : she will keep no fool, sir, till she be married ; and fools are as like husbands as pilchards are to herrings ; the husband's the bigger : I am indeed not her fool, but her corrupter of words.

Viola. I saw thee late at the Count Orsino's.

Clown. Foolery, sir, does walk about the orb like the sun, it shines every where. I would be sorry, sir, but the fool should be as oft with your master as with my mistress : I think I saw your wisdom there.

Viola. Nay, an thou pass upon me, I 'll no more with thee. Hold, there 's expenses for thee.

Clown. Now Jove, in his next commodity of hair, send thee a beard !

Viola. By my troth, I 'll tell thee, I am almost sick for one ; [*Aside*] though I would not have it grow on my chin. Is thy lady within ?

Clown. Would not a pair of these have bred, sir ?

Viola. Yes, being kept together and put to use.

Clown. I would play Lord Pandarus of Phrygia

sir, to bring a Cressida to this Troilus.
Viola. I understand you, sir ; 'tis well begged.
Clown. The matter I hope, is not great. sir,
begging but a beggar Cressida was a beggar. My
lady is within, sir. I will construe to them whence
you come ; who you are and what you would are
out of my welkin, I might say element.' but the
word is over-worn.   [*Exit.*
Viola. This fellow is wise enough to play the
fool ;
And to do that well craves a kind of wit :
He must observe their mood on whom he jests,
The quality of persons and the time,
And, like the haggard, check at every feather
That comes before his eye.   This is a practice
As full of labour as a wise man's art :
For folly that he wisely shows is fit ;
But wise men, folly-fall'n. quite taint their wit.

Enter SIR TOBY *and* SIR ANDREW.

Sir Toby. Save you, gentleman.
Viola. And you, sir
Sir Andrew. Dieu vous garde, monsieur.
Viola. Et vous aussi : votre serviteur.
Sir Andrew. I hope, sir. you are : and I am
yours.
Sir Toby. Will you encounter the house ? my
niece is desirous you should enter, if your trade be
to her.
Viola. I am bound to your niece, sir ; I mean,
she is the list of my voyage.
Sir Toby. Taste your legs, sir ; put them to
motion.
Viola. My legs do better understand me, sir,
than I understand what you mean by bidding me
taste my legs.
Sir Toby. I mean, to go, sir, to enter.
Viola. I will answer you with gait and entrance.
But we are prevented.

Enter OLIVIA *and* MARIA.

Most excellent accomplished lady, the heavens
rain odours on you !
Sir Andrew. That youth's a rare courtier : ' Rain
odours ; ' well.
Viola. My matter hath no voice, lady, but to
your own most pregnant and vouchsafed ear.
Sir Andrew. ' Odours,' ' pregnant ' and ' vouch-
safed : ' I 'll get 'em all three all ready.
Olivia. Let the garden door be shut, and leave
me to my hearing. [*Exeunt Sir Toby, Sir Andrew,
and Maria.*] Give me your hand, sir.
Viola. My duty, madam, and most humble
service.
Olivia. What is your name ?
Viola. Cesario is your servant's name, 'fair
princess.
Olivia. My servant, sir ! 'Twas never merry
world
Since lowly feigning was call'd compliment :
You 're servant to the Count Orsino, youth.
Viola. And he is yours, and his must needs be
yours :
Your servant's servant is your servant, madam.
Olivia. For him, I think not on him : for his
thoughts,
Would they were blanks, rather than fill'd with me !
Viola. Madam, I come to whet your gentle
thoughts
On his behalf.

Olivia. O, by your leave, I pray you,
I bade you never speak again of him :
But, would you undertake another suit,
I had rather hear you to solicit that
Than music from the spheres.
Viola.   Dear lady,—
Olivia. Give me leave, beseech you. I did send,
After the last enchantment you did here,
A ring in chase of you : so did I abuse
Myself, my servant and, I fear me, you :
Under your hard construction must I sit,
To force that on you, in a shameful cunning,
Which you knew none of yours : what might you
think ?
Have you not set mine honour at the stake
And baited it with all the unmuzzled thoughts
That tyrannous heart can think ? To one of your
receiving
Enough is shown : a cypress, not a bosom,
Hideth my heart. So, let me hear you speak.
Viola. I pity you.
Olivia.   That 's a degree to love.
Viola. No, not a grize ; for 'tis a vulgar proof,
That very oft we pity enemies.
Olivia. Why, then, methinks 'tis time to smile
again.
O world, how apt the poor are to be proud !
If one should be a prey, how much the better
To fall before the lion than the wolf !   [*Clock strikes.*
The clock upbraids me with the waste of time.
Be not afraid, good youth, I will not have you :
And yet, when wit and youth is come to harvest,
Your wife is like to reap a proper man :
There lies your way, due west.
Viola.   Then westward-ho ! Grace and good
disposition
Attend your ladyship !
You 'll nothing, madam, to my lord by me ?
Olivia. Stay :
I prithee, tell me what thou think'st of me.
Viola. That you do think you are not what you
are.
Olivia. If I think so, I think the same of you.
Viola. Then think you right : I am not what I am.
Olivia. I would you were as I would have you be !
Viola. Would it be better, madam, than I am ?
I wish it might, for now I am your fool.
Olivia. O, what a deal of scorn looks beautiful
In the contempt and anger of his lip !
A murderous guilt shows not itself more soon
Than love that would seem hid : love's night is
noon.
Cesario, by the roses of the spring,
By maidhood, honour, truth and every thing,
I love thee so, that, maugre all thy pride,
Nor wit nor reason can my passion hide.
Do not extort thy reasons from this clause,
For that I woo, thou therefore hast no cause ;
But rather reason thus with reason fetter,
Love sought is good, but given unsought is better.
Viola. By innocence I swear, and by my youth,
I have one heart, one bosom and one truth,
And that no woman has ; nor never none
Shall mistress be of it, save I alone.
And so adieu, good madam : never more
Will I my master's tears to you deplore.
Olivia. Yet come again ; for thou perhaps mayst
move
That heart, which now abhors, to like his love.
[*Exeunt.*

SCENE II. OLIVIA'S *house.*

Enter SIR TOBY, SIR ANDREW, *and* FABIAN.

Sir Andrew. No, faith, I 'll not stay a jot longer.
Sir Toby. Thy reason, dear venom, give thy reason.
Fabian. You must needs yield your reason, Sir Andrew.
Sir Andrew. Marry, I saw your niece do more favours to the count's serving-man than ever she bestowed upon me ; I saw 't i' the orchard.
Sir Toby. Did she see thee the while, old boy ? tell me that.
Sir Andrew. As plain as I see you now.
Fabian. This was a great argument of love in her toward you.
Sir Andrew. 'Slight, will you make an ass o' me ?
Fabian. I will prove it legitimate, sir, upon the oaths of judgement and reason.
Sir Toby. And they have been grand-jurymen since before Noah was a sailor.
Fabian. She did show favour to the youth in your sight only to exasperate you, to awake your dormouse valour, to put fire in your heart, and brimstone in your liver. You should then have accosted her ; and with some excellent jests, fire-new from the mint, you should have banged the youth into dumbness. This was looked for at your hand, and this was balked : the double gilt of this opportunity you let time wash off, and you are now sailed into the north of my lady's opinion ; where you will hang like an icicle on a Dutchman's beard, unless you do redeem it by some laudable attempt either of valour or policy.
Sir Andrew. An 't be any way, it must be with valour ; for policy I hate : I had as lief be a Brownist as a politician.
Sir Toby. Why, then, build me thy fortunes upon the basis of valour. Challenge me the count's youth to fight with him ; hurt him in eleven places : my niece shall take note of it ; and assure thyself, there is no love-broker in the world can more prevail in man's commendation with woman than report of valour.
Fabian. There is no way but this, Sir Andrew.
Sir Andrew. Will either of you bear me a challenge to him ?
Sir Toby. Go, write it in a martial hand ; be curst and brief ; it is no matter how witty, so it be eloquent and full of invention : taunt him with the license of ink : if thou thou'st him some thrice, it shall not be amiss ; and as many lies as will lie in thy sheet of paper, although the sheet were big enough for the bed of Ware in England, set 'em down : go, about it. Let there be gall enough in thy ink, though thou write with a goose-pen, no matter : about it.
Sir Andrew. Where shall I find you ?
Sir Toby. We 'll call thee at the cubiculo : go.
   [*Exit Sir Andrew.*
Fabian. This is a dear manakin to you, Sir Toby.
Sir Toby. I have been dear to him, lad, some two thousand strong, or so.
Fabian. We shall have a rare letter from him : but you 'll not deliver 't ?
Sir Toby. Never trust me, then : and by all means stir on the youth to an answer. I think oxen and wainropes cannot hale them together. For Andrew, if he were opened, and you find so much blood in his liver as will clog the foot of a flea, I 'll eat the rest of the anatomy.
Fabian. And his opposite, the youth, bears in his visage no great presage of cruelty.

Enter MARIA.

Sir Toby. Look, where the youngest wren of nine comes.
Maria. If you desire the spleen, and will laugh yourselves into stitches, follow me. Yond gull Malvolio is turned heathen, a very renegado ; for there is no Christian, that means to be saved by believing rightly, can ever believe such impossible passages of grossness. He 's in yellow stockings.
Sir Toby. And cross-gartered ?
Maria. Most villanously ; like a pedant that keeps a school i' the church. I have dogged him, like his murderer. He does obey every point of the letter that I dropped to betray him : he does smile his face into more lines than is in the new map with the augmentation of the Indies : you have not seen such a thing as 'tis. I can hardly forbear hurling things at him. I know my lady will strike him : if she do, he 'll smile and take 't for a great favour.
Sir Toby. Come, bring us, bring us where he is.
   [*Exeunt.*

SCENE III. *A street.*

Enter SEBASTIAN *and* ANTONIO.

Sebastian. I would not by my will have troubled you ;
But, since you make your pleasure of your pains,
I will no further chide you.
Antonio. I could not stay behind you : my desire,
More sharp than filed steel, did spur me forth ;
And not all love to see you, though so much
As might have drawn one to a longer voyage,
But jealousy what might befall your travel,
Being skilless in these parts ; which to a stranger,
Unguided and unfriended, often prove
Rough and unhospitable : my willing love,
The rather by these arguments of fear,
Set forth in your pursuit.
Sebastian.   My kind Antonio,
I can no other answer make but thanks,
† And thanks ; and ever......oft good turns
Are shuffled off with such uncurrent pay :
But, were my worth as is my conscience firm,
You should find better dealing. What 's to do ?
Shall we go see the reliques of this town ?
Antonio. To-morrow, sir : best first go see your lodging.
Sebastian. I am not weary, and 'tis long to night :
I pray you, let us satisfy our eyes
With the memorials and the things of fame
That do renown this city.
Antonio.   Would you 'ld pardon me :
I do not without danger walk these streets :
Once, in a sea-fight, 'gainst the count his galleys
I did some service ; of such note indeed,
That were I ta'en here it would scarce be answer'd.
Sebastian. Belike you slew great number of his people.
Antonio. The offence is not of such a bloody nature ;
Albeit the quality of the time and quarrel
Might well have given us bloody argument.
It might have since been answer'd in repaying

What we took from them ; which, for traffic's sake,
Most of our city did : only myself stood out ;
For which, if I be lapsed in this place,
I shall pay dear.
  Sebastian. Do not then walk too open.
  Antonio. It doth not fit me. Hold, sir, here 's my
purse.
In the south suburbs, at the Elephant,
Is best to lodge ; I will bespeak our diet,
Whiles you beguile the time and feed your knowledge
With viewing of the town : there shall you have me.
  Sebastian. Why I your purse ?
  Antonio. Haply your eye shall light upon some
toy
You have desire to purchase ; and your store,
I think, is not for idle markets, sir.
  Sebastian. I 'll be your purse-bearer and leave
you
For an hour.
  Antonio. To the Elephant.
  Sebastian. I do remember. [*Exeunt.*

SCENE IV. Olivia's *garden.*

Enter Olivia *and* Maria.

  Olivia. I have sent after him : he says he 'll
come ;
How shall I feast him ? what bestow of him ?
For youth is bought more oft than begg'd or bor-
row'd.
I speak too loud.
Where is Malvolio ? he is sad and civil,
And suits well for a servant with my fortunes :
Where is Malvolio ?
  Maria. He 's coming, madam ; but in very
strange manner. He is, sure, possessed, madam.
  Olivia. Why, what 's the matter ? does he rave ?
  Maria. No, madam, he does nothing but smile :
your ladyship were best to have some guard about
you, if he come ; for, sure, the man is tainted in 's
wits.
  Olivia. Go call him hither. [*Exit Maria.*] I
am as mad as he,
If sad and merry madness equal be.

Re-enter Maria, *with* Malvolio.

How now, Malvolio !
  Malvolio. Sweet lady, ho, ho.
  Olivia. Smilest thou ?
I sent for thee upon a sad occasion.
  Malvolio. Sad, lady ! I could be sad : this does
make some obstruction in the blood, this cross-
gartering ; but what of that ? if it please the eye
of one, it is with me as the very true sonnet is, ' Please
one, and please all.'
  Olivia. Why, how dost thou, man ? what is the
matter with thee ?
  Malvolio. Not black in my mind, though yellow
in my legs. It did come to his' hands and commands shall be executed : I think we do know the
sweet Roman hand.
  Olivia. Wilt thou go to bed, Malvolio ?
  Malvolio. To bed ! ay, sweet-heart, and I 'll
come to thee.
  Olivia. God comfort thee ! Why dost thou
smile so and kiss thy hand so oft ?
  Maria. How do you, Malvolio ?
  Malvolio. At your request ! yes ; nightingales
answer daws.

  Maria. Why appear you with this ridiculous
boldness before my lady ?
  Malvolio. ' Be not afraid of greatness :' 'twas
well writ.
  Olivia. What meanest thou by that, Malvolio ?
  Malvolio. ' Some are born great,'—
  Olivia. Ha !
  Malvolio. ' Some achieve greatness,'—
  Olivia. What sayest thou ?
  Malvolio. ' And some have greatness thrust upon
them.'
  Olivia. Heaven restore thee !
  Malvolio. ' Remember who commended thy
yellow stockings,'—
  Olivia. Thy yellow stockings !
  Malvolio. ' And wished to see thee cross-gartered.'
  Olivia. Cross-gartered !
  Malvolio. ' Go to, thou art made, if thou desirest
to be so ; '—
  Olivia. Am I made ?
  Malvolio. ' If not, let me see thee a servant still.'
  Olivia. Why, this is very midsummer madness.

Enter Servant.

  Servant. Madam, the young gentleman of the
Count Orsino's is returned : I could hardly entreat
him back : he attends your ladyship's pleasure.
  Olivia. I 'll come to him. [*Exit Servant.*] Good
Maria, let this fellow be looked to. Where 's my
cousin Toby ? Let some of my people have a special
care of him : I would not have him miscarry for
the half of my dowry. [*Exeunt Olivia and Maria.*
  Malvolio. O, ho ! do you come near me now ? no
worse man than Sir Toby to look to me ! This con-
curs directly with the letter : she sends him on
purpose, that I may appear stubborn to him ; for
she incites me to that in the letter. ' Cast thy humble
slough,' says she ; ' be opposite with a kinsman,
surly with servants ; let thy tongue tang with arguments of state ; put thyself into the trick of singularity ;' and consequently sets down the manner how ;
as, a sad face, a reverend carriage, a slow tongue,
in the habit of some sir of note, and so forth. I
have limed her ; but it is Jove's doing, and Jove
make me thankful ! And when she went away now,
' Let this fellow be looked to :' fellow ! not Malvolio, nor after my degree, but fellow. Why, everything adheres together, that no dram of a scruple,
no scruple of a scruple, no obstacle, no incredulous
or unsafe circumstance—What can be said ? Nothing
that can be can come between me and the full prospect of my hopes. Well, Jove, not I, is the doer
of this, and he is to be thanked.

Re-enter Maria, *with* Sir Toby *and* Fabian.

  Sir Toby. Which way is he, in the name of
sanctity ? If all the devils of hell be drawn in little,
and Legion himself possessed him, yet I 'll speak
to him.
  Fabian. Here he is, here he is. How is 't with
you, sir ? how is 't with you, man ?
  Malvolio. Go off ; I discard you : let me enjoy
my private : go off.
  Maria. Lo, how hollow the fiend speaks within
him ! did not I tell you ? Sir Toby, my lady prays
you to have a care of him.
  Malvolio. Ah, ha ! does she so ?
  Sir Toby. Go to, go to : peace, peace ; we must
deal gently with him : let me alone. How do you,

Malvolio ? how is 't with you ? What, man ! defy the devil : consider, he 's an enemy to mankind.

Malvolio. Do you know what you say ?

Maria. La you, an you speak ill of the devil, how he takes it at heart ! Pray God, he be not bewitched !

Fabian. Carry his water to the wise woman.

Maria. Marry, and it shall be done to-morrow morning, if I live. My lady would not lose him for more than I 'll say.

Malvolio. How now, mistress !

Maria. O Lord !

Sir Toby. Prithee, hold thy peace ; this is not the way : do you not see you move him ? let me alone with him.

Fabian. No way but gentleness ; gently, gently : the fiend is rough, and will not be roughly used.

Sir Toby. Why, how now, my bawcock ! how dost thou, chuck ?

Malvolio. Sir !

Sir Toby. Ay, Biddy, come with me. What, man ! 'tis not for gravity to play at cherry-pit with Satan : hang him, foul collier !

Maria. Get him to say his prayers, good Sir Toby, get him to pray.

Malvolio. My prayers, minx !

Maria. No, I warrant you, he will not hear of godliness.

Malvolio. Go, hang yourselves all ! you are idle shallow things : I am not of your element : you shall know more hereafter.   [*Exit.*

Sir Toby. Is 't possible ?

Fabian. If this were played upon a stage now, I could condemn it as an improbable fiction.

Sir Toby. His very genius hath taken the infection of the device, man.

Maria. Nay, pursue him now, lest the device take air and taint.

Fabian. Why, we shall make him mad indeed.

Maria. The house will be the quieter.

Sir Toby. Come, we 'll have him in a dark room and bound. My niece is already in the belief that he 's mad : we may carry it thus, for our pleasure and his penance, till our very pastime, tired out of breath, prompt us to have mercy on him : at which time we will bring the device to the bar and crown thee for a finder of madmen. But see, but see.

Enter SIR ANDREW.

Fabian. More matter for a May morning.

Sir Andrew. Here 's the challenge, read it : I warrant there 's vinegar and pepper in 't.

Fabian. Is 't so saucy ?

Sir Andrew. Ay, is 't, I warrant him : do but read.

Sir Toby. Give me. [*Reads*] ' Youth, whatsoever thou art, thou arbut art scurvy fellow.'

Fabian. Good, and valiant.

Sir Toby. [*Reads*] 'Wonder not, nor admire not in thy mind, why I do call thee so, for I will show thee no reason for 't.'

Fabian. A' good note ; that keeps you from the blow of the law.

Sir Toby. [*Reads*] ' Thou comest to the lady Olivia, and in my sight she uses thee kindly : but thou liest in thy throat ; that is not the matter I challenge thee for.'

Fabian. Very brief, and to exceeding good sense —less.

Sir Toby. [*Reads*] ' I will waylay thee going home ; where if it be thy chance to kill me,'—

Fabian. Good.

Sir Toby. [*Reads*] ' Thou killest me like a rogue and a villain.'

Fabian. Still you keep o' the windy side of the law : good.

Sir Toby. [*Reads*] ' Fare thee well ; and God have mercy upon one of our souls ! He may have mercy upon mine ; but my hope is better, and so look to thyself. Thy friend, as thou usest him, and thy sworn enemy,

ANDREW AGUECHEEK.'

If this letter move him not, his legs cannot : I 'll give 't him.

Maria. You may have very fit occasion for 't : he is now in some commerce with my lady, and will by and by depart.

Sir Toby. Go, Sir Andrew ; scout me for him at the corner of the orchard like a bum-baily : so soon as ever thou seest him, draw ; and, as thou drawest, swear horrible ; for it comes to pass oft that a terrible oath, with a swaggering accent sharply twanged off, gives manhood more approbation than ever proof itself would have earned him. Away !

Sir Andrew. Nay, let me alone for swearing. [*Exit.*

Sir Toby. Now will not I deliver his letter : for the behaviour of the young gentleman gives him out to be of good capacity and breeding ; his employment between his lord and my niece confirms no less : therefore this letter, being so excellently ignorant, will breed no terror in the youth : he will find it comes from a clodpole. But, sir, I will deliver his challenge by word of mouth ; set upon Aguecheek a notable report of valour ; and drive the gentleman, as I know his youth will aptly receive it, into a most hideous opinion of his rage, skill, fury and impetuosity. This will so fright them both that they will kill one another by the look, like cockatrices.

Re-enter OLIVIA, *with* VIOLA.

Fabian. Here he comes with your niece : give them way till he take leave, and presently after him.

Sir Toby. I will meditate the while upon some horrid message for a challenge.

[*Exeunt Sir Toby, Fabian, and Maria.*

Olivia. I have said too much unto a heart of stone

And laid mine honour too unchary out :

There 's something in me that reproves my fault ;

But such a headstrong potent fault it is,

That it but mocks reproof.

Viola. With the same 'haviour that your passion bears

Goes on my master's grief.

Olivia. Here, wear this jewel for me, 'tis my picture ;

Refuse it not ; it hath no tongue to vex you ;

And I beseech you come again to-morrow.

What shall you ask of me that I 'll deny,

That honour saved may upon asking give ?

Viola. Nothing but this ; your true love for my master.

Olivia. How with mine honour may I give him that

Which I have given to you ?

Viola.   I will acquit you.

Olivia. Well, come again to-morrow : fare thee well :

A fiend like thee might bear my soul to hell.   [*Exit.*

Re-enter Sir Toby *and* Fabian.

Sir Toby. Gentleman, God save thee.

Viola. And you, sir.

Sir Toby. That defence thou hast, betake thee to 't : of what nature the wrongs are thou hast done him, I know not ; but thy intercepter, full of despite, bloody as the hunter, attends thee at the orchard-end : dismount thy tuck, be yare in thy preparation, for thy assailant is quick, skilful and deadly.

Viola. You mistake, sir ; I am sure no man hath any quarrel to me : my remembrance is very free and clear from any image of offence done to any man.

Sir Toby. You 'll find it otherwise, I assure you : therefore, if you hold your life at any price, betake you to your guard ; for your opposite hath in him what youth, strength, skill and wrath can furnish man withal.

Viola. I pray you, sir, what is he ?

Sir Toby. He is knight, dubbed with unhatched rapier and on carpet consideration ; but he is a devil in private brawl : souls and bodies hath he divorced three ; and his incensement at this moment is so implacable, that satisfaction can be none but by pangs of death and sepulchre. Hob, nob, is his word ; give 't or take 't.

Viola. I will return again into the house and desire some conduct of the lady. I am no fighter. I have heard of some kind of men that put quarrels purposely on others, to taste their valour : belike this is a man of that quirk.

Sir Toby. Sir, no, his indignation derives itself out of a very competent injury : therefore, get you on and give him his desire. Back you shall not to the house, unless you undertake that with me which with as much safety you might answer him : therefore, on, or strip your sword stark naked ; for meddle you must, that 's certain, or forswear to wear iron about you.

Viola. This is as uncivil as strange. I beseech you, do me this courteous office, as to know of the knight what my offence to him is : it is something of my negligence, nothing of my purpose.

Sir Toby. I will do so. Signior Fabian, stay you by this gentleman till my return.   [*Exit.*

Viola. Pray you, sir, do you know of this matter ?

Fabian. I know the knight is incensed against you, even to a mortal arbitrement ; but nothing of the circumstance more.

Viola. I beseech you, what manner of man is he ?

Fabian. Nothing of that wonderful promise, to read him by his form, as you are like to find him in the proof of his valour. He is, indeed, sir, the most skilful, bloody and fatal opposite that you could possibly have found in any part of Illyria. Will you walk towards him ? I will make your peace with him if I can.

Viola. I shall be much bound to you for 't : I am one that had rather go with sir priest than sir knight : I care not who knows so much of my mettle.   [*Exeunt.*

Re-enter Sir Toby, *with* Sir Andrew.

Sir Toby. Why, man, he 's a very devil ; I have not seen such a firago. I had a pass with him, rapier, scabbard and all, and he gives me the stuck in with such a mortal motion, that it is inevitable ; and on the answer, he pays you as surely as your feet hit the ground they step on. They say he has been fencer to the Sophy.

Sir Andrew. Pox on 't, I 'll not meddle with him.

Sir Toby. Ay, but he will not now be pacified : Fabian can scarce hold him yonder.

Sir Andrew. Plague on 't, an I thought he had been valiant and so cunning in fence, I 'ld have seen him damned ere I 'ld have challenged him. Let him let the matter slip, and I 'll give him my horse, grey Capilet.

Sir Toby. I 'll make the motion : stand here, make a good show on 't : this shall end without the perdition of souls. [*Aside*] Marry, I 'll ride your horse as well as I ride you.

Re-enter Fabian *and* Viola.

[*To Fabian*] I have his horse to take up the quarrel : I have persuaded him the youth 's a devil.

Fabian. He is as horribly conceited of him ; and pants and looks pale, as if a bear were at his heels.

Sir Toby. [*To Viola*] There 's no remedy, sir ; he will fight with you, for 's oath sake : marry, he hath better bethought him of his quarrel, and he finds that now scarce to be worth talking of : therefore draw ; for the supportance of his vow ; he protests he will not hurt you.

Viola. [*Aside*] Pray God defend me ! A little thing would make me tell them how much I lack of a man.

Fabian. Give ground, if you see him furious.

Sir Toby. Come, Sir Andrew, there's no remedy ; the gentleman will, for his honour's sake, have one bout with you ; he cannot by the duello avoid it : but he has promised me, as he is a gentleman and a soldier, he will not hurt you. Come on : to 't.

Sir Andrew. Pray God, he keep his oath !

Viola. I do assure you, 'tis against my will.
[*They draw.*

Enter Antonio.

Antonio. Put up your sword. If this young gentleman
Have done offence, I take the fault on me :
If you offend him, I for him defy you.

Sir Toby. You, sir ! why, what are you ?

Antonio. One, sir, that for his love dares yet do more
Than you have heard him brag to you he will.

Sir Toby. Nay, if you be an undertaker, I am for you.
[*They draw.*

Enter Officers.

Fabian. O good Sir Toby, hold ! here come the officers.

Sir Toby. I 'll be with you anon.

Viola. Pray, sir, put your sword up, if you please.

Sir Andrew. Marry, will I, sir ; and, for that I promised you, I 'll be as good as my word : he will bear you easily and reins well.

First Officer. This is the man ; do thy office.

Second Officer. Antonio, I arrest thee at the suit of Count Orsino.

Antonio. You do mistake me, sir.

First Officer. No, sir, no jot ; I know your favour well,

Though now you have no sea-cap on your head.
Take him away : he knows I know him well.

Antonio. I must obey. [*To Viola*] This comes
      with seeking you :
But there 's no remedy ; I shall answer it.
What will you do, now my necessity
Makes me to ask you for my purse ? It grieves me
Much more for what I cannot do for you
Than what befalls myself. You stand amazed ;
But be of comfort.

Second Officer. Come, sir, away.

Antonio. I must entreat of you some of that
      money.

Viola. What money, sir ?
For the fair kindness you have show'd me here,
And, part, being prompted by your present trouble,
Out of my lean and low ability
I 'll lend you something : my having is not much ;
I 'll make division of my present with you :
Hold, there 's half my coffer.

Antonio.   Will you deny me now ?
Is 't possible that my deserts to you
Can lack persuasion ? Do not tempt my misery,
Lest that it make me so unsound a man
As to upbraid you with those kindnesses
That I have done for you.

Viola.   I know of none ;
Nor know I you by voice or any feature :
I hate ingratitude more in a man
Than lying, vainness, babbling, drunkenness,
Or any taint of vice whose strong corruption
Inhabits our frail blood.

Antonio.   O heavens themselves !

Second Officer. Come, sir, I pray you, go.

Antonio. Let me speak a little. This youth that
      you see here
I snatch'd one half out of the jaws of death,
Relieved him with such sanctity of love,
And to his image, which methought did promise
Most venerable worth, did I devotion.

First Officer. What 's that to us ? The time
      goes by : away !

Antonio. But O how vile an idol proves this god !
Thou hast, Sebastian, done good feature shame.
In nature there 's no blemish but the mind ;
None can be call'd deform'd but the unkind :
Virtue is beauty, but the beauteous evil
Are empty trunks o'erflourish'd by the devil.

First Officer. The man grows mad : away with
      him ! Come, come, sir.

Antonio. Lead me on.   [*Exit with Officers.*

Viola. Methinks his words do from such passion
      fly,
That he believes himself : so do not I.
Prove true, imagination, O, prove true,
That I, dear brother, be now ta'en for you !

Sir Toby. Come hither, knight ; come hither,
Fabian : we 'll whisper o'er a couplet or two of most
sage saws.

Viola. He named Sebastian : I my brother know
Yet living in my glass ; even such and so
In favour was my brother, and he went
Still in this fashion, colour, ornament,
For him I imitate : O, if it prove,
Tempests are kind and salt waves fresh in love.
                                    [*Exit.*

Sir Toby. A very dishonest paltry boy, and
more a coward than a hare : his dishonesty appears
in leaving his friend here in necessity and denying
him ; and for his cowardship, ask Fabian.

Fabian. A coward, a most devout coward, religious in it.

Sir Andrew. 'Slid, I 'll after him again and beat
him.

Sir Toby. Do ; cuff him soundly, but never draw
thy sword.

Sir Andrew. An I do not,—   [*Exit.*

Fabian. Come, let 's see the event.

Sir Toby. I dare lay any money 'twill be nothing
yet.   [*Exeunt.*

ACT IV.

SCENE I. *Before OLIVIA'S house.*

Enter SEBASTIAN and CLOWN.

Clown.

WILL you make me believe that I am not
      sent for you ?

Sebastian. Go to, go to, thou art a foolish
fellow :
Let me be clear of thee.

Clown. Well held out, i' faith ! No, I do not
know you ; nor I am not sent to you by my lady,
to bid you come speak with her ; nor your name is
not Master Cesario ; nor this is not my nose neither.
Nothing that is so is so.

Sebastian. I prithee, vent thy folly somewhere else :
Thou know'st not me.

Clown. Vent my folly ! he has heard that word
of some great man and now applies it to a fool.
Vent my folly ! I am afraid this great lubber, the
world, will prove a cockney. I prithee now, ungird
thy strangeness and tell me what I shall vent to my
lady : shall I vent to her that thou art coming ?

Sebastian. I prithee, foolish Greek, depart from
me :
There 's money for thee : if you tarry longer,
I shall give worse payment.

Clown. By my troth, thou hast an open hand.
These wise men that give fools money get themselves a good report—after fourteen years' purchase.

Enter SIR ANDREW, SIR TOBY, and FABIAN.

Sir Andrew. Now, sir, have I met you again ?
there 's for you.

Sebastian. Why, there 's for thee, and there, and
there.
Are all the people mad ?

Sir Toby. Hold, sir, or I 'll throw your dagger
o'er the house.

Clown. This will I tell my lady straight : I
would not be in some of your coats for two pence.
                                    [*Exit.*

Sir Toby. Come on, sir hold.

Sir Andrew. Nay, let him alone : I 'll go another
way to work with him ; I 'll have an action of
battery against him, if there be any law in Illyria :
though I struck him first, yet it 's no matter for that.

Sebastian. Let go thy hand.

Sir Toby. Come, sir, I will not let you go. Come,
my young soldier, put up your iron : you are well
fleshed ; come on.

Sebastian. I will be free from thee. What wouldst
      thou now ?
If thou darest tempt me further, draw thy sword.

Sir Toby. What, what ? Nay, then I must have
an ounce or two of this malapert blood from you.

Enter OLIVIA.

Olivia. Hold, Toby ; on thy life I charge thee,
  hold !
Sir Toby. Madam !
Olivia. Will it be ever thus ? Ungracious wretch,
Fit for the mountains and the barbarous caves,
Where manners ne'er were preach'd ! out of my
  sight !
Be not offended, dear Cesario.
Rudesby, be gone !
      [*Exeunt Sir Toby, Sir Andrew, and Fabian.*
      I prithee, gentle friend,
Let thy fair wisdom, not thy passion, sway
In this uncivil and unjust extent
Against thy peace. Go with me to my house,
And hear thou there how many fruitless pranks
This ruffian hath botch'd up, that thou thereby
Mayst smile at this : thou shalt not choose but
  go :
Do not deny. Beshrew his soul for me,
He started one poor heart of mine in thee.
Sebastian. What relish is in this ? how runs the
  stream ?
Or I am mad, or else this is a dream :
Let fancy still my sense in Lethe steep ;
If it be thus to dream, still let me sleep !
Olivia. Nay, come, I prithee ; would thou 'ldst
  be ruled by me !
Sebastian. Madam, I will.
Olivia. O, say so, and so be ! [*Exeunt.*

SCENE II. OLIVIA'S *house.*

Enter MARIA *and* CLOWN.

Maria. Nay, I prithee, put on this gown and
this beard ; make him believe thou art Sir Topas
the curate : do it quickly ; I 'll call Sir Toby the
whilst.   [*Exit.*
Clown. Well, I 'll put it on, and I will dissemble
myself in 't ; and I would I were the first that ever
dissembled in such a gown. I am not tall enough
to become the function well, nor lean enough to be
thought a good student ; but to be said an honest
man and a good housekeeper goes as fairly as to
say a careful man and a great scholar. The competitors enter.

Enter SIR TOBY *and* MARIA.

Sir Toby. Jove bless thee, master Parson.
Clown. Bonos dies, Sir Toby : for, as the old
hermit of Prague, that never saw pen and ink, very
wittily said to a niece of King Gorboduc, ' That
that is is ; ' so I, being master Parson, am master
Parson ; for, what is ' that ' but ' that,' and ' is '
but ' is ' ?
Sir Toby. To him, Sir Topas.
Clown. What, ho, I say ! peace in this prison !
Sir Toby. The knave counterfeits well ; a good
knave.
Malvolio. [*Within*] Who calls there ?
Clown. Sir Topas the curate, who comes to visit
Malvolio the lunatic.
Malvolio. Sir Topas, Sir Topas, good Sir Topas,
go to my lady.
Clown. Out, hyperbolical fiend ! how vexest
thou this man ! talkest thou nothing but of ladies ?
Sir Toby. Well said, master Parson.
Malvolio. Sir Topas, never was man thus wronged:

good Sir Topas, do not think I am mad : they have
laid me here in hideous darkness.
Clown. Fie, thou dishonest Satan ! I call thee
by the most modest terms ; for I am one of those
gentle ones that will use the devil himself with
courtesy : sayest thou that house is dark ?
Malvolio. As hell, Sir Topas.
Clown. Why, it hath bay windows transparent
as barricadoes, and the clearstores toward the south
north are as lustrous as ebony ; and yet complainest
thou of obstruction ?
Malvolio. I am not mad, Sir Topas : I say to you,
this house is dark.
Clown. Madman, thou errest : I say, there is no
darkness but ignorance ; in which thou art more
puzzled than the Egyptians in their fog.
Malvolio. I say, this house is as dark as ignorance, though ignorance were as dark as hell ; and
I say, there was never man thus abused. I am no
more mad than you are : make the trial of it in
any constant question.
Clown. What is the opinion of Pythagoras concerning wild fowl ?
Malvolio. That the soul of our grandam might
haply inhabit a bird.
Clown. What thinkest thou of his opinion ?
Malvolio. I think nobly of the soul, and no way
approve his opinion.
Clown. Fare thee well. Remain thou still in
darkness : thou shalt hold the opinion of Pythagoras ere I will allow of thy wits, and fear to kill
a woodcock, lest thou dispossess the soul of thy
grandam. Fare thee well.
Malvolio. Sir Topas, Sir Topas !
Sir Toby. My most exquisite Sir Topas !
Clown. Nay, I am for all waters.
Maria. Thou mightst have done this without
thy beard and gown : he sees thee not.
Sir Toby. To him in thine own voice, and bring
me word how thou findest him : I would we were
well rid of this knavery. If he may be conveniently
delivered, I would he were, for I am now so far in
offence with my niece that I cannot pursue with
any safety this sport to the upshot. Come by and
by to my chamber.   [*Exeunt Sir Toby and Maria.*
Clown. [*Singing*] ' Hey, Robin, jolly Robin,
                Tell me how thy lady does.'
Malvolio. Fool !
Clown. ' My lady is unkind, perdy.'
Malvolio. Fool !
Clown. ' Alas, why is she so ? '
Malvolio. Fool, I say !
Clown. ' She loves another '—Who calls, ha ?
Malvolio. Good fool, as ever thou wilt deserve
well at my hand, help me to a candle, and pen, ink
and paper : as I am a gentleman, I will live to be
thankful to thee for 't.
Clown. Master Malvolio ?
Malvolio. Ay, good fool.
Clown. Alas, sir, how fell you besides your five
wits ?
Malvolio. Fool, there was never man so notor-
iously abused : I am as well in my wits, fool, as
thou art.
Clown. But as well ? then you are mad indeed,
if you be no better in your wits than a fool.
Malvolio. They have here propertied me ; keep
me in darkness, send ministers to me, asses, and do
all they can to face me out of my wits.
Clown. Advise you what you say ; the minister
is here. Malvolio, Malvolio, thy wits the heavens

restore ! endeavour thyself to sleep, and leave thy vain bibble babble.

Malvolio. Sir Topas !

Clown. Maintain no words with him, good fellow. Who, I, sir ? not I, sir. God be wi' you, good Sir Topas. Marry, amen. I will, sir, I will.

Malvolio. Fool, fool, fool, I say !

Clown. Alas, sir, be patient. What say you, sir ? I am shent for speaking to you.

Malvolio. Good fool, help me to some light and some paper : I tell thee, I am as well in my wits as any man in Illyria.

Clown. Well-a-day that you were, sir !

Malvolio. By this hand, I am. Good fool, some ink, paper and light ; and convey what I will set down to my lady : it shall advantage thee more than ever the bearing of letter did.

Clown. I will help you to 't. But tell me true, are you not mad indeed ? or do you but counterfeit ?

Malvolio. Believe me, I am not ; I tell thee true.

Clown. Nay, I 'll ne'er believe a madman till I see his brains. I will fetch you light and paper and ink.

Malvolio. Fool, I 'll requite it in the highest degree : I prithee, be gone.

Clown. [*Singing*] I am gone, sir,
And anon, sir,
I 'll be with you again,
In a trice,
Like to the old Vice,
Your need to sustain ;
Who, with dagger of lath,
In his rage and his wrath,
Cries, ah, ha ! to the devil :
Like a mad lad,
Pare thy nails, dad ;
† Adieu, good man devil.   [*Exit.*

SCENE III. OLIVIA's *garden.*

Enter SEBASTIAN.

Sebastian. This is the air ; that is the glorious sun ;
This pearl she gave me, I do feel 't and see 't ;
And though 'tis wonder that enwraps me thus,
Yet 'tis not madness. Where 's Antonio, then ?
I could not find him at the Elephant :
Yet there he was ; and there I found this credit,
That he did range the town to seek me out.
His counsel now might do me golden service ;
For though my soul disputes well with my sense,
That this may be some error, but no madness,
Yet doth this accident and flood of fortune
So far exceed all instance, all discourse,
That I am ready to distrust mine eyes
And wrangle with my reason that persuades me
To any other trust but that I am mad
Or else the lady 's mad ; yet, if 'twere so,
She could not sway her house, command her followers,
Take and give back affairs and their dispatch
With such a smooth, discreet and stable bearing
As I perceive she does : there 's something in 't
That is deceiveable. But here the lady comes.

Enter OLIVIA *and* Priest.

Olivia. Blame not this haste of mine. If you mean well,
Now go with me and with this holy man
Into the chantry by : there, before him,
And underneath that consecrated roof,

Plight me the full assurance of your faith ;
That my most jealous and too doubtful soul
May live at peace. He shall conceal it
Whiles you are willing it shall come to note,
What time we will our celebration keep
According to my birth. What do you say ?

Sebastian. I 'll follow this good man, and go with you :
And, having sworn truth, ever will be true.

Olivia. Then lead the way, good father ; and heavens so shine,
That they may fairly note this act of mine !
[*Exeunt.*

ACT V.

SCENE 1. *Before* OLIVIA's *house.*

Enter CLOWN *and* FABIAN.

Fabian.
Now, as thou lovest me, let me see his letter.

Clown. Good Master Fabian, grant me another request.

Fabian. Any thing.

Clown. Do not desire to see this letter.

Fabian. This is, to give a dog, and in recompense desire my dog again.

Enter DUKE, VIOLA, CURIO, *and* Lords.

Duke. Belong you to the Lady Olivia, friends ?

Clown. Ay, sir ; we are some of her trappings.

Duke. I know thee well : how dost thou, my good fellow ?

Clown. Truly, sir, the better for my foes and the worse for my friends.

Duke. Just the contrary ; the better for thy friends.

Clown. No, sir, the worse.

Duke. How can that be ?

Clown. Marry, sir, they praise me and make an ass of me ; now my foes tell me plainly I am an ass : so that by my foes, sir, I profit in the knowledge of myself, and by my friends I am abused : so that, conclusions to be as kisses, if your four negatives make your two affirmatives, why then, the worse for my friends and the better for my foes.

Duke. Why, this is excellent.

Clown. By my troth, sir, no ; though it please you to be one of my friends.

Duke. Thou shalt not be the worse for me : there 's gold.

Clown. But that it would be double-dealing, sir, I would you could make it another.

Duke. O, you give me ill counsel.

Clown. Put your grace in your pocket, sir, for this once, and let your flesh and blood obey it.

Duke. Well, I will be so much a sinner, to be a double-dealer : there 's another.

Clown. Primo, secundo, tertio, is a good play ; and the old saying is, the third pays for all : the triplex, sir, is a good tripping measure ; or the bells of Saint Bennet, sir, may put you in mind ; one, two, three.

Duke. You can fool no more money out of me at this throw : if you will let your lady know I am here to speak with her, and bring her along with you, it may awake my bounty further.

Clown. Marry, sir, lullaby to your bounty till I come again. I go, sir ; but I would not have you

to think that my desire of having is the sin of covetousness : but, as you say, sir, let your bounty take a nap, I will awake it anon.   [*Exit.*
Viola. Here comes the man, sir, that did rescue me.

Enter ANTONIO *and* Officers.

Duke. That face of his I do remember well ;
Yet, when I saw it last, it was besmear'd
As black as Vulcan in the smoke of war :
A bawbling vessel was he captain of,
For shallow draught and bulk unprizable ;
With which such scathful grapple did he make
With the most noble bottom of our fleet,
That very envy and the tongue of loss
Cried fame and honour on him. What 's the matter ?
First Officer. Orsino, this is that Antonio
That took the Phœnix and her fraught from Candy ;
And this is he that did the Tiger board,
When your young nephew Titus lost his leg :
Here in the streets, desperate of shame and state,
In private brabble did we apprehend him.
Viola. He did me kindness, sir, drew on my side ;
But in conclusion put strange speech upon me :
I know not what 'twas but distraction.
Duke. Notable pirate ! thou salt-water thief !
What foolish boldness brought thee to their mercies,
Whom thou, in terms so bloody and so dear,
Hast made thine enemies ?
Antonio.   Orsino, noble sir,
Be pleased that I shake off these names you give me :
Antonio never yet was thief or pirate,
Though I confess, on base and ground enough,
Orsino's enemy. A witchcraft drew me hither :
That ingrateful boy there by your side,
From the rude sea's enraged and foamy mouth
Did I redeem ; a wreck past hope he was :
His life I gave him and did thereto add
My love, without retention or restraint,
All his in dedication ; for his sake
Did I expose myself, pure for his love,
Into the danger of this adverse town ;
Drew to defend him when he was beset :
Where being apprehended, his false cunning,
Not meaning to partake with me in danger,
Taught him to face me out of his acquaintance,
And grew a twenty years removed thing
While one would wink ; denied me mine own purse,
Which I had recommended to his use
Not half an hour before.
Viola.   How can this be ?
Duke. When came he to this town ?
Antonio. To-day, my lord ; and for three months before,
No interim, not a minute's vacancy,
Both day and night did we keep company.

Enter OLIVIA *and* Attendants.

Duke. Here comes the countess : now heaven walks on earth.
But for thee, fellow ; fellow, thy words are madness :
Three months this youth hath tended upon me ;
But more of that anon. Take him aside.
Olivia. What would my lord, but that he may not have,
Wherein Olivia may seem serviceable ?
Cesario, you do not keep promise with me.
Viola. Madam !

Duke. Gracious Olivia,—
Olivia. What do you say, Cesario ? Good my lord,—
Viola. My lord would speak ; my duty hushes me.
Olivia. If it be aught to the old tune, my lord,
It is as fat and fulsome to mine ear
As howling after music.
Duke.   Still so cruel ?
Olivia. Still so constant, lord.
Duke. What, to perverseness ? you uncivil lady,
To whose ingrate and unauspicious altars
My soul the faithfull'st offerings hath breathed out
That e'er devotion tender'd ! What shall I do ?
Olivia. Even what it please my lord, that shall become him.
Duke. Why should I not, had I the heart to do it,
Like to the Egyptian thief at point of death
Kill what I love ?—a savage jealousy
That sometime savours nobly. But hear me this :
Since you to non-regardance cast my faith,
And that I partly know the instrument
That screws me from my true place in your favour,
Live you the marble-breasted tyrant still ;
But this your minion, whom I know you love,
And whom, by heaven I swear, I tender dearly,
Him will I tear out of that cruel eye,
Where he sits crowned in his master's spite.
Come, boy, with me ; my thoughts are ripe in mischief :
I 'll sacrifice the lamb that I do love,
To spite a raven's heart within a dove.
Viola. And I, most jocund, apt and willingly,
To do you rest, a thousand deaths would die.
Olivia. Where goes Cesario ?
Viola.   After him I love
More than I love these eyes, more than my life,
More, by all mores, than e'er I shall love wife.
If I do feign, you witnesses above
Punish my life for tainting of my love !
Olivia. Ay me, detested ! how am I beguiled !
Viola. Who does beguile you ? who does do you wrong ?
Olivia. Hast thou forgot thyself ? is it so long ?
Call forth the holy father.
Duke.   Come, away !
Olivia. Whither, my lord ? Cesario, husband, stay.
Duke. Husband !
Olivia.   Ay, husband : can he that deny ?
Duke. Her husband, sirrah !
Viola.   No, my lord, not I.
Olivia. Alas, it is the baseness of thy fear
That makes thee strangle thy propriety :
Fear not, Cesario ; take thy fortunes up ;
Be that thou know'st thou art, and then thou art
As great as that thou fear'st.

Enter Priest.

O, welcome, father !
Father, I charge thee, by thy reverence,
Here to unfold, though lately we intended
To keep in darkness what occasion now
Reveals before 'tis ripe, what thou dost know
Hath newly pass'd between this youth and me.
Priest. A contract of eternal bond of love,
Confirm'd by mutual joinder of your hands,
Attested by the holy close of lips,
Strengthen'd by interchangement of your rings ;
And all the ceremony of this compact

Seal'd in my function, by my testimony:
Since when, my watch hath told me, toward my
    grave
I have travell'd but two hours.
  Duke. O thou dissembling cub! what wilt
    thou be
When time hath sow'd a grizzle on thy case?
Or will not else thy craft so quickly grow,
That thine own trip shall be thine overthrow?
Farewell, and take her; but direct thy feet
Where thou and I henceforth may never meet.
  Viola. My lord, I do protest—
  Olivia.   O, do not swear!
Hold little faith, though thou hast too much fear.

Enter Sir Andrew.

  Sir Andrew. For the love of God, a surgeon!
Send one presently to Sir Toby.
  Olivia. What's the matter?
  Sir Andrew. He has broke my head across and
has given Sir Toby a bloody coxcomb too: for the
love of God, your help! I had rather than forty
pound I were at home.
  Olivia. Who has done this, Sir Andrew?
  Sir Andrew. The count's gentleman, one Cesario:
we took him for a coward, but he's the very devil
incardinate.
  Duke. My gentleman, Cesario?
  Sir Andrew. 'Od's lifelings, here he is! You
broke my head for nothing; and that that I did,
I was set on to do 't by Sir Toby.
  Viola. Why do you speak to me? I never hurt
    you:
You drew your sword upon me without cause;
But I bespake you fair, and hurt you not.
  Sir Andrew. If a bloody coxcomb be a hurt,
you have hurt me: I think you set nothing by a
bloody coxcomb.

Enter Sir Toby *and* Clown.

Here comes Sir Toby halting: you shall hear more:
but if he had not been in drink, he would have
tickled you othergates than he did.
  Duke. How now, gentleman! how is 't with
you?
  Sir Toby. That's all one: has hurt me, and
there's the end on 't. Sot, didst see Dick surgeon,
sot?
  Clown. O, he's drunk, Sir Toby, an hour agóne;
his eyes were set at eight i' the morning.
  Sir Toby. Then he's a rogue, †and a passy
measures panyn: I hate a drunken rogue.
  Olivia. Away with him! Who hath made this
havoc with them?
  Sir Andrew. I'll help you, Sir Toby, because
we'll be dressed together.
  Sir Toby. Will you help? an ass-head and a
coxcomb and a knave, a thin-faced knave, a gull! I
  Olivia. Get him to bed, and let his hurt be
look'd to. [*Exeunt Clown, Fabian, Sir Toby, and*
                          Sir Andrew.

Enter Sebastian.

  Sebastian. I am sorry, madam, I have hurt your
    kinsman;
But, had it been the brother of my blood,
I must have done no less with wit and safety.

You throw a strange regard upon me, and by that
I do perceive it hath offended you:
Pardon me, sweet one, even for the vows
We made each other but so late ago.
  Duke. One face, one voice, one habit, and two
    persons,
A natural perspective, that is and is not!
  Sebastian. Antonio, O my dear Antonio!
How have the hours rack'd and tortured me,
Since I have lost thee!
  Antonio. Sebastian are you?
  Sebastian.   Fear'st thou that, Antonio?
  Antonio. How have you made division of your-
    self?
An apple, cleft in two, is not more twin
Than these two creatures. Which is Sebastian?
  Olivia. Most wonderful!
  Sebastian. Do I stand there? I never had a
    brother;
Nor can there be that deity in my nature,
Of here and every where. I had a sister.
Whom the blind waves and surges have devour'd.
Of charity, what kin are you to me?
What countryman? what name? what parentage?
  Viola. Of Messaline; Sebastian was my father;
Such a Sebastian was my brother too,
So went he suited to his watery tomb:
If spirits can assume both form and suit
You come to fright us.
  Sebastian.   A spirit I am indeed;
But am in that dimension grossly clad
Which from the womb I did participate.
Were you a woman, as the rest goes even,
I should my tears let fall upon your cheek,
And say 'Thrice-welcome, drowned Viola!'
  Viola. My father had a mole upon his brow.
  Sebastian. And so had mine.
  Viola. And died that day when Viola from her
    birth
Had number'd thirteen years.
  Sebastian. O, that record is lively in my soul!
He finished indeed his mortal act
That day that made my sister thirteen years.
  Viola. If nothing lets to make us happy both
But this my masculine usurp'd attire,
Do not embrace me till each circumstance
Of place, time, fortune, do cohere and jump
That I am Viola: which to confirm,
I'll bring you to a captain in this town,
Where lie my maiden weeds; by whose gentle help
I was preserved to serve this noble count,
All the occurrence of my fortune since
Hath been between this lady and this lord.
  Sebastian. [*To Olivia*] So comes it, lady, you have
    been mistook:
But nature to her bias drew in that.
You would have been contracted to a maid;
Nor are you therein, by my life, deceived,
You are betroth'd both to a maid and man.
  Duke. Be not amazed; right noble is his blood.
If this be so, as yet the glass seems true,
I shall have share in this most happy wreck.
[*To Viola*] Boy, thou hast said to me a thousand
    times
Thou never shouldst love woman like to me.
  Viola. And all those sayings will I over-swear;
And all those swearings keep as true in soul
As doth that orbed continent the fire
That severs day from night.
  Duke.   Give me thy hand;
And let me see thee in thy woman's weeds.

Viola. The captain that did bring me first on shore
Hath my maid's garments : he upon some action
Is now in durance, at Malvolio's suit,
A gentleman, and follower of my lady's.
Olivia. He shall enlarge him : fetch Malvolio
hither :
And yet, alas, now I remember me,
They say, poor gentleman, he 's much distract.

Re-enter CLOWN *with a letter, and* FABIAN.

A most extracting frenzy of mine own
From my remembrance clearly banish'd his.
How does he, sirrah ?
Clown. Truly, madam, he holds Belzebub at the
stave's end as well as a man in his case may do :
has here writ a letter to you ; I should have given 't
you to-day morning, but as a madman's epistles
are no gospels, so it skills not much when they
are delivered.
Olivia. Open 't, and read it.
Clown. Look then to be well edified when the
fool delivers the madman. [*Reads*] ' By the Lord,
madam,'—
Olivia. How now ! art thou mad ?
Clown. No, madam, I do but read madness : an
your ladyship will have it as it ought to be, you
must allow Vox.
Olivia. Prithee, read i' thy right wits.
Clown. So I do, madonna ; but to read this right
wits is to read thus : therefore perpend, my princess,
and give ear.
Olivia. Read it you, sirrah.   [*To Fabian.*
Fabian. [*Reads*] ' By the Lord, madam, you wrong
me, and the world shall know it : though you have
put me into darkness and given your drunken cousin
rule over me. yet have I the benefit of my senses as
well as your ladyship. I have your own letter
that induced me to the semblance I put on ; with
the which I doubt not but to do myself much right,
or you much shame. Think of me as you please.
I leave my duty a little unthought of and speak out
of my injury.
            THE MADLY-USED MALVOLIO.'
Olivia. Did he write this ?
Clown. Ay, madam.
Duke. This savours not much of distraction.
Olivia. See him deliver'd, Fabian ; bring him
hither.   [*Exit Fabian.*
My lord, so please you, these things further thought
on,
To think me as well a sister as a wife,
One day shall crown the alliance on 't, so please you,
Here at my house and at my proper cost.
Duke. Madam, I am most apt to embrace your
offer.
[*To Viola*] Your master quits you ; and for your
service done him,
So much against the mettle of your sex,
So far beneath your soft and tender breeding,
And since you call'd me master for so long,
Here is my hand ; you shall from this time be
Your master's mistress.
Olivia.   A sister ! you are she.

Re-enter FABIAN, *with* MALVOLIO.

Duke. Is this the madman ?
Olivia.   Ay, my lord, this same.
How now, Malvolio !
Malvolio.   Madam, you have done me wrong,
Notorious wrong.

Olivia.   Have I, Malvolio ? no.
Malvolio. Lady, you have.   Pray you, peruse
that letter.
You must not now deny it is your hand :
Write from it, if you can, in hand or phrase ;
Or say 'tis not your seal, not your invention :
You can say none of this : well, grant it then
And tell me, in the modesty of honour,
Why have you given me such clear lights of favour,
Bade me come smiling and cross-garter'd to you,
To put on yellow stockings and to frown
Upon Sir Toby and the lighter people ;
And, acting this in an obedient hope,
Why have you suffer'd me to be imprison'd,
Kept in a dark house, visited by the priest,
And made the most notorious geck and gull
That e'er invention play'd on ? tell me why.
Olivia. Alas, Malvolio, this is not my writing,
Though, I confess, much like the character :
But out of question 'tis Maria's hand.
And now I do bethink me, it was she
First told me thou wast mad ; then camest in smiling,
And in such forms which here were presupposed
Upon thee in the letter.   Prithee, be content :
This practice hath most shrewdly pass'd upon
thee ;
But when we know the grounds and authors of it,
Thou shalt be both the plaintiff and the judge
Of thine own cause.
Fabian.   Good madam, hear me speak,
And let no quarrel nor no brawl to come
Taint the condition of this present hour,
Which I have wonder'd at.   In hope it shall not,
Most freely I confess, myself and Toby
Set this device against Malvolio here,
Upon some stubborn and uncourteous parts
We had conceived against him : Maria writ
The letter at Sir Toby's great importance ; .
In recompense whereof he hath married her.
How with a sportful malice it was follow'd,
May rather pluck on laughter than revenge ;
If that the injuries be justly weigh'd
That have on both sides pass'd.
Olivia. Alas, poor fool, how have they baffled
thee !
Clown. Why, ' some are born great, some achieve
greatness, and some have greatness thrown upon
them.' I was one, sir, in this interlude ; one Sir
Topas, sir ; but that's all one. ' By the Lord,
fool, I am not mad.' But do you remember ?
' Madam, why laugh you at such a barren rascal ?'
an you smile not, he 's gagged : ' and thus the whirli-
gig of time brings in his revenges.
Malvolio. I 'll be revenged on the whole pack
of you.   [*Exit.*
Olivia. He hath been most notoriously abused.
Duke. Pursue him, and entreat him to a peace :
He hath not told us of the captain yet :
When that is known and golden time convents,
A solemn combination shall be made
Of our dear souls. Meantime, sweet sister,
We will not part from hence. Cesario, come ;
For so you shall be, while you are a man ;
But when in other habits you are seen,
Orsino's mistress and his fancy's queen.
                    [*Exeunt all, except Clown.*

Clown. [*Sings*]
    When that I was and a little tiny boy,
        With hey, ho, the wind and the rain,
    A foolish thing was but a toy,
        For the rain it raineth every day.

But when I came to man's estate,
  With hey, ho, &c.
'Gainst knaves and thieves men shut their gate,
  For the rain, &c.

But when I came, alas ! to wive,
  With hey, ho, &c.
By swaggering could I never thrive,
  For the rain, &c.

But when I came unto my beds,
  With hey, ho, &c.
With toss-pots still had drunken heads,
  For the rain, &c.

A great while ago the world begun,
  With hey, ho, &c.
But that 's all one, our play is done,
  And we 'll strive to please you every day.

                    [*Exit.*

THE

WINTER'S TALE

DRAMATIS PERSONÆ

LEONTES, king of Sicilia.
MAMILLIUS, *young prince of Sicilia*
CAMILLO,
ANTIGONUS,
CLEOMENES,   } *Four Lords of Sicilia.*
DION,
POLIXENES, *king of Bohemia.*
FLORIZEL, *prince of Bohemia.*
ARCHIDAMUS, *a Lord of Bohemia.*
Old Shepherd. *reputed·father of* Perdita.
Clown, *his son.*
AUTOLYCUS, *a rogue.*
A Mariner.
A Gaoler.

HERMIONE, queen to LEONTES.
PERDITA, *daughter to* Leontes *and* Hermione.
PAULINA, *wife to* Antigonus.
EMILIA, *a lady attending on* Hermione.
MOPSA,
DORCAS,   } *Shepherdesses.*

Other Lords *and* Gentlemen, Ladies, Officers,
and Servants, Shepherds, *and* Shepherdesses.

Time, as Chorus.

SCENE : Sicilia, and Bohemia.

ACT I

SCENE I. *Antechamber in* LEONTES' *palace.*

Enter CAMILLO *and* ARCHIDAMUS.

Archidamus.

I f you shall chance, Camillo, to visit Bohemia, on
the like occasion whereon my services are now
on foot, you shall see, as I have said, great
difference betwixt our Bohemia and your Sicilia.
Camillo. I think, this coming summer, the King
of Sicilia means to pay Bohemia the visitation which
he justly owes him.
Archidamus. Wherein our entertainment shall
shame us we will be justified in our loves ; for
indeed—
Camillo. Beseech you,—
Archidamus. Verily, I speak it in the freedom of
my knowledge : we cannot with such magnifi-
cence—in so rare—I know not what to say. We
will give you sleepy drinks, that your senses, unin-
telligent of our insufficience, may, though they

cannot praise us, as little accuse us.
Camillo. You pay a great deal too dear for
what 's given freely.
Archidamus. Believe me, I speak as my understanding instructs me and as mine honesty puts
it to utterance.
Camillo. Sicilia cannot show himself over-kind
to Bohemia. They were trained together in their
childhoods ; and there rooted betwixt them then
such an affection, which cannot choose but branch
now. Since their more mature dignities and royal
necessities made separation of their society, their
encounters, though not personal, have been royally
attorneyed with interchange of gifts, letters, loving
embassies ; that they have seemed to be together,
though absent, shook hands, as over a vast, and
embraced, as it were, from the ends of opposed
winds. The heavens continue their loves !
Archidamus. I think there is not in the world
either malice or matter to alter it. You have an
unspeakable comfort of your young prince Mamillius : it is a gentleman of the greatest promise that
ever came into my note.
Camillo. I very well agree with you in the hopes
of him : it is a gallant child ; one that indeed physics
the subject, makes old hearts fresh : they that
went on crutches ere he was born desire yet their
life to see him a man.
Archidamus. Would they else be content to die ?
Camillo. Yes ; if there were no other excuse
why they should desire to live.
Archidamus. If the king had no son, they would
desire to live on crutches till he had one.
                                                  [*Exeunt.*

SCENE II. *A room of state in the same.*

Enter LEONTES, HERMIONE, MAMILLIUS,
POLIXENES, CAMILLO, *and* Attendants.

Polixenes. Nine changes of the watery star hath
        been
The shepherd's note since we have left our throne
Without a burthen : time as long again
Would be fill'd up, my brother, with our thanks ;
And yet we should, for perpetuity,
Go hence in debt : and therefore, like a cipher,
Yet standing in rich place, I multiply
With one ' We thank you ' many thousands moe
That go before it.
Leontes.   Stay your thanks a while ;
And pay them when you part.
Polixenes.   Sir, that 's to-morrow.
I am question'd by my fears, of what may chance
Or breed upon our absence ; that may blow
No sneaping winds at home, to make us say
' This is put forth too truly : ' besides, I have stay'd
To tire your royalty.
Leontes.   We are tougher, brother,
Than you can put us to 't.

Polixenes.   No longer stay.
Leontes. One seven-night longer.
Polixenes.   Very sooth, to-morrow.
Leontes. We 'll part the time between 's then ;
and in that
I 'll no gainsaying.
Polixenes.   Press me not, beseech you, so.
There is no tongue that moves, none, none i' the
world,
So soon as yours could win me : so it should now,
Were there necessity in your request, although
'Twere needful I denied it. My affairs
Do even drag me homeward : which to hinder
Were in your love a whip to me ; my stay
To you a charge and trouble : to save both,
Farewell, our brother.
Leontes.   Tongue-tied our queen ? speak you.
Hermione. I had thought, sir, to have held my
peace until
You had drawn oaths from him not to stay.
You, sir,
Charge him too coldly. Tell him, you are sure
All in Bohemia 's well ; this satisfaction
The by-gone day proclaim'd : say this to him,
He 's beat from his best ward.
Leontes.   Well said, Hermione.
Hermione. To tell, he longs to see his son, were
strong :
But let him say so then, and let him go ;
But let him swear so, and he shall not stay,
We 'll thwack him hence with distaffs.
Yet of your royal presence I 'll adventure
The borrow of a week. When at Bohemia
You take my lord, I 'll give him my commission
To let him there a month behind the gest
Prefix'd for 's parting : yet, good deed, Leontes,
I love thee not a jar o' the clock behind
What lady-she her lord. You 'll stay ?
Polixenes.   No, madam.
Hermione. Nay, but you will ?
Polixenes.   I may not, verily.
Hermione. Verily !
You put me off with limber vows ; but I,
Though you would seek to unsphere the stars with
oaths,
Should yet say ' Sir, no going.' Verily,
You shall not go : a lady's ' Verily ' 's
As potent as a lord's. Will you go yet ?
Force me to keep you as a prisoner,
Not like a guest ; so you shall pay your fees
When you depart, and save your thanks. How
say you ?
My prisoner ? or my guest ? by your dread ' Verily,'
One of them you shall be.
Polixenes.   Your guest, then, madam ;
To be your prisoner should import offending ;
Which is for me less easy to commit
Than you to punish.
Hermione.   Not your gaoler, then,
But your kind hostess. Come, I 'll question you
Of my lord's tricks and yours when you were boys :
You were pretty lordings then ?
Polixenes.   We were, fair queen,
Two lads that thought there was no more behind
But such a day to-morrow as to-day.
And to be boy eternal.
Hermione.   Was not my lord
The verier wag o' the two ?
Polixenes. We were as twinn'd lambs that did
frisk i' the sun,
And bleat the one at the other : what we changed

Was innocence for innocence ; we knew not
The doctrine of ill-doing, nor dream'd
That any did. Had we pursued that life,
And our weak spirits ne'er been higher rear'd
With stronger blood, we should have answer'd
heaven
Boldly ' not guilty ; ' the imposition clear'd
Hereditary ours.
Hermione.   By this we gather
You have tripp'd since.
Polixenes.   O my most sacred lady !
Temptations have since then been born to 's ; for
In those unfledged days was my wife a girl ;
Your precious self had then not cross'd the eyes
Of my young play-fellow.
Hermione.   Grace to boot ! ·
Of this make no conclusion, lest you say
Your queen and I are devils : yet go on ;
The offences we have made you do we 'll answer,
If you first sinn'd with us and that with us
You did continue fault and that you slipp'd not
With any but with us.
Leontes.   Is he won yet ?
Hermione. He 'll stay, my lord.
Leontes.   At my request he would not.
Hermione, my dearest, thou never spokest
To better purpose.
Hermione.   Never ?
Leontes.   Never, but once.
Hermione. What ! have I twice said well ? when
was 't before ?
I prithee tell me ; cram 's with praise, and make 's
As fat as tame things : one good deed dying tongueless
Slaughters a thousand waiting upon that. .
Our praises are our wages : you may ride 's
With one soft kiss a thousand furlongs ere
With spur we heat an acre. But to the goal :
My last good deed was to entreat his stay :
What was my first ? it has an elder sister,
Or I mistake you : O, would her name were Grace !
But once before I spoke to the purpose : when ?
Nay, let me have 't ; I long.
Leontes.   Why, that was when
Three crabbed months had sour'd themselves to
death,
Ere I could make thee open thy white hand
And clap thyself my love : then didst thou utter
' I am yours for ever.'
Hermione.   'Tis grace indeed.
Why, lo you now, I have spoke to the purpose twice :
The one for ever earn'd a royal husband ;
The other for some while a friend.
Leontes.   [*Aside*] Too hot, too hot !
To mingle friendship far is mingling bloods.
I have tremor cordis on me : my heart dances ;
But not for joy ; not joy. This entertainment
May a free face put on, derive a liberty
From heartiness, from bounty, fertile bosom,
And well become the agent ; 't may, I grant ;
But to be paddling palms and pinching fingers,
As now they are, and making practised smiles,
As in a looking-glass, and then to sigh, as 'twere
The mort o' the deer ; O, that is entertainment
My bosom likes not, nor my brows ! Mamillius,
Art thou my boy ?
Mamillius.   Ay, my good lord.
Leontes.   I' fecks !
Why, that 's my bawcock. What, hast smutch'd
thy nose ?
They say it is a copy out of mine. Come, captain,
We must be neat ; not neat, but cleanly, captain :

And yet the steer, the heifer and the calf
Are all call'd neat.—Still virginalling
Upon his palm !—How now, you wanton calf !
Art thou my calf ?
Mamillius.   Yes, if you will, my lord.
Leontes. Thou want'st a rough pash and the
   shoots that I have,
To be full like me : yet they say we are
Almost as like as eggs ; women say so,
That will say any thing : but were they false
As o'er-dyed blacks, as wind, as waters, false
As dice are to be wish'd by one that fixes
No bourn 'twixt his and 'mine, yet were it true
To say this boy were like me. Come, sir page,
Look on me with your welkin eye : sweet villain !
Most dear'st ! my collop ! can thy dam ?—may 't
   be ?—
Affection ! thy intention stabs the centre :
Thou dost make possible things not so held,
Communicatest with dreams ;—how can this be ?—
With what 's unreal thou coactive art,
And fellow'st nothing : then 'tis very credent
Thou mayst co-join with something ; and thou dost,
And that beyond commission, and I find it,
And that to the infection of my brains
And hardening of my brows.
Polixenes.   What means Sicilia ?
Hermione. He something seems unsettled.
Polixenes.   How, my lord !
What cheer ? how is 't with you, best brother ?
Hermione.   You look
As if you held a brow of much distraction :
Are you moved, my lord ?
Leontes.   No, in good earnest.
How sometimes nature will betray its folly,
Its tenderness, and make itself a pastime
To harder bosoms ! Looking on the lines
Of my boy's face, methoughts I did recoil
Twenty-three years, and saw myself unbreech'd,
In my green velvet coat, my dagger muzzled,
Lest it should bite its master, and so prove,
As ornaments oft do, too dangerous :
How like, methought, I then was to this kernel,
This squash, this gentleman. Mine honest friend,
Will you take eggs for money ?
Mamillius. No, my lord, I 'll fight.
Leontes. You will ! why, happy man be 's dole !
My brother,
Are you so fond of your young prince as we
Do seem to be of ours ?
Polixenes.   If at home, sir,
He 's all my exercise, my mirth, my matter,
Now my sworn friend and then mine enemy,
My parasite, my soldier, statesman, all :
He makes a July's day short as December,
And with his varying childness cures in me
Thoughts that would thick my blood.
Leontes.   So stands this squire
Officed with me : we two will walk, my lord,
And leave you to your graver steps. Hermione,
How thou lovest us, show in our brother's welcome ;
Let what is dear in Sicily be cheap :
Next to thyself and my young rover, he 's
Apparent to my heart.
Hermione.   If you would seek us,
We are yours i' the garden : shall 's attend you
   there ?
Leontes. To your own bents dispose you : you 'll
   be found,
Be you beneath the sky. [*Aside*] I am angling
   now,

Though you perceive me not how I give line.
Go to, go to !
How she holds up the neb, the bill to him !
And arms her with the boldness of a wife
To her allowing husband !
          [*Exeunt Polixenes, Hermione, and
                              Attendants.*
          Gone already !
Inch-thick, knee-deep, o'er head and ears a fork'd
   one !
Go, play, boy, play : thy mother plays, and I
Play too, but so disgraced a part, whose issue
Will hiss me to my grave : contempt and clamour
Will be my knell. Go, play, boy, play. There
   have been,
Or I am much deceived, cuckolds ere now ;
And many a man there is, even at this present,
Now while I speak this, holds his wife by the arm,
That little thinks she has been sluiced in 's absence
And his pond fish'd by his next neighbour, by
Sir Smile, his neighbour : nay, there 's comfort
   in 't
Whiles other men have gates and those gates open'd,
As mine, against their will. Should all despair
That have revolted wives, the tenth of mankind
Would hang themselves. Physic for 't there is none ;
It is a bawdy planet, that will strike
Where 'tis predominant ; and 'tis powerful, think it,
From east, west, north and south : be it concluded,
No barricado for a belly ; know 't ;
It will let in and out the enemy
With bag and baggage : many thousand on 's
Have the disease, and feel 't not. How now, boy !
Mamillius. I am like you, they say.
Leontes.   Why, that 's some comfort.
What, Camillo there ?
Camillo. Ay, my good lord.
Leontes. Go play, Mamillius ; thou 'rt an honest
   man.   [*Exit Mamillius.*
Camillo, this great sir will yet stay longer.
Camillo. You had much ado to make his anchor
   hold :
When you cast out, it still came home.
Leontes.   Didst note it ?
Camillo. He would not stay at your petitions ;
   made
His business more material.
Leontes.   Didst perceive it ?
[*Aside*] They 're here with me already, whispering,
   rounding
' Sicilia is a so-forth : ' 'tis far gone,
When I shall gust it last. How came 't, Camillo,
That he did stay ?
Camillo.   At the good queen's entreaty.
Leontes. At the queen's be 't : ' good ' should
   be pertinent ;
But, so it is, it is not. Was this taken
By any understanding pate but thine ?
For thy conceit is soaking, will draw in
More than the common blocks : not noted, is 't,
But of the finer natures ? by some severals
Of head-piece extraordinary ? lower messes
Perchance are to this business purblind ? say.

Camillo. Business, my lord ! I think most un-
   derstand
Bohemia stays here longer.
Leontes.   Ha !
Camillo.   Stays here longer.
Leontes. Ay, but why ?

Camillo. To satisfy your highness and the en-
treaties
Of our most gracious mistress.
Leontes.   Satisfy !
The entreaties of your mistress ! satisfy !
Let that suffice. I have trusted thee, Camillo
With all the nearest things to my heart, as well
My chamber-councils, wherein, priest-like, thou
Hast cleansed my bosom, I from thee departed
Thy penitent reform'd : but we have been
Deceived in thy integrity, deceived
In that which seems so.
Camillo.   Be it forbid, my lord !
Leontes. To bide upon 't, thou art not honest, or,
If thou inclinest that way, thou art a coward,
Which hoxes honesty behind, restraining
From course required ; or else thou must be counted
A servant grafted in my serious trust
And therein negligent ; or else a fool
That seest a game play'd home, the rich stake drawn,
And takest it all for jest.
Camillo.   My gracious lord,
I may be negligent, foolish and fearful ;
In every one of these no man is free,
But that his negligence, his folly, fear,
Among the infinite doings of the world,
Sometime puts forth. In your affairs, my lord,
If ever I were wilful-negligent,
It was my folly ; if industriously
I play'd the fool, it was my negligence,
Not weighing well the end ; if ever fearful
To do a thing, where I the issue doubted,
Whereof the execution did cry out
Against the non-performance, 'twas a fear
Which oft infects the wisest : these, my lord,
Are such allow'd infirmities that honesty
Is never free of. But, beseech your grace,
Be plainer with me ; let me know my trespass
By its own visage : if I then deny it,
'Tis none of mine.
Leontes.   Ha' not you seen, Camillo,—
But that 's past doubt, you have, or your eye-glass
Is thicker than a cuckold's horn,—or heard,—
For to a vision so apparent rumour
Cannot be mute,—or thought,—for cogitation
Resides not in that man that does not think,—
My wife is slippery ? If thou wilt confess,
Or else be impudently negative,
To have nor eyes nor ears nor thought, then say
My wife 's a hobby-horse, deserves a name
As rank as any flax-wench that puts to
Before her troth-plight : say 't and justify 't.
Camillo. I would not be a stander-by to hear
My sovereign mistress clouded so, without
My present vengeance taken : 'shrew my heart,
You never spoke what did become you less
Than this ; which to reiterate were sin
As deep as that, though true.
Leontes.   Is whispering nothing ?
Is leaning cheek to cheek ? is meeting noses ?
Kissing with inside lip ? stopping the career
Of laughter with a sigh ?—a note infallible
Of breaking honesty—horsing foot on foot ?
Skulking in corners ? wishing clocks more swift ?
Hours, minutes ? noon, midnight ? and all eyes
Blind with the pin and web but theirs, theirs only,
That would unseen be wicked ? is this nothing ?
Why, then the world and all that 's in 't is nothing ;
The covering sky is nothing ; Bohemia nothing ;
My wife is nothing ; nor nothing have these nothings,
If this be nothing.

Camillo.   Good my lord, be cured
Of this diseased opinion, and betimes ;
For 'tis most dangerous.
Leontes.   Say it be, 'tis true.
Camillo. No, no, my lord.
Leontes.   It is ; you lie, you lie :
I say thou liest, Camillo, and I hate thee,
Pronounce thee a gross lout, a mindless slave,
Or else a hovering temporizer, that
Canst with thine eyes at once see good and evil,
Inclining to them both : were my wife's liver
Infected as her life, she would not live
The running of one glass.
Camillo.   Who does infect her ?
Leontes. Why, he that wears her like her medal,
hanging
About his neck, Bohemia : who, if I
Had servants true about me, that bare eyes
To see alike mine honour as their profits,
Their own particular thrifts, they would do that
Which should undo more doing : ay, and thou,
His cupbearer,—whom I from meaner form
Have bench'd and rear'd to worship, who mayst
see
Plainly as heaven sees earth and earth sees heaven.
How I am galled,—mightst bespice a cup
To give mine enemy a lasting wink ;
Which draught to me were cordial.
Camillo.   Sir, my lord,
I could do this, and that with no rash potion,
But with a lingering dram that should not work
Maliciously like poison : but I cannot
Believe this crack to be in my dread mistress,
So sovereignly being honourable.
I have loved thee,—
Leontes. † Make that thy question, and go rot !
Dost think I am so muddy, so unsettled,
To appoint myself in this vexation, sully
The purity and whiteness of my sheets,
Which to preserve is sleep, which being spotted
Is goads, thorns, nettles, tails of wasps,
Give scandal to the blood o' the prince my son,
Who I do think is mine and love as mine,
Without ripe moving to 't ? Would I do this ?
Could man so blench ?
Camillo.   I must believe you, sir :
I do ; and will fetch off Bohemia for 't ;
Provided that, when he 's removed, your highness
Will take again your queen as yours at first,
Even for your son's sake ; and thereby for sealing
The injury of tongues in courts and kingdoms
Known and allied to yours.
Leontes.   Thou dost advise me
Even as I mine own course have set down :
I 'll give no blemish to her honour, none.
Camillo. My lord,
Go then ; and with a countenance as clear
As friendship wears at feasts, keep with Bohemia
And with your queen. I am his cupbearer :
If from me he have wholesome beverage,
Account me not your servant.
Leontes.   This is all :
Do 't and thou hast the one half of my heart ;
Do 't not, thou split'st thine own.
Camillo.   I 'll do 't, my lord.
Leontes. I will seem friendly, as thou hast advised
me.   [*Exit.*
Camillo. O miserable lady ! But, for me,
What case stand I in ? I must be the poisoner
Of good Polixenes ; and my ground to do 't
Is the obedience to a master, one

Who in rebellion with himself will have
All that are his so too. To do this deed,
Promotion follows. If I could find example
Of thousands that had struck anointed kings
And flourish'd after, I 'ld not do 't ; but since
Nor brass nor stone nor parchment bears not
 one,
Let villany itself forswear't. I must
Forsake the court : to do 't, or no, is certain
To me a break-neck. Happy star reign now !
Here comes Bohemia.

Re-enter POLIXENES.

Polixenes. This is strange : methinks
My favour here begins to warp. Not speak ?
Good day, Camillo.
 Camillo. Hail, most royal sir !
 Polixenes. What is the news i' the court ?
 Camillo. None rare, my lord.
 Polixenes. The king hath on him such a counte-
nance
As he had lost some province and a region
Loved as he loves himself : even now I met him
With customary compliment ; when he,
Wafting his eyes to the contrary and falling
A lip of much contempt, speeds from me and
So leaves me to consider what is breeding
That changeth thus his manners.
 Camillo. I dare not know, my lord.
 Polixenes. How ! dare not ! do not. Do you
know, and dare not ?
Be intelligent to me : 'tis thereabouts ;
For, to yourself, what you do know, you must,
And cannot say, you dare not. Good Camillo,
Your changed complexions are to me a mirror
Which shows me mine changed too ; for I must be
A party in this alteration, finding
Myself thus alter'd with 't.
 Camillo. There is a sickness
Which puts some of us in distemper, but
I cannot name the disease ; and it is caught
Of you that yet are well.
 Polixenes. How ! caught of me !
Make me not sighted like the basilisk :
I have look'd on thousands, who have sped the
 better
By my regard, but kill'd none so. Camillo,—
As you are certainly a gentleman, thereto
Clerk-like experienced, which no less adorns
Our gentry than our parents' noble names,
In whose success we are gentle,—I beseech you,
If you know aught which does behove my know-
 ledge
Thereof to be inform'd, imprison 't not
In ignorant concealment.
 Camillo. I may not answer.
 Polixenes. A sickness caught of me, and yet I
 well !
I must be answer'd. Dost thou hear, Camillo ?
I conjure thee, by all the parts of man
Which honour does acknowledge, whereof the least
Is not this suit of mine, that thou declare
What incidency thou dost guess of harm
Is creeping toward me ; how far off, how near ;
Which way to be prevented, if to be ;
If not, how best to bear it.
 Camillo. Sir, I will tell you ;
Since I am charged in honour and by him
That I think honourable : therefore mark my
 counsel,

Which must be even as swiftly follow'd as
I mean to utter it, or both yourself and me
Cry lost, and so good night !
 Polixenes. On, good Camillo.
 Camillo. I am appointed him to murder you.
 Polixenes. By whom, Camillo ?
 Camillo. By the king.
 Polixenes. For what ?
 Camillo. He thinks, nay, with all confidence he
 swears,
As he had seen 't or been an instrument
To vice you to 't, that you have touch'd his queen
Forbiddenly.
 Polixenes. O, then my best blood turn
To an infected jelly and my name
Be yoked with his that did betray the Best !
Turn then my freshest reputation to
A savour that may strike the dullest nostril
Where I arrive, and my approach be shunn'd,
Nay, hated too, worse than the great'st infection
That e'er was heard or read !
 Camillo. Swear his thought over
By each particular star in heaven and
By all their influences, you may as well
Forbid the sea for to obey the moon
As or by oath remove or counsel shake
The fabric of his folly, whose foundation
Is piled upon his faith and will continue
The standing of his body.
 Polixenes. How should this grow ?
 Camillo. I know not : but I am sure 'tis safer to
Avoid what 's grown than question how 'tis born.
If therefore you dare trust my honesty,
That lies enclosed in this trunk which you
Shall bear along impawn'd, away to-night !
Your followers I will whisper to the business,
And will by twos and threes at several posterns
Clear them o' the city. For myself, I 'll put
My fortunes to your service, which are here
By this discovery lost. Be not uncertain ;
For, by the honour of my parents, I
Have utter'd truth : which if you seek to prove,
I dare not stand by ; nor shall you be safer
Than one condemn'd by the king's own mouth,
 thereon
His execution sworn.
 Polixenes. I do believe thee :
I saw his heart in 's face. Give me thy hand :
Be pilot to me and thy places shall
Still neighbour mine. My ships are ready and
My people do expect my hence departure
Two days ago. This jealousy
Is for a precious creature : as she 's rare,
Must it be great, and as his person 's mighty,
Must it be violent, and as he does conceive
He is dishonour'd by a man which ever
Profess'd to him, why, his revenges must
In that be made more bitter. Fear o'ershades me :
Good expedition be my friend, and comfort
† The gracious queen, part of his theme, but nothing
Of his ill-ta'en suspicion ! Come, Camillo ;
I will respect thee as a father if
Thou bear'st my life off hence : let us avoid.
 Camillo. It is in mine authority to command
The keys of all the posterns : please your highness
To take the urgent hour. Come, sir, away.
             [*Exeunt.*

ACT II

SCENE I. *A room in* Leontes' *palace.*

Enter Hermione, Mamillius, *and* Ladies.

Hermione.

Take the boy to you : he so troubles me,
'Tis past enduring.
 First Lady. Come, my gracious lord,
Shall I be your playfellow ?
 Mamillius.   No, I 'll none of you.
 First Lady. Why, my sweet lord ?
 Mamillius. You 'll kiss me hard and speak to
me as if
I were a baby still. I love you better.
 Second Lady. And why so, my lord ?
 Mamillius.   Not for because
Your brows are blacker ; yet black brows, they say,
Become some women best, so that there be not
Too much hair there, but in a semicircle,
Of a half-moon made with a pen.
 Second Lady. Who taught you this ?
 Mamillius. I learnt it out of women's faces.
Pray now
What colour are your eyebrows ?
 First Lady. Blue, my lord.
 Mamillius. Nay, that 's a mock : I have seen a
lady's nose
That has been blue, but not her eyebrows.
 First Lady. Hark ye ;
The queen your mother rounds apace : we shall
Present our services to a fine new prince
One of these days ; and then you 'ld wanton with
us,
If we would have you.
 Second Lady. She is spread of late
Into a goodly bulk : good time encounter her !
 Hermione. What wisdom stirs amongst you ?
Come, sir, now
I am for you again : pray you, sit by us,
And tell 's a tale.
 Mamillius. Merry or sad shall 't be ?
 Hermione. As merry as you will.
 Mamillius. A sad tale 's best for winter : I have
one
Of sprites and goblins.
 Hermione. Let 's have that, good sir.
Come on, sit down : come on, and do your best
To fright me with your sprites ; you 're powerful
at it.
 Mamillius. There was a man—
 Hermione. Nay, come, sit down ; then on.
 Mamillius. Dwelt by a churchyard : I will tell it
softly ;
Yond crickets shall not hear it.
 Hermione. Come on, then,
And give 't me in mine ear.

Enter Leontes, *with* Antigonus, Lords,
and others.

 Leontes. Was he met there ? his train ? Camillo
with him ?
 First Lord. Behind the tuft of pines I met them ;
never
Saw I men scour so on their way : I eyed them
Even to their ships.
 Leontes. How blest am I
In my just censure, in my true opinion !
Alack, for lesser knowledge ! how accursed

In being so blest ! There may be in the cup
A spider steep'd, and one may drink, depart,
And yet partake no venom, for his knowledge
Is not infected : but if one present
The abhorr'd ingredient to his eye, make known
How he hath drunk, he cracks his gorge, his sides,
With violent hefts. I have drunk, and seen the
spider.
Camillo was his help in this, his pandar :
There is a plot against my life, my crown ;
All 's true that is mistrusted : that false villain
Whom I employ'd was pre-employ'd by him :
He has discover'd my design, and I
Remain a pinch'd thing ; yea, a very trick
For them to play at will. How came the posterns
So easily open ?
 First Lord. By his great authority ;
Which often hath no less prevail'd than so
On your command.
 Leontes. I know 't too well.
Give me the boy : I am glad you did not nurse him :
Though he does bear some signs of me, yet you
Have too much blood in him.
 Hermione. What is this ? sport ?
 Leontes. Bear the boy hence ; he shall not come
about her ;
Away with him ! and let her sport herself
With that she 's big with ; for 'tis Polixenes
Has made thee swell thus.
 Hermione. But I 'ld say he had not,
And I 'll be sworn you would believe my saying,
Howe'er you lean to the nayward.
 Leontes. You, my lords,
Look on her, mark her well ; be but about
To say ' she is a goodly lady,' and
The justice of your hearts will thereto add
' 'Tis pity she 's not honest, honourable : '
Praise her but for this her without-door form,
Which on my faith deserves high speech, and straight
The shrug, the hum or ha, these petty brands
That calumny doth use—O, I am out—
That mercy does, for calumny will sear
Virtue itself : these shrugs, these hums and ha's,
When you have said ' she 's goodly,' come between
Ere you can say ' she 's honest : ' but be 't known,
From him that has most cause to grieve it should be,
She 's an adulteress.
 Hermione. Should a villain say so,
The most replenish'd villain in the world,
He were as much more villain : you, my lord,
Do but mistake.
 Leontes. You have mistook, my lady,
Polixenes for Leontes : O thou thing
Which I 'll not call a creature of thy place,
Lest barbarism, making me the precedent,
Should a like language use to all degrees
And mannerly distinguishment leave out
Betwixt the prince and beggar : I have said
She 's an adulteress ; I have said with whom :
More, she 's a traitor and Camillo is
A federary with her, and one that knows
What she should shame to know herself
But with her most vile principal, that she 's
A bed-swerver, even as bad as those
That vulgars give bold'st titles, ay, and privy
To this their late escape.
 Hermione. No, by my life,
Privy to none of this. How will this grieve you,
When you shall come to clearer knowledge, that
You thus have publish'd me ! Gentle my lord,
You scarce can right me throughly then to say

You did mistake.

Leontes.   No ; if I mistake
In those foundations which I build upon,
The centre is not big enough to bear
A school-boy s top.   Away with her ! to prison !
He who shall speak for her is afar off guilty
But that he speaks.

Hermione.   There 's some ill planet reigns :
I must be patient till the heavens look
With an aspect more favourable.   Good my lords,
I am not prone to weeping, as our sex
Commonly are ; the want of wh:ch vain dew
Perchance shall dry your pities : but I have
That honourable grief lodged here which burns
Worse than tears drown : beseech you all, my lords,
With thoughts so qualified as your charities
Shall best instruct you, measure me ; and so
The king's will be perform'd !

Leontes.   Shall I be heard ?

Hermione. Who is 't that goes with me ? Beseech
your highness,
My women may be with me ; for you see
My plight requires it.   Do not weep, good fools ;
There is no cause : when you shall know your
    mistress
Has deserved prison, then abound in tears
As I come out : this action I now go on
Is for my better grace.   Adieu, my lord :
I never wish'd to see you sorry ; now
I trust I shall.   My women, come ; you have leave.

Leontes. Go, do our bidding ; hence !
            [*Exit Queen, guarded ; with Ladies.*

First Lord. Beseech your highness, call the
queen again.

Antigonus. Be certain what you do, sir, lest your
justice
Prove violence ; in the which three great ones suffer,
Yourself, your queen, your son.

First Lord.   For her, my lord,
I dare my life lay down and will do 't, sir,
Please you to accept it, that the queen is spotless
I' the eyes of heaven and to you ; I mean,
In this which you accuse her.

Antigonus.   If it prove
† She 's otherwise, I 'll keep my stables where
I lodge my wife ; I 'll go in couples with her ;
Than when I feel and see her no farther trust her ;
For every inch of woman in the world,
Ay, every dram of woman's flesh is false,
If she be.

Leontes. Hold your peaces.

First Lord.   Good my lord,—

Antigonus. It is for you we speak, not for our-
selves :
You are abused and by some putter-on
That will be damn'd for 't ; would I knew the
villain,
† I would land-damn him.   Be she honour-flaw'd,
I have three daughters ; the eldest is eleven ;
The second and the third, nine, and some five ;
If this prove true, they 'll pay for 't : by mine honour,
I 'll geld 'em all ; fourteen they shall not see,
To bring false generations : they are co-heirs ;
And I had rather glib myself than they
Should not produce fair issue.

Leontes.   Cease ; no more.
You smell this business with a sense as cold
As is a dead man's nose : but I do see 't and feel 't,
As you feel doing thus ; and see withal
The instruments that feel.

Antigonus.   If it be so,

We need no grave to bury honesty :
There 's not a grain of it the face to sweeten
Of the whole dungy earth.

Leontes.   What ! lack I credit ?

First Lord. I had rather you did lack than I,
my lord,
Upon this ground ; and more it would content me
To have her honour true than your suspicion,
Be blamed for 't how you might.

Leontes.   Why, what need we
Commune with you of this, but rather follow
Our forceful instigation ? Our prerogative
Calls not your counsels, but our natural goodness
Imparts this ; which if you, or stupified
Or seeming so in skill, cannot or will not
Relish a truth like us, inform yourselves
We need no more of your advice : the matter,
The loss, the gain, the ordering on 't, is all
Properly ours.

Antigonus. And I wish, my liege,
You had only in your silent judgment tried it,
Without more overture.

Leontes.   How could that be ?
Either thou art most ignorant by age,
Or thou wert born a fool.   Camillo's flight,
Added to their familiarity,
Which was as gross as ever touch'd conjecture,
That lack'd sight only, nought for approbation
But only seeing, all other circumstances
Made up to the deed, doth push on this proceeding:
Yet, for a greater confirmation,
For in an act of this importance 'twere
Most piteous to be wild, I have dispatch'd in post
To sacred Delphos, to Apollo's temple,
Cleomenes and Dion, whom you know
Of stuff'd sufficiency : now from the oracle
They will bring all ; whose spiritual counsel had.
Shall stop or spur me.   Have I done well ?

First Lord. Well done, my lord.

Leontes. Though I am satisfied and need no more
Than what I know, yet shall the oracle
Give rest to the minds of others, such as he
Whose ignorant credulity will not
Come up to the truth.   So have we thought it good
From our free person she should be confined,
Lest that the treachery of the two fled hence
Be left her to perform.   Come, follow us ;
We are to speak in public ; for this business
Will raise us all.

Antigonus. [*Aside*] To laughter, as I take it,
If the good truth were known.   [*Exeunt.*

SCENE II.   *A prison.*

Enter PAULINA, *a Gentleman, and* Attendants.

Paulina. The keeper of the prison, call to him ;
Let him have knowledge who I am. [*Exit Gentleman.*
            Good lady,
No court in Europe is too good for thee ;
What dost thou then in prison ?

Re-enter Gentleman, *with the* Gaoler.

            Now, good sir,
You know me, do you not ?

Gaoler.   For a worthy lady
And one whom much I honour.

Paulina.   Pray you then,
Conduct me to the queen.

Gaoler.   I may not, madam :

To the contrary, I have express commandment.
Paulina. Here 's ado,
To lock up honesty and honour from
The access of gentle visitors ! Is 't lawful, pray you,
To see her women ? any of them ? Emilia ?
Gaoler. So please you, madam,
To put apart these your attendants, I
Shall bring Emilia forth.
Paulina. I pray now, call her.
Withdraw yourselves.
　　　　　　　[Exeunt Gentleman and Attendants.
Gaoler. And, madam,
I must be present at your conference.
Paulina. Well, be 't so, prithee. [*Exit Gaoler.*
Here 's such ado to make no stain a stain
As passes colouring.

Re-enter Gaoler, *with* EMILIA.

　　　　　　Dear gentlewoman,
How fares our gracious lady ?
Emilia. As well as one so great and so forlorn
May hold together : on her frights and griefs,
Which never tender lady hath borne greater,
She is something before her time deliver'd.
Paulina. A boy ?
Emilia. A daughter, and a goodly babe,
Lusty and like to live : the queen receives
Much comfort in 't ; says ' My poor prisoner,
I am innocent as you.'
Paulina. I dare be sworn :
These dangerous unsafe lunes i' the king, beshrew
　them !
He must be told on 't, and he shall : the office
Becomes a woman best ; I 'll take 't upon me :
If I prove honey-mouth'd, let my tongue blister
And never to my red-look'd anger be
The trumpet any more. Pray you, Emilia,
Commend my best obedience to the queen :
If she dares trust me with her little babe,
I 'll show 't the king and undertake to be
Her advocate to the loud'st. We do not know
How he may soften at the sight o' the child :
The silence often of pure innocence
Persuades when speaking fails.
Emilia. Most worthy madam,
Your honour and your goodness is so evident
That your free undertaking cannot miss
A thriving issue : there is no lady living
So meet for this great errand. Please your ladyship
To visit the next room, I 'll presently
Acquaint the queen of your most noble offer ;
Who but to-day hammer'd of this design,
But durst not tempt a minister of honour,
Lest she should be denied.
Paulina. Tell her, Emilia,
I 'll use that tongue I have : if wit flow from 't
As boldness from my bosom, let 't not be doubted
I shall do good.
Emilia. Now be you blest for it !
I 'll to the queen : please you, come something
　nearer.
Gaoler. Madam, if 't please the queen to send
　the babe,
I know not what I shall incur to pass it,
Having no warrant.
Paulina. You need not fear it, sir :
This child was prisoner to the womb and is
By law and process of great nature thence
Freed and enfranchised, not a party to
The anger of the king nor guilty of,

If any be, the trespass of the queen.
Gaoler. I do believe it.
Paulina. Do not you fear : upon mine honour, I
Will stand betwixt you and danger. [*Exeunt.*

SCENE III. *A room in* LEONTES' *palace.*

Enter LEONTES, ANTIGONUS, Lords, *and*
Servants.

Leontes. Nor night nor day no rest : it is but
　weakness
To bear the matter thus ; mere weakness. If
The cause were not in being,—part o' the cause,
She the adulteress ; for the harlot king
Is quite beyond mine arm, out of the blank
And level of my brain, plot-proof ; but she
I can hook to me : say that she were gone,
Given to the fire, a moiety of my rest
Might come to me again. Who 's there ?
First Servant. My lord ?
Leontes. How does the boy ?
First Servant. He took good rest to-night ;
'Tis hoped his sickness is discharged.
Leontes. To see his nobleness !
Conceiving the dishonour of his mother,
He straight declined, droop'd, took it deeply,
Fasten'd and fix'd the shame on 't in himself,
Threw off his spirit, his appetite, his sleep,
And downright languish'd. Leave me solely : go,
See how he fares. [*Exit Servant*] Fie, fie ! no
　thought of him :
The very thought of my revenges that way
Recoil upon me : in himself too mighty,
And in his parties, his alliance ; let him be
Until a time may serve : for present vengeance,
Take it on her. Camillo and Polixenes
Laugh at me, make their pastime at my sorrow :
They should not laugh if I could reach them, nor
Shall she within my power.

Enter PAULINA, *with a child.*

First Lord. You must not enter.
Paulina. Nay, rather, good my lords, be second
　to me :
Fear you his tyrannous passion more, alas,
Than the queen's life ? a gracious innocent soul,
More free than he is jealous.
Antigonus. That 's enough.
Second Servant. Madam, he hath not slept to-
　night ; commanded
None should come at him.
Paulina. Not so hot, good sir :
I come to bring him sleep. 'Tis such as you,
That creep like shadows by him and do sigh
At each his needless heavings, such as you
Nourish the cause of his waking : I
Do come with words as medicinal as true,
Honest as either, to purge him of that humour
That presses him from sleep.
Leontes. What noise there, ho ?
Paulina. No noise, my lord ; but needful con-
　ference
About some gossips for your highness.
Leontes. How !
Away with that audacious lady ! Antigonus,
I charged thee that she should not come about me :
I knew she would.
Antigonus. I told her so, my lord,
On your displeasure's peril and on mine,
She should not visit you.

Leontes.   What, canst not rule her ?
Paulina. From all dishonesty he can : in this,
Unless he take the course that you have done,
Commit me for committing honour, trust it,
He shall not rule me.
Antigonus.   La you now, you hear :
When she will take the rein I let her run :
But she 'll not stumble.
Paulina.   Good my liege, I come ;
And, I beseech you, hear me, who profess
Myself your loyal servant, your physician,
Your most obedient counsellor, yet that dare
Less appear so in comforting your evils,
Than such as most seem yours : I say, I come
From your good queen.
Leontes.   Good queen !
Paulina.   Good queen, my lord,
Good queen ; I say good queen ;
And would by combat make her good, so were I
A man, the worst about you.
Leontes.   Force her hence.
Paulina. Let him that makes but trifles of his
     eyes
First hand me : on mine own accord I 'll off ;
But first I 'll do my errand. The good queen,
For she is good, hath brought you forth a daughter ;
Here 'tis ; commends it to your blessing.
                    [*Laying down the child.*
Leontes.   Out !
A mankind witch ! Hence with her, out o' door :
A most intelligencing bawd !
Paulina.   Not so :
I am as ignorant in that as you
In so entitling me, and no less honest
Than you are mad ; which is enough, I 'll warrant,
As this world goes, to pass for honest.
Leontes.   Traitors !
Will you not push her out ? Give her the bastard.
Thou dotard ! thou art woman-tired, unroosted
By thy dame Partlet here. Take up the bastard ;
Take 't up, I say ; give 't to thy crone.
Paulina.   For ever
Unvenerable be thy hands, if thou
Takest up the princess by that forced baseness
Which he has put upon 't !
Leontes.   He dreads his wife.
Paulina. So I would you did ; then 'twere past
all doubt
You 'ld call your children yours.
Leontes.   A nest of traitors !
Antigonus. I am none, by this good light.
Paulina.   Nor I, nor any
But one that 's here, and that 's himself, for he
The sacred honour of himself, his queen's,
His hopeful son's, his babe's, betrays to slander,
Whose sting is sharper than the sword's ; and will
not—
For, as the case now stands, it is a curse
He cannot be compell'd to 't—once remove
The root of his opinion, which is rotten
As ever oak or stone was sound.
Leontes.   A callet
Of boundless tongue, who late hath beat her husband
And now baits me ! This brat is none of mine ;
It is the issue of Polixenes :
Hence with it, and together with the dam
Commit them to the fire !
Paulina.   It is yours ;
And, might we lay the old proverb to your charge,
So like you, 'tis the worse. Behold, my lords,
Although the print be little, the whole matter

And copy of the father, eye, nose, lip,
The trick of 's frown, his forehead, nay, the valley,
The pretty dimples of his chin and cheek,
His smiles,
The very mould and frame of hand, nail, finger :
And thou, good goddess Nature, which hast made it
So like to him that got it, if thou hast
The ordering of the mind too, 'mongst all colours
No yellow in 't, lest she suspect, as he does,
Her children not her husband's !
Leontes.   A gross hag !
And, lozel, thou art worthy to be hang'd,
That wilt not stay her tongue.
Antigonus.   Hang all the husbands
That cannot do that feat, you 'll leave yourself
Hardly one subject.
Leontes. Once more, take her hence.
Paulina. A most unworthy and unnatural lord
Can do no more.
Leontes.   I 'll ha' thee burnt.
Paulina.   I care not :
It is an heretic that makes the fire,
Not she which burns in 't. I 'll not call you tyrant ;
But this most cruel usage of your queen,
Not able to produce more accusation
Than your own weak-hinged fancy, something
     savours
Of tyranny and will ignoble make you,
Yea, scandalous to the world.
Leontes.   On your allegiance,
Out of the chamber with her ! Were I a tyrant,
Where were her life ? she durst not call me so,
If she did know me one. Away with her !
Paulina. I pray you, do not push me ; I 'll be
gone.
Look to your babe, my lord ; 'tis yours : Jove
send her
A better guiding spirit ! What needs these hands ?
You, that are thus so tender o'er his follies,
Will never do him good, not one of you.
So, so : farewell ; we are gone.   [*Exit.*
Leontes. Thou, traitor, hast set on thy wife to this.
My child ? away with 't ! Even thou, that hast
A heart as tender o'er it, take it hence
And see it instantly consumed with fire ;
Even thou and none but thou. Take it up straight :
Within this hour bring me word 'tis done,
And by good testimony, or I 'll seize thy life,
With what thou else call'st thine. If thou refuse
And wilt encounter with my wrath, say so ;
The bastard brains with these my proper hands
Shall I dash out. Go, take it to the fire ;
For thou set'st on thy wife.
Antigonus.   I did not, sir ;
These lords, my noble fellows, if they please,
Can clear me in 't.
Lords. We can : my royal liege,
He is not guilty of her coming hither.
Leontes. You 're liars all.
First Lord. Beseech your highness, give us better
     credit :
We have always truly served you, and beseech you
So to esteem of us, and on our knees we beg,
As recompense of our dear services
Past and to come, that you do change this purpose,
Which being so horrible, so bloody, must
Lead on to some foul issue : we all kneel.
Leontes. I am a feather for each wind that blows :
Shall I live on to see this bastard kneel
And call me father ? better burn it now
Than curse it then. But be it ; let it live.

It shall not neither. You, sir, come you hither ;
You that have been so tenderly officious
With Lady Margery, your midwife there,
To save this bastard's life,—for 'tis a bastard,
So sure as this beard's grey,—what will you ad-
   venture
To save this brat's life ?
   Antigonus.   Any thing, my lord,
That my ability may undergo
And nobleness impose : at least thus much :
I 'll pawn the little blood which I have left
To save the innocent : any thing possible.
   Leontes. It shall be possible. Swear by this
   sword
Thou wilt perform my bidding.
   Antigonus.   I will, my lord.
   Leontes. Mark and perform it, see'st thou ? for
   the fail
Of any point in 't shall not only be
Death to thyself but to thy lewd-tongued wife,
Whom for this time we pardon. We enjoin thee,
As thou art liege-man to us, that thou carry
This female bastard hence and that thou bear it
To some remote and desert place quite out
Of our dominions, and that there thou leave it,
Without more mercy, to it own protection
And favour of the climate. As by strange fortune
It came to us, I do in justice charge thee,
On thy soul's peril and thy body's torture,
That thou commend it strangely to some place
Where chance may nurse or end it. Take it up.
   Antigonus. I swear to do this, though a present
   death
Had been more merciful. Come on, poor babe :
Some powerful spirit instruct the kites and ravens
To be thy nurses ! Wolves and bears, they say,
Casting their savageness aside have done
Like offices of pity. Sir, be prosperous
In more than this deed does require ! And blessing
Against this cruelty fight on thy side,
Poor thing, condemn'd to loss !
                         [*Exit with the child.*
   Leontes.   No, I 'll not rear
Another's issue.

      Enter a Servant.

   Servant. Please your highness, posts
From those you sent to the oracle are come
An hour since : Cleomenes and Dion,
Being well arrived from Delphos, are both landed,
Hasting to the court.
   First Lord.   So please you, sir, their speed
Hath been beyond account.
   Leontes.   Twenty three days
They have been absent : 'tis good speed ; foretells
The great Apollo suddenly will have
The truth of this appear. Prepare you, lords ;
Summon a session, that we may arraign
Our most disloyal lady, for, as she hath
Been publicly accused, so shall she have
A just and open trial. While she lives
My heart will be a burthen to me. Leave me,
And think upon my bidding.   [*Exeunt.*

ACT III

SCENE I. *A sea-port in Sicilia.*

      Enter CLEOMENES *and* DION.

Cleomenes.

The climate 's delicate, the air most sweet,
   Fertile the isle, the temple much surpassing
   The common praise it bears.
   Dion.   I shall report,
For most it caught me, the celestial habits,
Methinks I so should term them, and the reverence
Of the grave wearers. O, the sacrifice !
How ceremonious, solemn and unearthly
It was i' the offering !
   Cleomenes.   But of all, the burst
And the ear-deafening voice o' the oracle,
Kin to Jove's thunder, so surprised my sense,
That I was nothing.
   Dion.   If the event o' the journey
Prove as successful to the queen,—O be 't so!—
As it hath been to us rare, pleasant, speedy,
The time is worth the use on 't.
   Cleomenes.   Great Apollo
Turn all to the best ! These proclamations,
So forcing faults upon Hermione,
I little like.
   Dion. The violent carriage of it
Will clear or end the business : when the oracle,
Thus by Apollo's great divine seal'd up,
Shall the contents discover, something rare
Even then will rush to knowledge. Go : fresh
   horses !
And gracious be the issue !   [*Exeunt.*

SCENE II. *A court of Justice.*

      Enter LEONTES, Lords, *and* Officers.

   Leontes. This sessions, to our great grief we
   pronounce,
Even pushes 'gainst our heart : the party tried
The daughter of a king, our wife, and one
Of us too much beloved. Let us be clear'd
Of being tyrannous, since we so openly
Proceed in justice, which shall have due course,
Even to the guilt or the purgation.
Produce the prisoner.
   Officer. It is his highness' pleasure that the queen
Appear in person here in court. Silence !

      Enter HERMIONE *guarded ;* PAULINA *and*
            Ladies *attending.*

   Leontes. Read the indictment.
   Officer. [*Reads*] Hermione, queen to the worthy
Leontes, king of Sicilia, thou art here accused and
arraigned of high treason, in committing adultery
with Polixenes, king of Bohemia, and conspiring
with Camillo to take away the life of our sovereign
lord the king, thy royal husband : the pretence
whereof being by circumstances partly laid open,
thou, Hermione, contrary to the faith and allegiance
of a true subject, didst counsel and aid them, for
their better safety, to fly away by night.
   Hermione. Since what I am to say must be but
   that
Which contradicts my accusation and
The testimony on my part no other
But what comes from myself, it shall scarce boot me
To say ' not guilty :' mine integrity
Being counted falsehood, shall, as I express it,
Be so received. But thus : if powers divine
Behold our human actions, as they do,
I doubt not then but innocence shall make
False accusation blush and tyranny

Tremble at patience. You, my lord, best know,
Who least will seem to do so, my past life
Hath been as continent, as chaste, as true,
As I am now unhappy ; which is more
Than history can pattern, though devised
And play'd to take spectators. For behold me
A fellow of the royal bed, which owe
A moiety of the throne, a great king's daughter,
The mother to a hopeful prince, here standing
To prate and talk for life and honour 'fore
Who please to come and hear. For life, I prize it
As I weigh grief, which I would spare : for honour,
'Tis a derivative from me to mine,
And only that I stand for. I appeal
To your own conscience, sir, before Polixenes
Came to your court, how I was in your grace,
How merited to be so ; since he came,
With what encounter so uncurrent I
Have strain'd to appear thus : if one jot beyond
The bound of honour, or in act or will
That way inclining, harden'd be the hearts
Of all that hear me, and my near'st of kin
Cry fie upon my grave !
Leontes.   I ne'er heard yet
That any of these bolder vices wanted
Less impudence to gainsay what they did
Than to perform it first.
Hermione.   That 's true enough ;
Though 'tis a saying, sir, not due to me.
Leontes. You will not own it.
Hermione.   † More than mistress of
Which comes to me in name of fault, I must not
At all acknowledge. For Polixenes,
With whom I am accused, I do confess
I loved him as in honour he required,
With such a kind of love as might become
A lady like me, with a love even such,
So and no other, as yourself commanded :
Which not to have done I think had been in me
Both disobedience and ingratitude
To you and toward your friend, whose love had
    spoke,
Even since it could speak, from an infant, freely
That it was yours. Now, for conspiracy,
I know not how it tastes ; though it be dish'd
For me to try how : all I know of it
Is that Camillo was an honest man;
And why he left your court, the gods themselves,
Wotting no more than I, are ignorant.
Leontes. You knew of his departure, as you
    know
What you have underta'en to do in 's absence.
Hermione. Sir,
You speak a language that I understand not :
My life stands in the level of your dreams,
Which I 'll lay down.
Leontes.   Your actions are my dreams ;
You had a bastard by Polixenes,
And I but dream'd it. As you were past all shame,—
Those of your fact are so—so past all truth :
Which to deny concerns more than avails ; for as
Thy brat hath been cast out, like to itself,
No father owning it,—which is, indeed,
More criminal in thee than it,—so thou
Shalt feel our justice, in whose easiest passage
Look for no less than death.
Hermione.   Sir, spare your threats:
The bug which you would fright me with I seek.
To me can life be no commodity :
The crown and comfort of my life, your favour,
I do give lost ; for I do feel it gone,

But know not how it went. My second joy
And first-fruits of my body, from his presence
I am barr'd, like one infectious. My third comfort,
Starr'd most unluckily, is from my breast,
The innocent milk in it most innocent mouth,
Haled out to murder : myself on every post
Proclaim'd a strumpet : with immodest hatred
The child-bed privilege denied, which 'longs
To women of all fashion ; lastly, hurried
Here to this place, i' the open air, before
I have got strength of limit. Now, my liege,
Tell me what blessings I have here alive,
That I should fear to die ? Therefore proceed.
But yet hear this ; mistake me not ; no life,
I prize it not a straw, but for mine honour,
Which I would free, if I shall be condemn'd
Upon surmises, all proofs sleeping else
But what your jealousies awake, I tell you
'Tis rigour and not law. Your honours all,
I do refer me to the oracle :
Apollo be my judge !
First Lord.   This your request
Is altogether just : therefore bring forth,
And in Apollo's name, his oracle.
                    [*Exeunt certain Officers.*
Hermione. The Emperor of Russia was my father :
O that he were alive, and here beholding
His daughter's trial ! that he did but see
The flatness of my misery, yet with eyes
Of pity, not revenge !

Re-enter Officers, *with* CLEOMENES *and* DION.

Officer. You here shall swear upon this sword
    of justice,
That you, Cleomenes and Dion, have
Been both at Delphos, and from thence have brought
This seal'd-up oracle, by the hand deliver'd
Of great Apollo's priest and that since then
You have not dared to break the holy seal
Nor read the secrets in 't.
Cleomenes. Dion.   All this we swear.
Leontes. Break up the seals and read.
Officer. [*Reads*] Hermione is chaste ; Polixenes
blameless ; Camillo a true subject ; Leontes a
jealous tyrant ; his innocent babe truly begotten ;
and the king shall live without an heir, if that which
is lost be not found.
Lords. Now blessed be the great Apollo !
Hermione.   Praised !
Leontes. Hast thou read truth ?
Officer.   Ay, my lord ; even so
As it is here set down.
Leontes. There is no truth at all i' the oracle :
The sessions shall proceed : this is mere falsehood.

Enter Servant.

Servant. My lord the king, the king !
Leontes.   What is the business ?
Servant. O sir, I shall be hated to report it !
The prince your son, with mere conceit and fear
Of the queen's speed, is gone.
Leontes.   How ! gone !
Servant.   Is dead.
Leontes. Apollo 's angry ; and the heavens
    themselves
Do strike at my injustice.   [*Hermione swoons.*]
    How now there !
Paulina. This news is mortal to the queen :
    look down

And see what death is doing.
　Leontes.　　　　　　Take her hence :
Her heart is but o'ercharged : she will recover :
I have too much believed mine own suspicion :
Beseech you, tenderly apply to her
Some remedies for life.
　　　　[*Exeunt Paulina and Ladies, with Hermione.*
　　　　　Apollo, pardon
My great profaneness 'gainst thine oracle !
I 'll reconcile me to Polixenes,
New woo my queen, recall the good Camillo,
Whom I proclaim a man of truth, of mercy ;
For, being transported by my jealousies
To bloody thoughts and to revenge, I chose
Camillo for the minister to poison
My friend Polixenes : which had been done,
But that the good mind of Camillo tardied
My swift command, though I with death and with
Reward did threaten and encourage him,
Not doing 't and being done : he, most humane
And fill'd with honour, to my kingly guest
Unclasp'd my practice, quit his fortunes here,
Which you knew great, and to the hazard
Of all incertainties himself commended,
No richer than his honour : how he glisters
Thorough my rust ! and how his piety
Does my deeds make the blacker !

Re-enter PAULINA.

　Paulina.　　　　　　Woe the while !
O, cut my lace, lest my heart, cracking it,
Break too !
　First Lord.　What fit is this, good lady ?
　Paulina.　What studied torments, tyrant, hast
　　for me ?
What wheels ? racks ? fires ? what flaying ? boil-
　　ing ?
In leads or oils ? what old or newer torture
Must I receive, whose every word deserves
To taste of thy most worst ? Thy tyranny
Together working with thy jealousies,
Fancies too weak for boys, too green and idle
For girls of nine, O, think what they have done
And then run mad indeed, stark mad ! for all
Thy by-gone fooleries were but spices of it.
That thou betray'dst Polixenes, 'twas nothing ;
That did but show thee, of a fool, inconstant
And damnable ingrateful : nor was 't much,
Thou wouldst have poison'd good Camillo's honour,
To have him kill a king ; poor trespasses,
More monstrous standing by : whereof I reckon
The casting forth to crows thy baby-daughter
To be or none or little ; though a devil
Would have shed water out of fire ere done 't :
Nor is 't directly laid to thee, the death
Of the young prince, whose honourable thoughts,
Thoughts high for one so tender, cleft the heart
That could conceive a gross and foolish sire
Blemish'd his gracious dam : this is not, no,
Laid to thy answer : but the last,—O lords,
When I have said, cry ' woe ! '—the queen, the
　　queen,
The sweet'st, dear's creature 's dead. and ven-
　　geance for 't
Not dropp'd down yet.
　First Lord.　　　The higher powers forbid !
　Paulina.　I say she 's dead ; I 'll swear 't. If
　　word nor oath
Prevail not, go and see : if you can bring
Tincture or lustre in her lip, her eye,

Heat outwardly or breath within, I 'll serve you
As I would do the gods. But, O thou tyrant !
Do not repent these things, for they are heavier
Than all thy woes can stir : therefore betake thee
To nothing but despair. A thousand knees
Ten thousand years together, naked, fasting,
Upon a barren mountain, and still winter
In storm perpetual, could not move the gods
To look that way thou wert.
　Leontes.　　　　　Go on, go on :
Thou canst not speak too much ; I have deserved
All tongues to talk their bitterest.
　First Lord.　　　　　Say no more :
Howe'er the business goes, you have made fault
I' the boldness of your speech.
　Paulina.　　　　I am sorry for 't :
All faults I make, when I shall come to know them,
I do repent. Alas ! I have show'd too much
The rashness of a woman : he is touch'd
To the noble heart. What 's gone and what 's
　　past help
Should be past grief : do not receive affliction
At my petition ; I beseech you, rather
Let me be punish'd, that have minded you
Of what you should forget. Now, good my liege,
Sir, royal sir, forgive a foolish woman :
The love I bore your queen—lo, fool again !—
I 'll speak of her no more, nor of your children ;
I 'll not remember you of my own lord,
Who is lost too : take your patience to you,
And I 'll say nothing.
　Leontes.　　　Thou didst speak but well
When most the truth ; which I receive much better
Than to be pitied of thee. Prithee, bring me
To the dead bodies of my queen and son :
One grave shall be for both : upon them shall
The causes of their death appear, unto
Our shame perpetual. Once a day I 'll visit
The chapel where they lie, and tears shed there
Shall be my recreation : so long as nature
Will bear up with this exercise, so long
I daily vow to use it. Come and lead me
Unto these sorrows.　　　　　[*Exeunt.*

SCENE III. *Bohemia.*　*A desert country near*
　　　　　the sea.

Enter ANTIGONUS *with a Child, and a*
　　　　　Mariner.

　Antigonus.　Thou art perfect then, our ship hath
　　touch'd upon
The deserts of Bohemia ?
　Mariner.　　　Ay, my lord ; and fear
We have landed in ill time : the skies look grimly
And threaten present blusters. In my conscience,
The heavens with that we have in hand are angry
And frown upon 's.
　Antigonus.　Their sacred wills be done ! Go, get
　　aboard ;
Look to thy bark : I 'll not be long before
I call upon thee.
　Mariner.　Make your best haste, and go not
Too far i' the land : 'tis like to be loud weather ;
Besides, this place is famous for the creatures
Of prey that keep upon 't.
　Antigonus.　　　　Go thou away :
I 'll follow instantly.
　Mariner.　　　I am glad at heart
To be so rid o' the business.　　　　　[*Exit.*
　Antigonus.　　　　Come, poor babe :

I have heard, but not believed, the spirits o' the dead
May walk again : if such thing be, thy mother
Appear'd to me last night, for ne'er was dream
So like a waking. To me comes a creature,
Sometimes her head on one side, some another ;
I never saw a vessel of like sorrow,
So fill'd and so becoming : in pure white robes,
Like very sanctity, she did approach
My cabin where I lay ; thrice bow'd before me,
And gasping to begin some speech, her eyes
Became two spouts : the fury spent, anon
Did this break from her : ' Good Antigonus,
Since fate, against thy better disposition,
Hath made thy person for the thrower-out
Of my poor babe, according to thine oath,
Places remote enough are in Bohemia,
There weep and leave it crying ; and, for the babe
Is counted lost for ever, Perdita,
I prithee, call 't. For this ungentle business,
Put on thee by my lord, thou ne'er shalt see
Thy wife Paulina more.' And so, with shrieks,
She melted into air. Affrighted much,
I did in time collect myself and thought
This was so and no slumber. Dreams are toys :
Yet for this once, yea, superstitiously,
I will be squared by this. I do believe
Hermione hath suffer'd death, and that
Apollo would, this being indeed the issue
Of King Polixenes, it should here be laid,
Either for life or death, upon the earth
Of its right father. Blossom, speed thee well !
There lie, and there thy character : there these ;
Which may, if fortune please, both breed thee,
    pretty,
And still rest thine. The storm begins : poor
    wretch,
That for thy mother's fault art thus exposed
To loss and what may follow ! Weep I cannot,
But my heart bleeds ; and most accursed am I
To be by oath enjoin'd to this. Farewell !
The day frowns more and more : thou 'rt like to
    have
A lullaby too rough : I never saw
The heavens so dim by day. A savage clamour !
Well may I get aboard ! This is the chase :
I am gone for ever.   [Exit, pursued by a bear.

Enter a Shepherd.

Shepherd. I would there were no age between
sixteen and three-and-twenty, or that youth would
sleep out the rest ; for there is nothing in the between but getting wenches with child, wronging the
ancientry, stealing, fighting—Hark you now !
Would any but these boiled brains of nineteen and
two-and-twenty hunt this weather ? They have
scared away two of my best sheep, which I fear the
wolf will sooner find than the master : if any where
I have them, 'tis by the seaside, browsing of ivy.
Good luck, an 't be thy will ! what have we here ?
Mercy on 's, a barne ; a very pretty barne ! A boy
or a child, I wonder ? A pretty one ; a very pretty
one : sure, some 'scape : though I am not bookish,
yet I can read waiting-gentlewoman in the 'scape.
This has been some stair-work, some trunk-work,
some behind-door-work : they were warmer that
got this than the poor thing is here. I 'll take it
up for pity : yet I 'll tarry till my son come ; he
hallooed but even now. Whoa, ho, hoa !

Enter Clown.

Clown. Hilloa, loa !
Shepherd. What, art so near ? If thou 'lt see a
thing to talk on when thou art dead and rotten,
come hither. What ailest thou, man ?
Clown. I have seen two such sights, by sea and
by land ! but I am not to say it is a sea, for it is
now the sky : betwixt the firmament and it you
cannot thrust a bodkin's point.
Shepherd. Why, boy, how is it ?
Clown. I would you did but see how it chafes,
how it rages, how it takes up the shore ! but that 's
not to the point. O, the most piteous cry of the
poor souls ! sometimes to see 'em, and not to see
'em ; now the ship boring the moon with her main-
mast, and anon swallowed with yest and froth, as
you 'ld thrust a cork into a hogshead. And then
for the land-service, to see how the bear tore out
his shoulder-bone ; how he cried to me for help
and said his name was Antigonus, a nobleman.
But to make an end of the ship, to see how the sea
flap-dragoned it : but, first, how the poor souls
roared, and the sea mocked them ; and how the poor
gentleman roared and the bear mocked him, both
roaring louder than the sea or weather.
Shepherd. Name of mercy, when was this, boy ?
Clown. Now, now : I have not winked since I
saw these sights : the men are not yet cold under
water, nor the bear half dined on the gentleman :
he 's at it now.
Shepherd. Would I had been by, to have helped
the old man !
Clown. I would you had been by the ship side,
to have helped her : there your charity would
have lacked footing.
Shepherd. Heavy matters ! heavy matters ! but
look thee here, boy. Now bless thyself : thou
mettest with things dying, I with things new-born.
Here 's a sight for thee ; look thee, a bearing-
cloth for a squire's child ! look thee here ; take
up, take up, boy ; open 't. So, let 's see : it was
told me I should be rich by the fairies. This is
some changeling : open 't. What 's within, boy ?
Clown. You 're a made old man : if the sins of
your youth are forgiven you, you 're well to live.
Gold ! all gold !
Shepherd. This is fairy gold, boy, and 'twill
prove so : up with 't, keep it close : home, home,
the next way. We are lucky, boy ; and to be so
still requires nothing but secrecy. Let my sheep
go : come, good boy, the next way home.
Clown. Go you the next way with your findings.
I 'll go see if the bear be gone from the gentleman
and how much he hath eaten : they are never curst
but when they are hungry : if there be any of him
left, I 'll bury it.
Shepherd. That 's a good deed. If thou mayest
discern by that which is left of him what he is,
fetch me to the sight of him.
Clown. Marry, will I ; and you shall help to
put him i' the ground.
Shepherd. 'Tis a lucky day, boy, and we 'll do
good deeds on 't.   [Exeunt.

ACT IV.

SCENE I.

Enter TIME, *the* Chorus.

Time.

I that please some, try all, both joy and terror
Of good and bad, that makes and unfolds error,
Now take upon me, in the name of Time,
To use my wings. Impute it not a crime
To me or my swift passage, that I slide
O'er sixteen years and leave the growth untried
Of that wide gap, since it is in my power
To o'erthrow law and in one self-born hour
To plant and o'erwhelm custom. Let me pass
The same I am, ere ancient'st order was
Or what is now received : I witness to
The times that brought them in ; so shall I do
To the freshest things now reigning and make stale
The glistering of this present, as my tale
Now seems to it. Your patience this allowing,
I turn my glass and give my scene such growing
As you had slept between : Leontes leaving,
The effects of his fond jealousies so grieving
That he shuts up himself, imagine me,
Gentle spectators, that i now may be
In fair Bohemia ; and remember well,
I mentioned a son o' the king's, which Florizel
I now name to you ; and with speed so pace
To speak of Perdita, now grown in grace
Equal with wondering : what of her ensues
I list not prophesy ; but let Time's news
Be known when 'tis brought forth. A shepherd's
  daughter,
And what to her adheres, which follows after,
Is the argument of Time. Of this allow,
If ever you have spent time worse ere now ;
If never, yet that Time himself doth say
He wishes earnestly you never may. [*Exit.*

SCENE II. *Bohemia. The palace of* POLIXENES.

Enter POLIXENES *and* CAMILLO.

Polixenes. I pray thee, good Camillo, be no more
importunate : 'tis a sickness denying thee any
thing ; a death to grant this.

Camillo. It is fifteen years since I saw my country :
though I have for the most part been aired abroad,
I desire to lay my bones there. Besides, the penitent
king, my master, hath sent for me ; to whose
feeling sorrows I might be some allay, or I o'erween
to think so, which is another spur to my departure.

Polixenes. As thou lovest me, Camillo, wipe not
out the rest of thy services by leaving me now :
the need I have of thee thine own goodness hath
made ; better not to have had thee than thus to
want thee : thou, having made me businesses which
none without thee can sufficiently manage, must
either stay to execute them thyself or take away
with thee the very services thou hast done ; which
if I have not enough considered, as too much I
cannot, to be more thankful to thee shall be my study,
and my profit therein the heaping friendships. Of
that fatal country, Sicilia, prithee speak no more ;
whose very naming punishes me with the remembrance of that penitent, as thou callest him, and
reconciled king, my brother ; whose loss of his
most precious queen and children are even now to
be afresh lamented. Say to me, when sawest thou
the Prince Florizel, my son ? Kings are no less

unhappy, their issue not being gracious, than they
are in losing them when they have approved their
virtues.

Camillo. Sir, it is three days since I saw the
prince. What his happier affairs may be, are to
me unknown : but I have missingly noted, he is
of late much retired from court and is less frequent
to his princely exercises than formerly he hath
appeared.

Polixenes. I have considered so much, Camillo,
and with some care ; so far that I have eyes under
my service which look upon his removedness ;
from whom I have this intelligence, that he is seldom
from the house of a most homely shepherd ; a
man, they say, that from very nothing, and beyond
the imagination of his neighbours, is grown into
an unspeakable estate.

Camillo. I have heard, sir, of such a man, who
hath a daughter of most rare note : the report of
her is extended more than can be thought to begin
from such a cottage.

Polixenes. That 's likewise part of my intelligence ; but, I fear, the angle that plucks our son
thither. Thou shalt accompany us to the place ;
where we will, not appearing what we are, have
some question with the shepherd ; from whose
simplicity I think it not uneasy to get the cause of
my son's resort thither. Prithee, be my present
partner in this business, and lay aside the thoughts
of Sicilia.

Camillo. I willingly obey your command.

Polixenes. My best Camillo ! We must disguise
ourselves. [*Exeunt.*

SCENE III. *A road near the* Shepherd's *cottage.*

Enter AUTOLYCUS, *singing.*

When daffodils begin to peer,
  With heigh ! the doxy over the dale,
Why, then comes in the sweet o' the year ;
  For the red blood reigns in the winter's pale.

The white sheet bleaching on the hedge,
  With heigh ! the sweet birds, O, how they sing !
Doth set my pugging tooth on edge ;
  For a quart of ale is a dish for a king.

The lark, that tirra-lyra chants,
  With heigh ! with heigh ! the thrush and the jay,
Are summer songs for me and my aunts,
  While we lie tumbling in the hay.

I have served Prince Florizel and in my time
wore three-pile ; but now I am out of service :

But shall I go mourn for that, my dear ?
  The pale moon shines by night :
And when I wander here and there,
  I then do most go right.

If tinkers may have leave to live,
  And bear the sow-skin budget,
Then my account I well may give,
  And in the stocks avouch it.

My traffic is sheets ; when the kite builds, look to
lesser linen. My father named me Autolycus ;
who being, as I am, littered under Mercury, was
likewise a snapper-up of unconsidered trifles. With
die and drab I purchased this caparison, and my

revenue is the silly cheat. Gallows and knock are too powerful on the highway : beating and hanging are terrors to me : for the life to come, I sleep out the thought of it. A prize ! a prize !

Enter Clown.

Clown. Let me see : every 'leven wether tods ; every tod yields pound and odd shilling ; fifteen hundred shorn, what comes the wool to ?

Autolycus. [*Aside*] If the springe hold, the cock's mine.

Clown. I cannot do 't without counters. Let me see ; what am I to buy for our sheep-shearing feast ? Three pound of sugar, five pound of currants, rice,—what will this sister of mine do with rice ? But my father hath made her mistress of the feast, and she lays it on. She hath made me four and twenty nosegays for the shearers, three-man-song-men all, and very good ones ; but they are most of them means and bases ; but one puritan amongst them, and he sings psalms to hornpipes. I must have saffron to colour the warden pies ; mace ; dates ?—none, that's out of my note ; nutmegs, seven ; a race or two of ginger, but that I may beg ; four pound of prunes, and as many of raisins o' the sun.

Autolycus. O that ever I was born !

[*Grovelling on the ground.*

Clown. I' the name of me—

Autolycus. O, help me, help me ! pluck but off these rags ; and then, death, death !

Clown. Alack, poor soul ! thou hast need of more rags to lay on thee, rather than have these off.

Autolycus. O sir, the loathsomeness of them offends me more than the stripes I have received, which are mighty ones and millions.

Clown. Alas, poor man ! a million of beating may come to a great matter.

Autolycus. I am robbed, sir, and beaten ; my money and apparel ta'en from me, and these detestable things put upon me.

Clown. What, by a horseman, or a footman ?

Autolycus. A footman, sweet sir, a footman.

Clown. Indeed, he should be a footman by the garments he has left with thee : if this be a horseman's coat, it hath seen very hot service. Lend me thy hand, I'll help thee : come, lend me thy hand.

Autolycus. O, good sir, tenderly, O !

Clown. Alas, poor soul !

Autolycus. O, good sir, softly, good sir ! I fear, sir, my shoulder-blade is out.

Clown. How now ! canst stand ?

Autolycus. [*Picking his pocket*] Softly, dear sir ; good sir, softly. You ha' done me a charitable office.

Clown. Dost lack any money ? I have a little money for thee.

Autolycus. No, good sweet sir ; no, I beseech you, sir : I have a kinsman not past three quarters of a mile hence, unto whom I was going ; I shall there have money, or any thing I want : offer me no money, I pray you ; that kills my heart.

Clown. What manner of fellow was he that robbed you ?

Autolycus. A fellow, sir, that I have known to go about with troll-my-dames : I knew him once a servant of the prince : I cannot tell, good sir, for which of his virtues it was, but he was certainly whipped out of the court.

Clown. His vices, you would say ; there's no

virtue whipped out of the court : they cherish it to make it stay there ; and yet it will no more but abide.

Autolycus. Vices, I would say, sir. I know this man well : he hath been since an ape-bearer ; then a process-server, a baliff ; then he compassed a motion of the Prodigal Son, and married a tinker's wife within a mile where my land and living lies ; and, having flown over many knavish professions, he settled only in rogue : some call him Autolycus.

Clown. Out upon him ! prig, for my life, prig : he haunts wakes, fairs and bear-baitings.

Autolycus. Very true, sir ; he, sir, he ; that's the rogue that put me into this apparel.

Clown. Not a more cowardly rogue in all Bohemia : if you had but looked big and spit at him, he'ld have run.

Autolycus. I must confess to you, sir, I am no fighter : I am false of heart that way ; and that he knew, I warrant him.

Clown. How do you now ?

Autolycus. Sweet sir, much better than I was ; I can stand and walk : I will even take my leave of you, and pace softly towards my kinsman's.

Clown. Shall I bring thee on the way ?

Autolycus. No, good-faced sir ; no, sweet sir.

Clown. Then fare thee well : I must go buy spices for our sheep-shearing.

Autolycus. Prosper you, sweet sir ! [*Exit Clown.* Your purse is not hot enough to purchase your spice. I'll be with you at your sheep-shearing too : if I make not this cheat bring out another and the shearers prove sheep, let me be unrolled and my name put in the book of virtue !

[*Sings*] Jog on, jog on, the foot-path way,
    And merrily hent the stile-a :
    A merry heart goes all the day,
    Your sad tires in a mile-a.   [*Exit.*

SCENE IV. *The Shepherd's cottage.*

Enter FLORIZEL *and* PERDITA.

Florizel. These your unusual weeds to each part
  of you
Do give a life : no shepherdess, but Flora
Peering in April's front. This your sheep-shearing
Is as a meeting of the petty gods,
And you the queen on 't.

Perdita.   Sir, my gracious lord,
To chide at your extremes it not becomes me :
O, pardon, that I name them ! Your high self,
The gracious mark o' the land, you have obscured
With a swain's wearing, and me, poor lowly maid,
Most goddess-like prank'd up : but that our feasts
In every mess have folly and the feeders
Digest it with a custom, I should blush
To see you so attired, sworn, I think,
To show myself a glass.

Florizel.   I bless the time
When my good falcon made her flight across
Thy father's ground.

Perdita.   Now Jove afford you cause !
To me the difference forges dread ; your greatness
Hath not been used to fear. Even now I tremble
To think your father, by some accident,
Should pass this way as you did : O, the Fates !
How would he look, to see his work so noble
Vilely bound up ? What would he say ? Or how
Should I, in these my borrow'd flaunts, behold
The sternness of his presence ?

Florizel.   Apprehend
Nothing but jollity. The gods themselves,
Humbling their deities to love, have taken
The shapes of beasts upon them : Jupiter
Became a bull, and bellow'd ; the green Neptune
A ram, and bleated ; and the fire-robed god,
Golden Apollo, a poor humble swain,
As I seem now. Their transformations
Were never for a piece of beauty rarer,
Nor in a way so chaste, since my desires
Run not before mine honour, nor my lusts
Burn hotter than my faith.
Perdita.   O, but, sir,
Your resolution cannot hold, when 'tis
Opposed, as it must be, by the power of the king :
One of these two must be necessities,
Which then will speak, that you must change this
          purpose,
Or I my life.
Florizel.   Thou dearest Perdita,
With these forced thoughts, I prithee, darken not
The mirth o' the feast. Or I 'll be thine, my fair,
Or not my father's. For I cannot be
Mine own, nor any thing to any, if
I be not thine. To this I am most constant,
Though destiny say no. Be merry, present
Strangle such thoughts as these with any thing
That you behold the while. Your guests are coming :
Lift up your countenance, as it were the day
Of celebration of that nuptial which
We two have sworn shall come.
Perdita.   O lady Fortune,
Stand you auspicious !
Florizel.   See, your guests approach :
Address yourself to entertain them sprightly,
And let 's be red with mirth.

Enter Shepherd, Clown, MOPSA, DORCAS, *and
 others, with* POLIXENES *and* CAMILLO *disguised.*

Shepherd. Fie, daughter ! when my old wife
          lived, upon
This day she was both pantler, butler, cook,
Both dame and servant ; welcomed all, served all ;
Would sing her song and dance her turn ; now here,
At upper end o' the table, now i' the middle ;
On his shoulder, and his ; her face o' fire
With labour and the thing she took to quench it,
She would to each one sip. You are retired,
As if you were a feasted one and not
The hostess of the meeting : pray you, bid
These unknown friends to 's welcome ; for it is
A way to make us better friends, more known.
Come, quench your blushes and present yourself
That which you are, mistress o' the feast : come on,
And bid us welcome to your sheep-shearing,
As your good flock shall prosper.
Perdita.   [*To* Polixenes] Sir, welcome :
It is my father's will I should take on me
The hostess-ship o' the day. [*To* Camillo] You 're
          welcome, sir.
Give me those flowers there, Dorcas. Reverend sirs,
For you there 's rosemary and rue ; these keep
Seeming and savour all the winter long :
Grace and remembrance be to you both,
And welcome to our shearing !
Polixenes.   Shepherdess,—
A fair one are you—well you fit our ages
With flowers of winter.
Perdita.   Sir, the year growing ancient,

Not yet on summer's death, nor on the birth
Of trembling winter, the fairest flowers o' the season
Are our carnations and streak'd gillyvors,
Which some call nature's bastards : of that kind
Our rustic garden 's barren ; and I care not
To get slips of them.
Polixenes.   Wherefore, gentle maiden,
Do you neglect them ?
Perdita.   For I have heard it said
There is an art which in their piedness shares
With great creating nature.
Polixenes.   Say there be ;
Yet nature is made better by no mean
But nature makes that mean : so, over that art
Which you say adds to nature, is an art
That nature makes. You see, sweet maid, we
          marry
A gentler scion to the wildest stock,
And make conceive a bark of baser kind
By bud of nobler race : this is an art
Which does mend nature, change it rather, but
The art itself is nature.
Perdita.   So it is.
Polixenes. Then make your garden rich in gilly-
          vors,
And do not call them bastards.
Perdita.   I 'll not put
The dibble in earth to set one slip of them ;
No more than were I painted I would wish
This youth should say 'twere well and only therefore
Desire to breed by me. Here 's flowers for you :
Hot lavender, mints, savory, marjoram ;
The marigold, that goes to bed wi' the sun
And with him rises weeping : these are flowers
Of middle summer, and I think they are given
To men of middle age. You 're very welcome.
Camillo. I should leave grazing, were I of your
          flock,
And only live by gazing.
Perdita.   Out, alas !
You 'ld be so lean, that blasts of January
Would blow you through and through. Now, my
          fair'st friend,
I would I had some flowers o' the spring that might
Become your time of day ; and yours, and yours,
That wear upon your virgin branches yet
Your maidenheads growing : O Proserpina,
For the flowers now, that frighted thou let'st fall
From Dis's waggon ! daffodils,
That come before the swallow dares, and take
The winds of March with beauty ; violets dim,
But sweeter than the lids of Juno's eyes
Or Cytherea's breath ; pale primroses,
That die unmarried, ere they can behold
Bright Phœbus in his strength—a malady
Most incident to maids ; bold oxlips and
The crown imperial ; lilies of all kinds,
The flower-de-luce being one ! O, these I lack,
To make you garlands of, and my sweet friend,
To strew him o'er and o'er !
Florizel.   What, like a corse ?
Perdita. No, like a bank for love to lie and play
          on ;
Not like a corse ; or if, not to be buried,
But quick and in mine arms. Come, take your
          flowers :
Methinks I play as I have seen them do
In Whitsun pastorals : sure this robe of mine
Does change my disposition.
Florizel.   What you do
Still betters what is done. When you speak, sweet,

I 'ld have you do it ever : when you sing,
I 'ld have you buy and sell so, so give alms,
Pray so ; and, for the ordering your affairs,
To sing them too : when you do dance, I wish you
A wave o' the sea, that you might ever do
Nothing but that ; move still, still so,
And own no other function : each your doing,
So singular in each particular,
Crowns what you are doing in the present deed,
That all your acts are queens.
   Perdita.   O Doricles,
Your praises are too large : but that your youth,
And the true blood which peepeth fairly through 't,
Do plainly give you out an unstain'd shepherd,
With wisdom I might fear, my Doricles.
You woo'd me the false way.
   Florizel.   I think you have
As little skill to fear as I have purpose
To put you to 't. But come ; our dance, I pray :
Your hand, my Perdita : so turtles pair,
That never mean to part.
   Perdita.   I 'll swear for 'em.
   Polixenes. This is the prettiest low-born lass that
      ever
Ran on the green-sward : nothing she does or seems
But smacks of something greater than herself,
Too noble for this place.
   Camillo.   He tells her something
That makes her blood look out : good sooth,
      she is
The queen of curds and cream.
   Clown.   Come on, strike up!
   Dorcas. Mopsa must be your mistress : marry,
      garlic,
To mend her kissing with !
   Mopsa.   Now, in good time !
   Clown. Not a word, a word ; we stand upon our
      manners.
Come, strike up !
   [*Music. Here a dance of Shepherds and
                   Shepherdesses.*
   Polixenes. Pray, good shepherd, what fair swain
      is this
Which dances with your daughter ?
   Shepherd. They call him Doricles ; and boasts
      himself
To have a worthy feeding : but I have it
Upon his own report and I believe it ;
He looks like sooth. He says he loves my daughter :
I think so, too ; for never gazed the moon
Upon the water as he 'll stand and read
As 'twere my daughter's eyes : and, to be plain,
I think there is not half a kiss to choose
Who loves another best.
   Polixenes.   She dances featly.
   Shepherd. So she does any thing ; though I
      report it,
That should be silent : if young Doricles
Do light upon her, she shall bring him that
Which he not dreams of.

            Enter Servant.

   Servant. O master, if you did but hear the pedlar at the door, you would never dance again after
a tabor and pipe ; no, the bagpipe could not move
you : he sings several tunes faster than you 'll tell
money ; he utters them as he had eaten ballads
and all men's ears grew to his tunes.
   Clown. He could never come better ; he shall
come in. I love a ballad but even too well, if it

be doleful matter merrily set down, or a very pleasant
thing indeed and sung lamentably.
   Servant. He hath songs for man or woman, of
all sizes ; no milliner can so fit his customers with
gloves : he has the prettiest love-songs for maids ;
so without bawdry, which is strange ; with such
delicate burthens of dildos and fadings, 'jump
her and thump her ; ' and where some stretch-
mouthed rascal would, as it were, mean mischief
and break a foul gap into the matter, he makes
the maid to answer ' Whoop, do me no harm,
good man ; ' puts him off, slights him, with ' Whoop,
do me no harm, good man.'
   Polixenes. This is a brave fellow.
   Clown. Believe me, thou talkest of an admirable
conceited fellow. Has he any unbraided wares ?
   Servant. He hath ribbons of all the colours i'
the rainbow ; points more than all the lawyers
in Bohemia can learnedly handle, though they come
to him by the gross : inkles, caddisses, cambrics,
lawns : why, he sings 'em over as they were gods
or goddesses ; you would think a smock were a
she-angel, he so chants to the sleeve-hand and the
work about the square on 't.
   Clown. Prithee bring him in ; and let him
approach singing.
   Perdita. Forewarn him that he use no scurrilous
words in 's tunes.   [*Exit Servant.*
   Clown. You have of these pedlars, that have
more in them than you 'ld think, sister.
   Perdita. Ay, good brother, or go about to think.

        Enter Autolycus, *singing.*

Lawn as white as driven snow ;
Cyprus black as e'er was crow ;
Gloves as sweet as damask roses ;
Masks for faces and for noses ;
Bugle bracelet, necklace amber,
Perfume for a lady's chamber ;
Golden quoifs and stomachers,
For my lads to give their dears ;
Pins and poking-sticks of steel,
What maids lack from head to heel :
Come buy of me, come ; come buy, come buy ;
Buy, lads, or else your lasses cry :
Come buy.
   Clown. If I were not in love with Mopsa, thou
shouldst take no money of me ; but being en-
thralled as I am, it will also be the bondage of
certain ribbons and gloves.
   Mopsa. I was promised them against the feast ;
but they come not too late now.
   Dorcas. He hath promised you more than that.
or there be liars.
   Mopsa. He hath paid you all he promised you :
may be, he has paid you more, which will shame
you to give him again.
   Clown. Is there no manners left among maids ?
will they wear their plackets where they should
bear their faces ? Is there not milking-time, when
you are going to bed, or kiln-hole, to whistle off
these secrets, but you must be tittle-tattling before
all our guests ? 'tis well they are whispering :
clamour your tongues, and not a word more.
   Mopsa. I have done. Come, you promised
me a tawdry-lace and a pair of sweet gloves.
   Clown. Have I not told thee how I was cozened
by the way and lost all my money ?
   Autolycus. And indeed, sir, there are cozeners a-
broad ; therefore it behoves men to be wary.

Clown. Fear not thou, man, thou shalt lose nothing here.

Autolycus. I hope so, sir ; for I have about me many parcels of charge.

Clown. What hast here ? ballads ?

Mopsa. Pray now, buy some : I love a ballad in print o' life, for then we are sure they are true.

Autolycus. Here 's one to a very doleful tune, how a usurer's wife was brought to bed of twenty money-bags at a burthen and how she longed to eat adders' heads and toads carbonadoed.

Mopsa. Is it true, think you ?

Autolycus. Very true, and but a month old.

Dorcas. Bless me from marrying a usurer !

Autolycus. Here 's the midwife's name to 't, one Mistress Tale-porter, and five or six honest wives that were present. Why should I carry lies abroad ?

Mopsa. Pray you now, buy it.

Clown. Come on, lay it by : and let 's first see moe ballads ; we 'll buy the other things anon.

Autolycus. Here 's another ballad of a fish, that appeared upon the coast on Wednesday the four-score of April, forty thousand fathom above water, and sung this ballad against the hard hearts of maids : it was thought she was a woman and was turned into a cold fish for she would not exchange flesh with one that loved her : the ballad is very pitiful and as true.

Dorcas. Is it true too, think you ?

Autolycus. Five justices' hands at it, and witnesses more than my pack will hold.

Clown. Lay it by too : another.

Autolycus. This is a merry ballad, but a very pretty one.

Mopsa. Let 's have some merry ones.

Autolycus. Why, this is a passing merry one and goes to the tune of ' Two maids wooing a man : ' there 's scarce a maid westward but she sings it ; 'tis in request, I can tell you.

Mopsa. We can both sing it : if thou 'lt bear a part, thou shalt hear ; 'tis in three parts.

Dorcas. We had the tune on 't a month ago.

Autolycus. I can bear my part ; you must know 'tis my occupation ; have at it with you.

SONG.

A. Get you hence, for I must go
     Where it fits not you to know.
     D. Whither ? *M.* O, whither ? *D.* Whither ?
M. It becomes thy oath full well,
     Thou to me thy secrets tell.
     D. Me too, let me go thither.
M. Or thou goest to the grange or mill.
D. If to either, thou dost ill.
A. Neither. *D.* What, neither ? *A.* Neither.
D. Thou hast sworn my love to be.
M. Thou hast sworn it more to me :
     Then whither goest ? say, whither ?

Clown. We 'll have this song out anon by our-selves : my father and the gentlemen are in sad talk, and we 'll not trouble them. Come, bring away my pack after me. Wenches, I 'll buy for you both. Pedlar, let 's have the first choice. Follow me. girls.

[Exit with Dorcas and Mopsa.

Autolycus. And you shall pay well for 'em.

[Follows singing.

Will you buy any tape,
     Or lace for your cape,
My dainty duck. my dear-a ?

Any silk, any thread,
     Any toys for your head,
Of the new'st and finest, finest wear-a
Come to the pedlar ;
     Money 's a medler,
That doth utter all men's ware-a.   *[Exit.*

Re-enter Servant.

Servant. Master, there is three carters, three shepherds, three neat-herds, three swine-herds, that have made themselves all men of hair, they call themselves Saltiers, and they have a dance which the wenches say is a gallimaufry of gambols, because they are not in 't ; but they themselves are o' the mind, if it be not too rough for some that know little but bowling, it will please plenti-fully.

Shepherd. Away ! we 'll none on 't : here has been too much homely foolery already. I know, sir, we weary you.

Polixenes. You weary those that refresh us : pray, let 's see these four threes of herdsmen.

Servant. One three of them, by their own report, sir, hath danced before the king : and not the worst of the three but jumps twelve foot and a half by the squier.

Shepherd. Leave your prating : since these good men are pleased, let them come in ; but quickly now.

Servant. Why, they stay at door, sir.   *[Exit.*

Here a dance of twelve Satyrs.

Polixenes. O, father, you 'll know more of that hereafter.
[*To Camillo*] Is it not too far gone ? 'Tis time
     to part them.
He 's simple and tells much. [*To Florizel*] How
     now, fair shepherd !
Your heart is full of something that does take
Your mind from feasting. Sooth, when I was
     young
And handed love as you do, I was wont
To load my she with knacks : I would have ran-
     sack'd
The pedlar's silken treasury and have pour'd it
To her acceptance ; you have let him go
And nothing marted with him. If your lass
Interpretation should abuse and call this
Your lack of love or bounty, you were straited
For a reply, at least if you make a care
Of happy holding her.
     Florizel.   Old sir, I know
She prizes not such trifles as these are :
The gifts she looks from me are pack'd and lock'd
Up in my heart ; which I have given already,
But not deliver'd. O, hear me breathe my life
Before this ancient sir, who, it should seem,
Hath sometime loved ! I take thy hand, this hand,
As soft as dove's down and as white as it,
Or Ethiopian's tooth, or the fann'd snow that 's
     bolted
By the northern blasts twice o'er.
     Polixenes.   What follows this ?
How prettily the young swain seems to wash
The hand was fair before ! I have put you out :
But to your protestation ; let me hear
What you profess.
     Florizel.   Do, and be witness to 't.
Polixenes. And this my neighbour too ?

Florizel.   And he, and more
Than he, and men, the earth, the heavens, and all :
That, were I crown'd the most imperial monarch,
Thereof most worthy, were I the fairest youth
That ever made eye swerve, had force and knowledge
More than was ever man's, I would not prize them
Without her love ; for her employ them all ;
Commend them and condemn them to her service
Or to their own perdition.
Polixenes.   Fairly offer'd.
Camillo.   This shows a sound affection.
Shepherd.   But, my daughter,
Say you the like to him ?
Perdita.   I cannot speak
So well, nothing so well ; no, nor mean better :
By the pattern of mine own thoughts I cut out
The purity of his.
Shepherd.   Take hands, a bargain !
And, friends unknown, you shall bear witness
    to 't :
I give my daughter to him, and will make
Her portion equal his.
Florizel.   O, that must be
I' the virtue of your daughter : one being dead,
I shall have more than you can dream of yet ;
Enough then for your wonder. But, come on,
Contract us 'fore these witnesses.
Shepherd.   Come, your hand ;
And, daughter, yours.
Polixenes.   Soft, swain, awhile, beseech you ;
Have you a father ?
Florizel.   I have : but what of him ?
Polixenes.   Knows he of this ?
Florizel.   He neither does nor shall.
Polixenes.   Methinks a father
Is at the nuptial of his son a guest
That best becomes the table. Pray you once more,
Is not your father grown incapable
Of reasonable affairs ? is he not stupid
With age and altering rheums ? can he speak ?
    hear ?
Know man from man ? dispute his own estate ?
Lies he not bed-rid ? and again does nothing
But what he did being childish ?
Florizel.   No, good sir ;
He has his health and ampler strength indeed
Than most have of his age.
Polixenes.   By my white beard,
You offer him, if this be so, a wrong
Something unfilial : reason my son
Should choose himself a wife, but as good reason
The father, all whose joy is nothing else
But fair posterity, should hold some counsel
In such a business.
Florizel.   I yield all this ;
But for some other reasons, my grave sir,
Which 'tis not fit you know, I not acquaint
My father of this business.
Polixenes.   Let him know 't.
Florizel.   He shall not.
Polixenes.   Prithee, let him.
Florizel.   No, he must not.
Shepherd.   Let him, my son : he shall not need
    to grieve
At knowing of thy choice.
Florizel.   Come, come, he must not.
Mark our contract.
Polixenes.   Mark your divorce, young sir,
                    [*Discovering himself.*
Whom son I dare not call ; thou art too base
To be acknowledged : thou a sceptre's heir,

That thus affect'st a sheep-hook ! Thou old traitor,
I am sorry that by hanging thee I can
But shorten thy life one week. And thou, fresh piece
Of excellent witchcraft, who of force must know
The royal fool thou copest with,—
Shepherd.   O, my heart !
Polixenes.   I 'll have thy beauty scratch'd with
    briers, and made
More homely than thy state. For thee, fond boy,
If I may ever know thou dost but sigh
That thou no more shalt see this knack, as never
I mean thou shalt, we 'll bar thee from succession ;
Not hold thee of our blood, no, not our kin,
Far than Deucalion off : mark thou my words :
Follow us to the court. Thou churl, for this time,
Though full of our displeasure, yet we free thee
From the dead blow of it. And you, enchantment,—
Worthy enough a herdsman ; yea, him too,
That makes himself but for our honour therein
Unworthy thee,—if ever henceforth thou
These rural latches to his entrance open,
Or hoop his body more with thy embraces.
I will devise a death as cruel for thee
As thou art tender to 't.   [*Exit.*
Perdita.   Even here undone !
I was not much afeard ; for once or twice
I was about to speak and tell him plainly,
The selfsame sun that shines upon his court
Hides not his visage from our cottage but
Looks on alike. Will 't please you, sir, be gone ?
I told you what would come of this : beseech you,
Of your own state take care : this dream of mine, —
Being now awake, I 'll queen it no inch farther,
But milk my ewes and weep.
Camillo.   Why, how now, father !
Speak ere thou diest.
Shepherd.   I cannot speak, nor think,
Nor dare to know that which I know. O sir !
You have undone a man of fourscore three,
That thought to fill his grave in quiet, yea,
To die upon the bed my father died,
To lie close by his honest bones : but now
Some hangman must put on my shroud and lay me
Where no priest shovels in dust. O cursed wretch,
That knew'st this was the prince, and wouldst
    adventure
To mingle faith with him ! Undone ! undone !
If I might die within this hour, I have lived
To die when I desire.   [*Exit.*
Florizel.   Why look you so upon me ?
I am but sorry, not afeard ; delay'd,
But nothing alter'd : what I was, I am ;
More straining on for plucking back, not following
My leash unwillingly.
Camillo.   Gracious my lord,
You know your father's temper : at this time
He will allow no speech, which I do guess
You do not purpose to him ; and as hardly
Will he endure your sight as yet, I fear :
Then, till the fury of his highness settle,
Come not before him.
Florizel.   I not purpose it
I think, Camillo ?
Camillo.   Even he, my lord.
Perdita.   How often have I told you 'twould be
    thus !
How often said, my dignity would last
But till 'twere known !
Florizel.   It cannot fail but by
The violation of my faith ; and then
Let nature crush the sides o' the earth together

And mar the seeds within ! Lift up thy looks :
From my succession wipe me, father ; I
Am heir to my affection.
  Camillo.   Be advised.
  Florizel. I am, and by my fancy : if my reason
Will thereto be obedient, I have reason ;
If not, my senses, better pleased with madness,
Do bid it welcome.
  Camillo.   This is desperate, sir.
  Florizel.   So call it : but it does fulfil my vow ;
I needs must think it honesty. Camillo,
Not for Bohemia, nor the pomp that may
Be thereat glean'd, for all the sun sees or
The close earth wombs or the profound seas hide
In unknown fathoms, will I break my oath
To this my fair beloved : therefore, I pray you,
As you have ever been my father's honour'd friend,
When he shall miss me,—as, in faith, I mean not
To see him any more,—cast your good counsels
Upon his passion : let myself and fortune
Tug for the time to come. This you may know
And so deliver, I am put to sea
With her whom here I cannot hold on shore ;
And most opportune to our need I have
A vessel rides fast by, but not prepared
For this design. What course I mean to hold
Shall nothing benefit your knowledge, nor
Concern me the reporting.
  Camillo.   O my lord !
I would your spirit were easier for advice,
Or stronger for your need.
  Florizel. Hark, Perdita.   [*Drawing her aside.*
I 'll hear you by and by.
  Camillo.   He 's irremoveable,
Resolved for flight. Now were I happy, if
His going I could frame to serve my turn,
Save him from danger, do him love and honour,
Purchase the sight again of dear Sicilia
And that unhappy king, my master. whom
I so much thirst to see.
  Florizel.   Now, good Camillo ;
I am so fraught with curious business that
I leave out ceremony.
  Camillo.   Sir, I think
You have heard of my poor services, i' the love
That I have borne your father ?
  Florizel.   Very nobly
Have you deserved : it is my father's music
To speak your deeds, not little of his care
To have them recompensed as thought on.
  Camillo.   Well, my lord,
If you may please to think I love the king
And through him what is nearest to him, which is
Your gracious self, embrace but my direction :
If your more ponderous and settled project
May suffer alteration. on mine honour,
I 'll point you where you shall have such receiving
As shall become your highness ; where you may
Enjoy your mistress, from the whom, I see,
There 's no disjunction to be made, but by—
As heavens forfend !—your ruin ; marry her,
And, with my best endeavours in your absence.
Your discontenting father strive to qualify
And bring him up to liking.
  Florizel.   How, Camillo
May this, almost a miracle, be done ?
That I may call thee something more than man
And after that trust to thee.
  Camillo.   Have you thought on
A place whereto you 'll go ?
  Florizel.   Not any yet :

But as the unthought-on accident is guilty
To what we wildly do, so we profess
Ourselves to be the slaves of chance and flies
Of every wind that blows.
  Camillo.   Then list to me :
This follows, if you will not change your purpose
But undergo this flight, make for Sicilia,
And there present yourself and your fair princess,
For so I see she must be, 'fore Leontes :
She shall be habited as it becomes
The partner of your bed. Methinks I see
Leontes opening his free arms and weeping
His welcomes forth ; asks thee the son forgiveness,
As 'twere i' the father's person ; kisses the hands
Of your fresh princess ; o'er and o'er divides him
'Twixt his unkindness and his kindness ; the one
He chides to hell and bids the other grow
Faster than thought or time.
  Florizel.   Worthy Camillo,
What colour for my visitation shall I
Hold up before him ?
  Camillo.   Sent by the king your father
To greet him and to give him comforts. Sir,
The manner of your bearing towards him, with
What you as from your father shall deliver,
Things known betwixt us three, I 'll write you down :
The which shall point you forth at every sitting
What you`must say ; that he shall not perceive
But that you have your father's bosom there
And speak his very heart.
  Florizel.   I am bound to you :
There is some sap in this.
  Camillo.   A course more promising
Than a wild dedication of yourselves
To unpath'd waters, undream'd shores, most certain
To miseries enough ; no hope to help you,
But as you shake off one to take another ;
Nothing so certain as your anchors, who
Do their best office, if they can but stay you
Where you 'll be loath to be : besides you know
Prosperity's the very bond of love,
Whose fresh complexion and whose heart together
Affliction alters.
  Perdita.   One of these is true :
I think affliction may subdue the cheek,
But not take in the mind.
  Camillo.   Yea, say you so ?
There shall not at your father's house these seven
    years
Be born another such.
  Florizel.   My good Camillo,
She is as forward of her breeding as
† She is i' the rear our birth.
  Camillo.   I cannot say 'tis pity
She lacks instructions, for she seems a mistress
To most that teach.
  Perdita.   Your pardon, sir : for this
I 'll blush you thanks.
  Florizel.   My prettiest Perdita !
But O, the thorns we stand upon ! Camillo,
Preserver of my father, now of me,
The medicine of our house, how shall we do ?
We are not furnish'd like Bohemia's son,
Nor shall appear in Sicilia.
  Camillo.   My lord,
Fear none of this : I think you know my fortunes
Do all lie there : it shall be so my care
To have you royally appointed as if
The scene you play were mine. For instance, sir,
That you may know you shall not want, one word.
               [*They talk aside.*

Re-enter AUTOLYCUS.

Autolycus. Ha, ha ! what a fool Honesty is !
and Trust, his sworn brother, a very simple gentleman ! I have sold all my trumpery ; not a counterfeit stone, not a ribbon, glass, pomander, brooch,
table-book, ballad, knife, tape, glove, shoe-tie,
bracelet, horn-ring, to keep my pack from fasting :
they throng who should buy first, as if my trinkets
had been hallowed and brought a benediction to
the buyer : by which means I saw whose purse was
best in picture ; and what I saw, to my good use
I remembered.   My clown, who wants but something to be a reasonable man, grew so in love with
the wenches' song, that he would not stir his pettitoes
till he had both tune and words ; which so drew
the rest of the herd to me that all their other senses
stuck in ears : you might have pinched a placket,
it was senseless ; 'twas nothing to geld a codpiece
of a purse ; I could have filed keys off that hung in
chains : no hearing, no feeling, but my sir's song,
and admiring the nothing of it.   So that in this time
of lethargy I picked and cut most of their festival
purses ; and had not the old man come in with a
whoo-bub against his daughter and the king's son
and scared my choughs from the chaff, I had not
left a purse alive in the whole army.

[*Camillo, Florizel, and Perdita come forward.*
Camillo. Nay, but my letters, by this means
    being there
So soon as you arrive, shall clear that doubt.
Florizel. And those that you 'll procure from
    King Leontes—
Camillo. Shall satisfy your father.
Perdita.   Happy be you !
All that you speak shows fair.
Camillo.   Who have we here ?
    [*Seeing* Autolycus.
We 'll make an instrument of this, omit
Nothing may give us aid.
Autolycus. If they have overheard me now, why,
hanging.
Camillo. How now, good fellow ! why shakest
thou so ? Fear not, man ; here 's no harm intended
to thee.
Autolycus. I am a poor fellow, sir.
Camillo. Why, be so still ; here 's nobody will
steal that from thee : yet for the outside of thy
poverty we must make an exchange ; therefore
discase thee instantly,—thou must think there 's
a necessity in 't,—and change garments with this
gentleman : though the pennyworth on his side
be the worst, yet hold thee, there 's some boot.
Autolycus. I am a poor fellow, sir. [*Aside*] I
know ye well enough.
Camillo. Nay, prithee, dispatch : the gentleman
is half flayed already.
Autolycus. Are you in earnest, sir ? [*Aside*] I
smell the trick on 't.
Florizel. Dispatch, I prithee.
Autolycus. Indeed, I have had earnest ; but I
cannot with conscience take it.
Camillo. Unbuckle, unbuckle.
    [*Florizel and Autolycus exchange garments.*
Fortunate mistress,—let my prophecy
Come home to ye !—you must retire yourself
Into some covert : take your sweetheart's hat
And pluck it o'er your brows, muffle your face,
Dismantle you, and, as you can, disliken
The truth of your own seeming ; that you may—
For I do fear eyes over—to shipboard

Get undescried.
Perdita.   I see the play so lies
That I must bear a part.
Camillo.   No remedy,
Have you done there ?
Florizel.   Should I now meet my father
He would not call me son.
Camillo.   Nay, you shall have no hat.
    [*Giving it to Perdita.*
Come, lady, come.   Farewell, my friend.
Autolycus.   Adieu, sir.
Florizel. O Perdita, what have we twain forgot !
Pray you, a word.
Camillo. [*Aside*] What I do next, shall be to
    tell the king
Of this escape and whither they are bound ;
Wherein my hope is I shall so prevail
To force him after : in whose company
I shall review Sicilia, for whose sight
I have a woman's longing.
Florizel.   Fortune speed us !
Thus we set on, Camillo, to the sea-side.
Camillo. The swifter speed the better.
    [*Exeunt Florizel, Perdita, and Camillo.*
Autolycus. I understand the business, I hear it :
to have an open ear, a quick eye, and a nimble
hand, is necessary for a cut-purse ; a good nose is
requisite also, to smell out work for the other
senses.   I see this is the time that the unjust man
doth thrive.   What an exchange had this been without boot ! What a boot is here with this exchange !
Sure the gods do this year connive at us, and we
may do any thing extempore.   The prince himself
is about a piece of iniquity, stealing away from
his father with his clog at his heels : if I thought
it were a piece of honesty to acquaint the king
withal, I would not do 't : I hold it the more knavery
to conceal it ; and therein am I constant to my
profession.

Re-enter Clown *and* Shepherd.

Aside, aside ; here is more matter for a hot brain :
every lane's end, every shop, church, session,
hanging, yields a careful man work.
Clown. See, see ; what a man you are now !
There is no other way but to tell the king she 's a
changeling and none of your flesh and blood.
Shepherd. Nay, but hear me.
Clown. Nay, but hear me.
Shepherd. Go to, then.
Clown. She being none of your flesh and blood,
your flesh and blood has not offended the king ;
and so your flesh and blood is not to be punished
by him. Show those things you found about her,
those secret things, all but what she has with her :
this being done, let the law go whistle : I warrant
you.
Shepherd. I will tell the king all, every word,
yea, and his son's pranks too ; who, I may say,
is no honest man, neither to his father nor to me,
to go about to make me the king's brother-in-law.
Clown. Indeed, brother-in-law was the farthest
off you could have been to him and then your
blood had been the dearer by I know how much an
ounce.
Autolycus. [*Aside*] Very wisely, puppies !
Shepherd. Well, let us to the king : there is that
in this fardel will make him scratch his beard.
Autolycus. [*Aside*] I know not what impediment
this complaint may be to the flight of my master.
Clown. Pray heartily he be at palace.

Autolycus. [*Aside*] Though I am not naturally honest, I am so sometimes by chance : let me pocket up my pedlar's excrement. [*Takes off his false beard.*] How now rustics ! whither are you bound ?

Shepherd. To the palace, an it like your worship.

Autolycus. Your affairs there, what, with whom, the condition of that fardel, the place of your dwelling, your names, your ages, of what having breeding, and any thing that is fitting to be known discover.

Clown. We are but plain fellows, sir.

Autolycus. A lie ; you are rough and hairy. Let me have no lying : it becomes none but tradesmen, and they often give us soldiers the lie : but we pay them for it with stamped coin, not stabbing steel ; therefore they do not give us the lie.

Clown. Your worship had like to have given us one if you had not taken yourself with the manner.

Shepherd. Are you a courtier, an 't like you, sir ?

Autolycus. Whether it like me or no I am a courtier. Seest thou not the air of the court in these enfoldings ? hath not my gait in it the measure of the court ? receives not thy nose court-odour from me ? reflect I not on thy baseness court-contempt ? Thinkest thou, for that I insinuate, or †toaze from thee thy business, I am therefore no courtier ? I am courtier cap-a-pe : and one that will either push on or pluck back thy business there : whereupon I command thee to open thy affair.

Shepherd. My business, sir, is to the king.

Autolycus. What advocate hast thou to him ?

Shepherd. I know not, an 't like you.

Clown. Advocate 's the court-word for a pheasant say you have none.

Shepherd. None. sir : I have no pheasant, cock nor hen.

Autolycus. How blessed are we that are not simple men !
Yet nature might have made me as these are.
Therefore I will not disdain.

Clown. This cannot be but a great courtier.

Shepherd. His garments are rich. but he wears them not handsomely

Clown. He seems to be the more noble in being fantastical : a great man, I 'll warrant : I know by the picking on 's teeth.

Autolycus. The fardel there ? what 's i' the fardel ? Wherefore that box ?

Shepherd. Sir, there lies such secrets in this fardel and box, which none must know but the king ; and which he shall know within this hour, if I may come to the speech of him.

Autolycus. Age, thou hast lost thy labour.

Shepherd. Why, sir ?

Autolycus. The king is not at the palace ; he is gone aboard a new ship to purge melancholy and air himself : for, if thou beest capable of things serious, thou must know the king is full of grief.

Shepherd. So 'tis said. sir ; about his son, that should have married a shepherd's daughter.

Autolycus. If that Shepherd be not in hand-fast, let him fly : the curses he shall have, the tortures he shall feel, will break the back of man. the heart of monster.

Clown. Think you so, sir ?

Autolycus. Not he alone shall suffer what wit can make heavy and vengeance bitter ; but those that are germane to him, though removed fifty times, shall all come under the hangman : which though it be great pity yet it is necessary. An old sheep-

whistling rogue, a ram-tender to offer to have his daughter come into grace ! Some say he shall be stoned ; but that death is too soft for him, say I : draw our throne into a sheep-cote ! all deaths are too few, the sharpest too easy.

Clown. Has the old man e'er a son, sir, do you hear, an 't like you, sir ?

Autolycus. He has a son, who shall be flayed alive, then 'nointed over with honey, set on the head of a wasp's nest, then stand till he be three quarters and a dram dead ; then recovered again with aqua-vitæ or some other hot infusion : then, raw as he is, in the hottest day prognostication proclaims, shall he be set against a brick-wall, the sun looking with a southward eye upon him, where he is to behold him with flies blown to death. But what talk we of these traitorly rascals, whose miseries are to be smiled at their offences being so capital ? Tell me, for you seem to be honest plain men, what you have to the king : being something gently considered, I 'll bring you where he is aboard, tender your persons to his presence, whisper him in your behalfs ; and if it be in man besides the king to effect your suits, here is man shall do it.

Clown. He seems to be of great authority : close with him, give him gold ; and though authority be a stubborn bear, yet he is oft led by the nose with gold : show the inside of your purse to the outside of his hand, and no more ado Remember ' stoned,' and ' flayed alive.'

Shepherd. An 't please you, sir, to undertake the business for us, here is that gold I have : I 'll make it as much more and leave this young man in pawn till I bring it you.

Autolycus. After I have done what I promised ?

Shepherd. Ay, sir.

Autolycus. Well, give me the moiety. Are you a party in this business ?

Clown. In some sort, sir : but though my case be a pitiful one, I hope I shall not be flayed out of it.

Autolycus. O that 's the case of the shepherd's son : hang him, he 'll be made an example.

Clown. Comfort, good comfort ! We must to the king and show our strange sights : he must know 'tis none of your daughter nor my sister ; we are gone else. Sir, I will give you as much as this old man does when the business is performed, and remain, as he says, your pawn till it be brought you.

Autolycus. I will trust you. Walk before toward the sea-side ; go on the right hand : I will but look upon the hedge and follow you.

Clown. We are blest in this man. as I may say, even blest.

Shepherd. Let 's before as he bids us : he was provided to do us good.

[*Exeunt Shepherd and Clown.*

Autolycus. If I had a mind to be honest, I see Fortune would not suffer me she drops booties in my mouth. I am courted now with a double occasion, gold and a means to do the prince my master good : which who knows how that may turn back to my advancement ? I will bring these two moles, these blind ones, aboard him : if he think it fit to shore them again and that the complaint they have to the king concerns him nothing. let him call me rogue for being so far officious ; for I am proof against that title and what shame else belongs to 't. To him will I present them : there may be matter in it.

[*Exit.*

ACT V.

SCENE I. *A room in* LEONTES' *palace.*

Enter LEONTES, CLEOMENES, DION, PAULINA,
and Servants.

Cleomenes.

Sir, you have done enough, and have perform'd
A saint-like sorrow : no fault could you make,
  Which you have not redeem'd ; indeed, paid
        down
More penitence than done trespass : at the last,
Do as the heavens have done, forget your evil ;
With them forgive yourself.
Leontes.   Whilst I remember
Her and her virtues, I cannot forget
My blemishes in them, and so still think of
The wrong I did myself ; which was so much,
That heirless it hath made my kingdom and
Destroy'd the sweet'st companion that e'er man
Bred his hopes out of.
Paulina.   True, too true, my lord :
If. one by one, you wedded all the world,
Or from the all that are took something good,
To make a perfect woman, she you kill'd
Would be unparallel'd.
Leontes.   I think so. Kill'd !
She I kill'd ! I did so : but thou strikest me
Sorely, to say I did ; it is as bitter
Upon thy tongue as in my thought : now, good now,
Say so but seldom.
Cleomenes.   Not at all, good lady :
You might have spoken a thousand things that
        would
Have done the time more benefit and graced
Your kindness better.
Paulina.   You are one of those
Would have him wed again.
Dion.   If you would not so,
You pity not the state, nor the remembrance
Of his most sovereign name ; consider little
What dangers, by his highness' fail of issue,
May drop upon his kingdom and devour
Incertain lookers on. What were more holy
Than to rejoice the former queen is well ?
What holier than, for royalty's repair,
For present comfort and for future good,
To bless the bed of majesty again
With a sweet fellow to 't ?
Paulina.   There is none worthy,
Respecting her that 's gone. Besides, the gods
Will have fulfill'd their secret purposes ;
For has not the divine Apollo said,
Is 't not the tenour of his oracle,
That King Leontes shall not have an heir
Till his lost child be found ? which that it shall,
Is all as monstrous to our human reason
As my Antigonus to break his grave
And come again to me ; who, on my life,
Did perish with the infant. 'Tis your counsel
My lord should to the heavens be contrary,
Oppose against their wills. [*To Leontes.*] Care not
        for issue ;
The crown will find an heir : great Alexander
Left his to the worthiest ; so his successor
Was like to be the best.
Leontes.   Good Paulina,
Who hast the memory of Hermione,
I know, in honour, O, that ever I
Had squared me to thy counsel ! then, even now,

I might have look'd upon my queen's full eyes,
Have taken treasure from her lips—
Paulina.   And left them
More rich for what they yielded.
Leontes.   Thou speak'st truth.
No more such wives ; therefore, no wife : one
        worse,
And better used, would make her sainted spirit
Again possess her corpse, and on this stage,
Where we 're offenders now, appear soul-vex'd,
†And begin, ' Why to me ? '
Paulina.   Had she such power,
She had just cause.
Leontes.   She had ; and would incense me
To murder her I married.
Paulina.   I should so.
Were I the ghost that walk'd, I 'ld bid you mark
Her eye, and tell me for what dull part in 't
You chose her ; then I 'ld shriek, that even your
        ears
Should rift to hear me ; and the words that follow'd
Should be ' Remember mine.'
Leontes.   Stars, stars,
And all eyes else dead coals ! Fear thou no wife ;
I 'll have no wife, Paulina.
Paulina.   Will you swear
Never to marry but by my free leave ?
Leontes. Never, Paulina ; so be blest my spirit !
Paulina. Then, good my lords, bear witness to
        his oath.
Cleomenes. You tempt him over-much.
Paulina.   Unless another,
As like Hermione as is her picture,
Affront his eye.
Cleomenes. Good madam,—
Paulina.   I have done.
Yet, if my lord will marry,—if you will, sir,
No remedy, but you will,—give me the office
To choose you a queen : she shall not be so young
As was your former ; but she shall be such
As, walk'd your first queen's ghost, it should take
        joy
To see her in your arms.
Leontes.   My true Paulina,
We shall not marry till thou bid'st us.
Paulina.   That
Shall be when your first queen 's again in breath ;
Never till then.

Enter a Gentleman.

Gentleman. One that gives out himself Prince
        Florizel,
Son of Polixenes, with his princess, she
The fairest I have yet beheld, desires access
To your high presence.
Leontes.   What with him ? he comes not
Like to his father's greatness : his approach,
So out of circumstance and sudden, tells us
'Tis not a visitation framed, but forced
By need and accident. What train ?
Gentleman.   But few,
And those but mean.
Leontes.   His princess, say you, with him ?
Gentleman. Ay, the most peerless piece of earth,
        I think,
That e'er the sun shone bright on.
Paulina.   O Hermione,
As every present time doth boast itself
Above a better gone, so must thy grave
Give way to what 's seen now ! Sir, you yourself

Have said and writ so, but your writing now
Is colder than that theme, ' She had not been,
Nor was not to be equall'd ;'—thus your verse
Flow'd with her beauty once : 'tis shrewdly ebb'd,
To say you have seen a better.
   Gentleman.   Pardon, madam :
The one I have almost forgot,—your pardon,—
The other, when she has obtain'd your eye,
Will have your tongue too. This is a creature,
Would she begin a sect, might quench the zeal
Of all professors else, make proselytes
Of who she but bid follow.
   Paulina.   How ! not women ?
   Gentleman. Women will love her. that she is a
woman
More worth than any man ; men, that she is
The rarest of all women.
   Leontes.   Go, Cleomenes ;
Yourself, assisted with your honour'd friends,
Bring them to our embracement. Still. 'tis strange
          [*Exeunt Cleomenes and others.*
He thus should steal upon us.
   Paulina.   Had our prince,
Jewel of children. seen this hour, he had pair'd
Well with this lord : there was not full a month
Between their births.
   Leontes. Prithee, no more ; cease ; thou know'st
He dies to me again when talk'd of : sure,
When I shall see this gentleman, thy speeches
Will bring me to consider that which may
Unfurnish me of reason. They are come.

    Re-enter CLEOMENES *and others, with*
      FLORIZEL *and* PERDITA.

Your mother was most true to wedlock, prince ;
For she did print your royal father off,
Conceiving you : were I but twenty one,
Your father's image is so hit in you,
His very air, that I should call you brother,
As I did him, and speak of something wildly
By us perform'd before. Most dearly welcome !
And your fair princess,—goddess !—O, Alas !
I lost a couple, that 'twixt heaven and earth
Might thus have stood begetting wonder as
You, gracious couple, do : and then I lost—
All mine own folly—the society,
Amity too, of your brave father, whom,
Though bearing misery, I desire my life
Once more to look on him.
   Florizel.   By his command
Have I here touch'd Sicilia and from him
Give you all greetings that a king, at friend,
Can send his brother : and, but infirmity
Which waits upon worn times hath something seized
His wish'd ability, he had himself
The lands and waters 'twixt your throne and his
Measured to look upon you ; whom he loves—
He bade me say so—more than all the sceptres
And those that bear them living.
   Leontes.   O my brother,
Good gentleman ! the wrongs I have done thee stir
Afresh within me, and these thy offices,
So rarely kind, are as interpreters
Of my behind-hand slackness. Welcome hither,
As is the spring to the earth. And hath he too
Exposed this paragon to the fearful usage,
At least ungentle, of the dreadful Neptune,
To greet a man not worth her pains, much less
The adventure of her person ?
   Florizel.   Good my lord,

She came from Libya.
   Leontes.   Where the warlike Smalus,
That noble honour'd lord, is fear'd and loved ?
   Florizel. Most royal sir. from thence : from him,
      whose daughter
His tears proclaim'd his, parting with her : thence,
A prosperous south-wind friendly, we have cross'd,
To execute the charge my father gave me
For visiting your highness : my best train
I have from your Sicilian shores dismiss'd ;
Who for Bohemia bend, to signify
Not only my success in Libya, sir,
But my arrival and my wife's in safety
Here where we are.
   Leontes.   The blessed gods
Purge all infection from our air whilst you
Do climate here ! You have a holy father
A graceful gentleman ; against whose person,
So sacred as it is, I have done sin :
For which the heavens, taking angry note,
Have left me issueless ; and your father 's blest,
As he from heaven merits it, with you
Worthy his goodness. What might I have been,
Might I a son and daughter now have look'd on,
Such goodly things as you !

        Enter a Lord.

   Lord.   Most noble sir,
That which I shall report will bear no credit,
Were not the proof so nigh. Please you, great sir,
Bohemia greets you from himself by me ;
Desires you to attach his son, who has—
His dignity and duty both cast off—
Fled from his father, from his hopes, and with
A shepherd's daughter.
   Leontes.   Where 's Bohemia ? speak.
   Lord. Here in your city ; I now came from
      him :
I speak amazedly ; and it becomes
My marvel and my message. To your court
Whiles he was hastening, in the chase, it seems,
Of this fair couple, meets he on the way
The father of this seeming lady and
Her brother, having both their country quitted
With this young prince.
   Florizel. Camillo has betray'd me ;
Whose honour and whose honesty till now
Endured all weathers.
   Lord.   Lay 't so to his charge :
He 's with the king your father.
   Leontes.   Who ? Camillo ?
   Lord. Camillo, sir ; I spake with him ; who now
Has these poor men in question. Never saw I
Wretches so quake : they kneel, they kiss the earth ;
Forswear themselves as often as they speak :
Bohemia stops his ears, and threatens them
With divers deaths in death.
   Perdita.   O my poor father !
The heaven sets spies upon us, will not have
Our contract celebrated.
   Leontes.   You are married ?
   Florizel. We are not, sir, nor are we like to be ;
The stars, I see, will kiss the valleys first :
The odds for high and low 's alike.
   Leontes.   My lord,
Is this the daughter of a king ?
   Florizel.   She is,
When once she is my wife.
   Leontes. That ' once,' I see by your good father's
      speed,

Will come on very slowly. I am sorry,
Most sorry, you have broken from his liking
Where you were tied in duty, and as sorry
Your choice is not so rich in worth as beauty,
That you might well enjoy her.
    Florizel.   Dear, look up :
Though Fortune, visible an enemy
Should chase us with my father, power no jot
Hath she to change our loves. Beseech you, sir,
Remember since you owed no more to time
Than I do now : with thought of such affections,
Step forth mine advocate ; at your request
My father will grant precious things as trifles.
    Leontes. Would he do so, I 'ld beg your precious
        mistress,
Which he counts but a trifle.
    Paulina.   Sir, my liege,
Your eye hath too much youth in 't : not a month
'Fore your queen died, she was more worth such
        gazes
Than what you look on now.
    Leontes.   I thought of her,
Even in these looks I made.   [*To Florizel.*]
    But your petition
Is yet unanswer'd. I will to your father :
Your honour not o'erthrown by your desires,
I am friend to them and you : upon which errand
I now go toward him ; therefore follow me
And mark what way I make : come, good my lord.
                        [*Exeunt.*

SCENE II. *Before* LEONTES' *palace.*

Enter AUTOLYCUS *and a* Gentleman.

    Autolycus. Beseech you, sir, were you present
at this relation ?
    First Gentleman. I was by at the opening of the
fardel, heard the old shepherd deliver the manner
how he found it : whereupon, after a little amazedness, we were all commanded out of the chamber ;
only this methought I heard the shepherd say, he
found the child.
    Autolycus. I would most gladly know the issue
of it.
    First Gentleman. I make a broken delivery of the
business ; but the changes I perceived in the king
and Camillo were very notes of admiration : they
seemed almost, with staring on one another, to
tear the cases of their eyes ; there was speech in
their dumbness, language in their very gesture ;
they looked as they had heard of a world ransomed,
or one destroyed : a notable passion of wonder
appeared in them ; but the wisest beholder, that
knew no more but seeing, could not say if the importance were joy or sorrow ; but in the extremity
of the one, it must needs be.

Enter another Gentleman.

Here comes a gentleman that haply knows more.
The news, Rogero ?
    Second Gentleman. Nothing but bonfires : the
oracle is fulfilled ; the king's daughter is found :
such a deal of wonder is broken out within this
hour that ballad-makers cannot be able to express it.

Enter a third Gentleman.

Here comes the Lady Paulina's steward : he can
deliver you more. How goes it now, sir ? this

news which is called true is so like an old tale, that
the verity of it is in strong suspicion : has the king
found his heir ?
    Third Gentleman. Most true, if ever truth were
pregnant by circumstance : that which you hear
you 'll swear you see, there is such unity in the
proofs. The mantle of Queen Hermione's, her
jewel about the neck of it, the letters of Antigonus
found with it which they know to be his character,
the majesty of the creature in resemblance of the
mother the affection of nobleness which nature
shows above her breeding, and many other evidences
proclaim her with all certainty to be the king's
daughter. Did you see the meeting of the two kings ?
    Second Gentleman. No.
    Third Gentleman. Then have you lost a sight,
which was to be seen, cannot be spoken of. There
might you have beheld one joy crown another, so
and in such manner that it seemed sorrow wept to
take leave of them, for their joy waded in tears.
There was casting up of eyes, holding up of hands,
with countenance of such distraction that they were
to be known by garment, not by favour. Our
king, being ready to leap out of himself for joy of
his found daughter, as if that joy were now become
a loss, cries ' O, thy mother, thy mother ! ' then asks
Bohemia forgiveness ; then embraces his son-in-
law ; then again worries he his daughter with
clipping her ; now he thanks the old shepherd,
which stands by like a weather-bitten conduit of
many kings' reigns. I never heard of such another
encounter, which lames report to follow it and
undoes description to do it.
    Second Gentleman. What, pray you, became of
Antigonus, that carried hence the child ?
    Third Gentleman. Like an old tale still, which
will have matter to rehearse, though credit be asleep
and not an ear open. He was torn to pieces with a
bear : this avouches the shepherd's son ; who has
not only his innocence, which seems much, to justify
him, but a handkerchief and rings of his that Paulina
knows.
    First Gentleman. What became of his bark and
his followers ?
    Third Gentleman. Wrecked the same instant of
their master's death and in the view of the shepherd :
so that all the instruments which aided to expose
the child were even then lost when it was found.
But O, the noble combat that 'twixt joy and sorrow
was fought in Paulina ! She had one eye declined
for the loss of her husband, another elevated that
the oracle was fulfilled : she lifted the princess
from the earth, and so locks her in embracing, as
if she would pin her to her heart that she might no
more be in danger of losing.
    First Gentleman. The dignity of this act was
worth the audience of kings and princes ; for by
such was it acted.
    Third Gentleman. One of the prettiest touches
of all and that which angled for mine eyes, caught
the water though not the fish, was when, at the
relation of the queen's death, with the manner how
she came to 't bravely confessed and lamented by
the king, how attentiveness wounded his daughter ;
till, from one sign of dolour to another, she did,
with an ' Alas,' I would fain say, bleed tears, for I
am sure my heart wept blood. Who was most
marble there changed colour ; some swooned, all
sorrowed : if all the world could have seen 't, the
woe had been universal.
    First Gentleman. Are they returned to the court ?

Third Gentleman. No: the princess hearing of her mother's statue, which is in the keeping of Paulina,—a piece many years in doing and now newly performed by that rare Italian master, Julio Romano, who, had he himself eternity and could put breath into his work, would beguile Nature of her custom, so perfectly he is her ape : he so near to Hermione hath done Hermione that they say one would speak to her and stand in hope of answer : thither with all greediness of affection are they gone, and there they intend to sup.

Second Gentleman. I thought she had some great matter there in hand ; for she hath privately twice or thrice a day, ever since the death of Hermione, visited that removed house. Shall we thither and with our company piece the rejoicing ?

First Gentleman. Who would be thence that has the benefit of access ? every wink of an eye some new grace will be born : our absence makes us unthrifty to our knowledge. Let 's along.

[*Exeunt Gentlemen.*

Autolycus. Now, had I not the dash of my former life in me, would preferment drop on my head. I brought the old man and his son aboard the prince ; told him I heard them talk of a fardel and I know not what : but he at that time, over-fond of the shepherd's daughter, so he then took her to be, who began to be much sea-sick, and himself little better, extremity of weather continuing, this mystery remained undiscovered. But 'tis all one to me ; for had I been the finder out of this secret, it would not have relished among my other discredits.

Enter Shepherd *and* Clown.

Here come those I have done good to against my will, and already appearing in the blossoms of their fortune.

Shepherd. Come, boy ; I am past moe children, but thy sons and daughters will be all gentlemen born.

Clown. You are well met, sir. You denied to fight with me this other day, because I was no gentleman born. See you these clothes ? say you see them not and think me still no gentleman born : you were best say these robes are not gentlemen born : give me the lie, do, and try whether I am not now a gentleman born.

Autolycus. I know you are now, sir, a gentleman born.

Clown. Ay, and have been so any time these four hours.

Shepherd. And so have I, boy.

Clown. So you have : but I was a gentleman born before my father ; for the king's son took me by the hand, and called me brother ; and then the two kings called my father brother ; and then the prince my brother and the princess my sister called my father father ; and so we wept, and there was the first gentleman-like tears that ever we shed.

Shepherd. We may live, son, to shed many more.

Clown. Ay ; or else 'twere hard luck, being in so preposterous estate as we are.

Autolycus. I humbly beseech you, sir, to pardon me all the faults I have committed to your worship and to give me your good report to the prince my master.

Shepherd. Prithee, son, do ; for we must be gentle, now we are gentlemen.

Clown. Thou wilt amend thy life ?

Autolycus. Ay, an it like your good worship.

Clown. Give me thy hand : I will swear to the prince thou art as honest a true fellow as any is in Bohemia.

Shepherd. You may say it, but not swear it.

Clown. Not swear it, now I am a gentleman ? Let boors and franklins say it, I 'll swear it.

Shepherd. How if it be false, son ?

Clown. If it be ne'er so false, a true gentleman may swear it in the behalf of his friend : and I 'll swear to the prince thou art a tall fellow of thy hands and that thou wilt not be drunk ; but I know thou art no tall fellow of thy hands and that thou wilt be drunk : but I 'll swear it and I would thou wouldst be a tall fellow of thy hands.

Autolycus. I will prove so, sir, to my power.

Clown. Ay, by any means prove a tall fellow : if I do not wonder how thou darest venture to be drunk, not being a tall fellow, trust me not. Hark ! the kings and the princes, our kindred, are going to see the queen's picture. Come, follow us : we 'll be thy good masters.

[*Exeunt.*

SCENE III. *A chapel in* PAULINA'S *house.*

Enter LEONTES, POLIXENES, FLORIZEL, PERDITA, CAMILLO, PAULINA, Lords, *and* Attendants.

Leontes. O grave and good Paulina, the great comfort
That I have had of thee !

Paulina. What, sovereign sir,
I did not well I meant well. All my services
You have paid home : but that you have vouch-safed,
With your crown'd brother and these your con-tracted
Heirs of your kingdoms, my poor house to visit,
It is a surplus of your grace, which never
My life may last to answer.

Leontes. O Paulina,
We honour you with trouble : but we came
To see the statue of our queen : your gallery
Have we pass'd through, not without much content
In many singularities ; but we saw not
That which my daughter came to look upon,
The statue of her mother

Paulina. As she lived peerless,
So her dead likeness, I do well believe,
Excels whatever yet you look'd upon
Or hand of man hath done ; therefore I keep it
Lonely, apart. But here it is : prepare
To see the life as lively mock'd as ever
Still sleep mock'd death : behold, and say 'tis well.

[*Paulina draws a curtain, and discovers Hermione standing like a statue.*

I like your silence, it the more shows off
Your wonder : but yet speak ; first, you, my liege.
Comes it not something near ?

Leontes. Her natural posture !
Chide me, dear stone, that I may say indeed
Thou art Hermione ; or rather, thou art she
In thy not chiding, for she was as tender
As infancy and grace. But yet, Paulina,
Hermione was not so much wrinkled, nothing
So aged as this seems.

Polixenes. O, not by much.

Paulina. So much the more our carver's excel-lence ;
Which lets go by some sixteen years and makes her
As she lived now.

Leontes.   As now she might have done,
So much to my good comfort, as it is
Now piercing to my soul. O, thus she stood,
Even with such life of majesty, warm life,
As now it coldly stands, when first I woo'd her !
I am ashamed : does not the stone rebuke me
For being more stone than it ? O royal piece,
There 's magic in thy majesty, which has
My evils conjured to remembrance and
From thy admiring daughter took the spirits,
Standing like stone with thee.
Perdita.   And give me leave.
And do not say 'tis superstition, that
I kneel and then implore her blessing. Lady,
Dear queen, that ended when I but began,
Give me that hand of yours to kiss.
Paulina.   O, patience !
The statue is but newly fix'd, the colour 's
Not dry.
Camillo.   My lord, your sorrow was too sore
laid on,
Which sixteen winters cannot blow away,
So many summers dry : scarce any joy
Did ever so long live ; no sorrow
But kill'd itself much sooner.
Polixenes.   Dear my brother,
Let him that was the cause of this have power
To take off so much grief from you as he
Will piece up in himself.
Paulina.   Indeed, my lord,
If I had thought the sight of my poor image
Would thus have wrought you,—for the stone is
mine—
I 'ld not have show'd it.
Leontes.   Do not draw the curtain.
Paulina.   No longer shall you gaze on 't, lest
your fancy
May think anon it moves.
Leontes.   Let be, let be.
Would I were dead, but that, methinks, already—
What was he that did make it ? See, my lord,
Would you not deem it breathed ? and that those
veins
Did verily bear blood ?
Polixenes.   Masterly done :
The very life seems warm upon her lip.
Leontes.   The fixure of her eye has motion in 't,
As we are mock'd with art.
Paulina.   I 'll draw the curtain :
My lord 's almost so far transported that
He 'll think anon it lives.
Leontes.   O sweet Paulina,
Make me to think so twenty years together !
No settled senses of the world can match
The pleasure of that madness. Let 't alone.
Paulina.   I am sorry, sir, I have thus far stirr'd
you : but
I could afflict you farther.
Leontes.   Do, Paulina ;
For this affliction has a taste as sweet
As any cordial comfort. Still, methinks,
There is an air comes from her : what fine chisel
Could ever yet cut breath ? Let no man mock me,
For I will kiss her.
Paulina.   Good my lord, forbear :
The ruddiness upon her lip is wet ;
You 'll mar it if you kiss it, stain your own
With oily painting. Shall I draw the curtain ?
Leontes.   No, not these twenty years.
Perdita.   So long could I
Stand by, a looker on.

Paulina.   Either forbear,
Quit presently the chapel, or resolve you
For more amazement. If you can behold it,
I 'll make the statue move indeed, descend
And take you by the hand : but then you 'll think—
Which I protest against—I am assisted
By wicked powers.
Leontes.   What you can make her do,
I am content to look on : what to speak,
I am content to hear ; for 'tis as easy
To make her speak as move.
Paulina.   It is required
You do awake your faith. Then all stand still ;
On : those that think it is unlawful business
I am about, let them depart.
Leontes.   Proceed :
No foot shall stir.
Paulina.   Music, awake her ; strike !   *(Music.*
'Tis time ; descend ; be stone no more ; approach ;
Strike all that look upon with marvel. Come,
I 'll fill your grave up : stir, nay, come away,
Bequeath to death your numbness, for from him
Dear life redeems you. You perceive she stirs :
                    [*Hermione comes down.*
Start not ; her actions shall be holy as
You hear my spell is lawful : do not shun her
Until you see her die again ; for then
You kill her double. Nay, present your hand :
When she was young you woo'd her ; now in age
Is she become the suitor ?
Leontes.   O, she 's warm !
If this be magic, let it be an art
Lawful as eating.
Polixenes.   She embraces him.
Camillo.   She hangs about his neck :
If she pertain to life let her speak too.
Polixenes.   Ay, and make 't manifest where she
has lived,
Or how stolen from the dead.
Paulina.   That she is living,
Were it but told you, should be hooted at
Like an old tale : but it appears she lives,
Though yet she speak not. Mark a little while.
Please you to interpose, fair madam : kneel
And pray your mother's blessing. Turn, good lady ;
Our Perdita is found.
Hermione.   You gods, look down
And from your sacred vials pour your graces
Upon my daughter's head ! Tell me, mine own,
Where hast thou been preserved ? where lived ?
how found
Thy father's court ? for thou shalt hear that I,
Knowing by Paulina that the oracle
Gave hope thou wast in being, have preserved
Myself to see the issue.
Paulina.   There 's time enough for that ;
Lest they desire upon this push to trouble
Your joys with like relation. Go together,
You precious winners all ; your exultation
Partake to every one. I, an old turtle,
Will wing me to some wither'd bough and there
My mate, that 's never to be found again,
Lament till I am lost.
Leontes.   O, peace, Paulina !
Thou shouldst a husband take by my consent,
As I by thine a wife : this is a match,
And made between 's by vows. Thou hast found
mine ;
But how, is to be question'd ; for I saw her,
As I thought, dead, and have in vain said many
A prayer upon her grave. I 'll not seek far—

For him, I partly know his mind—to find thee
An honourable husband. Come, Camillo,
And take her by the hand, whose worth and honesty
Is richly noted and here justified
By us, a pair of kings. Let 's from this place.
What ! look upon my brother : both your pardons,
That e'er I put between your holy looks

My ill suspicion. This is your son-in-law
And son unto the king, who, heavens directing,
Is troth-plight to your daughter   Good Paulina,
Lead us from hence, where we may leisurely
Each one demand and answer to his part
Perform'd in this wide gap of time since first
We were dissever'd : hastily lead away. [*Exeunt.*